# FICTION

## An Introduction
## to Reading and Writing

# FICTION

## An Introduction to Reading and Writing

EDGAR V. ROBERTS

*Lehman College,*
*The City University of New York*

HENRY E. JACOBS

*The University of Alabama*

PRENTICE-HALL, INC.   ENGLEWOOD CLIFFS, NEW JERSEY 07632

*Library of Congress Cataloging-in-Publication Data*

ROBERTS, EDGAR V.
   Fiction: an introduction to reading and writing.

      Rev. ed. of: Literature.  c1986.
      Includes indexes.
      1. Fiction.   2. Fiction—Collections.
   3. Exposition (Rhetoric).   4. College readers.
   I. Jacobs, Henry E.   II. Roberts, Edgar V.   Literature.
   III. Title.
   PN3353.R615 1987      808'.0668      86-22535
   ISBN  0-13-314378-3

Editorial and production supervision: **Lisa A. Domínguez**
Interior design: **Marjorie Borden**
Cover design: **Bruce D. Kenselaar**
Manufacturing buyer: **Ray Keating**
Developmental editor: **Raymond Mullaney**

Much of this material was previously published in *Literature: An Introduction to Reading and Writing.*

Credits and copyrights appear at the back of the book on pp. 509–512, which constitute an extension of the copyright page.

Printed in the United States of America

10  9  8  7  6  5  4  3  2  1

ISBN 0-13-314378-3   01

Prentice-Hall International (UK) Limited, *London*
Prentice-Hall of Australia Pty. Limited, *Sydney*
Prentice-Hall Canada Inc., *Toronto*
Prentice-Hall Hispanoamericana, S. A., *Mexico*
Prentice-Hall of India Private Limited, *New Delhi*
Prentice-Hall of Japan, Inc., *Tokyo*
Prentice-Hall of Southeast Asia Pte. Ltd., *Singapore*
Editora Prentice-Hall do Brasil, Ltda., *Rio de Janeiro*

In Memoriam, Henry E. Jacobs, 1936–1986

*Henry Jacobs, my co-worker, died suddenly in July, 1986, when this book was in production. He was a person of great intelligence, creativity, adaptability, and comprehensiveness. Despite difficulties of ill health, he was always helpful and good-humored.*
*His untimely passing is cause of regret and the deepest sorrow.*

—*Edgar V. Roberts*

# Contents

# Preface

*Fiction: An Introduction to Reading and Writing* is a unique book. It is not only an excellent anthology of short fiction, but it is also a comprehensive guide to writing essays about fiction. It therefore has a broader sense of mission than do most anthologies. Indeed, it was with the aim of combining literary selections with a comprehensive guide to writing that we began. As we planned and wrote this book, we thus had two related goals: to teach students how to read short fiction with understanding and how to write about it with skill and conviction.

In order to fulfill the first goal, we offer an anthology of great short stories and a guide to reading them. The selections are drawn from diverse periods and cultures ranging from ancient Greece and Palestine to contemporary England, America, and Canada. Because the short story is a distinctly modern phenomenon, however, most of the selections of this text were written in the nineteenth and twentieth centuries.

We have also sought to provide a broad range of authors from a variety of cultural and ethnic groups. Thus, there are works by men and women, blacks and whites, Hispanics and American Indians, conservatives and liberals, people with strong religious convictions, and others who have no apparent concern for spiritual matters. We have included works by well-known writers who have secure places in the history of literature as well as works by writers who are much less well known.

In order to place each writer and work in historical context, we have included the author's date of birth (and death) where possible. In addition, we have attempted to provide a date of composition, publication, or both for each work in the text. In most cases, a date of publication is provided, and when possible, it is followed by a date of composition in parentheses.

With the exception of the first two introductory chapters, each chapter in this book deals with a particular element of fiction, such as plot, point of view, or theme. We chose this approach rather than, for example, a historical approach because we feel that it permits the reader to analyze particular aspects of fiction one at a time and in depth. Most chapters begin with a general discussion of the topic or technique under consideration. Within this discussion, key terms and concepts are highlighted in bold type. The discussions often include some analysis or explanation of a story included in the chapter. Such analysis highlights the significant features of individual works. We do not mean to suggest, however, that our ideas about a story are the only right ones. To the contrary, a work of literature can be understood and experienced in many different ways, all of which can be considered absolutely "correct" so long as they are supported by the work itself. This is one of the features that separates literature from mathematics or chemistry; a math problem has one right answer, but a literary work can have many different and valid interpretations, all supported by the text.

The introductory material in each chapter is followed by selections of short stories to be read, studied, enjoyed, and thought about. To aid intelligent reading, we have included some explanatory notes; words that are defined or explained in notes are highlighted by small degree signs (°) in the text. Following each selection are study questions meant to awaken the reader's feelings and ideas. Some of these questions are easily answered; others may provoke extended thought.

Our second (but not secondary) goal in this book is to teach students how to write about short stories with skill and conviction. For us, writing about fiction is not a minor topic that can be addressed in twenty pages at the back of the book. It is a coequal concern that deserves and receives consideration in every chapter. The approaches to writing, developed from tested principles of studying literature together with our own experience in the classroom, have been presented for more than twenty years in *Writing Themes About Literature* by Edgar V. Roberts.

The skills needed for writing effective essays about literature do not represent a completely separate or distinct body of knowledge. Rather, careful reading and effective writing are integrated: Both ask that the student make important decisions and discoveries about the story under consideration, and both require that the student be able to point to specific features in the literary work at hand to justify his or her conclusions.

To this end, we have attempted to supply road maps that can show the way to move from reading to responding and thinking, and then to planning and writing. Each chapter of the text ends with an extensive discussion on writing about short stories. These focus on the topic or element of literature being studied in the chapter. For example, the chapter on setting deals with strategies for planning, organizing, developing, and writing an essay about the relationship between setting and meaning.

These discussions of the prewriting and writing processes are carefully designed to help the student proceed confidently to the task of writing. Each writing section contains suggestions and questions for planning an essay, developing a central idea, selecting supporting details from the story, organizing thoughts most effectively, and beginning the writing process and bringing it to a conclusion.

In these sections we do not simply *say* what can be done with a topic of literary study, we also *show* one way in which it might be done. Each chapter includes a sample essay (sometimes more than one) to exemplify the methods and strategies discussed. Thus, the general guidelines are combined with specific examples to make the writing process as open and clear as possible. Following each essay is a brief commentary that explains the focus and strategies employed in the essay.

Reading and writing skills are not useful only with literature; effective and careful reading and writing techniques will help students in virtually every college course and in any profession. Students may never read another short story by Eudora Welty or Ralph Ellison, but they will certainly read—newspapers, legal documents, magazine articles, technical reports, business proposals, and much more. Similarly, students may never write about character or plot in a short story again, but they will certainly find future situations requiring that they write. The more effectively a person can write about literature, the better he or she will be able to write about anything.

This book is designed both to teach and to delight. Sometimes students and teachers forget that these form a natural pair of processes. We hope that the prose fiction in this text will teach students about humanity, about their own life and feelings, and about timeless patterns of human existence. We hope that they will take delight in such discoveries. We also hope that the commentary and discussions in the text will contribute to their learning about literature and their enjoyment of it. We present this book in the hope that it will be thought of not as an end, but as the beginning of lifelong understanding and joy in great literature.

## ACKNOWLEDGMENTS

This book has been a long time in the making, and many people have offered helpful advice and suggestions along the way. At the University of Alabama, we wish to express our gratitude to Professors Robert Halli, Claudia Johnson, Matthew Marino, and Mathew Winston, and to Christel Bell, Angela Bramlett, Linda Bridgers, Catherine Davis, Edward Hoeppner, Anna F. Jacobs, Marlene H. McKenzie, and Eleanor Tubbs. At Lehman College, we thank Professors David Bady, Billy Collins, Alice Griffin, Gerhard Joseph, Francis Kearns, Ruth Milberg-Kaye, and Michael Paull, and to Nanette Roberts, Virginia Scott, and Eve Zarin. We also want to thank

Professors Anne S. Agee, Anne Arundel Community College; Vivian Brown, Laredo Junior College; Sara Burroughs, Northwestern State University; Iain Crawford, Berry College; Peter B. DeBlois, Syracuse University; C. R. Embry, Truckee Meadows Community College; Delryn R. Fleming, Brookhaven College; Patricia H. Graves, Georgia State University; George F. Hayhoe, formerly Virginia Tech; Ronald Janssen, Hofstra University; Alexander J. Kucsma, County College of Morris; Dallas Lacy, University of Texas at Arlington; Marylou Lewandowski, San Jose State University; Joanne H. McCarthy, Tacoma Community College; Lee McKnight, Stillman College; Ellis Marie Melder, Northwestern State University; Louis E. Murphy, Bucks County Community College; Georgia A. Newman, Polk Community College; Ghita P. Orth, University of Vermont; Richard M. Sippel, Community College of Allegheny County; Louie Skipper, Shelton State College; Ken M. Symes, Western Washington University; William B. Thesing, University of South Carolina; Charles Workman, Samford University. A word of special thanks goes to Bill Oliver, formerly of Prentice-Hall, and to Phil Miller, of Prentice-Hall, for their imagination, foresight, support, and patience in the development of this project. We are also grateful to Ray Mullaney, of Prentice-Hall's Product Development Department, for his wide knowledge, extra energy, tolerance, and special organizing skill. His efforts on our behalf have been invaluable and immeasurable. Additional thanks go to our copyeditor, Chrystena Chrzanowski. Finally, extra thanks go to Jon Roberts for special assistance at various stages in the project.

*Edgar V. Roberts*
*Henry E. Jacobs*

# FICTION

## An Introduction to Reading and Writing

# 1

# Introduction: Reading and Writing about Fiction

## THE VALUE OF LITERATURE

The question "What is literature?" is not easily answered; whole books have been devoted to the topic. No single definition can satisfy everyone; furthermore, once a definition has been made, the limits that it imposes often make it inadequate for at least some writing that some people may want to call *literature*. Nevertheless, we can say many things about literature that will help us begin to understand what it might be.

Technically, anything spoken or written may be called literature. By this definition, both a grocery list and a Shakespearean sonnet would qualify. It is clear, however, that a grocery list does not do those things that we expect from a literary work. It does not interest, entertain, stimulate, broaden, or ennoble us. Even though it may be structured according to the areas in a supermarket (dairy, frozen foods, produce, and so on), just as a Shakespearean sonnet is structured by three four-line stanzas and a concluding set of two lines, it is not designed to engage our emotions or imagination. A grocery list, in short, is simply useful; it is not literature. Rather, we will confine our definition to works that, like Shakespeare's sonnets, invite our emotional and intellectual involvement and response.

The literature that we are concerned about here is in written form, even though it may be performed on stage, in film, or on radio or television. The first advantage of written literature is flexibility. You can choose to read a work at any time according to your mood, and you may read and reread for your own comprehension and appreciation. You can stop at a word, should you wish, and you can go back to look at an earlier sentence. All you need to do is turn a page and fix your eyes on the desired spot. But can't we do much the same thing with a video cassette recorder? It is of course possible to backtrack with a VCR, but to go back to a previous part of a show, you need to operate machinery, and you can never stop at a particular point and still get motion or sound; all you will have is a still picture. On the other hand, with a book you can see a number of words at a glance and can comprehend them all at the same time.

When you read, you depend only on your own effort and imagination. There are no actors, no settings, no photographic or musical techniques to supersede your own reconstruction of the author's ideas. Some might consider this aspect a weakness of reading, but remember that the spectacle of performance, while graphic and stimulating, is also limiting. Even though reading is more demanding than passively watching images on a screen, it allows you to do your own thinking; you can achieve independence more readily by savoring the written word. With reading you may take the time to reflect and digest. You can stop reading and think for a while about what you have just read. You can leave a text and then return to it hours or days later and continue it just where you stopped. The book will always wait for you and will not change during the time you are gone. You can carry it around with you, and you may browse in it during private moments or when riding public transportation.

This is not to belittle the "warmer" media of television and film, but only to contrast them with written forms of literature. All literature, no matter what the form, has many things to offer, and the final word on the value of literary study has not been written. Quite often, in fact, people read literature without explaining, even to themselves, why they enjoy it, because goals and ideals are not easily defined. There are, however, areas of general agreement about some of the things that reading great works of literature can do.

Literature helps us grow, both personally and intellectually; it provides an objective base for our knowledge and understanding; it helps us to connect ourselves to the cultural context of which we are a part; it enables us to recognize human dreams and struggles in different societies that we would never otherwise get to know; it helps us to develop mature sensibility and compassion for the condition of *all* living things—human, animal, and vegetable; it gives us the knowledge and perception needed to appreciate the beauty of order and arrangement, just as a well-structured song or a beautifully done painting can; it provides the comparative basis from which we can see worthiness in the aims of all people, and it therefore helps us see beauty in the world around us; it exercises our emotions through the arousal of interest, concern, tension, excitement, hope, fear, regret, laughter, and sympathy. Through a process of cumulative experience, great literature can shape our goals and values by helping us clarify our own identities, both positively, through identification with the admirable in human life, and negatively, through rejection of the sinister. It can help us to shape our judgments through the constant comparison of the good against the bad. It enables us, both in our everyday activities and in the decisions we are responsible for making as citizens, to develop a perspective on the events that are occurring in the world. It encourages us to assist creative, talented people who are in need. It is one of the things that shape our lives. It helps to make us human.

## TYPES OF LITERATURE: THE GENRES

We usually classify imaginative literature into (1) prose fiction, (2) poetry, and (3) drama. These three forms have many common characteristics. While none of the genres is designed primarily to convey information, for example, all do to some degree. All are art forms, each with its own requirements of structure and style. In varying degrees, all the genres are dramatic and imaginative; they have at least some degree of action or are based in part on a dramatic situation.

Imaginative literature differs from textbooks, historical and biographical works, and news articles, all of which are based on fact or recount facts. Imaginative literature, while related to the truths of human life, may be based upon situations that never have and never may occur. This is not to say that literature is not truthful, but rather that the truth of literature is true to life and human nature, not necessarily to the world of historical and scientific facts.

Although the three main genres have much in common, they also differ in many ways. **Prose fiction,** or **narrative fiction,** is in prose form and includes *novels*, *short stories*, *myths*, *parables*, *romances*, and *epics*. These works generally focus on one or a few major characters who undergo some kind of change as they meet other characters or deal with problems or difficulties in their lives. **Poetry,** in contrast to prose fiction, is much more economical in the use of words and relies heavily on *imagery*, *figurative language*, *rhythm*, and *sound*. **Drama,** or **plays,** are meant to be performed on stage by actors. The goal of this text is to explore the ways in which writers create impact and meaning in fiction. To that end, it discusses many aspects of prose fiction and many short stories. Keep in mind, however, that many of these observations remain equally true for poetry and drama.

## READING AND STUDYING FICTION

There is obviously a difference between just reading prose fiction and studying it. We read many things in the course of daily life, but we do not read everything the same way. For example, reading a menu, reading a comic page, reading a news article, and reading an editorial require different attention and involvement and also evoke different responses. The menu requires a decision about what food to order; the comic page requires a coordination of picture and the ballon-enclosed speeches. The article requires that we assimilate details and also that we begin to form a response. The editorial requires that we understand the subject under discussion together with the political views of the writer so that we can decide to agree or disagree with the position. All these reading tasks require different amounts of time and thought.

By the same token, the *study* of a short story requires a larger investment of thought than a simple *reading*, yet many people assume that reading alone is a sufficient form of study. One can read a work casually, without being able to say much about the lives of the characters, the events, the form, or the ideas. Although such an offhand process might be called "reading the material," there is no way to support a claim that a job of studying has been done.

Studying is something else. It is a process of reading, reading again while taking notes, going back over material, practicing writing about it, and reading it again until it is fairly well fixed in the mind. We have presumed that the reader of this book is going to *study* in preparation for classroom discussion and either in-class or out-of-class writing. Many educators believe that you should spend two hours of study for every period you spend in class. We have therefore provided study questions for many of the stories contained here. We assume that you will be developing your own systematic way of recording and testing your responses to literature so that you can become a *disciplined* rather than a casual reader.

The tasks that make up the process of study are not difficult. Your objective should be to develop as complete an understanding as possible. If a particular study method has worked for you in the past, keep using it. Most study methods, however, will follow similar patterns: first, a general reading to get an overview of the work, and then as many subsequent readings as you need to develop fuller understanding. As you read, mark off interesting or noteworthy passages, and later give these crucial passages the time and thought they require. From that point on, you should try to follow this set of general procedures:

1.  Use a dictionary for words that are new or unfamiliar. When you find a passage that you do not readily understand, determine whether the problem arises from words that you cannot define easily. Once you have used your dictionary, be sure to compare the definitions with the passage where the word occurs, so that your understanding of the words in context is clear.

2.  Consider your thoughts and responses as you read. Did you laugh, smile, worry, get scared, feel a thrill, learn a great deal, feel proud, find a lot to think about? Try to describe how the various parts of the work caused your reactions.

3.  Make notes on interesting characterizations, events, techniques, and ideas. If you like a character, try to describe what you like. If you dislike an idea, try to put your reasons for dislike into your own words.

4.  Try to see patterns developing. Make an outline or scheme for the plot or the main ideas. What are the conflicts in the story? How does the author resolve them? Is one force, idea, or side the winner? Why? How do you respond to the winner, or the loser?

5.  Is there anything you do not understand? Make a note of the difficulty so that you may ask your instructor about it.

6.  For further study, think further about any passages you have underlined or marked out in the margins.

7.  Make a practice of writing one or more paragraphs describing your thoughts and responses after reading and considering the story. If you are reading the work in preparation for writing a specific type of essay, your paragraphs may be useful later. Even if you are making only a general preparation, however, try to continue the practice of committing your thoughts to paper.

## WRITING ESSAYS ABOUT FICTION

Writing is the sharpened, focused expression of thought and study. As you develop your writing skills, you will also improve your perceptions and increase your critical abilities. Although no one can ever reach a point of being a perfect master of the art of writing, the attempt to achieve such a state is worthwhile, and everyone can improve writing to the best of his or her ability.

The subject of this book is fiction: you will study it, ask questions about it, and write about it. The development of your ability to think and to write about short stories will also prepare you to write about any other topic. Literature contains the subject material of philosophy, religion, psychology, sociology, and politics. As you learn to analyze and write about stories, you will also be improving your perception of these other disciplines. You can bring your capacity for analysis to bear on future problems as well.

Writing ultimately boils down to the development of an idea. Some ideas are better than others. Getting good ideas is an acquired skill that grows out of your development as a thinker and writer. You will discover that your thinking will improve the longer you engage in the analysis of literature. In the same way, the quality of your ideas will improve as you go through the process of originating ideas, seeing the flaws in some of your thinking, proposing new avenues of development, securing new data to support ideas, and creating new aspects of an idea. Your objective always will be to convince a person reading your essays that your considerations are based on facts and that your conclusions are valid.

Unlike ordinary conversation and classroom discussion, writing must stick with great determination to a specific point of development. Ordinary conversation is usually random and disorganized; it shifts frequently from topic to topic—sometimes without clear cause—and it is sometimes repetitive. Classroom discussion is more organized, but there may be digressions and irrelevancies. Thus classroom discussion, while formal, is free and spontaneous. Writing, by contrast, is the most concise and highly organized form of expression that will ever be required of you.

## WHAT IS AN ESSAY?

It needs to be emphasized again and again that writing demands tight organization and control. The first requirement of the finished essay— although it is *not* the first requirement in the writing *process*—is that it have a **central idea.** Thus, an **essay** can be defined as a fully developed set of interconnected paragraphs that grow systematically out of a central idea. Everything in the essay should be directly related to the idea or should contribute to the reader's understanding of the idea.

Let us consider this definition in relation to essays about fiction. Such an essay should be a brief examination rather than an exhaustive treatment of a particular subject. It might be a character study or an analysis of point of view. Unity in the essay is achieved through the consistent reference to the central idea throughout the essay. Typical central ideas might be (1) that a character is strong and tenacious, as in Guy De Maupassant's "The Necklace" (p. 75), or (2) that the point of view makes the action seem "up close" and personal, as in Frank O'Connor's "First Confession" (p. 172). Everything in the essay is to be related to the central idea. Thus, it is a fact that Mathilde Loisel in "The Necklace" spends ten years working almost like a slave to repay a debt. This fact is not relevant to an essay on character unless you show that the hard work reveals Mathilde's strength and tenacity. Similarly, in an essay about point of view in "First Confession" it is not important to say that Jackie and Nora speak to each other unless you relate their conversations to the personal quality of the story resulting from the first-person point of view. By the same token, any attempt to show that "First Confession" reveals more about character than "The Necklace" must be introduced as part of an argument that O'Connor's story is different from or superior to De Maupassant's in regard to the development of character.

All these principles should be your goal when you are planning and writing your essay, and they should all hold in your finished essay. Here they are again:

1. The essay should cover the assigned topic such as those described in the various chapters of this book (e.g., character or point of view).

2.  The essay should have a central idea that governs its development.
3.  The essay should be organized so that every part contributes something to the reader's understanding of the central idea.

## THE PROCESS OF WRITING AN ESSAY

There are a number of things you can do to make systematic the process of writing an essay about literature. Two are **invention** and **prewriting.** Invention is the process of discovering or creating the things you want to say. Prewriting is the process of studying, thinking, raising and answering questions, planning, developing tentative ideas and first drafts, crossing out, erasing, changing, rearranging, and adding. In a way, prewriting and invention are merely different words for planning and thinking. They both acknowledge the sometimes uncertain way in which the mind works and also the fact that ideas are often not known until they get written down. Writing, at any stage, should always be thought of as a process of discovery and creation. There is always something more to develop.

The following description of the planning and writing process is presented as an approximation of what you should be doing in planning and writing an essay. You may change the order or omit some steps. In the overall process, however, you will probably not vary the steps widely.

Not every single step in the various stages of composition can be detailed here. There is not enough space to illustrate the development of various drafts before the final draft. If you compare the original notes with early drafts of observations and paragraphs, however, you can see that many changes take place and that one step really merges with another.

1. *Read the story through at least once for general understanding*. It is important that you have a general knowledge of the work before you try to start developing materials for your theme. Be sure, in this reading, to follow all the general principles outlined earlier (pp. 4–5).

2. *Take notes with your specific assignment in mind*. If you are to write about a character, for example, take notes on things done, said, and thought about by that character. The same applies if your assignment is on setting, ideas, and so on. By concentrating your notes in this way, and by excluding other elements of the work, you are already focusing on the subject at hand.

3. *Use a pen, pencil, typewriter, or word processor as an extension of your thought*. Writing, together with actually *seeing* the things written, is for most people a vital part of thinking. Therefore, you must get your thoughts into a visible form so that you may develop them further. For many people, the hand is a psychological necessity in this process. For others, thought may proceed through the fingers into a typewriter or a word processor. The important thing is that unwritten thought is still incomplete thought. Get it out onto something you can see and work with.

In addition, at some advanced step in your composing process, prepare a complete draft of what you have written thus far. Even with a word processor, you cannot lay everything out in front of you at once but can see only a small part on your screen. A clean, readable draft gives you the chance to see everything together and to make even more improvements. Sight is vital.

4. *Use the questions in the chapter on which the assignment is based.* Your answers to these questions, together with your notes and ideas, can often serve as the basis for parts of an essay.

5. *For all your preliminary materials, use cards or only one side of the paper.* In this way, you may spread out everything and get an overview as you plan and write your essay. Do not write on both sides of the paper, for ideas that are out of sight are often out of mind.

6. *Once you have put everything together in this way, try to develop a central idea.* This will serve as the focus of your planning and writing.

### Finding a Central Idea or a Thesis

You cannot find a central idea in a hat. It comes about as a result of the steps just described. In a way, you might think of discovering a central idea as a major goal in the prewriting process. Once you have the idea, you have a guide for accepting some of your materials, rejecting others, rearranging, changing, and rewording. It is therefore necessary to see how the central idea may be developed and how it may be used.

MAKING NOTES.    Let us assume that your assignment is an essay about the character Jackie in O'Connor's story "First Confession." (To read the complete story, see p. 172.) The following is a collection of notes and observations that you might write when reading the story. Notice that page numbers are noted so that you can easily go back to the story at any time to refresh your memory on any details.

> Jackie blames others, mainly his grandmother, for his troubles. He hates her bare feet and her eating and drinking habits. He dislikes his sister, Nora for "sucking up" to the grandmother. Also, Nora tells on him. He is ashamed to bring a friend home to play because of grandmother. (p. 173)
>
> He likes money rather than Mrs. Ryan's talk of hell.
> He is shocked by the story about the "fellow" who "made a bad confession." (p. 174)
> After learning to examine his conscience, he believes that he has broken all ten commandments because of the grandmother.
> He lies about a toothache to avoid confession. A kid's lie. (p. 174)
>
> He believes his sister is a "raging malicious devil." He remembers her "throwing" him through the church door. (p. 175)
> Very imaginative. Believes that he will make a "bad confession and then die in the night and be continually coming back and burning people's furniture."

This is funny, and also childish. He thinks women are hypocrites. (p. 176)
He is frightened by the dark confessional. (p. 175)

Curious and adventurous. He gets up on the shelf and kneels.
He is also frightened by the tone of the priest's voice. He falls out on the church floor and gets whacked by his sister. (p. 176)

Note: All the things about Jackie as a child are told by Jackie as an older person. The man is sort of telling a joke on himself.

Jackie is smart, can think about himself as a sinner once the priest gives him a clue. He likes the kind words of the priest, is impressed with him.
He begins reacting against the words of Mrs. Ryan and Nora, calling them "cackling." (p. 176)

He has sympathy for his mother. Calls her "poor soul." Seems to fear his father, who has given him the "flaking." (p. 173)

Note: Jackie is a child, and easily swayed. He says some things that are particularly childish and cute, such as coming back to burn furniture. His fears show that he is childish and naive. He is gullible. His memory of his anger against his sister shows a typical attitude of brother and sister.

**WRITING OBSERVATIONS FROM YOUR NOTES: "BRAINSTORMING."**     Once you have a set of notes like these, your job is to make something out of them. The notes do not make up an essay; they are disorganized and unfocused. However, they represent a starting point from which ideas may be organized and developed. Since the imaginary assignment we are discussing concerns character (rather than plot, imagery, symbolism, or the like), you should go back over your notes and extract single-sentence observations that relate specifically to character traits and development. Care must be taken to ensure that these sentences focus on the subject at hand—character—and do not offer plot summary or digressions. Such a reformulated list of sentences about Jackie's character might look like this:

Jackie likes thinking about money (the half crown) rather than hell. Is he irreligious, or does this show his childish nature?

He seems to be older when he is telling the story.

He has a dislike for his sister that seems to be normal brother-and-sister rivalry.

He tells a fib about the toothache, but he tells everything else to the priest. He is not a liar.

He blames his gran for his troubles. Is he irresponsible? No, he is just behaving like a child.

He is curious and adventurous, as much as a seven-year-old can be.

He is easily scared and impressed (see his response to the bad confession story, and his first response to the priest).

He says cute things, the sort of things a child would say (the old man in the pew, coming back to burn the furniture). He seems real as a child.

These are all observations that might or might not turn out to be worth much in your essay. It is not possible to tell until you do some further thinking about them. These basic ideas, however, are worth working up further, along with additional substantiating details.

**DEVELOPING YOUR OBSERVATIONS AS PARAGRAPHS.**   As you develop these basic ideas, you should be consulting the original set of notes and also looking at the text to make sure that all your facts are correct. As you write, you should bring in any new details that seem relevant. Here are some paragraphs that expand upon some of the observations presented above. You might consider this paragraph-writing phase a "second step" in the brainstorming needed for the essay:

1. Jackie comes to life. He seems real. His experiences are those that a child might have, and his reactions are lifelike. All brothers and sisters fight. All kids are "heart scalded" when they get a "flaking."

2. Jackie shows a great amount of anger. He kicks his grandmother on the shin and won't eat her cooking. He is mad at Nora for the penny that she gets from grandmother, and he "lashes out" at Nora with the bread knife. He blames his troubles on his grandmother. He talks about the "hypocrisy of women." He thinks that the stories of Mrs. Ryan and the religion of his sister are the "cackle of old women and girls." (p. 176)

3. Everything about Jackie as a child that we get in the story is told by Jackie when he is older, probably a grown man. The story is comic, and part of the comedy comes because the man is telling a jokelike story about himself.

4. Jackie's main characteristic is that he is a child and does many childish things. He remembers his anger with his sister. He also remembers being shocked by Mrs. Ryan's stories about hell. He crawls onto the ledge in the confessional. He is so impressed with the bad confession story that he says twice that he fears burning furniture. Some of these things are charming and cute, such as the observation about the old man having a grandmother and his thinking about the money when Mrs. Ryan offers the coin to the first boy who holds his finger in the candle flame.

**DETERMINING YOUR CENTRAL IDEA.**   Once you have reached this stage in your thinking, you are ready to pull the materials together and form a central idea or a thesis for the essay. To do this, look for a common thread or term that runs through many of your observations. In the notes, sentences, and paragraphs developed in the hypothetical assignment on character in "First Confession," one common thread is the term "childish." The anger, the sibling rivalry, the attraction to the coin, the fear of burning someone's furniture, the fib about the toothache—all these can be seen as signs of childishness. Once you have found this common thread (and it could easily have been some other point, such as Jackie's anger, or his attitude toward the females around him), it can be used as the central idea in an evolving essay.

Because the central idea is so vital in shaping an essay, it should be formed as carefully as possible in a complete sentence. Just the word "childishness" would not give us as much as any of the following sentences:

1. The main trait of Jackie is his childishness.
2. Jackie is bright and sensitive, but above all childlike.
3. Jackie is no more than a typical child.
4. Jackie is above all a child, with all the beauties of childhood.

Each one of these ideas would make a different kind of essay. The first would promote an essay showing that Jackie's actions and thoughts are childish. The third would do much the same thing but would also stress Jackie's limitations as a child. The second would try to show Jackie's better qualities and would show how they are limited by his age. The fourth might try to emphasize the charm and "cuteness" that were pointed out in some of the notes and observations.

You might try phrasing the central idea several different ways before you choose the one that will yield the most focused essay. Once you have a central idea (let us use the first one), you will be able to use it to bring your observations and conclusions into focus.

Let's take paragraph two in the brainstorming phase, the one about Jackie's anger. With childishness as our central idea, we can use the topic of anger as a way of illustrating Jackie's childish character. Is his anger adult or childish? Is it normal or psychotic? Is it sudden or deliberate? In the light of these questions, we may conclude that all the examples of angry action and thought can be seen as the normal responses or reflections of a child. With the material thus "arranged" in this way, we can reshape the second paragraph as follows:

*ORIGINAL PARAGRAPH*

Jackie shows a great amount of anger. He kicks his grandmother on the shin and won't eat her cooking. He is mad at Nora for the penny that she gets from grandmother, and he "lashes out" at Nora with the bread knife. He blames his troubles on his grandmother. He talks about the "hypocrisy of women." He thinks the stories of Mrs. Ryan and the religion of his sister are the "cackle of old women and girls." (p. 176)

*RESHAPED PARAGRAPH*

Jackie's great amount of anger is childish. Kicking his grandmother, refusing to eat her cooking, and lashing out at Nora with the bread knife are instances of childish anger. His jealousy of Nora and his distrust of women (as hypocrites) are the results of immature and childish thought. His anger at religion, evident in his claim that the fears of Mrs. Ryan and Nora are the "cackle of old women and girls" (p. 176), is also childish.

Notice here that the materials in each paragraph are substantially the same but that the central idea has shaped the right-hand paragraph. The left-hand column describes Jackie's anger, while the one on the right makes the claim that all the examples of angry action and thought are childish and immature. Once our paragraph has been shaped in this way, it is almost ready for placement into the emerging essay.

### The Thesis Sentence

Using the central idea as a guide, we can now go back to the earlier materials for arrangement. The goal is to establish a number of points to be developed as paragraphs in support of the central idea. The paragraphs written as the second step of brainstorming will serve us well. Paragraph 2, the one we have just "shaped," discusses childish anger. Paragraph 3 has material that could be used in an introduction (since it does not directly discuss any precise characteristics but instead describes how the reader gets the information about Jackie). Paragraph 1 has material that might be good in a conclusion. Paragraph 4 has two topics (it is not a unified paragraph), which may be labeled "responses" and "outlook." We may put these points into a list:

1.   Responses
2.   Outlook
3.   Anger

Once we have established this list, we may use it as the basic order for the development of our essay.

For the benefit of the reader, however, we should also use this ordering for the writing of our **thesis sentence.** This sentence is the operative sentence in the first part of the following general plan for most essays:

Tell what you are going to say.
Say it.
Tell what you've said.

The thesis sentence tells your reader what to expect. It is a plan for your essay: it connects the central idea and the list of topics in the order in which you plan to present them. Thus, if we put the central idea at the left and our list of topics at the right, we have the shape of a thesis sentence:

| *CENTRAL IDEA* | *TOPICS* |
|---|---|
| The main trait of Jackie is his childishness. | 1. Responses |
| | 2. Outlook |
| | 3. Anger |

From this arrangement we can write the following thesis sentence, which should usually be the concluding sentence before the body of the essay (that section in which you "say it," that is, in which you develop your central idea):

The childishness is emphasized in his responses, outlook, and anger.

With any changes made necessary by the context of your final essay, this thesis sentence and your central idea can go directly into your introduction. The central idea, as we have seen, is the glue of the essay. The thesis sentence shows the parts that are to be fastened together, that is, the topics in which the central idea will be demonstrated.

### The Body of the Essay: Topic Sentences

The term regularly used in this book for the development of the central idea is **body.** The body is the section where you present the materials you have been working up in your planning. You may rearrange or even reject some of what you have developed, as you wish, as long as you change your thesis sentence to account for the changes. Since the thesis sentence we have generated contains three topics, we will use these to form the essay.

Just as the organization of the entire essay is based on the thesis sentence, the organization of each paragraph is based on its **topic sentence.** The topic sentence is made up of one of the topics listed in the thesis sentence, combined with some assertion about how the topic will support the central idea. The first topic in our example is Jackie's responses, and the topic sentence should show how these responses illustrate a phase of Jackie's childishness. Suppose we choose the phase of the child's gullibility or impressionability. We can put together the topic and the phase, to get the following topic sentence:

Jackie's responses show childish impressionability.

The details that will be used to develop the paragraph will then show how Jackie's responses illustrate the impressionability and gullibility associated with children.

You should follow the same process in forming the other topic sentences, so that when you finish them you can use them in writing your essay.

### The Outline

All along we have actually been developing an **outline** to shape and organize the essay. Some writers never use a formal outline at all, whereas others find one to be quite helpful to them as they write. Still other writers insist that they cannot produce an outline until they have finished their essay. All of these views can be reconciled if you realize that finished essays should have a tight structure. At some point, therefore, you should create an outline as a guide. It may be early in your prewriting, or it may be late. What is important is that your final essay follow an outline form.

The kind of outline we have been developing here is the "analytical sentence outline." This type is easier to create than it sounds, for it is nothing more than a graphic form, a skeleton, of your essay. It consists of the following:

1. Title
2. Introduction
   a. Central idea
   b. Thesis sentence
3. Body
   a.
   b. } points announced in the thesis sentence
   c. etc.
4. Conclusion

The conclusion is optional in this scheme. Because the topic of the conclusion is a separate item, it is technically independent of the body, but it is part of the thematic organization and hence should be closely tied to the central idea. It may be a summary of the main points in the essay ("tell what you've said"). It may also be an evaluation of the ideas, or it may suggest further points of analysis that you did not write about in the body. Each of the following chapters offers suggestions to help you develop materials for your conclusions.

Remember that your outline should be a guide for organizing many thoughts and already completed paragraphs. Throughout our discussion of the process of writing the essay, we have seen that writing is discovery. At the right point, your outline can help you in this discovery. That is, the need to make your essay conform to the plan of the outline may help you to reshape, reposition, and reword some of your ideas.

When completed, the outline should have the following appearance (using the character study of Jackie in "First Confession"):

1. Title: "Jackie's Childish Character in O'Connor's 'First Confession' "
2. Introduction. Paragraph 1
   a. Central idea: The main trait of Jackie is his childishness.
   b. Thesis sentence: This childishness is emphasized in his responses, outlook, and anger.
3. Body: Topic sentences for paragraphs 2–4
   a. Jackie's responses show childish impressionability.
   b. His outlook reflects the simplicity of a child.
   c. His anger is also that of a child.
4. Conclusion. Paragraph 5
   Topic sentence: Jackie seems real as a child.

By the time you have created an outline like this one, you will have been planning and drafting your essay for quite some time. The outline will thus be a guide for *finishing* and *polishing* your essay, not for actually developing it. Usually you will have already completed the main parts of the body and will use the outline for the introduction and conclusion.

Briefly, here is the way to use the outline:

1. Include both the central idea and the thesis sentence in your introduction. (Some instructors require a fusion of the two in the final draft of the essay. Therefore, make sure you know what your instructor expects.) Use the suggestions in the chapter assignment to determine what else might be included in the introduction.

2. Include the various topic sentences at the beginning of your paragraphs, changing them as necessary to provide transitions or qualifications. Throughout this book the various topics are confined to separate paragraphs. However, it is also acceptable to divide the topic into two or more paragraphs, particularly if the topic is difficult or highly detailed. Should you make this division, your topic then is really a *section*, and your second and third paragraphs should each have their own topic sentences.

In paragraphs designed to demonstrate the validity of an assertion, the topic sentence usually begins the paragraph. The details then illustrate the truth of the assertion in the topic sentence. (Details about the use of evidence will follow below, pp. 19–21.) It is also acceptable to have the topic sentence elsewhere in the paragraph, particularly if your paragraph is a "thought paragraph," in which you use details to lead up to your topic idea.

Throughout this book, for illustrative purposes, all the central ideas, thesis sentences, and topic sentences are underlined so that you may distinguish them clearly as guides for your own writing.

## THE SAMPLE ESSAY

The following essay is a sample of the finished product of the process we have been illustrating. You will recognize the various organizing sentences because they are underlined. These are the sentences from the outline, with changes made to incorporate them into the essay and to provide transitions from paragraph to paragraph. You will also see that some of the paragraphs and thoughts have been taken from the prewriting stages, with necessary changes to bring them into tune with the central idea. (See the illustration of this change on p. 11.)

In each of the chapters in this book there are similar sample essays. It would be impossible to show the complete writing process for each of these, but you may assume that each one was completed more or less like the one that has been illustrated here. There were many good starts, and many false ones. Much was changed and rearranged, and much was redone once the outline for the essay was established. The materials for each essay were developed in the light of the issues introduced and exemplified in the first parts of each of the chapters. The plan for each essay corresponds to an outline, and its length is within the limits of many of the essays you will be assigned to write.

## SAMPLE ESSAY

### Jackie's Childish Character in O'Connor's "First Confession"*

[1] Jackie, the main character in O'Connor's "First Confession," is a child at the time of the action. All the things we learn about him, however, are told by him as an older person. The story is funny, and part of the humor is produced because the narrator is telling what amounts to a joke on himself. For this reason he brings out his own childhood childishness. That is, if Jackie were mature, the joke would not work because so much depends on his being young, powerless, and gullible. The main thing about Jackie, then, is his childishness.° This quality is emphasized in his responses, outlook, and anger.▫

[2] Jackie's responses show the ease with which a child may be impressed. His grandmother embarasses him with her drinking, eating, and unpleasant habits. He is so "shocked" by the story about the bad confession that twice he states his fear of saying a bad confession and coming back to burn furniture. He is quickly impressed by the priest and is able to change his mind about his sins (to his own favor) after no more than a few words with this man.

[3] His outlook above all reflects the limitations and the simplicity of a child. He is not old enough to know anything about the outside world, and therefore he supposes that the old man next to him at confession has also had problems with a grandmother. This same limited view causes him to think only about the half crown when Mrs. Ryan talks about punishment. It is just like a child to see everything in personal terms, without the detached, broad views of an experienced adult.

[4] His anger is also that of a child, although an intelligent one. Kicking his grandmother and lashing out against Nora with the bread knife are the reflexive actions of childish anger. He also has anger that he thinks about. His jealousy of Nora and his claim that women are hypocrites are the results of thought, even though this thought is immature and childish. His thinking about religion after first speaking to the priest makes him claim that the fears of Mrs. Ryan

---

* See p. 172 for this story.
° Central idea
▫ Thesis sentence

and Nora are the "cackle of old women and girls" (p. 176). He is intelligent, but he is also childish.

[5] Jackie therefore seems real as a child. His reactions are the right ones for a child to have. All brothers and sisters fight, and all children are "heart scalded" when they get a "flaking." The end of life and eternal punishment are remote for a child, whose first concern is the pleasure that money can buy. Therefore, Jackie's thoughts about the half crown are truly those of a child, as are all his thoughts and actions. The strength of "First Confession" is the reality and consistency of Jackie as a child.

### Essay Commentaries

Throughout this book, short commentaries follow each sample essay. Each discussion points out how the assignment is handled and how the instruction provided in the first part of the chapter is incorporated into the essay. For essays in which several approaches are suggested, the commentary points out which one is employed. When a sample essay uses two or more approaches, the commentary makes this fact clear. It is hoped that the commentaries will help you develop the insight necessary to use the sample essays as aids in your own study and writing.

## SOME COMMON PROBLEMS IN WRITING ESSAYS

The fact that you understand the early stages of the composition process and can apply the principles of developing a central idea and organizing with an outline and thesis sentence does not mean that you will have no problems in writing well. It is not hard to recognize good writing when you see it, but it can be difficult to explain why it is superior.

The most difficult and perplexing questions you will ask as you write are: (1) "How can I improve my writing?" (2) "If I got a C on my last essay, why wasn't the grade a B or an A? How can I get higher grades?" These are really the same question, but each has a different emphasis. Another way to ask this question is: "When I first read a work, I have a hard time following it. Yet when my instructor explains it, my understanding is greatly increased. How can I develop the ability to understand the work and write about it well without my instructor's help? How can I become an independent, confident reader and writer?"

The chapter discussions accompanying the readings in this book are designed to help you do just that. One of the major flaws in many essays about literature is that, despite the writer's best intentions and plans, they do no more than retell a story or describe an idea. Retelling the story shows only that you have read the work, not that you have thought about it. Writing a good essay, however, shows that you have digested the material and have been able to put it into an analytical pattern of thought.

### Establishing an Order in Making References

There are a number of ways in which you may set up patterns of development to show your understanding. One is to refer to events or passages in an order that you yourself establish. You do not have to present them in the order in which they occurred but can change them around to make them fit into your own thematic plans. Rarely, if ever, should you begin your essay by describing the opening of the work; it is better to talk about the conclusion or the middle of the work first. Beginning the body of your essay by referring to later parts of the work will almost force you to discuss your own central idea rather than to retell a story. If you look back at paragraph 3 of the sample essay on "First Confession," you will see that this technique has been used. The two references there are presented in reverse order from the story. This reversal shows the essay writer's own organization, not the organization of the work being analyzed.

### Your Mythical Reader: A Student Who Has Read but Not Thought

Consider the "mythical reader" for whom you are writing your essay. Imagine that you are writing to other students. They have read the assigned story, just as you have, but they have not thought about it. It is easy to imagine how to write for such mythical readers. They know the events or have followed the thread of the argument. They know who says what and when it is said. As a result, you do not need to tell these readers about everything in the work, but should think of your role as that of an *explainer* or *interpreter*. Tell them what things mean in relationship to your central idea. *Do not, however, just retell the story.*

To look at the situation in still another way, let us refer to Sir Arthur Conan Doyle's detective story "The Adventure of the Speckled Band," featuring Sherlock Holmes. Both Dr. Watson and Holmes are together when they examine the room of the potential murder victim, and both are able to see the same things. As the two men discuss their observations, Watson says, "You have evidently seen more in these rooms than was visible to me." To this, Holmes makes a telling and famous response: "No, but I fancy that I may have deduced a little more. I imagine that you saw all that I did." You should consider your role as a writer to be like that of Holmes as a detective. Thus, you explain and interpret facts and draw conclusions that your mythical readers, like Watson, are unable to draw for themselves even though they can see the same things that you do. If you look back at the sample essay on "First Confession," you will notice that everywhere *the assumption has been made that the reader has read the story already*. References to the story are thus made primarily to remind the reader of something he or she already knows, but *the principal emphasis of the essay is to draw conclusions and develop arguments*.

### Using Literary Material as Evidence

The comparison with Sherlock Holmes should remind you that whenever you write on any topic, your position is much like that of a detective using clues as evidence for building a case, or of a lawyer using evidence as support for arguments. If you argued in favor of securing a greater voice for students in college government, for example, you would introduce such evidence as past successes with student government, increased maturity of modern-day students, the constitutional amendment granting 18-year-olds the right to vote, and so on.

Writing about fiction requires evidence as well. *For practical purposes only*, when you are writing an essay, you may conveniently regard the story assigned as evidence for your arguments. You should make references to the work only as a part of the logical development of your discourse. Your objective is to convince your reader of your own knowledge and reasonableness, just as lawyers attempt to convince a jury of the reasonableness of their arguments.

The proper use of evidence in literary studies, as in law, psychology, or physics, is important and complex. Would it be accurate, for example, to deduce from the "evidence" of Doyle's "The Adventure of the Speckled Band" that Dr. Roylott is a good and kind man? The story gives us four pieces of evidence: (1) Roylott murdered a servant in India; (2) he is continually in a violent rage; (3) he probably murdered Helen Stoner's sister; (4) he is trying to murder Helen. The evidence, ladies and gentlemen of the literary jury, is clear: Roylott is not a pleasant individual. Instead, the only logical conclusion we can reach from Doyle's presentation of Roylott is that the man is dangerous and evil. We can see a similar use of literary "evidence" in the sample essay on "First Confession." The fourth paragraph, which focuses on Jackie's anger as an aspect of his childishness, introduces four pieces of "evidence" from the story as support. These details are not introduced to summarize plot or retell the story; they explicitly relate to the topic of Jackie's anger and childishness.

The correct and effective use of such literary evidence is vital to good writing. Look, for example, at these two paragraphs; both are from essays about the structure in "The Adventure of the Speckled Band":

| *1* | *2* |
|---|---|
| Midway in this conversation, Dr. Grimesby Roylott, Helen Stoner's step-father, bursts into the room. Before this point we had learned that he was an unpleasant, violent man. He had beaten a servant to death in India, and back in England had become known as a brawler and a man to avoid. The impression he gives in the scene with Holmes and Dr. Watson confirms all these stories of menace and anger that Helen had told Holmes earlier in the day. Roylott is a giant of a man, big enough to throw even a blacksmith into a stream, as Helen had related about him. His evil nature is shown in his face, also a fact which confirms Helen's story about his many angry quarrels with people who lived in his neighborhood. His appearance is not only evil, but it is also threatening. Dr. Watson says he resembles a bird of prey. Roylott, after stating his name, immediately demands to know what Helen had been saying to Holmes. When the great detective refuses to tell him, Roylott makes a number of insults, calling Holmes a meddler, a busy body, and a "Scotland Yard Jack-in-office." Then he threatens Holmes and anyone else who meddles in his affairs, and, to show his strength, he seizes a poker and bends it. After throwing the bent poker in the fireplace, he angrily leaves. Holmes then straightens the poker itself, while asserting that he, too, has strength. | Doyle uses the entry of Dr. Grimesby Roylott as a pivot point in the story. Roylott is the villain and will soon try to murder Helen Stoner, but at his first appearance the readers do not know that. Instead, he has been no more than a stormy, angry figure in Helen's narration. With his entry, however, Doyle makes him real. His rudeness, threats, and demonstration of brute strength with the poker confirm what Helen had said about him, even though at first his mad behavior could easily be explained as that of an angry stepfather and guardian rather than of a guilty murderer. In light of the ending of the story, however, in which Doyle, for the sake of the mystery, has Roylott work out his scheme of murder in darkness and concealment, the confrontation with Holmes is the only first-hand view we get of Roylott's evil character. By dramatizing this potential for violence in this way, Doyle makes it believable that Roylott could indeed be a murderer. Thus, this brief interruption and encounter are pivotal to Doyle's plot, for they confirm the earlier part of the story and establish the credibility of the latter part. |

Although the first example has more words than the second (240 in passage 1, 196 in 2), it is not adequate, for the writer is just restating things that the reader already should know. The paragraph is cluttered with details, and its conclusions and observations are minimal. If you judge it for what you might learn about Conan Doyle's actual *use* of the episode from "The Speckled Band," you cannot avoid concluding that it does not give you a single piece of new information and that it is no help at all in understanding the story. The writer did not have to think much in order to write the paragraph.

On the other hand, the second passage is responsive to the reader's needs, and it required a good deal of thought to write. Phrases like "Doyle uses" and "Doyle makes it believable" show that the writer of passage 2 has assumed the reader knows the story and now wants help in interpretation. Passage 2 therefore leads readers into a new and informative pattern of thought and analysis. It uses details from the story only to furnish evidence for a topic idea (the "pivotal" role of the episode) but excludes irrelevant details. Passage 1 includes nothing but raw, undirected actions. Passage 2 has a point; passage 1 does not.

The answer to the difficult question at how to turn *C*-grade writing into *A*-grade writing is to be found in the comparison of the two passages. Besides using English correctly, superior writers always allow their minds to play upon the materials. They try to give readers the results of their thoughts. They dare to trust their responses and are not afraid to make judgments about the literary work they are considering. Their principal aim in referring to events in a work is to develop their own thematic pattern. Observe this quality again by comparing two sentences that deal with the same details from the story:

| 1 | 2 |
|---|---|
| Midway in this conversation, Dr. Grimesby Roylott, Helen Stoner's step-father, bursts into the room. | Doyle uses the entry of Dr. Grimesby Roylott as a pivot point in the story. |

Sentence 1 is detailed and accurate but no more. Sentence 2 is admittedly less detailed, but it links the essential detail of the entry to a major idea about the plot of the story. The words "Doyle uses" and "as a pivot point" indicate the writer's thoughtful use of detail as a part of an argument or observation, not just as an undigested passing on of detail. There are many things that make good writing good, but perhaps the most important is the way in which a writer uses known and accepted facts as evidence in an original pattern of thought. Always try to achieve this quality in your writing.

### Keeping to Your Point

Whenever you write an essay about a story, then, you must pay great attention to the proper organization and to the proper use of references to the work assigned. As you write, you should try constantly to keep your material unified, for should you go off on a tangent, you are following the material rather than leading it. It is all too easy to start with your point but then wander off into a retelling of events or ideas. Once again, resist the tendency to be a narrator rather than an interpreter.

Let us look at another example. The following paragraph is taken from an essay on "The value of methodical intelligence in Doyle's 'The

Adventure of the Speckled Band.' " In this paragraph the writer attempts to demonstrate the importance of this idea to the section of the story where Holmes and Watson investigate the house in which Helen Stoner feels threatened.

> It is in the direct examination of the Roylott building, Stoke Moran, that the power of active intelligence is seen to be most practical and effective. Holmes and Watson first examine the outside of the right wing, where Helen Stoner is temporarily sleeping next to the room of Dr. Roylott. Then they go inside, where Holmes examines Helen's room, even using a magnifying glass to see things closely. He discovers that the bell rope is a dummy and that the ventilator opens not to the outside but to Dr. Roylott's room next door. Then they examine Roylott's room and discover a number of seemingly strange and unexplainable things, such as the large iron safe, the saucer of milk, the wooden chair, and a strange dog leash. It is then that Holmes truly realizes the danger and forms a plan of protection, action, and discovery.

This paragraph shows how easily writers may be diverted from their objective. The first sentence is an effective topic sentence that suggests that the writer began with a good plan. The remainder of the paragraph, however, does not follow through. It is simply an accurate account of what happens in the story but does not get tied in to the topic set forth in the opening sentence. The material is relevant to the topic, but the writer does not point out its relevance. Writers should not rely on detail alone to make meanings clear. They must make the connections between details and conclusions explicit.

Let us see how the problem shown in the paragraph may be corrected through revision. If the ideal paragraph could be schematized with line drawings, we might say that the paragraph's topic should be a straight line, moving directly toward a specific goal (explicit meaning), with an exemplifying line moving away from the straight line briefly in order to bring in evidence but returning to the line after each new fact in order to demonstrate the relevance of this fact. Thus, the ideal scheme would look like this:

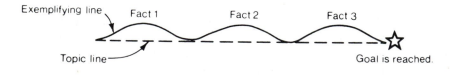

Notice that the exemplifying line always returns to the topic line. A scheme for the above paragraph on "The Adventure of the Speckled Band," however, would look like this:

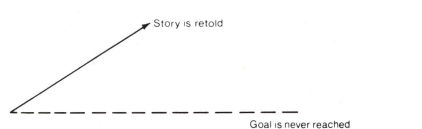

Story is retold

Goal is never reached

How might this paragraph be revised and improved? The best way is to reintroduce the topic again and again throughout the paragraph to keep reminding the reader of the relevance of the exemplifying material. Each time you mention the topic you are bringing yourself back to the line, and this practice should prevail no matter what the topic. If you are analyzing point of view, for example, you should keep pointing out the relevance of your material to the point of view of the work, and the same applies to *character* or whatever aspect of literature you are studying. According to this principle, we might revise the paragraph on "The Adventure of the Speckled Band" as follows, keeping as much of the original wording as we can. (Parts of sentences stressing the relationship of the examples to the topic of the paragraph are underlined.)

It is in the direct examination of the Roylott building, Stoke Moran, that the power of active intelligence is seen to be most practical and effective. In examining the outside of the right wing, where Helen Stoner is temporarily sleeping next to the room of Dr. Roylott, Holmes rules out the threat of forceful entry by the Gypsies. It is clear then, but only in the retrospect of the entire story, that Holmes concludes that the threat is internal, from Roylott himself. The inside examination of Helen's room and then Roylott's room is a discovery of the nature and method of Roylott's threat, or attack. It is clear that the physical details of both rooms—such as the dummy bell rope, the misdirected ventilator, the large iron safe, the saucer of milk, the wooden chair, and the strange dog leash—form the basis of Holmes's intelligent deductions. Once he has formulated his analysis of the danger, he almost instantly devotes his mind to form a plan of protection, action, and discovery. The idea that intelligence can be practically and effectively applied could hardly be more strongly illustrated.

The paragraph has been lengthened and improved. You might object that if all your paragraphs were lengthened in this way your essay would grow too long. The answer to this objection is that *it is better to develop a few topics fully than many scantily*. Such revision might require you to throw away some of your topics or else to incorporate them as subpoints in the topics you keep. This process can only improve your essay. But the result of greater length here is that the exemplifying detail points toward the topic, and the paragraph reaches its goal.

### Insight, Newness, Growth

Another important quality of excellence is making the central idea expand and grow. The word *growth* is a metaphor for development, the creation of new insights, the disclosure of ideas that were not at first noticeable, the expression of new, fresh, and original interpretations.

You might suppose that it is difficult to be original when you are writing about someone else's work. "The author has said everything," you might argue, "and therefore I can do little more than follow the story." This claim assumes that there is no choice whatever in the selection of material for an essay, and no opportunity for individual thoughts and original contributions. However, there is. The author has presented the work to you, and you can, if you look hard, find layer upon layer of meaning. One obvious area where you can exert your power of originality is the development and formulation of the central idea for your essay. For example, a first thought about Edgar Allan Poe's "The Masque of the Red Death" (p. 194) might be that it is about death. Just this topic does not carry you very far, however, and an additional idea might be developed from the idea that people want to escape death. This idea is regrettably not very original either. A more original insight can be provided if the topic is related directly to the bizarre setting of the story. Then a useful central idea might be that "the setting complements Prospero's crazed attempts to control and escape death." With this idea, it is possible to create a fresher, more original essay dealing with the colorful and macabre aspects of the story than one might create with the simple topic "death."

You can also develop your ability to treat your subject freshly and originally if you plan the body of the essay to build up to what you think is your most important, most incisive, and best-conceived idea. The following arrangement of topics illustrates how a central idea may be built up. Let us assume the central idea is "The power of intelligence in Doyle's 'The Adventure of the Speckled Band.'" The following paragraphs are presented not as a finished essay but rather as a set of thoughts in an ascending order of importance to show how the exemplification of a central idea may also allow for originality and growth:

1.    Holmes as a mental power

   Holmes's methods show his great power of observation and deduction. When he first meets Helen Stoner he deduces much about her from her appearance.

His questions to her show that his mind is working, searching for possible answers to the questions raised by her fears. When he goes to her home for an on-the-spot inspection, his investigation is thorough and intelligent. Always his mind is applied to the problem, and he solves the crime early, well before he and Watson begin their evening's vigil.

2.    Holmes as a power for helping individuals

To Helen Stoner, Holmes is a natural source of help. She acknowledges that she is unable to get out of danger by herself, for she cannot identify the forces against her. Holmes therefore represents the power of systematic knowledge when it is applied to the solution of difficult and dangerous problems. He is an agent of investigative action and therefore of improvement on the side of right and justice. For all these reasons, Holmes is a force for optimism and the belief that problems should not crush human beings.

3.    Holmes as a force of security and stability in civilization

Just as Holmes represents the power of applied knowledge, so he represents the hope to achieve civilized security and stability. At the end of the story, Holmes has made all his deductions, has made a plan of action, has defeated Dr. Roylott, and has explained his procedure. All danger is overcome and security is restored. Thus, Holmes is the means by which the world may be improved. All his mental effort is designed to ease fear and to restore security. The character of Sherlock Holmes therefore appeals to basic human desires. He is not simply a clever detective; his character is rooted in the same earth which causes people to pray, to dream, and to work toward a better future.

These examples suggest a thread of development from personal, to social, to cosmic. An essay along this line would attempt to show that Doyle's apparently conventional detective story is actually an embodiment of universal human needs. The topic has definitely grown. Details from the story are included as a part of this developing pattern of growth, and in no way are they introduced simply to retell the story. The pattern shows how two primary standards of excellence in essays—organization and growth—can be met. Without these qualities, there is no totally successful writing, just as there is no successful thinking.

It should be clear that whenever you write, an important goal should be the development of your central idea. You should try to go somewhere with your idea, to give your readers insights that they did not have before they started reading. To the degree that you can learn to develop your ideas, you will receive recognition for increasingly superior writing achievements.

Admittedly, in a short essay you will be able to move only a short distance with an idea, but you should never be satisfied to leave the idea exactly where you found it. Constantly adhere to your topic and constantly develop it. Nurture it and make it grow.

### Using Accurate and Forceful Language

The best writing has a quality of accuracy and force. Quite often the first products of our minds are rather weak, and they need to be rethought, recast, and reworded. Sometimes this process cannot be carried out immediately, for it may take days or even months for us to gain objectivity about what we say. As a student you usually do not have that kind of time, and thus you must acquire the habit of challenging your own statements almost as soon as you write them. Ask yourself whether they really mean what you want, or if you can make a stronger statement than you have.

As an example, consider the following statement, put forward as a central idea about Doyle's "The Adventure of the Speckled Band":

> The central idea in this story is about how Sherlock Holmes solves the mystery of the story.

This statement could not carry anyone very far in the development of an essay, because it promises nothing more than a retelling of the story. It needs further thought. Here are two possible central ideas developed from this sentence that might be more productive bases for an essay:

1.  In the story Doyle embodies the idea that careful observation is a necessary step in the solution of problems.
2.  Doyle makes Holmes's solution of the mystery a tribute to orderly methodology.

Although both these sentences might produce similar essays, the first would probably emphasize the investigative part of the story: the listening, the checking, the close observing. The direction the essay would likely take would be toward the need for getting details right before any accurate conclusions can be drawn. The second sentence points toward an essay that would likely cover Holmes's entire procedure, not just the observing and concluding, but the planning to thwart Dr. Roylott. The second essay, since it includes the word *tribute*, would probably also emphasize all the powers of Holmes as exhibited in the story. In any event, either of the two sentences would be more helpful as a statement of a central idea than the original sentence.

Sometimes, in seeking to say something, we wind up saying nothing.

Consider these two sentences from essays about Eudora Welty's "A Worn Path" (p. 101):

1. The straightforward plot structure of "A Worn Path" shows us the way that the story unfolds during Phoenix's long journey to Natchez.

2. Phoenix Jackson's long and difficult journey is what the story is all about; her conquest of the woods, the barbed-wire fence, the scarecrow, the ditch, and the hunter create a strong response in the reader.

The vagueness and circularity of sentences like these must be avoided. The first begins well, but wanders off into redundancy ("the plot shows us the plot"). It does not come to grips with an idea and it would probably lead the writer into plot summary rather than analysis. It should be revised so that it makes a clear assertion about plot. Such a revision might assert that "the straightforward plot structure of 'A Worn Path' shows us the courage and determination of Phoenix Jackson to overcome the negative forces of age, poverty, and environment." The revision expresses an idea; it would allow the writer to go on and consider specific aspects of the plot.

The second sentence is equally vague and confusing; it hints at ideas and responses, but it does not name them. If we adopt the principle that it is always better to name the specific things we are talking about, perhaps the second sentence might be revised as follows:

Phoenix Jackson's long and difficult journey is a demonstration of courage; her conquest of natural and social opposition, such as the ditch and the hunter, causes us to respect her for her determination, courage, love, and pride.

When you write your own sentences, you might test them in a similar way. Are you referring to an idea? State the idea directly. Are you mentioning a response or impression? Do not say simply, "The story left me with a definite impression," but describe the impression: "The story left me with an impression of sympathy," or "of understanding the hard lot of the migrant farmer." Similarly, do not rest with a statement such as "I found this story interesting," but try to describe what was interesting and why it was interesting. If you always confront your impressions and responses by trying to name them and to pin them down, your sentences should take on exactness and force. Your instructor will probably also tell you whatever you have accomplished or failed to accomplish. Good writing habits that you develop from these criticisms of your work, and from discussions with your instructor, will help you to write more forcefully and accurately.

Whenever you write an essay, then, keep these ideas in mind. Keep returning to the point you wish to make; regard the material of the work you have read as evidence to substantiate your arguments, not as material to be described. Keep demonstrating that all exemplifying detail is relevant to your main point. Keep trying to develop your topic; make it bigger than it was when you began writing. Constantly try to make your statements accurate and forceful. If you observe these precepts, you should be well on the way toward the successful handling of any assignments derived from the chapter discussions and study questions included in this book.

## GAIUS PETRONIUS (d. 66 A.D.)

*The Widow of Ephesus*                                                *(1st Century A.D.)*

From *The Satyricon*, Chs. 108–112
An English version by Edgar V. Roberts

We shook hands and congratulated ourselves, while the entire ship we were riding on rang with our songs and choruses. Seagulls landed on the yard-arms, and the poet Eumolpus, slightly drunk with wine, began cracking some bawdy jokes. He was determined that our cheerfulness should be buoyed up by a few of his stories, so he started attacking the character of women. He told about their lack of resistance in falling in love, and about their negligence, while having an affair, even of their own children. Moreover, he claimed that absolutely no woman he had ever known possessed a high enough moral character to save her from getting involved with a handsome man. He assured us that he was not relying for his claims upon old-fashioned melodramas or the typical women described by historians. He himself had seen what he was talking about, and he offered to tell us a true story if we were willing to hear. All of us on board were eager, and we watched and listened to him attentively. This is how Eumolpus began his tale:

"Once upon a time there lived in the city of Ephesus, on the Coast of Asia Minor, a certain woman whose virtue and faithfulness to her husband were so widely recognized that women from nearby and even distant towns and villages flocked to Ephesus just to get a glimpse of her. Unfortunately, her husband got sick and died, and this lady herself arranged for his funeral and burial. After the service she was not satisfied just with following the cortège in the usual way, with her hair torn and frizzed while she beat her naked breast for all to see. She actually accompanied the dead body right into the mausoleum, and when the coffin had been placed in the vault in the custom of the Greeks, she began a vigil beside it, weeping and wailing constantly both day and night. In fact she was starving herself to death and making herself weaker by the hour, but neither her parents nor her closest relatives could persuade her to come back home. Even the local politicians and judges could not win out against her; she snubbed them, and so, with their dignity ruffled, they gave up trying.

"By this time this most amazing woman was already in the fifth day of her fasting, to the sorrow of everyone in town, who believed that her death would come at any moment. At her side was her faithful handmaiden, who shed as many tears as the mournful Widow did. This maiden took care of the torch in the tomb; she refueled and relit it whenever it showed signs of going out. Through all the city of Ephesus, from one end to another, no one talked about anything else. All the people from the richest to the poorest claimed that the Widow had shown herself to be a supreme, shining example of wifely love and fidelity. They had never seen or heard of anyone like her.

"At this time the provincial governor commanded that a gang of local hoodlums should be executed by being crucified near the mausoleum in which the Widow was standing vigil. On the night of the crucifixion a soldier was stationed there to guard the crosses; his duty was to keep away all friends or relatives who wanted to take down the bodies in order to give them a proper burial. As he stood, he happened to notice a bright light shining from inside one of the tombs, and at the same time he heard the moans of someone in great sorrow.

"Curiosity is a weakness of humankind, and this soldier was typically human. So he went down the stairs into the vault of the Widow and her husband to take a look. Imagine his shock at seeing this pretty woman; at first he was as frightened as if he had seen a ghost, or an apparition out of hell. But he soon saw the corpse of the husband, and when he saw the Widow's tears and her nail-scarred face, he correctly concluded that this woman was in the grips of an insupportable sorrow. Therefore he ran up to his station to get his supper, which he brought down into the sepulchre. He then pleaded with the mourning woman to give up her fruitless sorrow and to stop tearing herself apart with ineffective sobs. 'The same inescapable fate stands waiting for all human beings,' he said, 'the final trip of everyone to the home of the dead.' He racked his brain for the usual words of condolence and consolation which are intended to knit together the broken hearts of those who are bereaved. But the lady, who was upset rather than consoled by these words of this strange man, only tore at her bosom more violently and ripped out some of her hair and threw it on the corpse. The soldier kept making his point with her, however, and repeated his soothing words, while at the same time he tried to tempt her with tasty bits of food. At last the handmaiden, her resistance broken by the aromatic bouquet of the wine, held out her hand and accepted the soldier's generous offer.

"Brought back to life by the wine and the food, she also joined the soldier in his siege against the fortress of her mistress's resolve. She cried out, 'What good can it do anyone if you let yourself starve to death, if you bury yourself alive, or if you speed up the day of your last breath before your time has truly come? Remember what Virgil says:

Do you believe that ashes or buried ghosts can feel?°

My Lady, come back to life, please! Give up this misguided idea of wifely faithfulness and, as long as you are able, enjoy the light of the sun once more. Even the

5

Virgil, *Aeneid*, IV. 34.

body of your dead husband, if it could speak, would advise you to get on with living.'

"Nobody is deaf when told to eat or continue living, and so the Widow, starving after her long days of fast, allowed her resolution to be overcome. She refreshed herself with the food just as greedily as the handmaiden who had surrendered first.

"But everybody knows that one appetite follows another. The soldier soon began wooing the Widow with the same tempting words he had used to bring her back from the brink of starvation. He was a strapping young man, and she was not unaware of his handsome good looks, even though she was as modest as they come. He was also persuasive, and her handmaiden aided him in his suit. This little maiden finally quoted a line by Virgil:

Would you hold out against a pleasure-giving passion?°

"Why make the story last longer? This Widow quickly gave up all resistance,    10
and the young soldier brought her to bed just as he had brought her to eat. So they spent the night together—and not just this first night, but the next night, and the next. Naturally they kept the door of the tomb barred and bolted so that if any people passing by, either strangers or friends, should come near the sepulchre, they would conclude that the ever-faithful wife had died and fallen upon the body of her dead husband. The soldier was enchanted both by the beauty of his new sweetheart and by their secret affair, and out of his small wage he bought a few little nothings for her. As soon as night came he took his presents to the tomb.

"The result of his absence from his post was that the parents of one of the crucified thieves assumed that the close guard had been withdrawn. They saw their chance, took down the body of their son from the cross, and had the final ceremony for the dead performed over it. The soldier was thus tricked because of his own dereliction of duty while enjoying his night of love. The next morning he saw that one corpse was gone, and he fell into a cold sweat at the thought of the punishment he knew would come to him. He told the story to the Widow. He swore that he could not wait for a court-martial and a sentence, but that he would punish himself for his folly by committing suicide on his own sword. He then asked her to set aside a place for his corpse and permit the sepulchre to be the final resting place not only for her husband, but also for him, her lover. The Widow, however, was just as sympathetic as she was virtuous.

" 'No,' she cried, 'heaven forbid that I should be forced by nothing but bad luck to stand vigil at the same time beside the bodies of the only two men in the world that I ever loved. I would rather hang up a dead man on the cross than permit a living man to die.'

"After these words she told him to take her husband's corpse from the vault, carry it to the empty cross, and nail it up. The next day everyone in town was asking how on earth the dead man had been able to climb onto the cross."

Virgil, *Aeneid*, IV. 38.

# QUESTIONS

1. Who tells the story of the widow of Ephesus? What is his attitude toward women? How is his attitude brought out in the story? How is he introduced as the narrator?

2. What virtue is the widow known for? How does she demonstrate this virtue upon her husband's death? How much do you learn about her as a person? What does her abandonment of her intention of self-sacrifice show about her?

3. What kind of person is the soldier? Why do you think he wanted to offer food to the widow and her servant? In what ways does he show both earnestness and fidelity?

4. Consider the widow's plan to substitute the body of her dead husband for that of the dead thief. Does her explanation defending her plan seem acceptable as a genuine expression of her feelings and needs?

5. Should the story be taken as a joke, as it apparently was intended, at the expense of the female protagonist? What values might make it still seem a joke? What values might make it seem more serious than it was originally intended?

6. In light of the misogynistic theme, to what degree are you able to like the story?

7. Consider the locations of the story. How well are they described? Does the location in the tomb help to make the story seem more realistic than it otherwise might seem? How normal does it seem that the crucifixions of the thieves were carried out in public and that the dead thieves were left on open exhibition so that the soldier would need to be posted as a guard?

# SIR ARTHUR CONAN DOYLE (1859–1930)

## The Adventure of the Speckled Band                    *1883*

On glancing over my notes of the seventy odd cases in which I have during the last eight years studied the methods of my friend Sherlock Holmes, I find many tragic, some comic, a large number merely strange, but none commonplace; for, working as he did rather for the love of his art than for the acquirement of wealth, he refused to associate himself with any investigation which did not tend towards the unusual, and even the fantastic. Of all these varied cases, however, I cannot recall any which presented more singular features than that which was associated with the well-known Surrey family of the Roylotts of Stoke Moran. The events in question occurred in the early days of my association with Holmes, when we were sharing rooms as bachelors in Baker Street. It is possible that I might have placed them upon record before, but a promise of secrecy was made at the time, from which I have only been freed during the last month by the untimely death of the lady to whom the pledge was given. It is perhaps as well that the facts should now come to light, for I have reasons to know that there are widespread rumours as to the death of Dr. Grimesby Roylott which tend to make the matter even more terrible than the truth.

It was early in April in the year '83 that I woke one morning to find Sherlock Holmes standing, fully dressed, by the side of my bed. He was a late riser, as a rule, and as the clock on the mantelpiece showed me that it was only a quarter-past seven, I blinked up at him in some surprise, and perhaps just a little resentment, for I was myself regular in my habits.

"Very sorry to knock you up,° Watson," said he, "but it's the common lot this morning. Mrs. Hudson has been knocked up, she retorted upon me, and I on you."

"What is it, then—a fire?"

"No; a client. It seems that a young lady has arrived in a considerable state    5
of excitement, who insists upon seeing me. She is waiting now in the sitting-room. Now, when young ladies wander about the metropolis at this hour of the morning, and knock sleepy people up out of their beds, I presume that it is something very pressing which they have to communicate. Should it prove to be an interesting case, you would, I am sure, wish to follow it from the outset. I thought, at any rate, that I should call you and give you the chance."

"My dear fellow, I would not miss it for anything."

I had no keener pleasure than in following Holmes in his professional investigations, and in admiring the rapid deductions, as swift as intuitions, and yet always founded on a logical basis, with which he unravelled the problems which were submitted to him. I rapidly threw on my clothes and was ready in a few minutes to accompany my friend down to the sitting-room. A lady dressed in black and heavily veiled, who had been sitting in the window, rose as we entered.

"Good-morning, madam," said Holmes cheerily. "My name is Sherlock Holmes. This is my intimate friend and associate, Dr. Watson, before whom you can speak as freely as before myself. Ha! I am glad to see that Mrs. Hudson has had the good sense to light the fire. Pray draw up to it, and I shall order you a cup of hot coffee, for I observe that you are shivering."

"It is not cold which makes me shiver," said the woman in a low voice, changing her seat as requested.

"What, then?"    10

"It is fear, Mr. Holmes. It is terror." She raised her veil as she spoke, and we could see that she was indeed in a pitiable state of agitation, her face all drawn and gray, with restless, frightened eyes, like those of some hunted animal. Her features and figure were those of a woman of thirty, but her hair was shot with premature gray, and her expression was weary and haggard. Sherlock Holmes ran her over with one of his quick, all-comprehensive glances.

"You must not fear," said he soothingly, bending forward and patting her forearm. "We shall soon set matters right, I have no doubt. You have come in by train this morning, I see."

"You know me, then?"

"No, but I observe the second half of a return ticket in the palm of your left glove. You must have started early, and yet you had a good drive in a dog-cart,° along heavy roads, before you reached the station."

*knock you up*: to wake up, a custom whereby a person was designated to make the rounds of a neighborhood and wake people up by knocking at their doors.
*dog-cart*: an open, horse-drawn cart with back-to-back seats.

The lady gave a violent start and stared in bewilderment at my companion.  15

"There is no mystery, my dear madam," said he, smiling. "The left arm of your jacket is spattered with mud in no less than seven places. The marks are perfectly fresh. There is no vehicle save a dog-cart which throws up mud in that way, and then only when you sit on the left-hand side of the driver."

"Whatever your reasons may be, you are perfectly correct," said she. "I started from home before six, reached Leatherhead at twenty past, and came in by the first train to Waterloo.° Sir, I can stand this strain no longer; I shall go mad if it continues. I have no one to turn to—none, save only one, who cares for me, and he, poor fellow, can be of little aid. I have heard of you, Mr. Holmes; I have heard of you from Mrs. Farintosh, whom you helped in the hour of her sore need. It was from her that I had your address. Oh, sir, do you not think that you could help me, too, and at least throw a little light through the dense darkness which surrounds me? At present it is out of my power to reward you for your services, but in a month or six weeks I shall be married, with the control of my own income, and then at least you shall not find me ungrateful."

Holmes turned to his desk and, unlocking it, drew out a small casebook, which he consulted.

"Farintosh," said he. "Ah yes, I recall the case; it was concerned with an opal tiara. I think it was before your time, Watson. I can only say, madam, that I shall be happy to devote the same care to your case as I did to that of your friend. As to reward, my profession is its own reward; but you are at liberty to defray whatever expenses I may be put to, at the time which suits you best. And now I beg that you will lay before us everything that may help us in forming an opinion upon the matter."

"Alas!" replied our visitor, "the very horror of my situation lies in the fact  20 that my fears are so vague, and my suspicions depend so entirely upon small points, which might seem trivial to another, that even he to whom of all others I have a right to look for help and advice looks upon all that I tell him about it as the fancies of a nervous woman. He does not say so, but I can read it from his soothing answers and averted eyes. But I have heard, Mr. Holmes, that you can see deeply into the manifold wickedness of the human heart. You may advise me how to walk amid the dangers which encompass me."

"I am all attention, madam."

"My name is Helen Stoner, and I am living with my stepfather, who is the last survivor of one of the oldest Saxon families in England, the Roylotts of Stoke Moran, on the western border of Surrey."

Holmes nodded his head. "The name is familiar to me," said he.

"The family was at one time among the richest in England, and the estates extended over the borders into Berkshire in the north, and Hampshire in the west. In the last century, however, four successive heirs were of a dissolute and wasteful disposition, and the family ruin was eventually completed by a gambler in the days of the Regency.° Nothing was left save a few acres of ground, and the two-hundred-year-old house, which is itself crushed under a heavy mortgage.

*Waterloo*: Waterloo Station in west London, the station for trains going to western England.

*The Regency*: the period from 1811 to 1820, when George III was declared incompetent and the Prince of Wales, later George IV (1820–1830), ruled as regent.

The last squire dragged out his existence there, living the horrible life of an aristocratic pauper; but his only son, my stepfather, seeing that he must adapt himself to the new conditions, obtained an advance from a relative, which enabled him to take a medical degree and went out to Calcutta, where, by his professional skill and his force of character, he established a large practice. In a fit of anger, however, caused by some robberies which had been perpetrated in the house, he beat his native butler to death and narrowly escaped a capital sentence. As it was, he suffered a long term of imprisonment and afterwards returned to England a morose and disappointed man.

"When Dr. Roylott was in India he married my mother, Mrs. Stoner, the     25
young widow of Major-General Stoner, of the Bengal Artillery. My sister Julia and I were twins, and we were only two years old at the time of my mother's remarriage. She had a considerable sum of money—not less than £1000 a year°— and this she bequeathed to Dr. Roylott entirely while we resided with him, with a provision that a certain annual sum should be allowed to each of us in the event of our marriage. Shortly after our return to England my mother died—she was killed eight years ago in a railway accident near Crewe. Dr. Roylott then abandoned his attempts to establish himself in practice in London and took us to live with him in the old ancestral house at Stoke Moran. The money which my mother had left was enough for all our wants, and there seemed to be no obstacle to our happiness.

"But a terrible change came over our stepfather about this time. Instead of making friends and exchanging visits with our neighbours, who had at first been overjoyed to see a Roylott of Stoke Moran back in the old family seat, he shut himself up in his house and seldom came out save to indulge in ferocious quarrels with whoever might cross his path. Violence of temper approaching to mania has been hereditary in the men of the family, and in my stepfather's case it had, I believe, been intensified by his long residence in the tropics. A series of disgraceful brawls took place, two of which ended in the police-court, until at last he became the terror of the village, and the folks would fly at his approach, for he is a man of immense strength, and absolutely uncontrollable in his anger.

"Last week he hurled the local blacksmith over a parapet into a stream, and it was only by paying over all the money which I could gather together that I was able to avert another public exposure. He had no friends at all save the wandering gypsies, and he would give these vagabonds leave to encamp upon the few acres of bramble-covered land which represent the family estate, and would accept in return the hospitality of their tents, wandering away with them sometimes for weeks on end. He has a passion also for Indian animals, which are sent over to him by a correspondent, and he has at this moment a cheetah and a baboon, which wander freely over his grounds and are feared by the villagers almost as much as their master.

"You can imagine from what I say that my poor sister Julia and I had no great pleasure in our lives. No servant would stay with us, and for a long time we did all the work of the house. She was but thirty at the time of her death, and yet her hair had already begun to whiten, even as mine has."

"Your sister is dead, then?"

"She died just two years ago, and it is of her death that I wish to speak to     30

*£1000*: worth perhaps $100,000.00 or more today.

you. You can understand that, living the life which I have described, we were
little likely to see anyone of our own age and position. We had, however, an aunt,
my mother's maiden sister, Miss Honoria Westphail, who lives near Harrow, and
we were occasionally allowed to pay short visits at this lady's house. Julia went
there at Christmas two years ago, and met there a half-pay major of marines, to
whom she became engaged. My stepfather learned of the engagement when my
sister returned and offered no objection to the marriage; but within a fortnight
of the day which had been fixed for the wedding, the terrible event occurred which
has deprived me of my only companion."

Sherlock Holmes had been leaning back in his chair with his eyes closed
and his head sunk in a cushion, but he half opened his lids now and glanced
across at his visitor.

"Pray be precise as to details," he said.

"It is easy for me to be so, for every event of that dreadful time is seared
into my memory. The manor-house is, as I have already said, very old, and only
one wing is now inhabited. The bedrooms in this wing are on the ground floor,
the sitting-rooms being in the central block of the buildings. Of these bedrooms
the first is Dr. Roylott's, the second my sister's, and the third my own. There is
no communication between them, but they all open out into the same corridor.
Do I make myself plain?"

"Perfectly so."

"The windows of the three rooms open out upon the lawn. That fatal night      35
Dr. Roylott had gone to his room early, though we knew that he had not retired
to rest, for my sister was troubled by the smell of the strong Indian cigars which
it was his custom to smoke. She left her room, therefore, and came into mine,
where she sat for some time, chatting about her approaching wedding. At eleven
o'clock she rose to leave me, but she paused at the door and looked back.

" 'Tell me, Helen,' said she, 'have you ever heard anyone whistle in the
dead of the night?'

" 'Never,' said I.

" 'I suppose that you could not possibly whistle, yourself, in your sleep?'

" 'Certainly not. But why?'

" 'Because during the last few nights I have always, about three in the morning,      40
heard a low, clear whistle. I am a light sleeper, and it has awakened me. I cannot
tell where it came from—perhaps from the next room, perhaps from the lawn. I
thought that I would just ask you whether you had heard it.'

" 'No, I have not. It must be those wretched gypsies in the plantation.'

" 'Very likely. And yet if it were on the lawn, I wonder that you did not
hear it also.'

" 'Ah, but I sleep more heavily than you.'

" 'Well, it is of no great consequence, at any rate.' She smiled back at me,
closed my door, and a few moments later I heard her key turn in the lock."

"Indeed," said Holmes. "Was it your custom always to lock yourselves in      45
at night?"

"Always."

"And why?"

"I think that I mentioned to you that the doctor kept a cheetah and a baboon.
We had no feeling of security unless our doors were locked."

"Quite so. Pray proceed with your statement."

"I could not sleep that night. A vague feeling of impending misfortune im-    50
pressed me. My sister and I, you will recollect, were twins, and you know how
subtle are the links which bind two souls which are so closely allied. It was a
wild night. The wind was howling outside, and the rain was beating and splashing
against the windows. Suddenly, amid all the hubbub of the gale, there burst forth
the wild scream of a terrified woman. I knew that it was my sister's voice. I sprang
from my bed, wrapped a shawl round me, and rushed into the corridor. As I
opened my door I seemed to hear a low whistle, such as my sister described,
and a few moments later a clanging sound, as if a mass of metal had fallen. As I
ran down the passage, my sister's door was unlocked, and revolved slowly upon
its hinges. I stared at it horror-stricken, not knowing what was about to issue
from it. By the light of the corridor-lamp I saw my sister appear at the opening,
her face blanched with terror, her hands groping for help, her whole figure swaying
to and fro like that of a drunkard. I ran to her and threw my arms round her,
but at that moment her knees seemed to give way and she fell to the ground.
She writhed as one who is in terrible pain, and her limbs were dreadfully convulsed.
At first I thought that she had not recognized me, but as I bent over her she
suddenly shrieked out in a voice which I shall never forget, 'Oh, my God! Helen!
It was the band! The speckled band!' There was something else which she would
fain have said, and she stabbed with her finger into the air in the direction of
the doctor's room, but a fresh convulsion seized her and choked her words.
I rushed out, calling loudly for my stepfather, and I met him hastening from
his room in his dressing-gown. When he reached my sister's side she was unconscious, and though he poured brandy down her throat and sent for medical aid
from the village, all efforts were in vain, for she slowly sank and died without
having recovered her consciousness. Such was the dreadful end of my beloved
sister."

"One moment," said Holmes; "are you sure about this whistle and metallic
sound? Could you swear to it?"

"That was what the county coroner asked me at the inquiry. It is my strong
impression that I heard it, and yet, among the crash of the gale and the creaking
of an old house, I may possibly have been deceived."

"Was your sister dressed?"

"No, she was in her night-dress. In her right hand was found the charred
stump of a match, and in her left a match-box."

"Showing that she had struck a light and looked about her when the alarm    55
took place. That is important. And what conclusions did the coroner come to?"

"He investigated the case with great care, for Dr. Roylott's conduct had
long been notorious in the county, but he was unable to find any satisfactory
cause of death. My evidence showed that the door had been fastened upon the
inner side, and the windows were blocked by old-fashioned shutters with broad
iron bars, which were secured every night. The walls were carefully sounded and
were shown to be quite solid all round, and the flooring was also thoroughly examined, with the same result. The chimney is wide, but is barred up by four large
staples. It is certain, therefore, that my sister was quite alone when she met her
end. Besides, there were no marks of any violence upon her."

"How about poison?"

"The doctors examined her for it, but without success."

"What do you think that this unfortunate lady died of, then?"

"It is my belief that she died of pure fear and nervous shock, though what 60
it was that frightened her I cannot imagine."

"Were there gypsies in the plantation at the time?"

"Yes, there are nearly always some there."

"Ah, and what did you gather from this allusion to a band—a speckled band?"

"Sometimes I have thought that it was merely the wild talk of delirium, sometimes that it may have referred to some band of people, perhaps to these very
gypsies in the plantation. I do not know whether the spotted handkerchiefs which
so many of them wear over their heads might have suggested the strange adjective
which she used."

Holmes shook his head like a man who is far from being satisfied. 65

"These are very deep waters," said he; "pray go on with your narrative."

"Two years have passed since then, and my life has been until lately lonelier
than ever. A month ago, however, a dear friend, whom I have known for many
years, has done me the honour to ask my hand in marriage. His name is Armitage—
Percy Armitage—the second son of Mr. Armitage, of Crane Water, near Reading.
My stepfather has offered no opposition to the match, and we are to be married
in the course of the spring. Two days ago some repairs were started in the west
wing of the building, and my bedroom wall has been pierced, so that I have had
to move into the chamber in which my sister died, and to sleep in the very bed
in which she slept. Imagine, then, my thrill of terror when last night, as I lay
awake, thinking over her terrible fate, I suddenly heard in the silence of the night
the low whistle which had been the herald of her own death. I sprang up and lit
the lamp, but nothing was to be seen in the room. I was too shaken to go to
bed again, however, so I dressed, and as soon as it was daylight I slipped down,
got a dog-cart at the Crown Inn, which is opposite, and drove to Leatherhead,
from whence I have come on this morning with the one object of seeing you
and asking your advice."

"You have done wisely," said my friend. "But have you told me all?"

"Yes, all."

"Miss Roylott, you have not. You are screening your stepfather." 70

"Why, what do you mean?"

For answer Holmes pushed back the frill of black lace which fringed the
hand that lay upon our visitor's knee. Five little livid spots, the marks of four
fingers and a thumb, were printed upon the white wrist.

"You have been cruelly used," said Holmes.

The lady coloured deeply and covered over her injured wrist. "He is a hard
man," she said, "and perhaps he hardly knows his own strength."

There was a long silence, during which Holmes leaned his chin upon his 75
hands and stared into the crackling fire.

"This is a very deep business," he said at last. "There are a thousand details
which I should desire to know before I decide upon our course of action. Yet we
have not a moment to lose. If we were to come to Stoke Moran to-day, would it
be possible for us to see over these rooms without the knowledge of your stepfather?"

"As it happens, he spoke of coming into town to-day upon some most important business. It is probable that he will be away all day, and that there would be

nothing to disturb you. We have a housekeeper now, but she is old and foolish, and I could easily get her out of the way."

"Excellent. You are not averse to this trip, Watson?"

"By no means."

"Then we shall both come. What are you going to do yourself?" 80

"I have one or two things which I would wish to do now that I am in town. But I shall return by the twelve o'clock train, so as to be there in time for your coming."

"And you may expect us early in the afternoon. I have myself some small business matters to attend to. Will you not wait and breakfast?"

"No, I must go. My heart is lightened already since I have confided my trouble to you. I shall look forward to seeing you again this afternoon." She dropped her thick black veil over her face and glided from the room.

"And what do you think of it all, Watson?" asked Sherlock Holmes, leaning back in his chair.

"It seems to me to be a most dark and sinister business." 85

"Dark enough and sinister enough."

"Yet if the lady is correct in saying that the flooring and walls are sound, and that the door, window, and chimney are impassable, then her sister must have been undoubtedly alone when she met her mysterious end."

"What becomes, then, of these nocturnal whistles, and what of the very peculiar words of the dying woman?"

"I cannot think."

"When you combine the ideas of whistles at night, the presence of a band 90 of gypsies who are on intimate terms with this old doctor, the fact that we have every reason to believe that the doctor has an interest in preventing his stepdaughter's marriage, the dying allusion to a band, and, finally, the fact that Miss Helen Stoner heard a metallic clang, which might have been caused by one of those metal bars that secured the shutters falling back into its place, I think that there is good ground to think that the mystery may be cleared along those lines."

"But what, then, did the gypsies do?"

"I cannot imagine."

"I see many objections to any such theory."

"And so do I. It is precisely for that reason that we are going to Stoke Moran this day. I want to see whether the objections are fatal, or if they may be explained away. But what in the name of the devil!"

The ejaculation had been drawn from my companion by the fact that our 95 door had been suddenly dashed open, and that a huge man had framed himself in the aperture. His costume was a peculiar mixture of the professional and of the agricultural, having a black tophat, a long frock-coat, and a pair of high gaiters,° with a hunting-crop swinging in his hand. So tall was he that his hat actually brushed the cross bar of the doorway, and his breadth seemed to span it across from side to side. A large face, seared with a thousand wrinkles, burned yellow with the sun, and marked with every evil passion, was turned from one to the other of us, while his deep-set, bile-shot eyes, and his high, thin, fleshless nose, gave him somewhat the resemblance to a fierce old bird of prey.

*gaiters*: leggings.

"Which of you is Holmes?" asked this apparition.

"My name, sir; but you have the advantage of me," said my companion quietly.

"I am Dr. Grimesby Roylott, of Stoke Moran."

"Indeed, Doctor," said Holmes blandly. "Pray take a seat."

"I will do nothing of the kind. My stepdaughter has been here. I have traced    100
her. What has she been saying to you?"

"It is a little cold for the time of the year," said Holmes.

"What has she been saying to you?" screamed the old man furiously.

"But I have heard that the crocuses promise well," continued my companion
imperturbably.

"Ha! You put me off, do you?" said our new visitor, taking a step forward
and shaking his hunting-crop. "I know you, you scoundrel! I have heard of you
before. You are Holmes, the meddler."

My friend smiled.    105

"Holmes, the busybody!"

His smile broadened.

"Holmes, the Scotland Yard Jack-in-office!"

Holmes chuckled heartily. "Your conversation is most entertaining," said
he. "When you go out close the door, for there is a decided draught."

"I will go when I have said my say. Don't you dare to meddle with my affairs.    110
I know that Miss Stoner has been here. I traced her! I am a dangerous man to
fall foul of! See here." He stepped swiftly forward, seized the poker, and bent it
into a curve with his huge brown hands.

"See that you keep yourself out of my grip," he snarled, and hurling the
twisted poker into the fireplace he strode out of the room.

"He seems a very amiable person," said Holmes, laughing. "I am not quite
so bulky, but if he had remained I might have shown him that my grip was not
much more feeble than his own." As he spoke he picked up the steel poker and,
with a sudden effort, straightened it out again.

"Fancy his having the insolence to confound me with the official detective
force! This incident gives zest to our investigation, however, and I only trust that
our little friend will not suffer from her imprudence in allowing this brute to trace
her. And now, Watson, we shall order breakfast, and afterwards I shall walk down
to Doctors' Commons,° where I hope to get some data which may help us in
this matter."

It was nearly one o'clock when Sherlock Holmes returned from his excursion.
He held in his hand a sheet of blue paper, scrawled over with notes and figures.

"I have seen the will of the deceased wife," said he. "To determine its exact    115
meaning I have been obliged to work out the present prices of the investments
with which it is concerned. The total income, which at the time of the wife's death
was little short of £1100, is now, through the fall in agricultural prices, not more
than £750. Each daughter can claim an income of £250, in case of marriage. It is
evident, therefore, that if both girls had married, this beauty would have had a
mere pittance, while even one of them would cripple him to a very serious extent.

*Doctors' Commons*: the place in London where records of wills and other deeds were
kept in official storage.

My morning's work has not been wasted, since it has proved that he has the very strongest motives for standing in the way of anything of the sort. And now, Watson, this is too serious for dawdling, especially as the old man is aware that we are interesting ourselves in his affairs; so if you are ready, we shall call a cab and drive to Waterloo. I should be very much obliged if you would slip your revolver into your pocket. An Eley's No. 2° is an excellent argument with gentlemen who can twist steel pokers into knots. That and a tooth-brush are, I think, all that we need."

At Waterloo we were fortunate in catching a train for Leatherhead, where we hired a trap° at the station inn and drove for four or five miles through the lovely Surrey lanes. It was a perfect day, with a bright sun and a few fleecy clouds in the heavens. The trees and wayside hedges were just throwing out their first green shoots, and the air was full of the pleasant smell of the moist earth. To me at least there was a strange contrast between the sweet promise of the spring and this sinister quest upon which we were engaged. My companion sat in the front of the trap, his arms folded, his hat pulled down over his eyes, and his chin sunk upon his breast, buried in the deepest thought. Suddenly, however, he started, tapped me on the shoulder, and pointed over the meadows.

"Look there!" said he.

A heavily timbered park stretched up in a gentle slope, thickening into a grove at the highest point. From amid the branches there jutted out the gray gables and high roof-tree of a very old mansion.

"Stoke Moran?" said he.

"Yes, sir, that be the house of Dr. Grimesby Roylott," remarked the driver.    120

"There is some building going on there," said Holmes; "that is where we are going."

"There's the village," said the driver, pointing to a cluster of roofs some distance to the left; "but if you want to get to the house, you'll find it shorter to get over this stile, and so by the foot-path over the fields. There it is, where the lady is walking."

"And the lady, I fancy, is Miss Stoner," observed Holmes, shading his eyes. "Yes, I think we had better do as you suggest."

We got off, paid our fare, and the trap rattled back on its way to Leatherhead.

"I thought it as well," said Holmes as we climbed the stile, "that this fellow    125 should think we had come here as architects, or on some definite business. It may stop his gossip. Good-afternoon, Miss Stoner. You see that we have been as good as our word."

Our client of the morning had hurried forward to meet us with a face which spoke her joy. "I have been waiting so eagerly for you," she cried, shaking hands with us warmly. "All has turned out splendidly. Dr. Roylott has gone to town, and it is unlikely that he will be back before evening."

"We have had the pleasure of making the doctor's acquaintance," said Holmes, and in a few words he sketched out what had occurred. Miss Stoner turned white to the lips as she listened.

"Good heavens!" she cried, "he has followed me, then."

*Eley's No. 2*: a handgun.
*trap*: a small horse-drawn coach.

"So it appears."

"He is so cunning that I never know when I am safe from him. What will 130
he say when he returns?"

"He must guard himself, for he may find that there is someone more cunning
than himself upon his track. You must lock yourself up from him to-night. If he
is violent, we shall take you away to your aunt's at Harrow. Now, we must make
the best use of our time, so kindly take us at once to the rooms which we are to
examine."

The building was of gray, lichen-blotched stone, with a high central portion
and two curving wings, like the claws of a crab, thrown out on each side. In one
of these wings the windows were broken and blocked with wooden boards, while
the roof was partly caved in, a picture of ruin. The central portion was in little
better repair, but the right-hand block was comparatively modern, and the blinds
in the windows, with the blue smoke curling up from the chimneys, showed that
this was where the family resided. Some scaffolding had been erected against the
end wall, and the stone-work had been broken into, but there were no signs of
any workmen at the moment of our visit. Holmes walked slowly up and down
the ill-trimmed lawn and examined with deep attention the outsides of the windows.

"This, I take it, belongs to the room in which you used to sleep, the centre
one to your sister's, and the one next to the main building to Dr. Roylott's chamber?"

"Exactly so. But I am now sleeping in the middle one."

"Pending the alterations, as I understand. By the way, there does not seem 135
to be any very pressing need for repairs at that end wall."

"There were none. I believe that it was an excuse to move me from my
room."

"Ah! that is suggestive. Now, on the other side of this narrow wing runs
the corridor from which these three rooms open. There are windows in it, of
course?"

"Yes, but very small ones. Too narrow for anyone to pass through."

"As you both locked your doors at night, your rooms were unapproachable
from that side. Now, would you have the kindness to go into your room and bar
your shutters?"

Miss Stoner did so, and Holmes, after a careful examination through the 140
open window, endeavoured in every way to force the shutter open, but without
success. There was no slit through which a knife could be passed to raise the
bar. Then with his lens he tested the hinges, but they were of solid iron, built
firmly into the massive masonry. "Hum!" said he, scratching his chin in some
perplexity, "my theory certainly presents some difficulties. No one could pass these
shutters if they were bolted. Well, we shall see if the inside throws any light upon
the matter."

A small side door led into the whitewashed corridor from which the three
bedrooms opened. Holmes refused to examine the third chamber, so we passed
at once to the second, that in which Miss Stoner was now sleeping, and in which
her sister had met with her fate. It was a homely little room, with a low ceiling
and a gaping fireplace, after the fashion of old country-houses. A brown chest of
drawers stood in one corner, a narrow white-counterpaned bed in another, and a
dressing-table on the left-hand side of the window. These articles, with two small

wicker-work chairs, made up all the furniture in the room save for a square of Wilton carpet in the centre. The boards round and the panelling of the walls were of brown, worm-eaten oak, so old and discoloured that it may have dated from the original building of the house. Holmes drew one of the chairs into a corner and sat silent, while his eyes travelled round and round and up and down, taking in every detail of the apartment.

"Where does that bell communicate with?" he asked at last, pointing to a thick bell-rope° which hung down beside the bed, the tassel actually lying upon the pillow.

"It goes to the housekeeper's room."

"It looks newer than the other things?"

"Yes, it was only put there a couple of years ago."                                                145

"Your sister asked for it, I suppose?"

"No, I never heard of her using it. We used always to get what we wanted for ourselves."

"Indeed, it seemed unnecessary to put so nice a bell-pull there. You will excuse me for a few minutes while I satisfy myself as to this floor." He threw himself down upon his face with his lens in his hand and crawled swiftly backward and forward, examining minutely the cracks between the boards. Then he did the same with the wood-work with which the chamber was panelled. Finally he walked over to the bed and spent some time in staring at it and in running his eye up and down the wall. Finally he took the bell-rope in his hand and gave it a brisk tug.

"Why, it's a dummy," said he.

"Won't it ring?"                                                                                   150

"No, it is not even attached to a wire. This is very interesting. You can see now that it is fastened to a hook just above where the little opening for the ventilator is."

"How very absurd! I never noticed that before."

"Very strange!" muttered Holmes, pulling at the rope. "There are one or two very singular points about this room. For example, what a fool a builder must be to open a ventilator into another room, when, with the same trouble, he might have communicated with the outside air!"

"That is also quite modern," said the lady.

"Done about the same time as the bell-rope?" remarked Holmes.                                       155

"Yes, there were several little changes carried out about that time."

"They seem to have been of a most interesting character—dummy bell-ropes, and ventilators which do not ventilate. With your permission, Miss Stoner, we shall now carry our researches into the inner apartment."

Dr. Grimesby Roylott's chamber was larger than that of his stepdaughter, but was as plainly furnished. A camp-bed, a small wooden shelf full of books, mostly of a technical character, an armchair beside the bed, a plain wooden chair against the wall, a round table, and a large iron safe were the principal things which met the eye. Holmes walked slowly round and examined each and all of them with the keenest interest.

"What's in here?" he asked, tapping the safe.

---

*bell rope*: a rope attached to a bell in the quarters of a servant so that the master or mistress could use it as a demand for instant service.

"My stepfather's business papers."

"Oh! you have seen inside, then?"

"Only once, some years ago. I remember that it was full of papers."

"There isn't a cat in it, for example?"

"No. What a strange idea!"

"Well, look at this!" He took up a small saucer of milk which stood on the top of it.

"No; we don't keep a cat. But there is a cheetah and a baboon."

"Ah, yes, of course! Well, a cheetah is just a big cat, and yet a saucer of milk does not go very far in satisfying its wants, I daresay. There is one point which I should wish to determine." He squatted down in front of the wooden chair and examined the seat of it with the greatest attention.

"Thank you. That is quite settled," said he, rising and putting his lens in his pocket. "Hello! Here is something interesting!"

The object which had caught his eye was a small dog lash° hung on one corner of the bed. The lash, however, was curled upon itself and tied so as to make a loop of whipcord.

"What do you make of that, Watson?"

"It's a common enough lash. But I don't know why it should be tied."

"That is not quite so common, is it? Ah, me! it's a wicked world, and when a clever man turns his brains to crime it is the worst of all. I think that I have seen enough now, Miss Stoner, and with your permission we shall walk out upon the lawn."

I had never seen my friend's face so grim or his brow so dark as it was when we turned from the scene of this investigation. We had walked several times up and down the lawn, neither Miss Stoner nor myself liking to break in upon his thoughts before he roused himself from his reverie.

"It is very essential, Miss Stoner," said he, "that you should absolutely follow my advice in every respect."

"I shall most certainly do so."

"The matter is too serious for any hesitation. Your life may depend upon your compliance."

"I assure you that I am in your hands."

"In the first place, both my friend and I must spend the night in your room."

Both Miss Stoner and I gazed at him in astonishment.

"Yes, it must be so. Let me explain. I believe that that is the village inn over there?"

"Yes, that is the Crown."

"Very good. Your windows would be visible from there?"

"Certainly."

"You must confine yourself to your room, on pretence of a headache, when your stepfather comes back. Then when you hear him retire for the night, you must open the shutters of your window, undo the hasp, put your lamp there as a signal to us, and then withdraw quietly with everything which you are likely to want into the room which you used to occupy. I have no doubt that, in spite of the repairs, you could manage there for one night."

"Oh, yes, easily."

*lash*: leash

"The rest you will leave in our hands."

"But what will you do?"

"We shall spend the night in your room, and we shall investigate the cause of this noise which has disturbed you."

"I believe, Mr. Holmes, that you have already made up your mind," said Miss Stoner, laying her hand upon my companion's sleeve.

"Perhaps I have."                                                                                    190

"Then, for pity's sake, tell me what was the cause of my sister's death."

"I should prefer to have clearer proofs before I speak."

"You can at least tell me whether my own thought is correct, and if she died from some sudden fright."

"No, I do not think so. I think that there was probably some more tangible cause. And now, Miss Stoner, we must leave you, for if Dr. Roylott returned and saw us our journey would be in vain. Good-bye, and be brave, for if you will do what I have told you you may rest assured that we shall soon drive away the dangers that threaten you."

Sherlock Holmes and I had no difficulty in engaging a bedroom and sitting-     195
room at the Crown Inn. They were on the upper floor, and from our window we could command a view of the avenue gate, and of the inhabited wing of Stoke Moran Manor House. At dusk we saw Dr. Grimesby Roylott drive past, his huge form looming up beside the little figure of the lad who drove him. The boy had some slight difficulty in undoing the heavy iron gates, and we heard the hoarse roar of the doctor's voice and saw the fury with which he shook his clinched fists at him. The trap drove on, and a few minutes later we saw a sudden light spring up among the trees as the lamp was lit in one of the sitting-rooms.

"Do you know, Watson," said Holmes as we sat together in the gathering darkness, "I have really some scruples as to taking you to-night. There is a distinct element of danger."

"Can I be of assistance?"

"Your presence might be invaluable."

"Then I shall certainly come."

"It is very kind of you."                                                                           200

"You speak of danger. You have evidently seen more in these rooms than was visible to me."

"No, but I fancy that I may have deduced a little more. I imagine that you saw all that I did."

"I saw nothing remarkable save the bell-rope, and what purpose that could answer I confess is more than I imagine."

"You saw the ventilator, too?"

"Yes, but I do not think that it is such a very unusual thing to have a small      205
opening between two rooms. It was so small that a rat could hardly pass through."

"I knew that we should find a ventilator before ever we came to Stoke Moran."

"My dear Holmes!"

"Oh, yes, I did. You remember in her statement she said that her sister could smell Dr. Roylott's cigar. Now, of course that suggested at once that there must be a communication between the two rooms. It could only be a small one, or it would have been remarked upon at the coroner's inquiry. I deduced a ventilator."

"But what harm can there be in that?"

"Well, there is at least a curious coincidence of dates. A ventilator is made, a cord is hung, and a lady who sleeps in the bed dies. Does not that strike you?" 210

"I cannot as yet see any connection."

"Did you observe anything very peculiar about that bed?"

"No."

"It was clamped to the floor. Did you ever see a bed fastened like that before?"

"I cannot say that I have." 215

"The lady could not move her bed. It must always be in the same relative position to the ventilator and to the rope—or so we may call it, since it was clearly never meant for a bell-pull."

"Holmes," I cried, "I seem to see dimly what you are hinting at. We are only just in time to prevent some subtle and horrible crime."

"Subtle enough and horrible enough. When a doctor does go wrong he is the first of criminals. He has nerve and he has knowledge. Palmer and Pritchard were among the heads of their profession.° This man strikes even deeper, but I think, Watson, that we shall be able to strike deeper still. But we shall have horrors enough before the night is over; for goodness' sake let us have a quiet pipe and turn our minds for a few hours to something more cheerful."

About nine o'clock the light among the trees was extinguished, and all was dark in the direction of the Manor House. Two hours passed slowly away, and then, suddenly, just at the stroke of eleven, a single bright light shone out right in front of us.

"That is our signal," said Holmes, springing to his feet; "it comes from the middle window." 220

As we passed out he exchanged a few words with the landlord, explaining that we were going on a late visit to an acquaintance, and that it was possible that we might spend the night there. A moment later we were out on the dark road, a chill wind blowing in our faces, and one yellow light twinkling in front of us through the gloom to guide us on our sombre errand.

There was little difficulty in entering the grounds, for unrepaired breaches gaped in the old park wall. Making our way among the trees, we reached the lawn, crossed it, and were about to enter through the window when out from a clump of laurel bushes there darted what seemed to be a hideous and distorted child, who threw itself upon the grass with writhing limbs and then ran swiftly across the lawn into the darkness.

"My God!" I whispered; "did you see it?"

Holmes was for the moment as startled as I. His hand closed like a vise upon my wrist in his agitation. Then he broke into a low laugh and put his lips to my ear.

"It is a nice household," he murmured. "That is the baboon." 225

I had forgotten the strange pets which the doctor affected. There was a cheetah, too; perhaps we might find it upon our shoulders at any moment. I confess that I felt easier in my mind when, after following Holmes's example and slipping off my shoes, I found myself inside the bedroom. My companion noiselessly closed the shutters, moved the lamp onto the table, and cast his eyes round the room.

*Palmer and Pritchard*: Both were doctors and notorious murderers; both poisoned their wives. Additionally, Palmer (executed 1856) poisoned his brother and also a friend, and Pritchard (executed 1865) poisoned his mother-in-law.

All was as we had seen it in the daytime. Then creeping up to me and making a trumpet of his hand, he whispered into my ear again so gently that it was all that I could do to distinguish the words:

"The least sound would be fatal to our plans."

I nodded to show that I had heard.

"We must sit without light. He would see it through the ventilator."

I nodded again.                                                                                                230

"Do not go asleep; your very life may depend upon it. Have your pistol ready in case we should need it. I will sit on the side of the bed, and you in that chair."

I took out my revolver and laid it on the corner of the table.

Holmes had brought up a long thin cane, and this he placed upon the bed beside him. By it he laid the box of matches and the stump of a candle. Then he turned down the lamp, and we were left in darkness.

How shall I ever forget that dreadful vigil? I could not hear a sound, not even the drawing of a breath, and yet I knew that my companion sat open-eyed, within a few feet of me, in the same state of nervous tension in which I was myself. The shutters cut off the least ray of light, and we waited in absolute darkness. From outside came the occasional cry of a night-bird, and once at our very window a long drawn catlike whine, which told us that the cheetah was indeed at liberty. Far away we could hear the deep tones of the parish clock, which boomed out every quarter of an hour. How long they seemed, those quarters! Twelve struck, and one and two and three, and still we sat waiting silently for whatever might befall.

Suddenly there was the momentary gleam of a light up in the direction of       235
the ventilator, which vanished immediately, but was succeeded by a strong smell of burning oil and heated metal. Someone in the next room had lit a dark-lantern. I heard a gentle sound of movement, and then all was silent once more, though the smell grew stronger. For half an hour I sat with straining ears. Then suddenly another sound became audible—a very gentle, soothing sound, like that of a small jet of steam escaping continually from a kettle. The instant that we heard it, Holmes sprang from the bed, struck a match, and lashed furiously with his cane at the bell-pull.

"You see it, Watson?" he yelled. "You see it?"

But I saw nothing. At the moment when Holmes struck the light I heard a low, clear whistle, but the sudden glare flashing into my weary eyes made it impossible for me to tell what it was at which my friend lashed so savagely. I could, however, see that his face was deadly pale and filled with horror and loathing.

He had ceased to strike and was gazing up at the ventilator when suddenly there broke from the silence of the night the most horrible cry to which I have ever listened. It swelled up louder and louder, a hoarse yell of pain and fear and anger all mingled in the one dreadful shriek. They say that away down in the village, and even in the distant parsonage, that cry raised the sleepers from their beds. It struck cold to our hearts, and I stood gazing at Holmes, and he at me, until the last echoes of it had died away into the silence from which it rose.

"What can it mean?" I gasped.

"It means that it is all over," Holmes answered. "And perhaps, after all, it       240
is for the best. Take your pistol, and we will enter Dr. Roylott's room."

With a grave face he lit the lamp and led the way down the corridor. Twice he struck at the chamber door without any reply from within. Then he turned the handle and entered, I at his heels, with the cocked pistol in my hand.

It was a singular sight which met our eyes. On the table stood a dark-lantern with the shutter half open, throwing a brilliant beam of light upon the iron safe, the door of which was ajar. Beside this table, on the wooden chair, sat Dr. Grimesby Roylott, clad in a long gray dressing-gown, his bare ankles protruding beneath, and his feet thrust into red heelless Turkish slippers. Across his lap lay the short stock with the long lash which we had noticed during the day. His chin was cocked upward and his eyes were fixed in a dreadful, rigid stare at the corner of the ceiling. Round his brow he had a peculiar yellow band, with brownish speckles, which seemed to be bound tightly round his head. As we entered he made neither sound nor motion.

"The band! the speckled band!" whispered Holmes.

I took a step forward. In an instant his strange headgear began to move, and there reared itself from among his hair the squat diamond-shaped head and puffed neck of a loathsome serpent.

"It is a swamp adder!" cried Holmes; "the deadliest snake in India. He has died within ten seconds of being bitten. Violence does, in truth, recoil upon the violent, and the schemer falls into the pit which he digs for another. Let us thrust this creature back into its den, and we can then remove Miss Stoner to some place of shelter and let the county police know what has happened."

245

As he spoke he drew the dog-whip swiftly from the dead man's lap, and throwing the noose round the reptile's neck he drew it from its horrid perch and, carrying it at arm's length, threw it into the iron safe, which he closed upon it.

Such are the true facts of the death of Dr. Grimesby Roylott, of Stoke Moran. It is not necessary that I should prolong a narrative which has already run to too great a length by telling how we broke the sad news to the terrified girl, how we conveyed her by the morning train to the care of her good aunt at Harrow, of how the slow process of official inquiry came to the conclusion that the doctor met his fate while discreetly playing with a dangerous pet. The little which I had yet to learn of the case was told me by Sherlock Holmes as we travelled back next day.

"I had," said he, "come to an entirely erroneous conclusion which shows, my dear Watson, how dangerous it always is to reason from insufficient data. The presence of the gypsies, and the use of the word 'band,' which was used by the poor girl, no doubt to explain the appearance which she had caught a hurried glimpse of by the light of her match, were sufficient to put me upon an entirely wrong scent. I can only claim the merit that I instantly reconsidered my position when, however, it became clear to me that whatever danger threatened an occupant of the room could not come either from the window or the door. My attention was speedily drawn, as I have already remarked to you, to this ventilator, and to the bell-rope which hung down to the bed. The discovery that this was a dummy, and that the bed was clamped to the floor, instantly gave rise to the suspicion that the rope was there as bridge for something passing through the hole and coming to the bed. The idea of a snake instantly occurred to me, and when I coupled it with my knowledge that the doctor was furnished with a supply of creatures from India, I felt that I was probably on the right track. The idea of using a form of poison which could not possibly be discovered by any chemical test was just such a one as would occur to a clever and ruthless man who had had an Eastern training. The rapidity with which such a poison would take effect would also, from his point of view, be an advantage. It would be a sharp-eyed coroner, indeed, who could distinguish the two little dark punctures which would show where the poison fangs had done their work. Then I thought of the whistle. Of course he must recall the snake before the morning light revealed it to the victim. He had trained it, probably by the use of the milk which we saw, to return to him when summoned. He would put it through this ventilator at the hour that he thought best, with the certainty that it would crawl down the rope and land on the bed. It might or might not bite the occupant, perhaps she might escape every night for a week, but sooner or later she must fall a victim.

"I had come to these conclusions before ever I had entered his room. An inspection of his chair showed me this: he had been in the habit of standing on it, which of course would be necessary in order that he should reach the ventilator. The sight of the safe, the saucer of milk, and the loop of whipcord were enough to finally dispel any doubts which may have remained. The metallic clang heard by Miss Stoner was obviously caused by her stepfather hastily closing the door of his safe upon its terrible occupant. Having once made up my mind, you know the steps which I took in order to put the matter to the proof. I heard the creature hiss as I have no doubt that you did also, and I instantly lit the light and attacked it."

"With the result of driving it through the ventilator."                                   250

"And also with the result of causing it to turn upon its master at the other side. Some of the blows of my cane came home and roused its snakish temper, so that it flew upon the first person it saw. In this way I am no doubt indirectly responsible for Dr. Grimesby Roylott's death, and I cannot say that it is likely to weigh very heavily upon my conscience."

## QUESTIONS

1. Who tells us the story of "The Adventure of the Speckled Band"? Doyle? Doctor Watson? Sherlock Holmes? Who is the "I" in the first sentence?

2. What do the first four or five paragraphs of the story tell us about the relationship between Watson and Holmes? How well do they know each other? What sort of regard do they have for each other? Why does Watson admire Holmes?

3. How does Watson get drawn into the case? What qualities does he have as a storyteller? Could the story be effectively told if, for example, Sherlock Holmes himself had been the teller? What can Watson say that Holmes could not say?

4. What does the discussion about the ticket and the mud indicate about Holmes's ability as an observer? Why do you think that Doyle includes the discussion as early in the story as he does?

5. According to Helen Stoner, what sort of person is Dr. Roylott? What sort of reputation does he have locally? How does he impress Holmes when he comes in? Has he been kind or cruel to Helen?

6. Why is the detail important about the impending marriages of, first, Julia and, second, Helen?

7. Why are the references to the nearby gypsies introduced?

8. Describe Holmes's method as an investigator. At what point do you think he concludes that Roylott is the murderer?

9. Describe Holmes's plan to foil Roylott. How do you learn about it?

10. Is the story more about the mystery or about Holmes? Is Holmes only a one-dimensional person, or do you learn more about his character as the story progresses?

11. Do you like this story? Try to explain reasons for either liking or disliking it.

## RESPONDING TO FICTION: LIKES AND DISLIKES

As we read short stories, we respond to them emotionally as well as intellectually, and we should be able to describe our responses. Reduced to their simplest form, these emotional responses take the form of pleasure or pain: we like or we dislike a specific piece of literature. There are, of course, many different levels and expressions of approval or disapproval; we might like one work very much indeed, be unmoved by another, and be thoroughly repulsed by a third. These are first reactions; they do not really convey much information about the story itself. In expressing likes or dislikes, we should seek to present responses that are *informed* and *informative* rather than *uninformed* and *unexplained*.

Sometimes the first response that readers express about a work of fiction is that it is "boring." This reaction is often simply a mask to cover an incomplete and superficial first reading of a work; it is neither informative nor informed. As you study most stories, however, you will discover that you will invariably get drawn into them. One word that describes this process is *interest*—literally, to be in it, inside it; that is, to be taken right into the work emotionally. Another word is *involvement*, referring to having one's emotions become almost rolled into the story, to get taken up by the characters, problems, and outcomes. Sometimes both of these words are used defensively, just like the word *boring*; it is easy to say that something you read was "interesting" or that you got "involved" in it, and you might say these things with a hope that no one will ask you what you mean. Both interest and involvement do describe genuine responses to reading, however. Once you become interested, your reading becomes less of a task than a pleasure, and, although you may undertake some assignments rather grudgingly because of the time and effort they may take, your deepening study will start to become its own reward.

Often you can equate your interest in a work with liking it. You can carry the specifics of liking further, however, by considering some of the following as reasons for your favorable responses:

You like and admire the characters and approve of what they do and stand for.

You learn more about topics that are important to you.

You learn something you had never known or thought before.

You gain new insights into things you had already known.

You learn about characters from different ways of life.

You are involved and interested in the outcome of the action or ideas and do not want to put the story down until you have finished it.

You feel happy because of reading the story.

You are amused and laugh often as you read.

You like the presentation.

You find that some of the ideas and expressions are beautiful and worth remembering.

Obviously, if you find none of these things in the work, or find something that is distasteful, you will not like the work.

### Keeping a Notebook for First Responses

Of course no one can tell you what you should or should not like; liking is your own concern. In any consideration of your responses, therefore, you should begin by keeping a notebook record of your thoughts immediately after finishing a work, or even while you are reading it. Be absolutely frank in your opinion. Write down your likes and dislikes, and try to explain the reasons for your response, even if these are not completely thought through. If later you change or modify your first impressions with more thought and fuller understanding, record these changes too. Here is such a notebook entry about Doyle's "The Adventure of the Speckled Band."

> I liked "The Speckled Band" because of the way Sherlock Holmes took charge to solve the mystery. He began by knowing nothing about what was happening to Helen Stoner, but he used the record office (the Doctors' Commons) and also the observations of the house, inside and outside, to learn. And learn he does. It was this example of his going from zero to a hundred that impressed me. By knowing what to do, he mastered the situation.

This paragraph could easily be expanded with further study and discussion. The virtue of it is that it is a clear statement of the student's liking, followed by the major reasons for this response. This pattern, which might best be phrased as "I like [dislike] this work because . . . ," can be quite helpful in your notebook entries.

The challenge in considering positive or negative reactions to literature is that you must eventually consider some of the "because" areas more fully. For this reason it is important to pinpoint some of the specific things you like or dislike while your informed first impressions are still fresh. If you cannot come up with full sentences detailing the causes of your responses, at least make a brief list of those things that you like or dislike. If you write nothing, you will likely forget your responses, and recovering them later, when you will need them for discussion or writing, will be difficult.

### What Do You Do with Dislikes?

Although so far we have dismissed *boring* and stressed *interest, involvement*, and *liking*, it is important to know that disliking an entire work, or something in it, is normal and acceptable. You do not need to hide this response. Here, for example, are three short notebook responses expressing dislike for the tale by Petronius, "The Widow of Ephesus" (p. 28).

1.  I didn't like "The Widow of Ephesus" because the widow seemed hypocritical and too quickly accepted the first man, the soldier, who came along.

2.  "The Widow of Ephesus" is not exciting like Doyle's "The Adventure of the Speckled Band," and I like reading only exciting mystery or adventure stories.

3.  I found "The Widow of Ephesus" distasteful because it is sexist and prejudiced. It began with a false generalization about women and then went on to "prove" it with a single example.

These are all legitimate responses because they are based on a clearly expressed standard of judgment. The first stems from a distaste for an unlikable trait shown by the main character; the second, from a preference for mystery or adventure stories, which contain rapid action to evoke interest in the dangers faced and overcome by main characters; the third, from the offense taken to the sexist tone of the work and from a criticism of its faulty logic.

Here is a notebook-type entry that might be developed from the first response. What is important is that the reasons for dislike are explained. They would need only slightly more development to be expressed later in classroom discussion or in an essay form.

> I do not like "The Widow of Ephesus" because the widow seems hypocritical. She too quickly accepts the first man, the soldier, who comes along. Even though she is shown as faithful to her husband, she is faithful only to a point. She seems concerned with nothing but outward show to impress the townspeople around her, and therefore she goes right into the tomb with her dead husband because that is the showy thing to do. Once she is there, and no one can see what is going on, she becomes the mistress of the soldier. Some fidelity. She is so hypocritical that she even suggests putting

her husband's body on the cross to cover up the soldier's neglect of his guard duty. I don't like this sudden shift in loyalty and don't like the story because of it.

Thus, if you list your reasons for dislike right away, you can later study and consider them further. You might even change your mind. However, it is better to record your honest responses of dislike than to force yourself into a position of liking which you do not hold.

### Putting Dislikes into a Larger Context

Even though one can honestly dislike a given work, one should try to expand one's taste. For example, the dislike for "The Widow of Ephesus" based on a preference for mystery or adventure stories could cause a person to dislike most works of literature.

If a person can put negative responses into a larger context, it is possible to expand his or her likes in line with very personal responses. A woman might be deeply involved in personal concerns and therefore be uninterested in seemingly remote literary figures. However, if by reading about literary characters she can gain insight into general problems of life, and therefore her own concerns, she might find something to like in just about any work of literature. A man might like sports events and therefore not care for reading anything but sports magazines. But what interests him in sports might be the competition. If he can find competition, or conflict, in a work of literature, he might come to appreciate that work. The principle here is that already established reasons for liking something may be stimulated by works that at first did not seem to bring them out.

As an example, let us consider again the dislike based on a preference for mystery stories and see if this preference can be analyzed. Here are some reasons for liking mysteries:

1. Mysteries get your attention by creating a puzzle. To get the solution, you need to keep reading to the end.
2. Mysteries involve danger.
3. Mysteries have characters who are active.
4. Mysteries have characters who are also clever, resourceful, and daring.
5. Mysteries present difficult obstacles that the characters must work hard to overcome.

No one could claim that "The Widow of Ephesus" can be completely described by any of these points, but the fourth point is promising. If we consider the widow as a character, she is indeed clever and resourceful, for she thinks of the plan to use her husband's body to cover up the soldier's neglect of duty. If a student likes mystery stories because the characters are clever in finding solutions to difficult problems, perhaps this student can also like "The Widow of Ephesus" because of this same quality in the Widow. A comparison like this one can become the basis for a thoughtful favorable response.

The following paragraph shows how the thought processes of the comparison might work:

> I usually like only mystery stories, and at first I disliked "The Widow of Ephesus" because it is not a mystery. But one of the reasons for which I like mysteries is that the characters in them are clever, resourceful, and daring. The widow has these qualities, because she is quick-witted and resourceful enough to suggest the use of her husband's body to substitute for the one of the thief that was taken away. In this way she uses one loved one, who is dead, to rescue another loved one, who is living. She is also daring, because the misuse of the dead in this way was probably a risky thing to do. Although she does not seem likable for much of the story, at the end these qualities come out, almost as a surprise, and therefore I came to like the story.

Thus an accepted principle of liking can be applied to a different work. A person who adapts principles in this open-minded way can, no matter how slowly, redefine dislikes and expand the ability to like and appreciate many kinds of literature.

An equally open-minded way to develop understanding and widen taste is to try to put dislikes in the following light: An author's creation of an unlikable character, situation, attitude, or expression may be deliberate. Your dislike might then result from the author's *intentions*. A first task of study therefore becomes the attempt to understand and explain the intention or plan. As you put the plan into your own words, you may find that you can like a work with unlikable things in it.

Neither of these two methods of broadening the contexts of dislike is dishonest to the original negative reactions. In the first instance, the thinker applies one of his principles of liking to include "The Widow of Ephesus." In the second, the thinker considers the impact of unlikable aspects of a story in terms of her total response and the ideas awakened through such revulsion. The main concern in both responses is to keep an open mind despite initial dislike and then to see if the unfavorable response can be more fully and broadly considered.

However, if, after consideration, you decide that your dislike outweighs any reasons you can find for liking, then you should be prepared to detail and defend your dislike of the work. As long as you are able to relate your response accurately to details in the work, and to measure it against a clearly stated standard of judgment, your dislike of even a commonly liked story will be acceptable.

## WRITING ABOUT YOUR LIKES AND DISLIKES

In planning an essay about why you like or dislike a story, you should rely on your initial informed reactions. Because it is not easy to reconstruct responses after a lapse of time, be sure to use your notes as your guide in the prewriting stage. Develop your essay in terms of what made you get interested, or not interested, in the work.

In your essay, be sure to relate the details of the work to the point you are making about your ongoing negative or positive responses. If you begin by indicating that you like the work and then you describe what it is that you like, it is easy to forget your basic response as you enumerate details. It is therefore necessary to keep stressing your involvement in the work as you develop your ideas. You can show your attitudes by indicating approval (or disapproval), by commenting favorably (or unfavorably) on the details, by indicating things that seem new (or shopworn) and particularly instructive (or wrong), and by giving assent to (or dissent from) ideas or expressions of feeling.

### Organizing Your Essay

**INTRODUCTION.**   You should open by describing briefly the conditions that influenced your response. Your central idea should be whether you like or dislike the story. The thesis sentence should list the major causes of your response, to be developed in the body of your essay.

**BODY.**   The most common approach is to consider the thing or things about the work that you like or dislike (for a list of possible reasons for liking a work, see p. 50). You may like a particular character, or maybe you got so interested in the story that you could not put it down. Also, it may be that a major idea, a fresh insight, or a particular outcome is the major point that you wish to develop. A sample notebook paragraph earlier (p. 50) shows how the positive example of the use of intelligence can be the source of a favorable response to Doyle's "The Adventure of the Speckled Band." The sample essay (p. 55) expands upon the thoughts in this paragraph.

Another approach is to give details about how your responses occurred or changed in your reading of the work. This method of development requires that you pinpoint, in order, the various good (or bad) parts of the work and how you responded to them. Your aim here should be not to retell the story, but to discuss those details that caused you to like or dislike it. The greatest pitfall to avoid here is a mere retelling of a story or summary of an argument. If you emphasize how the details brought out your responses, however, and if you stress these responses, your essay should rise above the level of a summary.

Two other approaches bring out a shift or development of response, either from negative to positive (most common) or vice versa. The first approach allows the writer to show that a principle for liking one kind of literature may be applied to the work being discussed. The second suggests that a writer may have first responded unfavorably to something about the work, but that on further consideration she or he has been able to establish a larger context which permitted a favorable response. (These responses were discussed earlier, pp. 52–53.)

CONCLUSION.   Here you might briefly summarize the reasons for your major response. You might also try to face any issues brought up by a change in your responses, if there is one. That is, if you have always held certain assumptions about your taste but like the work despite these assumptions, you may wish to talk about your own change or development. This topic is personal, but in an essay about likes or dislikes, discovery about yourself is something toward which you should aim.

## SAMPLE ESSAY

### Some Reasons for Liking A. Conan Doyle's "The Adventure of the Speckled Band"*

[1]   Mystery stories are good reading because the solution to a baffling problem is not known until the end. It might be hard for a reader to get into the mystery, however, because many of the characters are totally enmeshed in circumstances and therefore do not become fully interesting people. For this reason it seems necessary that a mystery focus first on a mastermind of some sort—a kind of friend of the reader—who creates immediate interest in himself or herself before the mystery plot thickens. "The Adventure of the Speckled Band," by A. Conan Doyle, is exactly this kind of mystery. I like the story because I like its master detective, Sherlock Holmes, and like to follow him.° From beginning to end, Holmes is presented as an admirable model of skill, resourcefulness, and bravery.□

[2]   Holmes's skill is an admirable demonstration of his intelligence. At the beginning of the story, he knows nothing about what is happening to Helen Stoner. But he knows what to do once he starts listening to her. So, for example, he immediately goes to the records office in Doctors' Commons to determine something about her estate. In this way, he learns about any possible financial motive that someone might have to kill her. Similar is his exacting method of examining the Roylott house, both inside and out, to narrow suspicion on Roylott himself as the murderer. By this exertion of his skill and the application of his method, Holmes earns the reader's confidence and approval.

---

\* See p. 31 for this story.
° Central idea.
□ Thesis sentence.

[3]

Holmes's excellence is shown not only in his skill, but in his resourcefulness. Once his examination of the premises is complete, it is clear that he knows exactly how Roylott's plot is designed to work. His plan, although we as readers do not learn it until he carries it out in practice, shows his ability to improvise with what is available to him. His warning to Watson about the danger, and his caution about the need for stealth, secrecy, darkness, and silence, all show that he has planned and is able to coordinate all the events of the night in order to save Helen and beat Roylott at his own game. Such resourcefulness is admirable.

[4]

The most admirable quality of Holmes is his bravery. When Roylott enters the London apartment and tries to browbeat him, Holmes speaks coolly and bravely. Even when Roylott turns to threats, Holmes faces the angry opponent down by asking him to leave. This same bravery enables Holmes to devise the plan to beat back the snake once Roylott has pushed the creature into Helen's room. The bite of the "speckled band" could be almost instantly fatal, but Holmes takes the risk, and his success is an example for all.

[5]

Holmes has just about everything that can arouse the reader's liking. Through all the mystery and the danger, he is center stage, and he performs his role well. He is the trusted one, who notices things that others pass over in ignorance. Because of his superiority, he controls and manages everything. With Holmes out in front as he is, it is impossible not to like "The Adventure of the Speckled Band." I certainly like it, and I recommend it highly.

### Commentary on the Essay

This essay demonstrates the first approach described on p. 54, and it is drawn from the first reason for liking a work as listed on p. 50. The opening paragraph explains why a mystery story needs a central figure as a focal point of interest and concern. Then the paragraph asserts that Holmes, the master detective in "The Adventure of the Speckled Band," is this central figure and therefore that he is the major cause for which the writer likes the story. The thesis sentence ends the paragraph.

Paragraph 2 points out that Holmes's method as a detective is the first reason for liking the story. The reason brought out in the third paragraph is Holmes's resourcefulness—that is, his development of a plan to stop the murderer and his foresight and control in making sure that his plan works. The fourth paragraph refers to Holmes's bravery. Because this quality is "most admirable," the essay brings it out as the climax of the three traits for which Holmes is likable.

The conclusion pulls everything together, once again stressing the idea brought out in the opening paragraph that Holmes is the major focus of interest and admiration in the story.

Throughout the essay, the central idea that the story is liked is brought out in words and expressions like "admirable," "knows what to do," "shows his ability," "is able to coordinate," and "success," among others. These expressions, mixed as they are with references to many details from the story, create thematic continuity that shapes and develops the essay. It is the thematic development, together with the use of the details from the story as supporting evidence, that distinguishes the sample essay from a summary.

# Fiction:
# An Overview
# of the Elements

**Fiction** originally meant anything made up, crafted, or shaped. As we understand the word today, it means a prose story based in the imagination of the author, not in literal facts. In English the first recorded use of the word in this sense was in the year 1599. The original meaning of the word in reference to things made up or crafted is helpful to us in focusing on the fact that fiction is to be distinguished from works that it has often imitated, such as reports, historical accounts, biographies, autobiographies, collections of letters, and personal memoirs and meditations. While writers of fiction may deliberately design their works to resemble these forms, fiction has a separate identity because of its origin in the creative, shaping powers of the writers. It is a fact that writers of fiction may include true and historically accurate details in their works, but they create their main stories not because of a wish to be faithful to history but rather because of a hope to say something significant about human life.

The essence of fiction, as opposed to drama, is **narration,** the relating or recounting of a sequence of events or actions. The earliest works of fiction relied almost exclusively on narration, with speeches and dialogue being reported rather than quoted directly. Many recent works of fiction include extended passages of dialogue, thereby rendering the works more dramatic even though narration is still the primary mode.

Fiction had its roots in ancient myths and folk tales. In primitive civilizations, stories were circulated by word of mouth, and often traveling storytellers would appear in a court or village to entertain eager listeners with tales based on the exploits of heroes and gods. Although many of these were heavily fictionalized accounts of events and people who may or may not ever have existed, they were largely accepted by the people as fact or history. An especially long tale, an **epic,** was recited over a period of days, and to aid their memories the storytellers delivered these works in poetic lines, perhaps also impressing and entertaining their listeners by playing stringed instruments.

Although the retelling of myths and legends was meant in part to be entertainment, these stories made a point or taught a lesson considered important either for the local religion or the dominant power structure. Myths of gods like Zeus and Athena (Greece), or Jupiter and Minerva (Rome) abounded, together with stories of famous men and women like Jason, Helen of Troy, Agamemnon, Hercules, Andromeda, Achilles, Odysseus, and Penelope. The ancient Macedonian king and conqueror Alexander the Great (356–323 B.C.) developed many of his ideas about nobility and valor from his boyhood learning of Homer's epic *The Iliad*, which told of the Trojan War. Perhaps nowhere is the moralistic-argumentative aspect of storytelling better illustrated than in the **fables** of Aesop, a Greek who wrote in the sixth century, B.C., and in the **parables** of Jesus as told in the Gospels of the New Testament. In these works, a short narrative is clearly directed to a religious, philosophic, or psychological conclusion. "The Widow of Ephesus" by Petronius illustrates this type of persuasive intention. Whether you agree with the author's conclusion or not, the subordination of the narrative events to a rhetorical and moralizing purpose is made clear right at the beginning of the story.

Beginning about 800 years ago, storytelling was developed to a fine art by writers such as Marie de France, a Frenchwoman who wrote in England near the end of the twelfth century, Giovanni Boccaccio (Italian, 1313–1375), and Geoffrey Chaucer (English, c. 1340–1400). William Shakespeare (1564–1616) drew heavily on history and legend for the stories and characters in his plays.

## MODERN FICTION

Fiction in the modern sense of the word did not begin to flourish until the late seventeenth and eighteenth centuries, when human beings of all social stations and ways of life became important literary topics. As one writer put it in 1709, human nature could not be explained simply, but only with reference to many complex motives like "passion, humor, caprice, zeal, faction, and a thousand other springs."[1] Thus fiction moved toward the characteristic concerns that it has today—the psychological and the highly individual. Indeed, fiction gains its strength from being grounded in the concrete and particular. Most characters have both first and last names; the cities and villages in which they live and move are modeled on real places; and the events and responses recounted are like those that readers themselves have experienced, could experience, or could easily imagine themselves experiencing.

[1] Anthony Ashley Cooper, Third Earl of Shaftesbury, *Sensus Communis*, pt. III, sec. iii.

The first true works of fiction as we know it were the lengthy Spanish and French **romances** written in the sixteenth and seventeenth centuries. (The French word for "novel" is still *roman*.) In English the word **novel** was borrowed from French and Italian to describe these works and to distinguish them from medieval and classical romances as something that was *new* (the meaning of *novel*). In England the word **story** was used along with *novel* in reference to this new literary form.

It was natural that increased levels of general education and literacy in the eighteenth century would make possible the further development of fiction. In Shakespeare's time the only way a writer could make money out of writing was to write a play and then receive either a percentage of the admissions or the proceeds from an "author's benefit" performance. The audiences, however, were limited to people who lived within a short distance of the theater (or who could afford the cost of travel to a performance) and who had the leisure time to attend a play. Once great numbers of people could read, the paying audience for literature expanded. A writer could write a novel and have it printed by a publisher, who could then sell it widely to many people, giving a portion of the proceeds to the writer. Readers could pick up the book at their leisure and finish it as they chose. Reading a novel could even be a social event: people read to each other as a means of sharing the experience. With this wider audience, authors could make a career out of writing. Fiction had arrived as a major genre of literature.

## THE SHORT STORY

Most novels were long, and reading them required many hours. It took an American writer, Edgar Allan Poe (1809–1849), to develop a theory of the **short story,** which he described in a review of Nathaniel Hawthorne's *Twice-Told Tales*. Poe was convinced that "worldly interests" prevented most readers from concentrating on their reading, and that as a result they lost the "totality" of comprehension and emotional reaction that careful reading should permit. He added to this practical consideration the belief that a short, concentrated story (which he called "a brief prose tale") could create a powerful, single impression on the reader. Thus he concluded that the best work of fiction was the short story that could be read at a single sitting of not more than an hour.

Once Poe had expressed his theory, the convenience if not the correctness of his recommendation prompted many later writers to work extensively in the short story form. Today, innumerable short stories are printed in weekly and monthly periodicals and in collections. Many writers who publish stories over a long period of time collect their works for inclusion in single volumes. Writers like William Faulkner, Ernest Hemingway, Shirley Jackson, Guy De Maupassant, Flannery O'Connor, Frank O'Connor, and Eudora Welty, to name only a small number, have had their works collected in this way.

## ELEMENTS OF FICTION

Modern fiction is in a sense similar to myth and epic in that it may teach a lesson or make a point that the writer views as important. Even works purportedly written with a goal of simply entertaining are based in an idea or position. Thus, writers of comic works are usually committed to the belief that human difficulties can be ironed out by discussion and humor. More serious works may instruct by involving characters in difficult moral choices, with the underlying assumption that in losing situations the only winner is the one who can maintain honor and self-respect. Works designed to create mystery and suspense are based in the belief that problems have solutions, even if they may not at first seem apparent. In the creation of stories, writers may deal with the triumphs and defeats of life, the admirable and the despicable, the humorous and the pathetic, but whatever their goal, they always have something to say about the human experience. If they are successful as writers, they will communicate their vision directly to us through their stories.

As a first aspect of this vision, fiction, along with drama, has a basis in **realism** or **verisimilitude.** That is, the situations or characters, though they are the **invention** of writers, are similar to those that many human beings know or experience in their lives. Even **fantasy,** the creation of events that are dreamlike or fantastic (and in this sense a counter to realism), is derived from a perception of life and action that is ultimately real. This similarity of art to life has led some critics to label fiction, and also drama, as an art of **imitation.** Shakespeare's Hamlet states that an actor attempts to portray real human beings in realistic situations (to "hold a mirror up to Nature"). That might also be said of the writer of fiction.

In accord with the idea of verisimilitude or imitation, therefore, everything in fiction is related in one way or another to the reality of everyday life. Some stories are told as though they actually occurred in life, not unlike reports of actual news events in a newspaper. Eudora Welty's "A Worn Path" is such a story. It recounts a woman's walking journey through a wooded area, to the streets of a town, and then to the interior of a building. The events of the story are on the level of the real: They could actually happen in life just as Welty tells about them.

Other levels of reality may also be offered in fiction. Shirley Jackson's "The Lottery," for example, seems at first to be happening on a plane of absolute, small-town reality. By the story's end, however, it is apparent that something else is happening, that the realistic level has changed into a more symbolic one. Such a story suggests that fiction may have many kinds of connections with reality. This link with reality in "The Lottery" may be regarded as a **postulate,** a given **premise,** what Henry James called a *donnée* (something given). Here the premise is this: "What would happen if a small, ordinary town held a lottery in which the 'winner' would be ritually stoned to death?" Everything follows from this given idea. The connection with reality can become remote, or fanciful, as in Poe's "The Masque of the Red Death," in which the given idea is, "What would happen if Death could actually attend a party in person and claim all the party-goers?" The connection can become symbolic or even miraculous, as in Marjorie Pickthall's "The Worker in Sandalwood," in which Jesus, who in life had worked as a carpenter, returns to earth and builds masterly furniture. In Shirley Jackson's "About Two Nice People" the given situation is farcical but romantic, and disputes lead not to hatred but to love. In Walter Clark's "A Portable Phonograph" the events occur in a possible future after much of the world's civilization has been destroyed in a terrible war. As you read works such as these, in which the actions and scenes do not seem realistic in our ordinary sense of the word, you should not dismiss the works as unreal. Instead, you should seek meaning in the actions as caused by the given situation. Always, you may judge a work by the standard of whether it is true if one grants the premises, or the *données*, created by the writer.

Indeed, you may accurately say that in fiction there is always some element of control that shapes the actions the author depicts. Even an apparently everyday level of reality disguises the craft and selectivity of the author. This control may be an occasion (such as the social worker calling the mother and expressing concern about the daughter in Tillie Olsen's "I Stand Here Ironing"). It may be a level of behavior (the boy's reactions to the people around him in O'Connor's "First Confession"). It may be an environment and a social situation, as in Crane's "The Bride Comes to Yellow Sky." Some controls apply to particular types of fiction. There are, for example, "love stories." In the simplest love story two people meet and overcome an obstacle of some sort (usually not a really serious one) on the way to falling in love. Interesting variations on this type may be seen in D. H. Lawrence's "The Horse Dealer's Daughter" and Anton Chekhov's "Lady with Lapdog." In James Joyce's "Araby" only one of the major characters is in love; this is the narrator, who is telling about his boyhood crush on the sister of a friend. In another type of story, the "detective story" like Doyle's "The Adventure of the Speckled Band," a mysterious event is posited, and then the detective (Sherlock Holmes, in this case) draws conclusions based on the available evidence. Most stories, however, resist easy classification into types like these. They are stories about characters similar to people you find in real life, characters who undergo experiences that are sometimes difficult and painful, other times happy and successful, sometimes a mixture of many emotions. In short, stories represent the full range of human experience.

## CHARACTER, PLOT, AND STRUCTURE

All works of fiction share a number of common elements which will be discussed in detail in the various chapters. The more apparent ones, for reference here, are *character*, *plot*, and *structure*.

### Character

Stories, like drama, are about characters—characters who, though not real people, are drawn from life. A character (see Chapter 4, p. 119) is a reasonable facsimile of a human being, with all the good and bad traits of being human.[2] A story is usually concerned with a major problem that a character must face. This may involve interaction with another character, with a difficult situation, or with an idea or general circumstances that force action. The character may win, lose, or tie. He or she may learn and be the better for the experience or may miss the point and be unchanged despite what has happened.

Earlier we mentioned that modern fiction rose coincidentally with the development of a psychological interest in human beings. Psychology itself has grown out of the philosophical and religious idea that people are not necessarily evil, but rather that they have an inborn capacity for goodness. They are not free of problems, and they make many mistakes in their lives, but they nevertheless are of independent interest and they are therefore worth writing about in literature, whether they are male or female; white, black, tan, or yellow; rich or poor; worker or industrialist; farmer, secretary, shepherd, clerk, or salesperson.

It would therefore seem that there is virtually nothing in the modern world that is beyond the scope of fiction. The plight of a married couple struggling under an enormous debt, the meditation of a woman about the growth of her daughter, the experience of a boy learning about sin and forgiveness, the solution to a personality clash in a business, the pathos of a woman surrounded by insensitive and self-seeking men, the development of power and the grounds for domination in a marriage of Mexican

---

[2] Even the beings from other worlds and the lifelike robots and computers that we meet in science fiction, along with animals who populate beast fables and modern comics and films, interest us only as they exhibit human characteristics. Thus, Yogi Bear prefers honey to berries; a supremely intelligent computer with a conflicting program turns destructive; and an alien of superhuman strength riding on a spaceship tries to destroy all the human passengers. But we all know human beings with a sweet tooth; we all know that internal conflicts can produce unpredictable and sometimes destructive results; and who would say that the desire for power is not human?

peasants—all of these are important because human beings are important. In fiction, you may expect characters from every area of life, and, because we all share the same human capacities for concern, involvement, sympathy, happiness, sorrow, exhilaration, and disappointment, you should be able to become interested in the plights of characters and in how they try to handle the world around them.

### Plot

Fictional characters, imitated from life, must go through a series of lifelike **actions,** or **incidents,** which in total make up the story. The interrelationship of incidents and character within a total design is the **plot** of the story. Plot has been compared to a map, scheme, or blueprint. In a carefully worked plot, all the actions, speeches, thoughts, and observations are inextricably linked to make up an entirety, sometimes called an **organic unity.** The essence of this unity of plot is the development and resolution of a **conflict,** in which a **protagonist,** or central character, is engaged in a struggle of some sort. Often this struggle is directed against another character, an **antagonist,** or group of antagonists. Just as often, however, the struggle may occur between opposing forces, ideas, and choices. The conflict may be carried out wherever human beings spend their lives, such as in open nature, communities, houses, courts of law, or mountain resorts. The conflict may also take place internally, within the mind of the protagonist.

Plot in its simplest stage is worked out in a pattern of **cause and effect** that can be traced in a **sequence** or **chronology.** That is, the incidents happen over a period of time, but chronology alone is not the cause of the sequence of actions. Instead, time enters into the cause-and-effect pattern to give the opportunity for effects to follow causes.

### Structure

Whereas a plot is related to chronology, the **structure** of a story may be different because authors often choose to present their stories in something other than direct chronological order. If a story is told in straightforward narrative from beginning to end, then plot and structure are virtually identical, but if the story gets pieced together through out-of-sequence events, speeches, remembrances, fragments of letters, descriptions of actions, overheard conversations, and the like, then the actual arrangement or structure of the story may diverge from the plot. Also, whereas the plot refers to the entire pattern of conflict as evidenced through cause and effect in the story, the study of structure may be directed toward a smaller aspect of arrangement. Structure, in other words, refers to the way in which the plot is assembled, either in whole or in part.

*Theme*

We have said that writers write because they have things to say about life. One of the elements unifying a story is the existence of an underlying **theme** or **central idea,** which is present throughout the work. The theme is somewhat comparable to a scaffold that is used by workers in the construction of a large building; once the building is complete, it is removed, but the effect of the scaffold is still apparent.

The comparison is not totally valid, however, because authors may sometimes leave some of the "scaffolding" in their stories in the form of a direct statement. Thus de Maupassant, in "The Necklace," indicates that people may be destroyed or made fortunate by the most insignificant of events. The accidental loss of the necklace is just such an event; this misfortune ruins the lives of both Mathilde and her husband for a period of ten years. Here the author has presented us with a direct statement of an idea—as it were, a part of his scaffold. There are many other ideas, however, that we might also locate in the story, such as that adversity may bring out worth, or that good fortune is never recognized until it is lost. With each of these alternatives, the story can be seen as being a consistent embodiment of an idea.

The process of determining and describing ideas in stories is probably never complete; there is always another idea that is equally valid and applicable. Such wide opportunity for discussion and interpretation is one of the things that makes fiction interesting and valuable.

## THE WRITER'S TOOLS

*Narration*

Writers have a number of modes of presentation, or "tools," with which they may create their stories. The principal of these tools (and the heart of fiction) is **narration,** the reporting of actions in chronological sequence. The object of narration is, as much as possible, to *render* the story, to make it clear and to bring it alive to the reader's imagination.

*Style*

The medium of fiction and of all literature is language, and the manipulation of language—the **style**—is a primary skill of the writer of fiction. A mark of a good writer's style is the use of *active verbs*, and the use of nouns that are *specific* and *concrete*. Even with the most active and graphic diction possible, writers can never make an exact rendering of their incidents and scenes, but they can indeed be judged on the extent to which they make their narration vivid.

### Point of View

One of the most important ways in which writers knit their stories together, and also an important way in which they try to interest and engage readers, is the careful control of **point of view** (see Chapter 5). Point of view is the voice of the story, the speaker who is doing the narration. It is the means by which the reality and truthfulness of a story are made to seem authentic. It may be regarded as the *focus* of the story, the *angle of vision* from which things are not only seen and reported but also judged.

A story may be told by a fictitious "observer" who tells us what he or she saw, heard, concluded, and thought. This **speaker** or observer may sometimes seem to be the author speaking directly using an authorial voice, but just as often the speaker is a **persona** with characteristics that separate him or her from the author. Sometimes the speaker is a fictitious actor or participant in the story. Stories told in either of these ways have **first-person** points of view, for the speaker usually uses the "I" personal pronoun in referring to his or her position as an observer or commentator.

The other point of view is the **third person.**[3] The third-person point of view may be (1) **limited,** with the focus being on one particular character and what he or she does, says, hears, thinks, and otherwise experiences, (2) **omniscient,** with the thoughts and behaviors of all the characters being open and fully known by the speaker, and (3) **dramatic,** or **objective,** with the story being confined *only* to essential reporting of actions and speeches, with no commentary and no revelation of the thoughts of any of the characters.

Point of view is often quite subtle—indeed, it may be one of the most difficult of all concepts in the study of literature. In fuller perspective, therefore, it may be considered as the position from which things are viewed, understood, and then communicated. It is point of view that makes fiction lifelike, although the author arranges the point of view so that the reader may be properly guided to learn of actions and dialogue. But point of view raises some of the same questions that are found in life. For example, we cannot always be sure of the reliability of what people tell us; we often need to know what their position is. In life, all people have their own limitations, attitudes, and opinions, so that their description of any event, and their attributions or conclusions about such events, will invariably be colored by these attitudes. For example, would the testimony of a near-sighted person who witnessed a distant incident while not wearing glasses be accurate? Would someone's report be reliable if the person were inter-

---

[3] Note Chapter 5, pp. 165–66, where the possibilities of a second-person point of view are discussed.

preting an activity of someone he or she did not like? The same applies to the speakers that we encounter in fiction. For readers, the perception of a fictional point of view can be as complex as life itself, and it may be as difficult to find and rely upon proper sources of information.

### Description

Together with narration, an important aspect of fiction is the use of **description,** which brings scenes and feelings to the imagination of readers. Description can be both physical (places and persons) and psychological (an emotion or set of emotions). As an end in itself, description can interrupt action, so that many writers include only as much as is necessary for the highlighting of important actions. In Olsen's "I Stand Here Ironing," for example, there is a minimum of physical description, although all of us can imagine where a woman doing the week's ironing might be and what she might look like. Other writers may make lavish descriptions in their works. Joseph Conrad, for example, provides extensive descriptions in his novels and stories. His scenes are not only places in which the characters act, but are so evocative that they provide a backdrop designed to give philosophical and even a semireligious perspective to the actions. Edgar Allan Poe used descriptions extensively. In "The Fall of the House of Usher" he attempted to evoke an impression of decay and doom; in "The Masque of the Red Death" his descriptions suggest a mood of macabre festivity.

**Mood** and **atmosphere** are important adjuncts of descriptive writing, and to the degree that descriptions evoke ideas and actions beyond those they stand for on the surface, they may reach the level of **metaphor** and **symbolism.** These characteristics of fiction are a property of all literature, and you will also encounter them in your considerations of poetry and drama.

### Dialogue

Another major tool of the writer of fiction is the creation of **dialogue.** At its simplest, dialogue is the conversation of two people, but more characters may participate, depending on their importance, the number present, and also the circumstances of the scene and action. The major medium of the dramatist, dialogue is just one of the means by which the fiction writer makes a story vivid and dramatic. Straight narration and description can do no more than say that a character's thoughts and responses exist, but dialogue makes eveything real and firsthand. Dialogue is hence a means of *rendering* rather than presenting. If characters feel pain or declare love, their speeches can be the exact expressions (or inexact, depending on the degree of their articulateness) of what is on their minds, in their own words. Some dialogue may be terse and minimal, like that found in Hemingway. Other dialogue may be expanded, depending on the situation, the personalities of the characters, and the author's intent. Dialogue may be about virtually anything, including future plans and goals, reactions, indications of emotion, and political, social, philosophical, or religious ideas.

The language of dialogue indicates the intelligence, articulateness, educational levels, or emotional states of the speakers. Hence the author might use *grammatical mistakes*, *faulty pronunciation*, or *slang* to show a character of limited or disadvantaged background or a character who is trying to be seen in that light. *Dialect* clearly shows the regional location from which the speaker came, just as an accent indicates the place of national origin. *Jargon* and *cliché* suggest a person who is pretentious—usually an infallible directive for the reader's laughter. The use of *private*, *intimate expressions* might show people who are close to each other emotionally. Speech that is interrupted with *voiced pauses* ("er," "ah," "um," "you know," and so on) and speech that is characterized by *inappropriate words* might show a character who is unsure or is not in control. There are many possibilities in dialogue, but no matter what specific qualities you observe, writers include dialogue in order to enable you better to know the characters peopling the scenes and the experiences they face.

### Commentary

Writers may also include **commentary, analysis,** or **interpretation** in the expectation that readers need at least some insight or illumination about the characters and actions. We have already spoken of "scaffolding" in relation to the ideas in fiction. Commentary is the use of scaffolding as a means of showing how things are put together. When fiction was new, authors often expressed such commentary. Henry Fielding (1707–1754), for example, divided his novels into "books" and included a chapter of philosophical or artistic commentary at the beginning of each book. In the next century George Eliot (1819–1880) included many extensive passages of commentary in her novels.

Later writers have kept commentary at a minimum, preferring instead to concentrate on direct action and dialogue. They have left it to readers to draw their own conclusions about meaning—to erect their own scaffolding, as it were. One is likely, however, to encounter something like interpretive observations in first-person narrations, particularly where the speaker not only is a storyteller but also has been a participant. Joseph Conrad's "Youth" is such a work, as is Olsen's "I Stand Here Ironing." Observations made by dramatic speakers in works like these may be accepted at face value, but you should recognize that anything the speakers say is also a mode of character disclosure. Such commentary is therefore just as much a part of the story as the narrative incidents.

### Tone and Irony

In every story one may consider **tone,** that is, an attitude or attitudes that the author conveys about the material in the story and also toward the readers of the story. In "The Necklace," for example, De Maupassant presents the bitter plight of Mathilde and her husband. Pity is thus an appropriate way of describing the attitude that the author conveys in this section of the story, and pity is indeed an appropriate response for the reader. But De Maupassant also shows that to a great degree Mathilde has brought her misfortune directly on herself, so the attitude is one of at least partial satisfaction that justice has been done. But Mathilde works hard and unselfishly; hence admiration tempers any inclination that the reader might have had to condemn her. But then the story's conclusion shows that Mathilde's virtual enslavement was unnecessary. Hence regret enters into the response. In a discussion of the tone of the story, it would be necessary to describe this mixture or complexity of attitudes. Usually, tone is complex in this way.

Because Mathilde's sacrifice for a period of ten years is unnecessary, her situation is ironic. **Irony** is the use of language and situations that are widely inappropriate or opposite from what might be ordinarily expected. **Situational irony** is a means by which authors create a strong emotional impact by presenting circumstances in which punishments do not fit crimes, or in which rewards are not earned. Forces, in other words, are beyond human control or comprehension. The characteristic of **dramatic irony** is that a character may perceive his or her situation in a limited way while the reader sees things more broadly and comprehensively. In John Collier's "The Chaser," for example, the main character believes that he is about to embark upon lifelong ecstasy and romance, but Collier makes the reader aware that the character's life will be sinister and not ecstatic. In **verbal irony,** which applies to language, what is *meant* is different from, or opposite to, what is *said*. Thus, De Maupassant in "The Necklace" does not directly say that Mathilde's husband is a crashing bore during the big party, but by asserting ironically that he had been sleeping "in a little empty room with three other men whose wives had also been enjoying themselves," De Maupassant conveys this idea with amusing force.

### Symbolism and Allegory

Because fiction impresses itself upon the human imagination, it is almost a necessary consequence that the incidents, speeches, and characters acquire an underlying idea or value. To this degree, even an apparently ordinary thing may be construed as a **symbol;** that is, the thing may be understood to mean something beyond itself, something bigger than itself. Because Sammy in Updike's "A & P" walks out on his job in protest against the way the girls in swimsuits are treated, he might easily serve as a symbol standing for freedom of personal behavior. To consider Sammy as a symbol, however, depends on the reader's willingness to make the necessary connection and justification. Many other symbols do not need such explanation, for sometimes writers deliberately create symbols. The cane in Hawthorne's "Young Goodman Brown" is such an example, for Hawthorne describes it as resembling the serpent associated with Satan. The cane therefore is a symbol showing that Brown's woodland companion is actually the Devil himself.

When a story, in addition to maintaining its own narrative integrity, may be clearly applied to another, parallel, set of situations, it is an **allegory.** "Young Goodman Brown" may be considered as an allegory of the development of hatred, distrust, and paranoia. Stories are usually not like "Young Goodman Brown," however, even though they may contain sections that have allegorical parallels. Thus, the narrative of Mathilde's long servitude in De Maupassant's "The Necklace" is similar to the lives and activities of many people who carry out tasks for reasons that are incorrect or even meaningless. For this reason, "The Necklace" may be considered allegorically, even though it is not a complete allegory.


These, then, are the major tools of writers of fiction. For analytical purposes, one or another of them may be discussed so that the artistic achievement of a particular author may be recognized. It is important to realize, however, that in a story everything is happening at once. The story may be told by a character who is a witness, and thus there is a *first-person point of view*. The major *character*, the *protagonist*, goes through a series of *actions* as a result of a carefully arranged *plot*. Because of this plot, together with the author's chosen method of narration, the story will exhibit an organization, or *structure*. One of the things that the actions may demonstrate will be the *theme* or *central idea* of the story. The writer's *style* may be manifested in *ironic* expressions. The description of the character's activity may reveal *irony of situation*, while at the same time this situation is made vivid through *dialogue* in which the character is a participant. Because the plight of the character is like the plight of many persons in the world, it may be considered as an *allegory*, and the character herself or himself may be a *symbol*.

Throughout the story, no matter what characteristics one is considering at the moment, it is most important to realize that a work of fiction is an entirety, a unity. Any reading of a story should be undertaken not to break things down into parts, but to understand and assimilate the work as a whole. The separate analysis of various topics, to which this book is committed, is thus the means to that end, not the end itself. Finally, the study of fiction, like the study of all literature, is designed to foster growth and understanding and to encourage the ultimate improvement of life.

# JOHN UPDIKE (b. 1932)

*A & P*°                                                                              *1961*

In walks these three girls in nothing but bathing suits. I'm in the third checkout slot, with my back to the door, so I don't see them until they're over by the bread. The one that caught my eye first was the one in the plaid green two-piece. She was a chunky kid, with a good tan and a sweet broad soft-looking can with those two crescents of white just under it, where the sun never seems to hit, at the top of the backs of her legs. I stood there with my hand on a box of HiHo crackers trying to remember if I rang it up or not. I ring it up again and the customer starts giving me hell. She's one of these cash-register-watchers, a witch about fifty with rouge on her cheekbones and no eyebrows, and I know it made her day to trip me up. She'd been watching cash registers for fifty years and probably never seen a mistake before.

By the time I got her feathers smoothed and her goodies into a bag—she gives me a little snort in passing, if she'd been born at the right time they would have burned her over in Salem—by the time I get her on her way the girls had circled around the bread and were coming back, without a pushcart, back my way along the counters, in the aisle between the checkouts and the Special bins. They didn't even have shoes on. There was this chunky one, with the two-piece—it was bright green and the seams on the bra were still sharp and her belly was still pretty pale so I guessed she just got it (the suit)—there was this one, with one of those chubby berry-faces, the lips all bunched together under her nose, this one, and a tall one, with black hair that hadn't quite frizzed right, and one of these sunburns right across under the eyes, and a chin that was too long—you know, the kind of girl other girls think is very "striking" and "attractive" but never quite makes it, as they very well know, which is why they like her so much—and then the third one, that wasn't quite so tall. She was the queen. She kind of led them, the other two peeking around and making their shoulders round. She didn't look around, not this queen, she just walked straight on slowly, on these long white prima-donna legs. She came down a little hard on her heels, as if she didn't walk in her bare feet that much, putting down her heels and then letting the weight move along to her toes as if she was testing the floor with every step, putting a little deliberate extra action into it. You never know for sure how girls' minds work (do you really think it's a mind in there or just a little buzz like a bee in a glass jar?) but you got the idea she had talked the other two into coming in here with her, and now she was showing them how to do it, walk slow and hold yourself straight.

She had on a kind of dirty-pink—beige maybe, I don't know—bathing suit with a little nubble all over it and, what got me, the straps were down. They were off her shoulders looped loose around the cool tops of her arms, and I guess as a result the suit had slipped a little on her, so all around the top of the cloth there was this shining rim. If it hadn't been there you wouldn't have known there could have been anything whiter than those shoulders. With the straps pushed off, there was nothing between the top of the suit and the top of her head except just *her*, this clean bare plane of the top of her chest down from the shoulder

*A & P*: "The Great Atlantic and Pacific Tea Company," a large grocery chain still operating in many states.

bones like a dented sheet of metal tilted in the light. I mean, it was more than pretty.

She had sort of oaky hair that the sun and salt had bleached, done up in a bun that was unraveling, and a kind of prim face. Walking into the A & P with your straps down, I suppose it's the only kind of face you *can* have. She held her head so high her neck, coming up out of those white shoulders, looked kind of stretched, but I didn't mind. The longer her neck was, the more of her there was.

She must have felt in the corner of her eye me and over my shoulder Stokesie in the second slot watching, but she didn't tip. Not this queen. She kept her eyes moving across the racks, and stopped, and turned so slow it made my stomach rub the inside of my apron, and buzzed to the other two, who kind of huddled against her for relief, and then they all three of them went up the cat-and-dog-food-breakfast-cereal-macaroni-rice-raisins-seasonings-spreads-spaghetti-soft-drinks-crackers-and-cookies aisle. From the third slot I look straight up this aisle to the meat counter, and I watched them all the way. The fat one with the tan sort of fumbled with the cookies, but on second thought she put the package back. The sheep pushing their carts down the aisle—the girls were walking against the usual traffic (not that we have one-way signs or anything)—were pretty hilarious. You could see them, when Queenie's white shoulders dawned on them, kind of jerk, or hop, or hiccup, but their eyes snapped back to their own baskets and on they pushed. I bet you could set off dynamite in an A & P and the people would by and large keep reaching and checking oatmeal off their lists and muttering "Let me see, there was a third thing, began with A, asparagus, no ah, yes, applesauce!" or whatever it is they do mutter. But there was no doubt, this jiggled them. A few houseslaves in pin curlers even looked around after pushing their carts past to make sure what they had seen was correct.

You know, it's one thing to have a girl in a bathing suit down on the beach, where what with the glare nobody can look at each other much anyway, and another thing in the cool of the A & P, under the fluorescent lights, against all those stacked packages, with her feet paddling along naked over our checkerboard green-and-cream rubber-tile floor.

"Oh Daddy," Stokesie said beside me. "I feel so faint."

"Darling," I said. "Hold me tight." Stokesie's married, with two babies chalked up on his fuselage already, but as far as I can tell that's the only difference. He's twenty-two, and I was nineteen this April.

"Is it done?" he asks, the responsible married man finding his voice. I forgot to say he thinks he's going to be manager some sunny day, maybe in 1990 when it's called the Great Alexandrov and Petrooshki Tea Company or something.

What he meant was, our town is five miles from a beach, with a big summer colony out on the Point, but we're right in the middle of town, and the women generally put on a shirt or shorts or something before they get out of the car into the street. And anyway these are usually women with six children and varicose veins mapping their legs and nobody, including them, could care less. As I say, we're right in the middle of town, and if you stand at our front doors you can see two banks and the Congregational church and the newspaper store and three real-estate offices and about twenty-seven old freeloaders tearing up Central Street because the sewer broke again. It's not as if we're on the Cape°; we're north of

*Cape*: Cape Cod, the southeastern area of Massachusetts, a place of many resorts and beaches.

Boston and there's people in this town haven't seen the ocean for twenty years.

The girls had reached the meat counter and were asking McMahon something. He pointed, they pointed, and they shuffled out of sight behind a pyramid of Diet Delight peaches. All that was left for us to see was old McMahon patting his mouth and looking after them sizing up their joints. Poor kids, I began to feel sorry for them, they couldn't help it.

Now here comes the sad part of the story, at least my family says it's sad, but I don't think it's so sad myself. The store's pretty empty, it being Thursday afternoon, so there was nothing much to do except lean on the register and wait for the girls to show up again. The whole store was like a pinball machine and I didn't know which tunnel they'd come out of. After a while they come around out of the far aisle, around the light bulbs, records at discount of the Caribbean Six or Tony Martin Sings or some such gunk you wonder they waste the wax on, sixpacks of candy bars, and plastic toys done up in cellophane that fall apart when a kid looks at them anyway. Around they come, Queenie still leading the way, and holding a little gray jar in her hand. Slots Three through Seven are unmanned and I could see her wondering between Stokes and me, but Stokesie with his usual luck draws an old party in baggy gray pants who stumbles up with four giant cans of pineapple juice (what do these bums *do* with all that pineapple juice? I've often asked myself) so the girls come to me. Queenie puts down the jar and I take it into my fingers icy cold. Kingfish Fancy Herring Snacks in Pure Sour Cream: 49¢. Now her hands are empty, not a ring or a bracelet, bare as God made them, and I wonder where the money's coming from. Still with that prim look she lifts a folded dollar bill out of the hollow at the center of her nubbled pink top. The jar went heavy in my hand. Really, I thought that was so cute.

Then everybody's luck begins to run out. Lengel comes in from haggling with a truck full of cabbages on the lot and is about to scuttle into that door marked MANAGER behind which he hides all day when the girls touch his eye. Lengel's pretty dreary, teaches Sunday school and the rest, but he doesn't miss that much. He comes over and says, "Girls, this isn't the beach."

Queenie blushes, though maybe it's just a brush of sunburn I was noticing for the first time, now that she was so close. "My mother asked me to pick up a jar of herring snacks." Her voice kind of startled me, the way voices do when you see the people first, coming out so flat and dumb yet kind of tony, too, the way it ticked over "pick up" and "snacks." All of a sudden I slid right down her voice into her living room. Her father and the other men were standing around in ice-cream coats and bow ties and the women were in sandals picking up herring snacks on toothpicks off a big glass plate and they were all holding drinks the color of water with olives and sprigs of mint in them. When my parents have somebody over they get lemonade and if it's a real racy affair Schlitz in tall glasses with "They'll Do It Every Time"° cartoons stenciled on.

"That's all right," Lengel said. "But this isn't the beach." His repeating this struck me as funny, as if it had just occurred to him, and he had been thinking all these years the A & P was a great big dune and he was the head lifeguard. He didn't like my smiling—as I say he doesn't miss much—but he concentrates on giving the girls that sad Sunday-school-superintendent stare.

15

*"They'll Do It Every Time"*: A syndicated daily and Sunday cartoon created by Jimmy Hatlo.

Queenie's blush is no sunburn now, and the plump one in plaid, that I liked better from the back—a really sweet can—pipes up, "We weren't doing any shopping. We just came in for the one thing."

"That makes no difference," Lengel tells her, and I could see from the way his eyes went that he hadn't noticed she was wearing a two-piece before. "We want you decently dressed when you come in here."

"We *are* decent," Queenie says suddenly, her lower lip pushing, getting sore now that she remembers her place, a place from which the crowd that runs the A & P must look pretty crummy. Fancy Herring Snacks flashed in her very blue eyes.

"Girls, I don't want to argue with you. After this come in here with your shoulders covered. It's our policy." He turns his back. That's policy for you. Policy is what the kingpins want. What the others want is juvenile delinquency.

All this while, the customers had been showing up with their carts but, you know, sheep, seeing a scene, they had all bunched up on Stokesie, who shook open a paper bag as gently as peeling a peach, not wanting to miss a word. I could feel in the silence everybody getting nervous, most of all Lengel, who asks me, "Sammy, have you rung up their purchase?"    20

I thought and said "No" but it wasn't about that I was thinking. I go through the punches, 4, 9, GROC, TOT—it's more complicated than you think, and after you do it often enough, it begins to make a little song, that you hear words to, in my case "Hello (*bing*) there, you (*gung*) hap-py *pee*-pul (*splat*)!"—the *splat* being the drawer flying out. I uncrease the bill, tenderly as you may imagine, it just having come from between the two smoothest scoops of vanilla I had ever known were there, and pass a half and a penny into her narrow pink palm, and nestle the herrings in a bag and twist its neck and hand it over, all the time thinking.

The girls, and who'd blame them, are in a hurry to get out, so I say "I quit" to Lengel quick enough for them to hear, hoping they'll stop and watch me, their unsuspected hero. They keep right on going, into the electric eye; the door flies open and they flicker across the lot to their car, Queenie and Plaid and Big Tall Goony-Goony (not that as raw material she was so bad), leaving me with Lengel and a kink in his eyebrow.

"Did you say something, Sammy?"

"I said I quit."

"I thought you did."    25

"You didn't have to embarrass them."

"It was they who were embarrassing us."

I started to say something that came out "Fiddle-de-doo." It's a saying of my grandmother's, and I know she would have been pleased.

"I don't think you know what you're saying," Lengel said.

"I know you don't," I said. "But I do." I pull the bow at the back of my    30
apron and start shrugging it off my shoulders. A couple customers that had been heading for my slot begin to knock against each other, like scared pigs in a chute.

Lengel sighs and begins to look very patient and old and gray. He's been a friend of my parents for years. "Sammy, you don't want to do this to your Mom and Dad," he tells me. It's true, I don't. But it seems to me that once you begin a gesture it's fatal not to go through with it. I fold the apron, "Sammy" stitched in red on the pocket, and put it on the counter, and drop the bow tie on top of it. The bow tie is theirs, if you've ever wondered. "You'll feel this for the rest of your life," Lengel says, and I know that's true, too, but remembering how he made that pretty girl blush makes me so scrunchy inside I punch the No Sale tab and the machine whirs "pee-pul" and the drawer splats out. One advantage to this scene taking place in summer, I can follow this up with a clean exit, there's no fumbling around getting your coat and galoshes, I just saunter into the electric eye in my white shirt that my mother ironed the night before, and the door heaves itself open, and outside the sunshine is skating around on the asphalt.

I look around for my girls, but they're gone, of course. There wasn't anybody but some young married screaming with her children about some candy they didn't get by the door of a powder-blue Falcon° station wagon. Looking back in the big windows, over the bags of peat moss and aluminum lawn furniture stacked on the pavement, I could see Lengel in my place in the slot, checking the sheep through. His face was dark gray and his back stiff, as if he'd just had an injection of iron, and my stomach kind of fell as I felt how hard the world was going to be to me hereafter.

## QUESTIONS

1. Describe Updike's exposition in this story. That is, how does he introduce Sammy, let you know something about his character, and lead up to the major conflict?

2. From Sammy's language what do you learn about his view of himself? About his educational and class level? The first sentence, for example, is grammatically incorrect in Standard English but not uncommon in colloquial English. Point out similar passages. Do they suggest that he violates Standard English deliberately or unwittingly?

3. Indicate evidence in the narration that Sammy is an experienced "girl watcher." What is his estimation of the intelligence of most girls? Is this judgment consistent with what he finally does?

4. Describe the community in which the A & P is located.

5. What is the role of Lengel in the development of the conflict of the story? What values does he represent? What values does Sammy attach, in conflict, to his perception of the rights of the girls?

6. Why does Sammy say "I quit" so abruptly? Does it seem to him at the time that his gesture is meaningful? What do you think he means at the end by saying that the world is going to be hard to him afterwards?

7. Why does Sammy think about the fact that the summer season will permit him to make a "clean exit"? Does this thought in any way affect the value of his gesture?

## GUY DE MAUPASSANT (1850–1893)

*The Necklace*                                                                1884

Translated by Edgar V. Roberts

She was one of those pretty and charming women, born, as if by an error of destiny, into a family of clerks and copyists. She had no dowry, no prospects, no way of getting known, courted, loved, married by a rich and distinguished man.

*Falcon*: A small car that had recently been introduced by the Ford Motor Company.

She finally settled for a marriage with a minor clerk in the Ministry of Education.

She was a simple person, without the money to dress well, but she was as unhappy as if she had gone through bankruptcy, for women have neither rank nor race. In place of high birth or important family connections, they can rely only on their beauty, their grace, and their charm. Their inborn finesse, their elegant taste, their engaging personalities, which are their only power, make working-class women the equals of the grandest duchesses.

She suffered constantly, feeling herself destined for all delicacies and luxuries. She suffered because of her grim apartment with its drab walls, threadbare furniture, ugly curtains. All such things, which most other women in her situation would not even have noticed, tortured her and filled her with despair. The sight of the young country girl who did her simple housework awakened in her only a sense of desolation and lost hopes. She daydreamed of large, silent anterooms, decorated with oriental tapestries and lighted by high bronze floor lamps, with two elegant valets in short culottes dozing in large armchairs under the effects of forced-air heaters. She visualized large drawing rooms draped in the most expensive silks, with fine end tables on which were placed knickknacks of inestimable value. She dreamed of the perfume of dainty private rooms, which were designed only for intimate tête-à-têtes with the closest friends, who because of their achievements and fame would make her the envy of all other women.

When she sat down to dinner at her round little table covered with a cloth that had not been washed for three days, in front of her husband who opened the kettle while declaring ecstatically, "Oh boy, beef stew, my favorite," she dreamed of expensive banquets with shining placesettings, and wall hangings depicting ancient heroes and exotic birds in an enchanted forest. She imagined a gourmet-prepared main course carried on the most exquisite trays and served on the most beautiful dishes, with whispered gallantries which she would hear with a sphinxlike smile as she dined on the pink meat of a trout or the delicate wing of a quail.

She had no decent dresses, no jewels, nothing. And she loved nothing but 5 these; she believed herself born only for these. She burned with the desire to please, to be envied, to be attractive and sought after.

She had a rich friend, a comrade from convent days, whom she did not want to see anymore because she suffered so much when she returned home. She would weep for the entire day afterward with sorrow, regret, despair, and misery.

Well, one evening, her husband came home glowing and carrying a large envelope.

"Here," he said, "this is something for you."

She quickly tore open the envelope and took out a card engraved with these words:

> The Chancellor of Education and Mrs. George Ramponneau request
> that Mr. and Mrs. Loisel do them the honor of coming to dinner
> at the Ministry of Education on the evening of January 8.

Instead of being delighted, as her husband had hoped, she threw the invitation 10 spitefully on the table while muttering:

"What do you expect me to do with this?"

"But Honey, I thought you'd be glad. You never get to go out, and this is a special occasion! I had a lot of trouble getting the invitation. Everyone wants one; the demand is high and not many clerks get invited. Everyone important will be there."

She looked at him angrily and stated impatiently:

"What do you want me to wear to go there?"

He had not thought of that. He stammered:

"But your theatre dress. That seems nice to me . . ."

He stopped, amazed and bewildered, as his wife began to cry. Large tears fell slowly from the corners of her eyes to her mouth. He said falteringly:

"What's wrong? What's wrong?"

But with a strong effort she had recovered, and she answered calmly as she wiped her damp cheeks:

"Nothing, except that I have nothing to wear and therefore can't go to the party. Give your invitation to someone else at the office whose wife will have nicer clothes than mine."

Distressed, he responded:

"Well, okay, Mathilde. How much would a new dress cost, something you could use at other times, but not anything fancy?"

She thought for a few moments, adding things up and thinking also of an amount that she could ask without getting an immediate refusal and a frightened outcry from the frugal clerk.

Finally she responded tentatively:

"I don't know exactly, but it seems to me that I could get by on four hundred francs."

He blanched slightly at this, because he had set aside just that amount to buy a shotgun and go with a few friends to Nanterre on Sundays the next summer to shoot larks.

However, he said:

"Okay, you've got four hundred francs, but make it a pretty dress."

As the day of the party drew near, Mrs. Loisel seemed sad, uneasy, anxious, even though her dress was all ready. One evening her husband said to her:

"What's up? You've been acting strangely for several days."

She answered:

"It's awful, but I don't have any jewels, not a single stone, nothing for matching jewelry. I'm going to look impoverished. I'd almost rather not go to the party."

He responded:

"You can wear a corsage of cut flowers. This year that's really the *in* thing. For no more than ten francs you can get two or three gorgeous roses."

She was not convinced.

"No . . . there's nothing more humiliating than to look ragged in the middle of rich women."

But her husband exclaimed:

"God, but you're silly! Go to your friend Mrs. Forrestier, and ask her to lend you some jewelry. You know her well enough to do that."

She uttered a cry of joy:

"That's right. I hadn't thought of that."

The next day she went to her friend's house and described her problem.

Mrs. Forrestier went to her glass-plated wardrobe, took out a large jewel box, opened it, and said to Mrs. Loisel:

"Choose, my dear."

She saw bracelets, then a pearl necklace, then a Venetian cross of finely worked gold and gems. She tried on the jewelry in front of a mirror, and hesitated, unable to make up her mind about which ones to give back. She kept asking:

"Do you have anything else?"                                                  45

"Certainly. Look to your heart's content. I don't know what will please you most."

Suddenly she found, in a black satin box, a superb diamond necklace, and her heart throbbed with desire for it. Her hands shook as she took it up. She fastened it around her neck, watched it gleam at her throat, and looked at herself ecstatically.

Then she asked, haltingly and anxiously:

"Could you lend me this, nothing but this?"

"Why yes, certainly."                                                          50

She jumped up, hugged her friend joyfully, then hurried away with her treasure.

The day of the party came. Mrs. Loisel was a success. She was prettier than anyone else, stylish, graceful, smiling, and wild with joy. All the men saw her, asked her name, and sought to be introduced. All the important administrators stood in line to waltz with her. The Chancellor himself eyed her.

She danced joyfully, passionately, intoxicated with pleasure, thinking of nothing but the moment, in the triumph of her beauty, in the glory of her success, in a cloud-nine of happiness made up of all the admiration, of all the aroused desire, of this victory so complete and so sweet to the heart of any woman.

She did not leave until four o'clock in the morning. Her husband, since midnight, had been sleeping in a little empty room with three other men whose wives had also been enjoying themselves.

He threw over her shoulders the shawl that he had brought for the trip     55
home, modest clothing from everyday life, the poverty of which contrasted sharply with the elegance of the party dress. She felt it and hurried away to avoid being noticed by the other women who luxuriated in rich furs.

Liosel tried to hold her back:

"Wait a while. You'll catch cold outdoors. I'll call a cab."

But she paid no attention and hurried down the stairs. When they reached the street they found no carriages. They began to look for one, shouting at cabmen passing by at a distance.

They walked toward the Seine, desperate, shivering. Finally, on a quay, they found one of those old night-going buggies that are seen in Paris only after dark, as if they were ashamed of their wretched appearance in daylight.

It took them to their door, on the Street of Martyrs, and they sadly climbed   60
the stairs to their flat. For her, it was finished. As for him, he could think only that he had to begin work at the Ministry of Education at ten o'clock.

She took the shawl off her shoulders, in front of the mirror, to see herself once more in her glory. But suddenly she cried out. The necklace was no longer around her neck!

Her husband, already half undressed, asked:

"What's wrong with you?"

She turned toward him frantically:

"I . . . I . . . I no longer have Mrs. Forrestier's necklace."                    65

He stood up, bewildered:

"What! . . . How! . . . It's not possible!"

And they looked in the folds of the dress, in the creases of the shawl, in the pockets, everywhere. They found nothing.

He asked:

"You're sure you still had it when you left the party?"                    70

"Yes. I checked it in the vestibule of the Ministry."

"But if you had lost it in the street, we would have heard it fall. It must be in the cab."

"Yes, probably. Did you notice the number?"

"No. Did you see it?"

"No."                    75

Overwhelmed, they looked at each other. Finally, Loisel got dressed again:

"I'm going out to retrace all our steps," he said, "to see if I can find the necklace that way."

And he went out. She stayed in her evening dress, without the energy to get ready for bed, prostrated in a chair, drained of strength and thought.

Her husband came back at about seven o'clock. He had found nothing.

He went to Police Headquarters and to the newspapers to announce a reward.                    80 He went to the small cab companies, and finally he followed up even the slightest hopeful lead.

She waited the entire day, in the same enervated state, in the face of this frightful disaster.

Loisel came back in the evening, his face pale and haggard. He had found nothing.

"You'll have to write to your friend," he said, "that you broke a fastening on her necklace and that you will have it fixed. That will give us time to look around."

She wrote as he dictated.

At the end of a week they had lost all hope.                    85

And Loisel, seemingly five years older, declared:

"We'll have to see about replacing the jewels."

The next day, they took the case which had contained the necklace, and went to the jeweler whose name was inside. He looked at his books:

"I wasn't the one, Madam, who sold the necklace. I only made the case."

Then they went from jeweler to jeweler, searching for a necklace like the                    90 other one, racking their memories, both of them sick with worry and anguish.

In a shop in the Palais-Royal, they found a string of diamonds that seemed to them exactly like the one they were seeking. It was priced at forty thousand francs. They could buy it for thirty-six thousand.

They got the jeweler to promise not to sell it for three days. And they made an agreement that he would buy it back for thirty-four thousand frances if the original was recovered before the end of February.

Loisel had saved eighteen thousand francs that his father had left him. He would have to borrow the rest.

He borrowed, asking a thousand francs from one, five hundred from another, five louis° here, three louis here. He made promissory notes, undertook ruinous obligations, did business with finance companies and the whole tribe of loan sharks. He compromised himself for the remainder of his days, risked his signature without knowing whether he would be able to honor it, and, terrified by anguish over the future, by the black misery that was about to descend on him, by the prospect of all kinds of physical deprivations and moral tortures, he went to get the new necklace, and put down thirty-six thousand francs on the jeweler's counter.

Mrs. Loisel took the necklace back to Mrs. Forrestier, who said with an of-    95
fended tone:

"You should have brought it back sooner, because I might have needed it."

She did not open the case, as her friend feared she might. If she had noticed the substitution, what would she have thought? What would she have said? Would she not have taken her for a thief?

Mrs. Loisel soon discovered the horrible life of the needy. She did her share, however, completely, heroically. That horrifying debt had to be paid. She would pay. They dismissed the maid; they changed their address; they rented an attic flat.

She learned to do heavy housework, dirty kitchen jobs. She washed the dishes, wearing away her manicured fingernails on greasy pots and encrusted baking dishes. She handwashed dirty linen, shirts, and dish towels that she hung out on the line to dry. Each morning, she took the garbage down to the street, and she carried up water, stopping at each floor to catch her breath. And, dressed in cheap house dresses, she went to the fruit dealer, the grocer, the butchers, with her basket under her arms, haggling, insulting, defending her measly cash penny by penny.

They had to make installment payments every month, and, to buy more    100
time, to refinance loans.

The husband worked evenings to make fair copies of tradesmen's accounts, and late into the night he made copies at five cents a page.

And this life lasted ten years.

At the end of ten years, they had paid back everything—everything—including the extra charges imposed by loan sharks and the accumulation of compound interest.

Mrs. Loisel seemed old now. She had become the strong, hard, and rude woman of poor households. Her hair unkempt, with uneven skirts and rough, red hands, she spoke loudly, washed floors with large buckets of water. But sometimes, when her husband was at work, she sat down near the window, and she dreamed of that evening so long ago, of that party, where she had been so beautiful and so admired.

What would life have been like if she had not lost that necklace? Who knows?    105
Who knows? Life is so peculiar, so uncertain. How little a thing it takes to destroy you or to save you!

---

*louis*: a twenty-franc coin.

Well, one Sunday, as she had gone on a stroll along the Champs-Elysées to relax from the cares of the week, she suddenly noticed a woman walking with a child. It was Mrs. Forrestier, always youthful, always beautiful, always attractive.

Mrs. Loisel felt moved. Would she speak to her? Yes, certainly. And now that she had paid, she could tell all. Why not?

She walked closer.

"Hello, Jeanne."

The other did not recognize her at all, being astonished to be addressed    110
so intimately by this working woman. She stammered:

"But . . . Madam! . . . I don't know. . . . You must have made a mistake."

"No. I'm Mathilde Loisel."

Her friend cried out:

"Oh! . . . My poor Mathilde, you've changed so much."

"Yes. I've had some hard times since I saw you last; in fact, miseries . . .    115
and all this because of you! . . ."

"Of me . . . how so?"

"You remember the diamond necklace that you lent me to go to the party at the Ministry of Education?"

"Yes. What then?"

"Well, I lost it."

"How, since you gave it back to me?"    120

"I brought back another exactly like it. And for ten years we've been paying for it. You understand that this wasn't easy for us, who have nothing. . . . Finally it's over, and I'm mighty damned glad."

Mrs. Forrestier stopped her.

"You say that you bought a diamond necklace to replace mine?"

"Yes, You didn't notice it, eh? They were exactly like yours."

And she smiled with proud and childish joy.    125

Mrs. Forrestier, deeply moved, took both her hands.

"Oh, my poor Mathilde! But mine was false. At the most, it was worth five hundred francs! . . ."

# QUESTIONS

1. Describe the character of Mathilde. On balance, is she as negative as she might seem at first? Why does De Maupassant describe her efforts to cooperate in paying the debt as "heroic"? How does her character as first described create the situation that causes the financial penance the Loisels must undergo?

2. Are Mathilde's daydreams unusual for a woman in her station? Do you think that De Maupassant fashioned the ironic conclusion to demonstrate that Mathilde somehow deserved her misfortune?

3. What sort of person is Loisel? How does his character contribute to the financial disaster?

4. Describe the relationship between Mathilde and Loisel as shown in their

conversations. Does their relationship seem to be intimate or is it less personal?

5. De Maupassant's speaker states that small things save or destroy people. Do you think that "The Necklace" bears out this idea? Does there seem to be any role for a concept of fate in such a view of existence, or is chance the governing influence?

6. Can an argument be made that De Maupassant is presenting a view in the story that might be described as econmic determinism? That is, to what degree does he relate economic status, either positively or negatively, to happiness and character fulfillment?

## HOW TO WRITE A PRÉCIS

The words *précis* and *precise* are closely related, and this connection is helpful in enabling an understanding of the nature of a précis—namely, a cutting down of a long story into its *precise,* essential parts. The object is to make a very short encapsulation of a story. Other words describing the précis are *abridgment*, *paraphrase*, *abstract*, *condensation*, and *epitome*. Epitome is particularly helpful as a description for a précis, for an epitome is a cutting away of inessentials so that only the important, most vital parts remain.

The technique of writing a précis of a story can be significant not only in reading fiction, but in undertaking many other areas of study. Précis writing can be used for taking notes, preparing for exams, establishing and clarifying facts for any body of discourse, studying for classroom discussion, and reinforcing things learned in the past. The object of a précis should be not to tell *everything*, but only to give the highlights, so that any reader would be able to know the main points of the story.

Some guidelines to follow in the development of a précis are discussed in the following sections.

### Selection

Only essential details belong in a précis. For example, at the opening of the story "The Necklace," De Maupassant describes the pleasing daydreams of Mathilde Loisel. She is preoccupied with visions of what wealth could bring, such as large anterooms, tapestries, lamps, valets, silks, end tables, expensive bric-a-brac, private rooms, and elegant and exotic meals. Including references to all these would needlessly lengthen a précis of "The Necklace." Instead, it is sufficient to say something like "Mathilde daydreams of wealth," which gets at the vital facts about her dissatisfaction with her life and her dreams for a wealthier one.

This concentration on only essentials allows a précis to be shortened. A 5,000-word story might be epitomized in 100, 200, or 400 words. It is clear that more details might be selected for inclusion in the longer précis than in the shorter ones. Whatever the length of the final précis, however, selection of detail is to be based on the importance of the material in the story being described.

### Accuracy

There should be no mistakes in a précis, so all details should be correctly recorded. Because the essay is an abbreviation of a lengthy story, there is a risk not just of factual misstatement, but also of using words that might give a misleading impression of the original. Thus, in "The Necklace," Mathilde Loisel cooperates with her husband for ten long years to repay their 36,000-franc debt. It would be easy just to say that she "works" during this time, but this word might mislead, for some readers might assume that it refers to outside employment. What De Maupassant actually tells us is that Mathilde does heavy housework as a part of her general economizing in her *own* household, not in the houses of others.

The need to condense long sections of a story necessarily produces the need for comprehensive words that accurately account for sections of the story. Thus, in "The Necklace" Loisel needs to borrow money to pay for half of the 36,000 francs the replacement will cost. Just to say "he borrows money," however, does not convey the usurious rates of interest he must accept to get 18,000 francs from various lenders and loansharks. An accurate précis description of this borrowing must include some account of these desperate promises to pay. Thus, a clause like "he almost literally mortgages his future to get the needed loans" would cover not only the borrowing but also the high rates of interest. For any précis, the choice of proper wording should be made with comprehensive accuracy in mind.

### Diction

The précis is to be an original work, and therefore it should be written in words that are not taken directly from the story. The best way to ensure original wording is to read the story, record the major things that happen, and then put the story out of sight during the writing process. That way the temptation to borrow words directly can be avoided.

However, if some of the story's words find their way into the précis even after a careful try to be totally original, it is important to put these words into quotation marks. As long as direct quotations are kept at a minimum, they are satisfactory. Too many quoted words, however, indicate that the précis is not really original writing.

### Objectivity

A précis should be scrupulously factual. It must avoid explanatory or introductory material unless that is actually a part of the story. As much effort should be made to *avoid* conclusions in a précis as is exerted to *include* them in other kinds of writing about fiction. Here is a comparative example of what to do and what to avoid:

| WHAT TO DO | WHAT TO AVOID |
| --- | --- |
| Mathilde Loisel, a French housewife married to a minor clerk, is unhappy with her poor household possessions. She daydreams about wealth and is even more dissatisfied after visiting Jeane Forrestier, a rich woman who is a former schoolmate. One day Loisel, Mathilde's husband, brings home an invitation to an exclusive dinner dance. Mathilde angrily claims that she has nothing to wear, but Loisel gives her all his money to buy a party dress. | De Maupassant opens the story by introducing the dissatisfaction that ultimately will propel Mathilde Loisel and her husband to their ten-year disaster. Mathilde's unhappiness with her own household possessions, and her dreams about wealth, lead her naturally to reproach her husband when he brings home the invitation to the dinner at the Ministry of Education. It is clear that her unhappiness leads her to spend beyond their means for a special party dress. |

The right-hand column contains a guiding topic sentence, to which the following sentences adhere. Such writing is commendable everywhere else, but not in a précis. The left-hand column is better writing *as a précis*, for it presents a selection of details only as they appear in the story, without introductory sentences, because in the story there are no such introductions.

### Paragraphs

The normal principle of devoting a paragraph to only one topic may also be applied to a précis. If each major division, episode, scene, action, or section of the story is considered a topic, then the précis may be divided into paragraphs devoted to each of the divisions. Thus the first paragraph of the sample précis of "The Necklace" includes the material leading up to the dinner dance, while the last is devoted to the meeting near the Champs-Elysées. In most stories similar divisions into scenes and episodes may serve as natural topics which limit the extent of paragraphs.

### Arrangement and Sequence

In a précis the arrangement and sequence are to remain as in the order of the original story. Thus, if the story has a surprise ending, like that in "The Necklace," the conclusion is also withheld until the end of the précis. By contrast, in an analysis of an idea, say, or in the study of a character, the surprise ending might be included whenever it becomes important. It is proper, however, to introduce names, places, and other essential details of circumstance at the beginning of the précis, even though these details are not brought out immediately in the story. For example, De Maupassant does not name Mathilde right away, and he never says that she is French, but a précis of "The Necklace" would be obscure if these details were withheld.

### Sentences

Because of the precise, factual nature of the précis, it is tempting to write choppy sentences, comparable to short bursts of machine gun fire. Here is an example of choppy sentences:

> Mathilde gives up her nice apartment. She works hard for ten years. She climbs stairs. She cleans the floors. She uses big buckets of water. She gets coarse and loud. She haggles with shopkeepers. She is no longer young and beautiful.

An entire essay consisting of sentences like these might make readers feel as though they actually have been machine gunned. The problem is to include detail but also to remember to shape and organize sentences. Here is a more acceptable set of sentences revised to contain the same information:

> She gives up her nice apartment and devotes herself to hard work for the entire ten years. At home she climbs many stairs and throws buckets of water to clean the floors. When marketing, she haggles with shopkeepers for bargains. At the end of the time this hard work has made her loud and coarse, and her youthful beauty is gone.

This revision blends the shorter sentences together and makes a contrast between the second and third sentences. Even though sentences in a précis are to be almost rigidly factual, there should be an effort to make them as graceful as possible.

## SAMPLE ESSAY

### A Précis of De Maupassant's "The Necklace"*

[1]    Mathilde Loisel, a French housewife married to a minor clerk, is unhappy with her poor household possessions. She daydreams about wealth and is even more dissatisfied after visiting Jeanne Forrestier. a rich woman who is a former schoolmate. One day Loisel, Mathilde's husband, brings home an invitation to an exclusive dinner dance. Mathilde angrily claims that she has nothing to wear, but Loisel gives her all his money to buy a party dress. With no jewelry to match, she is ready to give up the affair, but at Loisel's suggestion she borrows a beautiful necklace from Jeanne.

---

* See p. 75 for this story.

[2] At the party Mathilde is a huge success, but afterward she and Loisel hurry away because she is ashamed to be seen in her everyday shawl. Upon arriving home she is horrified to discover that she has lost the necklace.

[3] In desperation, Loisel and she spend a week looking for the necklace. Unable to find it, Loisel buys another for 36,000 francs. He uses his entire inheritance for half of this sum and borrows the rest wherever he can, almost literally mortgaging his future to get the needed loans.

[4] For the next ten years Mathilde and Loisel make sacrifices to pay back all the loans. She gives up her nice apartment and devotes herself to hard work for the entire ten years. At home she climbs many stairs and throws buckets of water to clean the floors. When marketing, she haggles with shopkeepers for bargains. At the end of the time this hard work has made her loud and coarse, and her youthful beauty is gone.

[5] One Sunday she takes a walk and sees Jeanne, who does not recognize her at first because of her changed appearance. Mathilde tells Jeanne of her ten years of sacrifice. Sympathetically, Jeanne responds by explaining that the original necklace had been false, and worth no more than 500 francs.

### Commentary on the Essay

This précis, about 300 words long, illustrates the selection of major actions and the omission of interesting but inessential detail. Thus, the clause "she daydreams about wealth" contains four words, and it condenses more than 150 words of detailed description in the story. The next clause about the rich friend, Jeanne Forrestier, is longer, and it condenses a relatively short passage in the story. The clause is important, however, because it related Mathilde's increased dissatisfaction upon seeing Jeanne, and Jeanne is doubly important, for she is the owner of the false necklace which is the cause of the Loisel family's downfall. The principle here is this: The selection of what to include in a précis depends not so much upon the length as upon the significance of parts in the original.

Each of the five paragraphs in the précis is devoted to a comparable episode of "The Necklace." Paragraph 1 describes the story up to the party; paragraph 2, the events of the party leading up to the discovery of the loss. The third and fourth paragraphs deal with the borrowing of money to restore the necklace and with the ten-year sacrifice to pay back the loans. The last paragraph describes the scene in which Mathilde learns that the sacrifice was unnecessary.

The basis for determining the appropriateness of episode for paragraph is not time but unity. Thus, paragraph 2 describes an episode that takes place within a few hours, but the unifying element is the party and the discovery of the loss immediately after it. The events of paragraph 4, on the other hand, take ten years, and the unifying principle is the coarsening of Mathilde's character because of her hard work.

# 3

# Plot and Structure

Just as the people or characters in fiction are derived from life, so are the **actions.** The actions, as we have observed, occur in sequence, or in chronological order. Once we have established the narrative or sequential order, we consider **plot,** or the plan of development of the actions.

## WHAT IS PLOT?

Without a plot, we do not have a story. A plot is a plan or groundwork for a story, based in conflicting human motivations, with the actions resulting from believable and realistic human response. In a well-plotted story, nothing is irrelevant; everything is related. The British novelist E. M. Forster, in *Aspects of the Novel*, presents a memorable illustration of plot. As a bare minimum narration of actions in contrast to a story with a plot, he uses the following: "The king died, and then the queen died." This sentence describes a sequence, a chronological order, but it is no more. To have a plot, a sequence must be integrated with human motivation. Thus the following sentence qualifies as fiction with a plot: "The king died, and then the queen died of grief." Once the narrative introduces the operative element "of grief," which shows that one thing (grief over the king's death) produces or overcomes another (the death of the queen), there is a plot. Thus, in a story, time is important not simply because one thing happens *after* another but because one thing happens *because* of another. It is response, interaction, opposition, and causation that make a plot out of a simple series of actions.

### Conflict

Fictional human responses are brought out to their highest degree in the development of a **conflict.** In its most elemental form, a conflict is the opposition of two people. They may fight, argue, enlist help against each other, and otherwise carry on their opposition. Conflicts may also exist between larger groups of people, although in fiction conflicts between individuals are more identifiable and therefore more interesting. Conflict may also exist between an individual and larger forces, such as natural objects, ideas, modes of behavior, public opinion, and the like. The existence of difficult *choices* within an individual's mind may also be presented as conflict, or **dilemma.** In addition, the conflict may be presented not as direct opposition, but rather as a set of comparative or contrastive ideas or values. In short, there are many ways to bring out a conflict in fiction.

CONFLICT, DOUBT, TENSION, AND INTEREST.    The reason that conflict is the major ingredient in plot is that once two forces are in opposition, there may be doubt about the outcome. The doubt, if the reader becomes interested and engaged with the characters, produces curiosity and tension. The same concern furnishes the lifeblood of athletic competition. For just a moment, consider which kind of football game is more interesting: (1) one in which the score goes back and forth and there is doubt about the outcome right up to the last second, or (2) one in which one of the teams gets so far ahead in the first quarter that there is no more doubt about who will win. The interest that a highly contested game provides is also generated by a conflict in a story. The conflict should be a genuine contest, an engagement between characters or forces of approximately equal strength. It should never be a "walkaway," "mismatch," "rout," or "laugher," to use terminology from the sports world. Unless there is doubt, there is no tension, and unless there is tension, there is no interest.

CONFLICT IN PLOT.    To see a plot in operation, let us build on Forster's description. Here is a bare plot for a story: "John and Jane meet, fall in love, and get married." This plot would probably not get many readers, for it lacks any conflict. Now, using this same essential narrative of "boy meets girl," let us introduce some elements of conflict:

> John and Jane meet at school and fall in love. They go together for two years, and they plan to marry, but a problem arises. Jane wants to develop a career first, and after marriage she wants to be an equal contributor to the family. John understands Jane's desire for a career, but he wants to marry first and let her continue her studies afterward in preparation for her goal. Jane believes that this solution will not work, insisting instead that it is a trap from which she will never escape. This conflict interrupts their plans, and they part in regret and anger. Going their separate ways even though they still love each other, both marry other people and build their lives and careers. Neither is completely happy even though they like and respect their spouses. Many years later, after they have children and grandchildren of their own, they meet again. John is now a widower and Jane has divorced. Their earlier conflict no longer being a barrier, they marry and live successfully together. During their marriage, however, even their new happiness is

tinged with reproach and regret because of their earlier conflict, their increasing age, and the lost years that they might have spent with each other.

Here we have a plot, with a conflict that takes a number of shapes. The (1) initial conflict is resolved by a (2) separation leading each of the characters to a new life that is (3) satisfactory but not totally happy. The final marriage produces (4) not unqualified happiness, but a note of regret and (5) a sense of time lost that cannot be restored. It is the establishment of these contrasting or conflicting situations and responses that produces the interest the short-short story contains. The situation is lifelike; the conflict stems out of realistic values; the outcome is true to life. The imposition of the various conflicts and contrasts has made an interesting plot out of what could have been a common "boy meets girl" sequence.

## THE STRUCTURE OF FICTION

Thus the plot of a story is the establishment of a conflict and the consequences, variations, and developments that stem from it. To the degree that the plot requires a set of events that may be laid out in a chronological order, which may have a clearly formed shape, it may be termed a major *structure* of the story.

**Structure** describes the arrangement and placement of the story's materials. The word *structure* belongs to a whole family of words that are concerned with spreading and ordering, including *instruct*, *construct*, *street*, *streusel* (*a layering of dough in a pastry*), and *stratagem*. The study of structure in fiction is a study of the causes and reasons (*stratagem* here is a helpful related word) behind matters such as placement, balance, recurring themes, juxtapositions, true and misleading conclusions, suspense, and the imitation of models or forms (like letters, conversations, confessions, and the like). Thus a story may be divided into parts, or it might be arranged according to principal actions that occur outdoors or indoors, or it might be laid out according to the pattern of movement of a vehicle such as a train. Structure relates to these arrangements and the purposes for which they are made.

### Formal Categories of Structure

Many aspects of structure are common to all genres of literature, and often the structure of fiction is parallel to that of drama. In any story, however, there will be the following aspects that form the backbone, skeleton, or pattern of development.

EXPOSITION. **Exposition** is the *laying out*, the putting forth, of the materials in the story: the main characters, their backgrounds, their characteristics, goals, limitations, and potentials. It presents everything that is going to be important in the story. It is not necessarily limited to the beginning of a story, but it may be found anywhere. Thus, there may be intricacies, twists, turns, false leads, blind alleys, surprises, and other quirks introduced in order to perplex, intrigue, please, and otherwise interest readers. Whenever something new arises, to the degree that it is new it is a part of exposition. At a certain point, however, the introduction of new materials must cease and the story must proceed to a conclusion with only those elements that have already been included.

COMPLICATION.    The **complication** marks the onset of the major conflict in the story. The participants are the protagonist and the antagonist, together with whatever ideas and values they represent, such as good and evil, individualism and collectivization, childhood and age, love and hate, intelligence and stupidity, knowledge and ignorance, freedom and slavery, desire and resistance, and the like.

CRISIS.    The **crisis** is the turning point, the separation between what has gone before and what will come after. In practice, the crisis is usually a decision or action undertaken in an effort to *resolve* the conflict. It is important to stress, however, that the crisis, though a result of operating forces and decisions, may not produce the intended results. That situation is the next part of the formal structure, the climax.

CLIMAX.    The **climax** (from the Greek for *ladder*) is the *high point* in the action, in which the conflict and the consequent tension are brought out to the fullest extent. Another way to think of climax is to define it as that point in a story in which all the rest of the action becomes inevitable. This inevitability does not, of course, occur in an instant but happens as a result of the fact that once the high point is reached, there must be an action or development that brings the climax to a conclusion. For example, in Stephen Crane's "The Bride Comes to Yellow Sky" the climax is the confrontation of Potter and Scratchy Wilson. Since Scratchy is alcoholic and therefore unpredictable, there is at least some doubt about the outcome. Once Potter declares that he is not carrying his gun, however, Scratchy's primitive sense of honor demands that he back down from his wanted shootout. Thus the declaration is the end of the climax and the point which marks the beginning of the end of the story.

RESOLUTION OR DENOUEMENT.    The **resolution** (a releasing or untying) or **denouement** (untying) is the set of actions bringing the story to its conclusion. Scratchy Wilson's brief queries into the truth of Potter's declaration, for example, and his learning about Potter's marriage, are the resolution of the conflict of "The Bride Comes to Yellow Sky." Once the "untying" has been done, the author usually concludes the story as quickly as possible. Both "The Bride Comes to Yellow Sky" and Eudora Welty's

"A Worn Path," for example, end with characters walking away. The major actions are completed and the final action, the walking, underscores the note of finality.

### Formal and Actual Structure

The formal structure just described is an ideal one, a pattern that is almost identical to the plot and that takes place in straightforward, chronological order. In practice, however, the structure of a story will usually vary the ideal pattern, even though all the elements will be present. Mystery stories, for example, postpone climaxes until the last possible moment and also necessarily delay crucial exposition, inasmuch as the goal is to mystify. In a story where the exposition allows readers to know who a wrongdoer is, by contrast, the goal of the story is often to create suspense about whether the protagonist can maintain life while seeking the wrongdoer out. More realistic, less "artificial" stories might also embody structural variations. In Welty's "A Worn Path," for example, a memorable variation is produced by the information introduced at the very end. During most of the story the complication seems to be that Phoenix Jackson's major conflict is with (1) her age and (2) the natural environment. At the end, however, we learn the additional detail that she is the sole guardian and caretaker of an invalid grandson. Thus, even at the end we get exposition and complication, so much so that our previous understanding of the conflict is augmented. The anguish of our reponse is made more acute, for Phoenix's antagonist is not just age and environment but also hopeless illness. The *structure* of the story is designed to withhold an essential detail to maximize impact. The resolution of the story, coming at the same moment as this crucial complication, points toward the final, inevitable defeat of Phoenix while it also demonstrates her determined character.

Variants in structure are almost as numerous as the stories you will encounter. There might be a "flashback" method, for example: The moment at which the flashback is taking place might actually be during the resolution of the plot, and the flashback might lead you into a moment of climax but then go on to develop the details that are more properly part of the exposition. Let us again consider our brief plot about John and Jane, and develop a possible flashback way of structuring the story.

> Jane is now old, and a noise outside causes her to think of the argument that forced her to part with John many years before. Then she thinks of the years she and John spent happily together after they married. She then contrasts her happiness with her earlier, less happy marriage, and from there she reflects on her years of courtship with John before their conflict over career plans developed. Then she looks over at John, reading in a chair, and smiles. John smiles back, and the story ends.

This structure suggests one way of telling the story, but there might be others. Let us suppose that John is in a sickbed at the time Jane thinks about their past, or he might be dead in his coffin. These variables would produce different stories. Or, let us suppose that Jane is a widow of many years, either thinking about her past or giving advice to a son or daughter. Then, too, she might be looking back as a divorcee from her first marriage, having just met John again, with the final action being their wedding. The years of happiness might then be introduced as anticipation, or as a resolution described by a narrator, who might have heard about things later from a friend. In short, the possibilities of structuring our story are great. Using the flashback method such as the one demonstrated here, we would necessarily bring out all the formal elements of plot, but the actual arrangement—the real structure—would be unique.

There are, of course, many other ways to structure a story. A plot might be developed by a group of persons, each one with a part of the details; by the time all finish making their contribution, all the necessary complications and resolutions would be clear. If a story is structured as though it is a dream, elements of exposition and complication might naturally be introduced out of the sequence that the ideal structure might require. Parts of a story might also be arranged in fragments of overheard conversation, or portions of letters. Another story might develop with partial narration and partial dialogue, and still another might be total dialogue.

### Questions for the Study of Structure

In the determination of the structure of any story, there are a number of questions that one might ask. What does the reader need to know in order to understand the story? Are all these things actually included? How are these things ordered? Do they come at a point when they might be expected, in the light of the story's plot? What comes first, and why? What comes afterward, and why? If the second and following things preceded the first thing, how would the story be different? How does the present ordering of actions, scenes, speeches, and narration contribute to the completion of the story? How are these placements influential in the effect produced by the story?

## STEPHEN CRANE (1871–1900)

*The Bride Comes to Yellow Sky*                                        *1898*

### I

The great pullman was whirling onward with such dignity of motion that a glance from the window seemed simply to prove that the plains of Texas were pouring eastward. Vast flats of green grass, dull-hued spaces of mesquite and cactus, little groups of frame houses, woods of light and tender trees, all were sweeping into the east, sweeping over the horizon, a precipice.

A newly married pair had boarded this coach at San Antonio. The man's face was reddened from many days in the wind and sun, and a direct result of his new black clothes was that his brick-coloured hands were constantly performing in a most conscious fashion. From time to time he looked down respectfully at his attire. He sat with a hand on each knee, like a man waiting in a barber's shop. The glances he devoted to other passengers were furtive and shy.

The bride was not pretty nor was she very young. She wore a dress of blue cashmere, with small reservations of velvet here and there, and with steel buttons abounding. She continually twisted her head to regard her puff sleeves, very stiff, straight, and high. They embarrassed her. It was quite apparent that she had cooked, and that she expected to cook, dutifully. The blushes caused by the careless scrutiny of some passengers as she had entered the car were strange to see upon this plain, under-class countenance, which was drawn in placid, almost emotionless lines.

They were evidently very happy. "Ever been in a parlour-car before?" he asked, smiling with delight.

"No," she answered; "I never was. It's fine, ain't it?"    5

"Great! And then after a while we'll go forward to the diner, and get a big lay-out. Finest meal in the world. Charge a dollar."

"Oh, do they?" cried the bride. "Charge a dollar? Why, that's too much—for us—ain't it, Jack?"

"Not this trip, anyhow," he answered bravely. "We're going to go the whole thing."

Later he explained to her about the trains. "You see, it's a thousand miles from one end of Texas to the other; and this train runs right across it, and never stops but four times." He had the pride of an owner. He pointed out to her the dazzling fittings of the coach; and in truth her eyes opened wider as she contemplated the sea-green figured velvet, the shining brass, silver, and glass, the wood that gleamed as darkly brilliant as the surface of a pool of oil. At one end a bronze figure sturdily held a support for a separated chamber, and at convenient places on the ceiling were frescos in olive and silver.

To the minds of the pair, their surroundings reflected the glory of their    10 marriage that morning in San Antonio; this was the environment of their new estate; and the man's face in particular beamed with an elation that made him appear ridiculous to the negro porter. This individual at times surveyed them from afar with an amused and superior grin. On other occasions he bullied them with skill in ways that did not make it exactly plain to them that they were being bullied. He subtly used all the manners of the most unconquerable kind of snobbery. He oppressed them; but of this oppression they had small knowledge, and they speedily forgot that infrequently a number of travellers covered them with stares of derisive enjoyment. Historically there was supposed to be something infinitely humorous in their situation.

"We are due in Yellow Sky at 3:42," he said, looking tenderly into her eyes.

"Oh, are we?" she said, as if she had not been aware of it. To evince surprise at her husband's statement was part of her wifely amiability. She took from a pocket a little silver watch; and as she held it before her, and stared at it with a frown of attention, the new husband's face shone.

"I bought it in San Anton' from a friend of mine," he told her gleefully.

"It's seventeen minutes past twelve," she said, looking up at him with a kind of shy and clumsy coquetry. A passenger, noting this play, grew excessively sardonic, and winked at himself in one of the numerous mirrors.

At last they went to the dining-car. Two rows of negro waiters, in glowing     15
white suits, surveyed their entrance with the interest, and also the equanimity, of men who had been forewarned. The pair fell to the lot of a waiter who happened to feel pleasure in steering them through their meal. He viewed them with the manner of a fatherly pilot, his countenance radiant with benevolence. The patronage, entwined with the ordinary deference, was not plain to them. And yet, as they returned to their coach, they showed in their faces a sense of escape.

To the left, miles down a long purple slope, was a little ribbon of mist where moved the keening Rio Grande. The train was approaching it at an angle, and the apex was Yellow Sky. Presently it was apparent that, as the distance from Yellow Sky grew shorter, the husband became commensurately restless. His brick-red hands were more insistent in their prominence. Occasionally he was even rather absent-minded and far-away when the bride leaned forward and addressed him.

As a matter of truth, Jack Potter was beginning to find a shadow of a deed weigh upon him like a leaden slab. He, the town marshal of Yellow Sky, a man known, liked, and feared in his corner, a prominent person, had gone to San Antonio to meet a girl he believed he loved, and there, after the usual prayers, had actually induced her to marry him, without consulting Yellow Sky for any part of the transaction. He was now bringing his bride before an innocent and unsuspecting community.

Of course people in Yellow Sky married as it pleased them, in accordance with a general custom; but such was Potter's thought of his duty to his friends, or of their idea of his duty, or of an unspoken form which does not control men in these matters, that he felt he was heinous. He had committed an extraordinary crime. Face to face with this girl in San Antonio, and spurred by his sharp impulse, he had gone headlong over all the social hedges. At San Antonio he was like a man hidden in the dark. A knife to sever any friendly duty, any form, was easy to his hand in that remote city. But the hour of Yellow Sky—the hour of daylight—was approaching.

He knew full well that his marriage was an important thing to his town. It could only be exceeded by the burning of the new hotel. His friends could not forgive him. Frequently he had reflected on the advisability of telling them by telegraph, but a new cowardice had been upon him. He feared to do it. And now the train was hurrying him toward a scene of amazement, glee, and reproach. He glanced out of the window at the line of haze swinging slowly in toward the train.

Yellow Sky had a kind of brass band, which played painfully, to the delight     20
of the populace. He laughed without heart as he thought of it. If the citizens could dream of his prospective arrival with his bride, they would parade the band at the station and escort them, amid cheers and laughing congratulations, to his adobe home.

He resolved that he would use all the devices of speed and plainscraft in making the journey from the station to his house. Once within that safe citadel, he could issue some sort of vocal bulletin, and then not go among the citizens until they had time to wear off a little of their enthusiasm.

The bride looked anxiously at him. "What's worrying you, Jack?"

He laughed again. "I'm not worrying, girl; I'm only thinking of Yellow Sky."

She flushed in comprehension.

A sense of mutual guilt invaded their mind and developed a finer tenderness.   25
They looked at each other with eyes softly aglow. But Potter often laughed the same nervous laugh; the flush upon the bride's face seemed quite permanent.

The traitor to the feelings of Yellow Sky narrowly watched the speeding landscape. "We're nearly there," he said.

Presently the porter came and announced the proximity of Potter's home. He held a brush in his hand, and, with all his airy superiority gone, he brushed Potter's new clothes as the latter slowly turned this way and that way. Potter fumbled out a coin and gave it to the porter, as he had seen others do. It was a heavy and muscle-bound business, as that of a man showing his first horse.

The porter took their bag, and as the train began to slow they moved forward to the hooded platform of the car. Presently the two engines and their long string of coaches rushed into the station of Yellow Sky.

"They have to take water here," said Potter, from a constricted throat and in mournful cadence, as one announcing death. Before the train stopped his eye had swept the length of the platform, and he was glad and astonished to see there was none upon it but the station-agent, who, with a slightly hurried and anxious air, was walking toward the water-tanks. When the train had halted, the porter alighted first, and placed in position a little temporary step.

"Come on, girl," said Potter, hoarsely. As he helped her down they each   30
laughed on a false note. He took the bag from the negro, and bade his wife cling to his arm. As they slunk rapidly away, his hang-dog glance perceived that they were unloading the two trunks, and also that the station-agent, far ahead near the baggage-car, had turned and was running toward him, making gestures. He laughed, and groaned as he laughed, when he noted the first effect of his marital bliss upon Yellow Sky. He gripped his wife's arm firmly to his side, and they fled. Behind them the porter stood, chuckling fatuously.

## II

The California express on the Southern Railway was due at Yellow Sky in twenty-one minutes. There were six men at the bar of the Weary Gentleman saloon. One was a drummer° who talked a great deal and rapidly; three were Texans who did not care to talk at that time; and two were Mexican sheep-herders, who did not talk as a general practice in the Weary Gentleman saloon. The barkeeper's dog lay on the board walk that crossed in front of the door. His head was on his paws, and he glanced drowsily here and there with the constant vigilance of a dog that is kicked on occasion. Across the sandy street were some vivid green grassplots, so wonderful in appearance, amid the sands that burned near them in a blazing sun, that they caused a doubt in the mind. They exactly resembled the grass mats used to represent lawns on the stage. At the cooler end of the railway station, a man without a coat sat in a tilted chair and smoked his pipe. The fresh-

*drummer*: salesman

cut bank of the Rio Grande circled near the town, and there could be seen beyond it a great plum-coloured plain of mesquite.

Save for the busy drummer and his companions in the saloon, Yellow Sky was dozing. The new-comer leaned gracefully upon the bar, and recited many tales with the confidence of a bard who has come upon a new field.

"—and at the moment that the old man fell downstairs with the bureau in his arms, the old woman was coming up with two scuttles of coal, and of course—"

The drummer's tale was interrupted by a young man who suddenly appeared in the open door. He cried: "Scratchy Wilson's drunk, and has turned loose with both hands." The two Mexicans at once set down their glasses and faded out of the rear entrance of the saloon.

The drummer, innocent and jocular, answered: "All right, old man. S'pose   35
he has? Come in and have a drink, anyhow."

But the information had made such an obvious cleft in every skull in the room that the drummer was obliged to see its importance. All had become instantly solemn. "Say," said he, mystified, "what is this?" His three companions made the introductory gesture of eloquent speech; but the young man at the door fore-stalled them.

"It means, my friend," he answered, as he came into the saloon, "that for the next two hours this town won't be a health resort."

The barkeeper went to the door, and locked and barred it; reaching out of the window, he pulled in heavy wooden shutters, and barred them. Immediately a solemn, chapel-like gloom was upon the place. The drummer was looking from one to another.

"But say," he cried, "what is this, anyhow? You don't mean there is going to be a gun-fight?"

"Don't know whether there'll be a fight or not," answered one man, grimly;   40
"but there'll be some shootin'—some good shootin'."

The young man who had warned them waved his hand. "Oh, there'll be a fight fast enough, if any one wants it. Anybody can get a fight out there in the street. There's a fight just waiting."

The drummer seemed to be swayed between the interest of a foreigner and a perception of personal danger.

"What did you say his name was?" he asked.

"Scratchy Wilson," they answered in chorus.

"And will he kill anybody? What are you going to do? Does this happen   45
often? Does he rampage around like this once a week or so? Can he break in that door?"

"No; he can't break down the door," replied the barkeeper. "He's tried it three times. But when he comes you'd better lay down on the floor, stranger. He's dead sure to shoot at it, and a bullet may come through."

Therafter the drummer kept a strict eye upon the door. The time had not yet been called for him to hug the floor, but, as a minor precaution, he sidled near to the wall. "Will he kill anybody?" he said again.

The men laughed low and scornfully at the question.

"He's out to shoot, and he's out for trouble. Don't see any good in experimen-tin' with him."

"But what do you do in a case like this? What do you do?"                    50
A man responded: "Why, he and Jack Potter—"
"But," in chorus the other men interrupted, "Jack Potter's in San Anton'."
"Well, who is he? What's he got to do with it?"
"Oh, he's the town marshal. He goes out and fights Scratchy when he gets
on one of these tears."
"Wow!" said the drummer, mopping his brow. "Nice job he's got."             55
The voices had toned away to mere whisperings. The drummer wished to
ask further questions, which were born of an increasing anxiety and bewilderment;
but when he attempted them, the men merely looked at him in irritation and
motioned him to remain silent. A tense waiting hush was upon them. In the deep
shadows of the room their eyes shone as they listened for sounds from the street.
One man made three gestures at the barkeeper; and the latter, moving like a ghost,
handed him a glass and a bottle. The man poured a full glass of whisky, and set
down the bottle noiselessly. He gulped the whisky in a swallow, and turned again
toward the door in immovable silence. The drummer saw that the barkeeper, without
a sound, had taken a Winchester from beneath the bar. Later he saw this individual
beckoning to him, so he tiptoed across the room.
"You better come with me back of the bar."
"No, thanks," said the drummer, perspiring; "I'd rather be where I can make
a break for the back door."
Whereupon the man of bottles made a kindly but peremptory gesture. The
drummer obeyed it, and, finding himself seated on a box with his head below
the level of the bar, balm was laid upon his soul at sight of various zinc and
copper fittings that bore a resemblance to armour-plate. The barkeeper took a
seat comfortably upon an adjacent box.
"You see," he whispered, "this here Scratchy Wilson is a wonder with a        60
gun—a perfect wonder; and when he goes on the war-trail, we hunt our holes—
naturally. He's about the last one of the old gang that used to hang out along
the river here. He's a terror when he's drunk. When he's sober he's all right—
kind of simple—wouldn't hurt a fly—nicest fellow in town. But when he's drunk—
whoo!"
There were periods of stillness. "I wish Jack Potter was back from San Anton',"
said the barkeeper. "He shot Wilson up once—in the leg—and he would sail in
and pull out the kinks in this thing."
Presently they heard from a distance the sound of a shot, followed by three
wild yowls. It instantly removed a bond from the men in the darkened saloon.
There was a shuffling of feet. They looked at each other. "Here he comes," they
said.


### III

A man in a maroon-coloured flannel shirt, which had been purchased for
purposes of decoration, and made principally by some Jewish women on the East
Side of New York, rounded a corner and walked into the middle of the main
street of Yellow Sky. In either hand the man held a long, heavy, blue-black revolver.
Often he yelled, and these cries rang through a semblance of a deserted village,

shrilly flying over the roofs in a volume that seemed to have no relation to the
ordinary vocal strength of a man. It was as if the surrounding stillness formed
the arch of a tomb over him. These cries of ferocious challenge rang against walls
of silence. And his boots had red tops with gilded imprints, of the kind beloved
of winter by little sledding boys on the hillsides of New England.

The man's face flamed in a rage begot of whisky. His eyes, rolling, and yet
keen for ambush, hunted the still doorways and windows. He walked with the
creeping movement of the midnight cat. As it occurred to him, he roared menacing
information. The long revolvers in his hands were as easy as straws; they were
moved with an electric swiftness. The little fingers of each hand played sometimes
in a musician's way. Plain from the low collar of the shirt, the cords of his neck
straightened and sank, straightened and sank, as passion moved him. The only
sounds were his terrible invitations. The calm adobes preserved their demeanour
at the passing of this small thing in the middle of the street.

There was no offer of fight—no offer of fight. The man called to the sky.    65
There were no attractions. He bellowed and fumed and swayed his revolvers here
and everywhere.

The dog of the barkeeper of the Weary Gentleman saloon had not appreciated
the advance of events. He yet lay dozing in front of his master's door. At sight
of the dog, the man paused and raised his revolver humorously. At sight of the
man, the dog sprang up and walked diagonally away, with a sullen head, and growling. The man yelled, and the dog broke into a gallop. As it was about to enter
an alley, there was a loud noise, a whistling, and something spat the ground directly
before it. The dog screamed, and, wheeling in terror, galloped headlong in a new
direction. Again there was a noise, a whistling, and sand was kicked viciously before
it. Fear-stricken, the dog turned and flurried like an animal in a pen. The man
stood laughing, his weapons at his hips.

Ultimately the man was attracted by the closed door of the Weary Gentleman
saloon. He went to it and, hammering with a revolver, demanded drink.

The door remaining imperturbable, he picked a bit of paper from the walk,
and nailed it to the framework with a knife. He then turned his back contemptuously
upon this popular resort and, walking to the opposite side of the street and spinning
there on his heel quickly and lithely, fired at the bit of paper. He missed it by a
half-inch. He swore at himself, and went away. Later he comfortably fusilladed
the windows of his most intimate friend. The man was playing with this town; it
was a toy for him.

But still there was no offer of fight. The name of Jack Potter, his ancient
antagonist, entered his mind, and he concluded that it would be a glad thing if
he should go to Potter's house, and by bombardment induce him to come out
and fight. He moved in the direction of his desire, chanting Apache scalp-music.

When he arrived at it, Potter's house presented the same still front as had    70
the other adobes. Taking up a strategic position, the man howled a challenge.
But this house regarded him as might a great stone god. It gave no sign. After a
decent wait, the man howled further challenges, mingling with them wonderful
epithets.

Presently there came the spectacle of a man churning himself into deepest
rage over the immobility of a house. He fumed at it as the winter wind attacks a

prairie cabin in the North. To the distance there should have gone the sound of a tumult like the fighting of two hundred Mexicans. As necessity bade him, he paused for breath or to reload his revolvers.

## IV

Potter and his bride walked sheepishly and with speed. Sometimes they laughed together shamefacedly and low.

"Next corner, dear," he said finally.

They put forth the efforts of a pair walking bowed against a strong wind. Potter was about to raise a finger to point the first appearance of the new home when, as they circled the corner, they came face to face with a man in a maroon-coloured shirt, who was feverishly pushing cartridges into a large revolver. Upon the instant the man dropped his revolver to the ground and, like lightning, whipped another from its holster. The second weapon was aimed at the bridegroom's chest.

There was a silence. Potter's mouth seemed to be merely a grave for his   75
tongue. He exhibited an instinct to at once loosen his arm from the woman's grip, and he dropped the bag to the sand. As for the bride, her face had gone as yellow as old cloth. She was a slave to hideous rites, gazing at the apparitional snake.

The two men faced each other at a distance of three paces. He of the revolver smiled with a new and quiet ferocity.

"Tried to sneak up on me," he said. "Tried to sneak up on me!" His eyes grew more baleful. As Potter made a slight movement, the man thrust his revolver venomously forward. "No; don't you do it, Jack Potter. Don't you move a finger toward a gun just yet. Don't you move an eyelash. The time has come for me to settle with you, and I'm goin' to do it my own way, and loaf along with no interferin'. So if you don't want a gun bent on you, just mind what I tell you."

Potter looked at his enemy. "I ain't got a gun on me Scratchy," he said. "Honest, I ain't." He was stiffening and steadying, but yet somewhere at the back of his mind a vision of the Pullman floated: the sea-green figured velvet, the shining brass, silver, and glass, the wood that gleamed as darkly brilliant as the surface of a pool of oil—all the glory of the marriage, the environment of the new estate. "You know I fight when it comes to fighting, Scratchy Wilson; but I ain't got a gun on me. You'll have to do all the shootin' yourself."

His enemy's face went livid. He stepped forward, and lashed his weapon to and fro before Potter's chest. "Don't you tell me you ain't got no gun on you, you whelp. Don't tell me no lie like that. There ain't a man in Texas ever seen you without no gun. Don't take me for no kid." His eyes blazed with light, and his throat worked like a pump.

"I ain't takin' you for no kid," answered Potter. His heels had not moved   80
an inch backward. "I'm takin' you for a damn fool. I tell you I ain't got a gun, and I ain't. If you're goin' to shoot me up, you better begin now; you'll never get a chance like this again."

So much enforced reasoning had told on Wilson's rage; he was calmer. "If you ain't got a gun, why ain't you got a gun?" he sneered. "Been to Sunday-school?"

"I ain't got a gun because I've just come from San Anton' with my wife. I'm married," said Potter. "And if I'd thought there was going to be any galoots like you prowling around when I brought my wife home, I'd had a gun, and don't you forget it."

"Married!" said Scratchy, not at all comprehending.

"Yes, married. I'm married," said Potter, distinctly.

"Married?" said Scratchy. Seemingly for the first time, he saw the drooping,    85
drowning woman at the other man's side. "No!" he said. He was like a creature allowed a glimpse of another world. He moved a pace backward, and his arm, with the revolver, dropped to his side. "Is this the lady?" he asked.

"Yes; this is the lady," answered Potter.

There was another period of silence.

"Well," said Wilson at last, slowly, "I s'pose it's all off now."

"It's all off if you say so, Scratchy. You know I didn't make the trouble." Potter lifted his valise.

"Well, I 'low it's off, Jack," said Wilson. He was looking at the ground.    90
"Married!" He was not a student of chivalry; it was merely that in the presence of this foreign condition he was a simple child of the earlier plains. He picked up his starboard revolver, and, placing both weapons in their holsters, he went away. His feet made funnel-shaped tracks in the heavy sand.

## QUESTIONS

1.  What is a Pullman? Why are Jack Potter and his new bride on it? What is the attitude of the other people in the car to the newly married couple? Why? Is it possible for you to be amused, too?

2.  Describe the plot in terms of the principal conflict between Potter and Scratchy, and also of the various related conflicts.

3.  Where is the crisis of the story? How extended is it? At what point does it become clear that there will be a peaceful resolution?

4.  Describe the structural relationship of each of the four sections of the story to the development of the plot.

5.  Why is Potter apprehensive about returning to Yellow Sky? What is the relationship between his concern and his later showdown with Scratchy Wilson? Describe the "code" that previously governed the gunslinging conduct of Jack and Scratchy. How does the presence of Potter's wife affect Scratchy's perception of his new role with regard to Potter?

6.  What is the scene in the Weary Gentleman saloon? Is there any expository purpose for which Crane has included a drummer (a traveling salesman who is unfamiliar with life in Yellow Sky) in the group of men?

7.  The story is designed to be comic. Because of this intention, how seriously is Scratchy Wilson, with his gun, to be taken? How do the speeches of the men in the bar contribute to your understanding of the danger Scratchy poses?

## EUDORA WELTY (b. 1909)

*A Worn Path*                                                                    *1941*

It was December—a bright frozen day in the early morning. Far out in the country there was an old Negro woman with her head tied in a red rag, coming along a path through the pinewoods. Her name was Phoenix Jackson. She was very old and small and she walked slowly in the dark pine shadows, moving a little from side to side in her steps, with the balanced heaviness and lightness of a pendulum in a grandfather clock. She carried a thin, small cane made from an umbrella, and with this she kept tapping the frozen earth in front of her. This made a grave and persistent noise in the still air, that seemed meditative like the chirping of a solitary little bird.

She wore a dark striped dress reaching down to her shoe tops, and an equally long apron of bleached sugar sacks, with a full pocket: all neat and tidy, but every time she took a step she might have fallen over her shoelaces, which dragged from her unlaced shoes. She looked straight ahead. Her eyes were blue with age. Her skin had a pattern all its own of numberless branching wrinkles and as though a whole little tree stood in the middle of her forehead, but a golden color ran underneath, and the two knobs of her cheeks were illumined by a yellow burning under the dark. Under the rag her hair came down on her neck in the frailest of ringlets, still black, and with an odor like copper.

Now and then there was a quivering in the thicket. Old Phoenix said, "Out of my way, all you foxes, owls, beetles, jack rabbits, coons and wild animals! . . . Keep out from under these feet, little bob-whites. . . . Keep the big wild hogs out of my path. Don't let none of those come running my direction. I got a long way." Under her small black-freckled hand her cane, limber as a buggy whip, would switch at the brush as if to rouse up any hiding things.

On she went. The woods were deep and still. The sun made the pine needles almost too bright to look at, up where the wind rocked. The cones dropped as light as feathers. Down in the hollow was the mourning dove—it was not too late for him.

The path ran up a hill. "Seem like there is chains about my feet, time I get     5
this far," she said, in the voice of argument old people keep to use with themselves. "Something always take a hold of me on this hill—pleads I should stay."

After she got to the top she turned and gave a full, severe look behind her where she had come. "Up through pines," she said at length. "Now down through oaks."

Her eyes opened their widest, and she started down gently. But before she got to the bottom of the hill a bush caught her dress.

Her fingers were busy and intent, but her skirts were full and long, so that before she could pull them free in one place they were caught in another. It was not possible to allow the dress to tear. "I in the thorny bush," she said. "Thorns, you doing your appointed work. Never want to let folks pass, no sir. Old eyes thought you was a pretty little *green* bush."

Finally, trembling all over, she stood free, and after a moment dared to stoop for her cane.

"Sun so high!" she cried, leaning back and looking, while the thick tears          10
went over her eyes. "The time getting all gone here."

At the foot of this hill was a place where a log was laid across the creek.

"Now comes the trial," said Phoenix.

Putting her right foot out, she mounted the log and shut her eyes. Lifting
her skirt, leveling her cane fiercely before her, like a festival figure in some parade,
she began to march across. Then she opened her eyes and she was safe on the
other side.

"I wasn't as old as I thought," she said.

But she sat down to rest. She spread her skirts on the bank around her          15
and folded her hands over her knees. Up above her was a tree in a pearly cloud
of mistletoe. She did not dare to close her eyes, and when a little boy brought
her a plate with a slice of marble-cake on it she spoke to him. "That would be
acceptable," she said. But when she went to take it there was just her own hand
in the air.

So she left that tree, and had to go through a barbed-wire fence. There
she had to creep and crawl, speading her knees and stretching her fingers like a
baby trying to climb the steps. But she talked loudly to herself: she could not let
her dress be torn now, so late in the day, and she could not pay for having her
arm or her leg sawed off if she got caught fast where she was.

At last she was safe through the fence and risen up out in the clearing. Big
dead trees, like black men with one arm, were standing in the purple stalks of
the withered cotton field. There sat a buzzard.

"Who you watching?"

In the furrow she made her way along.

"Glad this not the season for bulls," she said, looking sideways, "and the          20
good Lord made his snakes to curl up and sleep in the winter. A pleasure I don't
see no two-headed snake coming around that tree, where it come once. It took a
while to get by him, back in the summer."

She passed through the old cotton and went into a field of dead corn. It
whispered and shook and was taller than her head. "Through the maze now,"
she said, for there was no path.

Then there was something tall, black, and skinny there, moving before her.

At first she took it for a man. It could have been a man dancing in the
field. But she stood still and listened, and it did not make a sound. It was as
silent as a ghost.

"Ghost," she said sharply, "who be you the ghost of? For I have heard of
nary death close by."

But there was no answer—only the ragged dancing in the wind.          25

She shut her eyes, reached out her hand, and touched a sleeve. She found
a coat and inside that an emptiness, cold as ice.

"You scarecrow," she said. Her face lighted. "I ought to be shut up for
good," she said with laughter. "My senses is gone. I too old. I the oldest people
I ever know. Dance, old scarecrow," she said, "while I dancing with you."

She kicked her foot over the furrow, and with mouth drawn down, shook
her head once or twice in a little strutting way. Some husks blew down and whirled
in streamers about her skirts.

Then she went on, parting her way from side to side with the cane, through
the whispering field. At last she came to the end, to a wagon track where the

silver grass blew between the red ruts. The quail were walking around like pullets, seeming all dainty and unseen.

"Walk pretty," she said. "This is the easy place. This the easy going." 30

She followed the track, swaying through the quiet bare fields, through the little strings of trees silver in their dead leaves, past cabins silver from weather, with the doors and windows boarded shut, all like old women under a spell sitting there. "I walking in their sleep," she said, nodding her head vigorously.

In a ravine she went where a spring was silently flowing through a hollow log. Old Phoenix bent and drank. "Sweet-gum makes the water sweet," she said, and drank more. "Nobody know who made this well, for it was here when I was born."

The track crossed a swampy part where the moss hung as white as lace from every limb. "Sleep on, alligators, and blow your bubbles." Then the track went into the road.

Deep, deep the road went down between the high green-colored banks. Overhead the live-oaks met, and it was as dark as a cave.

A black dog with a lolling tongue came up out of the weeds by the ditch. 35 She was meditating, and not ready, and when he came at her she only hit him a little with her cane. Over she went in the ditch, like a little puff of milkweed.

Down there, her senses drifted away. A dream visited her, and she reached her hand up, but nothing reached down and gave her a pull. So she lay there and presently went to talking. "Old woman," she said to herself, "that black dog come up out of the weeds to stall you off, and now there he sitting on his fine tail smiling at you."

A white man finally came along and found her—a hunter, a young man, with his dog on a chain.

"Well, Granny!" he laughed. "What are you doing there?"

"Lying on my back like a June-bug waiting to be turned over, mister," she said, reaching up her hand.

He lifted her up, gave her a swing in the air, and set her down. "Anything 40 broken, Granny?"

"No sir, them old dead weeds is springy enough," said Phoenix, when she had got her breath. "I thank you for your trouble."

"Where do you live, Granny?" he asked, while the two dogs were growling at each other.

"Away back yonder, sir, behind the ridge. You can't even see it from here."

"On your way home?"

"No sir, I going to town." 45

"Why, that's too far! That's as far as I walk when I come out myself, and I get something for my trouble." He patted the stuffed bag he carried, and there hung down a little closed claw. It was one of the bob-whites, with its beak hooked bitterly to show it was dead. "Now you go on home, Granny!"

"I bound to go to town, mister," said Phoenix. "The time come around."

He gave another laugh, filling the whole landscape. "I know you old colored people! Wouldn't miss going to town to see Santa Claus!"

But something held old Phoenix very still. The deep lines in her face went into a fierce and different radiation. Without warning, she had seen with her own eyes a flashing nickel fall out of the man's pocket onto the ground.

"How old are you, Granny?" he was saying. 50

"There is no telling, mister," she said, "no telling."

Then she gave a little cry and clapped her hands and said, "Git on away from here, dog! Look! Look at that dog!" She laughed as if in admiration. "He ain't scared of nobody. He a big black dog." She whispered, "Sic him!"

"Watch me get rid of that cur," said the man. "Sic him, Pete! Sic him!"

Phoenix heard the dogs fighting, and heard the man running and throwing sticks. She even heard a gunshot. But she was slowly bending forward by that time, further and further forward, the lids stretched down over her eyes, as if she were doing this in her sleep. Her chin was lowered almost to her knees. The yellow palm of her hand came out from the fold of her apron. Her fingers slid down and along the ground under the piece of money with the grace and care they would have in lifting an egg from under a setting hen. Then she slowly straightened up, she stood erect, and the nickel was in her apron pocket. A bird flew by. Her lips moved. "God watching me the whole time. I come to stealing."

The man came back, and his own dog panted about them. "Well, I scared    55
him off that time," he said, and then he laughed and lifted his gun and pointed it at Phoenix.

She stood straight and faced him.

"Doesn't the gun scare you?" he said, still pointing it.

"No, sir, I seen plenty go off closer by, in my day, and for less than what I done," she said, holding utterly still.

He smiled, and shouldered the gun. "Well, Granny," he said, "you must be a hundred years old, and scared of nothing. I'd give you a dime if I had any money with me. But you take my advice and stay home, and nothing will happen to you."

"I bound to go on my way, mister," said Phoenix. She inclined her head in    60
the red rag. Then they went in different directions, but she could hear the gun shooting again and again over the hill.

She walked on. The shadows hung from the oak trees to the road like curtains. Then she smelled wood-smoke, and smelled the river, and she saw a steeple and the cabins on their steep steps. Dozens of little black children whirled around her. There ahead was Natchez shining. Bells were ringing. She walked on.

In the paved city it was Christmas time. There were red and green electric lights strung and crisscrossed everywhere, and all turned on in the daytime. Old Phoenix would have been lost if she had not distrusted her eyesight and depended on her feet to know where to take her.

She paused quietly on the sidewalk where people were passing by. A lady came along in the crowd, carrying an armful of red-, green- and silver-wrapped presents; she gave off perfume like the red roses in hot summer, and Phoenix stopped her.

"Please, missy, will you lace up my shoe?" She held up her foot.

"What do you want, Grandma?"    65

"See my shoe," said Phoenix. "Do all right for out in the country, but wouldn't look right to go in a big building."

"Stand still then, Grandma," said the lady. She put her packages down on the sidewalk beside her and laced and tied both shoes tightly.

"Can't lace 'em with a cane," said Phoenix. "Thank you, missy. I doesn't mind asking a nice lady to tie up my shoe, when I gets out on the street."

Moving slowly and from side to side, she went into the big building, and into a tower of steps, where she walked up and around and around until her feet knew to stop.

She entered a door, and there she saw nailed up on the wall the document that had been stamped with the gold seal and framed in the gold frame, which matched the dream that was hung up in her head. 70

"Here I be," she said. There was a fixed and ceremonial stiffness over her body.

"A charity case, I suppose," said an attendant who sat at the desk before her.

But Phoenix only looked above her head. There was sweat on her face, the wrinkles in her skin shone like a bright net.

"Speak up, Grandma," the woman said. "What's your name? We must have your history, you know. Have you been here before? What seems to be the trouble with you?"

Old Phoenix only gave a twitch to her face as if a fly were bothering her. 75

"Are you deaf?"cried the attendant.

But then the nurse came in.

"Oh, that's just old Aunt Phoenix," she said. "She doesn't come for herself— she has a little grandson. She makes these trips just as regular as clockwork. She lives away back off the Old Natchez Trace." She bent down. "Well, Aunt Phoenix, why don't you just take a seat? We won't keep you standing after your long trip." She pointed.

The old woman sat down, bolt upright in the chair.

"Now, how is the boy?" asked the nurse. 80

Old Phoenix did not speak.

"I said, how is the boy?"

But Phoenix only waited and stared straight ahead, her face very solemn and withdrawn into rigidity.

"Is his throat any better?" asked the nurse. "Aunt Phoenix, don't you hear me? Is your grandson's throat any better since the last time you came for the medicine?"

With her hands on her knees, the old woman waited, silent, erect and motion- 85 less, just as if she were in armor.

"You mustn't take up our time this way, Aunt Phoenix," the nurse said. "Tell us quickly about your grandson, and get it over. He isn't dead, is he?"

At last there came a flicker and then a flame of comprehension across her face, and she spoke.

"My grandson. It was my memory had left me. There I sat and forgot why I made my long trip."

"Forgot?" the nurse frowned. "After you came so far?"

Then Phoenix was like an old woman begging a dignified forgiveness for 90 waking up frightened in the night. "I never did go to school, I was too old at the Surrender," she said in a soft voice. "I'm an old woman without an education. It was my memory fail me. My little grandson, he is just the same, and I forgot it in the coming."

"Throat never heals, does it?" said the nurse, speaking in a loud, sure voice to old Phoenix. By now she had a card with something written on it, a little list. "Yes. Swallowed lye. When was it—January—two, three years ago—"

Phoenix spoke unasked now. "No, missy, he not dead, he just the same.

Every little while his throat begin to close up again, and he not able to swallow. He not get his breath. He not able to help himself. So the time come around, and I go on another trip for the soothing medicine."

"All right. The doctor said as long as you came to get it, you could have it," said the nurse. "But it's an obstinate case."

"My little grandson, he sit up there in the house all wrapped up, waiting by himself," Phoenix went on. "We is the only two left in the world. He suffer and it don't seem to put him back at all. He got a sweet look. He going to last. He wear a little patch quilt and peep out holding his mouth open like a little bird. I remembers so plain now. I not going to forget him again, no, the whole enduring time. I could tell him from all the others in creation."

"All right." The nurse was trying to hush her now. She brought her a bottle    95
of medicine. "Charity," she said, making a check mark in a book.

Old Phoenix held the bottle close to her eyes, and then carefully put it into her pocket.

"I thank you," she said.

"It's Christmas time, Grandma," said the attendant. "Could I give you a few pennies out of my purse?"

"Five pennies is a nickel," said Phoenix stiffly.

"Here's a nickel," said the attendant.    100

Phoenix rose carefully and held out her hand. She received the nickel and then fished the other nickel out of her pocket and laid it beside the new one. She stared at her palm closely, with her head on one side.

Then she gave a tap with her cane on the floor.

"This is what come to me to do," she said. "I going to the store and buy my child a little windmill they sells, made out of paper. He going to find it hard to believe there such a thing in the world. I'll march myself back where he waiting, holding it straight up in this hand."

She lifted her free hand, gave a little nod, turned around, and walked out of the doctor's office. Then her slow step began on the stairs, going down.


## QUESTIONS

1. From the fact that Phoenix wears an apron of "bleached sugar sacks" and ties her hair with a red rag, what do you conclude about her economic condition? Has she taken the path through the woods before? How do you know? Is she accustomed to being alone? What do you make of her speaking to animals, and of her imagining a boy offering her a piece of cake? What does her speech show about her education and general background?

2. Describe the plot of the story. With Phoenix as the protagonist, what are the antagonisms ranged against her? Are they malevolent to any degree? How might Phoenix be considered to be in the grip of large and indifferent social and political forces?

3. Describe the structure of the story according to the classes of exposition, complication, crisis, climax, and resolution. Does the actual structure correspond to this orderly arrangement? Wherein does it depart? Why?

4. Comment on the meaning of this dialogue between Phoenix and the hunter:

> "Doesn't the gun scare you?" he said, still pointing it.
> "No, sir, I seen plenty go off closer by, in my day, and for less than what I done," she said, holding utterly still.

5. A number of responses might be made to this story, among them admiration for Phoenix, pity for her and her grandson and for the downtrodden generally, anger at her impoverished condition, and apprehension about her approaching senility. Do you share in any of these responses? Do you have any others?


# TOM WHITECLOUD (b. ca. 1918)

*Blue Winds Dancing*                                                    (*1938*)

There is a moon out tonight. Moon and stars and clouds tipped with moonlight. And there is a fall wind blowing in my heart. Ever since this evening, when against a fading sky I saw geese wedge southward. They were going home. . . . Now I try to study, but against the pages I see them again, driving southward. Going home.

Across the valley there are heavy mountains holding up the night sky, and beyond the mountains there is home. Home, and peace, and the beat of drums, and blue winds dancing over snow fields. The Indian lodge will fill with my people, and our gods will come and sit among them. I should be there then. I should be at home.

But home is beyond the mountains, and I am here. Here where fall hides in the valleys, and winter never comes down from the mountains. Here where all the trees grow in rows; the palms stand stiffly by the roadsides, and in the groves' the orange trees line in military rows, and endlessly bear fruit. Beautiful, yes; there is always beauty in order, in rows of growing things! But it is the beauty of captivity. A pine fighting for existence on a windy knoll is much more beautiful.

In my Wisconsin, the leaves change before the snows come. In the air there is the smell of wild rice and venison cooking; and when the winds come whispering through the forests, they carry the smell of rotting leaves. In the evenings, the loon calls, lonely; and birds sing their last songs before leaving. Bears dig roots and eat late fall berries, fattening for their long winter sleep. Later, when the first snows fall, one awakens in the morning to find the world white and beautiful and clean. Then one can look back over his trail and see the tracks following. In the woods there are tracks of deer and snowshoe rabbits, and long streaks where partridges slide to alight. Chipmunks make tiny footprints on the limbs; and one can hear squirrels busy in hollow trees, sorting acorns. Soft lake waves wash the shores, and sunsets burst each evening over the lakes, and make them look as if they were afire.

That land which is my home! Beautiful, calm—where there is no hurry to get anywhere, no driving to keep up in a race that knows no ending and no goal.

5

No classes where men talk and talk, and then stop now and then to hear their own words come back to them from the students. No constant peering into the maelstrom of one's mind; no worries about grades and honors; no hysterical preparing for life until that life is half over; no anxiety about one's place in the thing they call Society.

I hear again the ring of axes in deep woods, the crunch of snow beneath my feet. I feel again the smooth velvet of ghost-birch bark. I hear the rhythm of the drums. . . . I am tired. I am weary of trying to keep up this bluff of being civilized. Being civilized means trying to do everything you don't want to, never doing anything you want to. It means dancing to the strings of custom and tradition; it means living in houses and never knowing or caring who is next door. These civilized white men want us to be like them—always dissatisfied—getting a hill and wanting a mountain.

Then again, maybe I am not tired. Maybe I'm licked. Maybe I am just not smart enough to grasp these things that go to make up civilization. Maybe I am just too lazy to think hard enough to keep up.

Still, I know my people have many things that civilization has taken from the whites. They know how to give; how to tear one's piece of meat in two and share it with one's brother. They know how to sing—how to make each man his own songs and sing them; for their music they do not have to listen to other men singing over a radio. They know how to make things with their hands, how to shape beads into design and make a thing of beauty from a piece of birch bark.

But we are inferior. It is terrible to have to feel inferior; to have to read reports of intelligence tests, and learn that one's race is behind. It is terrible to sit in classes and hear men tell you that your people worship sticks of wood— that your gods are all false, that the Manitou forgot your people and did not write them a book.

I am tired. I want to walk again among the ghost-birches. I want to see the    10
leaves turn in autumn, the smoke rise from the lodgehouses, and to feel the blue winds. I want to hear the drums; I want to hear the drums and feel the blue whispering winds.

There is a train wailing into the night. The trains go across the mountains. It would be easy to catch a freight. They will say he has gone back to the blanket; I don't care. The dance at Christmas. . . .

A bunch of bums warming at a tiny fire talk politics and women and joke about the Relief and the WPA and smoke cigarettes. These men in caps and over-coats and dirty overalls living on the outskirts of civilization are free, but they pay the price of being free in civilization. They are outcasts. I remember a sociology professor lecturing on adjustment to society; hobos and prostitutes and criminals are individuals who never adjusted, he said. He could learn a lot if he came and listened to a bunch of bums talk. He would learn that work and a woman and a place to hang his hat are all the ordinary man wants. These are all he wants, but other men are not content to let him want only these. He must be taught to want radios and automobiles and a new suit every spring. Progress would stop if he did not want these things. I listen to hear if there is any talk of communism or socialism in the hobo jungles. There is none. At best there is a sort of disgusted philosophy about life. They seem to think there should be a better distribution of wealth, or more work, or something. But they are not rabid about it. The radicals live in the cities.

I find a fellow headed for Albuquerque, and talk road-talk with him. "It is hard to ride fruit cars. Bums break in. Better to wait for a cattle car going back to the Middle West, and ride that." We catch the next east-bound and walk the tops until we find a cattle car. Inside, we crouch near the forward wall, huddle, and try to sleep. I feel peaceful and content at last. I am going home. The cattle car rocks. I sleep.

Morning and the desert. Noon and the Salton Sea, lying more lifeless than a mirage under a somber sun in a pale sky. Skeleton mountains rearing on the skyline, thrusting out of the desert floor, all rock and shadow and edges. Desert. Good country for an Indian reservation. . . .

Yuma and the muddy Colorado. Night again, and I wait shivering for the dawn.                                                                                              15

Phoenix. Pima country. Mountains that look like cardboard sets on a forgotten stage. Tucson. Papago country. Giant cacti that look like petrified hitchhikers along the highways. Apache country. At El Paso my road-buddy decides to go on to Houston. I leave him, and head north to the mesa country. Las Cruces and the terrible Organ Mountains, jagged peaks that instill fear and wondering. Albuquerque. Pueblos along the Rio Grande. On the boardwalk there are some Indian women in colored sashes selling bits of pottery. The stone age offering its art to the twentieth century. They hold up a piece and fix the tourists with black eyes until, embarrassed, he buys or turns away. I feel suddenly angry that my people should have to do such things for a living. . . .

Santa Fe trains are fast, and they keep them pretty clean of bums. I decide to hurry and ride passenger coaltenders. Hide in the dark, judge the speed of the train as it leaves, and then dash out, and catch it. I hug the cold steel wall of the tender and think of the roaring fire in the engine ahead, and of the passengers back in the dining car reading their papers over hot coffee. Beneath me there is a blur of rails. Death would come quick if my hands should freeze and I fall. Up over the Sangre De Cristo range, around cliffs and through canyons to Denver. Bitter cold here, and I must watch out for Denver Bob. He is a railroad bull who has thrown bums from fast freights. I miss him. It is too cold, I suppose. On north to the Sioux country.

Small towns lit for the coming Christmas. On the streets of one I see a beam-shouldered young farmer gazing into a window filled with shining silver toasters. He is tall and wears a blue shirt buttoned, with no tie. His young wife by his side looks at him hopefully. He wants decorations for his place to hang his hat to please his woman. . . .

Northward again. Minnesota, and great white fields of snow; frozen lakes, and dawn running into dusk without noon. Long forests wearing white. Bitter cold, and one night the northern lights. I am nearing home.

I reach Woodruff at midnight. Suddenly I am afraid, now that I am but twenty miles from home. Afraid of what my father will say, afraid of being looked on as a stranger by my own people. I sit by a fire and think about myself and all other young Indians. We just don't seem to fit in anywhere—certainly not among the whites, and not among the older people. I think again about the learned sociology professor and his professing. So many things seem to be clear now that I am away from school and do not have to worry about some                                                                                              20 man's opinion of my ideas. It is easy to think while looking at dancing flames.

Morning. I spend the day cleaning up, and buying some presents for my family with what is left of my money. Nothing much, but a gift is a gift, if a man buys it with his last quarter. I wait until evening, then start up the track toward home.

Christmas Eve comes in on a north wind. Snow clouds hang over the pines, and the night comes early. Walking along the railroad bed, I feel the calm peace of snowbound forests on either side of me. I take my time; I am back in a world where time does not mean so much now. I am alone; alone but not nearly so lonely as I was back on the campus at school. Those are never lonely who love the snow and the pines; never lonely when the pines are wearing white shawls and snow crunches coldly underfoot. In the woods I know there are the tracks of deer and rabbit; I know that if I leave the rails and go into the woods I shall find them. I walk along feeling glad because my legs are light and my feet seem to know that they are home. A deer comes out of the woods just ahead of me, and stands silhouetted on the rails. The North, I feel, has welcomed me home. I watch him and am glad that I do not wish for a gun. He goes into the woods quietly, leaving only the design of his tracks in the snow. I walk on. Now and then I pass a field, white under the night sky, with houses at the far end. Smoke comes from the chimneys of the houses, and I try to tell what sort of wood each is burning by the smoke; some burn pine, others aspen, others tamarack. There is one from which comes black coal smoke that rises lazily and drifts out over the tops of the trees. I like to watch houses and try to imagine what might be happening in them.

Just as a light snow begins to fall I cross the reservation boundary; somehow it seems as though I have stepped into another world. Deep woods in a white-and-black winter night. A faint trail leading to the village.

The railroad on which I stand comes from a city sprawled by a lake—a city with a million people who walk around without seeing one another; a city sucking the life from all the country around; a city with stores and police and intellectuals and criminals and movies and apartment houses; a city with its politics and libraries and zoos.

Laughing, I go into the woods. As I cross a frozen lake I begin to hear the    25
drums. Soft in the night the drums beat. It is like the pulse beat of the world. The white line of the lake ends at a black forest, and above the trees the blue winds are dancing.

I come to the outlying houses of the village. Simple box houses, etched black in the night. From one or two windows soft lamplight falls on the snow. Christmas here, too, but it does not mean much; not much in the way of parties and presents. Joe Sky will get drunk. Alex Bodidash will buy his children red mittens and a new sled. Alex is a Carlisle man, and tries to keep his home up to white standards. White standards. Funny that my people should be ever falling farther behind. The more they try to imitate whites the more tragic the result. Yet they want us to be imitation white men. About all we imitate well are their vices.

The village is not a sight to instill pride, yet I am not ashamed; one can never be ashamed of his own people when he knows they have dreams as beautiful as white snow on a tall pine.

Father and my brother and sister are seated around the table as I walk in. Father stares at me for a moment, then I am in his arms, crying on his shoulder.

I give them the presents I have brought, and my throat tightens as I watch my sister save carefully bits of red string from the packages. I hide my feelings by wrestling with my brother when he strikes my shoulder in token of affection. Father looks at me, and I know he has many questions, but he seems to know why I have come. He tells me to go on alone to the lodge, and he will follow.

I walk along the trail to the lodge, watching the northern lights forming in the heavens. White waving ribbons that seem to pulsate with the rhythm of the drums. Clean snow creaks beneath my feet, and a soft wind sighs through the trees, singing to me. Everything seems to say "Be happy! You are home now— you are free. You are among friends—we are your friends; we, the trees, and the snow, and the lights." I follow the trail to the lodge. My feet are light, my heart seems to sing to the music, and I hold my head high. Across white snow fields blue winds are dancing.

Before the lodge door I stop, afraid. I wonder if my people will remember    30
me. I wonder—"Am I Indian, or am I white?" I stand before the door a long time. I hear the ice groan on the lake, and remember the story of the old woman who is under the ice, trying to get out, so she can punish some runaway lovers. I think to myself, "If I am white I will not believe that story; if I am Indian, I will know that there is an old woman under the ice." I listen for a while, and I know that there is an old woman under the ice. I look again at the lights, and go in.

Inside the lodge there are many Indians. Some sit on benches around the walls, others dance in the center of the floor around a drum. Nobody seems to notice me. It seems as though I were among a people I have never seen before. Heavy women with long black hair. Women with children on their knees—small children that watch with intent black eyes the movements of the dancers, whose small faces are solemn and serene. The faces of the old people are serene, too, and their eyes are merry and bright. I look at the old men. Straight, dressed in dark trousers and beaded velvet vests, wearing soft moccasins. Dark, lined faces intent on the music. I wonder if I am at all like them. They dance on, lifting their feet to the rhythm of the drums, swaying lightly, looking upward. I look at their eyes, and am startled at the rapt attention to the rhythm of the music.

The dance stops. The men walk back to the walls, and talk in low tones or with their hands. There is little conversation, yet everyone seems to be sharing some secret. A woman looks at a small boy wandering away, and he comes back to her.

Strange, I think, and then remember. These people are not sharing words— they are sharing a mood. Everyone is happy. I am so used to white people that it seems strange so many people could be together without someone talking. These Indians are happy because they are together, and because the night is beautiful outside, and the music is beautiful. I try hard to forget school and white people, and be one of these—my people. I try to forget everything but the night, and it is a part of me; that I am one with my people and we are all a part of something universal. I watch eyes, and see now that the old people are speaking to me. They nod slightly, imperceptibly, and their eyes laugh into mine. I look around the room. All the eyes are friendly; they all laugh. No one questions my being here. The drums begin to beat again, and I catch the invitation in the eyes of the old men. My feet begin to lift to the rhythm, and I look out beyond the walls into the night and see the lights. I am happy. It is beautiful. I am home.

## QUESTIONS

1.   Describe the first section of the story in terms of the plot. How much is exposition? How much complication? Could a case be made that this first section contains its own crisis and climax and that the rest of the story is really a resolution?

2.   What do you learn in the first section about the conflict in the attitudes of the young Indian narrator? What is his attitude about "civilization"? What values derived from his home make him think this way? If he is the protagonist, who or what is the antagonist?

3.   What does it mean to "catch a freight"? What is the narrator's judgment about the value of acquiring things and property? Is there any contradiction in the fact that he later buys Christmas presents for his family?

4.   What does the narrator mean by saying, "I am alone; alone but not nearly so lonely as I was back on the campus at school"?

5.   Do you believe that the author, Tom Whitecloud, wants you to think that the choice made by the narrator to return home is wise or foolish? Why?

6.   What is meant by the dancing of the blue winds? What kind of wisdom is represented by this perception? What is the place for such wisdom in a computerized, industrialized society?

7.   The narrator claims that the only things that Indians can imitate well from whites are their vices. In light of this assertion, and considering the rest of the story, what sorts of roles can Indians take in society so that they might be successful while preserving their identity and integrity?

8.   Is it absolutely necessary for civilized people to forsake their love of nature and family as they become "modern," as the narrator asserts?

## WRITING ABOUT THE PLOT OF A STORY

In planning an essay about a story's plot you will need to analyze the conflict and the developments and routes it takes. The goal is not just a straightforward chronological listing, as with the précis essay (see Chapter 2). The organization of an essay about plot is not based on parts of the story or principal events, because these would invite a chronological summary. Instead, plan on organization that is grounded in the various important elements of the conflict or conflicts.

### Organizing Your Essay

**INTRODUCTION.**    The introduction contains brief references to the principal characters, circumstances, and issues of the plot. It also states the central idea for the essay in a sentence formulating the plot or the principal conflict. The thesis sentence concludes the introduction.

**BODY.**   The body focuses on the major elements of the plot, emphasizing the plan of conflict in the story. Who is the main character? What are the qualities of this character that are important in the conflict? What strengths and weaknesses does the character have? What is the conflict? How is it embodied in the story? What person or persons are the antagonists? Is the conflict one of ideas or values? What are these? Does the character face a difficult decision of any sort? Are the effects of any decision the intended ones? In terms of success by personal, occupational, or political standards, does the conflict make the principal character rise or fall? In terms of personal integrity, does the character emerge from the conflict in triumph, defeat, or somewhere in the middle? Answers to questions like these form the basis of the body of the essay.

Because a description of elements in a plot can easily become long, it is necessary to be selective and also to decide on a particular aspect to emphasize. One kind of development might treat the aspects of the conflict equally. Such an essay on "The Bride Comes to Yellow Sky," for example, might contrast Potter's new values as a married man with his older values as a single man frequently involved with juvenile but dangerous showdowns like the one Scratchy Wilson wishes to have.

Another kind of development might emphasize the protagonist and his or her qualities and values. In "Blue Winds Dancing," for example, such an essay would stress the narrator's resentment, homesickness, and desire for an Indian identity. It might be possible, too, to emphasize more broadly the values of the Indian culture to which the narrator is returning, as a contrast to the values of the predominant "civilized" culture which he is leaving. It would be possible, of course, to make the same treatment for the antagonistic side of the plot.

It is thus important to realize that there are choices in the development of the body of the essay. The plot may be analyzed simply in terms of the persons involved in the conflict, or more broadly in terms of factors such as impulses, goals, ideas, values, issues, and historical perspectives.

**CONCLUSION.**   The conclusion might contain a brief summary of the points in the body. Also, quite often a study of plot necessarily leaves out one of the most important reasons for reading, and that is the impact of the plot. Thus the conclusion is a fitting location for a brief consideration of effect. Additional comments might concentrate on an evaluation of the plot, such as whether the author has contrived it in any way to tip the balance toward one side or the other, or whether it is realistic, true to life, fair, and impartial.

## SAMPLE ESSAY

### The Plot of Eudora Welty's "A Worn Path"*

[1]
At first, the plot complexity of Eudora Welty's "A Worn Path" is not clear. The main character is Phoenix Jackson, an old, poor, and frail black woman; the story seems to be no more than a record of her walk to Natchez through the woods from her rural home. By the story's end, however, the plot is clear: It presents the brave attempts of a courageous, valiant woman to carry on normally despite overwhelming negative forces.° It is the gap between her determination and the odds against her that gives the story its impact. The powers she opposes in the story are environment, poverty, and old age.▯

[2]
Environment is shown, during that portion of the story when Phoenix walks to town, as almost an active opponent. Thus she must contend against and overcome a long hill, a thornbush, a log across a creek that poses a threat of falling, and a barbed-wire fence. Also a part of the force is the dog which attacks her. Against these obstacles, Phoenix attempts to assert her determination by carrying on a cheerful monologue. She prevails, for the moment at least, because she finally reaches her destination, the city of Natchez.

[3]
The poverty against which Phoenix must contend is not evident in any one spot, but is shown throughout. She cannot take her trip to town by car, for example, but must walk alone on the long "worn path" wearing only tennis shoes. She has no money and keeps the nickel dropped by the hunter; at the medical office she asks for and gets another nickel. She is the recipient of charity and is given the "soothing syrup" for her grandson as a free service. Despite the boy's obvious need for advanced medical care, she does not have the means to provide it, and thus her guardianship is doomed to be a failure.

[4]
Old age as an opponent is shown in signs of Phoenix's increasing senility. It is not her mind but her feet, for example, that tell her where to find the medical office in Natchez. Despite her quiet inner strength, she is unable to state her purpose to the nursing attendant, instead sitting dumbly and unknowingly for a time. Against the power of advancing age, Phoenix is slowly losing. The implication is that she soon will lose entirely.

[5]
This brief description of the plot can only hint at the final power of the story. Phoenix emerges as strong and admirable, but with everything against her nothing can enable her ever to win. The story itself is layered to bring out the full range of the conditions against her. Welty saves the most hopeless fact, the condition of the invalid grandson, to the very end. It is this delayed final revelation of the plot that creates an almost overwhelming sympathy for Phoenix. The plot is powerful because it is so real, and Phoenix is a memorable protagonist struggling against overwhelming odds.

\* See p. 101 for this story.
° Central idea.
▯ Thesis sentence.

### Commentary on the Essay

In this essay on plot, emphasis is given to the major aspects of the conflict in "A Worn Path." The plot involves the protagonist, Phoenix, who is opposed not by any person, for the other persons in the story are nice to her, but by the forces of environment, poverty, and old age. The introduction points out how these forces cumulatively account for the story's impact. Paragraph 2 details the environmental obstacles of the conflict. Paragraph 3 examines Phoenix's poverty, and the fourth paragraph considers her old age. The concluding paragraph introduces one other major conflict—the invalid condition of the grandson—as another of the forces against which Phoenix contends. This paragraph also points out that in this set of conflicts the protagonist cannot win, except as she lives out her duty and her devotion to help her grandson. Continuing the theme of the introduction, the last paragraph also accounts for the power of the plot: By building up to Phoenix's personal affirmation against unbeatable forces, the story evokes both strong sympathy and great admiration.

## WRITING ABOUT STRUCTURE IN A STORY

An essay about the structure of a story is concerned with arrangement and shape. In form, the essay does not need to follow the pattern of the story part by part. Rather it explains why things are where they are. "Why is this here and not there?" is the fundamental question you should aim to answer in your prewriting and planning. Thus you may begin with the crisis of the story, and in explaining its position to consider how the author's manipulation of the exposition and complication have built up to it. Some vital piece of information, for example, might have been withheld in the earlier exposition and delayed until the crisis; thus the crisis might be heightened because there might have been less suspense if the detail had been introduced earlier. An essay might also consider the effect or impact of the story and then analyze how the structuring produced this effect.

### Organizing Your Essay

**Introduction.**   The introduction first presents a general overview of the story and then centers on the aspect or aspects of structure to be emphasized in the body of the essay. The central idea is a succinct statement about the structure. The thesis sentence points out the various main headings of the body.

**BODY.**    The body is best developed in the light of what the story contains. For example, suppose a story contains a number of separate scenes or settings, such as the countryside, city, and building in "A Worn Path." An essay based on the structural importance of these locations would try to explain the relationship of each to the development of the plot. Similarly, both "Blue Winds Dancing" and "The Bride Comes to Yellow Sky" involve characters riding trains and then arriving at their destinations. A structural study of these stories might stem out of these locations and their relationship to the resolution of the plot.

Other noteworthy characteristics of the story can be used to develop an essay on structure. For example, in "A Worn Path" a vital piece of exposition is withheld until the conclusion. An essay on structure might consider what effects this delay produces in the story, and therefore the benefit (or detriment) of this kind of mystery or suspense structure.

It is also possible to devote the body of the essay not to the entire structure of the story, but to a major part, character, or action. Thus the climax of a story might be the principal subject. Some questions to be explored might be these: Where does the climax begin? What events are included in it? Is any new piece of information introduced in the climax? Why then and not earlier? What is the apparent way in which the climax is going to be resolved? How and how soon does the reader learn what the resolution is going to be? Similar questions might be posed and answered if the topic of the essay were to be some other aspect of the structure. With such a concentration on only one aspect of the story's structure, naturally, the introduction would need to make clear that a part rather than the whole will be explored.

In writing about the author's structuring of particular characters, it would be important to establish how the characters are introduced, how information is brought out about them, how they figure in the plot, and how they are treated in the resolution. With an action, it might be that one seemingly minor event is introduced to show the importance of fate, chance, or casual happenings in life. Or it might be that the action is not the one intended by the character or by a group. Thus the event could be seen as it influences the structuring and arrangement of the story's outcome.

**CONCLUSION.**    Here any necessary summarizing is made. Also, the conclusion might deal briefly with the relationship of structure to the plot. Much can be learned from a brief statement about any departures the structure makes from the strict chronological sequence that elements of plot might ordinarily be expected to require.

## SAMPLE ESSAY

### The Structure of Eudora Welty's "A Worn Path"*

[1] On the surface, Eudora Welty's "A Worn Path" is structured simply. The narrative is not difficult to follow, and things go forward in straight chronology. The main character is Phoenix Jackson, an old, poor black woman. She walks from her rural home in Mississippi through the woods to Natchez to get a free bottle of medicine for her grandson, who is a hopeless invalid; everything takes place in just a few hours. This action is only the frame, however, for a more skillfully structured plot making for a story of great power.° The masterly control of structure is shown in the story's locations, delayed revelation, and complicated climax.□

[2] The locations in the story are arranged to coincide with the increasing difficulties set out against Phoenix. The first and most obvious "worn path," for example, is the rural woods with all its difficulties. For most people the obstacles would be natural and not especially difficult, but for an old woman they are formidable. In Natchez, the location of the next part of the story, Phoenix's inability to bend over to tie her shoe demonstrates the lack of flexibility of old age. In the medical office, where the final scene takes place, two major difficulties of the plot are brought out. One is Phoenix's increasing senility, and the other is the disclosure that her grandson is an incurable invalid. This set of oppositions, the major conflicts in the plot, thus coincide with the places or locations in the story to demonstrate the increasing insurmountability of the conditions against which Phoenix must contend.

[3] It is the delay of the important revelation about the grandson that makes the story something like a mystery. Because this detail is not known until the end, the reader is left wondering during most of the story what might happen next to Phoenix. In fact, some of the details that are presented to show the conflicting forces against Phoenix are really false leads in terms of the major reason for which she is walking to town. For example, the episode with the dog is threatening, but it leads nowhere; Phoenix, with the aid of the hunter, is unharmed by the animal. Her theft of the nickel might be cause for punishment, but the young hunter is ignorant of the missing coin, and he makes no accusations against her. Right up to the moment of her entering the medical building, therefore, there is no apparent pending resolution. The reader is still wondering what might happen.

[4] Hence the details about the grandson, carefully concealed as they are right until the end, heighten and intensify the climax of the story. The effect is that this information forces a reconsideration of the entire story—a double take. In view of the grandson's condition, Phoenix's walk into town and all her efforts have really been a mission of mercy, but also a totally hopeless one. The delayed final detail also causes a reevaluation of Phoenix's character. She is not just a funny old woman who speaks to the objects and animals around

---

* See p. 101 for this story.
° Central idea.
□ Thesis sentence.

her, but she is an amazingly brave although pathetic woman trying to carry on normally against crushing odds. These conclusions are not apparent for most of the story, and when the carefully concealed details are brought out, the story takes on added force and pathos.

[5] Thus the parts of "A Worn Path," while seemingly simple, are skillfully arranged. The key to the double take and reevaluation is Welty's withholding of the crucial detail of exposition right until the very end. As it were, parts of the exposition and complication merge with the climax at just about the same point near the end of the story. And in some respects, the detail makes it seem as though Phoenix's entire existence is actually a crisis, although she is not aware of this condition as she leaves the office to buy the little paper windmill. It is this complex buildup and emotional peak that make the structure of "A Worn Path" the creation of a master writer.

### Commentary on the Essay

To highlight the differences between essays on plot and structure, the topic of this sample essay is Welty's "A Worn Path," the same story analyzed in the sample essay on plot. While both essays are concerned with the conflicts of the story, the essay on plot concentrates on the forces involved, while the essay on structure focuses on the placement and arrangement of the plot elements.

The introduction of this essay points out that the masterly structure accounts for the story's power. The second paragraph develops the topic that the geographical locations are arranged climactically to demonstrate the forces against the major character. Paragraph 3 deals with the delayed revelation about the invalid grandson, pointing out that the suspended detail leaves the reader concerned but baffled about the ultimate climax and resolution of the plot. The fourth paragraph deals with the complexity brought about by the delayed information: The necessary reevaluation of Phoenix's character and her mission to town. The concluding paragraph deals further with this complexity, accounting for the story's power by pointing out the virtual merging of a number of plot elements near the very end to bring things out swiftly and powerfully.

# 4

# Characters:
# The People in Fiction

**Character** in literature generally, and in fiction specifically, is an extended verbal representation of a human being, the inner self that determines thought, speech, and behavior. Through dialogue, action, and commentary, authors capture some of the interactions of character and circumstance. Fiction makes these interactions interesting by portraying characters who are worth caring about, rooting for, and even loving, although there are also characters at whom you may laugh or whom you may dislike or even hate.

## CHOICE AND CHARACTER

The choices that people make indicate their characters, if we assume that they have freedom of choice. We always make silent comparisons with the choices made or rejected. Thus, if you know that John works twelve hours a day, while Tom puts in five, and Jim sleeps under a tree, you have a number of separate facts, but you do not conclude anything about their characters unless you have a basis for comparison. This basis is easy: The usual, average number of working hours is eight. With no more than this knowledge for comparison, you might conclude that John is a workaholic, Tom lazy, and Jim either unwell or a dropout. To be fair, you would need to know much more about the lives and financial circumstances of each character before your conclusions would be final.

In fiction you may expect such completeness of context. You may think of each action or speech, no matter how small or seemingly unusual, as an accumulating part of a total portrait. Whereas in life things may "just happen," in fiction the actions, interactions, speeches, and observations are all arranged to give you the details you need for conclusions about character. Thus you read about important events like a plan to discredit a disliked fellow worker (James Thurber's "The Catbird Seat"), an action of jealousy and revenge (Katherine Anne Porter's "María Concepción"), or an act of defiance (William Faulkner's "Barn Burning"). From these events in their contexts you draw conclusions about the characters involved.

## MAJOR CHARACTER TRAITS

In studying a literary character, you should try to determine the character's major trait or traits. As in life, characters may be lazy or ambitious, anxious or serene, aggressive or fearful, assertive or bashful, confident or self-doubting, adventurous or timid, noisy or quiet, visionary or practical, reasonable or hotheaded, careful or careless, fair or partial, straightforward or underhanded, "winners" or "losers," and so on.

With this sort of list, to which you may add at will, you can analyze and develop your own conclusions about character. For example, in studying Erwin Martin, the main character in Thurber's "The Catbird Seat" (and the subject of the sample essay at the end of this chapter), you would note that on the surface he is a quiet, unassuming man, one who is normally as unnoticeable as the furniture in the office where he works. Once Mrs. Barrows enters the business and upsets his normal placidity, however, his disturbance causes him to develop a dangerous scheme to eliminate her. It is out of conflicts and reactions such as this that you can get a "handle" on characters.

## APPEARANCE, ACTION, AND CHARACTER

When you study character, be sure to consider physical descriptions, but also be sure to relate the physical to the mental. Suppose your author stresses the neatness of one character and the sloppiness of another. Most likely, these descriptions can be related to your character study. The same also applies to your examination of what a character *does*. Go beyond the actions themselves and try to determine what they show *about* the character. Always try to get from the outside to the inside, for it is on the inside that character resides.

## TYPES OF CHARACTERS: ROUND AND FLAT

In fiction you will encounter two types of characters, which E. M. Forster (in *Aspects of the Novel*) called "round" and "flat." **Round chracters** are usually the major figures in a story. They have many realistic traits and are relatively fully developed by the author. For this reason they are often given the names **hero** or **heroine.** Because many major characters are anything but heroic, however, it is probably best to use the more descriptive term, which we have introduced before, **protagonist.** The protagonist is central to the action, moves against an **antagonist,** and usually exhibits the human attributes we expect of rounded characters.

To the degree that round characters possess many individual and unpredictable human traits they may be considered as **dynamic;** that is, they demonstrate their capacity to change or to grow. In Porter's "María Concepción," for example, María is a dynamic character. She begins the story as an apparently dutiful and devoted woman who attends faithfully to her chores and religious obligations. But events bring out some of her jealousy, coldness, and rage so that she commits a violent act of revenge. By the story's end, she is not a subservient but a dominant woman.

In considering a round character, you may decide for yourself whether such alterations are really *change* or whether they are *growth*. Is human character capable of change, or is change more accurately described as growth or development? If María is apparently dutiful and quiet, for example, but commits an act of vengeance, does this act show that she has changed, or does it show that firmness, resoluteness, personal honor, and ruthlessness are qualities of her character that were latent but that could be brought out by strong provocation? With round or full characters, a question of this type is appropriate, for round characters are just as complex and as difficult to understand as individual living people. A round character therefore stands out, totally identifiable within the class, occupation, or circumstances of which she or he is a part. Obviously, in a brief story we cannot learn everything there is to know about a major character, but if the author is skillful, there will be enough in the story to enable us to get the significant details that add up to a memorable character. Indeed, an author is to be judged by how fully he or she can bring round characters to life as memorable individuals.

As contrasted with round characters, **flat characters** are essentially undistinguishable from their group or class. Therefore they are not individual, but **representative.** They are usually minor characters, although not all minor characters are flat. They are mostly useful and structural in the stories. Usually they stay the same; they are **static,** and not dynamic like round characters. Thus, they make announcements, drive major characters to airports, describe duties or services they performed, serve meals, provide essential information, and perform the innumerable other tasks that are important in the development of a story. We learn little if anything about their traits and their lives. They are not developed, and because they are not central to the plot they do not change or grow.

Sometimes flat characters are prominent in certain types of fiction, such as cowboy, police, and detective stories, where the main characters need to be strong, tough, steadfast, and clever so that they may overcome the obstacles before them or solve the crime. These and other types of stories feature recurring situations and require characters to perform similar roles. The term **stock character** is used to refer to characters that perform in these repeating situations. Obviously, names, ages, and sexes are often changed, and places and offices are slightly different, but stock characters have many common traits. Some of the many stock characters are the clown, the revenger, the foolish boss, the bewildered parent, the macho male, the unfaithful husband or wife, the long-suffering wife, the angry police captain, the lovable drunk, the kid sister or brother, and the nice hotel keeper.

These characters are not necessarily flat, but they stay flat as long as they perform only their functions, exhibit conventional and unindividual characteristics, and then disappear from the story and from your memory. When stock characters possess no attitudes except those to be expected from their class, they are often given the label **stereotype,** because they all seem to be cast in the same mold. Often in highly conventionalized stories like the cowboy and police stories mentioned above, and in romances, even the major characters are flat and stereotypical even though they occupy center stage throughout.

Complications occur when round characters are in stock situations and might be expected to behave stereotypically. Thus Juan Villegas in "María Concepción" exhibits characteristics of the macho male and unfaithful husband. The plot of the story develops, however, because María Concepción does not accept the role of the stereotypical long-suffering wife, but takes on some of the qualities of a revenger. Because of this complication, and also because of her very human responses to the murder, she is dynamic, a fully realized and round individual. Had she simply looked the other way at Juan's philanderings, she would have been flat, representative, and stereotypical, and there would have been no story. Erwin Martin of "The Catbird Seat" is another character who emerges from a stock role as an office wallflower to assume status as a round character. The other people in the story have always taken him as quiet and unassuming, but by the story's end he has become individual, round, human, and therefore memorable.

## HOW IS CHARACTER DISCLOSED IN FICTION?

Authors use four different ways to convey information about characters in fiction. As you read, remember that you must use your own knowledge and experience with human beings to make judgments about the qualities—the flatness or roundness—of the characters being revealed.

1. *What the characters themselves say* (*and think, if the author expresses their thoughts*). On the whole, speeches may be accepted at face value to indicate the character of the speaker. Sometimes, however, a speech may be made offhand, or it may reflect a momentary emotional or intellectual state. Thus, if characters in deep despair say that life is worthless, you must balance this speech with what the same characters say when they are happy. You must also consider the situation or total context of a statement. Macbeth's despair at the end of Shakespeare's play *Macbeth* is voiced after he has been guilty of ruthless political suppression and assassination. His speech therefore reflects his own guilt and self-hatred. You should also consider whether speeches show change or development. A despairing character might say depressing things at the start but happy things at the end. Your analysis of such speeches should indicate how they show change in your character.

2. *What the characters do.* You have heard that "actions speak louder than words," and you should interpret actions as signs of character. Thus you might consider Phoenix's trip through the woods (Welty's "A Worn Path") as a sign of a loving, responsible character, even though Phoenix nowhere says that she is loving and responsible. The difficulty and hardship she goes through on the walk, however, justify such a conclusion about this character.

Often you will find that action is inconsistent with logic or expectation. Such behaviors may signal naiveté, weakness, deceit, a scheme or subterfuge, a change or realization of some sort, or strong inner conflict. For example, in Porter's "María Concepción" the medicine woman Lupe has overwhelming personal cause to turn María Concepción over to the police for murder. But she permits María to go free because of her realization: Her identification with her own community, María included, is stronger than her wish for personal revenge. Sarty, in Faulkner's "Barn Burning," warns de Spain because his commitment to truth is greater than his loyalty to his father. In Thurber's "The Catbird Seat," Erwin Martin indulges conspicuously in untypical behavior because he is scheming to overthrow Mrs. Barrows.

3. *What other characters say about them.* In stories and plays, as in life, people often talk about other people. If the speakers are shown as honest, you may usually accept their opinions as accurate descriptions of character. However, sometimes a person's prejudices and interests distort what that person says. You know, for example, that the word of a person's enemy is usually slanted, unfair, or even untrue. Therefore an author may give you a good impression of characters by having a bad character say bad things about them. Similarly, the word of a close friend may be biased in favor of a particular character. You must always consider the context and source of all remarks before you use them in your evaluation.

4. *What the author says about them, speaking as storyteller or observer.* What the author says about a character is usually to be accepted as truth. Natu-

rally, authors must be accepted on matters of fact. However, when they *interpret* the actions and characteristics of their characters, they themselves assume the critic's role, and their opinions may be either right or wrong. For this reason authors frequently avoid interpretations and devote their skill instead to arranging events and speeches so that the conclusions may be drawn by the reader.

## REALITY AND PROBABILITY: VERISIMILITUDE

You are entitled to expect that characters in literature will be true to life. That is, their actions, statements, and thoughts must all be what human beings are *likely* to do, say, and think under given conditions. This expectation is often called the standard of **probability, verisimilitude** ("similar to truth"), or **plausibility.** That is, there are often unusual persons in life who do exceptional things. Such characters in a work of fiction would not be true to life, however, because they are not within our judgment of *normal* human behavior. They are not probable or believable.

One should therefore distinguish between what can *possibly* happen and what would frequently or most usually happen. Some reactions do not belong in a story involving full, round characters. Thus, for example, in De Maupassant's "The Necklace," it is possible that Mathilde could have told Jeanne Forrestier that she had lost the necklace. In light of the sense of pride, honor, shame, and respectability of Mathilde and her husband, however, it is more normal for her to hide the fact, buy a replacement necklace, and endure the ten-year hardship needlessly. The probable here has overshadowed the possible.

Nevertheless, probability does not rule out surprise or even exaggeration. Thus in Thurber's "The Catbird Seat" the main character, Erwin Martin, improvises an outrageously clever and effective scheme to discredit Ulgine Barrows. This action is farcical and sudden, but it is not improbable given the energetic but secret private life of Martin and also the extremity of his original plot to murder her. Martin's later imperturbability is actually less probable than his enactment of his "confession" with Mrs. Barrows.

There are, of course, many ways of rendering the probable in literature. Fiction that attempts to mirror life—the realistic, naturalistic, or "slice of life" types of fiction—sets up conditions and raises expectations about the characters that are different from those of fiction that attempts to portray a romantic, fanciful world. A character's behavior and speech in the "realistic" setting would be out of place in the romantic setting.

But the situation is more complex than this, for within the romantic setting a character might reasonably be *expected* to behave and speak in a fanciful, dreamlike way. Speech and action under both conditions are therefore *probable* as we understand the word, although different aspects of human character are presented in these two different types of works.

It is also possible that within the same work you might find some characters who are realistic and others who are not. In such works you have contrasting systems of reality. Mathilde in "The Necklace" exhibits such a contrast. Her dream world at the beginning is so powerful that she makes unrealistic demands on her husband. When the borrowed necklace is lost, her character as a dreamer has effectively destroyed her life in the real world. You might also encounter works where there are *mythical* or *supernatural* figures who contrast with the reality of the other characters. Such a contrast may be found in Marjorie Pickthall's "The Worker in Sandalwood," where there is a young boy who is real and who is visited on Christmas Eve by the boy Jesus. The magic of the story results from the mingling of the real and the miraculous.

You may reasonably wonder about how you should judge the characters of gods, like the boy Jesus in Pickthall's story, or devils, like the woodland guide in Nathaniel Hawthorne's "Young Goodman Brown." Usually gods embody the qualities of the best human beings, whereas devils take on the attributes of the worst. However, one should also remember that the devil is often imagined as a character with many engaging traits, the easier to deceive poor sinners and lead them into hell. In judging characters of this or any type, the best guide is that of probability, consistency, and believability.

As you read, then, look carefully at the development of character. When comments are made about a figure, determine whether these are true. When characters go into action, consider what these actions tell about their natures. If there are unusual traits, determine what they show. Above all, try to conclude whether the characters come to life as round, individual, and dynamic, or whether they stay on the page as flat, static, and only representative.

## KATHERINE ANNE PORTER (1890–1980)

*María Concepción*                                                        *1930*

María Concepción walked carefully, keeping to the middle of the white dusty road, where the maguey thorns and the treacherous curved spines of organ cactus had not gathered so profusely. She would have enjoyed resting for a moment in the dark shade by the roadside, but she had no time to waste drawing cactus needles from her feet. Juan and his chief would be waiting for their food in the damp trenches of the buried city.

She carried about a dozen living fowls slung over her right shoulder, their feet fastened together. Half of them fell upon the flat of her back, the balance dangled uneasily over her breast. They wriggled their benumbed and swollen legs against her neck, they twisted their stupefied eyes and peered into her face inquiringly. She did not see them or think of them. Her left arm was tired with the weight of the food basket, and she was hungry after her long morning's work.

Her straight back outlined itself strongly under her clean bright blue cotton rebozo.° Instinctive serenity softened her black eyes, shaped like almonds, set far

*rebozo*: a long scarf or shawl.

apart, and tilted a bit endwise. She walked with the free, natural, guarded ease of the primitive woman carrying an unborn child. The shape of her body was easy, the swelling life was not a distortion, but the right inevitable proportions of a woman. She was entirely contented. Her husband was at work and she was on her way to market to sell her fowls.

Her small house sat half-way up a shallow hill, under a clump of pepper-trees, a wall of organ cactus enclosing it on the side nearest to the road. Now she came down into the valley, divided by the narrow spring, and crossed a bridge of loose stones near the hut where María Rosa the beekeeper lived with her old godmother, Lupe the medicine woman. María Concepción had no faith in the charred owl bones, the singed rabbit fur, the cat entrails, the messes and ointments sold by Lupe to the ailing of the village. She was a good Christian, and drank simple herb teas for headache and stomachache, or bought her remedies bottled, with printed directions that she could not read, at the drugstore near the city market, where she went almost daily. But she often bought a jar of honey from young María Rosa, a pretty, shy child only fifteen years old.

María Concepción and her husband, Juan Villegas, were each a little past their eighteenth year. She had a good reputation with the neighbors as an energetic religious woman who could drive a bargain to the end. It was commonly known that if she wished to buy a new rebozo for herself or a shirt for Juan, she could bring out a sack of hard silver coins for the purpose. 5

She had paid for the license, nearly a year ago, the potent bit of stamped paper which permits people to be married in the church. She had given money to the priest before she and Juan walked together up to the altar the Monday after Holy Week. It had been the adventure of the villagers to go, three Sundays one after another, to hear the banns called by the priest for Juan de Dios Villegas and María Concepción Manríquez, who were actually getting married in the church, instead of behind it, which was the usual custom, less expensive, and as binding as any other ceremony. But María Concepción was always as proud as if she owned a hacienda.

She paused on the bridge and dabbled her feet in the water, her eyes resting themselves from the sun-rays in a fixed gaze to the far-off mountains, deeply blue under their hanging drift of clouds. It came to her that she would like a fresh crust of honey. The delicious aroma of bees, their slow thrilling hum, awakened a pleasant desire for a flake of sweetness in her mouth.

"If I do not eat it now, I shall mark my child," she thought, peering through the crevices in the thick hedge of cactus that sheered up nakedly, like bared knife blades set protectingly around the small clearing. The place was so silent she doubted if María Rosa and Lupe were at home.

The leaning jacal° of dried rush-withes and corn sheaves, bound to tall sap-lings thrust into the earth, roofed with yellowed maguey leaves flattened and overlapping like shingles, hunched drowsy and fragrant in the warmth of noonday. The hives, similarly made, were scattered towards the back of the clearing, like small mounds of clean vegetable refuse. Over each mound there hung a dusty golden shimmer of bees.

A light gay scream of laughter rose from behind the hut; a man's short laugh joined in. "Ah, hahahaha!" went the voices together high and low, like a song. 10

*jacal*: a small, thatched-roof hut.

"So María Rosa has a man!" María Concepción stopped short, smiling, shifted her burden slightly, and bent forward shading her eyes to see more clearly through the spaces of the hedge.

María Rosa ran, dodging between beehives, parting two stunted jasmine bushes as she came, lifting her knees in swift leaps, looking over her shoulder and laughing in a quivering, excited way. A heavy jar, swung to her wrist by the handle, knocked against her thighs as she ran. Her toes pushed up sudden spurts of dust, her half-raveled braids showered around her shoulders in long crinkled wisps.

Juan Villegas ran after her, also laughing strangely, his teeth set, both rows gleaming behind the small soft black beard growing sparsely on his lips, his chin, leaving his brown cheeks girl-smooth. When he seized her, he clenched so hard her chemise gave way and ripped from her shoulder. She stopped laughing at this, pushed him away and stood silent, trying to pull up the torn sleeve with one hand. Her pointed chin and dark red mouth moved in an uncertain way, as if she wished to laugh again; her long black lashes flickered with the quick-moving lights in her hidden eyes.

María Concepción did not stir nor breathe for some seconds. Her forehead was cold, and yet boiling water seemed to be pouring slowly along her spine. An unaccountable pain was in her knees, as if they were broken. She was afraid Juan and María Rosa would feel her eyes fixed upon them and would find her there, unable to move, spying upon them. But they did not pass beyond the enclosure, nor even glance towards the gap in the wall opening upon the road.

Juan lifted one of María Rosa's loosened braids and slapped her neck with it playfully. She smiled softly, consentingly. Together they moved back through the hives of honey-comb. María Rosa balanced her jar on one hip and swung her long full petticoats with every step. Juan flourished his wide hat back and forth, walking proudly as a game-cock.

María Concepción came out of the heavy cloud which enwrapped her head and bound her throat, and found herself walking onward, keeping the road without knowing it, feeling her way delicately, her ears strumming as if all María Rosa's bees had hived in them. Her careful sense of duty kept her moving toward the buried city where Juan's chief, the American archeologist, was taking his midday rest, waiting for his food.

Juan and María Rosa! She burned all over now, as if a layer of tiny fig-cactus bristles, as cruel as spun glass, had crawled under her skin. She wished to sit down quietly and wait for her death, but not until she had cut the throats of her man and that girl who were laughing and kissing under the cornstalks. Once when she was a young girl she had come back from market to find her jacal burned to a pile of ash and her few silver coins gone. A dark empty feeling had filled her; she kept moving about the place, not believing her eyes, expecting it all to take shape again before her. But it was gone, and though she knew an enemy had done it, she could not find out who it was, and could only curse and threaten the air. Now here was a worse thing, but she knew her enemy. María Rosa, that sinful girl, shameless! She heard herself saying a harsh, true word about María Rosa, saying it aloud as if she expected someone to agree with her: "Yes, she is a whore! She has no right to live."

At this moment the gray untidy head of Givens appeared over the edges of

15

the newest trench he had caused to be dug in his field of excavations. The long deep crevasses, in which a man might stand without being seen, lay crisscrossed like orderly gashes of a giant scalpel. Nearly all of the men of the community worked for Givens, helping him to uncover the lost city of their ancestors. They worked all the year through and prospered, digging every day for those small clay heads and bits of pottery and fragments of painted walls for which there was no good use on earth, being all broken and encrusted with clay. They themselves could make better ones, perfectly stout and new, which they took to town and peddled to foreigners for real money. But the unearthly delight of the chief in finding these worn-out things was an endless puzzle. He would fairly roar for joy at times, waving a shattered pot or a human skull above his head, shouting for his photographer to come and make a picture of this!

Now he emerged, and his young enthusiast's eyes welcomed María Concepción from his old-man face, covered with hard wrinkles and burned to the color of red earth. "I hope you've brought me a nice fat one." He selected a fowl from the bunch dangling nearest him as María Concepción, wordless, leaned over the trench. "Dress it for me, there's a good girl, I'll broil it."

María Concepción took the fowl by the head, and silently, swiftly drew her     20
knife across its throat, twisting the head off with the casual firmness she might use with the top of a beet.

"Good God, woman, you do have nerve," said Givens, watching her. "I can't do that. It gives me the creeps."

"My home country is Guadalajara," explained María Concepción, without bravado, as she picked and gutted the fowl.

She stood and regarded Givens condescendingly, that diverting white man who had no woman of his own to cook for him, and moreover appeared not to feel any loss of dignity in preparing his own food. He squatted now, eyes squinted, nose wrinkled to avoid the smoke, turning the roasting fowl busily on a stick. A mysterious man, undoubtedly rich, and Juan's chief, therefore to be respected, to be placated.

"The tortillas are fresh and hot, señor," she murmured gently. "With your permission I will now go to market."

"Yes, yes, run along; bring me another of these tomorrow." Givens turned     25
his head to look at her again. Her grand manner sometimes reminded him of royalty in exile. He noticed her unnatural paleness. "The sun is too hot, eh?" he asked.

"Yes, sir. Pardon me, but Juan will be here soon?"

"He ought to be here now. Leave his food. The others will eat it."

She moved away; the blue of her rebozo became a dancing spot in the heat waves that rose from the gray-red soil. Givens liked his Indians best when he could feel a fatherly indulgence for their primitive childish ways. He told comic stories of Juan's escapades, of how often he had saved him, in the past five years, from going to jail, and even from being shot, for his varied and always unexpected misdeeds.

"I am never a minute too soon to get him out of one pickle or another," he would say. "Well, he's a good worker, and I know how to manage him."

After Juan was married, he used to twit him, with exactly the right shade     30
of condescension, on his many infidelities to María Concepción. "She'll catch you

yet, and God help you!" he was fond of saying, and Juan would laugh with immense pleasure.

It did not occur to María Concepción to tell Juan she had found him out. During the day her anger against him died, and her anger against María Rosa grew. She kept saying to herself, "When I was a young girl like María Rosa, if a man had caught hold of me so, I would have broken my jar over his head." She forgot completely that she had not resisted even so much as María Rosa, on the day that Juan had first taken hold of her. Besides she had married him afterwards in the church, and that was a very different thing.

Juan did not come home that night, but went away to war and María Rosa went with him. Juan had a rifle at his shoulder and two pistols at his belt. María Rosa wore a rifle also, slung on her back along with the blankets and the cooking pots. They joined the nearest detachment of troops in the field, and María Rosa marched ahead with the battalion of experienced women of war, which went over the crops like locusts, gathering provisions for the army. She cooked with them, and ate with them what was left after the men had eaten. After battles she went out on the field with the others to salvage clothing and ammunition and guns from the slain before they should begin to swell in the heat. Sometimes they would encounter the women from the other army, and a second battle as grim as the first would take place.

There was no particular scandal in the village. People shrugged, grinned. It was far better that they were gone. The neighbors went around saying that María Rosa was safer in the army than she would be in the same village with María Concepción.

María Concepción did not weep when Juan left her; and when the baby was born, and died within four days, she did not weep. "She is mere stone," said old Lupe, who went over and offered charms to preserve the baby.

"May you rot in hell with your charms," said María Concepción.

35

If she had not gone so regularly to church, lighting candles before the saints, kneeling with her arms spread in the form of a cross for hours at a time, and receiving holy communion every month, there might have been talk of her being devil-possessed, her face was so changed and blind-looking. But this was impossible when, after all, she had been married by the priest. It must be, they reasoned, that she was being punished for her pride. They decided that this was the true cause for everything: she was altogether too proud. So they pitied her.

During the year that Juan and María Rosa were gone María Concepción sold her fowls and looked after her garden and her sack of hard coins grew. Lupe had no talent for bees, and the hives did not prosper. She began to blame María Rosa for running away, and to praise María Concepción for her behavior. She used to see María Concepción at the market or at church, and she always said that no one could tell by looking at her now that she was a woman who had such a heavy grief.

"I pray God everything goes well with María Concepción from this out," she would say, "for she has had her share of trouble."

When some idle person repeated this to the deserted woman, she went down to Lupe's house and stood within the clearing and called to the medicine woman, who sat in her doorway stirring a mess of her infallible cure for sores: "Keep your prayers to yourself, Lupe, or offer them for others who need them. I will ask God for what I want in this world."

"And will you get it, you think, María Concepción?" asked Lupe, tittering    40 cruelly and smelling the wooden mixing spoon. "Did you pray for what you have now?"

Afterward everyone noticed that María Concepción went oftener to church, and even seldomer to the village to talk with the other women as they sat along the curb, nursing their babies and eating fruit, at the end of the market-day.

"She is wrong to take us for enemies," said old Soledad, who was a thinker and a peace-maker. "All women have these troubles. Well, we should suffer together."

But María Concepción lived alone. She was gaunt, as if something were gnawing her away inside, her eyes were sunken, and she would not speak a word if she could help it. She worked harder than ever, and her butchering knife was scarcely ever out of her hand.

Juan and María Rosa, disgusted with military life, came home one day without asking permission of anyone. The field of war had unrolled itself, a long scroll of vexations, until the end had frayed out within twenty miles of Juan's village. So he and María Rosa, now lean as a wolf, burdened with a child daily expected, set out with no farewells to the regiment and walked home.

They arrived one morning about daybreak. Juan was picked up on sight by    45 a group of military police from the small barracks on the edge of town, and taken to prison, where the officer in charge told him with impersonal cheerfulness that he would add one to a catch of ten waiting to be shot as deserters the next morning.

María Rosa, screaming and falling on her face in the road, was taken under the armpits by two guards and helped briskly to her jacal, now sadly run down. She was received with professional importance by Lupe, who helped the baby to be born at once.

Limping with foot soreness, a layer of dust concealing his fine new clothes got mysteriously from somewhere, Juan appeared before the captain at the barracks. The captain recognized him as head digger for his good friend Givens, and dispatched a note to Givens saying: "I am holding the person of Juan Villegas awaiting your further disposition."

When Givens showed up Juan was delivered to him with the urgent request that nothing be made public about so humane and sensible an operation on the part of military authority.

Juan walked out of the rather stifling atmosphere of the drumhead court, a definite air of swagger about him. His hat, of unreasonable dimensions and embroidered with silver thread, hung over one eyebrow, secured at the back by a cord of silver dripping with bright blue tassels. His shirt was of a checkerboard pattern in green and black, his white cotton trousers were bound by a belt of yellow leather tooled in red. His feet were bare, full of stone bruises, and sadly ragged as to toenails. He removed his cigarette from the corner of his full-lipped wide mouth. He removed the splendid hat. His black dusty hair, pressed moistly to his forehead, sprang up suddenly in a cloudy thatch on his crown. He bowed to the officer, who appeared to be gazing at a vacuum. He swung his arm wide in a free circle upsoaring towards the prison window, where forlorn heads poked over the window sill, hot eyes following after the lucky departing one. Two or three of the heads nodded, and a half dozen hands were flipped at him in an effort to imitate his own casual and heady manner.

Juan kept up this insufferable pantomine until they rounded the first clump of fig-cactus. Then he seized Givens' hand and burst into oratory. "Blessed be the day your servant Juan Villegas first came under your eyes. From this day my life is yours without condition, ten thousand thanks with all my heart!"

"For God's sake stop playing the fool," said Givens irritably. "Some day I'm going to be five minutes too late."

"Well, it is nothing much to be shot, my chief—certainly you know I was not afraid—but to be shot in a drove of deserters, against a cold wall, just in the moment of my home-coming, by order of that. . . ."

Glittering epithets tumbled over one another like explosions of a rocket. All the scandalous analogies from the animal and vegetable worlds were applied in a vivid, unique and personal way to the life, loves, and family history of the officer who had just set him free. When he had quite cursed himself dry, and his nerves were soothed, he added: "With your permission, my chief!"

"What will María Concepción say to all this?" asked Givens. "You are very informal, Juan, for a man who was married in the church."

Juan put on his hat.

"Oh, María Concepción! That's nothing. Look, my chief, to be married in the church is a great misfortune for a man. After that he is not himself any more. How can that woman complain when I do not drink even at fiestas enough to be really drunk? I do not beat her; never, never. We were always at peace. I say to her, Come here, and she comes straight. I say, Go there, and she goes quickly. Yet sometimes I looked at her and thought, Now I am married to that woman in the church, and I felt a sinking inside, as if something were lying heavy on my stomach. With María Rosa it is all different. She is not silent; she talks. When she talks too much, I slap her and say, Silence, thou simpleton! and she weeps. She is just a girl with whom I do as I please. You know how she used to keep those clean little bees in their hives? She is like their honey to me. I swear it. I would not harm María Concepción because I am married to her in the church; but also, my chief, I will not leave María Rosa, because she pleases me more than any other woman."

"Let me tell you, Juan, things haven't been going as well as you think. You be careful. Some day María Concepción will just take your head off with that carving knife of hers. You keep that in mind."

Juan's expression was the proper blend of masculine triumph and sentimental melancholy. It was pleasant to see himself in the role of hero to two such desirable women. He had just escaped from the threat of a disagreeable end. His clothes were new and handsome, and they had cost him just nothing. María Rosa had collected them for him here and there after battles. He was walking in the early sunshine, smelling the good smells of ripening cactus-figs, peaches, and melons, of pungent berries dangling from the pepper-trees, and the smoke of his cigarette under his nose. He was on his way to civilian life with his patient chief. His situation was ineffably perfect, and he swallowed it whole.

"My chief," he addressed Givens handsomely, as one man of the world to another, "women are good things, but not at this moment. With your permission,

50

55

I will now go to the village and eat. My God, *how* I shall eat! Tomorrow morning very early I will come to the buried city and work like seven men. Let us forget María Concepción and María Rosa. Each one in her place. I will manage them when the time comes."

News of Juan's adventure soon got abroad, and Juan found many friends  60
about him during the morning. They frankly commended his way of leaving the army. It was in itself the act of a hero. The new hero ate a great deal and drank somewhat, the occasion being better than a feast-day. It was almost noon before he returned to visit María Rosa.

He found her sitting on a clean straw mat, rubbing fat on her three-hour-old son. Before this felicitous vision Juan's emotions so twisted him that he returned to the village and invited every man in the "Death and Resurrection" pulque° shop to drink with him.

Having thus taken leave of his balance, he started back to María Rosa, and found himself unaccountably in his own house, attempting to beat María Concepción by way of reestablishing himself in his legal household.

María Concepción, knowing all the events of that unhappy day, was not in a yielding mood, and refused to be beaten. She did not scream nor implore; she stood her ground and resisted; she even struck at him. Juan, amazed, hardly knowing what he did, stepped back and gazed at her inquiringly through a leisurely whirling film which seemed to have lodged behind his eyes. Certainly he had not even thought of touching her. Oh, well, no harm done. He gave up, turned away, half-asleep on his feet. He dropped amiably in a shadowed corner and began to snore.

María Concepción, seeing that he was quiet, began to bind the legs of her fowls. It was market-day and she was late. She fumbled and tangled the bits of cord in her haste, and set off across the plowed fields instead of taking the accustomed road. She ran with a crazy panic in her head, her stumbling legs. Now and then she would stop and look about her, trying to place herself, then go on a few steps, until she realized that she was not going towards the market.

At once she came to her senses completely, recognized the thing that troubled  65
her so terribly, was certain of what she wanted. She sat down quietly under a sheltering thorny bush and gave herself over to her long devouring sorrow. The thing which had for so long squeezed her whole body into a tight dumb knot of suffering suddenly broke with shocking violence. She jerked with the involuntary recoil of one who receives a blow, and the sweat poured from her skin as if the wounds of her whole life were shedding their salt ichor. Drawing her rebozo over her head, she bowed her forehead on her updrawn knees, and sat there in deadly silence and immobility. From time to time she lifted her head where the sweat formed steadily and poured down her face, drenching the front of her chemise, and her mouth had the shape of crying, but there were no tears and no sound. All her being was a dark confused memory of grief burning in her at night, of deadly baffled anger eating at her by day, until her very tongue tasted bitter, and her feet were as heavy as if she were mired in the muddy roads during the time of rains.

After a great while she stood up and threw the rebozo off her face, and set out walking again.

*pulque*: a milky alcoholic drink.

Juan awakened slowly, with long yawns and grumblings, alternated with short relapses into sleep full of visions and clamors. A blur of orange light seared his eyeballs when he tried to unseal his lids. There came from somewhere a low voice weeping without tears, saying meaningless phrases over and over. He began to listen. He tugged at the leash of his stupor, he strained to grasp those words which terrified him even though he could not quite hear them. Then he came awake with frightening suddenness, sitting up and staring at the long sharpened streak of light piercing the corn-husk walls from the level disappearing sun.

María Concepción stood in the doorway, looming colossally tall to his betrayed eyes. She was talking quickly, and calling his name. Then he saw her clearly.

"God's name!" said Juan, frozen to the marrow, "here I am facing my death!" for the long knife she wore habitually at her belt was in her hand. But instead, she threw it away, clear from her, and got down on her knees, crawling toward him as he had seen her crawl many times toward the shrine at Guadalupe Villa. He watched her approach with such horror that the hair of his head seemed to be lifting itself away from him. Falling forward upon her face, she huddled over him, lips moving in a ghostly whisper. Her words became clear, and Juan understood them all.

For a second he could not move nor speak. Then he took her head between both his hands, and supported her in this way, saying swiftly, anxiously reassuring, almost in a babble:

"Oh, thou poor creature! Oh, madwoman! Oh, my María Concepción, unfortunate! Listen. . . . Don't be afraid. Listen to me! I will hide thee away, I thy own man will protect thee! Quiet! Not a sound!"

Trying to collect himself, he held her and cursed under his breath for a few moments in the gathering darkness. María Concepción bent over, face almost on the ground, her feet folded under her, as if she would hide behind him. For the first time in his life Juan was aware of danger. This was danger. María Concepción would be dragged away between two gendarmes, with him following helpless and unarmed, to spend the rest of her days in Belén Prison, maybe. Danger! The night swarmed with threats. He stood up and dragged her up with him. She was silent and perfectly rigid, holding to him with resistless strength, her hands stiffened on his arms.

"Get me the knife," he told her in a whisper. She obeyed, her feet slipping along the hard earth floor, her shoulders straight, her arms close to her side. He lighted a candle. María Concepción held the knife out to him. It was stained and dark even to the handle with drying blood.

He frowned at her harshly, noting the same stains on her chemise and hands.

"Take off thy clothes and wash thy hands," he ordered. He washed the knife carefully, and threw the water wide of the doorway. She watched him and did likewise with the bowl in which she had bathed.

"Light the brasero and cook food for me," he told her in the same peremptory tone. He took her garments and went out. When he returned, she was wearing an old soiled dress, and was fanning the fire in the charcoal burner. Seating himself cross-legged near her, he stared at her as at a creature unknown to him, who bewildered him utterly, for whom there was no possible explanation. She did not turn her head, but kept silent and still, except for the movements of her strong hands fanning the blaze which cast sparks and small jets of white smoke, flaring

70

75

and dying rhythmically with the motion of the fan, lighting her face and darkening it by turns.

Juan's voice barely disturbed the silence: "Listen to me carefully, and tell me the truth, and when the gendarmes come here for us, thou shalt have nothing to fear. But there will be something for us to settle between us afterward."

The light from the charcoal burner shone in her eyes; a yellow phosphorescence glimmered behind the dark iris.

"For me everything is settled now," she answered, in a tone so tender, so grave, so heavy with suffering, that Juan felt his vitals contract. He wished to repent openly, not as a man, but as a very small child. He could not fathom her, nor himself, nor the mysterious fortunes of life grown so instantly confused where all had seemed so gay and simple. He felt too that she had become invaluable, a woman without equal among a million women, and he could not tell why. He drew an enormous sigh that rattled in his chest.

"Yes, yes, it is all settled. I shall not go away again. We must stay here together."                                                                                        80

Whispering, he questioned her and she answered whispering, and he instructed her over and over until she had her lesson by heart. The hostile darkness of the night encroached upon them, flowing over the narrow threshold, invading their hearts. It brought with it sighs and murmurs, the pad of secretive feet in the near-by road, the sharp staccato whimper of wind through the cactus leaves. All these familiar, once friendly cadences were now invested with sinister terrors; a dread, formless and uncontrollable, took hold of them both.

"Light another candle," said Juan, loudly, in too resolute, too sharp a tone. "Let us eat now."

They sat facing each other and ate from the same dish, after their old habit. Neither tasted what they ate. With food half-way to his mouth, Juan listened. The sound of voices rose, spread, widened at the turn of the road along the cactus wall. A spray of lantern light shot through the hedge, a single voice slashed the blackness, ripped the fragile layer of silence suspended above the hut.

"Juan Villegas!"

"Pass, friends!" Juan roared back cheerfully.                                             85

They stood in the doorway, simple cautious gendarmes from the village, mixed-bloods themselves with Indian sympathies, well known to all the community. They flashed their lanterns almost apologetically upon the pleasant, harmless scene of a man eating supper with his wife.

"Pardon, brother," said the leader. "Someone has killed the woman María Rosa, and we must question her neighbors and friends." He paused, and added with an attempt at severity, "Naturally!"

"Naturally," agreed Juan. "You know that I was a good friend of María Rosa. This is bad news."

They all went away together, the men walking in a group, María Concepción following a few steps in the rear, near Juan. No one spoke.

The two points of candlelight at María Rosa's head fluttered uneasily; the shadows            90
shifted and dodged on the stained darkened walls. To María Concepción everything in the smothering enclosing room shared an evil restlessness. The watchful faces of those called as witnesses, the faces of old friends, were made alien by the look

of speculation in their eyes. The ridges of the rose-colored rebozo thrown over the body varied continually, as though the thing it covered was not perfectly in repose. Her eyes swerved over the body in the open painted coffin, from the candle tips at the head to the feet, jutting up thinly, the small scarred soles protruding, freshly washed, a mass of crooked, half-healed wounds, thornpricks and cuts of sharp stones. Her gaze went back to the candle flame, to Juan's eyes warning her, to the gendarmes talking among themselves. Her eyes would not be controlled.

With a leap that shook her her gaze settled upon the face of María Rosa. Instantly her blood ran smoothly again: there was nothing to fear. Even the restless light could not give a look of life to that fixed countenance. She was dead. María Concepción felt her muscles give way softly; her heart began beating steadily without effort. She knew no more rancor against the pitiable thing, lying indifferently in its blue coffin under the fine silk rebozo. The mouth drooped sharply at the corners in a grimace of weeping arrested half-way. The brows were distressed; the dead flesh could not cast off the shape of its last terror. It was all finished. María Rosa had eaten too much honey and had had too much love. Now she must sit in hell, crying over her sins and her hard death forever and ever.

Old Lupe's cackling voice arose. She had spent the morning helping María Rosa, and it had been hard work. The child had spat blood the moment it was born, a bad sign. She thought then that bad luck would come to the house. Well, about sunset she was in the yard at the back of the house grinding tomatoes and peppers. She had left mother and babe asleep. She heard a strange noise in the house, a choking and smothered calling, like someone wailing in sleep. Well, such a thing is only natural. But there followed a light, quick, thudding sound—

"Like the blows of a fist?" interrrupted an officer.

"No, not at all like such a thing."

"How do you know?"

"I am well acquainted with that sound, friends," retorted Lupe. "This was something else."

She was at a loss to describe it exactly. A moment later, there came the sound of pebbles rolling and slipping under feet; then she knew someone had been there and was running away.

"Why did you wait so long before going to see?"

"I am old and hard in the joints," said Lupe. "I cannot run after people. I walked as fast as I could to the cactus hedge, for it is only by this way that anyone can enter. There was no one in the road, sir, no one. Three cows, with a dog driving them; nothing else. When I got to María Rosa, she was lying all tangled up, and from her neck to her middle she was full of knife-holes. It was a sight to move the Blessed Image Himself! Her eyes were—"

"Never mind. Who came oftenest to her house before she went away? Did you know her enemies?"

Lupe's face congealed, closed. Her spongy skin drew into a network of secretive wrinkles. She turned withdrawn and expressionless eyes upon the gendarmes.

"I am an old woman. I do not see well. I cannot hurry on my feet. I know no enemy of María Rosa. I did not see anyone leave the clearing."

"You did not hear splashing in the spring near the bridge?"

"No, sir."

"Why, then, do our dogs follow a scent there and lose it?"

95

100

105

"God only knows, my friend. I am an old wo—"

"Yes. How did the footfalls sound?"

"Like the tread of an evil spirit!" Lupe broke forth in a swelling oracular tone that startled them. The Indians stirred uneasily, glanced at the dead, then at Lupe. They half expected her to produce the evil spirit among them at once.

The gendarme began to lose his temper.

"No, poor unfortunate; I mean, were they heavy or light? The footsteps of 110 a man or of a woman? Was the person shod or barefoot?"

A glance at the listening circle assured Lupe of their thrilled attention. She enjoyed the dangerous importance of her situation. She could have ruined that María Concepción with a word, but it was even sweeter to make fools of these gendarmes who went about spying on honest people. She raised her voice again. What she had not seen she could not describe, thank God! No one could harm her because her knees were stiff and she could not run even to seize a murderer. As for knowing the difference between footfalls, shod or bare, man or woman, nay, between devil and human, who ever heard of such madness?

"My eyes are not ears, gentlemen," she ended grandly, "but upon my heart I swear those footsteps fell as the tread of the spirit of evil!"

"Imbecile!" yapped the leader in a shrill voice. "Take her away, one of you! Now, Juan Villegas, tell me—"

Juan told his story patiently, several times over. He had returned to his wife that day. She had gone to market as usual. He had helped her prepare her fowls. She had returned about mid-afternoon, they had talked, she had cooked, they had eaten, nothing was amiss. Then the gendarmes came with the news about María Rosa. That was all. Yes, María Rosa had run away with him, but there had been no bad blood between him and his wife on this account, nor between his wife and María Rosa. Everybody knew that his wife was a quiet woman.

María Concepción heard her own voice answering without a break. It was 115 true at first she was troubled when her husband went away, but after that she had not worried about him. It was the way of men, she believed. She was a church-married woman and knew her place. Well, he had come home at last. She had gone to market but had come back early, because now she had her man to cook for. That was all.

Other voices broke in. A toothless old man said: "She is a woman of good reputation among us, and María Rosa was not." A smiling young mother, Anita, baby at breast, said: "If no one thinks so, how can you accuse her? It was the loss of her child and not of her husband that changed her so." Another: "María Rosa had a strange life, apart from us. How do we know who might have come from another place to do her evil?" And old Soledad spoke up boldly: "When I saw María Concepción in the market today, I said, 'Good luck to you, María Concepción, this is a happy day for you!' " and she gave María Concepción a long easy stare, and the smile of a born wise-woman.

María Concepción suddenly felt herself guarded, surrounded, upborne by her faithful friends. They were around her, speaking for her, defending her, the forces of life were ranged invincibly with her against the beaten dead. María Rosa had thrown away her share of strength in them, she lay forfeited among them. María Concepción looked from one to the other of the circling, intent faces. Their eyes gave back reassurance, understanding, a secret and mighty sympathy.

The gendarmes were at a loss. They, too, felt that sheltering wall cast impenetrably around her. They were certain she had done it, and yet they could not accuse her. Nobody could be accused; there was not a shred of true evidence. They shrugged their shoulders and snapped their fingers and shuffled their feet. Well, then, good night to everybody. Many pardons for having intruded. Good health!

A small bundle lying against the wall at the head of the coffin squirmed like an eel. A wail, a mere sliver of sound, issued. María Concepción took the son of María Rosa in her arms.

"He is mine," she said clearly, "I will take him with me."  120

No one assented in words, but an approving nod, a bare breath of complete agreement, stirred among them as they made way for her.

María Concepción, carrying the child, followed Juan from the clearing. The hut was left with its lighted candles and a crowd of old women who would sit up all night, drinking coffee and smoking and telling ghost stories.

Juan's exaltation had burned out. There was not an ember of excitement left in him. He was tired. The perilous adventure was over. María Rosa had vanished, to come no more forever. Their days of marching, of eating, of quarreling and making love between battles, were all over. Tomorrow he would go back to dull and endless labor, he must descend into the trenches of the buried city as María Rosa must go into her grave. He felt his veins fill up with bitterness, with black unendurable melancholy. Oh, Jesus! what bad luck overtakes a man!

Well, there was no way out of it now. For the moment he craved only to sleep. He was so drowsy he could scarcely guide his feet. The occasional light touch of the woman at his elbow was as unreal, as ghostly as the brushing of a leaf against his face. He did not know why he had fought to save her, and now he forgot her. There was nothing in him except a vast blind hurt like a covered wound.

He entered the jacal, and without waiting to light a candle, threw off his  125
clothing, sitting just within the door. He moved with lagging, half-awake hands, to strip his body of its heavy finery. With a long groaning sigh of relief he fell straight back on the floor, almost instantly asleep, his arms flung up and outward.

María Concepción, a small clay jar in her hand, approached the gentle little mother goat tethered to a sapling, which gave and yielded as she pulled at the rope's end after the farthest reaches of grass about her. The kid, tied up a few feet away, rose bleating, its feathery fleece shivering in the fresh wind. Sitting on her heels, holding his tether, she allowed him to suckle a few moments. Afterward—all her movements very deliberate and even—she drew a supply of milk for the child.

She sat against the wall of her house, near the doorway. The child, fed and asleep, was cradled in the hollow of her crossed legs. The silence overfilled the world, the skies flowed down evenly to the rim of the valley, the stealthy moon crept slantwise to the shelter of the mountains. She felt soft and warm all over; she dreamed that the newly born child was her own, and she was resting deliciously.

María Concepción could hear Juan's breathing. The sound vapored from the low doorway, calmly; the house seemed to be resting after a burdensome day. She breathed, too, very slowly and quietly, each inspiration saturating her with repose. The child's light, faint breath was a mere shadowy moth of sound in the silver air. The night, the earth under her, seemed to swell and recede together with a limitless, unhurried, benign breathing. She drooped and closed her eyes, feeling the slow rise and fall within her own body. She did not know what it was, but it eased her all through. Even as she was falling asleep, head bowed over the child, she was still aware of a strange, wakeful happiness.

## QUESTIONS

1. Characterize the society of which María Concepción and Juan Villegas are a part. To what ethnic group do the people belong? What is their economic status? How do the people form their attitudes, and what role do these play in the resolution of the story?

2. Describe María Concepción's character. What does her behavior show about her during the absence of Juan and María Rosa? What are her strengths, her weaknesses? What does her church affiliation signify? What values cause her to kill María Rosa, yet permit her to feel happy at the end of the story? To what extent does her use of her knife seem representative of her character? In what ways does she grow or change in the course of the story?

3. Describe Juan Villegas. Would you characterize him as responsible or irresponsible, caring or uncaring? Are any elements of his character more properly considered flat rather than round? What facet of his character is brought out in his behavior during the investigation about María Rosa's death? What do we learn about Juan during the encounter with María Concepción after she appears with the bloody knife?

4. Discuss your attitude toward María Concepción's murder of María Rosa. What do you think about the killer's going free? How do the circumstances of the story influence your responses?

5. What is the central conflict or conflicts in the story? Who is the protagonist? Is there only one antagonist, or are there more? Describe the crisis of the story, the climax. Whom does the resolution satisfy more, María Concepción or her husband?

6. Consider the characters of Givens and Lupe. They are lesser characters, but are they therefore flat? What static elements do they exhibit? Are there any elements of growth or dynamism evident in them?

7. What techniques does Porter use to reveal the character of María Concepción? How important is the voice of the narrator? The use of dialogue? The use of action? Reports of the opinions of others?

## JAMES THURBER (1894–1961)

*The Catbird Seat*                                                                      *1945*

Mr. Martin bought the pack of Camels on Monday night in the most crowded cigar store on Broadway. It was theater time and seven or eight men were buying cigarettes. The clerk didn't even glance at Mr. Martin, who put the pack in his overcoat pocket and went out. If any of the staff at F & S had seen him buy the cigarettes, they would have been astonished, for it was generally known that Mr. Martin did not smoke, and never had. No one saw him.

It was just a week to the day since Mr. Martin had decided to rub out Mrs. Ulgine Barrows.° The term "rub out" pleased him because it suggested nothing more than the correction of an error—in this case an error of Mr. Fitweiler. Mr. Martin had spent each night of the past week working out his plan and examining it. As he walked home now he went over it again. For the hundredth time he resented the element of imprecision, the margin of guesswork that entered into the business. The project as he had worked it out was casual and bold, the risks were considerable. Something might go wrong anywhere along the line. And therein lay the cunning of his scheme. No one would ever see in it the cautious, painstaking hand of Erwin Martin, head of the filing department at F & S, of whom Mr. Fitweiler had once said, "Man is fallible but Martin isn't." No one would see his hand, that is, unless it were caught in the act.

Sitting in his apartment, drinking a glass of milk, Mr. Martin reviewed his case against Mrs. Ulgine Barrows, as he had every night for seven nights. He began at the beginning. Her quacking voice and braying laugh had first profaned the halls of F & S on March 7, 1941 (Mr. Martin had a head for dates). Old Roberts, the personnel chief, had introduced her as the newly appointed special adviser to the president of the firm, Mr. Fitweiler. The woman had appalled Mr. Martin instantly, but he hadn't shown it. He had given her his dry hand, a look of studious concentration, and a faint smile. "Well," she had said, looking at the papers on his desk, "are you lifting the oxcart out of the ditch?" As Mr. Martin recalled that moment, over his milk, he squirmed slightly. He must keep his mind on her crimes as a special adviser, not on her peccadillos as a personality. This he found difficult to do, in spite of entering an objection and sustaining it. The faults of the woman as a woman kept chattering on in his mind like an unruly witness. She had, for almost two years now, baited him. In the halls, in the elevator, even in his own office, into which she romped now and then like a circus horse, she was constantly shouting these silly questions at him. "Are you lifting the oxcart out of the ditch? Are you tearing up the pea patch? Are you hollering down the rain barrel? Are you scraping around the bottom of the pickle barrel? Are you sitting in the catbird seat?"

It was Joey Hart, one of Mr. Martin's two assistants, who had explained what the gibberish meant. "She must be a Dodger fan," he had said. "Red Barber° announces the Dodger games over the radio and he uses those expressions—picked 'em up down South." Joey had gone on to explain one or two. "Tearing up the pea patch" meant going on a rampage; "sitting in the catbird seat" meant sitting pretty, like a batter with three balls and no strikes on him. Mr. Martin dismissed all this with an effort. It had been annoying, it had driven him near to distraction, but he was too solid a man to be moved to murder by anything so childish. It was fortunate, he reflected as he passed on to the important charges against Mrs. Barrows, that he had stood up under it so well. He had maintained always an outward appearance of polite tolerance. "Why, I even believe you like the woman," Miss Paird, his other assistant, had once said to him. He had simply smiled.

*Mrs. Ulgine Barrows*: Among other things, it means a castrated pig.
*Red Barber*: Walter Lanier ("Red") Barber (b. 1908), born in Mississippi and raised there and in Florida, announced Brooklyn Dodger games from 1939 to 1954.

A gavel rapped in Mr. Martin's mind and the case proper was resumed.    5
Mrs. Ulgine Barrows stood charged with willful, blatant, and persistent attempts
to destroy the efficiency and system of F & S. It was competent, material, and
relevant to review her advent and rise to power. Mr. Martin had got the story
from Miss Paird, who seemed always able to find things out. According to her,
Mrs. Barrows had met Mr. Fitweiler at a party, where she had rescued him from
the embraces of a powerfully built drunken man who had mistaken the president
of F & S for a famous retired Middle Western football coach. She had led him to
a sofa and somehow worked upon him a monstrous magic. The aging gentleman
had jumped to the conclusion there and then that this was a woman of singular
attainments, equipped to bring out the best in him and in the firm. A week later
he had introduced her into F & S as his special adviser. On that day confusion
got its foot in the door. After Miss Tyson, Mr. Brundage, and Mr. Bartlett had
been fired and Mr. Munson had taken his hat and stalked out, mailing in his resignation later, old Roberts had been emboldened to speak to Mr. Fitweiler. He mentioned that Mr. Munson's department had been "a little disrupted" and hadn't
they perhaps better resume the old system there? Mr. Fitweiler had said certainly
not. He had the greatest faith in Mrs. Barrow's ideas. "They require a little seasoning, a little seasoning, is all," he had added. Mr. Roberts had given it up. Mr.
Martin reviewed in detail all the changes wrought by Mrs. Barrows. She had begun
chipping at the cornices of the firm's edifice and now she was swinging at the
foundation stones with a pickaxe.

Mr. Martin came now, in his summing up, to the afternoon of Monday, November 2, 1942—just one week ago. On that day, at 3 P.M., Mrs. Barrows had bounced
into his office. "Boo!" she had yelled. "Are you scraping around the bottom of
the pickle barrel?" Mr. Martin had looked at her from under his green eyeshade,
saying nothing. She had begun to wander about the office, taking it in with her
great, popping eyes. "Do you really need *all* these filing cabinets?" she had demanded suddenly. Mr. Martin's heart had jumped. "Each of these files," he had
said, keeping his voice even, "plays an indispensable part in the system of F &
S." She had brayed at him, "Well, don't tear up the pea patch!" and gone to the
door. From there she had bawled, "But you sure have got a lot of fine scrap° in
here!" Mr. Martin could no longer doubt that the finger was on his beloved department. Her pickaxe was on the upswing, poised for the first blow. It had not come
yet; he had received no blue memo from the enchanted Mr. Fitweiler bearing
nonsensical instructions deriving from the obscene woman. But there was no doubt
in Mr. Martin's mind that one would be forthcoming. He must act quickly. Already
a precious week had gone by. Mr. Martin stood up in his living room, still holding
his milk glass. "Gentlemen of the jury," he said to himself, "I demand the death
penalty for this horrible person."

The next day Mr. Martin followed his routine, as usual. He polished his
glasses more often and once sharpened an already sharp pencil, but not even
Miss Paird noticed. Only once did he catch sight of his victim; she swept past

---

*scrap*: During World War II (1941–1945) the government constantly collected scrap
metal to be used in wartime manufacture. Saving scrap was considered patriotic.

him in the hall with a patronizing "Hi!" At five-thirty he walked home, as usual, and had a glass of milk, as usual. He had never drunk anything stronger in his life—unless you could count ginger ale. The late Sam Schlosser, the S of F & S, had praised Mr. Martin at a staff meeting several years before for his temperate habits. "Our most efficient worker neither drinks nor smokes," he had said. "The results speak for themselves." Mr. Fitweiler had sat by, nodding approval.

Mr. Martin was still thinking about that red-letter day as he walked over to the Schrafft's on Fifth Avenue near Forty-sixth Street. He got there, as he always did, at eight o'clock. He finished his dinner and the financial page of the *Sun* at a quarter to nine, as he always did. It was his custom after dinner to take a walk. This time he walked down Fifth Avenue at a casual pace. His gloved hands felt moist and warm, his forehead cold. He transferred the Camels from his overcoat to a jacket pocket. He wondered, as he did so, if they did not represent an unnecessary note of strain. Mrs. Barrows smoked only Luckies. It was his idea to puff a few puffs on a Camel (after the rubbing-out), stub it out in the ashtray holding her lipstick-stained Luckies, and thus drag a small red herring across the trail. Perhaps it was not a good idea. It would take time. He might even choke, too loudly.

Mr. Martin had never seen the house on West Twelfth Street where Mrs. Barrows lived, but he had a clear enough picture of it. Fortunately, she had bragged to everybody about her ducky first-floor apartment in the perfectly darling three-story red-brick. There would be no doorman or other attendants; just the tenants of the second and third floors. As he walked along, Mr. Martin realized that he would get there before nine-thirty. He had considered walking north on Fifth Avenue from Schrafft's to a point from which it would take him until ten o'clock to reach the house. At that hour people were less likely to be coming in or going out. But the procedure would have made an awkward loop in the straight thread of his casualness, and he had abandoned it. It was impossible to figure when people would be entering or leaving the house, anyway. There was a great risk at any hour. If he ran into anybody, he would simply have to place the rubbing-out of Ulgine Barrows in the inactive file forever. The same thing would hold true if there were someone in her apartment. In that case he would just say that he had been passing by, recognized her charming house and thought to drop in.

It was eighteen minutes after nine when Mr. Martin turned into Twelfth Street. A man passed him, and a man and a woman talking. There was no one within fifty paces when he came to the house, halfway down the block. He was up the steps in the small vestibule in no time, pressing the bell under the card that said "Mrs. Ulgine Barrows." When the clicking in the lock started, he jumped forward against the door. He got inside fast, closing the door behind him. A bulb in a lantern hung from the hall ceiling on a chain seemed to give a monstrously bright light. There was nobody on the stair, which went up ahead of him along the left wall. A door opened down the hall in the wall on the right. He went toward it swiftly, on tiptoe.

"Well, for God's sake, look who's here!" bawled Mrs. Barrows, and her braying laugh rang out like the report of a shotgun. He rushed past her like a football tackle, bumping her. "Hey, quit shoving!" she said, closing the door behind them. They were in her living room, which seemed to Mr. Martin to be lighted by a hundred lamps. "What's after you?" she said. "You're as jumpy as a goat." He found he was unable to speak. His heart was wheezing in his throat. "I—yes," he finally brought out. She was jabbering and laughing as she started to help him off with his coat. "No, no," he said. "I'll put it here." He took it off and put it on a chair near the door. "Your hat and gloves, too," she said. "You're in a lady's house." He put his hat on top of the coat. Mrs. Barrows seemed larger than he had thought. He kept his gloves on. "I was passing by," he said. "I recognized— is there anyone here?" She laughed louder than ever. "No," she said, "we're all alone. You're as white as a sheet, you funny man. Whatever *has* come over you? I'll mix you a toddy." She started toward a door across the room. "Scotch-and-soda be all right? But say, you don't drink, do you?" She turned and gave him her amused look. Mr. Martin pulled himself together. "Scotch-and-soda will be all right," he heard himself say. He could hear her laughing in the kitchen.

Mr. Martin looked quickly around the living room for the weapon. He had counted on finding one there. There were andirons and a poker and something in a corner that looked like an Indian club. None of them would do. It couldn't be that way. He began to pace around. He came to a desk. On it lay a metal paper knife with an ornate handle. Would it be sharp enough? He reached for it and knocked over a small brass jar. Stamps spilled out of it and it fell to the floor with a clatter. "Hey," Mrs. Barrows yelled from the kitchen, "are you tearing up the pea patch?" Mr. Martin gave a strange laugh. Picking up the knife, he tried its point against his left wrist. It was blunt. It wouldn't do.

When Mrs. Barrows reappeared, carrying two highballs, Mr. Martin, standing there with his gloves on, became acutely conscious of the fantasy he had wrought. Cigarettes in his pocket, a drink prepared for him—it was all too grossly improbable. It was more than that; it was impossible. Somewhere in the back of his mind a vague idea stirred, sprouted. "For heaven's sake, take off those gloves," said Mrs. Barrows. "I always wear them in the house," said Mr. Martin. The idea began to bloom, strange and wonderful. She put the glasses on a coffee table in front of a sofa and sat on the sofa. "Come over here, you odd little man," she said. Mr. Martin went over and sat beside her. It was difficult getting a cigarette out of the pack of Camels, but he managed it. She held a match for him, laughing. "Well," she said, handing him his drink, "this is perfectly marvelous. You with a drink and a cigarette."

Mr. Martin puffed, not too awkwardly, and took a gulp of the highball. "I drink and smoke all the time," he said. He clinked his glass against hers. "Here's nuts to that old windbag, Fitweiler," he said, and gulped again. The stuff tasted awful, but he made no grimace. "Really, Mr. Martin," she said, her voice and posture changing, "you are insulting our employer." Mrs. Barrows was now all special adviser to the president. "I am preparing a bomb," said Mr. Martin, "which will blow the old goat higher than hell." He had only had a little of the drink, which was not strong. It couldn't be that. "Do you take dope or something?" Mrs. Barrows asked coldly. "Heroin," said Mr. Martin. "I'll be coked to the gills when I bump that old buzzard off." "Mr. Martin!" she shouted, getting to her feet. "That will be all of that. You must go at once." Mr. Martin took another swallow of his drink. He tapped his cigarette out in the ashtray and put the pack of Camels on the coffee table. Then he got up. She stood glaring at him. He walked over and put on his hat and coat. "Not a word about this," he said, and laid an index finger against his lips. All Mrs. Barrows could bring out was "Really!" Mr. Martin put his hand on the doorknob. "I'm sitting in the catbird seat," he said. He stuck his tongue out at her and left. Nobody saw him go.

Mr. Martin got to his apartment, walking, well before eleven. No one saw     15 him go in. He had two glasses of milk after brushing his teeth, and he felt elated. It wasn't tipsiness, because he hadn't been tipsy. Anyway, the walk had worn off all effects of the whisky. He got in bed and read a magazine for a while. He was asleep before midnight.

Mr. Martin got to the office at eight-thirty the next morning, as usual. At a quarter to nine, Ulgine Barrows, who had never before arrived at work before ten, swept into his office. "I'm reporting to Mr. Fitweiler now!" she shouted. "If he turns you over to the police, it's no more than you deserve!" Mr. Martin gave her a look of shocked surprise. "I beg your pardon?" he said. Mrs. Barrows snorted and bounced out of the room, leaving Miss Paird and Joey Hart staring after her. "What's the matter with that old devil now?" asked Miss Paird. "I have no idea," said Mr. Martin, resuming his work. The other two looked at him and then at each other. Miss Paird got up and went out. She walked slowly past the closed door of Mr. Fitweiler's office. Mrs. Barrows was yelling inside, but she was not braying. Miss Paird could not hear what the woman was saying. She went back to her desk.

Forty-five minutes later, Mrs. Barrows left the president's office and went into her own, shutting the door. It wasn't until half an hour later that Mr. Fitweiler sent for Mr. Martin. The head of the filing department, neat, quiet, attentive, stood in front of the old man's desk. Mr. Fitweiler was pale and nervous. He took his glasses off and twiddled them. He made a small, bruffing sound in his throat. "Martin," he said, "you have been with us more than twenty years." "Twenty-two, sir," said Mr. Martin. "In that time," pursued the president, "your work and your—uh—manner have been exemplary." "I trust so, sir," said Mr. Martin. "I have understood, Martin," said Mr. Fitweiler, "that you have never taken a drink or smoked." "That is correct, sir," said Mr. Martin. "Ah, yes." Mr. Fitweiler polished his glasses. "You may describe what you did after leaving the office yesterday, Martin," he said. Mr. Martin allowed less than a second for his bewildered pause. "Certainly, sir," he said. "I walked home. Then I went to Schrafft's for dinner. Afterward I walked home again. I went to bed early, sir, and read a magazine for a while. I was asleep before eleven." "Ah, yes," said Mr. Fitweiler again. He was silent for a moment, searching for the proper words to say to the head of the filing department. "Mrs. Barrows," he said finally, "Mrs. Barrows has worked hard, Martin, very hard. It grieves me to report that she has suffered a severe breakdown. It has taken the form of a persecution complex accompanied by distressing hallucinations." "I am very sorry, sir," said Mr. Martin. "Mrs. Barrows is under the delusion," continued Mr. Fitweiler, "that you visited her last evening and behaved yourself in an—uh—unseemly manner." He raised his hand to silence Mr. Martin's little pained outcry. "It is the nature of these psychological diseases," Mr. Fitweiler said, "to fix upon the least likely and most innocent party as the—uh—source of persecution. These matters are not for the lay mind to grasp, Martin. I've just had my psychiatrist, Dr. Fitch, on the phone. He would not, of course, commit himself, but he made enough generalizations to substantiate my suspicions. I suggested to Mrs. Barrows when she had completed her—uh—story to me this morning, that she visit Dr. Fitch, for I suspected a condition at once. She flew, I regret to say, into a rage, and demanded—uh—requested that I call you on the carpet. You may not know, Martin, but Mrs. Barrows had planned a reorganization of your department—subject to my approval, of course, subject to my approval. This brought you, rather than anyone else, to her mind—but again that is a phenomenon for Dr. Fitch and not for us. So, Martin, I am afraid Mrs. Barrows' usefulness here is at an end." "I am dreadfully sorry, sir," said Mr. Martin.

It was at this point that the door to the office blew open with the suddenness of a gas-main explosion and Mrs. Barrows catapulted through it. "Is the little rat denying it?" she screamed. "He can't get away with that!" Mr. Martin got up and moved discreetly to a point beside Mr. Fitweiler's chair. "You drank and smoked at my apartment," she bawled at Mr. Martin, "and you know it! You called Mr. Fitweiler an old windbag and said you were going to blow him up when you got coked to the gills on your heroin!" She stopped yelling to catch her breath and a new glint came into her popping eyes. "If you weren't such a drab, ordinary little man," she said, "I'd think you'd planned it all. Sticking your tongue out at me, saying you were sitting in the catbird seat, because you thought no one would believe me when I told it! My God, it's really too perfect!" She brayed loudly and hysterically, and the fury was on her again. She glared at Mr. Fitweiler. "Can't you see how he has tricked us, you old fool? Can't you see his little game?" But Mr. Fitweiler had been surreptitiously pressing all the buttons under the top of his desk and employees of F & S began pouring into the room. "Stockton," said Mr. Fitweiler, "You and Fishbein will take Mrs. Barrows to her home. Mrs. Powell, you will go with them." Stockton, who had played a little football in high school, blocked Mrs. Barrows as she made for Mr. Martin. It took him and Fishbein together to force her out of the door into the hall, crowded with stenographers and office boys. She was still screaming imprecations at Mr. Martin, tangled and contradictory imprecations. The hubbub finally died out down the corridor.

"I regret that this has happened," said Mr. Fitweiler. "I shall ask you to dismiss it from your mind, Martin." "Yes, sir," said Mr. Martin, anticipating his chief's "That will be all" by moving to the door. "I will dismiss it." He went out and shut the door, and his step was light and quick in the hall. When he entered his department he had slowed down to his customary gait, and he walked quietly across the room to the W20 file, wearing a look of studious concentration.


## QUESTIONS

1.  Why does Erwin Martin change his plan? When do you learn completely what the full plan really is? What role does Martin's twenty-two–year employment with F & S play in Fitweiler's reaction? Why is the plan successful?

2.  Describe Martin's character. Is he round or flat? Do you learn enough about him to determine if he is dynamic? Does his character suggest that he is capable of going through with his original plan of murder? What does his use of the following terms indicate about some of the ways he has spent his time: "rub out," "old goat," "coked to the gills," and "buzzard"? What

do you learn about his inner life? What do his habits of milk drinking, regular dinner times, and general efficiency contribute to your understanding of his character? What is the catbird seat, and is Martin one of its occupants at the end of the story?

3. What is the effect upon Martin's plan of Fitweiler's experience with psychiatry? When Martin is in Mrs. Barrows's apartment and develops his plan, do you think he is predicting what Fitweiler's response will be to her report of his "confession"?

4. Summarize Mrs. Barrows's career at F & S. Does it seem to you that the "death penalty" is justifiable for her? What do phrases like "quacking voice and braying laugh" and "she romped now and then like a circus horse" contribute to your attitude toward her? How are you affected by her behavior in her home when Martin visits her? Is there any discrepancy in your responses? Do you think that Thurber is fair to her?

5. Is the story serious, farcical, or a little bit of both? What parts are funny (i.e., characters, the language of Mrs. Barrows, the plot, the climax, the resolution)? Even though there is much that is comic, what values embodied in the conflict between Martin and Mrs. Barrows might have a more serious implication?


## WILLIAM FAULKNER (1897–1962)

### Barn Burning                                                          *1939*

The store in which the Justice of the Peace's court was sitting smelled of cheese. The boy, crouched on his nail keg at the back of the crowded room, knew he smelled cheese, and more: from where he sat he could see the ranked shelves close-packed with the solid, squat, dynamic shapes of tin cans whose labels his stomach read, not from the lettering which meant nothing to his mind but from the scarlet devils and the silver curve of fish—this, the cheese which he knew he smelled and the hermetic meat which his intestines believes he smelled coming in intermittent gusts momentary and brief between the other constant one, the smell and sense just a little of fear because mostly of despair and grief, the old fierce pull of blood. He could not see the table where the Justice sat and before which his father and his father's enemy (*our enemy* he thought in that despair; *ourn! mine and hisn both! He's my father!*) stood, but he could hear them, the two of them that is, because his father had said no word yet:

"But what proof have you, Mr. Harris?"

"I told you. The hog got into my corn. I caught it up and sent it back to him. He had no fence that would hold it. I told him so, warned him. The next time I put the hog in my pen. When he came to get it I gave him enough wire to patch up his pen. The next time I put the hog up and kept it. I rode down to his house and saw the wire I gave him still rolled on to the spool in his yard. I told him he could have the hog when he paid me a dollar pound fee. That evening a nigger came with the dollar and got the hog. He was a strange nigger. He said, 'He say to tell you wood and hay kin burn.' I said, 'What?' 'That whut he say to tell you,' the nigger said. 'Wood and hay kin burn.' That night my barn burned. I got the stock out but I lost the barn.''

"Where is the nigger? Have you got him?"

"He was a strange nigger, I tell you. I don't know what became of him."    5

"But that's not proof. Don't you see that's not proof?"

"Get that boy up here. He knows." For a moment the boy thought too that the man meant his older brother until Harris said, "Not him. The little one. The boy," and, crouching, small for his age, small and wiry like his father, in patched and faded jeans even too small for him, with straight, uncombed, brown hair and eyes gray and wild as storm scud, he saw the men between himself and the table part and become a lane of grim faces, at the end of which he saw the Justice, a shabby, collarless, graying man in spectacles, beckoning him. He felt no floor under his bare feet; he seemed to walk beneath the palpable weight of the grim turning faces. His father, stiff in his black Sunday coat donned not for the trial but for the moving, did not even look at him. *He aims for me to lie*, he thought, again with that frantic grief and despair. *And I will have to do hit.*

"What's your name, boy?" the Justice said.

"Colonel Sartoris Snopes," the boy whispered.

"Hey?" the Justice said. "Talk louder. Colonel Sartoris? I reckon anybody    10 named for Colonel Sartoris in this country can't help but tell the truth, can they?" The boy said nothing. *Enemy! Enemy!* he thought; for a moment he could not even see, could not see that the Justice's face was kindly nor discern that his voice was troubled when he spoke to the man named Harris: "Do you want me to question this boy?" But he could hear, and during those subsequent long seconds while there was absolutely no sound in the crowded little room save that of quiet and intent breathing it was as if he had swung outward at the end of a grape vine, over a ravine, and at the top of the swing had been caught in a prolonged instant of mesmerized gravity, weightless in time.

"No!" Harris said violently, explosively. "Damnation! Send him out of here!" Now time, the fluid world, rushed beneath him again, the voices coming to him again through the smell of cheese and sealed meat, the fear and despair and the old grief of blood:

"This case is closed. I can't find against you, Snopes, but I can give you advice. Leave this country and don't come back to it."

His father spoke for the first time, his voice cold and harsh, level, without emphasis: "I aim to. I don't figure to stay in a country among people who . . ." he said something unprintable and vile, addressed to no one.

"That'll do," the Justice said, "Take your wagon and get out of this country before dark. Case dismissed."

His father turned, and he followed the stiff black coat, the wiry figure walking    15 a little stiffly from where a Confederate provost's man's musket ball had taken him in the heel on a stolen horse thirty years ago, followed the two backs now, since his older brother had appeared from somewhere in the crowd, no taller than the father but thicker, chewing tobacco steadily, between the two lines of grim-faced men and out of the store and across the worn gallery and down the sagging steps and among the dogs and half-grown boys in the mild May dust, where as he passed a voice hissed:

"Barn burner!"

Again he could not see, whirling; there was a face in a red haze, moonlike, bigger than the full moon, the owner of it half again his size, he leaping in the red haze toward the face, feeling no blow, feeling no shock when his head struck the earth, scrabbling up and leaping again, feeling no blow this time either and tasting no blood, scrabbling up to see the other boy in full flight and himself already leaping into pursuit as his father's hand jerked him back, the harsh, cold voice speaking above him: "Go get in the wagon."

It stood in a grove of locusts and mulberries across the road. His two hulking sisters in their Sunday dresses and his mother and her sister in calico and sunbonnets were already in it, sitting on and among the sorry residue of the dozen and more movings which even the boy could remember—the battered stove, the broken beds and chairs, the clock inlaid with mother-of-pearl, which would not run, stopped at some fourteen minutes past two o'clock of a dead and forgotten day and time, which had been his mother's dowry. She was crying, though when she saw him she drew her sleeve across her face and began to descend from the wagon. "Get back," the father said.

"He's hurt. I got to get some water and wash his . . ."

"Get back in the wagon," his father said. He got in too, over the tail-gate.  20 His father mounted to the seat where the older brother already sat and struck the gaunt mules two savage blows with the peeled willow, but without heat. It was not even sadistic; it was exactly that same quality which in later years would cause his descendants to over-run the engine before putting a motor car into motion, striking and reining back in the same movement. The wagon went on, the store with its quiet crowd of grimly watching men dropped behind; a curve in the road hid it. *Forever* he thought. *Maybe he's done satisfied now, now that he has . . .* stopping himself, not to say it aloud even to himself. His mother's hand touched his shoulder.

"Does hit hurt?" she said.

"Naw," he said. "Hit don't hurt. Lemme be."

"Can't you wipe some of the blood off before hit dries?"

"I'll wash tonight," he said. "Lemme be, I tell you."

The wagon went on. He did not know where they were going. None of  25 them ever did or ever asked, because it was always somewhere, always a house of sorts waiting for them a day or two days or even three days away. Likely his father had already arranged to make a crop on another farm before he . . . Again he had to stop himself. He (the father) always did. There was something about his wolflike independence and even courage when the advantage was at least neutral which impressed strangers, as if they got from his latent ravening ferocity not so much a sense of dependability as a feeling that his ferocious conviction in the rightness of his own actions would be of advantage to all whose interest lay with his.

That night they camped, in a grove of oaks and beeches where a spring ran. The nights were still cool and they had a fire against it, of a rail lifted from a nearby fence and cut into lengths—a small fire, neat, niggard almost, a shrewd fire; such fires were his father's habit and custom always, even in freezing weather. Older, the boy might have remarked this and wondered why not a big one; why should not a man who had not only seen the waste and extravagance of war, but who had in his blood an inherent voracious prodigality with material not his own, have burned everything in sight? Then he might have gone a step farther and thought that that was the reason: that niggard blaze was the living fruit of nights passed during those four years in the woods hiding from all men, blue or gray, with his strings of horses (captured horses, he called them). And older still, he might have divined the true reason: that the element of fire spoke to some deep mainspring of his father's being, as the element of steel or of powder spoke to other men, as the one weapon for the preservation of integrity, else breath were not worth the breathing, and hence to be regarded with respect and used with discretion.

But he did not think this now and he had seen those same niggard blazes all his life. He merely ate his supper beside it and was already half asleep over his iron plate when his father called him, and once more he followed the stiff back, the stiff and ruthless limp, up the slope and on to the starlit road where, turning, he could see his father against the stars but without face or depth—a shape black, flat, and bloodless as though cut from tin in the iron folds of the frockcoat which had not been made for him, the voice harsh like tin and without heat like tin:

"You were fixing to tell them. You would have told him." He didn't answer. His father struck him with the flat of his hand on the side of the head, hard but without heat, exactly as he had struck the two mules at the store, exactly as he would strike either of them with any stick in order to kill a horse fly, his voice still without heat or anger: "You're getting to be a man. You got to learn. You got to learn to stick to your own blood or you ain't going to have any blood to stick to you. Do you think either of them, any man there this morning, would? Don't you know all they wanted was a chance to get at me because they knew I had them beat? Eh?" Later, twenty years later, he was to tell himself, "If I had said they wanted only truth, justice, he would have hit me again." But now he said nothing. He was not crying. He just stood there. "Answer me," his father said.

"Yes," he whispered. His father turned.

"Get on to bed. We'll be there tomorrow."                                          30

Tomorrow they were there. In the early afternoon the wagon stopped before a paintless two-room house identical almost with the dozen others it had stopped before even in the boy's ten years, and again, as on the other dozen occasions, his mother and aunt got down and began to unload the wagon, although his two sisters and his father and brother had not moved.

"Likely hit ain't fitten for hawgs," one of the sisters said.

"Nevertheless, fit it will and you'll hog it and like it," his father said. "Get out of them chairs and help your Ma unload."

The two sisters got down, big, bovine, in a flutter of cheap ribbons; one of them drew from the jumbled wagon bed a battered lantern, the other a worn broom. His father handed the reins to the older son and began to climb stiffly over the wheel. "When they get unloaded, take the team to the barn and feed them." Then he said, and at first the boy thought he was still speaking to his brother: "Come with me."

"Me?" he said.                                                                     35

"Yes," his father said. "You."

"Abner," his mother said. His father paused and looked back—the harsh level stare beneath the shaggy, graying, irascible brows.

"I reckon I'll have a word with the man that aims to begin tomorrow owning me body and soul for the next eight months."

They went back up the road. A week ago—or before last night, that is—he would have asked where they were going, but not now. His father had struck him before last night but never before had he paused afterward to explain why; it was as if the blow and the following calm, outrageous voice still rang, repercussed, divulging nothing to him save the terrible handicap of being young, the light weight of his few years, just heavy enough to prevent his soaring free of the world as it seemed to be ordered but not heavy enough to keep him footed solid in it, to resist it and try to change the course of its events.

Presently he could see the grove of oaks and cedars and the other flowering trees and shrubs where the house would be, though not the house yet. They walked beside a fence massed with honeysuckle and Cherokee roses and came to a gate swinging open between two brick pillars, and now, beyond a sweep of drive, he saw the house for the first time and at that instant he forgot his father and the terror and despair both, and even when he remembered his father again (who had not stopped) the terror and despair did not return. Because, for all the twelve movings, they had sojourned until now in a poor country, a land of small farms and fields and houses, and he had never seen a house like this before. *Hit's big as a courthouse* he thought quietly, with a surge of peace and joy whose reason he could not have thought into words, being too young for that: *They are safe from him. People whose lives are a part of this peace and dignity are beyond his touch, he no more to them than a buzzing wasp: capable of stinging for a little moment but that's all; the spell of this peace and dignity rendering even the barns and stable and cribs which belong to it impervious to the puny flames he might contrive . . .* this, the peace and joy, ebbing for an instant as he looked again at the stiff black back, the stiff and implacable limp of the figure which was not dwarfed by the house, for the reason that it had never looked big anywhere and which now, against the serene columned backdrop, had more than ever that impervious quality of something cut ruthlessly from tin, depthless, as though, sidewise to the sun, it would cast no shadow. Watching him, the boy remarked the absolutely undeviating course which his father held and saw the stiff foot come squarely down in a pile of fresh droppings where a horse had stood in the drive and which his father could have avoided by a simple change of stride. But it ebbed only for a moment, though he could not have thought this into words either, walking on in the spell of the house, which he could even want but without envy, without sorrow, certainly never with that ravening and jealous rage which unknown to him walked in the ironlike black coat before him: *Maybe he will feel it too. Maybe it will even change him now from what maybe he couldn't help but be.*

They crossed the portico. Now he could hear his father's stiff foot as it came down on the boards with clocklike finality, a sound out of all proportion to the displacement of the body it bore and which was not dwarfed either by the white door before it, as though it had attained to a sort of vicious and ravening minimum not to be dwarfed by anything—the flat, wide, black hat, the formal coat of broadcloth which had once been black but which had now that friction-glazed greenish cast of the bodies of old house flies, the lifted sleeve which was too large, the lifted hand like a curled claw. The door opened so promptly that the boy knew the Negro must have been watching them all the time, an old man with neat grizzled

40

hair, in a linen jacket, who stood barring the door with his body, saying "Wipe yo foots, white man, fo you come in here. Major ain't home nohow."

"Get out of my way, nigger," his father said, without heat too, flinging the door back and the Negro also and entering, his hat still on his head. And now the boy saw the prints of the stiff foot on the doorsill and saw them appear on the pale rug behind the machinelike deliberation of the foot which seemed to bear (or transmit) twice the weight which the body compassed. The Negro was shouting "Miss Lula! Miss Lula!" somewhere behind them, then the boy, deluged as though by a warm wave by a suave turn of carpeted stair and a pendant glitter of chandeliers and a mute gleam of gold frames, heard the swift feet and saw her too, a lady—perhaps he had never seen her like before either—in a gray, smooth gown with lace at the throat and an apron tied at the waist and the sleeves turned back, wiping cake or biscuit dough from her hands with a towel as she came up the hall, looking not at his father at all but at the tracks on the blond rug with an expression of incredulous amazement.

"I tried," the Negro cried. "I tole him to . . ."

"Will you please go away?" she said in a shaking voice. "Major de Spain is not at home. Will you please go away?"

His father had not spoken again. He did not speak again. He did not even look at her. He just stood stiff in the center of the rug, in his hat, the shaggy iron-gray brows twitching slightly above the pebble-colored eyes as he appeared to examine the house with brief deliberation. Then with the same deliberation he turned; the boy watched him pivot on the good leg and saw the stiff foot drag round the arc of the turning, leaving a final long and fading smear. His father never looked at it, he never once looked down at the rug. The Negro held the door. It closed behind them, upon the hysteric and indistinguishable woman-wail. His father stopped at the top of the steps and scraped his boot clean on the edge of it. At the gate he stopped again. He stood for a moment, planted stiffly on the stiff foot, looking back at the house. "Pretty and white, ain't it?" he said. "That's sweat. Nigger sweat. Maybe it ain't white enough yet to suit him. Maybe he wants to mix some white sweat with it."

Two hours later the boy was chopping wood behind the house within which his mother and aunt and the two sisters (the mother and aunt, not the two girls, he knew that; even at this distance and muffled by walls the flat loud voices of the two girls emanated an incorrigible idle inertia) were setting up the stove to prepare a meal, when he heard the hooves and saw the linen-clad man on a fine sorrel mare, whom he recognized even before he saw the rolled rug in front of the Negro youth following on a fat bay carriage horse—a suffused, angry face vanishing, still at full gallop, beyond the corner of the house where his father and brother were sitting in the two tilted chairs; and a moment later, almost before he could have put the axe down, he heard the hooves again and watched the sorrel mare go back out of the yard, already galloping again. Then his father began to shout one of the sisters' names, who presently emerged backward from the kitchen door dragging the rolled rug along the ground by one end while the other sister walked behind it.

"If you ain't going to tote, go on and set up the wash pot," the first said.

"You, Sarty!" the second shouted. "Set up the wash pot!" His father appeared at the door, framed against that shabbiness, as he had been against that other

45

bland perfection, impervious to either, the mother's anxious face at his shoulder.

"Go on," the father said. "Pick it up." The two sisters stooped, broad, lethargic; stooping, they presented an incredible expanse of pale cloth and a flutter of tawdry ribbons.

"If I thought enough of a rug to have to git hit all the way from France I   50
wouldn't keep hit where folks coming in would have to tromp on hit," the first said. They raised the rug.

"Abner," the mother said. "Let me do it."

"You go back and git dinner," his father said. "I'll tend to this."

From the woodpile through the rest of the afternoon the boy watched them, the rug spread flat in the dust beside the bubbling wash pot, the two sisters stooping over it with that profound and lethargic reluctance, while the father stood over them in turn, implacable and grim, driving them though never raising his voice again. He could smell the harsh homemade lye they were using; he saw his mother come to the door once and look toward them with an expression not anxious now but very like despair; he saw his father turn, and he fell to with the axe and saw from the corner of his eye his father raise from the ground a flattish fragment of field stone and examine it and return to the pot, and this time his mother actually spoke: "Abner. Abner. Please don't. Please, Abner."

Then he was done too. It was dusk; the whippoorwills had already begun. He could smell coffee from the room where they would presently eat the cold food remaining from the mid-afternoon meal, though when he entered the house he realized they were having coffee again probably because there was a fire on the hearth, before which the rug now lay spread over the backs of the two chairs. The tracks of his father's foot were gone. Where they had been were now long, water-cloudy scoriations resembling the sporadic course of a Lilliputian mowing machine.

It still hung there while they ate the cold food and then went to bed, scattered   55
without order or claim up and down the two rooms, his mother in one bed, where his father would later lie, the older brother in the other, himself, the aunt, and the two sisters on pallets on the floor. But his father was not in bed yet. The last thing the boy remembered was the depthless, harsh silhouette of the hat and coat bending over the rug and it seemed to him that he had not even closed his eyes when the silhouette was standing over him, the fire almost dead behind it, the stiff foot prodding him awake. "Catch up the mule," his father said.

When he returned with the mule his father was standing in the black door, the rolled rug over his shoulder. "Ain't you going to ride?" he said.

"No. Give me your foot."

He bent his knee into his father's hand, the wiry, surprising power flowed smoothly, rising, he rising with it, on to the mule's bare back (they had owned a saddle once; the boy could remember it though not when or where) and with the same effortlessness his father swung the rug up in front of him. Now in the starlight they retraced the afternoon's path, up the dusty road rife with honeysuckle, through the gate and up the black tunnel of the drive to the lightless house, where he sat on the mule and felt the rough warp of the rug drag across his thighs and vanish.

"Don't you want me to help?" he whispered. His father did not answer and now he heard again that stiff foot striking the hollow portico with that wooden and clocklike deliberation, that outrageous overstatement of the weight it carried. The rug, hunched, not flung (the boy could tell that even in the darkness) from his father's shoulder, struck the angle of wall and floor with a sound unbelievably loud, thunderous, then the foot again, unhurried and enormous; a light came on in the house and the boy sat, tense, breathing steadily and quietly and just a little fast, though the foot itself did not increase its beat at all, descending the steps now; now the boy could see him.

"Don't you want to ride now?" he whispered. "We kin both ride now," the light within the house altering now, flaring up and sinking. *He's coming down the stairs now*, he thought. He had already ridden the mule up beside the horse block; presently his father was up behind him and he doubled the reins over and slashed the mule across the neck, but before the animal could begin to trot the hard, thin arm came round him, the hard, knotted hand jerking the mule back to a walk. 60

In the first red rays of the sun they were in the lot, putting plow gear on the mules. This time the sorrel mare was in the lot before he heard it at all, the rider collarless and even bareheaded, trembling, speaking in a shaking voice as the woman in the house had done, his father merely looking up once before stooping again to the hame he was buckling, so that the man on the mare spoke to his stooping back:

"You must realize you have ruined that rug. Wasn't there anybody here, any of your women . . ." He ceased, shaking, the boy watching him, the older brother leaning now in the stable door, chewing, blinking slowly and steadily at nothing apparently. "It cost a hundred dollars. But you never had a hundred dollars. You never will. So I'm going to charge you twenty bushels of corn against your crop. I'll add it in your contract and when you come to the commissary you can sign it. That won't keep Mrs. de Spain quiet but maybe it will teach you to wipe your feet off before you enter her house again."

Then he was gone. The boy looked at his father, who still had not spoken or even looked up again, who was now adjusting the logger-head in the hame.

"Pap," he said. His father looked at him—the inscrutable face, the shaggy brows beneath which the gray eyes glinted coldly. Suddenly the boy went toward him, fast, stopping as suddenly. "You done the best you could!" he cried. "If he wanted hit done different why didn't he wait and tell you how? He won't git no twenty bushels! He won't git none! We'll get hit and hide hit! I kin watch . . ."

"Did you put the cutter back in that straight stock like I told you?" 65

"No, sir," he said.

"Then go do it."

That was Wednesday. During the rest of that week he worked steadily, at what was within his scope and some which was beyond it, with an industry that did not need to be driven nor even commanded twice; he had this from his mother, with the difference that some at least of what he did he liked to do, such as splitting wood with the half-size axe which his mother and aunt had earned, or saved money somehow, to present him with at Christmas. In company with the two older women (and on one afternoon even one of the sisters), he built pens for the shoat and the cow which were a part of his father's contract with the landlord, and one afternoon, his father being absent, gone somewhere on one of the mules, he went to the field.

They were running a middle buster now, his brother holding the plow straight while he handled the reins, and walking beside the straining mule, the rich black soil shearing cool and damp against his bare ankles, he thought *Maybe this is the end of it. Maybe even that twenty bushels that seems hard to have to pay for just a rug will be a cheap price for him to stop forever and always from being what he used to be*; thinking, dreaming now, so that his brother had to speak sharply to him to mind the mule: *Maybe he even won't collect the twenty bushels. Maybe it will all add up and balance and vanish—corn, rug, fire; the terror and grief, the being pulled two ways like between two teams of horses—gone, done with forever and ever.*

Then it was Saturday; he looked up from beneath the mule he was harnessing    70
and saw his father in the black coat and hat. "Not that," his father said. "The wagon gear." And then, two hours later, sitting in the wagon bed behind his father and brother on the seat, the wagon accomplished a final curve, and he saw the weathered paintless store with its tattered tobacco- and patent-medicine posters and the tethered wagons and saddle animals below the gallery. He mounted the gnawed steps behind his father and brother, and there again was the lane of quiet, watching faces for the three of them to walk through. He saw the man in spectacles sitting at the plank table and he did not need to be told this was a Justice of the Peace; he sent one glare of fierce, exultant, partisan defiance at the man in collar and cravat now, whom he had seen but twice before in his life, and that on a galloping horse, who now wore on his face an expression not of rage but of amazed unbelief which the boy could not have known was at the incredible circumstance of being sued by one of his own tenants, and came and stood against his father and cried at the Justice: "He ain't done it! He ain't burnt . . ."

"Go back to the wagon," his father said.

"Burnt?" the Justice said. "Do I understand this rug was burned too?"

"Does anybody here claim it was?" his father said. "Go back to the wagon." But he did not, he merely retreated to the rear of the room, crowded as that other had been, but not to sit down this time, instead, to stand pressing among the motionless bodies, listening to the voices:

"And you claim twenty bushels of corn is too high for the damage you did to the rug?"

"He brought the rug to me and said he wanted the tracks washed out of it.    75
I washed the tracks out and took the rug back to him."

"But you didn't carry the rug back to him in the same condition it was in before you made the tracks on it."

His father did not answer, and now for perhaps half a minute there was no sound at all save that of breathing, the faint, steady suspiration of complete and intent listening.

"You decline to answer that, Mr. Snopes?" Again his father did not answer. "I'm going to find against you, Mr. Snopes. I'm going to find that you were responsible for the injury to Major de Spain's rug and hold you liable for it. But twenty bushels of corn seems a little high for a man in your circumstances to have to pay. Major de Spain claims it cost a hundred dollars. October corn will be worth about fifty cents. I figure that if Major de Spain can stand a ninety-five-dollar loss on something he paid cash for, you can stand a five-dollar loss you haven't earned yet. I hold you in damages to Major de Spain to the amount of ten bushels of corn over and above your contract with him, to be paid to him out of your crop at gathering time. Court adjourned."

It had taken no time hardly, the morning was but half begun. He thought they would return home and perhaps back to the field, since they were late, far behind all other farmers. But instead his father passed on behind the wagon, merely indicating with his hand for the older brother to follow with it, and crossed the road toward the blacksmith shop opposite, pressing on after his father, overtaking him, speaking, whispering up at the harsh, calm face beneath the weathered hat: "He won't git no ten bushels neither. He won't git one. We'll . . ." until his father glanced for an instant down at him, the face absolutely calm, the grizzled eyebrows tangled above the cold eyes, the voice almost pleasant, almost gentle:

"You think so? Well, we'll wait till October anyway."                                                                    80

The matter of the wagon—the setting of a spoke or two and the tightening of the tires—did not take long either, the business of the tires accomplished by driving the wagon into the spring branch behind the shop and letting it stand there, the mules nuzzling into the water from time to time, and the boy on the seat with the idle reins, looking up the slope and through the sooty tunnel of the shed where the slow hammer rang and where his father sat on an upended cypress bolt, easily, either talking or listening, still sitting there when the boy brought the dripping wagon up out of the branch and halted it before the door.

"Take them on to the shade and hitch," his father said. He did so and returned. His father and the smith and a third man squatting on his heels inside the door were talking, about crops and animals; the boy, squatting too in the ammoniac dust and hoof-parings and scales of rust, heard his father tell a long and unhurried story out of the time before the birth of the older brother even when he had been a professional horsetrader. And then his father came up beside him where he stood before a tattered last year's circus poster on the other side of the store, gazing rapt and quiet at the scarlet horses, the incredible poisings and convolutions of tulle and tights and the painted leers of comedians, and said, "It's time to eat."

But not at home. Squatting beside his brother against the front wall, he watched his father emerge from the store and produce from a paper sack a segment of cheese and divided it carefully and deliberately into three with his pocket knife and produce crackers from the same sack. They all three squatted on the gallery and ate slowly, without talking; then in the store again, they drank from a tin dipper tepid water smelling of the cedar bucket and of living beech trees. And still they did not go home. It was a horse lot this time, a tall rail fence upon and along which men stood and sat and out of which one by one horses were led, to be walked and trotted and then cantered back and forth along the road while the slow swapping and buying went on and the sun began to slant westward, they— the three of them—watching and listening, the older brother with his muddy eyes and his steady, inevitable tobacco, the father commenting now and then on certain of the animals, to no one in particular.

It was after sundown when they reached home. They ate supper by lamplight, then, sitting on the doorstep, the boy watched the night fully accomplish, listening to the whippoorwills and the frogs, when he heard his mother's voice: "Abner! No! No! Oh, God. Oh, God. Abner!" and he rose, whirled, and saw the altered light through the door where a candle stub now burned in a bottle neck on the table and his father, still in the hat and coat, at once formal and burlesque as though dressed carefully for some shabby and ceremonial violence, emptying the reservoir of the lamp back into the five-gallon kerosene can from which it had been filled, while the mother tugged at his arm until he shifted the lamp to the other hand and flung her back, not savagely or viciously, just hard, into the wall, her hands flung out against the wall for balance, her mouth open and in her face the same quality of hopeless despair as had been in her voice. Then his father saw him standing in the door.

"Go to the barn and get that can of oil we were oiling the wagon with," 85 he said. The boy did not move. Then he could speak.

"What . . ." he cried. "What are you . . ."

"Go get that oil," his father said. "Go."

Then he was moving, running, outside the house, toward the stable: this the old habit, the old blood which he had not been permitted to choose for himself, which had been bequeathed him willy nilly and which had run for so long (and who knew where, battening on what of outrage and savagery and lust) before it came to him. *I could keep on*, he thought. *I could run on and on and never look back, never need to see his face again. Only I can't. I can't*, the rusted can in his hand now, the liquid sploshing in it as he ran back to the house and into it, into the sound of his mother's weeping in the next room, and handed the can to his father.

"Ain't you going to even send a nigger?" he cried. "At least you sent a nigger before!"

This time his father didn't strike him. The hand came even faster than the 90 blow had, the same hand which had set the can on the table with almost excruciating care flashing from the can toward him too quick for him to follow it, gripping him by the back of his shirt and on to tiptoe before he had seen it quit the can, the face stooping at him in breathless and frozen ferocity, the cold, dead voice speaking over him to the older brother who leaned against the table, chewing with that steady, curious, sidewise motion of cows:

"Empty the can into the big one and go on. I'll catch up with you."

"Better tie him up to the bedpost," the brother said.

"Do like I told you," the father said. Then the boy was moving, his bunched shirt and the hard, bony hand between his shoulder-blades, his toes just touching the floor, across the room and into the other one, past the sisters sitting with spread heavy thighs in the two chairs over the cold hearth, and to where his mother and aunt sat side by side on the bed, the aunt's arms about his mother's shoulders.

"Hold him," the father said. The aunt made a startled movement. "Not you," the father said. "Lennie. Take hold of him. I want to see you do it." His mother took him by the wrist. "You'll hold him better than that. If he gets loose don't you know what he is going to do? He will go up yonder." He jerked his head toward the road. "Maybe I'd better tie him."

"I'll hold him," his mother whispered. 95

"See you do then." Then his father was gone, the stiff foot heavy and measured upon the boards, ceasing at last.

Then he began to struggle. His mother caught him in both arms, he jerking and wrenching at them. He would be stronger in the end, he knew that. But he had no time to wait for it. "Lemme go!" he cried. "I don't want to have to hit you!"

"Let him go!" the aunt said. "If he don't go, before God, I am going up there myself!"

"Don't you see I can't?" his mother cried. "Sarty! Sarty! No! No! Help me, Lizzie!"

Then he was free. His aunt grasped at him but it was too late. He whirled, 100
running, his mother stumbled forward on to her knees behind him, crying to the
nearer sister: "Catch him, Net! Catch him!" But that was too late too, the sister
(the sisters were twins, born at the same time, yet either of them now gave the
impression of being, encompassing as much living meat and volume and weight
as any other two of the family) not yet having begun to rise from the chair, her
head, face, alone merely turned, presenting to him in the flying instant an astonishing expanse of young female features untroubled by any surprise even, wearing
only an expression of bovine interest. Then he was out of the room, out of the
house, in the mild dust of the starlit road and the heavy rifeness of honeysuckle,
the pale ribbon unspooling with terrific slowness under his running feet, reaching
the gate at last and turning in, running, his heart and lungs drumming, on
up the drive toward the lighted house, the lighted door. He did not knock, he
burst in, sobbing for breath, incapable for the moment of speech; he saw the astonished face of the Negro in the linen jacket without knowing when the Negro had
appeared.

"De Spain!" he cried, panted. "Where's . . ." then he saw the white man
too emerging from a white door down the hall. "Barn!" he cried. "Barn!"

"What?" the white man said. "Barn?"

"Yes!" the boy cried. "Barn!"

"Catch him!" the white man shouted.

But it was too late this time too. The Negro grasped his shirt, but the entire 105
sleeve, rotten with washing, carried away, and he was out that door too and in
the drive again, and had actually never ceased to run even while he was screaming
into the white man's face.

Behind him the white man was shouting, "My horse! Fetch my horse!" and
he thought for an instant of cutting across the park and climbing the fence into
the road, but he did not know the park nor how high the vine-massed fence might
be and he dared not risk it. So he ran on down the drive, blood and breath roaring;
presently he was in the road again though he could not see it. He could not hear
either: the galloping mare was almost upon him before he heard her, and even
then he held his course, as if the very urgency of his wild grief and need must in
a moment more find him wings, waiting until the ultimate instant to hurl himself
aside and into the weed-choked roadside ditch as the horse thundered past and
on, for an instant in furious silhouette against the stars, the tranquil early summer
night sky which, even before the shape of the horse and rider vanished, strained
abruptly and violently upward: a long, swirling roar incredible and soundless, blot-
ting the stars, and he springing up and into the road again, running again, knowing
it was too late yet still running even after he heard the shot and, an instant later,
two shots, pausing now without knowing he had ceased to run, crying "Pap! Pap!,"
running again before he knew he had begun to run, stumbling, tripping over something and scrabbling up again without ceasing to run, looking backward over his
shoulder at the glare as he got up, running on among the invisible trees, panting,
sobbing, "Father! Father!"

At midnight he was sitting on the crest of a hill. He did not know it was
midnight and he did not know how far he had come. But there was no glare
behind him now and he sat now, his back toward what he had called home for
four days anyhow, his face toward the dark woods which he would enter when

breath was strong again, small, shaking steadily in the chill darkness, hugging himself into the remainder of his thin, rotten shirt, the grief and despair now no longer terror and fear but just grief and despair. *Father. My father*, he thought. "He was brave!" he cried suddenly, aloud but not loud, no more than a whisper: "He was! He was in the war! He was in Colonel Sartoris' cav'ry!" not knowing that his father had gone to that war a private in the fine old European sense, wearing no uniform, admitting the authority of and giving fidelity to no man or army or flag, going to war as Malbrouck° himself did: for booty—it meant nothing and less than nothing to him if it were enemy booty or his own.

The slow constellations wheeled on. It would be dawn and then sun-up after a while and he would be hungry. But that would be tomorrow and now he was only cold, and walking would cure that. His breathing was easier now and he decided to get up and go on, and then he found that he had been asleep because he knew it was almost dawn, the night almost over. He could tell that from the whippoorwills. They were everywhere now among the dark trees below him, constant and inflectioned and ceaseless, so that, as the instant for giving over to the day birds drew nearer and nearer, there was no interval at all between them. He got up. He was a little stiff, but walking would cure that too as it would the cold, and soon there would be the sun. He went on down the hill, toward the dark woods within which the liquid silver voices of the birds called unceasing—the rapid and urgent beating of the urgent and quiring heart of the late spring night. He did not look back.

## QUESTIONS

1. What is the story's setting (time and place)? How does Faulkner convey this information to the reader?

2. Who is telling the story? Why are the boy and his father in court?

3. Describe the Snopes family. How does Faulkner let us know that they have moved often from place to place? What does this tell us about the family? Are the mother and sisters round or flat? Explain.

4. What is Abner Snopes like as a character? How does his behavior in court help define his character? To what extent does his Civil War experience contribute to this definition? What is his attitude toward the de Spain family? To what extent does his behavior with the rug illustrate his attitude and help define his character?

5. What does Major de Spain expect Abner Snopes to do in order to pay for the rug? What does the court decide? How does Abner react to the court's decision? What does he plan to do to the de Spains? What does this sequence of events tell us about Abner Snopes?

6. What is Sarty (Colonel Sartoris Snopes) like? What is his attitude toward his father? Toward his father's decision to act against the de Spains? Why does Sarty leave and "not look back" at the end of the story?

7. Whose story is this: Abner's or Sarty's? In other words, which is the protagonist? Explain.

*Malbrouck*: The hero of an old French ballad ("Malbrouck s'en va-t-en guerre") about the uncertain fate of soldiers going to war.

8. What sorts of different conflicts are developed in the story? What is the central conflict? To what extent is this conflict resolved in the climax? To what extent does this resolution help us identify the protagonist of the story?

9. For what reasons might we argue that Sarty is a round (rather than flat) character and a dynamic (rather than static) character? In what ways does Sarty change and grow in the story? What does he learn?

10. In the old Testament book of 2 Samuel (Chapters 2 and 3), Abner, the cousin of King Saul, was a powerful commander, warrior, and king maker. He was loyal to the son of Saul and fought against the supporters of King David. When Abner died, it became possible for David to become uncontested king over the ancient holy land. Do you see any significance in Faulkner's selection of the name *Abner* as the father of the Snopes family? Why do you think that Faulkner, at the end of "Barn Burning," points out that Abner Snopes entered the Civil War purely "for booty"? Could you think of Abner as a hero without scruple, a hero in reverse, an antihero, a symbol of degeneration?

11. At the climax, who is the rider of the horse? Who fires the three shots? Why does Faulkner not tell us the result of the shooting? (In Book I of *The Hamlet*, we learn that Abner and his other son, Flem, escape.)

## WRITING ABOUT CHARACTER

Most likely your assignment for study in your essay will be a major character, although it is possible that it might be a minor character or characters. Either way, your prewriting procedures will be much the same. After your customary overview, begin taking notes. In light of the discussion about character beginning this chapter, try to determine as many traits as you can, and also determine how the story presents information about the character.

To assemble materials for writing, try to answer questions like these: Does the character come to life? Is he or she "round" or "flat," lifelike or wooden? Are there admirable qualities, or are there many shortcomings? What are they? Is the character central to the action and therefore the hero or protagonist of the story? What traits make the character genuinely major? Do you like him or her? Why? Who or what is the antagonist? How does reaction to the antagonist bring out qualities in your character? What are they? Does the character exhibit any stock or stereotypical qualities? If so, does he or she rise above them, and how? What is the relationship of the character to the other characters? What do the others say or think about him or her? How accurate are their observations?

Once you have gathered materials in response to these and other questions, it will be possible to go ahead to do the necessary classifying and sorting necessary for the composition of the essay.

### Organizing Your Essay

**INTRODUCTION.**   The introduction may begin with a brief identification of the character to be analyzed, which may be followed by reference to any noteworthy problems in defining the character's qualities. The central idea is a statement about the major trait or quality of the character. The thesis sentence is a brief sentence linking the central idea to the main sections to be covered in the body of the essay.

**BODY.**   The organization is designed to illustrate the central idea to make it convincing. There is much freedom in the approach you can take, such as the following:

1. *Organization around central traits or major habits and characteristics*, such as "kindness, gentleness, generosity, firmness," or "resoluteness of will frustrated by inopportune moments for action, resulting in despondency, doubt, and melancholy." A body containing this sort of structure would demonstrate how the story brings out each of these qualities. For example, there might be a particular speech in which one of the traits is studied, or an action in which the character himself or herself dramatizes the trait. With such specific topics of treatment, the task of speaking about character can be greatly facilitated.

2. *Organization around the growth of change of a character*. The beginning of such a body would establish the traits that the character possesses at the start of the story and then would describe the changes or developments that occur. It is important here to be careful to avoid a summary, and to stress the actual alterations as they emerge from the circumstances of the story. It is also important to determine whether the growth or change is genuine; do the traits belong clearly to the character, and are they logically produced, or are they manufactured as needed by the events of the story?

3. *Organizations around central incidents that reveal, even if they do not cause, primary characteristics*. Certain key incidents may stand out in a work, and the body of the essay might effectively be structured according to these as signposts for the discussion. As with the second organization just described, it is important to stress in the topic sentences that the purpose is to illuminate the character, not just develop a discussion of the incidents themselves. With this arrangement, the emphasis should be on the causal relationship of incident to trait, if there is one, or on the relationship of incident to the development of character.

4. *Organization around qualities of a flat character or characters*. If the assigned essay is on a character who is not round but flat, the body might treat topics like the plot function of the character, the group of which the character is representative, the relationship of the flat character to the round ones and the importance of this relationship, and any additional qualities or traits that are delineated by the writer.

CONCLUSION.    The conclusion is the place for statements about how the discussed characteristics are related to the story as a whole. If the person was good but came to a bad end, does this discrepancy elevate him or her to tragic stature? If the person was a nobody and came to a bad end, does this fact suggest any authorial attitudes about the class or type of which he or she is a part? Or does it seem to illustrate the author's general view of human life? Or both? Do the characteristics explain why the person helps or hinders other characters? Does the essay help in the clearing up of any misunderstandings that might have been present on a first reading? Questions like these may be raised and answered in the conclusion.

## SAMPLE ESSAY

### The Character of Erwin Martin in Thurber's "The Catbird Seat"*

[1]    Erwin Martin is the major character in "The Catbird Seat" by James Thurber. The action is reported as though it is seen over his shoulder if not through his eyes, and he is the constant subject, or focus, of the story. Although the action might be considered whimsical or farcical, Martin is nevertheless well realized and developed. As a character, he is fully round.° He is real because of his image in the eyes of others, his active inner life, and his clever plan of action."

[2]    Externally, as others see him, Martin has established himself as a model of withdrawn colorlessness. For plot purposes, in fact, this image is essential, but it seems that from Martin's viewpoint it is intentional. Thus Martin in the past has done nothing daring, for his purchase of cigarettes is unlike what people had ever seen him do. His present boss, Fitweiler, praises him for his "exemplary" work and manner. Fitweiler also says, "Man is fallible but Martin isn't." The earlier boss, Sam Schlosser, had praised Martin's teetotaling habits, and even Mrs. Barrows recognizes him as a "drab, ordinary little man." In every respect, Martin has developed a reputation for cooperation and reliability, even though he has also created a self-image of overstability and dullness. To achieve such recognition is perhaps by itself worthy of note.

[3]    It is his apparently vigorous inner life that makes him especially distinctive. It is clear from his conversation with Mrs. Barrows that there is more to him than appears on the surface. His use of terms like "bump off," "old goat," "coked to the gills," and "old buzzard" suggest that he has been responsive to the colorful world of popular culture around him. His own inner trial of Mrs. Barrows, with his concluding verdict of "the death penalty for this horrible per-

---

* See p. 138 for this story.
° Central idea.
" Thesis Sentence.

son,'' demonstrates not a withdrawn, flat, colorless person, but one with a vigorous imagination.

[4]
The greatest mark of his character, of course, is his impromptu development of his ''strange and wonderful'' idea about discrediting Mrs. Barrows. This scheme, which Thurber does not describe beforehand, but which is dramatized in the last 40 percent of the story, suggests not just imagination but also cleverness, nerve, control, effrontery, and bravery. To make the scheme work, Martin must be clever enough to predict how others—particularly Fitweiler with his reliance on psychoanalysis—will respond to the true story Mrs. Barrows will tell, and he must therefore be able to predict his own victory. It is this element of control that makes him round and memorable, a doer and not just a responder.

[5]
The story of course is not a fully realistic one, but it does rely on elements of reality. Thus Martin's triumph as a character is also a triumph of individuality over mere efficiency. His annoyance at the unpleasant expressions of Mrs. Barrows is like the annoyance of subordinate people everywhere who must listen to the unpleasant and even stupid words of superiors. To this degree, Martin is representative. But because of his outrageous scheme he becomes an individual, a major character who asserts himself against the pressures to cast him out of the niche which he has made for himself. He is not a hero, but he does have his moment of victory, and he is certainly a round, well-developed character.

### Commentary on the Essay

The essay demonstrates the study of a major character, based on a quality, habit, and idea. In this respect it illustrates the first approach described above. The introductory paragraph establishes the status of Martin as a round character despite the problem that the story itself is not completely realistic. Paragraph 2 deals with the apparent drabness of Martin's character. The topic is that even an apparently withdrawn individual can be seen as round if the details about him or her are believably presented. The third paragraph deals with Martin's vigorous inner life, a second major aspect of the character. Paragraph 4 considers the traits manifested in Martin's impromptu scheme. The conclusion treats the relationship of Martin to the large class of those who are annoyed and downtrodden. The central idea is again stressed, however, that Martin is round and well realized and not just a representative of that class.

# 5

# Point of View

Point of view is the position from which details in a work of fiction are perceived and related to the reader. It is a method of rendering, a means by which authors create a centralizing intelligence, a narrative personality, an intellectual filter through which you receive the narration or argument. Other terms describing point of view are *viewpoint*, *unifying voice*, *perspective*, *angle of vision*, *persona*, *mask*, *center of attention*, and *focus*. Another helpful term is *coign of vantage*, which implies a high spot or corner—a vantage point—from which things below may be seen.

In practice, you can think of point of view as the character or speaker who does the talking.

You might respond that our definition means that authors do not use their own "voices" when they write but somehow change themselves into another character, who may be a totally separate creation. This response is right. It is true that authors, as writers of their own works, are always in control of what gets written, but it does not follow that they always use their own voices. It is not easy to determine exactly what one's "own voice" is. Test yourself: When you speak to your instructor, to your friend, to a child, to a person you love, or to a distant relative, your voice always sounds the same, but the personality—or persona—that you employ changes according to the person you are talking to.

In examining point of view, therefore, you should try to determine the nature of the speaker. It is not helpful to deal vaguely with "the author's point of view," as though you were talking about opinions. What you need is to analyze the character and circumstances of the speaker who is relating the events of the story.

## POINT OF VIEW AND "THROWING THE VOICE"

A helpful way to consider point of view is to think of the speaker as a ventriloquist's dummy and the author not as the speaker but the ventriloquist. The author "throws" the voice into the dummy, whose written words you actually read. Although the dummy or speaker is the one who is talking, the author is the one who has made the speaker believable and consistent.

Often this speaker, or **voice,** is separate and totally independent, a character who is completely imagined and consistently maintained by the author. A problem of identifying the voice occurs when the speaker seems to be the author in person. To claim that authors are also speakers, however, assumes that we have *absolute* biographical and psychological knowledge about them. Authors, like all people, change. They may have been changing even as they were writing the works you are reading. In addition, they may have been creating a separate personality, or aspect of themselves, as the voice they used when they wrote. Beyond all that, there is the general problem that human personality is elusive. For all these reasons, in works where the author seems to be talking directly, it is more proper to refer to the author's **authorial** voice as the speaker rather than the author himself or herself.

In short, the author creates not only stories and ideas, but also the speakers or voices of their works. To study and discuss point of view is to consider these speakers, even the authorial voices.

It is most important to understand this fact. As an exercise, suppose for a moment that you are an author and are planning a set of stories. Try to imagine the speakers you would create for the following situations:

A happy niece who has just inherited $25 million from an uncle recalls a childhood experience with the uncle years ago.

A disappointed nephew who was cut off without a cent describes a childhood experience with the same uncle.

A ship's captain who is filled with ideas of personal honor, integrity, and responsibility describes the life of a sailor who has committed a cowardly act.

A person who has survived a youth of poverty and degradation describes a brother who has succumbed to drugs and crime.

An economist looks at problems of unemployment.

A person who has just lost a job looks at problems of unemployment.

In trying to create voices and stories for the various situations, you will recognize the importance of your *imagination* in the selection of point of view. You are always yourself, but your imagination can enable you to speak like someone else totally distinct from yourself. Point of view is hence an imaginative creation, just as much a part of the author's work as the events narrated or the ideas discussed.

## POINT OF VIEW AS A PHYSICAL POSITION

Thus far we have considered point of view as an interaction of personality and circumstance. There are also purely physical aspects, specifically (1) the actual place or position from which speakers or narrators see and hear the action, and (2) the capacities of the speakers as receivers of information from others. If narrators have been at the "scene" of an action, this position gives them credibility because they are reporting events they actually saw or heard. Some speakers may have been direct participants in the action; others may have been bystanders. It is possible that a speaker may have overheard a conversation, or may have witnessed a scene through a keyhole. If the speakers were not "on the spot," they must have gained their "facts" in a believable way. They could get them from someone else who was a witness or participant. They could receive letters, read newspaper articles, go through old papers in an attic or library, or hear things on a radio or television program. Sometimes the unidentified voice of the author comes from a person who seems to be hovering somehow right above the characters as they move and speak. Such a speaker, being present everywhere without being noticed, is a reliable source of all information presented in the narrative.

## KINDS OF POINTS OF VIEW

The kinds of points of view may be classified fairly easily. You may detect the point of view in any work by determining the grammatical voice of the speaker. Then, of course, you should go on to all the other considerations thus far discussed.

### First Person

If the story is told by an "I," the author is using the **first-person** point of view—the voice of a fictional narrator and not the author's own voice. First-person speakers report significant things that they see, hear, and think and, as they do so, they convey not only the action of the work, but also some of their own background, thinking, attitudes, and prejudices. The speaker's particular type of speech will have a great effect on the language of the work itself. Thus a sailor uses many seagoing terms, and a young boy may use much slang.

There are a number of possible first-person storytellers, depending on their involvement in the events being narrated. One kind of speaker has acquired information because he or she was a direct participant in the action as a major character (or "mover"). Marlow in Joseph Conrad's "Youth," for example, is such a narrator (even though his tale is reported verbatim by an unnamed recorder who introduces the story). Sammy, in Updike's "A & P," and Jackie, in O'Connor's "First Confession," are also narrators in this mold. One type of major participant deserves special mention. This is a speaker like Dr. Watson, who in "The Adventure of the Speckled Band" is involved in all the action but actually is an observer. Even though he is and must be a major participant, he is not a major mover, for that role is assigned to the brilliant master detective Sherlock Holmes. Watson's first-person narration, however, is essential to the authenticity of the story.

Both the age and the understanding of the narrators are significant in what they say and therefore in our perception of the stories they tell. A mature adult, like Marlow in "Youth," presents his or her recollection and also provides adult commentary on the nature of the experience. A less aware, naive narrator, like the narrator of Americo Paredes's "The Hammon and the Beans," actually presents a more dramatic account, because such a narrator is to be accepted as accurate on actions and conversations even though he or she does not make adult observations about them. Also, the narrator may have reached adulthood, but may not indicate an adult's understanding. Such speakers are Jackie in "First Confession" and the unnamed narrator in James Joyce's "Araby." With first-person points of view like these the reader must sort out details and also must judge the observations included by the narrator as commentary on the action.

One thing seems clear in regard to stories containing the first-person point of view. Whenever the speaker uses the "I" and comments on the action, that speaker is also an important part of the story. Everything we read is reported by the speaker. Therefore, his or her abilities, position as an observer, character, attitudes, and possible prejudices or self-interests are to be considered along with everything that is said. The first-person speaker of Tillie Olsen's "I Stand Here Ironing," for example, is the mother of the girl, and as she speaks we can follow her own attempts at self-explanation and justification. She, like virtually all first-person narrators, is as much a focus of interest as the events themselves.

### Second Person

Although a *second person* narration (in which the narrator tells a listener what he or she has done, using the "you" personal pronoun) is possible, it is rare because in effect the second-person actually requires a first-person voice. The viewpoint requires also that the listener be the character who lived through the narration. Thus a parent might be telling a child what the child did during infancy, for which the child has no memory. Or a doctor might tell a patient with amnesia about what occurred during the time when his or her memory was gone, or a lawyer might present a story of a crime directly to a defendant accused of the crime. In practice, the second-person point of view is of only passing use in most fiction, and it is so rarely used that it is almost negligible. A. A. Milne uses it for a time at the beginning of the children's story *Winnie the Pooh*, but drops it as soon as the events of Pooh Bear and the rest of the animals get under way. Jay McInerney uses it in *Bright Lights, Big City* (1984). The "you," however, is very clearly a colloquial substitute for "I," so that the point of view is not second person, but rather first.

### Third Person

If the narrator is not introduced as a character, and if everything in the work is described in the third person (that is, *he, she, it, they*), the author is using the **third-person** point of view. There are three variants: omniscient, limited omniscient, and dramatic or objective.

**OMNISCIENT.**    The third-person point of view is called **omniscient** (all-knowing) when the speaker not only describes the action and dialogue of the work, but also seems to know everything that goes on in the minds of the characters. In the third-person omniscient point of view authors take great responsibility: By delving into the minds of their characters, they assume a stance that exceeds our ordinary experience with other persons. The result is that an omniscient story is not realistic, according to our present way of seeing things. This viewpoint was much used when prose fiction was a relatively new genre. Because it is not probable that any narrator can truly know the inner workings of others' minds, however, there are few if any writers today who employ it.

**LIMITED OMNISCIENT.**    Most common is the **limited omniscient** point of view, in which the author uses the third person but confines the story to what one single character does, says, sees, and sometimes thinks. Often this viewpoint will use expressions that the point-of-view character might use, as in Katherine Mansfield's "Miss Brill." While the omniscient point of view can include thoughts of almost all the characters, the limited focuses on only one. Sarty of "Barn Burning," Erwin Martin of "The Catbird Seat" and Mathilde Loisel of "The Necklace" are such limited-point-of-view characters. Everything in these stories is there because these characters, like Miss Brill, experienced it, heard about it, and thought about it. Obviously there are variations in how deeply the limited omniscience may extend. Thus, we learn more about Miss Brill and Erwin Martin, for example, than about Mathilde, because Mansfield and Thurber present more of the inner thoughts of these characters than does De Maupassant.

**DRAMATIC OR OBJECTIVE.**   Writers using the dramatic point of view (also called **third-person objective**) confine the work mainly to quotations and descriptions of actions. They avoid telling that certain characters thought this or felt that but instead allow the characters themselves to state what is on their minds. Shirley Jackson's "The Lottery" is a prime example of the dramatic point of view in a story, as is John Collier's "The Chaser" and the "Prodigal Son" from the Gospel according to St. Luke. The narrator of the dramatic point of view perceives things and reports them in a way that is roughly analogous to a hovering or tracking motion-picture camera. Thus, characters in the out of doors may be seen at a distance or up close, and when they move indoors or into a conveyance of some sort, the speaker continues to observe and report their activities.

Though actions and dialogue are the main substance of the dramatic point of view, authors may allow certain characters to express their own attitudes and feelings, which then also become a part of the story. Old Man Warner in "The Lottery" is an example of the commentator who represents a conservative voice in favor of the institution of the lottery even as he notes that there are persons in other communities in favor of giving it up.

The key to the dramatic point of view is that the writer presents actions and dialogue and leaves any conclusions and interpretations up to the readers. Naturally, however, the author does not relinquish his or her shaping spirit with the choice of the dramatic viewpoint. Hence the reader's conclusions are shaped by the author's ordering of the materials of the story.

## MINGLING POINTS OF VIEW

In most stories there is a mingling of viewpoints. Hence a point of view may be limited omniscient when focused on the thoughts of a major character, but dramatic when focused on the actions and dialogue. The writer may tell most of the story in one type of point of view but then shift at an important point for the purpose of sustaining interest or creating suspense. For example, Thurber in "The Catbird Seat" ends his limited omniscient disclosure of the thoughts of Erwin Martin when Martin develops his plan in the apartment of Mrs. Barrows. After this point Thurber uses the dramatic point of view so that the reader will not know the plan until it has been fully enacted. As you analyze point of view in a story, you will find the following summary helpful.

*POINTS OF VIEW*

1.  First Person ("I") All these first-person narrators may have (1) complete understanding, (2) partial or incorrect understanding, or (3) no understanding at all.
    a.  Major participant
        i.   telling his or her own story as a major mover
        ii.  telling a story about others and also about herself or himself as one of the major inter-actors
        iii. telling a story mainly about others; this narrator is on the spot and completely involved but is not a major mover.
    b.  Minor participant, telling a story about events experienced and/or witnessed.
    c.  Uninvolved character, telling a story not witnessed but reported to the narrator by other means.
2.  Second person ("you") Occurs only when speaker has more authority on a character's actions than the character himself or herself; for example, parent, psychologist, lawyer. Occurs only in brief passages when necessary.
3.  Third person ("she," "he," "it," "they")
    a.  Omniscient. Omniscient speaker sees all, reports all, knows inner workings of minds of characters.
    b.  Limited omniscient. Action is focused on one major character.
    c.  Dramatic or third-person objective. Speaker reports only actions and speeches. Thoughts of characters can be expressed only as dialogue.

## POINT OF VIEW AND "EVIDENCE"

In considering point of view, you should try to analyze all aspects that bear on the presentation of the material in the work. You may imagine yourself somewhat like a member of a jury. Jury members cannot accept testimony uncritically, for some witnesses may have much to gain by misstatements, distortions, or outright lies. Before rendering a verdict, jury members must consider all these possibilities. Speakers in literary works are usually to be accepted as reliable witnesses, but it is true that their characters, interests, capacities, personal involvements, and positions to view action may have a bearing on the material they present. A classic example is the Japanese film *Rashomon* (1950), directed by Akira Kurosawa, in which four different people tell a story as evidence in a court, and each presents a version that makes that person seem more honorable than he or she actually was. While most stories are not as complex as this, you should always consider the character of the speaker before you render your verdict on what the story is about.

## KATHERINE MANSFIELD (1888–1923)

### Miss Brill°

*1920*

Although it was so brilliantly fine—the blue sky powdered with gold and great spots of light like white wine splashed over the Jardins Publiques° —Miss Brill was glad that she had decided on her fur. The air was motionless, but when you opened your mouth there was just a faint chill, like a chill from a glass of iced water before you sip, and now and again a leaf came drifting—from nowhere, from the sky. Miss Brill put up her hand and touched her fur. Dear little thing! It was nice to feel it again. She had taken it out of its box that afternoon, shaken out the moth-powder, given it a good brush, and rubbed the life back into the dim little eyes. "What has been happening to me?" said the sad little eyes. Oh, how sweet it was to see them snap at her again from the red eiderdown! . . . But the nose, which was of some black composition, wasn't at all firm. It must have had a knock, somehow. Never mind—a little dab of black sealing-wax when the time came—when it was absolutely necessary. . . . Little rogue! Yes, she really felt like that about it. Little rogue biting its tail just by her left ear. She could have taken it off and laid it on her lap and stroked it. She felt a tingling in her hands and arms, but that came from walking, she supposed. And when she breathed, something light and sad—no, not sad, exactly—something gentle seemed to move in her bosom.

There were a number of people out this afternoon, far more than last Sunday. And the band sounded louder and gayer. That was because the Season had begun. For although the band played all the year round on Sundays, out of season it was never the same. It was like some one playing with only the family to listen; it didn't care how it played if there weren't any strangers present. Wasn't the conductor wearing a new coat, too? She was sure it was new. He scraped with his foot and flapped his arms like a rooster about to crow, and the bandsmen sitting in the green rotunda blew out their cheeks and glared at the music. Now there came a little "flutey" bit—very pretty!—a little chain of bright drops. She was sure it would be repeated. It was; she lifted her head and smiled.

Only two people shared her "special" seat: a fine old man in a velvet coat, his hands clasped over a huge carved walking-stick, and a big old woman, sitting upright, with a roll of knitting on her embroidered apron. They did not speak. This was disappointing, for Miss Brill always looked forward to the conversation. She had become really quite expert, she thought, at listening as though she didn't listen, at sitting in other people's lives just for a minute while they talked round her.

She glanced, sideways, at the old couple. Perhaps they would go soon. Last Sunday, too, hadn't been as interesting as usual. An Englishman and his wife, he wearing a dreadful Panama hat and she button boots. And she'd gone on the whole time about how she ought to wear spectacles; she knew she needed them; but that it was no good getting any; they'd be sure to break and they'd never

---

*Miss Brill*: *Brill* is the name of a common deepsea flatfish.
*Jardins Publiques*: public gardens, or public park. The setting of the story is apparently a French seaside town.

keep on. And he'd been so patient. He'd suggested everything—gold rims, the kind that curved round your ears, little pads inside the bridge. No, nothing would please her. "They'll always be sliding down my nose!" Miss Brill had wanted to shake her.

The old people sat on the bench, still as statues. Never mind, there was     5
always the crowd to watch. To and fro, in front of the flower-beds and the band rotunda, the couples and groups paraded, stopped to talk, to greet, to buy a handful of flowers from the old beggar who had his tray fixed to the railings. Little children ran among them, swooping and laughing; little boys with big white silk bows under their chins, little girls, little French dolls, dressed up in velvet and lace. And sometimes a tiny staggerer came suddenly rocking into the open from under the trees, stopped, stared, as suddenly sat down "flop," until its small high-stepping mother, like a young hen, rushed scolding to its rescue. Other people sat on the benches and green chairs, but they were nearly always the same, Sunday after Sunday, and—Miss Brill had often noticed—there was something funny about nearly all of them. They were odd, silent, nearly all old, and from the way they stared they looked as though they'd just come from dark little rooms or even—even cupboards!

Behind the rotunda the slender trees with yellow leaves down drooping, and through them just a line of sea, and beyond the blue sky with gold-veined clouds.

Tum-tum-tum tiddle-um! tiddle-um! tum tiddley-um tum ta! blew the band.

Two young girls in red came by and two young soldiers in blue met them, and they laughed and paired and went off arm-in-arm. Two peasant women with funny straw hats passed, gravely, leading beautiful smoke-coloured donkeys. A cold, pale nun hurried by. A beautiful woman came along and dropped her bunch of violets, and a little boy ran after to hand them to her, and she took them and threw them away as if they'd been poisoned. Dear me! Miss Brill didn't know whether to admire that or not! And now an ermine toque° and a gentleman in grey met just in front of her. He was tall, stiff, dignified, and she was wearing the ermine toque she'd bought when her hair was yellow. Now everything, her hair, her face, even her eyes, was the same colour as the shabby ermine, and her hand, in its cleaned glove, lifted to dab her lips, was a tiny yellowish paw. Oh, she was so pleased to see him—delighted! She rather thought they were going to meet that afternoon. She described where she'd been—everywhere, here, there, along by the sea. The day was so charming—didn't he agree? And wouldn't he, perhaps? . . . But he shook his head, lighted a cigarette, slowly breathed a great deep puff into her face, and, even while she was still talking and laughing, flicked the match away and walked on. The ermine toque was alone; she smiled more brightly than ever. But even the band seemed to know what she was feeling and played more softly, played tenderly, and the drum beat, "The Brute! The Brute!" over and over. What would she do? What was going to happen now? But as Miss Brill wondered, the ermine toque turned, raised her hand as though she'd seen some one else, much nicer, just over there, and pattered away. And the band changed again and played more quickly, more gaily than ever, and the old couple on Miss Brill's seat got up and marched away, and such a funny old man with

---

*toque*: a hat. The phrase "ermine toque" refers to a woman wearing a hat made of the fur of a weasel.

long whiskers hobbled along in time to the music and was nearly knocked over by four girls walking abreast.

Oh, how fascinating it was! How she enjoyed it! How she loved sitting here, watching it all! It was like a play. It was exactly like a play. Who could believe the sky at the back wasn't painted? But it wasn't till a little brown dog trotted on solemn and then slowly trotted off, like a little "theatre" dog, a little dog that had been drugged, that Miss Brill discovered what it was that made it so exciting. They were all on the stage. They weren't only the audience, not only looking on; they were acting. Even she had a part and came every Sunday. No doubt somebody would have noticed if she hadn't been there; she was part of the performance after all. How strange she'd never thought of it like that before! And yet it explained why she made such a point of starting from home at just the same time each week—so as not to be late for the performance—and it also explained why she had quite a queer, shy feeling at telling her English pupils how she spent her Sunday afternoons. No wonder! Miss Brill nearly laughed out loud. She was on the stage. She thought of the old invalid gentleman to whom she read the newspaper four afternoons a week while he slept in the garden. She had got quite used to the frail head on the cotton pillow, the hollowed eyes, the open mouth and the high pinched nose. If he'd been dead she mightn't have noticed for weeks; she wouldn't have minded. But suddenly he knew he was having the paper read to him by an actress! "An actress!" The old head lifted; two points of light quivered in the old eyes. "An actress—are ye?" And Miss Brill smoothed the newspaper as though it were the manuscript of her part and said gently: "Yes, I have been an actress for a long time."

The band had been having a rest. Now they started again. And what they played was warm, sunny, yet there was just a faint chill—a something, what was it?—not sadness—no, not sadness—a something that made you want to sing. The tune lifted, lifted, the light shone; and it seemed to Miss Brill that in another moment all of them, all the whole company, would begin singing. The young ones, the laughing ones who were moving together, they would begin, and the men's voices, very resolute and brave, would join them. And then she too, she too, and the others on the benches—they would come in with a kind of accompaniment—something low, that scarcely rose or fell, something so beautiful—moving. . . . And Miss Brill's eyes filled with tears and she looked smiling at all the other members of the company. Yes, we understand, we understand, she thought—though what they understood she didn't know.

Just at that moment a boy and a girl came and sat down where the old couple had been. They were beautifully dressed; they were in love. The hero and heroine, of course, just arrived from his father's yacht. And still soundlessly singing, still with that trembling smile, Miss Brill prepared to listen.

"No, not now," said the girl. "Not here, I can't."

"But why? Because of that stupid old thing at the end there?" asked the boy. "Why does she come here at all—who wants her? Why doesn't she keep her silly old mug at home?"

"It's her fu-fur which is so funny," giggled the girl. "It's exactly like a fried whiting."

"Ah, be off with you!" said the boy in an angry whisper. Then: "Tell me, ma petite chérie—"

"No, not here," said the girl. "Not *yet*."

10

15

On her way home she usually bought a slice of honeycake at the baker's. It was her Sunday treat. Sometimes there was an almond in her slice, sometimes not. It made a great difference. If there was an almond it was like carrying home a tiny present—a surprise—something that might very well not have been there. She hurried on the almond Sundays and struck the match for the kettle in quite a dashing way.

But to-day she passed the baker's by, climbed the stairs, went into the little dark room—her room like a cupboard—and sat down on the red eiderdown. She sat there for a long time. The box that the fur came out of was on the bed. She unclasped the necklet quickly; quickly, without looking, laid it inside. But when she put the lid on she thought she heard something crying.

## QUESTIONS

1.  Describe the point of view of "Miss Brill." Is it in the third person limited, omniscient, or dramatic? Who says, in paragraph 1, "Dear little thing!" about the fur? How do you justify your conclusion about the source of this and similar insights that appear throughout the story?

2.  Would this story be possible if told in the first person by Miss Brill herself? What might it have been like if told by a walker in the park who observed Miss Brill and overheard the conversation about her by the boy and girl?

3.  A shift in the point of view occurs when the boy and girl sit down and Miss Brill overhears them. Describe the nature of this shift. Why do you think that Mansfield made the change at this point?

4.  In relation to the point of view, explain the last sentence of the story: "But when she put the lid on she thought she heard something crying." Is this sentence consistent with the point of view of the previous seven paragraphs, or with the great bulk of the story before that?

5.  Briefly describe the things that happen in the story. Are there many genuine actions? On the basis of your answers to these questions, would you say that "Miss Brill" is mainly active, or mainly reflective and psychological?

6.  In what ways does Miss Brill think of her presence in the park as her being on the stage? Describe her sense of *camaraderie* with the other people in the park.

7.  What is illustrated in the description of the woman wearing the ermine toque? Is there any parallel with the life of Miss Brill herself?

8.  Do you like Miss Brill? Do you feel sorry for her? How do you think Mansfield wanted you to feel about her?

## FRANK O'CONNOR (1903–1966)

*First Confession*                                                           1951

All the trouble began when my grandfather died and my grandmother—my father's mother—came to live with us. Relations in the one house are a strain at the best of times, but, to make matters worse, my grandmother was a real old countrywoman and quite unsuited to the life in town. She had a fat, wrinkled old face, and, to Mother's great indignation, went round the house in bare feet—the boots had her crippled, she said. For dinner she had a jug of porter° and a pot of potatoes with—sometimes—a bit of salt fish, and she poured out the potatoes on the table and ate them slowly, with great relish, using her fingers by way of a fork.

Now, girls are supposed to be fastidious, but I was the one who suffered most from this. Nora, my sister, just sucked up to the old woman for the penny she got every Friday out of the old-age pension, a thing I could not do. I was too honest, that was my trouble; and when I was playing with Bill Connell, the sergeant-major's son, and saw my grandmother steering up the path with the jug of porter sticking out from beneath her shawl I was mortified. I made excuses not to let him come into the house, because I could never be sure what she would be up to when we went in.

When Mother was at work and my grandmother made the dinner I wouldn't touch it. Nora once tried to make me, but I hid under the table from her and took the bread-knife with me for protection. Nora let on to be very indignant (she wasn't, of course, but she knew Mother saw through her, so she sided with Gran) and came after me. I lashed out at her with the bread-knife, and after that she left me alone. I stayed there till Mother came in from work and made my dinner, but when Father came in later Nora said in a shocked voice: "Oh, Dadda, do you know what Jackie did at dinnertime?" Then, of course, it all came out; Father gave me a flaking; Mother interfered, and for days after that he didn't speak to me and Mother barely spoke to Nora. And all because of that old woman! God knows, I was heart-scalded.

Then, to crown my misfortune, I had to make my first confession and communion. It was an old woman called Ryan who prepared us for these. She was about the one age with Gran; she was well-to-do, lived in a big house on Montenotte, wore a black cloak and bonnet, and came every day to school at three o'clock when we should have been going home, and talked to us of hell. She may have mentioned the other place as well, but that could only have been by accident, for hell had the first place in her heart.

She lit a candle, took out a new half-crown, and offered it to the first boy who would hold one finger—only one finger!—in the flame for five minutes by the school clock. Being always very ambitious I was tempted to volunteer, but I thought it might look greedy. Then she asked were we afraid of holding one finger—only one finger!—in a little candle flame for five minutes and not afraid of burning all over in roasting hot furnaces for all eternity. "All eternity! Just think of that! A whole lifetime goes by and it's nothing, not even a drop in the ocean of your sufferings." The woman was really interesting about hell, but my attention was all fixed on the half-crown. At the end of the lesson she put it back in her purse. It was a great disappointment; a religious woman like that, you wouldn't think she'd bother about a thing like a half-crown.

Another day she said she knew a priest who woke one night to find a fellow he didn't recognize leaning over the end of his bed. The priest was a bit frightened—naturally enough—but he asked the fellow what he wanted, and the fellow said in a deep, husky voice that he wanted to go to confession. The priest said it was

5

*porter*: beer.

an awkward time and wouldn't it do in the morning, but the fellow said that last time he went to confession, there was one sin he kept back, being ashamed to mention it, and now it was always on his mind. Then the priest knew it was a bad case, because the fellow was after making a bad confession and committing a mortal sin. He got up to dress, and just then the cock crew in the yard outside, and—lo and behold!—when the priest looked round there was no sign of the fellow, only a smell of burning timber, and when the priest looked at his bed didn't he see the print of two hands burned in it? That was because the fellow had made a bad confession. This story made a shocking impression on me.

But the worst of all was when she showed us how to examine our conscience. Did we take the name of the Lord, our God, in vain? Did we honour our father and our mother? (I asked her did this include grandmothers and she said it did.) Did we love our neighbours as ourselves? Did we covet our neighbour's goods? (I thought of the way I felt about the penny that Nora got every Friday.) I decided that, between one thing and another, I must have broken the whole ten commandments, all on account of that old woman, and so far as I could see, so long as she remained in the house I had no hope of ever doing anything else.

I was scared to death of confession. The day the whole class went I let on to have a toothache, hoping my absence wouldn't be noticed; but at three o'clock, just as I was feeling safe, along comes a chap with a message from Mrs. Ryan that I was to go to confession myself on Saturday and be at the chapel for communion with the rest. To make it worse, Mother couldn't come with me and sent Nora instead.

Now, that girl had ways of tormenting me that Mother never knew of. She held my hand as we went down the hill, smiling sadly and saying how sorry she was for me, as if she were bringing me to the hospital for an operation.

"Oh, God help us!" she moaned. "Isn't it a terrible pity you weren't a good      10
boy? Oh, Jackie, my heart bleeds for you! How will you ever think of all your sins? Don't forget you have to tell him about the time you kicked Gran on the shin."

"Lemme go!" I said, trying to drag myself free of her. "I don't want to go to confession at all."

"But sure, you'll have to go to confession, Jackie," she replied in the same regretful tone. "Sure, if you didn't, the parish priest would be up to the house, looking for you. 'Tisn't, God knows, that I'm not sorry for you. Do you remember the time you tried to kill me with the bread-knife under the table? And the language you used to me? I don't know what he'll do with you at all, Jackie. He might have to send you up to the bishop."

I remember thinking bitterly that she didn't know the half of what I had to tell—if I told it. I knew ı couldn't tell it, and understood perfectly why the fellow in Mrs. Ryan's story made a bad confession; it seemed to me a great shame that people wouldn't stop criticizing him. I remember that steep hill down to the church, and the sunlit hillsides beyond the valley of the river, which I saw in the gaps between the houses like Adam's last glimpse of Paradise.

Then, when she had manœuvered me down the long flight of steps to the chapel yard, Nora suddenly changed her tone. She became the raging malicious devil she really was.

"There you are!" she said with a yelp of triumph, hurling me through the church door. "And I hope he'll give you the penitential psalms, you dirty little caffler."

I knew then I was lost, given up to eternal justice. The door with the coloured-glass panels swung shut behind me, the sunlight went out and gave place to deep shadow, and the wind whistled outside so that the silence within seemed to crackle like ice under my feet. Nora sat in front of me by the confession box. There were a couple of old woman ahead of her, and then a miserable-looking poor devil came and wedged me in at the other side, so that I couldn't escape even if I had the courage. He joined his hands and rolled his eyes in the direction of the roof, muttering aspirations in an anguished tone, and I wondered had he a grandmother too. Only a grandmother could account for a fellow behaving in that heartbroken way, but he was better off than I, for he at least could go and confess his sins; while I would make a bad confession and then die in the night and be continually coming back and burning people's furniture.

Nora's turn came, and I heard the sound of something slamming, and then her voice as if butter wouldn't melt in her mouth, and then another slam, and out she came. God, the hypocrisy of women! Her eyes were lowered, her head was bowed, and her hands were joined very low down on her stomach, and she walked up the aisle to the side altar looking like a saint. You never saw such an exhibition of devotion, and I remembered the devilish malice with which she had tormented me all the way from our door, and wondered were all religious people like that, really. It was my turn now. With the fear of damnation in my soul I went in, and the confessional door closed of itself behind me.

It was pitch-dark and I couldn't see priest or anything else. Then I really began to be frightened. In the darkness it was a matter between God and me, and He had all the odds. He knew what my intentions were before I even started; I had no chance. All I had ever been told about confession got mixed up in my mind, and I knelt to one wall and said: "Bless me, father, for I have sinned; this is my first confession." I waited for a few minutes, but nothing happened, so I tried it on the other wall. Nothing happened there either. He had me spotted all right.

It must have been then that I noticed the shelf at about one height with my head. It was really a place for grown-up people to rest their elbows, but in my distracted state I thought it was probably the place you were supposed to kneel. Of course, it was on the high side and not very deep, but I was always good at climbing and managed to get up all right. Staying up was the trouble. There was room only for my knees, and nothing you could get a grip on but a sort of wooden moulding, a bit above it. I held on to the moulding and repeated the words a little louder, and this time something happened all right. A slide was slammed back; a little light entered the box, and a man's voice said: "Who's there?"

" 'Tis me, father," I said for fear he mightn't see me and go away again. I couldn't see him at all. The place the voice came from was under the moulding, about level with my knees, so I took a good grip of the moulding and swung myself down till I saw the astonished face of a young priest looking up at me. He had to put his head on one side to see me, and I had to put mine on one side to see him, so we were more or less talking to one another upside-down. It

15

20

struck me as a queer way of hearing confessions, but I didn't feel it my place to criticize.

"Bless me, father, for I have sinned; this is my first confession," I rattled off all in one breath, and swung myself down the least shade more to make it easier for him.

"What are you doing up there?" he shouted in an angry voice, and the strain the politeness was putting on my hold of the moulding, and the shock of being addressed in such an uncivil tone, were too much for me. I lost my grip, tumbled, and hit the door an unmerciful wallop before I found myself flat on my back in the middle of the aisle. The people who had been waiting stood up with their mouths open. The priest opened the door of the middle box and came out, pushing his biretta back from his forehead; he looked something terrible. Then Nora came scampering down the aisle.

"Oh, you dirty little caffler!" she said. "I might have known you'd do it. I might have known you'd disgrace me. I can't leave you out of my sight for one minute."

Before I could even get to my feet to defend myself she bent down and gave me a clip across the ear. This reminded me that I was so stunned I had even forgotten to cry, so that people might think I wasn't hurt at all, when in fact I was probably maimed for life. I gave a roar out of me.

"What's all this about?" the priest hissed, getting angrier than ever and    25
pushing Nora off me. "How dare you hit the child like that, you little vixen?"

"But I can't do my penance with him, father," Nora cried, cocking an outraged eye up to him.

"Well, go and do it, or I'll give you some more to do," he said, giving me a hand up. "Was it coming to confession you were, my poor man?" he asked me.

" 'Twas, father," said I with a sob.

"Oh," he said respectfully, "a big hefty fellow like you must have terrible sins. Is this your first?"

" 'Tis, father," said I.    30

"Worse and worse," he said gloomily. "The crimes of a lifetime. I don't know will I get rid of you at all today. You'd better wait now till I'm finished with these old ones. You can see by the looks of them they haven't much to tell."

"I will, father," I said with something approaching joy.

The relief of it was really enormous. Nora stuck out her tongue at me from behind his back, but I couldn't even be bothered retorting. I knew from the very moment that man opened his mouth that he was intelligent above the ordinary. When I had time to think, I saw how right I was. It only stood to reason that a fellow confessing after seven years would have more to tell than people that went every week. The crimes of a lifetime, exactly as he said. It was only what he expected, and the rest was the cackle of old women and girls with their talk of hell, the bishop, and the penitential psalms. That was all they knew. I started to make my examination of conscience, and barring the one bad business of my grandmother it didn't seem so bad.

The next time, the priest steered me into the confession box himself and left the shutter back the way I could see him get in and sit down at the further side of the grille from me.

"Well, now," he said, "what do they call you?"

"Jackie, father," said I.

"And what's a-trouble to you, Jackie?"

"Father," I said, feeling I might as well get it over while I had him in good humour, "I had it all arranged to kill my grandmother."

He seemed a bit shaken by that, all right, because he said nothing for quite a while.

"My goodness," he said at last, "that'd be a shocking thing to do. What put that into your head?"

"Father," I said, feeling very sorry for myself, "she's an awful woman."

"Is she?" he asked. "What way is she awful?"

"She takes porter, father," I said, knowing well from the way Mother talked of it that this was a mortal sin, and hoping it would make the priest take a more favourable view of my case.

"Oh, my!" he said, and I could see he was impressed.

"And snuff, father," said I.

"That's a bad case, sure enough, Jackie," he said.

"And she goes round in her bare feet, father," I went on in a rush of self-pity, "and she knows I don't like her, and she gives pennies to Nora and none to me, and my da sides with her and flakes me, and one night I was so heart-scalded I made up my mind I'd have to kill her."

"And what would you do with the body?" he asked with great interest.

"I was thinking I could chop that up and carry it away in a barrow I have," I said.

"Begor, Jackie," he said, "do you know you're a terrible child?"

"I know, father," I said, for I was just thinking the same thing myself. "I tried to kill Nora too with a bread-knife under the table, only I missed her."

"Is that the little girl that was beating you just now?" he asked.

"'Tis, father."

"Someone will go for her with a bread-knife one day, and he won't miss her," he said rather cryptically. "You must have great courage. Between ourselves, there's a lot of people I'd like to do the same to but I'd never have the nerve. Hanging is an awful death."

"Is it, father?" I asked with the deepest interest—I was always very keen on hanging. "Did you ever see a fellow hanged?"

"Dozens of them," he said solemnly. "And they all died roaring."

"Jay!" I said.

"Oh, a horrible death!" he said with great satisfaction. "Lots of the fellows I saw killed their grandmothers too, but they all said 'twas never worth it."

He had me there for a full ten minutes talking, and then walked out the chapel yard with me. I was genuinely sorry to part with him, because he was the most entertaining character I'd ever met in the religious line. Outside, after the shadow of the church, the sunlight was like the roaring of waves on a beach; it dazzled me; and when the frozen silence melted and I heard the screech of trams on the road my heart soared. I knew now I wouldn't die in the night and come back, leaving marks on my mother's furniture. It would be a great worry to her, and the poor soul had enough.

Nora was sitting on the railing, waiting for me, and she put on a very sour puss when she saw the priest with me. She was made jealous because a priest had never come out of the church with her.

"Well," she asked coldly, after he left me, "what did he give you?"

"Three Hail Marys," I said.

"Three Hail Marys," she repeated incredulously. "You mustn't have told him anything."

"I told him everything," I said confidently.

"About Gran and all?"                                                              65

"About Gran and all."

(All she wanted was to be able to go home and say I'd made a bad confession.)

"Did you tell him you went for me with the bread-knife?" she asked with a frown.

"I did to be sure."

"And he only gave you three Hail Marys?"                                           70

"That's all."

She slowly got down from the railing with a baffled air. Clearly, this was beyond her. As we mounted the steps back to the main road she looked at me suspiciously.

"What are you sucking?" she asked.

"Bullseyes."

"Was it the priest gave them to you?"                                             75

" 'Twas."

"Lord God," she wailed bitterly, "some people have all the luck! 'Tis no advantage to anybody trying to be good. I might just as well be a sinner like you."


## QUESTIONS

1.  Could this story be effective if it had been told in the third-person point of view limited to the character of Jackie? How might it have been different, or better or worse?

2.  Read the sample essay on the point of view in the story (p. 188). Do you agree or disagree with the assertion there that Jackie, from an adult perspective, lacks maturity? Might he be more easily explained if you judged him as an adolescent rather than as an adult?

3.  Describe the character of Jackie as a storyteller. What vestiges of childhood perception can you find in his narration? That is, what sorts of perceptiveness does he show with regard to Mrs. Ryan? His sister? The approaching confession? The nature of women? His ability to learn from experience?

4.  Is Jackie's confession a "good" one? What sort of religiosity is more appealing and effective, the sort represented by Mrs. Ryan or by the priest?

5.  Do you think that the relationships among members of Jackie's family seem unusual or potentially damaging? Does the sister, Nora, seem out of the ordinary at all in light of her treatment of her younger brother? Does the narrator's judgment of her, and of women generally, seem justified, coming from an adult? Why or why not?

6.  "First Confession" is a funny story. What makes it funny, and why?

## SHIRLEY JACKSON (1919–1965)

### The Lottery                                                   1948

The morning of June 27th was clear and sunny, with the fresh warmth of a full-summer day; the flowers were blossoming profusely and the grass was richly green. The people of the village began to gather in the square, between the post office and the bank, around ten o'clock; in some towns there were so many people that the lottery took two days and had to be started on June 26th, but in this village, where there were only about three hundred people, the whole lottery took less than two hours, so it could begin at ten o'clock in the morning and still be through in time to allow the villagers to get home for noon dinner.

The children assembled first, of course. School was recently over for the summer, and the feeling of liberty sat uneasily on most of them; they tended to gather together quietly for a while before they broke into boisterous play, and their talk was still of the classroom and the teacher, of books and reprimands. Bobby Martin had already stuffed his pockets full of stones, and the other boys soon followed his example, selecting the smoothest and roundest stones; Bobby and Harry Jones and Dickie Delacroix—the villagers pronounced this name "Dellacroy"—eventually made a great pile of stones in one corner of the square and guarded it against the raids of the other boys. The girls stood aside, talking among themselves, looking over their shoulders at the boys, and the very small children rolled in the dust or clung to the hands of their older brothers or sisters.

Soon the men began to gather, surveying their own children, speaking of planting and rain, tractors and taxes. They stood together, away from the pile of stones in the corner, and their jokes were quiet and they smiled rather than laughed. The women, wearing faded house dresses and sweaters, came shortly after their menfolk. They greeted one another and exchanged bits of gossip as they went to join their husbands. Soon the women, standing by their husbands, began to call to their children, and the children came reluctantly, having to be called four or five times. Bobby Martin ducked under his mother's grasping hand and ran, laughing, back to the pile of stones. His father spoke up sharply, and Bobby came quickly and took his place between his father and his oldest brother.

The lottery was conducted—as were the square dances, the teen-age club, the Halloween program—by Mr. Summers, who had time and energy to devote to civic activities. He was a round-faced, jovial man and he ran the coal business, and people were sorry for him, because he had no children and his wife was a scold. When he arrived in the square, carrying the black wooden box, there was a murmur of conversation among the villagers, and he waved and called, "Little late today, folks." The postmaster, Mr. Graves, followed him, carrying a three-legged stool, and the stool was put in the center of the square and Mr. Summers set the black box down on it. The villagers kept their distance, leaving a space between themselves and the stool, and when Mr. Summers said, "Some of you fellows want to give me a hand?" there was a hesitation before two men, Mr. Martin and his oldest son, Baxter, came forward to hold the box steady on the stool while Mr. Summers stirred up the papers inside it.

The original paraphernalia for the lottery had been lost long ago, and the          5
black box now resting on the stool had been put into use even before Old Man
Warner, the oldest man in town, was born. Mr. Summers spoke frequently to the
villagers about making a new box, but no one liked to upset even as much tradition
as was represented by the black box. There was a story that the present box had
been made with some pieces of the box that had preceded it, the one that had
been constructed when the first people settled down to make a village here. Every
year, after the lottery, Mr. Summers began talking again about a new box, but
every year the subject was allowed to fade off without anything's being done. The
black box grew shabbier each year; by now it was no longer completely black but
splintered badly along one side to show the original wood color, and in some
places faded or stained.

Mr. Martin and his oldest son, Baxter, held the black box securely on the
stool until Mr. Summers had stirred the papers thoroughly with his hand. Because
so much of the ritual had been forgotten or discarded, Mr. Summers had been
successful in having slips of paper substituted for the chips of wood that had been
used for generations. Chips of wood, Mr. Summers had argued, had been all very
well when the village was tiny, but now that the population was more than three
hundred and likely to keep on growing, it was necessary to use something that
would fit more easily into the black box. The night before the lottery, Mr. Summers
and Mr. Graves made up the slips of paper and put them in the box, and it was
then taken to the safe of Mr. Summers' coal company and locked up until Mr.
Summers was ready to take it to the square next morning. The rest of the year,
the box was put away, sometimes one place, sometimes another; it had spent one
year in Mr. Graves's barn and another year underfoot in the post office, and sometimes it was set on a shelf in the Martin grocery and left there.

There was a great deal of fussing to be done before Mr. Summers declared
the lottery open. There were the lists to make up—of heads of families, heads of
households in each family, members of each household in each family. There was
the proper swearing-in of Mr. Summers by the postmaster, as the official of the
lottery; at one time, some people remembered, there had been a recital of some
sort, performed by the official of the lottery, a perfunctory, tuneless chant that
had been rattled off duly each year; some people believed that the official of the
lottery used to stand just so when he said or sang it, others believed that he was
supposed to walk among the people, but years and years ago this part of the
ritual had been allowed to lapse. There had been, also, a ritual salute, which the
official of the lottery had had to use in addressing each person who came up to
draw from the box, but this also had changed with time, until now it was felt
necessary only for the official to speak to each person approaching. Mr. Summers
was very good at all this; in his clean white shirt and blue jeans, with one hand
resting carelessly on the black box, he seemed very proper and important as he
talked interminably to Mr. Graves and the Martins.

Just as Mr. Summers finally left off talking and turned to the assembled
villagers, Mrs. Hutchinson came hurriedly along the path to the square, her sweater
thrown over her shoulders, and slid into place in the back of the crowd. "Clean
forgot what day it was," she said to Mrs. Delacroix, who stood next to her, and
they both laughed softly. "Thought my old man was out back stacking wood,"
Mrs. Hutchinson went on, "and then I looked out the window and the kids was
gone, and then I remembered it was the twenty-seventh and came a-running."

She dried her hands on her apron, and Mrs. Delacroix said, "You're in time, though. They're still talking away up there."

Mrs. Hutchinson craned her neck to see through the crowd and found her husband and children standing near the front. She tapped Mrs. Delacroix on the arm as a farewell and began to make her way through the crowd. The people separated good-humoredly to let her through; two or three people said, in voices just loud enough to be heard across the crowd, "Here comes your Missus, Hutchinson," and "Bill, she made it after all." Mrs. Hutchinson reached her husband, and Mr. Summers, who had been waiting, said cheerfully, "Thought we were going to have to get on without you, Tessie." Mrs. Hutchinson said, grinning, "Wouldn't have me leave m'dishes in the sink, now, would you, Joe?," and soft laughter ran through the crowd as the people stirred back into position after Mrs. Hutchinson's arrival.

"Well, now," Mr. Summers said soberly, "guess we better get started, get    10
this over with, so's we can go back to work. Anybody ain't here?"

"Dunbar," several people said. "Dunbar, Dunbar."

Mr. Summers consulted his list. "Clyde Dunbar," he said. "That's right. He's broke his leg, hasn't he? Who's drawing for him?"

"Me, I guess," a woman said, and Mr. Summers turned to look at her. "Wife draws for her husband," Mr. Summers said. "Don't you have a grown boy to do it for you, Janey?" Although Mr. Summers and everyone else in the village knew the answer perfectly well, it was the business of the official of the lottery to ask such questions formally. Mr. Summers waited with an expression of polite interest while Mrs. Dunbar answered.

"Horace's not but sixteen yet," Mrs. Dunbar said regretfully. "Guess I gotta fill in for the old man this year."

"Right," Mr. Summers said. He made a note on the list he was holding.    15
Then he asked, "Watson boy drawing this year?"

A tall boy in the crowd raised his hand. "Here," he said. "I'm drawing for m'mother and me." He blinked his eyes nervously and ducked his head as several voices in the crowd said things like "Good fellow, Jack," and "Glad to see your mother's got a man to do it."

"Well," Mr. Summers said, "guess that's everyone. Old Man Warner make it?"

"Here," a voice said, and Mr. Summers nodded.

A sudden hush fell on the crowd as Mr. Summers cleared his throat and looked at the list. "All ready?" he called. "Now, I'll read the names—heads of families first—and the men come up and take a paper out of the box. Keep the paper folded in your hand without looking at it until everyone has had a turn. Everything clear?"

The people had done it so many times that they only half listened to the    20
directions; most of them were quiet, wetting their lips, not looking around. Then Mr. Summers raised one hand high and said, "Adams." A man disengaged himself from the crowd and came forward. "Hi, Steve," Mr. Summers said, and Mr. Adams said, "Hi, Joe." They grinned at one another humorlessly and nervously. Then Mr. Adams reached into the black box and took out a folded paper. He held it firmly by one corner as he turned and went hastily back to his place in the crowd, where he stood a little apart from his family, not looking down at his hand.

"Allen," Mr. Summers said. "Anderson. . . . Bentham."

"Seems like there's no time at all between lotteries any more," Mrs. Delacroix said to Mrs. Graves in the back row. "Seems like we got through with the last one only last week."

"Time sure goes fast," Mrs. Graves said.

"Clark. . . . Delacroix."

"There goes my old man," Mrs. Delacroix said. She held her breath while         25
her husband went forward.

"Dunbar," Mr. Summers said, and Mrs. Dunbar went steadily to the box while one of the women said, "Go on, Janey," and another said, "There she goes."

"We're next," Mrs. Graves said. She watched while Mr. Graves came around from the side of the box, greeted Mr. Summers gravely, and selected a slip of paper from the box. By now, all through the crowd there were men holding the small folded papers in their large hands, turning them over and over nervously. Mrs. Dunbar and her two sons stood together, Mrs. Dunbar holding the slip of paper.

"Harburt. . . . Hutchinson."

"Get up there, Bill," Mrs. Hutchinson said, and the people near her laughed.

"Jones."                                                                        30

"They do say," Mr. Adams said to Old Man Warner, who stood next to him, "that over in the north village they're talking of giving up the lottery."

Old Man Warner snorted. "Pack of crazy fools," he said. "Listening to the young folks, nothing's good enough for *them*. Next thing you know, they'll be wanting to go back to living in caves, nobody work any more, live *that* way for a while. Used to be a saying about 'Lottery in June, corn be heavy soon.' First thing you know, we'd all be eating stewed chickweed and acorns. There's *always* been a lottery," he added petulantly. "Bad enough to see young Joe Summers up there joking with everybody."

"Some places have already quit lotteries," Mrs. Adams said.

"Nothing but trouble in *that*," Old Man Warner said stoutly. "Pack of young fools."

"Martin." And Bobby Martin watched his father go forward. "Overdyke. . . .       35
Percy."

"I wish they'd hurry," Mrs. Dunbar said to her older son. "I wish they'd hurry."

"They're almost through," her son said.

"You get ready to run tell Dad," Mrs. Dunbar said.

Mr. Summers called his own name and then stepped forward precisely and selected a slip from the box. Then he called, "Warner."

"Seventy-seventh year I been in the lottery," Old Man Warner said as he          40
went through the crowd. "Seventy-seventh time."

"Watson." The tall boy came awkwardly through the crowd. Someone said, "Don't be nervous, Jack," and Mr. Summers said, "Take your time, son."

"Zanini."

After that, there was a long pause, a breathless pause, until Mr. Summers, holding his slip of paper in the air, said, "All right, fellows." For a minute, no one moved, and then all the slips of paper were opened. Suddenly, all the women began to speak at once, saying, "Who is it?" "Who's got it?" "Is it the Dunbars?" "Is it the Watsons?" Then the voices began to say, "It's Hutchinson. It's Bill," "Bill Hutchinson's got it."

"Go tell your father," Mrs. Dunbar said to her older son.

People began to look around to see the Hutchinsons. Bill Hutchinson was standing quiet, staring down at the paper in his hand. Suddenly, Tessie Hutchinson shouted to Mr. Summers, "You didn't give him time enough to take any paper he wanted. I saw you. It wasn't fair!"

"Be a good sport, Tessie," Mrs. Delacroix called, and Mrs. Graves said, "All of us took the same chance."                                                                  45

"Shut up, Tessie," Bill Hutchinson said.

"Well, everyone," Mr. Summers said, "that was done pretty fast, and now we've got to be hurrying a little more to get done in time." He consulted his next list. "Bill," he said, "you draw for the Hutchinson family. You got any other households in the Hutchinsons?"

"There's Don and Eva," Mrs. Hutchinson yelled. "Make *them* take their chance!"

"Daughters draw with their husbands' families, Tessie," Mr. Summers said gently. "You know that as well as anyone else."

"It wasn't *fair*," Tessie said.                                                                           50

"I guess not, Joe," Bill Hutchinson said regretfully. "My daughter draws with her husband's family, that's only fair. And I've got no other family except the kids."

"Then, as far as drawing for families is concerned, it's you," Mr. Summers said in explanation, "and as far as drawing for households is concerned, that's you, too. Right?"

"Right," Bill Hutchinson said.

"How many kids, Bill?" Mr. Summers asked formally.

"Three," Bill Hutchinson said. "There's Bill, Jr., and Nancy, and little Dave. And Tessie and me."                                                                       55

"All right, then," Mr. Summers said. "Harry, you got their tickets back?"

Mr. Graves nodded and held up the slips of paper. "Put them in the box, then," Mr. Summers directed. "Take Bill's and put it in."

"I think we ought to start over," Mrs. Hutchinson said, as quietly as she could. "I tell you it wasn't *fair*. You didn't give him time enough to choose. *Every-body* saw that."

Mr. Graves had selected the five slips and put them in the box, and he dropped all the papers but those onto the ground, where the breeze caught them and lifted them off.

"Listen, everybody," Mrs. Hutchinson was saying to the people around her.                                                                                               60

"Ready, Bill?" Mr. Summers asked, and Bill Hutchinson, with one quick glance around at his wife and children, nodded.

"Remember," Mr. Summers said, "take the slips and keep them folded until each person has taken one. Harry, you help little Dave." Mr. Graves took the hand of the little boy, who came willingly with him up to the box. "Take a paper out of the box, Davy," Mr. Summers said. Davy put his hand into the box and laughed. "Take just *one* paper," Mr. Summers said. "Harry, you hold it for him." Mr. Graves took the child's hand and removed the folded paper from the tight fist and held it while little Dave stood next to him and looked up at him wonderingly.

"Nancy next," Mr. Summers said. Nancy was twelve, and her school friends breathed heavily as she went forward, switching her skirt, and took a slip daintily from the box. "Bill, Jr.," Mr. Summers said, and Billy, his face red and his feet over-large, nearly knocked the box over as he got a paper out. "Tessie," Mr. Summers said. She hesitated for a minute, looking around defiantly, and then set her lips and went up to the box. She snatched a paper out and held it behind her.

"Bill," Mr. Summers said, and Bill Hutchinson reached into the box and felt around, bringing his hand out at last with the slip of paper in it.

The crowd was quiet. A girl whispered, "I hope it's not Nancy," and the    65
sound of the whisper reached the edges of the crowd.

"It's not the way it used to be," Old Man Warner said clearly. "People ain't the way they used to be."

"All right," Mr. Summers said. "Open the papers. Harry, you open little Dave's."

Mr. Graves opened the slip of paper and there was a general sigh through the crowd as he held it up and everyone could see that it was blank. Nancy and Bill, Jr., opened theirs at the same time, and both beamed and laughed, turning around to the crowd and holding their slips of paper above their heads.

"Tessie," Mr. Summers said. There was a pause, and then Mr. Summers looked at Bill Hutchinson, and Bill unfolded his paper and showed it. It was blank.

"It's Tessie," Mr. Summers said, and his voice was hushed. "Show us her    70
paper, Bill."

Bill Hutchinson went over to his wife and forced the slip of paper out of her hand. It had a black spot on it, the black spot Mr. Summers had made the night before with the heavy pencil in the coal-company office. Bill Hutchinson held it up, and there was a stir in the crowd.

"All right, folks," Mr. Summers said. "Let's finish quickly."

Although the villagers had forgotten the ritual and lost the original black box, they still remembered to use stones. The pile of stones the boys had made earlier was ready; there were stones on the ground with the blowing scraps of paper that had come out of the box. Mrs. Delacroix selected a stone so large she had to pick it up with both hands and turned to Mrs. Dunbar. "Come on," she said. "Hurry up."

Mrs. Dunbar had small stones in both hands, and she said, gasping for breath, "I can't run at all. You'll have to go ahead and I'll catch up with you."

The children had stones already, and someone gave little Davy Hutchinson    75
a few pebbles.

Tessie Hutchinson was in the center of a cleared space by now, and she held her hands out desperately as the villagers moved in on her. "It isn't fair," she said. A stone hit her on the side of the head.

Old Man Warner was saying, "Come on, come on, everyone." Steve Adams was in the front of the crowd of villagers with Mrs. Graves beside him.

"It isn't fair, it isn't right," Mrs. Hutchinson screamed, and then they were upon her.

## QUESTIONS

1.  Describe the point of view of the story. Is it best described as third-person limited, omniscient, or dramatic? What seems to be the position from which the narrator sees and describes the events? How much extra information does the narrator provide? Does the narrator anywhere express any opinion about the events connected with the lottery?

2.  What would the story be like if it were attempted with an omniscient point of view, or with the first person? Could the story be as suspenseful as it is? Would it be necessary to provide more information than is now present about the lottery? Why so? In what other ways might the story be different with a different point of view?

3.  Does the conclusion of "The Lottery" seem to come as a surprise? In retrospect, are there hints earlier in the story about what is to come? Discuss how you perceived these hints before and after you read the conclusion.

4.  A scapegoat, in the ritual of purification described in the Old Testament (Leviticus 16), was an actual goat that was released into the wilderness after having been ceremonially heaped with the "iniquities" of the people (Leviticus 16:22). What traces of such a ritual are suggested in "The Lottery" by references to things like the abandoned salute and the recital, and also the jingle "Lottery in June, corn be heavy soon"? Can you think of any other kinds of rituals that are retained today even though their basis in belief is now remote or even nonexistent?

5.  Is the story a horror story or a surprise story, or neither or both?

6.  What idea or ideas do you think Jackson is asserting by making the characters in "The Lottery" seem to be just plain, ordinary folks? What would the story have been like if the people had been criminals? If they had all been devil worshippers?

## WRITING ABOUT POINT OF VIEW

In prewriting activities for an essay on point of view, you must consider things like language, authority and opportunity for observation, selection of detail, characterization, interpretive commentaries, and narrative development. You might plan an analysis of one, a few, or all of these elements. Generally the essay should explain how the point of view has contributed to making the story uniquely as it is. One of the major purposes in an essay on point of view is to establish the nature and adherence to verisimilitude of the narration, the similarity to truth achieved by the way the events are presented. The basic question is whether the story's actions and speeches are reported authentically so that the telling of the story is just as "true" as the story itself.

### *Organizing Your Essay*

**INTRODUCTION.**    In your introduction you should get at the matters that you plan to develop. Which point of view is used in the work? What is the major influence of this point of view? (For example, "The omniscient point of view causes full, leisurely insights into many shades of character," or "The first-person point of view enables the work to resemble an exposé of back-room political deals.") To what extent does the selection of point of view make the work particularly interesting and effective, or uninteresting and ineffective? What particular aspects of the work (action, dialogue, characters, description, narration, analysis) do you wish to analyze in support of your central idea?

**BODY.**    The questions you raise here will of course depend on the work you have studied. It would be impossible to answer all of the following questions in your analysis, but going through them should make you aware of the sorts of things you can include in the body of your theme.

If you have read a work with the first-person point of view, your analysis will necessarily involve the speaker. Who is she (supposing, for the moment, a woman)? Is she a major or a minor character? What is her background? What is her relationship to the person listening to her (if there is a listener)? Does she speak directly to you, the reader, in such a way that you are a listener or an eavesdropper? How does the speaker describe the various situations? Is her method uniquely a function of her character? Or (supposing a man), how reliable is he as an observer? How did he acquire the information he is presenting? How much does he disclose? How much does he hide? Does he ever rely on the information of others for his material? How reliable are these other witnesses? Does the speaker undergo any changes in the course of the work that have any bearing on the ways he presents the material? Does he notice one kind of thing (for example, discussion) but miss others (for example, natural scenery)? What might have escaped him, if anything? Does the author put the speaker into situations that he can describe but not understand? Why? Is the speaker ever confused? Is he close to the action, or distant from it? Does he show emotional involvement in any situations? Are you sympathetic to his concerns or are you put off by them? If the speaker makes any commentary, are his thoughts valid? To what extent, if any, is the speaker of as much interest as the material he presents?

If you encounter any of the third-person points of view, try to determine the characteristics of the voice employed by the author. Does it seem that the author is speaking in an authorial voice, or that the narrator has a special voice? You can approach this problem by answering many of the questions that are relevant to the first-person point of view. Also try to determine the distance of the narrator to the action. How is the action described? How is the dialogue recorded? Is there any background information given? Do the descriptions reveal any bias toward any of the characters? Are the descriptions full or bare? Does the author include descriptions or analyses of a character's thoughts? What are these like? Do you see evidence of the author's own philosophy? Does the choice of words direct you toward any particular interpretations? What limitations or freedoms devolve upon the story as a result of the point of view?

CONCLUSION.    In your conclusion you should evaluate the success of the story's point of view: Was it consistent, effective, truthful? What did the writer gain (if anything) by the selection of point of view? What was lost (if anything)? How might a less skillful writer have handled similar material? After answering questions like these, you may end your theme.

### Problems

1. In considering point of view, you will encounter the problem of whether to discuss the author or the speaker as the originator of attitudes and ideas. If the author is employing the first-person point of view, there is no problem. Use the speaker's name, if he or she is given one (for example, Sammy from "A & P," Jackie from "First Confession"), or else talk about the "speaker" or "persona" if there is no name (for example, the speaker of Whitecloud's "Blue Winds Dancing" is unnamed). You face a greater problem with the third-person points of view, but even here it is safe for you to discuss the "speaker" rather than the "author," remembering always that the author is manipulating the narrative voice. Sometimes authors emphasize a certain phase of their own personalities in their authorial voices. Many ideas are therefore common to both the author and the speaker, but your statements about these must be inferential, not absolute.

2. You may have a tendency to wander away from point of view into retelling the story. Emphasize the presentation of the events and ideas, and the causes for this presentation. Do not emphasize the subject material itself, but use it only as it bears on your consideration of point of view. Your object is not just to interpret the work, but also to show how the point of view enables you to interpret the work.

Obviously you must talk about the material in the work, but use it only to illustrate your assertions about point of view. Avoid the following pattern of statement, which will always lead you astray: "The speaker says this, which means this." Instead, adhere to the following pattern, which will keep your emphasis always on your central idea: "The speaker says this, which shows this about her and her attitudes." If a particular idea is difficult, you might need to explain it, but do not do so unless it illustrates your central idea.

3. Remember that you are dealing with point of view in the *entire* work and not simply in single narrations and conversations. For example, an individual character has her own way of seeing things when she states something, but in relation to the entire work her speech is a function of the dramatic point of view. Thus, you should not talk about Character A's point of view, and Character B's, but instead should state that "Using the dramatic point of view, Author Z allows the various characters to argue their cases, in their own words and with their own limitations."

4. Be particularly careful to distinguish between point of view and opinions or beliefs. Point of view refers to the total position from which things are seen, heard, and reported, whereas an opinion is a thought about something. In this essay, you are to describe not the ideas, but the method of narration of an author.

## SAMPLE ESSAY

### Frank O'Connor's First-Person Point of View in "First Confession"*

[1]     In Frank O'Connor's "First Confession," a story based in early twentieth-century Ireland, the point of view is first person. The speaker is an adult named Jackie, who recalls the events leading up to and including his first confession as a boy of seven. Jackie has good recall and organizing ability, but has limited adult perspective.° These qualities make the story detailed, dramatic, and objective.□

[2]     The detail of the story seems vivid and real because O'Connor presents Jackie as a person with strong recall. Events such as the knife scene, the drinking and eating by the barefoot grandmother, and the stories of Mrs. Ryan are colorful. They seem like high points of childhood that an adult would truly remember. The entire confession is presented as if it just happened, not as if it were an almost forgotten event of the past. Such vivid details, which give the story great interest, depend on their being still alive in the narrator's memory.

[3]     Beyond simple recall, O'Connor's drama rests on the organizing skills of the narrator. The story is made up of scenes that are unified and connected. Thus the first part of the confession, ending with Jackie's falling out of the confessional and being whacked by Nora, is a short but complete farce. The burning handprints of the man of the bad confession become a theme in Jackie's mind as he waits for the priest. In the confession itself Jackie mentions even the dramatic pause before the priest responds to the confessed plan to kill the grandmother. The drama in all these scenes results from a good storytelling narrator.

---

* See p. 172 for this story.
° Central idea
□ Thesis sentence

[4] The objective quality of "First Confession," accounting for O'Connor's humor, is related to a flaw in the narrator. Jackie makes remarks about the action, but these are childish and not adult. A more mature narrator might comment about the fear the boy gains through his religious instruction, the difficulties of his family life, or the beauty of his first confession. But from the adult Jackie's point of view we get no such comments. O'Connor makes Jackie stick to the events, and therefore he keeps the story objective, simple, and funny.

[5] Thus O'Connor's selection of the first-person point of view gives the story strength and humor. Jackie the adult is faithful to his childhood feelings. We get everything from his side, and only his side. He never gives his father or his sister any credit. It is the consistent point of view that makes "First Confession" both comic and excellent. If Jackie showed more adult understanding, O'Connor's humor would be gone, and the story would not be such good entertainment.

### Commentary on the Essay

This essay emphasizes both the abilities and the flaw of the narrator and attempts to relate these qualities to the nature of "First Confession." The introduction provides a brief background of the story but gets right to the point of view. The qualification of Jackie as a first-person observer is mentioned, followed by the central idea and thesis sentence. The second paragraph states that the vivid detail of the story results from Jackie's powerful recall. The third paragraph connects the dramatic quality of the various scenes with his skill as a storyteller. In the fourth paragraph a flaw in Jackie's adult character—a lack of adult perceptiveness—is shown as the cause of the objectivity and humor in the story. The conclusion states that the point of view is consistent, even if it is immature. The last sentence goes back to paragraph 4: The humor depends on the narrator's having a lack of sympathy for, and understanding of, childhood antagonists. Throughout the essay, therefore, certain qualities of the story are connected directly to the character, ability, and limited perspective of the point of view or centralizing mind.

# 6

# Setting: Place and Objects in Fiction

**Setting** refers to the natural and artificial scenery or environment in which characters in literature live and move. Things such as the time of day and the amount of light, the trees and animals, the sounds described, the smells, and the weather are part of the setting. Paint brushes, apples, pitchforks, rafts, six-shooters, watches, automobiles, horses and buggies, and many other items belong to the setting. References to clothing, descriptions of physical appearance, and spatial relationships among the characters are also part of setting. In short, the setting of a work is the sum total of references to physical and temporal objects and artifacts.

The setting of a story or novel is much like the sets and properties of the stage or the location for a motion picture. The dramatist writing for the stage is physically limited by what can be constructed and moved or carried onto the stage. Writers of nondramatic works, however, are limited only by their imaginations. It is possible for them to include details of many places without the slightest external restraint. For our purposes, the references will be to stories that establish a setting either in nature or in manufactured things.

The action of a story may occur in more than one place. In a novel, the locale may shift constantly. There may be several settings in a work, and the term *setting* refers to all the places mentioned. If a story is short, all the scenes may be in one city or countryside.

## TYPES OF SETTINGS

### Natural

The setting for a great number of stories is the out-of-doors, and, naturally enough, Nature herself is seen as a force that shapes action and therefore directs and redirects lives. A deep woods may make walking difficult or

190

dangerous, or may be a place for a sinister meeting of devil worshippers. The open road may be a place where one person seeks flight, others face a showdown, and still others may meet their fate. A lake may be the location where one person literally rescues another and also silently and unconsciously makes a direct commitment to the saved person. Bushes may furnish places of concealment, while a mountain top is a spot protecting occupants from the outside world. The ocean may be the location of a test of youth but also may provide the environment for the memory of vanished dreams. Nature, in short, is one of the major forces governing the circumstances of characters who go about facing the conflicts on which the plots of stories depend.

### Manufactured

Manufactured things always reflect the people who make them. A building or a room tells about the people who built it and live in it, and ultimately about the social and political orders that maintain the conditions. A richly decorated house shows the expensive tastes and resources of the characters owning it. A few cracks in the plaster and some chips in the paint may show the same persons declining in fortune and power. Ugly and impoverished surroundings may contribute to the weariness, insensitivity, negligence, or even hostility of the characters living in them.

## STUDYING THE USES OF SETTING

In studying the setting of a story, your first concern should be to discover all the details that conceivably form a part of setting, and then to determine how the author has used these details. For example, as writers stress character, plot, or action, they may emphasize or minimize setting. At times a setting will be no more than a roughly sketched place where events occur. In other stories, the setting may be so prominent that it may almost be considered as a participant in the action. An instance of such "participation" is Welty's "A Worn Path," where the woods and roadway provide obstacles that are almost active antagonists against Phoenix as she pushes her way to Natchez.

### Setting and Credibility

One of the major purposes of setting is to lend realism or verisimilitude; to set a story in a particular place or time makes the action credible. Irwin Shaw's "Act of Faith" presents the realistic conditions of France as a genuine background in which authentic soldiers plan an actual trip to Paris so that they may have a truly great weekend. The more detailed the description of setting, the more believable the events of the story become. Because the details of the woodworking shop are well delineated in Marjorie Pickthall's "The Worker in Sandalwood" (p. 297), for example, they lend authenticity to the miraculous event that occurs there. Even futuristic, unrealistic, symbolic, and fantastic stories, as well as ghost stories, take on authenticity if the details of setting are presented as though the world of these stories is the one we normally see and experience. Walter Van Tilburg Clark's "The Portable Phonograph," Franz Kafka's "The Hunger Artist," Nathaniel Hawthorne's "Young Goodman Brown," and Edgar Allan Poe's "The Masque of the Red Death" are such stories. Without a basis in detailed settings, these works would lose some of their credibility even though they make no pretenses at actual realism.

### Setting and Statement

Setting may be a kind of pictorial language, a means by which the author makes statements much as a painter uses certain images as ideas in a painting. Thus the dwelling place of Dr. Jenkins in Clark's "The Portable Phonograph" is compared to "the mouth of a mine tunnel." In this respect it is also somewhat like a cave. Because the scene of the story is the dark, bleak, cold world after a catastrophic war, the visual effect is that the war has sent human beings back to the caves in which they presumably lived during the Stone Age, before our modern civilization.

### Setting and Character

In the same vein, setting may intersect with character as one of the means by which character is to be underscored and therefore understood. To refer again to Dr. Jenkins of "The Portable Phonograph," we must realize that he has come to his present circumstances as a mature, sophisticated person. Amid the hostile surroundings, his strength, tenacity, and love of music emerge, so that he clings to the past joys of life as represented by his meager record collection. But he is also adaptable, and hence he arranges things in his cave so that he can continue to exist even though the conditions are so grim. Here the setting is clearly designed to help shape our ideas of his character. A similar blending of the setting and the major character of Guy De Maupassant's "The Necklace" (p. 75) is explored in the sample essay. In virtually every story that you encounter, a comparable relationship may be found and studied.

### Setting and Organization

Authors might also use setting as a means of organizing their works. It is often comic, for example, to move a character from one setting to another (provided that no harm is done in the process). Thus, Stephen

Crane provokes smiles in the first part of "The Bride Comes to Yellow Sky" (p. 92) by shifting a backwoods town marshal into the plush setting of a Pullman railroad car. Crane's descriptions of the awkwardness of the marshal and the patronizing airs of the other characters are humorous. Poe achieves a grimly opposite effect in "The Masque of the Red Death" by transposing the specter of death, usually the inhabitant of cemeteries and mausoleums, into a large group of nobles at a masquerade party or revel.

Another organizational use of setting may be thought of as a **framing** or **enclosing method.** An author frames a story by opening with a description of a setting, and then returns to the description at the end. Like a picture frame, the setting constantly affects the reader's thoughts about the story. An example of this method is Irwin Shaw's "Act of Faith," which is set in France immediately after the victory against Germany in World War II but which also refers to many other locations. The story begins with two soldiers slogging through the mud with the hope of getting enough money to go on a weekend pass to Paris. At the end the same two soldiers, together with a third, are walking in "damp, dead grass"—the same activity over similar ground. The intention to go to town has not changed, but the stakes have changed dramatically, from a simple intention of having a good time to a major commitment in regard to the entire future of a Jew living in postwar America. Shaw's setting of muddy and slippery ground over which soldiers walk, in short, frames a story of remarkably serious importance.

### Setting and Atmosphere

Setting also affects the **atmosphere** or **mood** of stories. You might note that the description of an action requires no more than a functional description of setting. Thus, an action in a forest needs just the statement that the forest is there. However, if you read descriptions of the trees, the shapes, the light and shadows, the animals, the wind, and the sounds, you may be sure that the author is working to create an atmosphere or mood for the action. There are many ways of creating moods. Descriptions of "warm" colors (red, orange, yellow) may contribute to a mood of happiness. "Cooler" colors may suggest gloom. References to smells and sounds bring the setting even more to life by asking additional sensory responses from the reader. The setting of a story on a farm or in a city apartment may evoke a response to these habitats that may contribute to a story's atmosphere.

### Setting and Irony

Just as setting is present as an element of concurrence, agreement, reinforcement, and strengthening of character and theme, so it may work as an element of irony. The setting, in other words, may create an environment that is the opposite of what actually occurs in the story. Thus the setting of Shirley Jackson's "The Lottery" (p. 179) builds up the background of a small town in which seemingly a prize of money or gifts rather than death is to be won. This normal, rural America atmosphere makes the conclusion grimly ironic, for it is just real folks who cast the stones of ritual execution. Poe uses a similar ironic twist in "The Masque of the Red Death," where Prince Prospero seals off his palace from the outside world of pestilence and infection, but at the same moment he actually seals in Death himself and thereby ensures the end of all the revelers. The irony is that closed doors may just as easily prevent exit as entry. Mark Twain creates the same sort of irony of setting in the story "Luck" (p. 230), where the Russian army reinforcements are befuddled by the witless charge of the forces headed by the main character. Here, unlike the case in the stories of Poe and Jackson, the irony is used in a mode of comedy rather than grimness.

## EDGAR ALLAN POE (1809–1849)

*The Masque of the Red Death*                                            *1842*

The "Red Death" had long devastated the country. No pestilence had ever been so fatal, or so hideous. Blood was its Avatar° and its seal—the redness and the horror of blood. There were sharp pains, and sudden dizziness, and then profuse bleeding at the pores, with dissolution. The scarlet stains upon the body and especially upon the face of the victim, were the pest ban which shut him out from the aid and from the sympathy of his fellow-men. And the whole seizure, progress, and termination of the disease, were the incidents of half an hour.

But the Prince Prospero° was happy and dauntless and sagacious. When his dominions were half depopulated, he summoned to his presence a thousand hale and light-hearted friends from among the knights and dames of his court, and with these retired to the deep seclusion of one of his castellated abbeys. This was an extensive and magnificent structure, the creation of the prince's own eccentric yet august taste. A strong and lofty wall girdled it in. This wall had gates of iron. The courtiers, having entered, brought furnaces and massy hammers and welded the bolts. They resolved to leave means neither of ingress nor egress to the sudden impulses of despair or of frenzy from within. The abbey was amply provisioned. With such precautions the courtiers might bid defiance to contagion. The external world could take care of itself. In the meantime it was folly to grieve, or to think. The prince had provided all the appliances of pleasure. There were buffoons, there were improvisatori, there were ballet-dancers, there were musicians, there was Beauty, there was wine. All these and security were within. Without was the "Red Death."

It was toward the close of the fifth or sixth month of his seclusion, and

*Avatar*: model, incarnation, manifestation.
*Prospero*: that is, "prosperous." See Shakespeare's *The Tempest*, where the principal character is Prospero.

while the pestilence raged most furiously abroad, that the Prince Prospero entertained his thousand friends at a masked ball of the most unusual magnificence.

It was a voluptuous scene, that masquerade. But first let me tell of the rooms
in which it was held. There were seven—an imperial suite. In many palaces, however,
such suites form a long and straight vista, while the folding doors slide back nearly
to the walls on either hand, so that the view of the whole extent is scarcely impeded.
Here the case was very different; as might have been expected from the duke's
love of the *bizarre*. The apartments were so irregularly disposed that the vision
embraced but little more than one at a time. There was a sharp turn at every
twenty or thirty yards, and at each turn a novel effect. To the right and left, in
the middle of each wall, a tall and narrow Gothic window looked out upon a closed
corridor which pursued the windings of the suite. These windows were of stained
glass whose color varied in accordance with the prevailing hue of the decorations
of the chamber into which it opened. That at the eastern extremity was hung,
for example, in blue—and vividly blue were its windows. The second chamber
was purple in its ornaments and tapestries, and here the panes were purple. The
third was green throughout, and so were the casements. The fourth was furnished
and lighted with orange—the fifth with white—the sixth with violet. The seventh
apartment was closely shrouded in black velvet tapestries that hung all over the
ceiling and down the walls, falling in heavy folds upon a carpet of the same material
and hue. But in this chamber only, the color of the windows failed to correspond
with the decorations. The panes here were scarlet—a deep blood color. Now in
no one of the seven apartments was there any lamp or candelabrum, amid the
profusion of golden ornaments that lay scattered to and fro or depended from
the roof. There was no light of any kind emanating from lamp or candle within
the suite of chambers. But in the corridors that followed the suite, there stood,
opposite to each window, a heavy tripod, bearing a brazier of fire, that projected
its rays through the tinted glass and so glaringly illumined the room. And thus
were produced a multitude of gaudy and fantastic appearances. But in the western
or black chamber the effect of the fire-light that streamed upon the dark hangings
through the blood-tinted panes was ghastly in the extreme, and produced so wild
a look upon the countenances of those who entered, that there were few of the
company bold enough to set foot within its precincts at all.

It was in this apartment, also, that there stood against the western wall, a     5
gigantic clock of ebony. Its pendulum swung to and fro with a dull, heavy, monotonous clang; and when the minute-hand made the circuit of the face, and the hour
was to be stricken, there came from the brazen lungs of the clock a sound which
was clear and loud and deep and exceedingly musical, but of so peculiar a note
and emphasis that, at each lapse of an hour, the musicians of the orchestra were
constrained to pause, momentarily, in their performance, to hearken to the sound;
and thus the waltzers perforce ceased their evolutions; and there was a brief disconcert of the whole gay company; and, while the chimes of the clock yet rang, it
was observed that the giddiest grew pale, and the more aged and sedate passed
their hands over their brows as if in confused revery or meditation. But when
the echoes had fully ceased, a light laughter at once pervaded the assembly; the
musicians looked at each other and smiled as if at their own nervousness and
folly, and made whispering vows, each to the other, that the next chiming of the
clock should produce in them no similar emotion; and then, after the lapse of

sixty minutes (which embrace three thousand and six hundred seconds of the Time that flies), there came yet another chiming of the clock, and then were the same disconcert and tremulousness and meditation as before.

But, in spite of these things, it was a gay and magnificent revel. The tastes of the duke were peculiar. He had a fine eye for colors and effects. He disregarded the *decora*° of mere fashion. His plans were bold and fiery, and his conceptions glowed with barbaric lustre. There are some who would have thought him mad. His followers felt that he was not. It was necessary to hear and see and touch him to be *sure* that he was not.

He had directed, in great part, the movable embellishments of the seven chambers, upon occasion of this great fête,° and it was his own guiding taste which had given character to the masqueraders. Be sure they were grotesque. There were much glare and glitter and piquancy and phantasm—much of what has been since seen in "Hernani."° There were arabesque figures with unsuited limbs and appointments. There were delirious fancies such as the madman fashions. There were much of the beautiful, much of the wanton, much of the *bizarre*, something of the terrible, and not a little of that which might have excited disgust. To and fro in the seven chambers there stalked, in fact, a multitude of dreams. And these— the dreams—writhed in and about, taking hue from the rooms, and causing the wild music of the orchestra to seem as the echo of their steps. And, anon, there strikes the ebony clock which stands in the hall of the velvet. And then, for a moment, all is still, and all is silent save the voice of the clock. The dreams are stiff-frozen as they stand. But the echoes of the chime die away—they have endured but an instant—and a light, half-subdued laughter floats after them as they depart. And now again the music swells, and the dreams live, and writhe to and fro more merrily than ever, taking hue from the many-tinted windows through which stream the rays from the tripods. But to the chamber which lies most westwardly of the seven there are now none of the maskers who venture; for the night is waning away; and there flows a ruddier light through the blood-colored panes; and the blackness of the sable drapery appalls; and to him whose foot falls upon the sable carpet, there comes from the near clock of ebony a muffled peal more solemnly emphatic than any which reaches *their* ears who indulge in the more remote gaieties of the other apartments.

But these other apartments were densely crowded, and in them beat feverishly the heart of life. And the revel went whirlingly on, until at length there commenced the sounding of midnight upon the clock. And then the music ceased, as I have told; and the evolutions of the waltzers were quieted; and there was an uneasy cessation of all things as before. But now there were twelve strokes to be sounded by the bell of the clock; and thus it happened, perhaps that more of thought crept, with more of time, into the meditations of the thoughtful among those who revelled. And thus too, it happened, perhaps, that before the last echoes of the last chime had utterly sunk into silence, there were many individuals in the crowd who had found leisure to become aware of the presence of a masked figure which had arrested the attention of no single individual before. And the rumor of this new

*decora*: schemes, patterns.
*fête*: party, revel.
*Hernani*: a tragedy by Victor Hugo (1802–1885), a play with elaborate scenes and costumes.

presence having spread itself whisperingly around, there arose at length from the whole company a buzz, or murmur, expressive of disapprobation and surprise— then, finally, of terror, of horror, and of disgust.

In an assembly of phantasms such as I have painted, it may well be supposed that no ordinary appearance could have excited such sensation. In truth the masquerade license of the night was nearly unlimited; but the figure in question had out-Heroded Herod,° and gone beyond the bounds of even the prince's indefinite decorum. There are chords in the hearts of the most reckless which cannot be touched without emotion. Even with the utterly lost, to whom life and death are equally jests, there are matters of which no jest can be made. The whole company, indeed, seemed now deeply to feel that in the costume and bearing of the stranger neither wit nor propriety existed. The figure was tall and gaunt, and shrouded from head to foot in the habiliments of the grave. The mask which concealed the visage was made so nearly to resemble the countenance of a stiffened corpse that the closest scrutiny must have had difficulty in detecting the cheat. And yet all this might have been endured, if not approved, by the mad revellers around. But the mummer had gone so far as to assume the type of the Red Death. His vesture was dabbled in *blood*—and his broad brow, with all the features of the face, was besprinkled with the scarlet horror.

When the eyes of Prince Prospero fell upon this spectral image (which, with a slow and solemn movement, as if more fully to sustain its *rôle*, stalked to and fro among the waltzers) he was seen to be convulsed, in the first moment with a strong shudder either of terror or distaste; but, in the next, his brow reddened with rage.

"Who dares"—he demanded hoarsely of the courtiers who stood near him— "who dares insult us with this blasphemous mockery? Seize him and unmask him— that we may know whom we have to hang, at sunrise, from the battlements!"

It was in the eastern or blue chamber in which stood the Prince Prospero as he uttered these words. They rang throughout the seven rooms loudly and clearly, for the prince was a bold and robust man, and the music had become hushed at the waving of his hand.

It was in the blue room where stood the prince, with a group of pale courtiers by his side. At first, as he spoke, there was a slight rushing movement of this group in the direction of the intruder, who, at the moment was also near at hand, and now, with deliberate and stately step, made closer approach to the speaker. But from a certain nameless awe with which the mad assumptions of the mummer had inspired the whole party, there were found none who put forth hand to seize him; so that, unimpeded, he passed within a yard of the prince's person; and, while the vast assembly, as if with one impulse, shrank from the centres of the rooms to the walls, he made his way uninterruptedly, but with the same solemn and measured step which had distinguished him from the first, through the blue chamber to the purple—through the purple to the green—through the green to the orange—through this again to the white—and even thence to the violet, ere a decided movement had been made to arrest him. It was then, however, that the Prince Prospero, maddening with rage and the shame of his own momentary

10

*out-Heroded Herod*: quoted from Shakespeare's *Hamlet*, act 3, scene 2, in reference to extreme overacting.

cowardice, rushed hurriedly through the six chambers, while none followed him on account of a deadly terror that had seized upon all. He bore aloft a drawn dagger, and had approached, in rapid impetuosity, to within three or four feet of the retreating figure, when the latter, having attained the extremity of the velvet apartment, turned suddenly and confronted his pursuer. There was a sharp cry— and the dagger dropped gleaming upon the sable carpet, upon which, instantly afterward, fell prostrate in death the Prince Prospero. Then, summoning the wild courage of despair, a throng of the revellers at once threw themselves into the black apartment, and, seizing the mummer, whose tall figure stood erect and motionless within the shadow of the ebony clock, gasped in unutterable horror at finding the grave cerements and corpse-like mask, which they handled with so violent a rudeness, untenanted by any tangible form.

And now was acknowledged the presence of the Red Death. He had come like a thief in the night.° And one by one dropped the revellers in the blood-bedewed halls of their revel, and died each in the despairing posture of his fall. And the life of the ebony clock went out with that of the last of the gay. And the flames of the tripods expired. And Darkness and Decay and the Red Death held illimitable dominion over all.

## QUESTIONS

1. What is happening throughout the country in Poe's "Masque of the Red Death"? How does Prince Prospero react to these events? What does the Prince's reaction tell us about him?

2. How is the building in which Prince Prospero and his thousand nobles take shelter described? To what extent does the description of this "abbey" help us form an opinion of Prince Prospero?

3. How many rooms are used in the masquerade ball or revel in the story? In what ways might this number be significant? What is the dominant color of each room? How are the rooms lighted? How do these details help create the atmosphere and mood of the story?

4. What color is the last room? What color is its window? Why does this room make the revellers nervous? To what extent does this last room reflect the plot and ideas of the story?

5. What single object is located in this last room? How is this object described? What effect does it have on the revellers when it sounds? How might you explain this effect? What do you think Poe is suggesting symbolically with this object and its effects?

6. How are the nobles dressed for the masquerade? Why does the "masked figure" introduced near the end of the story stand out as remarkable? How does Prospero react to this masked figure? Can you explain Prospero's reaction? What does this figure represent?

7. What is the central conflict in this story? Who is the protagonist? The antagonist? Where is the climax of the story? How is the central conflict resolved at the climax?

*thief in the night*: 2 Peter 3:10.

8. What point of view is employed in the story? Explain why Poe uses this point of view.

## WALTER VAN TILBURG CLARK (1909–1971)

*The Portable Phonograph*                                              *1942*

The red sunset, with narrow, black cloud strips like threats across it, lay on the curved horizon of the prairie. The air was still and cold, and in it settled the mute darkness and greater cold of night. High in the air there was wind, for through the veil of the dusk the clouds could be seen gliding rapidly south and changing shapes. A sensation of torment, of two-sided, unpredictable nature, arose from the stillness of the earth air beneath the violence of the upper air. Out of the sunset, through the dead, matted grass and isolated weed stalks of the prairie, crept the narrow and deeply rutted remains of a road. In the road, in places, there were crusts of shallow, brittle ice. There were little islands of an old oiled pavement in the road too, but most of it was mud, now frozen rigid. The frozen mud still bore the toothed impress of great tanks, and a wanderer on the neighboring undulations might have stumbled, in this light, into large, partially filled-in and weed-grown cavities, their banks channeled and beginning to spread into badlands. These pits were such as might have been made by falling meteors, but they were not. They were the scars of gigantic bombs, their rawness already made a little natural by rain, seed and time. Along the road there were rakish remnants of fence. There was also, just visible, one portion of tangled and multiple barbed wire still erect, behind which was a shelving ditch with small caves, now very quiet and empty, at intervals in its back wall. Otherwise there was no structure or remnant of a structure visible over the dome of the darkling earth, but only, in sheltered hollows, the darker shadows of young trees trying again.

Under the wuthering arch of the high wind a V of wild geese fled south. The rush of their pinions sounded briefly, and the faint, plaintive notes of their expeditionary talk. Then they left a still greater vacancy. There was the smell and expectation of snow, as there is likely to be when the wild geese fly south. From the remote distance, toward the red sky, came faintly the protracted howl and quick yap-yap of a prairie wolf.

North of the road, perhaps a hundred yards, lay the parallel and deeply intrenched course of a small creek, lined with leafless alders and willows. The creek was already silent under ice. Into the bank above it was dug a sort of cell, with a single opening, like the mouth of a mine tunnel. Within the cell there was a little red of fire, which showed dully through the opening, like a reflection or a deception of the imagination. The light came from the chary burning of four blocks of poorly aged peat, which gave off a petty warmth and much acrid smoke. But the precious remnants of wood, old fence posts and timbers from the long-deserted dugouts, had to be saved for the real cold, for the time when a man's breath blew white, the moisture in his nostrils stiffened at once when he stepped out, and the expansive blizzards paraded for days over the vast open, swirling and settling and thickening, till the dawn of the cleared day when the sky was a thin blue-green and the terrible cold, in which a man could not live for three hours unwarmed, lay over the uniformly drifted swell of the plain.

Around the smoldering peat four men were seated cross-legged. Behind them, traversed by their shadows, was the earth bench, with two old and dirty army blankets, where the owner of the cell slept. In a niche in the opposite wall were a few tin utensils which caught the glint of the coals. The host was rewrapping in a piece of daubed burlap, four fine, leather-bound books. He worked slowly and very carefully, and at last tied the bundle securely with a piece of grass-woven cord. The other three looked intently upon the process, as if a great significance lay in it. As the host tied the cord, he spoke. He was an old man, his long, matted beard and hair gray to nearly white. The shadows made his brows and cheekbones appear gnarled, his eyes and cheeks deeply sunken. His big hands, rough with frost and swollen by rheumatism, were awkward but gentle at their task. He was like a prehistoric priest performing a fateful ceremonial rite. Also his voice had in it a suitable quality of deep, reverent despair, yet perhaps, at the moment, a sharpness of selfish satisfaction.

"When I perceived what was happening," he said, "I told myself, 'It is the 5 end. I cannot take much; I will take these.'

"Perhaps I was impractical," he continued. "But for myself, I do not regret, and what do we know of those who will come after us? We are the doddering remnant of a race of mechanical fools. I have saved what I love; the soul of what was good in us here; perhaps the new ones will make a strong enough beginning not to fall behind when they become clever."

He rose with slow pain and placed the wrapped volumes in the niche with his utensils. The others watched him with the same ritualistic gaze.

"Shakespeare, the Bible, *Moby Dick*,° *The Divine Comedy*,"° one of them said softly. "You might have done worse; much worse."

"You will have a little soul left until you die," said another harshly. "That is more than is true of us. My brain becomes thick, like my hands." He held the big, battered hands, with their black nails, in the glow to be seen.

"I want paper to write on," he said. "And there is none." 10

The fourth man said nothing. He sat in the shadow farthest from the fire, and sometimes his body jerked in its rags from the cold. Although he was still young, he was sick, and coughed often. Writing implied a greater future than he now felt able to consider.

The old man seated himself laboriously, and reached out, groaning at the movement, to put another block of peat on the fire. With bowed heads and averted eyes, his three guests acknowledged his magnanimity.

"We thank you, Doctor Jenkins, for the reading," said the man who had named the books.

They seemed then to be waiting for something. Doctor Jenkins understood, but was loath to comply. In an ordinary moment he would have said nothing. But the words of *The Tempest*,° which he had been reading, and the religious attention of the three, made this an unusual occasion.

---

*Moby Dick*: By Herman Melville (1819–1891), a classic American novel published in 1851.

*The Divine Comedy*: By Dante (1265–1321), regarded as the supreme poem of the Italian Renaissance, circulated about 1300.

*The Tempest*: Shakespeare's last play, first performed about 1611–1612.

"You wish to hear the phonograph,"° he said grudgingly.                    15

The two middle-aged men stared into the fire, unable to formulate and expose the enormity of their desire.

The young man, however, said anxiously, between suppressed coughs, "Oh, please," like an excited child.

The old man rose again in his difficult way, and went to the back of the cell. He returned and placed tenderly upon the packed floor, where the firelight might fall upon it, an old, portable phonograph in a black case. He smoothed the top with his hand, then opened it. The lovely green-felt-covered disk became visible.

"I have been using thorns as needles," he said. "But tonight, because we have a musician among us"—he bent his head to the young man, almost invisible in the shadow—"I will use a steel needle. There are only three left."

The two middle-aged men stared at him in speechless adoration. The one         20
with the big hands, who wanted to write, moved his lips, but the whisper was not audible.

"Oh, don't," cried the young man, as if he were hurt. "The thorns will do beautifully."

"No," the old man said. "I have become accustomed to the thorns—but they are not really good. For you, my young friend, we will have good music tonight.

"After all," he added generously, and beginning to wind the phonograph, which creaked, "they can't last forever."

"No, nor we," the man who needed to write said harshly. "The needle, by all means."

"Oh, thanks," said the young man. "Thanks," he said again, in a low, excited         25
voice, and then stifled his coughing with a bowed head.

"The records, though," said the old man when he had finished winding, "are a different matter. Already they are very worn. I do not play them more than once a week. One, once a week, that is what I allow myself.

"More than a week I cannot stand it; not to hear them," he apologized.

"No, how could you?" cried the young man. "And with them here like this."

"A man can stand anything," said the man who wanted to write, in his harsh, antagonistic voice.

"Please, the music," said the young man.                    30

"Only the one," said the old man. "In the long run we will remember more that way."

He had a dozen records with luxuriant gold and red seals. Even in that light the others could see that the threads of the records were becoming worn. Slowly he read out the titles, and the tremendous, dead names of the composers and the artists and the orchestras. The three worked upon the names in their minds, carefully. It was difficult to select from such a wealth what they would at

---

*phonograph*: a wind-up type in use before electrically driven record players. It played records at a speed of 78 revolutions per minute, and steel needles had to be changed after each side was played. The phonograph is especially valuable to the characters in the story because they have no electricity.

once most like to remember. Finally the man who wanted to write named Gershwin's "New York."°

"Oh, no," cried the sick young man, and then could say nothing more because he had to cough. The others understood him, and the harsh man withdrew his selection and waited for the musician to choose.

The musician begged Doctor Jenkins to read the titles again, very slowly, so that he could remember the sounds. While they were read, he lay back against the wall, his eyes closed, his thin, horny hand pulling at his light beard, and listened to the voices and the orchestras and the single instruments in his mind.

When the reading was done he spoke despairingly. "I have forgotten," he complained. "I cannot hear them clearly.                    35

"There are things missing," he explained.

"I know," said Doctor Jenkins. "I thought that I knew all of Shelley° by heart. I should have brought Shelley."

"That's more soul than we can use," said the harsh man. "*Moby Dick* is better.

"By God, we can understand that," he emphasized.

The doctor nodded.                    40

"Still," said the man who had admired the books, "we need the absolute if we are to keep a grasp on anything.

"Anything but these sticks and peat clods and rabbit snares," he said bitterly.

"Shelley desired an ultimate absolute," said the harsh man. "It's too much," he said. "It's no good; no earthly good."

The musician selected a Debussy° nocturne. The others considered and approved. They rose to their knees to watch the doctor prepare for the playing, so that they appeared to be actually in an attitude of worship. The peat glow showed the thinness of their bearded faces, and the deep lines in them, and revealed the condition of their garments. The other two continued to kneel as the old man carefully lowered the needle onto the spinning disk, but the musician suddenly drew back against the wall again, with his knees up, and buried his face in his hands.

At the first notes of the piano the listeners were startled. They stared at     45
each other. Even the musician lifted his head in amazement, but then quickly bowed it again, strainingly, as if he were suffering from a pain he might not be able to endure. They were all listening deeply, without movement. The wet, blue-green notes tinkled forth from the old machine, and were individual, delectable presences in the cell. The individual, delectable presences swept into a sudden tide of unbearably beautiful dissonance, and then continued fully the swelling and ebbing of that tide, the dissonant inpourings, and the resolutions, and the diminishments, and the little, quiet wavelets of interlude lapping between. Every sound was piercing and singularly sweet. In all the men except the musician, there occurred rapid

*George Gershwin* (1898–1937): an American composer who wrote in the idiom of jazz, not in the classical manner.

*Percy Bysshe Shelley* (1792–1822): English poet who wrote poems about the soul, intellectual beauty, and mutability.

*Claude Debussy* (1862–1918): French composer. A "nocturne" is a "night piece" of music.

sequences of tragically heightened recollection. He heard nothing but what was there. At the final, whispering disappearance, but moving quietly, so that the others would not hear him and look at him, he let his head fall back in agony, as if it were drawn there by the hair, and clenched the fingers of one hand over his teeth. He sat that way while the others were silent, and until they began to breathe again normally. His drawn-up legs were trembling violently.

Quickly Doctor Jenkins lifted the needle off, to save it, and not to spoil the recollection with scraping. When he had stopped the whirling of the sacred disk, he courteously left the phonograph open and by the fire, in sight.

The others, however, understood. The musician rose last, but then abruptly, and went quickly out at the door without saying anything. The others stopped at the door and gave their thanks in low voices. The doctor nodded magnificently.

"Come again," he invited, "in a week. We will have the 'New York.' "

When the two had gone together, out toward the rimmed road, he stood in the entrance, peering and listening. At first there was only the resonant boom of the wind overhead, and then, far over the dome of the dead, dark plain, the wolf cry lamenting. In the rifts of clouds the doctor saw four stars flying. It impressed the doctor that one of them had just been obscured by the beginning of a flying cloud at the very moment he heard what he had been listening for, a sound of suppressed coughing. It was not near by, however. He believed that down against the pale alders he could see the moving shadow.

With nervous hands he lowered the piece of canvas which served as his door, and pegged it at the bottom. Then quickly and quietly, looking at the piece of canvas frequently, he slipped the records into the case, snapped the lid shut, and carried the phonograph to his couch. There, pausing often to stare at the canvas and listen, he dug earth from the wall and disclosed a piece of board. Behind this there was a deep hole in the wall, into which he put the phonograph. After a moment's consideration, he went over and reached down his bundle of books and inserted it also. Then, guardedly, he once more sealed up the hole with the board and the earth. He also changed his blankets, and the grass-stuffed sack which served as a pillow, so that he could lie facing the entrance. After carefully placing two more blocks of peat on the fire, he stood for a long time watching the stretched canvas, but it seemed to billow naturally with the first gusts of a lowering wind. At last he prayed, and got in under his blankets, and closed his smoke-smarting eyes. On the inside of the bed, next the wall, he could feel with his hand, the comfortable piece of lead pipe.

50

## QUESTIONS

1.  Clark devotes the first three paragraphs of this story completely to description, thus establishing the general setting. What kind of environment is described? How would you characterize the scene? What has obviously happened before the story opens? To what extent do these paragraphs establish the tone and atmosphere of the entire story?

2.  The first three descriptive paragraphs are loaded with adjectives. In the first, for example, we find *narrow*, *black*, *still*, *cold*, *mute*, *dead*, *isolated*, *shallow*, *brittle*,

old, frozen, tangled, quiet, and empty. What do most of these adjectives have in common? How do they contribute to the establishment of setting and, in turn, mood?

3.  How is "the host's" home described? What adjectives and comparisons are employed? What objects and utensils are described? What do these specific details tell us about humanity and existence in the world of the story?

4.  Who is "the host"? What was his profession? What things does he seem to value most highly? What do his valued possessions tell us about him?

5.  What record do the men choose to hear? How do the listeners react to it? What do the phonograph and the music represent to these men?

6.  What does Dr. Jenkins do with the books, the phonograph, and records after the men leave? How does he readjust his bed? Why does he do these things? What do these actions imply?

7.  Who is the protagonist in this story? Who or what is the antagonist? What are the conflicts here? Which is the central conflict? To what extent is it resolved in the story?


## IRWIN SHAW (1913–1984)

### Act of Faith                                                                    1946

"Present it in a pitiful light," Olson was saying, as they picked their way through the mud toward the orderly room° tent. "Three combat-scarred veterans, who fought their way from Omaha Beach to—what was the name of the town we fought our way to?"

"Konigstein," Seeger said.

"Konigstein." Olson lifted his right foot heavily out of a puddle and stared admiringly at the three pounds of mud clinging to his overshoe. "The backbone of the army. The noncommissioned officer. We deserve better of our country. Mention our decorations in passing."

"What decorations should I mention?" Seeger asked. "The marksman's medal?"

"Never quite made it," Olson said. "I had a cross-eyed scorer at the butts.°     5 Mention the Bronze Star, the Silver Star, the Croix de Guerre, with palms, the unit citation, the Congressional Medal of Honor."

"I'll mention them all." Seeger grinned. "You don't think the CO° 'll notice that we haven't won most of them, do you?"

"Gad, sir," Olson said with dignity, "do you think that one southern military gentleman will dare doubt the word of another southern military gentleman in the hour of victory?"

"I come from Ohio," Seeger said.

"Welch comes from Kansas," Olson said, coolly staring down a second lieutenant who was passing. The lieutenant made a nervous little jerk with his hand

---

orderly room: administrative headquarters of an army unit.
butts: mound of dirt used as a backstop on a target range.
CO: abbreviation for "Commanding Officer."

as though he expected a salute, then kept it rigid, as a slight superior smile of scorn twisted at the corner of Olson's mouth. The lieutenant dropped his eyes and splashed on through the mud. "You've heard of Kansas," Olson said. "Magnolia-scented Kansas."

"Of course," said Seeger. "I'm no fool." 10

"Do your duty by your men, Sergeant." Olson stopped to wipe the rain off his face and lectured him. "Highest ranking noncom° present took the initiative and saved his comrades, at great personal risk, above and beyond the call of you-know-what, in the best traditions of the American army."

"I will throw myself in the breach,"° Seeger said.

"Welch and I can't ask more," said Olson, approvingly.

They walked heavily through the mud on the streets between the rows of tents. The camp stretched drearily over the Rheims plain, with the rain beating on the sagging tents. The division had been there over three weeks by now, waiting to be shipped home, and all the meager diversions of the neighborhood had been sampled and exhausted, and there was an air of watchful suspicion and impatience with the military life hanging over the camp now, and there was even reputed to be a staff sergeant in C Company who was laying odds they would not get back to America before July Fourth.

"I'm redeployable," Olson sang. "It's so enjoyable . . ." It was a jingle he 15 had composed to no recognizable melody in the early days after the victory in Europe, when he had added up his points and found they only came to 63. "Tokyo, wait for me . . ."

They were going to be discharged as soon as they got back to the States, but Olson persisted in singing the song, occasionally adding a mournful stanza about dengue fever° and brown girls with venereal disease. He was a short, round boy who had been flunked out of air cadets' school and transferred to the infantry, but whose spirits had not been damaged in the process. He had a high, childish voice and a pretty baby face. He was very good-natured, and had a girl waiting for him at the University of California, where he intended to finish his course at government expense when he got out of the army, and he was just the type who is killed off early and predictably and sadly in motion pictures about the war, but he had gone through four campaigns and six major battles without a scratch.

Seeger was a large lanky boy, with a big nose, who had been wounded at Saint Lô, but had come back to his outfit in the Siegfried Line,° quite unchanged. He was cheerful and dependable, and he knew his business and had broken in five or six second lieutenants who had been killed or wounded and the CO had tried to get him commissioned in the field, but the war had ended while the paper-work was being fumbled over at headquarters.

They reached the door of the orderly tent and stopped. "Be brave, Sergeant," Olson said. "Welch and I are depending on you."

"O.K." Seeger said, and went in.

The tent had the dank, army-canvas smell that had been so much a part of 20 Seeger's life in the past three years. The company clerk was reading a July, 1945,

---

*noncom*: a noncommissioned officer (corporal and above), distinguished from a commissioned officer (second lieutenant and above).
*breach*: Shakespeare, *Henry V*, 3.1.1
*dengue fever*: a tropical disease caused by mosquitoes.
*Siegfried Line*: a German line of fortifications against France.

issue of the *Buffalo Courier-Express*, which had just reached him, and Captain Taney, the company CO, was seated at a sawbuck table he used as a desk, writing a letter to his wife, his lips pursed with effort. He was a small, fussy man, with sandy hair that was falling out. While the fighting had been going on, he had been lean and tense and his small voice had been cold and full of authority. But now he had relaxed, and a little pot belly was creeping up under his belt and he kept the top button of his trousers open when he could do it without too public loss of dignity. During the war Seeger had thought of him as a natural soldier, tireless, fanatic about detail, aggressive, severely anxious to kill Germans. But in the past few months Seeger had seen him relapsing gradually and pleasantly into a small-town wholesale hardware merchant, which he had been before the war, sedentary and a little shy, and, as he had once told Seeger, worried, here in the bleak champagne fields of France, about his daughter, who had just turned twelve and had a tendency to go after the boys and had been caught by her mother kissing a fifteen-year-old neighbor in the hammock after school.

"Hello, Seeger," he said, returning the salute in a mild, offhand gesture. "What's on your mind?"

"Am I disturbing you, sir?"

"Oh, no. Just writing a letter to my wife. You married, Seeger?" He peered at the tall boy standing before him.

"No, sir."

"It's very difficult," Taney sighed, pushing dissatisfiedly at the letter before    25
him. "My wife complains I don't tell her I love her often enough. Been married fifteen years. You'd think she'd know by now." He smiled at Seeger. "I thought you were going to Paris," he said. "I signed the passes yesterday."

"That's what I came to see you about, sir."

"I suppose something's wrong with the passes." Taney spoke resignedly, like a man who has never quite got the hang of army regulations and has had requisitions, furloughs, requests for court-martial returned for correction in a baffling flood.

"No, sir," Seeger said. "The passes're fine. They start tomorrow. Well, it's just . . ." He looked around at the company clerk, who was on the sports page.

"This confidential?" Taney asked.

"If you don't mind, sir."    30

"Johnny," Taney said to the clerk, "go stand in the rain some place."

"Yes, sir," the clerk said, and slowly got up and walked out.

Taney looked shrewdly at Seeger, spoke in a secret whisper. "You pick up anything?" he asked.

Seeger grinned. "No, sir, haven't had my hands on a girl since Strasbourg."

"Ah, that's good." Taney leaned back, relieved, happy he didn't have to    35
cope with the disapproval of the Medical Corps.

"It's—well," said Seeger, embarrassed, "it's hard to say—but it's money."

Taney shook his head sadly. "I know."

"We haven't been paid for three months, sir, and . . ."

"Damn it!" Taney stood up and shouted furiously. "I would like to take every bloody chair-warming old lady in the Finance Department and wring their necks."

The clerk stuck his head into the tent. "Anything wrong? You call for me,    40
sir?"

"No," Taney shouted. "Get out of here."

The clerk ducked out.

Taney sat down again. "I suppose," he said, in a more normal voice, "they have their problems. Outfits being broken up, being moved all over the place. But it is rugged."

"It wouldn't be so bad," Seeger said. "But we're going to Paris tomorrow, Olson, Welch and myself. And you need money in Paris."

"Don't I know it." Taney wagged his head. "Do you know what I paid for a bottle of champagne on the Place Pigalle° in September . . . ?" He paused significantly. "I won't tell you. You won't have any respect for me the rest of your life."

Seeger laughed. "Hanging," he said, "is too good for the guy who thought up the rate of exchange."

"I don't care if I never see another franc as long as I live." Taney waved his letter in the air, although it had been dry for a long time.

There was silence in the tent and Seeger swallowed a little embarrassedly, watching the CO wave the flimsy sheet of paper in regular sweeping movements. "Sir," he said, "the truth is, I've come to borrow some money for Welch, Olson and myself. We'll pay it back out of the first pay we get, and that can't be too long from now. If you don't want to give it to us, just tell me and I'll understand and get the hell out of here. We don't like to ask, but you might just as well be dead as be in Paris broke."

Taney stopped waving his letter and put it down thoughtfully. He peered at it, wrinkling his brow, looking like an aged bookkeeper in the single gloomy light that hung in the middle of the tent.

"Just say the word, Captain," Seeger said, "and I'll blow . . ."

"Stay where you are, son," said Taney. He dug in his shirt pocket and took out a worn, sweat-stained wallet. He looked at it for a moment. "Alligator," he said, with automatic, absent pride. "My wife sent it to me when we were in England. Pounds don't fit in it. However . . ." He opened it and took out all the contents. There was a small pile of francs on the table in front of him. He counted them. "Four hundred francs," he said. "Eight bucks."

"Excuse me," Seeger said humbly. "I shouldn't have asked."

"Delighted," Taney said vigorously. "Absolutely delighted." He started dividing the francs into two piles. "Truth is, Seeger, most of my money goes home in allotments. And the truth is, I lost eleven hundred francs in a poker game three nights ago, and I ought to be ashamed of myself. Here . . ." he shoved one pile toward Seeger. "Two hundred francs."

Seeger looked down at the frayed, meretricious paper, which always seemed to him like stage money, anyway. "No, sir," he said, "I can't take it."

"Take it," Taney said. "That's a direct order."

Seeger slowly picked up the money, not looking at Taney. "Some time, sir," he said, "after we get out, you have to come over to my house and you and my father and my brother and I'll go on a real drunk."

"I'll regard that," Taney said, gravely, "as a solemn commitment."

*Place Pigalle*: A notorious spot in Paris, near Montmartre, mispronounced as "pig alley" by American soldiers. Whiskey and prostitutes were plentiful there.

*dry*: Taney is using a fountain pen with liquid ink. Ball-point pens were things of the future in 1945.

They smiled at each other and Seeger started out.

"Have a drink for me," said Taney, "at the Café de la Paix. A small drink."
He was sitting down to write his wife he loved her when Seeger went out of the
tent.

Olson fell into step with Seeger and they walked silently through the mud        60
between the tents.

"Well, *mon vieux*?"° Olson said finally.

"Two hundred francs," said Seeger.

Olson groaned. "Two hundred francs! We won't be able to pinch a whore's
behind on the Boulevard des Capucines° for two hundred francs. That miserable,
penny-loving Yankee!"

"He only had four hundred," Seeger said.

"I revise my opinion," said Olson.                                               65

They walked disconsolately and heavily back toward their tent.

Olson spoke only once before they got there. "These raincoats," he said,
patting his. "Most ingenious invention of the war. Highest saturation point of
any modern fabric. Collect more water per square inch, and hold it, than any
material known to man. All hail the quartermaster!"

Welch was waiting at the entrance of their tent. He was standing there peering
excitedly and short-sightedly out at the rain through his glasses, looking angry
and tough, like a big-city hack driver, individual and incorruptible even in the
ten-million colored uniform. Every time Seeger came upon Welch unexpectedly,
he couldn't help smiling at the belligerent stance, the harsh stare through the
steel-rimmed GI glasses, which had nothing at all to do with the way Welch really
was. "It's a family inheritance," Welch had once explained. "My whole family stands
as though we were getting ready to rap a drunk with a beer glass. Even my old
lady." Welch had six brothers, all devout, according to Welch, and Seeger from
time to time idly pictured them standing in a row, on Sunday mornings in church,
seemingly on the verge of general violence, amid the hushed Latin and Sabbath
millinery.

"How much?" Welch asked loudly.

"Don't make us laugh," Olson said, pushing past him into the tent.              70

"What do you think I could get from the French for my combat jacket?"
Seeger said. He went into the tent and lay down on his cot.

Welch followed them in and stood between the two of them, a superior
smile on his face. "Boys," he said, "on a man's errand."

"I can just see us now," Olson murmured, lying on his cot with his hands
clasped behind his head, "painting Montmartre red. Please bring on the naked
dancing girls. Four bucks worth."

"I am not worried," Welch announced.

"Get out of here.' Olson turned over on his stomach.                           75

"I know where we can put our hands on sixty-five bucks." Welch looked
triumphantly first at Olson, then at Seeger.

*Café de la Paix*: one of the best-known Parisian restaurants, on the Boulevard des Capu-
cines, which Olson mentions a few moments later.
    *mon vieux*: French for "my old"; i.e., "old boy," "old friend," "old fellow."
    *Boulevard des Capucines*: a street near the business district, extending from the Madeleine
to the Opéra.

Olson turned over slowly and sat up. "I'll kill you," he said, "if you're kidding."

"While you guys are wasting your time," Welch said, "fooling around with the infantry, I used my head. I went into Reems° and used my head."

"Rance," Olson said automatically. He had had two years of French in college and he felt, now that the war was over, that he had to introduce his friends to some of his culture.

"I got to talking to a captain in the air force," Welch said eagerly. "A little     80
fat old paddle-footed captain that never got higher off the ground than the second
floor of the Com Z headquarters, and he told me that what he would admire to
do more than anything else is to take home a nice shiny German Luger pistol
with him to show to the boys back in Pacific Grove, California."

Silence fell on the tent and Welch and Olson looked tentatively at Seeger.

"Sixty-five bucks for a Luger, these days," Olson said, "is a very good figure."

"They've been sellin' for as low as thirty-five," said Welch hesitantly. "I'll
bet," he said to Seeger, "you could sell yours now and buy another one back
when you get some dough and make a clear twenty-five on the deal."

Seeger didn't say anything. He had killed the owner of the Luger, an enormous
SS° major, in Coblenz, behind some paper bales in a warehouse, and the major
had fired at Seeger three times with it, once knicking his helmet, before Seeger
hit him in the face at twenty feet. Seeger had kept the Luger, a long, heavy, well-
balanced gun, very carefully since then, lugging it with him, hiding it at the bottom
of his bedroll, oiling it three times a week, avoiding all opportunities of selling
it, although he had been offered as much as a hundred dollars for it and several
times eighty and ninety, while the war was still on, before German weapons became
a glut on the market.

"Well," said Welch, "there's no hurry. I told the captain I'd see him tonight     85
around 8 o'clock in front of the Lion d'Or Hotel. You got five hours to make up
your mind. Plenty of time."

"Me," said Olson. after a pause. "I won't say anything."

Seeger looked reflectively at his feet and the other two men avoided looking
at him. Welch dug in his pocket. "I forgot," he said. "I picked up a letter for
you." He handed it to Seeger.

"Thanks," Seeger said. He opened it absently, thinking about the Luger.

"Me," said Olson, "I won't say a bloody word. I'm just going to lie here
and think about that nice fat air force captain."

Seeger grinned a little at him and went to the tent opening to read the     90
letter in the light. The letter was from his father, and even from one glance at
the handwriting, scrawly and hurried and spotted, so different from his father's
usual steady, handsome, professorial script, he knew that something was wrong.

"Dear Norman," it read, "sometime in the future, you must forgive me for
writing this letter. But I have been holding this in so long, and there is no one
here I can talk to, and because of your brother's condition I must pretend to be
cheerful and optimistic all the time at home, both with him and your mother,

---

*Reems*: Welch mispronounces *Reims*; Olson corrects him.
*SS*: The Schutzstaffel, a German military unit led by Heinrich Himmler, dreaded for
its ruthlessness and atrocities.

who has never been the same since Leonard was killed. You're the oldest now, and although I know we've never talked very seriously about anything before, you have been through a great deal by now, and I imagine you must have matured considerably, and you've seen so many different places and people. . . . Norman, I need help. While the war was on and you were fighting, I kept this to myself. It wouldn't have been fair to burden you with this. But now the war is over, and I no longer feel I can stand up under this alone. And you will have to face it some time when you get home, if you haven't faced it already, and perhaps we can help each other by facing it together. . . ."

"I'm redeployable," Olson was singing softly, on his cot. "It's so enjoyable, In the Pelilu° mud, With the tropical crud . . ." He fell silent after his burst of song.

Seeger blinked his eyes, at the entrance of the tent, in the wan rainy light, and went on reading his father's letter, on the stiff white stationery with the University letterhead in polite engraving at the top of each page.

"I've been feeling this coming on for a long time," the letter continued, "but it wasn't until last Sunday morning that something happened to make me feel it in its full force. I don't know how much you've guessed about the reason for Jacob's discharge from the army. It's true he was pretty badly wounded in the leg at Metz, but I've asked around, and I know that men with worse wounds were returned to duty after hospitalization. Jacob got a medical discharge, but I don't think it was for the shrapnel wound in his thigh. He is suffering now from what I suppose you call combat fatigue, and he is subject to fits of depression and hallucinations. Your mother and I thought that as time went by and the war and the army receded, he would grow better. Instead, he is growing worse. Last Sunday morning when I came down into the living room from upstairs he was crouched in his old uniform, next to the window, peering out . . ."

"What the hell," Olson was saying, "if we don't get the sixty-five bucks we    95 can always go to the Louvre. I understand the Mona Lisa is back."

"I asked Jacob what he was doing," the letter went on. "He didn't turn around. 'I'm observing,' he said. 'V-1's and V-2's.° Buzz-bombs and rockets. They're coming in by the hundreds.' I tried to reason with him and he told me to crouch and save myself from flying glass. To humor him I got down on the floor beside him and tried to tell him the war was over, that we were in Ohio, 4,000 miles away from the nearest spot where bombs had fallen, that America had never been touched. He wouldn't listen. 'These're the new rocket bombs,' he said, 'for the Jews.' "

"Did you ever hear of the Pantheon?" Olson asked loudly.

"No," said Welch.

"It's free."

"I'll go," said Welch.    100

Seeger shook his head a little and blinked his eyes before he went back to the letter.

"After that," his father went on, "Jacob seemed to forget about the bombs from time to time, but he kept saying that the mobs were coming up the street

*Pelilu:* Peleliu Island, in the Palau chain, part of the Caroline Islands, in the South Pacific.

*V-1s and V-2's:* The first rocket weapons, developed by the Germans near the end of World War II, and used against England.

armed with bazookas and Browning automatic rifles. He mumbled incoherently a good deal of the time and kept walking back and forth saying, 'What's the situation? Do you know what the situation is?' And he told me he wasn't worried about himself, he was a soldier and he expected to be killed, but he was worried about Mother and myself and Leonard and you. He seemed to forget that Leonard was dead. I tried to calm him and get him back to bed before your mother came down, but he refused and wanted to set out immediately to rejoin his division. It was all terribly disjointed and at one time he took the ribbon he got for winning the Bronze Star and threw it in the fireplace, then he got down on his hands and knees and picked it out of the ashes and made me pin it on him again, and he kept repeating, 'This is when they are coming for the Jews.' "

"The next war I'm in," said Olson, "they don't get me under the rank of colonel."

It had stopped raining by now and Seeger folded the unfinished letter and went outside. He walked slowly down to the end of the company street, and facing out across the empty, soaked French fields, scarred and neglected by various armies, he stopped and opened the letter again.

"I don't know what Jacob went through in the army," his father wrote, "that has done this to him. He never talks to me about the war and he refuses to go to a psychoanalyst, and from time to time he is his own bouncing, cheerful self, playing in tennis tournaments, and going around with a large group of girls. But he has devoured all the concentration camp reports, and I have found him weeping when the newspapers reported that a hundred Jews were killed in Tripoli some time ago.

"The terrible thing is, Norman, that I find myself coming to believe that it is not neurotic for a Jew to behave like this today. Perhaps Jacob is the normal one, and I, going about my business, teaching economics in a quiet classroom, pretending to understand that the world is comprehensible and orderly, am really the mad one. I ask you once more to forgive me for writing you a letter like this, so different from any letter or any conversation I've ever had with you. But it is crowding me, too. I do not see rockets and bombs, but I see other things.

"Wherever you go these days—restaurants, hotels, clubs, trains—you seem to hear talk about the Jews, mean, hateful, murderous talk. Whatever page you turn to in the newspapers you seem to find an article about Jews being killed somewhere on the face of the globe. And there are large, influential newspapers and well-known columnists who each day are growing more and more outspoken and more popular. The day that Roosevelt died I heard a drunken man yelling outside a bar, 'Finally, they got the Jew out of the White House.' And some of the people who heard him merely laughed and nobody stopped him. And on V-E Day,° in celebration, hoodlums in Los Angeles savagely beat a Jewish writer. It's difficult to know what to do, whom to fight, where to look for allies.

"Three months ago, for example, I stopped my Thursday night poker game, after playing with the same men for over ten years. John Reilly happened to say that the Jews were getting rich out of this war, and when I demanded an apology, he refused, and when I looked around at the faces of the men who had been my friends for so long, I could see they were not with me. And when I left the house

*V-E Day*: May 8, 1945, the day of *V*ictory in *E*urope.

105

no one said good night to me. I know the poison was spreading from Germany before the war and during it, but I had not realized it had come so close.

"And in my economics class, I find myself idiotically hedging in my lectures. I discover that I am loath to praise any liberal writer or any liberal act and find myself somehow annoyed and frightened to see an article of criticism of existing abuses signed by a Jewish name. And I hate to see Jewish names on important committees, and hate to read of Jews fighting for the poor, the oppressed, the cheated and hungry. Somehow, even in a country where my family has lived a hundred years, the enemy has won this subtle victory over me—he has made me disfranchise myself from honest causes by calling them foreign, Communist, using Jewish names connected with them as ammunition against them.

"And, most hateful of all, I find myself looking for Jewish names in the casualty lists and secretly being glad when I discover them there, to prove that there at least, among the dead and wounded, we belong. Three times, thanks to you and your brothers, I have found our name there, and, may God forgive me, at the expense of your blood and your brother's life, through my tears, I have felt that same twitch of satisfaction. . . .

"When I read the newspapers and see another story that Jews are still being killed in Poland, or Jews are requesting that they be given back their homes in France, or that they be allowed to enter some country where they will not be murdered, I am annoyed with them, I feel they are boring the rest of the world with their problems, they are making demands upon the rest of the world by being killed, they are disturbing everyone by being hungry and asking for the return of their property. If we could all fall through the crust of the earth and vanish in one hour, with our heroes and poets and prophets and martyrs, perhaps we would be doing the memory of the Jewish race a service. . . .

"This is how I feel today, son. I need some help. You've been to the war, you've fought and killed men, you've seen the people of other countries. Maybe you understand things that I don't understand. Maybe you see some hope somewhere. Help me. Your loving father."

Seeger folded the letter slowly, not seeing what he was doing because the tears were burning his eyes. He walked slowly and aimlessly across the dead autumn grass of the empty field, away from the camp.

He tried to wipe away his tears, because with his eyes full and dark, he kept seeing his father and brother crouched in the old-fashioned living room in Ohio and hearing his brother, dressed in the old, discarded uniform, saying, "These're the new rocket bombs. For the Jews."

He sighed, looking out over the bleak, wasted land. Now, he thought, now I have to think about it. He felt a slight, unreasonable twinge of anger at his father for presenting him with the necessity of thinking about it. The army was good about serious problems. While you were fighting, you were too busy and frightened and weary to think about anything, and at other times you were relaxing, putting your brain on a shelf, postponing everything to that impossible time of clarity and beauty after the war. Well, now, here was the impossible, clear, beautiful time, and here was his father, demanding that he think. There are all sorts of Jews, he thought, there are the sort whose every waking moment is ridden by

*pogrom*: an organized massacre of a minority, specifically Jews.

the knowledge of Jewishness, who see signs against the Jew in every smile on a streetcar, every whisper, who see pogroms° in every newspaper article, threats in every change of the weather, scorn in every handshake, death behind each closed door. He had not been like that. He was young, he was big and healthy and easy-going and people of all kinds had seemed to like him all his life, in the army and out. In America, especially, what was going on in Europe had seemed remote, unreal, unrelated to him. The chanting, bearded old men burning in the Nazi furnaces, and the dark-eyed women screaming prayers in Polish and Russian and German as they were pushed naked into the gas chambers had seemed as shadowy and almost as unrelated to him as he trotted out onto the Stadium field for a football game, as they must have been to the men named O'Dwyer and Wickersham and Poole who played in the line beside him.

They had seemed more related in Europe. Again and again in the towns that had been taken from the Germans, gaunt, gray-faced men had stopped him humbly, looking searchingly at him, and had asked, peering at his long, lined, grimy face, under the anonymous helmet, "Are you a Jew?" Sometimes they asked it in English, sometimes French, or Yiddish. He didn't know French or Yiddish, but he learned to recognize the phrase. He had never understood exactly why they had asked the question, since they never demanded anything from him, rarely even could speak to him, until, one day in Strasbourg, a little bent old man and a small, shapeless woman had stopped him, and asked, in English, if he was Jewish.

"Yes," he said, smiling at them.

The two old people had smiled widely, like children. "Look," the old man had said to his wife. "A young American soldier. A Jew. And so large and strong." He had touched Seeger's arm reverently with the tips of his fingers, then had touched the Garand° he was carrying. "And such a beautiful rifle . . ."

And there, for a moment, although he was not particularly sensitive, Seeger got an inkling of why he had been stopped and questioned by so many before. Here, to these bent, exhausted old people, ravaged of their families, familiar with flight and death for so many years, was a symbol of continuing life. A large young man in the uniform of the liberator, blood, as they thought, of their blood, but not in hiding, not quivering in fear and helplessness, but striding secure and victorious down the street, armed and capable of inflicting terrible destruction on his enemies.

Seeger had kissed the old lady on the cheek and she had wept and the old man had scolded her for it, while shaking Seeger's hand fervently and thankfully before saying good-bye.

And, thinking back on it, it was silly to pretend that, even before his father's letter, he had been like any other American soldier going through the war. When he had stood over the huge dead SS major with the face blown in by his bullets in the warehouse in Coblenz, and taken the pistol from the dead hand, he had tasted a strange little extra flavor of triumph. How many Jews, he'd thought, has this man killed, how fitting it is that I've killed him. Neither Olson nor Welch, who were like his brothers, would have felt that in picking up the Luger, its barrel still hot from the last shots its owner had fired before dying. And he had resolved that he was going to make sure to take this gun back with him to America, and

120

*Garand*: an American standard infantry rifle.

plug it and keep it on his desk at home, as a kind of vague, half-understood sign to himself that justice had once been done and he had been its instrument.

Maybe, he thought, maybe I'd better take it back with me, but not as a memento. Not plugged, but loaded. America by now was a strange country for him. He had been away a long time and he wasn't sure what was waiting for him when he got home. If the mobs were coming down the street toward his house, he was not going to die singing and praying.

When he was taking basic training he'd heard a scrawny, clerklike-looking soldier from Boston talking at the other end of the PX° bar, over the watered beer. "The boys at the office," the scratchy voice was saying, "gave me a party before I left. And they told me one thing. 'Charlie,' they said, 'hold onto your bayonet. We're going to be able to use it when you get back. On the Yids.' "°

He hadn't said anything then, because he'd felt it was neither possible nor desirable to fight against every random overheard voice raised against the Jews from one end of the world to another. But again and again, at odd moments, lying on a barracks cot, or stretched out trying to sleep on the floor of a ruined French farmhouse, he had heard that voice, harsh, satisfied, heavy with hate and ignorance, saying above the beery grumble of apprentice soldiers at the bar, "Hold onto your bayonet. . . ."

And the other stories—Jews collected stories of hatred and injustice and          125
inklings of doom like a special, lunatic kind of miser. The story of the naval officer, commander of a small vessel off the Aleutians, who, in the officers' wardroom, had complained that he hated the Jews because it was the Jews who had demanded that the Germans be beaten first and the forces in the Pacific had been starved in consequence. And when one of his junior officers, who had just come aboard, had objected and told the commander that he was a Jew, the commander had risen from the table and said, "Mister, the Constitution of the United States says I have to serve in the same navy with Jews, but it doesn't say I have to eat at the same table with them." In the fogs and the cold, swelling Arctic seas off the Aleutians, in a small boat, subject to sudden, mortal attack at any moment . . .

And the two young combat engineers in an attached company on D Day,° when they were lying off the coast right before climbing down into the landing barges. "There's France," one of them had said.

"What's it like?" the second one had asked, peering out across the miles of water toward the smoking coast.

"Like every place else," the first one had answered. "The Jews've made all the dough during the war."

"Shut up!" Seeger had said, helplessly thinking of the dead, destroyed, wandering, starving Jews of France. The engineers had shut up, and they'd climbed down together into the heaving boat, and gone into the beach together.

And the million other stories. Jews, even the most normal and best adjusted          130
of them, became living treasuries of them, scraps of malice and bloodthirstiness, clever and confusing and cunningly twisted so that every act by every Jew became suspect and blameworthy and hateful. Seeger had heard the stories, and had made

*PX*: Post Exchange, where military persons may buy at cost.
*Yids*: Jews.
*D Day*: June 6, 1944, the day on which the allied forces invaded France from the
sea.

an almost conscious effort to forget them. Now, holding his father's letter in his hand, he remembered them all.

He stared unseeingly out in front of him. Maybe, he thought, maybe it would've been better to have been killed in the war, like Leonard. Simpler. Leonard would never have to face a crowd coming for his mother and father. Leonard would not have to listen and collect these hideous, fascinating little stories that made of every Jew a stranger in any town, on any field, on the face of the earth. He had come so close to being killed so many times, it would have been so easy, so neat and final.

Seeger shook his head. It was ridiculous to feel like that, and he was ashamed of himself for the weak moment. At the age of twenty-one, death was not an answer.

"Seeger!" It was Olson's voice. He and Welch had sloshed silently up behind Seeger, standing in the open field. "Seeger, *mon vieux,* what're you doing—grazing?"

Seeger turned slowly to them. "I wanted to read my letter," he said.

Olson looked closely at him. They had been together so long, through so       135
many things, that flickers and hints of expression on each other's faces were recognized and acted upon. "Anything wrong?" Olson asked.

"No," said Seeger. "Nothing much."

"Norman," Welch said, his voice young and solemn. "Norman, we've been talking. Olson and me. We decided—you're pretty attached to that Luger, and maybe—if you— well . . ."

"What he's trying to say," said Olson, "is we withdraw the request. If you want to sell it, O.K. If you don't, don't do it for our sake. Honest."

Seeger looked at them, standing there, disreputable and tough and familiar. "I haven't made up my mind yet," he said.

"Anything you decide," Welch said oratorically, "is perfectly all right with       140
us. Perfectly."

They walked aimlessly and silently across the field, away from camp. As they walked, their shoes making a wet, sliding sound in the damp, dead grass, Seeger thought of the time Olson had covered him in the little town outside Cherbourg, when Seeger had been caught going down the side of a street by four Germans with a machine gun on the second story of a house on the corner and Olson had had to stand out in the middle of the street with no cover at all for more than a minute, firing continuously, so that Seeger could get away alive. And he thought of the time outside Saint Lô when he had been wounded and had lain in a mine field for three hours and Welch and Captain Taney had come looking for him in the darkness and found him and picked him up and run for it, all of them expecting to get blown up any second.

And he thought of all the drinks they'd had together and the long marches and the cold winter together, and all the girls they'd gone out with together, and he thought of his father and brother crouching behind the window in Ohio waiting for the rockets and the crowds armed with Browning automatic rifles.

"Say," he stopped and stood facing them. "Say, what do you guys think of the Jews?"

Welch and Olson looked at each other, and Olson glanced down at the letter in Seeger's hand.

"Jews?" Olson said finally. "What're they? Welch, you ever hear of the Jews?"       145

Welch looked thoughtfully at the gray sky. "No," he said. "But remember, I'm an uneducated fellow."

"Sorry, Bud," Olson said, turning to Seeger. "We can't help you. Ask us another question. Maybe we'll do better."

Seeger peered at the faces of his friends. He would have to rely upon them, later on, out of uniform, on their native streets, more than he had ever relied on them on the bullet-swept street and in the dark mine field in France. Welch and Olson stared back at him, troubled, their faces candid and tough and dependable.

"What time," Seeger asked, "did you tell that captain you'd meet him?"

"Eight o'clock," Welch said. "But we don't have to go. If you have any    150
feeling about that gun . . ."

"We'll meet him," Seeger said. "We can use that sixty-five bucks."

"Listen," Olson said, "I know how much you like that gun and I'll feel like a heel if you sell it."

"Forget it," Seeger said, starting to walk again. "What could I use it for in America?"

## QUESTIONS

1.  Why is it important to the story to include at the beginning the details about the states from which the various characters come? Even though the immediate setting is just after World War II, can a case be made that the setting is the entire United States?

2.  How many separate scenes are introduced as places for action in the story? What function and importance might these have as bases of organization?

3.  Why is the mud of the streets mentioned early in the story, and why is the wet grass mentioned at the end? Can you perceive any contrast between this drab setting and the ideas in the minds of the soldiers about the streets of Paris?

4.  Describe the significance of the German Luger in the story. How is it a source of possible conflict among the soldiers? In what way is it the cause of the story's resolution?

5.  What is the immediate central conflict in the story? How does the larger fear that Seeger has about the future figure into this conflict? How is the immediate conflict resolved?

6.  Describe the point of view of the story. How does it begin? At what point does it shift to become limited to Seeger? What issue becomes prominent with this shift?

7.  What stories does Seeger recall about prejudice toward Jews? What does he recall about his associations with Welch, Taney, and Olson? What is his act of faith? Does his question at the end, "What could I use it [the Luger] for in America?" seem to be an accurate assessment on which to base his decision?

8.  In what ways do Welch, Taney, and Olson all make acts of faith?

## WRITING ABOUT SETTING

In preparing to write about setting, you should take notes directed toward the locations and artifacts that figure prominently in the story. Generally you should determine if there is one location of action or more. Raise questions about how much detail is included: Are things described visually so that you can make a sketch or draw a plan (such a sketch might help you organize your essay), or are the locations left vague? Why? What influence do the locations have upon the characters in the story, if any? Do the locations bring characters together, push them apart, make it easy for them to be private, make intimacy and conversation difficult? What artifacts are important in the action, and how important are they? Are they well described? Are they vital to the action? Are things like shapes, colors, times of day, locations of the sun, conditions of light, seasons of the year, and conditions of vegetation described? Do characters respect or mistreat the environment around them?

With answers to questions like these, you can then formulate ideas for your essay. Remember to work toward a central idea so you avoid writing no more than a description of scenes and objects (such an essay would be analogous to doing no more than retelling the story). Emphasize the connection between setting and whatever aspect or aspects you choose about the story. A possible central idea might thus be, "The palatial setting not only is gaudily shown, but is also a force preventing the revelers from escaping their fate," or "The drab, cold, bleak setting underscores the elemental, barbaric conditions of life in this destroyed world." Emphasis on such central ideas would force you to use description only as illustration and evidence and not as an end in itself.

### Organizing Your Essay

**INTRODUCTION.** The introduction should give a brief description of the setting or scenes of the story, with a characterization of the degree of detail presented by the author (that is, a little, a lot; visual, aural; colorful, monochromatic, and so on). The central idea explains the relationship to be explored in the essay, and the thesis sentence determines the major topics in which the central idea will be traced.

**BODY.** Following are five possible approaches to essays about setting. Which one you choose is your decision, but you may find that some works almost invite you to pick one approach over the others. Although each approach outlines a major emphasis in your essay, you may wish to bring in details from one of the others if they seem important at any point.

1. *Setting and action.* Here you explore the use of setting in the various actions of the work. Among the questions to be answered are these: How detailed and extensive are the descriptions of the setting? Are the scenes related to the action? (Are they essential or incidental?) Does the setting serve as part of the action (places of flight or concealment; public places where people meet openly or out-of-the-way places where they meet

privately; natural or environmental obstacles; sociological obstacles; seasonal conditions such as searing heat or numbing cold, and so on)? Do details of setting get used regularly, or are they mentioned only when they become necessary to an action? Do any physical objects figure into the story as causes of aspiration or conflict (for example, a diamond necklace, a boat, a phonograph, a pistol, a bag of groceries, a sail, a dog, a blanket)?

2. *Setting and organization.*    A closely related way of writing about setting is to connect it to the organization of the work. Some questions to help you get started with this approach are these: Is the setting a frame, an enclosure? Is it mentioned at various parts, or at shifts in the action? Does the setting undergo any expected or unexpected changes as the action changes? Do any parts of the setting have greater involvement in the action than other parts? Do any objects, such as money or property, figure into the developing or changing motivation of the characters? Do descriptions made at the start become important in the action later on? If so, in what order?

3. *Setting and character.*    Your aim here is to pick those details that seem to have a bearing on character and to write about their effects. The major question is the degree to which the setting seems to interact with or influence character. You might get at this topic through additional questions: Are the characters happy or unhappy where they live? Do they express their feelings, or get into discussions or arguments about them? Do they seem adjusted? Do they want to stay or leave? Does the economic, cultural, or ethnic level of the setting make the characters think in any unique ways? What jobs do the characters perform because of their ways of life? What freedoms or restraints do these jobs cause? How does the setting influence their decisions, transportation, speech habits, eating habits, attitudes about love and honor, and general folkways?

4. *Setting and atmosphere.*    Here you should write about those aspects of setting that seem designed to evoke a mood. Some questions are: Does the detail of setting go beyond the minimum needed for action or character? Do clear details help make clear the conflicts in the story, or do vague and amorphous details help to make these conflicts problematic? Are descriptive words used mainly to paint verbal pictures, to evoke a mood through references to colors, shapes, sounds, smells, or tastes? Does the setting establish a mood, say, of joy or hopelessness, lushness or spareness? Do things happen in daylight or night? Are the movements of the characters permanent, or do the locations emphasize impermanence (like footsteps in the sand, or movement through water)? If temperatures are mentioned, are things warm and pleasant, or cold and harsh? Does the mood established seem to suggest that life, too, is this way?

5. *Other aspects.*    In an earlier section of this chapter, "Setting and Statement" and "Setting and Irony" were listed as important uses of setting.

Not all stories lend themselves to either treatment, but for stories that do, you could create an interesting essay. If the author has used setting as a means of underscoring the circumstances and ideas of the story, you might use the section on statement as a guide for the body of your essay. If you perceive a contrast between setting and content, that too could be the basis of an essay such as those described in the paragraph on "Setting and Irony."

CONCLUSION.   You always have the option of summarizing your major points as your conclusion, but you might also want to write about anything you neglected in the body of your essay. Thus, you might have been treating the relationship of the setting to the action and may wish to mention something about any ties the setting has with character or atmosphere. You might also wish to point out whether your central idea about the setting also applies to other major aspects of the work.

## SAMPLE ESSAY

### De Maupassant's Use of Setting in "The Necklace"* to Show the Character of Mathilde

[1]   In "The Necklace" De Maupassant does not give much detail about the setting. He does not describe even the necklace, which is the central object in the plot, but he says only that it is "superb." Rather he uses setting to reflect the character of the major figure, Mathilde Loisel.° He gives no more detail than is needed to explain her feelings. This carefully directed setting may be considered as the first apartment, the dream-life mansion rooms, and the attic flat.□

[2]   Details about the first walkup apartment on the Street of Martyrs are presented to explain Mathilde's unhappiness. The walls are "drab," the furniture "threadbare," and the curtains "ugly." There is only a country girl to do housework. The tablecloth is not cleaned, and the best dinner dish is beef stew boiled in a kettle. Mathilde has no pretty dresses, but only a theater dress which she does not like. These details show her dissatisfaction about life with her low-salaried husband.

[3]   The dream-life, mansionlike setting is like the apartment, because it too makes her unhappy. In Mathilde's daydreams, the rooms are large, filled with expensive furniture and bric-a-brac, and draped in silk. She imagines private rooms for intimate talks, and big dinners with delicacies like trout and quail. With dreams of such a rich home, she feels even more despair about her modest apartment.

* See p. 75 for this story.
° Central idea.
□ Thesis sentence.

[4]     Finally, the attic flat indicates the coarsening of her character. There is little detail about this flat except that it is cheap and that Mathilde must carry water up many stairs to reach it. De Maupassant emphasizes the drudgery that she must bear to keep up the flat, such as washing the floor using large pails of water. He indicates her loss of refinement by writing that she gives up caring for her hair and hands, wears cheap dresses, speaks loudly, and swears. In this setting, she no longer has her dreams of the mansionlike rooms. Thus the flat in the attic goes along with the loss of her youth and beauty.

[5]     In summary, De Maupassant focuses everything, including the setting, on Mathilde. Anything extra is not needed, and he does not include it. Thus he says little about the big party scene, but emphasizes the necessary detail that Mathilde was a great "success." In "The Necklace," De Maupassant uses setting as a means to his end—the story of Mathilde and her needless misfortune.

### Commentary on the Essay

This essay illustrates the approach of relating setting to character. The introduction makes the point that De Maupassant uses only as much detail as he needs, and no more. There is nothing to excess. The central idea is that the details of setting may be directly related to Mathilde's character and feelings. The thesis sentence does not indicate a plan to deal with all the aspects of setting in the story, but only two real ones and one imaginary one.

Paragraphs 2 and 3 show how Mathilde's real-life apartment and dream-life mansion fill her with despair about her life. The fourth paragraph relates her flat in the attic in a cheaper neighborhood to the dulling and coarsening of her character. The idea here is that while better surroundings at the start fill her with despair, the ugly attic flat does not seem to affect her at all. At least, De Maupassant says nothing about her unhappiness with the poorer conditions.

The conclusion makes the assertion that, in the light of the general concentration in the story on the character of Mathilde, the setting is typical of De Maupassant's technique in "The Necklace."

# 7

# Style: The Words That
# Tell the Story

The word **style,** derived from the Latin word *stilus* (a writing instrument),
is understood to mean the way in which writers assemble words to tell
the story, develop the argument, dramatize the play, or compose the poem.
Often the definition is extended to distinguish style from content. It is
probably wiser, however, not to make this separation but to consider style
as the placement of words in the *service* of content. The way a thing is
said, in other words, cannot be separated from the thing itself.

Style is also highly individualistic. It is a matter of the way in which
specific authors put words together under specific conditions in specific
works. It is therefore possible to speak of the style of Ernest Hemingway,
for example, and of Mark Twain, even though both writers at any time
are adapting their words to the situations imagined in their works. Thus
authors may actually have a separate style for narrative and descriptive
passages, and their style in dialogue is likely different from either of these.
Indeed, it would be a mark of an inferior style if a writer were to use
the same manner for all the varying purposes that must exist in a story.
It must therefore be emphasized that style is to be judged on the degree
of its adaptability. The better the writer, the more that writer's words
will fit the precise situation called for in the story. Jonathan Swift defined
style as the right words in the right places. We may add to this definition
that style is also the right words at the right time and in the right circumstances.

## DICTION: CHOICE OF WORDS

The study of style begins with words, and **diction** refers to a writer's selection of specific words. The selection should be accurate and explicit, so
that all actions and ideas are clear. It is perhaps difficult to judge accuracy

and completeness, inasmuch as often we do not have any basis of comparison. Nevertheless, if a passage comes across as effective, if it conveys an idea well or gets at the essence of an action vividly and powerfully, we may confidently say that the words have been the right ones. In a passage describing action, for example, there should be active verbs, whereas in a description of a place there should be nouns and adjectives that provide locations, relationships, colors, and shapes. An explanatory or reflective passage should include a number of words that convey thoughts, states of mind and emotion, and various conditions of human relationships.

### Formal, Neutral, and Informal Diction

Words fall naturally into three basic groups, or classes, that may be called **formal** or *high*, **neutral** or *middle*, and **informal** or *low*. Formal or high diction consists of standard and often elegant words (frequently polysyllabic), the retention of correct word order, and the absence of contractions. The sentence "It is I," for example, is formal. The following sentences from Poe's "The Masque of the Red Death" use formal language:

> They resolved to leave means neither of ingress nor egress to the sudden impulses of despair or of frenzy from within. The abbey was amply provisioned. With such precautions the courtiers might bid defiance to contagion.

Note here words like *ingress*, *egress*, *provisioned*, *bid defiance*, and *contagion*. These words are not in ordinary, everyday vocabulary and have what we may call elegance. Though they are used accurately and aptly, and though the sentences are brief and simple, the diction is high.

Neutral or middle diction is ordinary, everyday but still standard vocabulary, with a shunning of longer words but with the use of contractions when necessary. The sentence "It's me," for example, is neutral, the sort of thing many people say in preference to "It is I" when identifying themselves on the telephone. The following passage from Alice Munro's "The Found Boat" illustrates middle, neutral diction:

> What surprised them in the second place was that when the boys did actually see what boat was meant, this old flood-smashed wreck held up in the branches, they did not understand that they had been fooled, that a joke had been played on them. They did not show a moment's disappointment, but seemed as pleased at the discovery as if the boat had been whole and new. They were already barefoot, because they had been wading in the water to get lumber, and they waded in here without a stop, surrounding the boat and appraising it and paying no attention even of an insulting kind to Eva and Carol who bobbed up and down on their log. Eva and Carol had to call to them.

In this passage the words are ordinary and easy. Even the longer words, like *surprised*, *disappointment*, *surrounding*, *appraising*, and *insulting*, are not beyond the level of conversation, although *appraising* and *surrounding* would not be out of place in a more formal passage. Essentially, however, the words do not draw attention to themselves but are centered on the topic. In a way, such words in the neutral style are designed to be like clear windows, while words of the high style are more like stained glass.

Informal or low diction may range from colloquial—the language used by people in relaxed, common activities—to the level of substandard or slang expressions. A person speaking to a very close friend is likely to use diction and idiom that would not be appropriate in public and formal situations, and even in some social situations. Low language is thus appropriate for dialogue in stories, depending on the characters speaking, and for stories told in the first-person point of view as though the speaker is talking directly to a group of sympathetic and relaxed close friends. For example, Sammy's opening sentence in John Updike's "A & P" illustrates the informal, low style:

> In walks these three girls in nothing but bathing suits.

Note the idiomatic "In walks," a singular verb, followed by a plural subject. Note also the use of "these" girls, an idiom used indefinitely to refer to specific people. In Grace Paley's story "Good Bye, and Good Luck" the diction is informal; the uniqueness is caused by the omission of certain key words and the unusual positioning of phrases, as in this passage:

> Nowadays you could find me any time in a hotel, uptown or downtown. Who needs an apartment to live like a maid with a dustrag in the hand, sneezing?

Note here the misuse of *could* for *can*, the omission of *at* which more formally would begin the phrase *any time*. The second sentence is almost impossible to analyze except to note that it has been arranged with masterly skill to duplicate exactly the idiomatic speech of the Jewish woman who is the speaker.

### Specific–General and Concrete–Abstract Language

**Specific** refers to a real thing or things that may be readily perceived or imagined; "my pet dog" is specific. **General** statements refer to broad classes of persons or things. "Dogs make good pets" is a generalization. **Concrete** refers to words that describe qualities or conditions; in the phrase "a cold day" the word *cold* is concrete. You cannot see cold, but you know the exact difference between cold and hot, and therefore you understand the word readily in reference to the external temperature. **Abstract** refers to qualities that are more removed from the concrete, and abstract words can therefore refer to many classes of separate things. On a continuum of qualities, ice cream may be noted as being cold, sweet, and creamy.

If we go on to say that it is *good*, however, this word is so widely applicable that it is abstract and therefore difficult to apply. Anything may be good, including other food, scenes, actions, words, and ideas. If we say only that something is *good*, we indicate approval but very little else about our topic.

Usually, good narrative and descriptive writing features specific and concrete words in preference to those that are general and abstract. If a narrative passage contains much general and abstract diction, it is difficult to understand because it is not easy to apply the words to any imaginable reality. Let us look at two examples of prose, the first from Hemingway's novel *A Farewell to Arms*, the second from Theodore Dreiser's *The Titan*:

> In the late summer of that year we lived in a house in a village that looked across the river and the plain to the mountains. In the bed of the river there were pebbles and boulders, dry and white in the sun, and the water was clear and swiftly moving and blue in the channels. Troops went by the house and down the road and the dust they raised powdered the leaves of the trees. The trunks of the trees too were dusty and the leaves fell early that year and we saw the troops marching along the road and the dust rising and leaves, stirred by the breeze, falling and the soldiers marching and afterward the road bare and white except for the leaves.

> From New York, Vermont, New Hampshire, Maine had come a strange company, earnest, patient, determined, unschooled in even the primer of refinement, hungry for something the significance of which, when they had it, they could not even guess, anxious to be called great, determined so to be without ever knowing how.

Hemingway's diction is specific; that is, many of the words, such as *house*, *river*, *plain*, *mountains*, *dust*, *leaves*, and *trees*, describe something that can be seen or felt. In describing aspects of the scene, Hemingway uses concrete words, like *dry*, *clear*, *swiftly moving*, *dusty*, *stirred*, *falling*, *marching*, and *bare*. These words indicate clearly perceivable actions or states. Dreiser's words are in marked contrast. The names of states are specific, but *company* is a general word for a group of any sort, unlike Hemingway's *troops*. Dreiser's key descriptive words are *strange*, *earnest*, *patient*, *determined*, *hungry*, and *anxious*. Because none of these words describes anything that can be perceived, unlike *dry* and *dusty*, they are called *abstract*. Obviously the two passages are on different topics, and both are successful in their ways, but Hemingway's diction indicates an attempt to present a specific, concrete perception of things while Dreiser's indicates an attempt at psychological penetration.

### Denotation and Connotation

Another way of getting at style is to be alert for the author's management of *denotation* and *connotation*. **Denotation** refers to what a word means, and **connotation** to what the word suggests. It is one thing to call a person *skinny*, for example, another to use the word *thin*, and still something else to say *svelte* or *shapely*. Similarly, both *cat* and *kitten* are accurate words denotatively, but *kitten* connotes more playfulness and cuteness than one might associate with a cat. If a person in a social situation behaves in ways that are described as *friendly*, *warm*, *polite*, or *correct*, these words all suggest slight differences in behavior, not because the words are not approximately synonymous, but because the words have different connotations.

It is through the careful choice of words not only for denotation but also for connotation that authors create unique effects even though they might be describing similar or even identical situations. Let us look, for example, at the concluding paragraph of Joseph Conrad's novel *Nostromo* (1904). The hero of the novel, Nostromo, has just died, and the woman who loves him has cried out in grief:

> In that true cry of love and grief that seemed to ring aloud from Punta Mala to Azuera and away to the bright line of the horizon, overhung by a big white cloud shining like a mass of solid silver, the genius of the magnificent *capataz de cargadores* dominated the dark gulf containing his conquests of treasure and love.

This circumstance is not uncommon, for people die every day, and their loved ones grieve for them. But through connotative words like *bright line*, *shining*, *solid silver*, *genius*, *magnificent*, and *dominated*, Conrad suggests that Nostromo was more than ordinary, a person of great worth and power, a virtual demigod.

In contrast, here is the concluding paragraph of Hemingway's *A Farewell to Arms*:

> But after I had got them out and shut the door and turned off the light it wasn't any good. It was like saying good-by to a statue. After a while I went out and left the hospital and walked back to the hotel in the rain.

Hemingway's situation is similar to Conrad's. The heroine, Catherine Barclay, has died, and the hero, Frederick Henry, expresses his grief. He had loved her deeply, but their dreams for a happy future have been destroyed. Hemingway is interested in emphasizing the finality of the moment and he does so through phrases like *shut the door*, *turned off the light*, *went out*, and *walked back*. These expressions are all so common that you might at first be surprised to find them at so emotional a point in the book. But these flat, bare words serve a purpose; they suggest that death is as much a part of life as shutting a door and turning off a light. Both passages show clearly the ways in which control over connotation may create different effects.

## RHETORIC

Broadly, **rhetoric** refers to the art of persuasive writing and, even more broadly, to the general art of writing. Any passage can be studied for its rhetorical qualities. For this reason it is necessary to develop both the methods and the descriptive vocabulary with which to carry out an analysis. Some things that may easily be done involve counting various elements in a passage and analyzing the types of sentences the author uses.

### Counting

Doing a count of the number of words in a sentence; or the number of verbs, adjectives, prepositions, and adverbs; or the number of syllables in relation to the total number of words, can often lead to valuable conclusions about style, especially if the count is related to other aspects of the passage. The virtue of counting is that it is easy to do and therefore it provides a "quick opening" into at least one aspect of style. Always remember that conclusions based on a count will provide *tendencies* of a particular author rather than absolutes. For illustration, let us say that Author *A* uses words mainly of 1 or 2 syllables, while Author *B* includes many words of 3, 4, and 5 syllables. Going further, let us say that *A* uses an average of 12 words per sentence while *B* uses 35. It would be fair to conclude that Author *A* is brief while Author *B* is more expansive. This is not to say that Author *A*'s passage would be easier or superior, however, for a long string of short sentences with short words might become choppy and tiresome and might cause your mind to wander.

### Sentence Types

You can often learn much about a passage by determining the sorts of sentences it contains. Though you have probably learned the basic sentence types at one time or another, let's review them here:

1.  **Simple sentences** contain one subject and one verb, together with modifiers and complements. They are often short and are most appropriate for actions and declarations. Often they are idiomatic, particularly in dialogue.

2.  **Compound sentences** contain two simple sentences joined by a conjunction (*and*, *but*, *for*, *or*, *nor*, and so on) and a comma, or by a semicolon without a conjunction. Frequently, compound sentences are strung together as a series of three or four or more simple sentences.

3.  **Complex sentences** contain a main clause and a subordinate clause. Because of the subordinate clause, the complex sentence is often suitable for describing cause-and-effect relationships in narrative, and also for analysis and reflection.

4.   **Compound-complex sentences** contain two main clauses and a dependent clause. In practice, many authors produce sentences that may contain a number of subordinate clauses together with many more than two main clauses. Usually the more clauses, the more difficult the sentence.

### Loose and Periodic Sentences

A major way to describe sentences in terms of the development of their content is to use the terms *loose* and *periodic*. A **loose sentence** unfolds easily, with no surprises. Because it is fairly predictable, it is the most commonly used sentence in stories. Here is an example:

In America, the idea of equality was first applied only to white males.

**Periodic sentences** are arranged as much as possible in an order of climax, with the concluding information or thought being withheld to make the sentence especially interesting or surprising. Usually the periodic sentence begins with a dependent clause so that the content may be built up to the final detail, as in this sentence:

Although in America the idea of equality was first applied only to males of European ancestry, in this century, despite the reluctance and even the opposition of many men who have regarded equality as a mark of their own status and not as a right for everyone, it has been extended to women and to persons of all races.

In narrative prose, sentences of this type are usually carefully placed in spots of crucial importance. Often the sentence alone might be said to contain the crisis and resolution at the same moment, as in this sentence from Edgar Allan Poe's "The Fall of the House of Usher":

For a moment she remained trembling and reeling to and fro upon the threshold, then, with a low moaning cry, fell heavily inward upon the person of her brother, and in her violent and now final death-agonies, bore him to the floor a corpse, and a victim to the terrors he had anticipated.

### Parallelism

To create interest, authors often rely on the rhetorical device called **parallelism,** which is common and easily recognized. Parallelism is the repetition of the same grammatical form (nouns, verbs, phrases, clauses) to balance expressions, conserve words, and build up to climaxes. Here, for example, is another sentence from Poe, which occurs in the story "The Black Cat":

> I grew, day by day, more moody, more irritable, more regardless of the feelings of others.

Arrangements like this are called *parallel* because they may actually be laid out graphically, according to parts of speech, in parallel lines, as in the following (with the phrase "day by day" left out):

                more moody
I grew    more irritable
                more regardless of the feelings of others

Poe's sentence achieves an order of increasing severity of psychological depression developing from the personal to the social. Such an ascending order marks a deliberate attempt at climax, unlike the parallelism in the following sentence from the concluding paragraph of Clark's "The Portable Phonograph":

          1                    2                                                            1
Then quickly and quietly, looking at the piece of canvas frequently, he slipped
                              2                                3
the records into the case, snapped the lid shut, and carried the phonograph
to his couch.

Here there are two parallel adverbs at the beginning, both ending in *-ly*, and three past tense verbs ending in *-ed*, all of which have direct objects. The order here is time; in a short sentence, Clark conveys a great deal of information.

The same parallel arrangements may be seen also in individual sentences within a paragraph or longer unit. In the following passage from Alice Munro's "The Found Boat," for example, there are a number of sentences of identical structure which sum up the exhilaration of young people dashing naked to swim in a river. Parallel sentences begin "They felt," "They felt," "They thought," "They went running," and finally "They dipped and floated and separated":

> Nobody said a word this time, they all bent and stripped themselves. Eva, naked first, started running across the field, and then all the others ran, all five of them running bare through the knee-high hot grass, running towards the river. Not caring now about being caught but in fact leaping and yelling to call attention to themselves, if there was anybody to hear or see. They felt as if they were going to jump off a cliff and fly. They felt that something was happening to them different from anything that had happened before, and it had to do with the boat, the water, the sunlight, the dark ruined station, and each other. They thought of each other now hardly as names or people, but as echoing shrieks, reflections, all bold and white and loud and scandalous, and as fast as arrows. They went running without a break into the cold water and when it came almost to the tops of their legs they

fell on it and swam. It stopped their noise. Silence, amazement, came over them in a rush. They dipped and floated and separated, sleek as mink.

**Cumulatio or accumulation.** The paragraph from "The Found Boat" also illustrates another rhetorical device much used by writers, namely **cumulatio** or **accumulation.** While parallelism refers to grammatical constructions, cumulatio refers to the building up of details, such as the materials in the "they" sentences in Munro's paragraph.[1] The device is therefore a brief way of introducing much information, for once the parallel rhythm of the buildup begins, readers will readily accept new material directly into the pattern. The device thus acts as a series of quick glimpses or vignettes, and vividness is established through the parallel repetition.

**Chiasmus or Antimetabole.** Also fitting into the pattern of parallelism is a favorite device called **chiasmus** or **antimetabole.** This pattern is designed to create vividness through memorable repetition. The pattern is *A B B A*, which can be arranged graphically at the ends of an X (which is the same as the Greek letter *chi*):

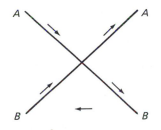

Mark Twain, in the story "Luck," creates a sentence that shows the pattern:

    *A*                 *B*                 *B*                *A*

I drilled him and crammed him, and crammed him and drilled him.

You may not always encounter such easily observed patterns, but you should always be alert to positions and arrangements that you think are particularly noticeable or effective. Even though you may not be able to use a technically correct name, your analysis should go well as long as you focus your attention on important aspects of effective writing in the stories that you read.

## STYLE IN GENERAL

If the work is successful, you probably will not think of the style as you read, for clear expressions and easy reading are marks of a writer's success. On consideration, however, you can begin to understand the author's

---

[1] For another example of cumulatio, by Jonathan Swift, see p. 258.

achievement through a study of style. The action described in a particular passage, the relationship of the passage to the entire work, the level of the diction, the vividness of the descriptions—all these can enter into an assessment of the passage.

In the paragraph quoted above from Munro's "The Found Boat," for example, great stylistic mastery can be perceived beyond the parallelism that we noted. The passage could readily be considered the climax of the story, which is, among other things, about emerging sexuality. In an almost ritualistic way, the paragraph describes young people running impetuously toward a river and diving in—an action that may be construed as having symbolic sexual overtones. Note that after the first two sentences describing action, Munro's narrator shifts the focus with four sentences of omniscient analysis describing the feelings of the young people. If her intention had been to create searching psychological scrutiny here, she might have selected words from the language of psychology (*libido, urge, sublimation*, and so on). Instead, Munro uses words that could genuinely have been in the vocabularies of the characters. Hence the young people feel "as if they were going to jump off a cliff and fly" and feel "that something was happening to them different from anything that had happened before." With these neutral words, the passage focuses on the excitement of the situation rather than upon any hidden psychological significance. In light of all these considerations, the style of the paragraph seems just right. Munro describes the actions adequately but not extensively, she objectivizes the feelings of the characters, and she avoids the sort of psychological analysis that here would interrupt rather than instruct.

Observations of this kind may not occur on first reading, but on reflection you will find that the style of just about any passage will yield relatively full material for study. As long as the focus is on the content and also on the relationship of words to content, fruitful analysis of style will result.

## MARK TWAIN (1835–1910)
## [SAMUEL LANGHORNE CLEMENS]

### Luck[1]                                                               *1891*

It was at a banquet in London in honor of one of the two or three conspicuously illustrious English military names of this generation. For reasons which will presently appear, I will withhold his real name and titles and call him Lieutenant-General Lord Arthur Scoresby, Y.C., K.C.B., etc., etc., etc. What a fascination there is in a renowned name! There sat the man, in actual flesh, whom I had heard of so many thousands of times since that day, thirty years before, when his name shot

---

[1] This is not a fancy sketch. I got it from a clergyman who was an instructor at Woolwich forty years ago, and who vouched for its truth. [Clemens' note.]

suddenly to the zenith from a Crimean battlefield, to remain forever celebrated. It was food and drink to me to look, and look, and look at that demi-god; scanning, searching, noting: the quietness, the reserve, the noble gravity of his countenance; the simple honesty that expressed itself all over him; the sweet unconsciousness of his greatness—unconsciousness of the hundreds of admiring eyes fastened upon him, unconsciousness of the deep, loving, sincere worship welling out of the breasts of those people and flowing toward him.

The clergyman at my left was an old acquaintance of mine—clergyman now, but had spent the first half of his life in the camp and field and as an instructor in the military school at Woolwich. Just at the moment I have been talking about a veiled and singular light glimmered in his eyes and he leaned down and muttered confidentially to me—indicating the hero of the banquet with a gesture:

"Privately—he's an absolute fool."

This verdict was a great surprise to me. If its subject had been Napoleon, or Socrates, or Solomon, my astonishment could not have been greater. Two things I was well aware of: that the Reverend was a man of strict veracity and that his judgment of men was good. Therefore I knew, beyond doubt or question, that the world was mistaken about this hero: he *was* a fool. So I meant to find out, at a convenient moment, how the Reverend, all solitary and alone, had discovered the secret.

Some days later the opportunity came, and this is what the Reverend told me:

About forty years ago I was an instructor in the military academy at Woolwich. I was present in one of the sections when young Scoresby underwent his preliminary examination. I was touched to the quick with pity, for the rest of the class answered up brightly and handsomely, while he—why, dear me, he didn't know *anything*, so to speak. He was evidently good, and sweet, and lovable, and guileless; and so it was exceedingly painful to see him stand there, as serene as a graven image, and deliver himself of answers which were veritably miraculous for stupidity and ignorance. All the compassion in me was aroused in his behalf. I said to myself, when he comes to be examined again he will be flung over, of course; so it will be simply a harmless act of charity to ease his fall as much as I can. I took him aside and found that he knew a little of Caesar's history; and as he didn't know anything else, I went to work and drilled him like a galley-slave on a certain line of stock questions concerning Caesar which I knew would be used. If you'll believe me, he went through with flying colors on examination day! He went through on that purely superficial "cram," and got compliments too, while others, who knew a thousand times more than he, got plucked. By some strangely lucky accident— an accident not likely to happen twice in a century—he was asked no question outside of the narrow limits of his drill.

It was stupefying. Well, all through his course I stood by him, with something of the sentiment which a mother feels for a crippled child; and he always saved himself—just by miracle, apparently.

Now, of course, the thing that would expose him and kill him at last was mathematics. I resolved to make his death as easy as I could; so I drilled him and crammed him, and crammed him and drilled him, just on the line of questions which the examiners would be most likely to use, and then launched him on his fate. Well, sir, try to conceive of the result: to my consternation, he took the first prize! And with it he got a perfect ovation in the way of compliments.

Sleep? There was no more sleep for me for a week. My conscience tortured me day and night. What I had done I had done purely through charity, and only to ease the poor youth's fall. I never had dreamed of any such preposterous results as the thing that had happened. I felt as guilty and miserable as Frankenstein. Here was a wooden-head whom I had put in the way of glittering promotions and prodigious responsibilities, and but one thing could happen: he and his responsibilities would all go to ruin together at the first opportunity.

The Crimean War had just broken out. Of course there had to be a war, I said to myself. We couldn't have peace and give this donkey a chance to die before he is found out. I waited for the earthquake. It came. And it made me reel when it did come. He was actually gazetted to a captaincy in a marching regiment! Better men grow old and gray in the service before they climb to a sublimity like that. And who could ever have foreseen that they would go and put such a load of responsibility on such green and inadequate shoulders? I could just barely have stood it if they had made him a cornet; but a captain—think of it! I thought my hair would turn white.

Consider what I did—I who so loved repose and inaction. I said to myself, I am responsible to the country for this, and I must go along with him and protect the country against him as far as I can. So I took my poor little capital that I had saved up through years of work and grinding economy, and went with a sigh and bought a cornetcy in his regiment, and away we went to the field.

And there—oh, dear, it was awful. Blunders?—why he never did anything *but* blunder. But, you see, nobody was in the fellow's secret. Everybody had him focused wrong, and necessarily misinterpreted his performance every time. Consequently they took his idiotic blunders for inspirations of genius. They did, honestly! His mildest blunders were enough to make a man in his right mind cry; and they did make me cry—and rage and rave, too, privately. And the thing that kept me always in a sweat of apprehension was the fact that every fresh blunder he made increased the luster of his reputation! I kept saying to myself, he'll get so high that when discovery does finally come it will be like the sun falling out of the sky.

He went right along, up from grade to grade, over the dead bodies of his superiors, until at last, in the hottest moment of the battle of ———— down went our colonel, and my heart jumped into my mouth, for Scoresby was next in rank! Now for it, said I; we'll all land in Sheol in ten minutes, sure.

The battle was awfully hot; the allies were steadily giving way all over the field. Our regiment occupied a position that was vital; a blunder now must be destruction. At this crucial moment, what does this immortal fool do but detach the regiment from its place and order a charge over a neighboring hill where there wasn't a suggestion of an enemy! "There you go!" I said to myself; "this *is* the end at last."

And away we did go, and were over the shoulder of the hill before the insane movement could be discovered and stopped. And what did we find? An entire and unsuspected Russian army in reserve! And what happened? We were eaten up? That is necessarily what would have happened in ninety-nine cases out of a hundred. But no; those Russians argued that no single regiment would come brows-

10

15

ing around there at such a time. It must be the entire English army, and that the sly Russian game was detected and blocked; so they turned tail, and away they went, pell-mell, over the hill and down into the field, in wild confusion, and we after them; they themselves broke the solid Russian center in the field, and tore through, and in no time there was the most tremendous rout you ever saw, and the defeat of the allies was turned into a sweeping and splendid victory! Marshal Canrobert looked on, dizzy with astonishment, admiration, and delight; and sent right off for Scoresby, and hugged him, and decorated him on the field in presence of all the armies!

And what was Scoresby's blunder that time? Merely the mistaking his right hand for his left—that was all. An order had come to him to fall back and support our right; and, instead, he fell *forward* and went over the hill to the left. But the name he won that day as a marvelous military genius filled the world with his glory, and that glory will never fade while history books last.

He is just as good and sweet and lovable and unpretending as a man can be, but he doesn't know enough to come in when it rains. Now that is absolutely true. He is the supremest ass in the universe; and until half an hour ago nobody knew it but himself and me. He has been pursued, day by day and year by year, by a most phenomenal astonishing luckiness. He has been a shining soldier in all our wars for a generation; he has littered his whole military life with blunders, and yet has never committed one that didn't make him a knight or a baronet or a lord or something. Look at his breast; why, he is just clothed in domestic and foreign decorations. Well, sir, every one of them is the record of some shouting stupidity or other; and, taken together, they are proof that the very best thing in all this world that can befall a man is to be born lucky. I say again, as I said at the banquet, Scoresby's an absolute fool.

## QUESTIONS

1. Describe Twain's style as a writer of narrative prose. What kinds of detail does he present? Does he give you enough detail about the battle during the Crimean War (1854–1856), for example, to justify an assertion that he describes action vividly? Or does he confine his detail to illuminate the life of Scoresby?

2. What elements in the story are amusing? Does Twain's style have any influence on laughter? If so, how does the development of humor depend on the arrangement of words?

3. Study the first paragraph for rhetorical effect. What does it seem that Twain intended after the "look, and look, and look" phrase? Why do you think that he begins the story with such a description that might even be called heroic? Contrast this paragraph with the rhetoric of paragraph 12, where the word "blunder" is repeated.

4. Who begins telling the story? Who finally tells the story? What is the effect of this change of point of view upon the debunking of Scoresby that is the main subject? How does the clergyman narrator learn about all that Scoresby does? How does he summarize Scoresby's career?

5. How does Twain explain things so as to make it believable that Scoresby

could have passed his exams? Why is it necessary to include this cramming as a first step in the great career?

6. Describe the organization of the story. What is the climax? Where does it occur? What is the relationship of the story's title to the resolution of the plot?

7. Describe the character of Scoresby. Aside from his luck, what things do you learn about him? Is there enough to justify the claim of the narrator that Scoresby is "an absolute fool"?

## ERNEST HEMINGWAY (1899–1961)

*A Clean, Well-Lighted Place*                                    1933

It was late and every one had left the café except an old man who sat in the shadow the leaves of the tree made against the electric light. In the day time the street was dusty, but at night the dew settled the dust and the old man liked to sit late because he was deaf and now at night it was quiet and he felt the difference. The two waiters inside the café knew that the old man was a little drunk, and while he was a good client they knew that if he became too drunk he would leave without paying, so they kept watch on him.

"Last week he tried to commit suicide," one waiter said.

"Why?"

"He was in despair."

"What about?"                                                     5

"Nothing."

"How do you know it was nothing?"

"He has plenty of money."

They sat together at a table that was close against the wall near the door of the café and looked at the terrace where the tables were all empty except where the old man sat in the shadow of the leaves of the tree that moved slightly in the wind. A girl and a soldier went by in the street. The street light shone on the brass number on his collar. The girl wore no head covering and hurried beside him.

"The guard will pick him up," one waiter said.                   10

"What does it matter if he gets what he's after?"

"He had better get off the street now. The guard will get him. They went by five minutes ago."

The old man sitting in the shadow rapped on his saucer with his glass. The younger waiter went over to him.

"What do you want?"

The old man looked at him. "Another brandy," he said.            15

"You'll be drunk," the waiter said. The old man looked at him. The waiter went away.

"He'll stay all night," he said to his colleague. "I'm sleepy now. I never get into bed before three o'clock. He should have killed himself last week."

The waiter took the brandy bottle and another saucer from the counter inside the café and marched out to the old man's table. He put down the saucer and poured the glass full of brandy.

"You should have killed yourself last week," he said to the deaf man. The old man motioned with his finger. "A little more," he said. The waiter poured on into the glass so that the brandy slopped over and ran down the stem into the top saucer of the pile. "Thank you," the old man said. The waiter took the bottle back inside the café. He sat down at the table with his colleague again.

"He's drunk now," he said.                                                      20

"He's drunk every night."

"What did he want to kill himself for?"

"How should I know."

"How did he do it?"

"He hung himself with a rope."                                                  25

"Who cut him down?"

"His niece."

"Why did they do it?"

"Fear for his soul."

"How much money has he got?"                                                    30

"He's got plenty."

"He must be eighty years old."

"Anyway I should say he was eighty."

"I wish he would go home. I never get to bed before three o'clock. What kind of hour is that to go to bed?"

"He stays up because he likes it."                                              35

"He's lonely. I'm not lonely. I have a wife waiting in bed for me."

"He had a wife once too."

"A wife would be no good to him now."

"You can't tell. He might be better with a wife."

"His niece looks after him. You said she cut him down."                         40

"I know."

"I wouldn't want to be that old. An old man is a nasty thing."

"Not always. This old man is clean. He drinks without spilling. Even now, drunk. Look at him."

"I don't want to look at him. I wish he would go home. He has no regard for those who must work."

The old man looked from his glass across the square, then over at the waiters.   45

"Another brandy," he said, pointing to his glass. The waiter who was in a hurry came over.

"Finished," he said, speaking with that omission of syntax stupid people employ when talking to drunken people or foreigners. "No more tonight. Close now."

"Another," said the old man.

"No. Finished." The waiter wiped the edge of the table with a towel and shook his head.

The old man stood up, slowly counted the saucers, took a leather coin purse   50
from his pocket and paid for the drinks, leaving half a peseta tip.

The waiter watched him go down the street, a very old man walking unsteadily but with dignity.

"Why didn't you let him stay and drink?" the unhurried waiter asked. They were putting up the shutters. "It is not half-past two."

"I want to go home to bed."

"What is an hour?"

"More to me than to him."                                                                                      55

"An hour is the same."

"You talk like an old man yourself. He can buy a bottle and drink at home."

"It's not the same."

"No, it is not," agreed the waiter with a wife. He did not wish to be unjust. He was only in a hurry.

"And you? You have no fear of going home before your usual hour?"        60

"Are you trying to insult me?"

"No, hombre, only to make a joke."

"No," the waiter who was in a hurry said, rising from pulling down the metal shutters. "I have confidence. I am all confidence."

"You have youth, confidence, and a job," the older waiter said. "You have everything."

"And what do you lack?"                                                                                          65

"Everything but work."

"You have everything I have."

"No. I have never had confidence and I am not young."

"Come on. Stop talking nonsense and lock up."

"I am of those who like to stay late at the café," the older waiter said. "With     70
all those who do not want to go to bed. With all those who need a light for the night."

"I want to go home and into bed."

"We are of two different kinds," the older waiter said. He was now dressed to go home. "It is not only a question of youth and confidence although those things are very beautiful. Each night I am reluctant to close up because there may be some one who needs the café."

"Hombre, there are bodegas° open all night long."

"You do not understand. This is a clean and pleasant café. It is well lighted. The light is very good and also, now, there are shadows of the leaves."

"Good night," said the younger waiter.                                                                      75

"Good night," the other said. Turning off the electric light he continued the conversation with himself. It is the light of course but it is necessary that the place be clean and pleasant. You do not want music. Certainly you do not want music. Nor can you stand before a bar with dignity although that is all that is provided for these hours. What did he fear? It was not fear or dread. It was a nothing that he knew too well. It was all a nothing and a man was nothing too. It was only that and light was all it needed and a certain cleanness and order. Some lived in it and never felt it but he knew it all was nada y pues nada° y nada y pues nada. Our nada who art in nada, nada be thy name thy kingdom nada thy will be nada in nada as it is in nada. Give us this nada our daily nada and nada us our nada as we nada our nadas and nada us not into nada but deliver us from nada; pues nada. Hail nothing full of nothing, nothing is with thee.

*bodega*: a store.
*nada y pues nada*: "nothing and then nothing."

He smiled and stood before a bar with a shining steam pressure coffee machine.

"What's yours?" asked the barman.

"Nada."

"Otro loco mas,"° said the barman and turned away.

"A little cup," said the waiter.                                                                                      80

The barman poured it for him.

"The light is very bright and pleasant but the bar is unpolished," the waiter said.

The barman looked at him but did not answer. It was too late at night for conversation.

"You want another copita?"° the barman asked.

"No, thank you," said the waiter and went out. He disliked bars and bodegas.   85
A clean, well-lighted café was a very different thing. Now, without thinking further, he would go home to his room. He would lie in the bed and finally, with daylight, he would go to sleep. After all, he said to himself, it is probably only insomnia. Many must have it.

> *otro loco mas*: "another [even] more crazy."
> *copita*: "little cup."

## QUESTIONS

1.  Describe the diction of the story. Can it be called high, middle, or low? Are there any unusual words? What is the effect of the Spanish words used in the story?

2.  Briefly characterize the two waiters and the circumstances of their lives that Hemingway includes. From their conversations, can you identify which one is speaking even though Hemingway does not introduce many of their speeches? Do you think that the speeches sufficiently identify the waiters, or should Hemingway have included introductions?

3.  Analyze paragraph 9 as an example of descriptive prose. How is each sentence used? Can you visualize the scene as a result of the description? Of the four sentences, why do you think the first is longer than the other three combined?

4.  What is the point of view of the story? Can you see any shift as the story follows the older waiter after he leaves the café?

5.  What is the conflict or conflicts of the story? Are there any antagonists? What problem is the old man facing? What problem does the older waiter face? What is the resolution of their conflicts?

6.  Describe the older waiter's parody of the first part of the Lord's Prayer and the opening of the Ave Maria. Why does the waiter substitute "nada" (nothing) for key words in the prayers? In view of this negativism, what is the meaning of the older waiter's sympathies for the old man and also of his assessment of human needs? What is the meaning of the title? Why are cleanliness and light stressed? Are the assertions about life made in the story accurate or overly negative?

7.  Describe the setting of the story. How much detail do you find? What things
    in the story are important, as things or artifacts? How does Hemingway tell
    you, for example, that there is a nearby streetlight? Are the settings best
    described as vivid or impressionistic?

## ALICE MUNRO (b. 1931)

*The Found Boat*                                                    *1974*

At the end of Bell Street, McKay Street, Mayo Street, there was the Flood. It
was the Wawanash River, which every spring overflowed its banks. Some springs,
say one in every five, it covered the roads on that side of town and washed over
the fields, creating a shallow choppy lake. Light reflected off the water made everything bright and cold, as it is in a lakeside town, and woke or revived in people
certain vague hopes of disaster. Mostly during the late afternoon and early evening,
there were people straggling out to look at it, and discuss whether it was still
rising, and whether this time it might invade the town. In general, those under
fifteen and over sixty-five were most certain that it would.

Eva and Carol rode out on their bicycles. They left the road—it was the
end of Mayo Street, past any houses—and rode right into a field, over a wire
fence entirely flattened by the weight of the winter's snow. They coasted a little
way before the long grass stopped them, then left their bicycles lying down and
went to the water.

"We have to find a log and ride on it," Eva said.

"Jesus, we'll freeze our legs off."

"Jesus, we'll freeze our legs off!" said one of the boys who were there too     5
at the water's edge. He spoke in a sour whine, the way boys imitated girls although
it was nothing like the way girls talked. These boys—there were three of them—
were all in the same class as Eva and Carol at school and were known to them
by name (their names being Frank, Bud and Clayton), but Eva and Carol, who
had seen and recognized them from the road, had not spoken to them or looked
at them or, even yet, given any sign of knowing they were there. The boys seemed
to be trying to make a raft, from lumber they had salvaged from the water.

Eva and Carol took off their shoes and socks and waded in. The water was
so cold it sent pain up their legs, like blue electric sparks shooting through their
veins, but they went on, pulling their skirts high, tight behind and bunched so
they could hold them in front.

"Look at the fat-assed ducks in wading."

"Fat-assed fucks."

Eva and Carol, of course, gave no sign of hearing this. They laid hold of a
log and climbed on, taking a couple of boards floating in the water for paddles.
There were always things floating around in the Flood—branches, fence-rails, logs,
road signs, old lumber; sometimes boilers, washtubs, pots and pans, or even a
car seat or stuffed chair, as if somewhere the Flood had got into a dump.

They paddled away from shore, heading out into the cold lake. The water     10
was perfectly clear, they could see the brown grass swimming along the bottom.
Suppose it was the sea, thought Eva. She thought of drowned cities and countries.
Atlantis. Suppose they were riding in a Viking boat—Viking boats on the Atlantic

were more frail and narrow than this log on the Flood—and they had miles of clear sea beneath them, then a spired city, intact as a jewel irretrievable on the ocean floor.

"This is a Viking boat," she said. "I am the carving on the front." She stuck her chest out and stretched her neck, trying to make a curve, and she made a face, putting out her tongue. Then she turned and for the first time took notice of the boys.

"Hey, you sucks!" she yelled at them. "You'd be scared to come out here, this water is ten feet deep!"

"Liar," they answered without interest, and she was.

They steered the log around a row of trees, avoiding floating barbed wire, and got into a little bay created by a natural hollow of the land. Where the bay was now, there would be a pond full of frogs later in the spring, and by the middle of summer there would be no water visible at all, just a low tangle of reeds and bushes, green, to show that mud was still wet around their roots. Larger bushes, willows, grew around the steep bank of this pond and were still partly out of the water. Eva and Carol let the log ride in. They saw a place where something was caught.

It was a boat, or part of one. An old rowboat with most of one side ripped    15
out, the board that had been the seat just dangling. It was pushed up among the branches, lying on what would have been its side, if it had a side, the prow caught high.

Their idea came to them without consultation, at the same time:

"You guys! Hey, you guys!"

"We found you a boat!"

"Stop building your stupid raft and come and look at the boat!"

What surprised them in the first place was that the boys really did come,    20
scrambling overland, half running, half sliding down the bank, wanting to see.

"Hey, where?"

"Where is it, I don't see no boat."

What surprised them in the second place was that when the boys did actually see what boat was meant, this old flood-smashed wreck held up in the branches, they did not understand that they had been fooled, that a joke had been played on them. They did not show a moment's disappointment, but seemed as pleased at the discovery as if the boat had been whole and new. They were already barefoot, because they had been wading in the water to get lumber, and they waded in here without a stop, surrounding the boat and appraising it and paying no attention even of an insulting kind to Eva and Carol who bobbed up and down on their log. Eva and Carol had to call to them.

"How do you think you're going to get it off?"

"It won't float anyway."    25

"What makes you think it will float?"

"It'll sink. Glub-blub-blub, you'll all be drownded."

The boys did not answer, because they were too busy walking around the boat, pulling at it in a testing way to see how it could be got off with the least possible damage. Frank, who was the most literate, talkative and inept of the three, began referring to the boat as *she*, an affectation which Eva and Carol acknowledged with fish-mouths of contempt.

"She's caught two places. You got to be careful not to tear a hole in her bottom. She's heavier than you'd think."

It was Clayton who climbed up and freed the boat, and Bud, a tall fat boy, who got the weight of it on his back to turn it into the water so that they could half float, half carry it to shore. All this took some time. Eva and Carol abandoned their log and waded out of the water. They walked overland to get their shoes and socks and bicycles. They did not need to come back this way but they came. They stood at the top of the hill, leaning on their bicycles. They did not go on home, but they did not sit down and frankly watch, either. They stood more or less facing each other, but glancing down at the water and at the boys struggling with the boat, as if they had just halted for a moment out of curiosity, and staying longer than they intended, to see what came of this unpromising project. 30

About nine o'clock, or when it was nearly dark—dark to people inside the houses, but not quite dark outside—they all returned to town, going along Mayo Street in a sort of procession. Frank and Bud and Clayton came carrying the boat, upside-down, and Eva and Carol walked behind, wheeling their bicycles. The boys' heads were almost hidden in the darkness of the overturned boat, with its smell of soaked wood, cold swampy water. The girls could look ahead and see the street lights in their tin reflectors, a necklace of lights climbing Mayo Street, reaching all the way up to the standpipe. They turned onto Burns Street heading for Clayton's house, the nearest house belonging to any of them. This was not the way home for Eva or for Carol either, but they followed along. The boys were perhaps too busy carrying the boat to tell them to go away. Some younger children were still out playing, playing hopscotch on the sidewalk though they could hardly see. At this time of year the bare sidewalk was still such a novelty and delight. These children cleared out of the way and watched the boat go by with unwilling respect; they shouted questions after it, wanting to know where it came from and what was going to be done with it. No one answered them. Eva and Carol as well as the boys refused to answer or even look at them.

The five of them entered Clayton's yard. The boys shifted weight, as if they were going to put the boat down.

"You better take it round to the back where nobody can see it," Carol said. That was the first thing any of them had said since they came into town.

The boys said nothing but went on, following a mud path between Clayton's house and a leaning board fence. They let the boat down in the back yard.

"It's a stolen boat, you know," said Eva, mainly for the effect. "It must've belonged to somebody. You stole it." 35

"You was the ones who stole it then," Bud said, short of breath. "It was you seen it first."

"It was you took it."

"It was all of us then. If one of us gets in trouble then all of us does."

"Are you going to tell anybody on them?" said Carol as she and Eva rode home, along the streets which were dark between the lights now and potholed from winter.

"It's up to you. I won't if you won't." 40

"I won't if you won't."

They rode in silence, relinquishing something, but not discontented.

The board fence in Clayton's back yard had every so often a post which supported it, or tried to, and it was on these posts that Eva and Carol spent several evenings sitting, jauntily but not very comfortably. Or else they just leaned against the fence while the boys worked on the boat. During the first couple of evenings neighborhood children attracted by the sound of hammering tried to get into the yard to see what was going on, but Eva and Carol blocked their way.

"Who said you could come in here?"

"Just us can come in this yard."                                        45

These evenings were getting longer, the air milder. Skipping was starting on the sidewalks. Further along the street there was a row of hard maples that had been tapped. Children drank the sap as fast as it could drip into the buckets. The old man and woman who owned the trees, and who hoped to make syrup, came running out of the house making noises as if they were trying to scare away crows. Finally, every spring, the old man would come out on his porch and fire his shotgun into the air, and then the thieving would stop.

None of those working on the boat bothered about stealing sap, though all had done so last year.

The lumber to repair the boat was picked up here and there, along back lanes. At this time of year things were lying around—old boards and branches, sodden mitts, spoons flung out with the dishwater, lids of pudding pots that had been set in the snow to cool, all the debris that can sift through and survive winter. The tools came from Clayton's cellar—left over, presumably, from the time when his father was alive—and though they had nobody to advise them the boys seemed to figure out more or less the manner in which boats are built, or rebuilt. Frank was the one who showed up with diagrams from books and *Popular Mechanics* magazines. Clayton looked at these diagrams and listened to Frank read the instructions and then went ahead and decided in his own way what was to be done. Bud was best at sawing. Eva and Carol watched everything from the fence and offered criticism and thought up names. The names for the boat that they thought of were: Water Lily, Sea Horse, Flood Queen, and Caro-Eve, after them because they had found it. The boys did not say which, if any, of these names they found satisfactory.

The boat had to be tarred. Clayton heated up a pot of tar on the kitchen stove and brought it out and painted slowly, his thorough way, sitting astride the overturned boat. The other boys were sawing a board to make a new seat. As Clayton worked, the tar cooled and thickened so that finally he could not move the brush any more. He turned to Eva and held out the pot and said, "You can go in and heat this on the stove."

Eva took the pot and went up the back steps. The kitchen seemed black          50
after outside, but it must be light enough to see in, because there was Clayton's mother standing at the ironing board, ironing. She did that for a living, took in wash and ironing.

"Please may I put the tar pot on the stove?" said Eva, who had been brought up to talk politely to parents, even wash-and-iron ladies, and who for some reason especially wanted to make a good impression on Clayton's mother.

"You'll have to poke up the fire then," said Clayton's mother, as if she doubted whether Eva would know how to do that. But Eva could see now, and she picked up the lid with the stove-lifter, and took the poker and poked up a flame. She stirred the tar as it softened. She felt privileged. Then and later. Before she went to sleep a picture of Clayton came to her mind; she saw him sitting astride the boat, tar-painting, with such concentration, delicacy, absorption. She thought of him speaking to her, out of his isolation, in such an ordinary peaceful taking-for-granted voice.

On the twenty-fourth of May, a school holiday in the middle of the week, the boat was carried out of town, a long way now, off the road over fields and fences that had been repaired, to where the river flowed between its normal banks. Eva and Carol, as well as the boys, took turns carrying it. It was launched in the water from a cow-trampled spot between willow bushes that were fresh out in leaf. The boys went first. They yelled with triumph when the boat did float, when it rode amazingly down the river current. The boat was painted black, and green inside, with yellow seats, and a strip of yellow all the way around the outside. There was no name on it, after all. The boys could not imagine that it needed any name to keep it separate from the other boats in the world.

Eva and Carol ran along the bank, carrying bags full of peanut butter-and-jam sandwiches, pickles, bananas, chocolate cake, potato chips, graham crackers stuck together with corn syrup and five bottles of pop to be cooled in the river water. The bottles bumped against their legs. They yelled for a turn.

"If they don't let us they're bastards," Carol said, and they yelled together, 55 "We found it! We found it!"

The boys did not answer, but after a while they brought the boat in, and Carol and Eva came crashing, panting down the bank.

"Does it leak?"

"It don't leak yet."

"We forgot a bailing can," wailed Carol, but nevertheless she got in, with Eva, and Frank pushed them off, crying, "Here's to a Watery Grave!"

And the thing about being in a boat was that it was not solidly bobbing, 60 like a log, but was cupped in the water, so that riding in it was not like being on something in the water, but like being in the water itself. Soon they were all going out in the boat in mixed-up turns, two boys and a girl, two girls and a boy, a girl and a boy, until things were so confused it was impossible to tell whose turn came next, and nobody cared anyway. They went down the river—those who weren't riding, running along the bank to keep up. They passed under two bridges, one iron, one cement. Once they saw a big carp just resting, it seemed to smile at them, in the bridge-shaded water. They did not know how far they had gone on the river, but things had changed—the water had got shallower, and the land flatter. Across an open field they saw a building that looked like a house, abandoned. They dragged the boat up on the bank and tied it and set out across the field.

"That's the old station," Frank said. "That's Pedder Station." The others had heard this name but he was the one who knew, because his father was the station agent in town. He said that this was a station on a branch line that had been torn up, and that there had been a sawmill here, but a long time ago.

Inside the station it was dark, cool. All the windows were broken. Glass lay in shards and in fairly big pieces on the floor. They walked around finding the larger pieces of glass and tramping on them, smashing them, it was like cracking ice on puddles. Some partitions were still in place, you could see where the ticket window had been. There was a bench lying on its side. People had been here, it looked as if people came here all the time, though it was so far from anywhere. Beer bottles and pop bottles were lying around, also cigarette packages, gum and candy wrappers, the paper from a loaf of bread. The walls were covered with dim and fresh pencil and chalk writings and carved with knives.

I LOVE RONNIE COLES

I WANT TO FUCK

KILROY WAS HERE

RONNIE COLES IS AN ASS-HOLE

WHAT ARE YOU DOING HERE?

WAITING FOR A TRAIN

DAWNA   MARY-LOU   BARBARA   JOANNE

It was exciting to be inside this large, dark, empty place, with the loud noise of breaking glass and their voices ringing back from the underside of the roof. They tipped the old beer bottles against their mouths. That reminded them that they were hungry and thirsty and they cleared a place in the middle of the floor and sat down and ate the lunch. They drank the pop just as it was, lukewarm. They ate everything there was and licked the smears of peanut butter and jam off the bread-paper in which the sandwiches had been wrapped.

They played Truth or Dare.

"I dare you to write on the wall, I am a Stupid Ass, and sign your name."    65

"Tell the truth—what is the worst lie you ever told?"

"Did you ever wet the bed?"

"Did you ever dream you were walking down the street without any clothes on?"

"I dare you to go outside and pee on the railway sign."

It was Frank who had to do that. They could not see him, even his back,    70 but they knew he did it, they heard the hissing sound of his pee. They all sat still, amazed, unable to think of what the next dare would be.

"I dare everybody," said Frank from the doorway, "I dare—Everybody."

"What?"

"Take off all our clothes."

Eva and Carol screamed.

"Anybody who won't do it has to walk—has to *crawl*—around this floor on    75 their hands and knees."

They were all quiet, till Eva said, almost complacently, "What first?"

"Shoes and socks."

"Then we have to go outside, there's too much glass here."

They pulled off their shoes and socks in the doorway, in the sudden blinding sun. The field before them was bright as water. They ran across where the tracks used to go.

That's enough, that's enough," said Carol. "Watch out for thistles!"    80

"Tops! Everybody take off their tops!"

"I won't! We won't, will we, Eva?"

But Eva was whirling round and round in the sun where the track used to be. "I don't care, I don't care! Truth or Dare! Truth or Dare!"

She unbuttoned her blouse as she whirled, as if she didn't know what her hand was doing, she flung it off.

Carol took off hers. "I wouldn't have done it, if you hadn't!"    85

"Bottoms!"

Nobody said a word this time, they all bent and stripped themselves. Eva, naked first, started running across the field, and then all the others ran, all five of them running bare through the knee-high hot grass, running towards the river. Not caring now about being caught but in fact leaping and yelling to call attention to themselves, if there was anybody to hear or see. They felt as if they were going to jump off a cliff and fly. They felt that something was happening to them different from anything that had happened before, and it had to do with the boat, the water, the sunlight, the dark ruined station, and each other. They thought of each other now hardly as names or people, but as echoing shrieks, reflections, all bold and white and loud and scandalous, and as fast as arrows. They went running without a break into the cold water and when it came almost to the tops of their legs they fell on it and swam. It stopped their noise. Silence, amazement, came over them in a rush. They dipped and floated and separated, sleek as mink.

Eva stood up in the water her hair dripping, water running down her face. She was waist deep. She stood on smooth stones, her feet fairly wide apart, water flowing between her legs. About a yard away from her Clayton also stood up, and they were blinking the water out of their eyes, looking at each other. Eva did not turn or try to hide; she was quivering from the cold of the water, but also with pride, shame, boldness, and exhilaration.

Clayton shook his head violently, as if he wanted to bang something out of it, then bent over and took a mouthful of river water. He stood up with his cheeks full and made a tight hole of his mouth and shot the water at her as if it was coming out of a hose, hitting her exactly, first one breast and then the other. Water from his mouth ran down her body. He hooted to see it, a loud self-conscious sound that nobody would have expected, from him. The others looked up from wherever they were in the water and closed in to see.

Eva crouched down and slid into the water, letting her head go right under.   90
She swam, and when she let her head out, downstream, Carol was coming after her and the boys were already on the bank, already running into the grass, showing their skinny backs, their white, flat buttocks. They were laughing and saying things to each other but she couldn't hear, for the water in her ears.

"What did he do?" said Carol.

"Nothing."

They crept in to shore. "Let's stay in the bushes till they go," said Eva. "I hate them anyway. I really do. Don't you hate them?"

"Sure," said Carol, and they waited, not very long, until they heard the boys still noisy and excited coming down to the place a bit upriver where they had left the boat. They heard them jump in and start rowing.

"They've got all the hard part, going back," said Eva, hugging herself and   95
shivering violently. "Who cares? Anyway. It never was our boat."

"What if they tell?" said Carol.

"We'll say it's all a lie."

Eva hadn't thought of this solution until she said it, but as soon as she did she felt almost light-hearted again. The ease and scornfulness of it did make them both giggle, and slapping themselves and splashing out of the water they set about developing one of those fits of laughter in which, as soon as one showed signs of exhaustion, the other would snort and start up again, and they would make helpless—soon genuinely helpless—faces at each other and bend over and grab themselves as if they had the worst pain.

## QUESTIONS

1. Consider the details used in passages of description in the story. What kinds of details are included? In the first paragraph, for example, what is the focus of interest, the flood or people's reactions to it?
2. What is the level of diction in the dialogue of the story? Do you see contractions? Slang? Grammatical mistakes? Profanity? From the dialogue what do you learn about the various speakers?
3. Study paragraph 10 as an example of the relationship of style to the character Eva as a limited-point-of-view center of interest. What does the paragraph tell you about her? How does it do so?
4. Consider the last paragraph in the story as an example of writing about action. How much action is selected for description? What verbs are used and how well do they help you visualize and imagine the sounds of the scene? What is the effect of the verb "snort"? How does the paragraph cause you to respond at the story's end?
5. What is "Truth or Dare"? What is the dare that concludes the game? To what degree is the game a guise under which boys and girls may develop their emotions toward each other?
6. Characterize the relationship between Eva and Clayton. How does this relationship help you focus on the main topic matter of the story?
7. What is the plot of the story? Who or what is in conflict? What elements are introduced as complication? What are the climax and resolution of the story?
8. How many details of setting are included? From the lifestyle and artifacts mentioned, what do you learn about the approximate time of the events in the story? About the economic level of the town? How well realized is the town? What is the effect of the facts that it is early springtime, that the water is still cold, but that in May the water is swimmable? Are there any implications for summer?
9. From the descriptions of the boys, try to characterize them. Which seems to be a planner but not a doer? Which seems competent and practical? Of Eva and Carol, which seems the leader and which the follower?

## WRITING ABOUT STYLE

In prewriting, you should consider the selected passage in the context of the entire story. What sort of passage is it? Narrative? Descriptive? Does it contain any dialogue? Is there a speaker with clearly established characteristics? How does the passage reflect his or her personality? Try to determine the level of the diction: Did you need to use a dictionary to discover the meaning of any of the words? Are there any unusual words? Any especially difficult or uncommon words? Do any of the words distract you as you read? Is there any slang? Are any words used only in particular occupations or ways of life (such as words used about drink, or automobiles, or horses, words from other languages, and so on)? Are there any contractions? Do they indicate a conversational, intimate level of speech? Are the words the most common ones that might be used? Can you think of more difficult ones? Easier ones? More accurate ones? Are there many short words? Long words?

Can you easily imagine the situations described by the words? If you have difficulty, can you find any reasons that stem out of the level of diction?

Are the sentences long, or short? Is there any variation in length? Can you observe any relationship between length and topic material? Are the sentences simple, compound, or complex? Does one type predominate? Why? Can you describe any noteworthy rhetorical devices? Are there any sentences that may be clearly established to be periodic as opposed to loose? What sort of effect is gained by this sentence or sentences? Are there any other noticeable devices? What are they? How are they used? What is their effect?

With answers to questions like these, you will readily assemble materials for your essay on the style of a passage from a story.

### Organizing Your Essay

**INTRODUCTION.**    In your introduction you should establish the particulars about the passage you are studying and should present a central idea that relates the style to these particulars. You should mention the place of the passage in the work, the general subject matter, any special ideas, the speaker, the apparent audience (if any except the general reader), and the basic method of presentation (that is, monologue, dialogue, or narration, all of which might be interspersed with argument, description, or comparison).

**BODY.**    In the body of your essay you should describe and evaluate the style of the passage. Always remember to consider the style in relationship to the circumstances of the work. For example, suppose the speaker is in a plane crashing to the ground, or in a racing car just approaching the finish line, or hurrying to meet a sweetheart; or suppose the speaker is recalling the past or considering the future. Such conditions must be kept foremost throughout your analysis.

To focus your essay, you might wish to single out one aspect of style, or to discuss everything, depending on the length of the assignment. Be sure to treat things like levels of diction, categories like specific–general and concrete–abstract, the degree of simplicity or complexity, length, numbers of words (an approach that is relatively easy for a beginning), and denotation–connotation. In discussing rhetorical aspects, go as far as you can with the nomenclature at your command. Consider things like sentence types and any specific rhetorical devices you notice and are able to describe. If you can draw attention to the elements in a parallel structure by using grammatical terms, do so. If you are able to detect the ways in which the sentences are kept simple or made complex, describe these ways. Be sure to use examples from the passage to illustrate your point; indent them and leave spaces between them and your own material.

The sort of essay envisaged here is designed to sharpen your levels of awareness at your own stage of development as a reader. Later, to the degree that you will have gained sharper perceptions and a wider descriptive vocabulary, you will be able to enhance the sophistication of your analyses.

**Conclusion.**   Whereas the body is the place for detailed descriptions and examples, your conclusion is the place where you can make evaluations of the author's style. To what extent have your discoveries in your analysis increased or reinforced your appreciation of the author's technique? Does the passage take on any added importance as a result of your study? Is there anything elsewhere in the work comparable to the content, words, or ideas that you have discussed in the passage?

### Numbers for Easy Reference

Include a copy of your passage at the beginning of your essay, as in the example. For your reader's convenience, number the sentences in the passage, and use these numbers as they become relevant in your essay.

## SAMPLE ESSAY

### O'Connor's Economy of Style in "First Confession"*

[1] Nora's turn came, and I heard the sound of something slamming, and then her voice as if butter wouldn't melt in her mouth, and then another slam, and out she came. [2] God, the hypocrisy of women. [3] Her eyes were lowered, her head was bowed, and her hands were joined very low down on her stomach, and she walked up the aisle to the side altar looking like a saint. [4] You never saw such an exhibition of devotion, and I remembered the devilish malice with which she had tormented me all the way from our door, and wondered were all religious people like that, really. [5] It was my turn now. [6] With the fear of damnation in my soul I went in, and the confessional door closed of itself behind me.

This paragraph from "First Confession" appears midway in the story. It is transitional, coming between the recollections by Jackie, the narrator, of

* See p. 172 for this story.

[1] his childhood troubles at home and his happier memory of his first confession. Though mainly narrative, the passage is punctuated by Jackie's personal reactions. While Jackie is an accurate observer, his reactions do not show much subtlety or understanding. O'Connor's economic but well-controlled style in the passage reflects both this accuracy and simplicity.° In all respects—accuracy, word level, brevity, concreteness, and grammatical control—the passage is typical of the directness and conciseness of the entire story.□

[2] The actions and responses in the paragraph are treated fully but also with great economy. The first four sentences are devoted to Nora's confession and Jackie's reactions to it. Sentence 1 refers to the sounds of Nora's confession, while the third sentence describes her show of devotion as she leaves the confessional. Each of these descriptive sentences is followed by Jackie's angry reactions. This depth of feeling is transformed to "fear of damnation" at the beginning of sentence 6, which describes Jackie's own entry into the confessional. In other words, the paragraph succinctly presents the sounds, reactions, sights, confusion, and fear inherent in the scene. O'Connor moves all these things along so swiftly and economically that the reader is hardly aware that so much is going on in so short a passage.

[3] Just as the passage is accurately observed, the level of diction is middle or neutral, enabling a full concentration on the subject. None of the words are unusual or difficult. What could be more ordinary, for example, than words like *butter*, *slam*, *hands*, *joined*, *low*, *people*, and *closed*? One may grant that *hypocrisy*, *exhibition*, *devilish malice*, *tormented*, and *damnation* are not in the speech of everyday life, but in this context they accurately describe Jackie's reactions against the religious forces which he believes are gaining control over him. Because of their aptness and because they are not excessive granted the situation, they enable the reader to focus entirely on Jackie's responses and in this respect are appropriate to the middle level of diction of the passage.

[4] In keeping with Jackie's powers of direct observation and narrative swiftness, most of the words are short. Over 78 percent have only one syllable. If one adds the nineteen two-syllable words to this total, the fraction of short words goes to 93 percent. The highest percentage of one-syllable words is in the narrative sentences (81 percent for number 1, 85 percent for 3, 100 percent for 5, and 80 percent for 6), while in the two responsive sentences, 2 and 4, the percentage of one-syllable words is lower (60 percent and 69 percent). The second sentence contains only five words, and therefore the percentage is on a small base. The percentage in the fourth sentence, however, is significant, because any expression of reactions, including Jackie's, are naturally expressed in longer, more abstract words.

Not only are the words accurate, common, and short, but most of them are specific and concrete. Nora's "turn" came, for example, and "something slammed," and Nora's "voice" was heard, and "another slam" happened and then "out she came." Equally specific is Nora's appearance while walking to the altar. Her eyes, her head, and her hands are all easily visualized. More

° Central idea.
□ Thesis sentence.

abstract are sentences 2 and 4, which detail Jackie's angry responses. Jackie's word *hypocrisy*, however (sentence 2), though an abstraction, has a clear meaning even if Jackie's attribution of the fault to women generally is not warranted by all his experiences with women in the story. Sentence 4 contains more abstractions which are highly connotative—first the "exhibition of devotion," and second the "devilish malice with which she had tormented me." But these are conclusions about the sister alone, and in context they are understandable. More problematic is Jackie's general doubt about "religious people." The observation is expressed as a child's question, and therefore, in the context, it lends itself to that aspect of the story's humor that Jackie brings directly on himself. In the last sentence, "fear of damnation" is abstract, but again it is meaningful in the light of the specific punishments described earlier in the communicants class taught by Mrs. Ryan. Despite these abstract and general words, however, most words in the paragraph are specific and concrete.

[5]

Grammatically, as well, there is great economy. Thus in the first sentence, the verb *heard* is used with three parallel direct objects (*sound*, *voice*, and *slam*), in this way cutting down on words while still detailing the major sounds of Nora's confession. Only three nouns in the paragraph are preceded by descriptive adjectives (*devilish* malice, *religious* people, and *confessional* door), and of these, only *devilish* is nonessential even though it is also colorful. Even here, however, *devilish* helps to characterize the narrator, Jackie, and therefore its presence can be justified as necessary. The third sentence best illustrates the swiftness and spareness of O'Connor's narrative style. Each of the first three clauses contains four words ("her eyes were lowered," "her head was bowed," and "her hands were joined"), with only the third being given a modifying phrase ("very low down on her stomach"). There could be no way to express these actions with fewer words, and this brevity is typical of the entire paragraph. While Jackie is an accurate observer, the skill here, of course, belongs to O'Connor.

[6]

In all respects, the passage seems to be a model of the right use of words in the right places. It is hard to imagine any other way to say what O'Connor says here. The speaker, Jackie, still retains a vivid memory of the incident as he is telling the story, and the words skillfully revive that. He also remembers his anger, and that, too, is accurately expressed. The words are direct and well chosen, and the sentences are brief and to the point, being shorter or longer as the need arises. In all respects the economic style is a means of rendering and displaying the content and is in no way a detraction of any sort. The paragraph is an example of accurate, concise narrative prose.

[7]

## Commentary on the Essay

The opening of the introductory paragraph demonstrates the way in which a passage being studied may be related to the entire work of which it is a part. Because the central idea is connected to a brief characterization of O'Connor's narrator, Jackie, the point is made that style and substance are integrated. The thesis sentence indicates five aspects of style to be considered in the essay. Any one of these, if necessary, could be more fully developed as a separate, complete essay.

Paragraph 2 treats that aspect of the style by which O'Connor covers much action and response with great economy. Paragraph 3 deals with the level of O'Connor's (or Jackie's) diction. In paragraph 4, which is closely tied to the idea in paragraph 3, the topic is the comparative shortness of most of the words. The paragraph shows how simple calculations may be used to support conclusions about diction. In paragraph 5 the topic is that the words are mostly concrete and specific, making for easy visualizing of the details. This paragraph also deals with the problem of why a slightly increased number of abstract and general words appear in those sentences in which Jackie is expressing his reactions.

Paragraph 6 treats some easily perceived aspects of grammar, always relating the discussion to the central idea. Noted in this paragraph are parallelism (and therefore the cutting down of words), the absence of descriptive adjectives, and the use of only essential words in the first three clauses of O'Connor's sentence 3. The concluding paragraph, 7, is a tribute to O'Connor's style, emphasizing again the connection of the speaker's character to the choice of words.

# 8

# Tone: Attitude and Control in Fiction

**Tone** refers to the methods by which writers convey attitudes, although the discussion of tone sometimes becomes focused on the attitudes themselves. For this reason, *tone* and *attitude* are often confused. You should remember, however, that tone refers not to attitudes but to those techniques and modes of presentation that *reveal* or *create* these attitudes.

## LITERARY TONE AND SPEAKING TONE OF VOICE

In literary study the word *tone* has been borrowed from the phrase *tone of voice*. Tone of voice in speech is a reflection of your control over your attitude toward whomever you are addressing and toward your subject matter. It is made up of many elements in addition to what you actually say: the speed with which you speak, the amount of enthusiasm that you project into your thoughts, the pitch and loudness of your speech, your facial expressions, the way you hold your body, and your distance from the person to whom you are speaking.

## TONE OF CHARACTERS WITHIN THE STORY

The idea underlying a study of tone is that all authors, like all real-life speakers, have a *choice* about what to say and how to say it, and that they make their choices in full consideration of their readers. One obvious judgment that authors make about their audience is that readers are intelligent human beings who can perceive the intricacies involved in both real and fictional human interchanges. As a specific example, John Collier, at the beginning of the grimly fanciful story "The Chaser" (the topic of the sample essay in this chapter), creates an extremely difficult situation: A young man, Alan Austen, comes to a chemist's shop seeking a love potion. The chemist, an old man, wants to tell Austen about a deadly and untraceable poison. Here the proper tone is absolutely essential. Collier must heed the integrity of his characters, which requires that not all things can be directly stated if the aims and goals of each are to be fulfilled. Therefore he has the old man speak indirectly about the poison, as follows:

> "I look at it like this," said the old man. "Please a customer with one article, and he will come back when he needs another. Even if it *is* more costly. He will save up for it, if necessary."

The indirect, veiled style of this speech shows the old chemist's assessment of the young man, Austen. If he were to say outright that Austen will eventually come back for the poison to kill the woman whom he now wants so desperately, Austen would flee immediately. So the old man uses the phrase "come back when he needs another" to suggest that in the future Austen may indeed remember these words and find himself in the category of men who want the poison. The tone of the speech, therefore, is right for the circumstances. The example shows how an author may judge and control the tone of speaking characters within a story.

## TONE AND THE AUTHOR'S ATTITUDE TOWARD READERS

The author is always aware that readers are virtual participants in the creative act and that therefore all elements of a story must be created with the audience in mind.

By controlling the style of the speech of the old man in "The Chaser," Collier also demonstrates a tone of confidence in the perceptiveness of his readers, who are able to judge whether the dialogue in the story is realistic. Suppose that Collier had written an interchange in which the old man does indeed tell Austen that someday he will return for the poison. Could one then expect sophisticated and intelligent readers to believe that Austen would still buy the love potion for which he came? Obviously Collier's answer is no. The point is that Austen, *at the moment of the story*, is young, romantic, and idealistic, but that *at a future time* he will become so cynical and so weary of his sweetheart that he will want to kill her, and that he will then remember that the old man can sell him the necessary poison. The story therefore goes forward as it does, with the old man speaking ambiguously and ominously, and with Austen hearing but not understanding the implications of what is said. Collier clearly wrote the story not only with due regard for the probability of the characters and situation, but also with a clear vision of the intelligence and perceptiveness of readers.

This example illustrates that aspect of tone involving the author's attitude toward his or her audience. Readers would instantly know that any departures from normally expected behavior—from verisimilitude— would strain credibility, as would any inappropriate language, settings, motivation, chronology, and so on.

## LITERARY ARTISTRY AS AN ASPECT OF TONE

It is possible for writers to deviate from what is ordinary—they can, should, and do—but they should never deviate from what is *human*. The task is enormous: to be sufficiently skilled to cause readers continuously to accept the story as plausible, no matter how initially implausible the outcome might seem, or how special or particular the ideas. Writers, like all speakers, may feel deeply about a subject, and they may wish to get their feelings across. If they simply express their feelings but neglect getting readers on their side, however, they are likely to create no more than an emotional display rather than a literary work. Writers must always control sentiment by tying it to objective, realistic details, because their appeal must be not only to their readers' sympathies, but also to their understandings.

With this idea in mind, let us consider the story "The Hammon and the Beans," by Américo Parédes. Underlying the story is a sense of outrage against the miseries of poverty among Mexican peasants, but the story is not an indignant diatribe; instead, the principal action is the death of a little Mexican peasant girl named Chonita. The problem is determining the control with which Parédes treats this event. The death of a poor, helpless child, serious as it is, could easily become an occasion for sentimentality. It could also be received indifferently unless the death can be related to other things about which we care. In view of these problems, Parédes controls his material skillfully in order to put the death in perspective and at the same time to cause deep concern in the reader. He uses a doctor to report Chonita's death. This doctor, conversing with the narrator's father, then discusses disease, the callous behavior of Chonita's stepfather, the wretched life of the local Mexican peasants, and other topics that are both political and historical. Their commentary, which includes the doctor's angry outburst, followed by the narrator's personal response of tears, provides a context for Chonita's death. She becomes not only an object of pathos, but a case study of the effects of injustice and political neglect. By thus providing a larger context of human, personal, medical, social, military, and political matters, Parédes has exhibited great artistic control over tone in "The Hammon and the Beans." His social and political ideas are clear, and the underlying note of indignation is also clear, but above all the story is effective, well controlled, and beautiful.


## LAUGHTER, COMEDY, AND FARCE

A major aspect of tone is laughter and the methods of comedy and farce. No two critics agree on what exactly makes people laugh, but all agree that laughter is essential in a person's psychological well-being. Laughter is an unpredictable action; what a person finds amusing today will not move him or her tomorrow. The causes of laughter are complicated and difficult to analyze and isolate. However, the major elements in laughter seem to be these:

1. *An object of laughter.*   There must be something to laugh at, whether a person, thing, situation, custom, habit of speech or dialect, or arrangement of words.

2. *Incongruity.*   Human beings have a sense of what to expect under given conditions, and anything that violates these expectations may be a cause of laughter. On a day when the temperature is 100°F., for example, you would reasonably expect people to dress lightly. But if you saw a person dressed in a heavy overcoat, a warm hat, a muffler, and large gloves, who was shivering, waving his arms, and stamping his feet as though to keep them warm, you would likely laugh because this person would have violated your expectation of what a sane person would do under the conditions. His response to the weather is inappropriate or *incongruous*, an incongruity of *situation*. The standup comedian's story that, "Yesterday afternoon I was walking down the street and turned into a drugstore," is funny because "turned into" can have two incompatible meanings. Here the language itself has furnished its own incongruity. A student once wrote that in high school he had enjoyed singing in the "archipelago choir." This is an inadvertent verbal mistake called a *malapropism*, after Mrs. Malaprop, a character in Richard Brinsley Sheridan's play *The Rivals*. In the student's report about the choir, you expect to see *a capella*—or at least a recognizable misspelling of the word—and when you see *archipelago*, a word that makes sense elsewhere and sounds something like *a capella*, you laugh, or at least smile. Incongruity is the quality common to all these instances of laughter. In the literary creation of such verbal slips, the tone is directed against the speaker, and the author and reader both share the enjoyment.

3. *Safety and/or goodwill.*   Seeing a person who has just slipped on a banana peel hurtling through the air and about to crack his or her skull may cause laughter as long as we ourselves are not that person, for our laughter depends on our being insulated from danger and pain. In farce,

where a great deal of physical abuse takes place, such as falling through trapdoors or being hit in the face by cream pies, the abuse never harms the participants. The incongruity of such situations causes laughter, and one's safety from personal consequences—together with the insulation from pain of the participants—prevents the interference of more grave or even horrified responses. The element of goodwill enters into laughter in romantic comedy or in works where you are drawn into general sympathy with the major figures, such as Walter and Ellen in Shirley Jackson's "About Two Nice People." Here the infectiousness of laughter and happiness influences your responses. As the author leads the characters toward success, your involvement with them will produce a general sense of happiness which may cause you to smile and also may cause you to laugh sympathetically.

4. *Unfamiliarity, newness, uniqueness, spontaneity.* Laughter depends on seeing something new or unique, or on experiencing a known thing freshly. Laughter usually occurs in a flash of insight or revelation, and the situation producing laughter must always possess spontaneity. This is not to say that ordinary situations are excluded as topics of humor. Indeed, the task of the comic writer is to develop ordinary materials to the point of instant recognition, when spontaneity enables laughter to proceed. For example, Jackson's "About Two Nice People" is, among other things, about the friction that develops between people living in adjoining apartments. There is nothing unusual here, but Jackson's artistry creates humor out of the ordinary. As a crisis of the situation between the young man, Walter, and the young woman, Ellen, Walter calls in his wealthy aunt, Mrs. Nesmith, to scare Ellen. However, this lady, who owns the apartment building, stops short in her badgering by refraining from threatening Ellen with eviction, because, she says, "Apartments are too hard to get these days. . . . That would have been too unkind." Here the author has developed a joke out of the housing shortage and in this way has created the spontaneity necessary for laughter.

### Irony

One of the most human traits is the capacity to have two or more attitudes toward something. You might love someone but on occasion express your affection by insults rather than praise. A large number of contemporary greeting cards feature witty insults, because many people cannot stand the sentimentality of the "straight" cards and send the insulting card in the expectation that the person receiving it will be amused and will recognize genuine fondness on the sender's part. Expressions in which one attitude is conveyed by its opposite are *ironic*. **Irony** is a mode of ambiguous or indirect expression; it is natural to human beings who are aware of the possibilities and complexities in life. Irony is a function of the realization that life does not always measure up to promise, that friends and loved ones may sometimes be angry and bitter toward each other, that the universe offers mysteries that human beings cannot comprehend, that doubt exists even in the face of certainty, and that character is built through chagrin, regret, and pain as much as through emulation and praise. In expressing an idea ironically, writers pay the greatest compliment to their readers, for they assume sufficient skill and understanding to see through the surface statement into the seriousness or levity beneath.

The major types of irony are *verbal*, *situational*, and *dramatic*. **Verbal irony** is a statement in which one thing is said and another is meant. For example, one of the American astronauts was once asked how he would feel if all his reentry safety equipment failed as he was coming back to earth. He answered, "A thing like that could ruin your whole day." His words would have been appropriate for day-to-day minor mishaps, but since failed safety equipment would cause his death, his answer was ironic. This form of verbal irony is **understatement.** By contrast, **overstatement** or **hyperbole** is exaggeration for effect, as in "I'll love you till the oceans go dry." Often verbal irony is ambiguous, having double meaning or **double-entendre.** At the end of Collier's "The Chaser," for example, the old man responds to Austen's "Good-bye" with the French farewell salutation "Au revoir." This phrase, meaning "Until I see you again," is not especially unusual, and on the surface it seems fairly innocent, but the context makes clear that the old man's final words are a dire prediction that Austen will return one day for the untraceable poison. In other words, the old man's statement has two meanings, one innocent and the other sinister. Ambiguity of course may be used in relation to any topic. Quite often *double-entendre* is used in statements about sexuality and love, usually for the amusement of listeners or readers.

The term **situational irony,** or **irony of situation,** refers to conditions that are measured against forces that transcend and overpower human capacities. These forces may be psychological, social, political, or environmental. The sample essay on Collier's "The Chaser" develops the idea that Collier's story is based on the irony of the situation in which an unrealistic desire for romantic possession leads people inevitably toward destructiveness rather than everlasting love. Situational irony that is connected with a pessimistic or fatalistic view of life is sometimes called **irony of fate** or **cosmic irony.** It is such an irony of fate that we find in "The Hammon and the Beans" by Parédes. In the setting of Mexican-American families living in poverty in Texas, the dead little girl, Chonita, is no more than a minor statistic; her life is only an insignificant part of a gigantic pattern of social and political neglect. If we consider that she had been a human being with a great potential for growth, however, we could justifiably conclude that she might have matured to be an engaging, bright adult who could lead a productive, happy life. She could have been important. However, under the circumstances of poverty, ill education, and poor nutrition and care she never has a chance. Her situation, and that of those like her, is ironically fatal, for the implication of "The Hammon and the Beans" is that human beings are caught in a web of circumstances from which they cannot escape.

Situational irony could of course work in a more optimistic context. For example, an average, or even blockheaded person could go through a set of difficult circumstances and be on the verge of losing everything in life, but, through someone's perversity or through luck, might emerge successfully, as does Scoresby in Mark Twain's story "Luck." Such a situation could reflect an author's conception of a benevolent universe, or, as in the case of Scoresby, a more arbitrarily comic one. Most often, however, situational irony is like that in the story by Parédes.

**Dramatic irony** is a special kind of situational irony; it applies when a character perceives a situation in a limited way while the audience, including other characters, may see it in greater perspective. The character therefore is able to understand things in only one way while the larger audience can perceive two. The character Austen in "The Chaser" is locked into such irony; he believes that the only potion he will ever need is the one that will win him love, while the old man and the readers know that he will one day return for the poison. The classic example of dramatic irony is found in the play *Oedipus Rex* by Sophocles. All his life Oedipus has been enclosed by fate, which he can never escape. As the play draws to its climax and Oedipus believes that he is about to discover the murderer of his father, the audience knows that he is drawing closer to the point of his own self-destruction: As he condemns the murderer, he is also condemning himself.

## READING FOR TONE

Because so many parts of a story—situation, character, style, audience—are relevant to a consideration of tone, it is important to read with alertness to the potential full impact of any particular passage. To see how everything can work at once, let us consider Jonathan Swift's novelistic satire *Gulliver's Travels* (1726), a work known for its control of tone. The following passage from the fourth voyage is readily approachable for modern readers, for it contains a list of weaponry and the horrors of warfare (alas). Swift's speaker is the protagonist Gulliver, who is describing eighteenth-century English military exploits with a certain degree of naive pride:

. . . being no stranger to the art of war, I gave . . . a description of cannons, culverins, muskets, carabines, pistols, bullets, powder, swords, bayonets, battles, sieges, retreats, attacks, undermines, countermines, bombardments, seafights; ships sunk with a thousand men, twenty thousand killed on each side; dying groans, limbs flying in the air, smoke, noise, confusion, trampling to death under horses' feet; flight, pursuit, victory; fields strewed with carcasses left for food to dogs, and wolves, and birds of prey; plundering, stripping, ravishing, burning and destroying. And to set forth the valour of my own dear countrymen, I assured him, that I had seen them blow up a hundred enemies at once in a siege, and as many in a ship, and beheld the dead bodies drop down in pieces from the clouds, to the great diversion of all the spectators.

The tone is that of condemnation, angry but cold. Swift is in control. He achieves his tone in a number of ways. First, Gulliver thinks he is praising war while the sensitive reader receives entirely different signals. The reader and Swift provide a humane political and moral context against which Gulliver's words are to be measured. Thus we have an example of situational irony. Second, the texture of the passage is one of accumulation. Swift has Gulliver list all the death-dealing weapons and all the horrible consequences of warfare. The condemnation of war is achieved by the multiplication of examples alone, virtually overcoming all possible opposing views. Third, there is verbal irony in phrases like "the valour of my own dear countrymen" and "to the great diversion of all the spectators." This is hyperbole that cuttingly exposes the callousness to suffering that usually accompanies war. Fourth, the passage is capable of producing laughter— not happy laughter, but laughter of amazement and repulsion at the incongruity caused by the common moral pretensions of many people and their dereliction of these pretensions during warfare. When you read the passage, you respond to everything at once, yet analysis reveals a passage of high complexity. Swift's control of tone is the cause of your responses.

As you read, then, remember that studying tone requires an awareness of everything in a work that contributes to more than denotative statement. To perceive tone you should be constantly aware of the general impressions that various passages leave you with and you should be analytical enough to study the ways the writers achieve these effects. It is necessary first to understand all the words and all the situations. Read the work carefully, and then study passages selected for discussion to determine matters such as the situations that prompt dialogue, the appropriateness of style (e.g., speech to character, descriptions to setting and action), the comparative freedom the characters may exert to control their fates, the presence of humor, and apparent attitudes toward readers. Because so much in the story may affect the tone, it is important not to overlook anything that can be relevant.

# AMÉRICO PARÉDES (b. 1915)

*The Hammon and the Beans*                                                    1963

Once we lived in one of my grandfather's houses near Fort Jones.° It was just a block from the parade grounds, a big frame house painted a dirty yellow. My mother hated it, especially because of the pigeons that cooed all day about the eaves. They had fleas, she said. But it was a quiet neighborhood at least, too far from the center of town for automobiles and too near for musical, night-roaming drunks.

At this time Jonesville-on-the Grande was not the thriving little city that it is today. We told off our days by the routine on the post. At six sharp the flag was raised on the parade grounds to the cackling of the bugles, and a field piece thundered out a salute. The sound of the shot bounced away through the morning mist until its echoes worked their way into every corner of town. Jonesville-on-the-Grande woke to the cannon's roar, as if to battle, and the day began.

At eight the whistle from the post laundry sent us children off to school. The whole town stopped for lunch with the noon whistle, and after lunch everybody went back to work when the post laundry said that it was one o'clock, except for those who could afford to be old-fashioned and took the siesta. The post was the town's clock, you might have said, or like some insistent elder person who was always there to tell you it was time.

At six the flag came down, and we went to watch through the high wire fence that divided the post from the town. Sometimes we joined in the ceremony, standing at salute until the sound of the cannon made us jump. That must have been when we had just studied about George Washington in school, or recited "The Song of Marion's Men"° about Marion the Fox and the British cavalry that chased him up and down the broad Santee. But at other times we stuck out our tongues and jeered at the soldiers. Perhaps the night before we had hung at the edges of a group of old men and listened to tales about Aniceto Pizaña and the "border troubles,"° as the local paper still called them when it referred to them gingerly in passing.

It was because of the border troubles, ten years or so before, that the soldiers        5
had come back to old Fort Jones. But we did not hate them for that; we admired them even, at least sometimes. But when we were thinking about the border troubles instead of Marion the Fox we hooted them and the flag they were lowering, which

---

*Fort Jones*: The setting of Fort Jones and Jonesville-on-the Grande in Texas is fictional. The story takes place in the mid-1920s, one of the most turbulent periods of Mexican history and only a few years after the deaths of two of the greatest heroes of the Mexican revolution— Pancho Villa (1877–1923) and Emiliano Zapata (ca. 1879–1919).

*"Song of Marion's Men"*: a poem by William Cullen Bryant (1794–1878) about Colonel Francis Marion (ca. 1732–1795), who was a leader of irregular guerilla forces in South Carolina during the Revolutionary War. Because of his hit-and-run tactics, involving his hiding in the swamps near the "broad Santee" river in South Carolina, Marion was given the name of the "Swamp Fox."

*border troubles*: The most serious border incidents occurred in 1916, when Pancho Villa was responsible for deaths of Americans on both sides of the border. He made repeated raids into New Mexico and Texas.

for the moment was theirs alone, just as we would have jeered an opposing ball team, in a friendly sort of way. On these occasions even Chonita would join in the mockery, though she usually ran home at the stroke of six. But whether we taunted or saluted, the distant men in khaki uniforms went about their motions without noticing us at all.

The last word from the post came in the night when a distant bugle blew. At nine it was all right because all the lights were on. But sometimes I heard it at eleven when everything was dark and still, and it made me feel that I was all alone in the world. I would even doubt that I was me, and that put me in such a fright that I felt like yelling out just to make sure I was really there. But next morning the sun shone and life began all over again. With its whistles and cannon shots and bugles blowing. And so we lived, we and the post, side by side with the wire fence in between.

The wandering soldiers whom the bugle called home at night did not wander in our neighborhood, and none of us ever went into Fort Jones. None except Chonita. Every evening when the flag came down she would leave off playing and go down towards what was known as the "lower" gate of the post, the one that opened not on Main Street but against the poorest part of town. She went into the grounds and to the mess halls and pressed her nose against the screens and watched the soldiers eat. They sat at long tables calling to each other through food-stuffed mouths.

"Hey bud, pass the coffee!"

"Give me the ham!"

"Yeah, give me the beans!"

10

After the soldiers were through the cooks came out and scolded Chonita, and then they gave her packages with things to eat.

Chonita's mother did our washing, in gratefulness—as my mother put it—for the use of a vacant lot of my grandfather's which was a couple of blocks down the street. On the lot was an old one-room shack which had been a shed long ago, and this Chonita's father had patched up with flattened-out pieces of tin. He was a laborer. Ever since the end of the border troubles there had been a development boom in the Valley, and Chonita's father was getting his share of the good times. Clearing brush and building irrigation ditches he sometimes pulled down as much as six dollars a week. He drank a good deal of it up, it was true. But corn was just a few cents a bushel in those days. He was the breadwinner, you might say, while Chonita furnished the luxuries.

Chonita was a poet too. I had just moved into the neighborhood when a boy came up to me and said, "Come on! Let's go hear Chonita make a speech."

She was already on top of the alley fence when we got there, a scrawny little girl of about nine, her bare dirty feet clinging to the fence almost like hands. A dozen other kids were there below her, waiting. Some were boys I knew at school; five or six were her younger brothers and sisters.

"Speech! Speech!" they all cried. "Let Chonita make a speech! Talk in English, Chonita!"

15

They were grinning and nudging each other except for her brothers and sisters, who looked up at her with proud serious faces. She gazed out beyond us all with a grand, distant air and then she spoke.

"Give me the hammon and the beans!" she yelled. "Give me the hammon and the beans!"

She leaped off the fence and everybody cheered and told her how good it was and how she could talk English better than the teachers at the grammar school.

I thought it was a pretty poor joke. Every evening almost, they would make her get up on the fence and yell, "Give me the hammon and the beans!" And everybody would cheer and make her think she was talking English. As for me, I would wait there until she got it over with so we could play at something else. I wondered how long it would be before they got tired of it all. I never did find out because just about that time I got the chills and fever, and when I got up and around Chonita wasn't there anymore.

In later years I thought of her a lot, especially during the thirties when I was growing up. Those years would have been just made for her. Many's the time I have seen her in my mind's eyes, in the picket lines demanding not bread, not cake, but the hammon and the beans. But it didn't work out that way.

One night Doctor Zapata came into our kitchen through the back door. He set his bag on the table and said to my father, who had opened the door for him, "Well, she is dead."

My father flinched. "What was it?" he asked.

The doctor had gone to the window and he stood with his back to us, looking out toward the light of Fort Jones. "Pneumonia, flu, malnutrition, worms, the evil eye," he said without turning around. "What the hell difference does it make?"

"I wish I had known how sick she was," my father said in a very mild tone. "Not that it's really my affair, but I wish I had."

The doctor snorted and shook his head.

My mother came in and I asked her who was dead. She told me. It made me feel strange but I did not cry. My mother put her arm around my shoulders. "She is in Heaven now," she said. "She is happy."

I shrugged her arm away and sat down in one of the kitchen chairs.

"They're like animals," the doctor was saying. He turned round suddenly and his eyes glistened in the light. "Do you know what that brute of a father was doing when I left? He was laughing! Drinking and laughing with his friends."

"There's no telling what the poor man feels," my mother said.

My father made a deprecatory gesture. "It wasn't his daughter anyway."

"No?" the doctor said. He sounded interested.

"This is the woman's second husband," my father explained. "First one died before the girl was born, shot and hanged from a mesquite limb. He was working too close to the tracks the day the Olmito train was derailed."

"You know what?" the doctor said. "In classical times they did things better. Take Troy, for instance. After they stormed the city they grabbed the babies by the heels and dashed them against the wall. That was more humane."

My father smiled. "You sound very radical. You sound just like your relative down there in Morelos."°

"No relative of mine," the doctor said. "I'm a conservative, the son of a conservative, and you know that I wouldn't be here except for that little detail."

"Habit," my father said. "Pure habit, pure tradition. You're a radical at heart."

"It depends on how you define radicalism," the doctor answered. "People tend to use words too loosely. A dentist could be called a radical, I suppose. He pulls up things by the roots."

*Morelos*: the home state of Zapata.

My father chuckled.

"Any bandit in Mexico nowadays can give himself a political label," the doctor went on, "and that makes him respectable. He's a leader of the people."

"Take Villa, now—" my father began.                                                    40

"Villa was a different type of man," the doctor broke in.

"I don't see any difference."

The doctor came over to the table and sat down. "Now look at it this way," he began, his finger in front of my father's face. My father threw back his head and laughed.

"You'd better go to bed and rest," my mother told me. "You're not completely well, you know."

So I went to bed, but I didn't go to sleep, not right away. I lay there for a         45
long time while behind my darkened eyelids Emiliano Zapata's cavalry charged down to the broad Santee, where there were grave men with hoary hairs.° I was still awake at eleven when the cold voice of the bugle went gliding in and out of the dark like something that couldn't find its way back to wherever it had been. I thought of Chonita in Heaven, and I saw her in her torn and dirty dress, with a pair of bright wings attached, flying round and round like a butterfly shouting, "Give me the hammon and the beans!"

Then I cried. And whether it was the bugle, or whether it was Chonita or what, to this day I do not know. But cry I did, and I felt much better after that.

*Grave men with hoary hairs*: Cf. lines 49–52 of Bryant's "Song of Marion's Men:"

> Grave Men there are by broad Santee,
>     Grave men with hoary hairs;
> Their hearts are all with Marion,
>     For Marion are their prayers.

# QUESTIONS

1.  How does Parédes establish the setting of the story? What is the significance of the fort? Of the "dirty yellow" paint? Of the vacant lot and the shack?

2.  What is the point of view in the story? Who is the narrator? About how old was the narrator when the events related in the story occurred? About how old is the narrator as he or she tells the story? What effect is produced by this difference in age?

3.  What effect does "Fort Jones" have on "Jonesville-on-the-Grande"? What two opposing attitudes do the children have toward the fort and the soldiers? How might you account for these two attitudes?

4.  Who is the protagonist in the story? Who (or what) is the antagonist?

5.  How is Chonita described? What is her family like? How do her actions at the mess hall and her "speeches" help characterize her and her family?

6.  Is Chonita a round or flat character? Dynamic or static? Individual or representative? To what extent do the author's choices about this character allow her to work as a symbol or representative of a whole ethnic group?

7.  What is the central conflict in the story? Where is the climax? To what extent is the central conflict resolved?

8. What is the tone of the story (some possibilities: joyful, sorrowful, ironic, cynical, resigned, bitter, resentful)? What techniques does Parédes use to control the tone?

9. To what extent does the characterization of Doctor Zapata (interesting name) help to control the tone? How does the doctor's own attitude toward Chonita's death and the words he uses to announce it help to control the tone?

10. Describe the concern in the story with political, social, and broadly human problems. How does the tale of Chonita's brief life and her death figure into the larger sociopolitical framework of the story?

11. Describe the irony of the situation in which the Mexican-American children learn in school about Washington, the American Revolutionary War, and the guerilla tactics of Marion but seem to be taught nothing about the political movements represented by Villa and Zapata?

12. Near the conclusion of Bryant's "Song of Marion's Men" the following four lines appear:

> And lovely ladies greet our band [i.e., of soldiers]
>   With kindliest welcoming,
> And smiles like those of summer,
>   And tears like those of spring.
>     —lines 53–56

Contrast the women of these lines with the narrator's vision of Chonita in heaven. How might this vision affect the narrator's thoughts about the meaning of Chonita's life in subsequent years (he says that he thought about her many times in the 1930's)?

# JOHN COLLIER (1901–1980)

*The Chaser*                                                           *1940*

Alan Austen, as nervous as a kitten, went up certain dark and creaky stairs in the neighborhood of Pell Street, and peered about for a long time on the dim landing before he found the name he wanted written obscurely on one of the doors.

He pushed open this door, as he had been told to do, and found himself in a tiny room, which contained no furniture but a plain kitchen table, a rocking-chair, and an ordinary chair. On one of the dirty buff-coloured walls were a couple of shelves, containing in all perhaps a dozen bottles and jars.

An old man sat in the rocking-chair, reading a newspaper. Alan, without a word, handed him the card he had been given. "Sit down, Mr. Austen," said the old man very politely. "I am glad to make your acquaintance."

"Is it true," asked Alan, "that you have a certain mixture that has—er—quite extraordinary effects?"

"My dear sir," replied the old man, "my stock in trade is not very large—I don't deal in laxatives and teething mixtures—but such as it is, it is varied. I think nothing I sell has effects which could be precisely described as ordinary."

"Well, the fact is . . ." began Alan.

"Here, for example," interrupted the old man, reaching for a bottle from

5

the shelf. "Here is a liquid as colourless as water, almost tasteless, quite imperceptible in coffee, wine, or any other beverage. It is also quite imperceptible to any
known method of autopsy."

"Do you mean it is a poison?" cried Alan, very much horrified.

"Call it a glove-cleaner if you like," said the old man indifferently. "Maybe
it will clean gloves. I have never tried. One might call it a life-cleaner. Lives need
cleaning sometimes.

"I want nothing of that sort," said Alan.                                           10

"Probably it is just as well," said the old man. "Do you know the price of
this? For one teaspoonful, which is sufficient, I ask five thousand dollars. Never
less. Not a penny less."

"I hope all your mixtures are not as expensive," said Alan apprehensively.

"Oh dear, no," said the old man. "It would be no good charging that sort
of price for a love potion, for example. Young people who need a love potion
very seldom have five thousand dollars. Otherwise they would not need a love
potion."

"I am glad to hear that," said Alan.

"I look at it like this," said the old man. "Please a customer with one article,    15
and he will come back when he needs another. Even if it *is* more costly. He will
save up for it, if necessary."

"So," said Alan, "you really do sell love potions?"

"If I did not sell love potions," said the old man, reaching for another bottle,
"I should not have mentioned the other matter to you. It is only when one is in
a position to oblige that one can afford to be so confidential."

"And these potions," said Alan. "They are not just—just—er—"

"Oh, no," said the old man. "Their effects are permanent, and extend far
beyond the mere casual impulse. But they include it. Oh, yes, they include it.
Bountifully, insistently. Everlastingly."

"Dear me!" said Alan, attempting a look of scientific detachment. "How          20
very interesting!"

"But consider the spiritual side," said the old man.

"I do, indeed," said Alan.

"For indifference," said the old man, "they substitute devotion. For scorn,
adoration. Give one tiny measure of this to the young lady—its flavour is imperceptible in orange juice, soup, or cocktails—and however gay and giddy she is, she
will change altogether. She will want nothing but solitude and you."

"I can hardly believe it," said Alan. "She is so fond of parties."

"She will not like them any more," said the old man. "She will be afraid of    25
the pretty girls you may meet."

"She will actually be jealous?" cried Alan in a rapture. "Of me?"

"Yes, she will want to be everything to you."

"She is, already. Only she doesn't care about it."

"She will, when she has taken this. She will care intensely. You will be her
sole interest in life."

"Wonderful!" cried Alan.                                                        30

"She will want to know all you do," said the old man. "All that has happened
to you during the day. Every word of it. She will want to know what you are
thinking about, why you smile suddenly, why you are looking sad."

"That is love!" cried Alan.

"Yes," said the old man. "How carefully she will look after you! She will never allow you to be tired, to sit in a draught, to neglect your food. If you are an hour late, she will be terrified. She will think you are killed, or that some siren has caught you."

"I can hardly imagine Diana like that!" cried Alan, overwhelmed with joy.

"You will not have to use your imagination," said the old man. "And, by the way, since there are always sirens, if by any chance you *should*, later on, slip a little, you need not worry. She will forgive you, in the end. She will be terribly hurt, of course, but she will forgive you—in the end." 35

"That will not happen," said Alan fervently.

"Of course not," said the old man. "But, if it did, you need not worry. She would never divorce you. Oh, no! And, of course, she will never give you the least, the very least, grounds for—uneasiness."

"And how much," said Alan, "is this wonderful mixture?"

"It is not as dear," said the old man, "as the glove-cleaner, or life-cleaner, as I sometimes call it. No. That is five thousand dollars, never a penny less. One has to be older than you are, to indulge in that sort of thing. One has to save up for it."

"But the love potion?" said Alan. 40

"Oh, that," said the old man, opening the drawer in the kitchen table, and taking out a tiny, rather dirty-looking phial. "That is just a dollar."

"I can't tell you how grateful I am," said Alan, watching him fill it.

"I like to oblige," said the old man. "Then customers come back, later in life, when they are better off, and want more expensive things. Here you are. You will find it very effective."

"Thank you again," said Alan. "Good-bye."

"Au revoir," said the old man. 45

## QUESTIONS

1. Summarize the plot of this story. What are the qualities of the poison that the old man tells Austen about? What are the powers of the love potion? What is the connection between the love potion and the "spot remover"?

2. Who is the protagonist in the story? What is his problem? What is the solution to his problem?

3. What is the central conflict in the story? How is this conflict resolved? To what extent is this resolution complete? What new problem or conflict is introduced at the end of the story?

4. Are the two characters in this story static or dynamic? Round or flat? Representative or individual? To what extent do these choices help focus the story and control the tone?

5. What type of person is Alan Austen? What does he think love should be? What is the old man's attitude toward love?

6. What is Diana like? What does Alan want her to be like? What does the old man say she will be like after drinking the love potion?

7.  How is the setting of the story described? What is the old man's apartment like? How does this description contribute to the mood of the story and the characterization of the old man?

8.  What point of view is used in the story? What is the effect of using this point of view? What does it force us to do?

9.  To what extent do the words of the story control the tone and attitude? What specific words help us form an attitude toward Alan Austen? Toward the old man?

10. To what extent is the story ironic? What do we and the old man know that Alan Austen doesn't?

11. How is the title of the story ironic? What is a "chaser"? How are the old man's last words in the story ironic?

12. What point does this story make about love? About youth? About human desire? How can the story be taken as a commentary about the need for developing love relationships that preserve individuality as well as romantic commitment?

## SHIRLEY JACKSON (1919–1965)

*About Two Nice People*                                                    *1951*

A problem of some importance, certainly, these days, is that of anger. When one half of the world is angry at the other half, or one half of a nation is angry at the rest, or one side of town feuds with the other side, it is hardly surprising, when you stop to think about it, that so many people lose their tempers with so many other people. Even if, as in this case, they are two people not usually angry, two people whose lives are obscure and whose emotions are gentle, whose smiles are amiable and whose voices are more apt to be cheerful than raised in fury. Two people, in other words, who would much rather be friends than not and who yet, for some reason, perhaps chemical or sociological or environmental, enter upon a mutual feeling of dislike so intense that only a very drastic means can bring them out of it.

Take two such people:

Ellen Webster was what is referred to among her friends as a "sweet" girl. She had pretty, soft hair and dark, soft eyes, and she dressed in soft colors and wore frequently a lovely old-fashioned brooch which had belonged to her grandmother. Ellen thought of herself as a very happy and very lucky person, because she had a good job, was able to buy herself a fair number of soft-colored dresses and skirts and sweaters and coats and hats; she had, by working hard at it evenings, transformed her one-room apartment from a bare, neat place into a charming little refuge with her sewing basket on the table and a canary at the window; she had a reasonable conviction that someday, perhaps soon, she would fall in love with a nice young man and they would be married and Ellen would devote herself wholeheartedly to children and baking cakes and mending socks. This not-very-unusual situation, with its perfectly ordinary state of mind, was a source of great happiness to Ellen. She was, in a word, not one of those who rail against their fate, who live in sullen hatred of the world. She was—her friends were right—a sweet girl.

On the other hand, even if you would not have called Walter Nesmith sweet, you would very readily have thought of him as a "nice" fellow, or an "agreeable" person, or even—if you happened to be a little old white-haired lady—a "dear boy." There was a subtle resemblance between Ellen Webster and Walter Nesmith. Both of them were the first resort of their friends in trouble, for instance. Walter's ambitions, which included the rest of his life, were refreshingly similar to Ellen's: Walter thought that someday he might meet some sweet girl, and would then devote himself wholeheartedly to coming home of an evening to read his paper and perhaps work in the garden on Sundays.

Walter thought that he would like to have two children, a boy and a girl.        5
Ellen thought that she would like to have three children, a boy and two girls. Walter was very fond of cherry pie, Ellen preferred Boston cream. Ellen enjoyed romantic movies, Walter preferred Westerns. They read almost exactly the same books.

In the ordinary course of events, the friction between Ellen and Walter would have been very slight. But—and what could cause a thing like this?—the ordinary course of events was shattered by a trifle like a telephone call.

Ellen's telephone number was 3—4126. Walter's telephone number was 3—4216. Ellen lived in apartment 3-A and Walter lived in apartment 3-B; these apartments were across the hall from each other and very often Ellen, opening her door at precisely quarter of nine in the morning and going toward the elevator, met Walter, who opened *his* door at precisely quarter of nine in the morning and went toward the elevator. On these occasions Ellen customarily said "Good morning" and looked steadfastly the other way. Walter usually answered "Good morning," and avoided looking in her direction. Ellen thought that a girl who allowed herself to be informal with strangers created a bad impression, and Walter thought that a man who took advantage of living in the same building to strike up an acquaintance with a girl was a man of little principle. One particularly fine morning, he said to Ellen in the elevator, "Lovely day," and she replied, "Yes, isn't it?" and both of them felt scarcely that they had been bold. How this mutual respect for each other's dignity could have degenerated into fury is a mystery not easily understood.

It happened that one evening—and, to do her strict justice, Ellen had had a hard day, she was coming down with a cold, it had rained steadily for a week, her stockings were unwashed, and she had broken a fingernail—the phone which had the number 3—4126 rang. Ellen had been opening a can of chicken soup in the kitchenette, and she had her hands full; she said "Darn," and managed to drop and break a cup in her hurry to answer the phone.

"Hello?" she said, thinking, *This is going to be something cheerful*.

"Hello, is Walter there?"        10

"Walter?"

"Walter Nesmith. I want to speak to Walter, please."

"This is the wrong number," Ellen said thinking with the self-pity that comes with the first stages of a head cold that no one ever called *her*.

"Is this three—four two one six?"

"This is three four one two six," Ellen said, and hung up.                                    15

At that time, although she knew that the person in the apartment across the hall was named Walter Nesmith, she could not have told the color of his hair or even of the outside of his apartment door. She went back to her soup and had a match in her hand to light the stove when the phone rang again.

"Hello?" Ellen said without enthusiasm; this *could* be someone cheerful, she was thinking.

"Hello, is Walter there?"

"This is the wrong number again," Ellen said; if she had not been such a very sweet girl she might have let more irritation show in her voice.

"I *want* to *speak* to Walter Nesmith, *please*."                                           20

"This is three—four one two six again," Ellen said patiently. "You want three—four two one six."

"What?" said the voice.

"This," said Ellen, "is number three—four one two six. The number you want is three—four two one six." Like anyone who has tried to say a series of numbers several times, she found her anger growing. Surely anyone of *normal* intelligence, she was thinking, surely anyone *ought* to be able to dial a phone, anyone who can't dial a phone shouldn't be allowed to have a nickel.

She got all the way back into the kitchenette and was reaching out for the can of soup before the phone rang again. This time when she answered she said "Hello?" rather sharply for Ellen, and with no illusions about who it was going to be.

"Hello, may I please speak to Walter?"                                                        25

At that point it started. Ellen had a headache and it was raining and she was tired and she was apparently not going to get any chicken soup until this annoyance was stopped.

"Just a minute," she said into the phone.

She put the phone down with an understandable bang on the table, and marched, without taking time to think, out of her apartment and up to the door across the hall. "Walter Nesmith" said a small card at the doorbell. Ellen rang the doorbell with what was, for her, a vicious poke. When the door opened she said immediately, without looking at him:

"Are you Walter Nesmith?"

Now Walter had had a hard day, too, and *he* was coming down with a cold,          30
and *he* had been trying ineffectually to make himself a cup of hot tea in which he intended to put a spoonful of honey to ease his throat, that being a remedy his aunt had always recommended for the first onslaught of a cold. If there had been one fraction less irritation in Ellen's voice, or if Walter had not taken off his shoes when he came home that night, it might very probably have turned out to be a pleasant introduction, with Walter and Ellen dining together on chicken soup and hot tea, and perhaps even sharing a bottle of cough medicine. But when Walter opened the door and heard Ellen's voice, he was unable to answer her cordially, and so he said briefly:

"I am. Why?"

"Will you please come and answer my phone?" said Ellen, too annoyed to realize that this request might perhaps bewilder Walter.

"Answer your phone?" said Walter stupidly.

"Answer my phone," said Ellen firmly. She turned and went back across the hall, and Walter stood in his doorway in his stocking feet and watched her numbly. "Come on," she said sharply, as she went into her own apartment, and Walter, wondering briefly if they allowed harmless lunatics to live alone as though they were just like other people, hesitated for an instant and then followed her, on the theory that it would be wiser to do what she said when she seemed so cross, and reassuring himself that he could leave the door open and yell for help if necessary. Ellen stamped into her apartment and pointed at the phone where it lay on the table. "There. Answer it."

Eying her sideways, Walter edged over to the phone and picked it up. "Hello," 35 he said nervously. Then, "Hello? Hello?" Looking at her over the top of the phone, he said, "What do you want me to do now?"

"Do you mean to say," said Ellen ominously, "that that terrible terrible person has hung up?"

"I guess so," said Walter, and fled back to his apartment.

The door had only just closed behind him when the phone rang again, and Ellen, answering it, heard, "May I speak to Walter, please?"

Not a very serious mischance, surely. But the next morning Walter pointedly avoided going down in the elevator with Ellen, and sometime during that day the deliveryman left a package addressed to Ellen at Walter's door.

When Walter found the package he took it manfully under his arm and went 40 boldly across the hall, and rang Ellen's doorbell. When Ellen opened her door she thought at first—and she may have been justified—that Walter had come to apologize for the phone call the evening before, and she even thought that the package under his arm might contain something delightfully unexpected, like a box of candy. They lost another chance then; if Walter had not held out the package and said "Here," Ellen would not have gone on thinking that he was trying to apologize in his own shy way, and she would certainly not have smiled warmly, and said, "You *shouldn't* have bothered."

Walter, who regarded transporting a misdelivered parcel across the hall as relatively little bother, said blankly, "No bother at all," and Ellen, still deceived, said, "But it really wasn't *that* important."

Walter went back into his own apartment convinced that this was a very odd girl indeed, and Ellen, finding that the package had been mailed to her and contained a wool scarf knitted by a cousin, was as much angry as embarrassed because, once having imagined that an apology is forthcoming, it is very annoying not to have one after all, and particularly to have a wool scarf instead of a box of candy.

How this situation disintegrated into the white-hot fury which rose between these two is a puzzle, except for the basic fact that when once a series of misadventures has begun between two people, everything tends to contribute further to a state of misunderstanding. Thus, Ellen opened a letter of Walter's by mistake, and Walter dropped a bottle of milk—he was still trying to cure his cold, and thought that perhaps milk toast was the thing—directly outside Ellen's door, so that even after his nervous attempts to clear it up, the floor was still littered with fragments of glass, and puddled with milk.

Then Ellen—who believed by now that Walter had thrown the bottle of milk against her door—allowed herself to become so far confused by this succession of small annoyances that she actually wrote and mailed a letter to Walter, asking politely that he try to turn down his radio a little in the evenings. Walter replied with a frigid letter to the effect that certainly if he had known that she was bothered by his radio, he should surely never have dreamed—

That evening, perhaps by accident, his radio was so loud that Ellen's canary 45 woke up and chirped hysterically, and Ellen, pacing her floor in incoherent fury, might have been heard—if there had been anyone to hear her, and if Walter's radio had not been so loud—to say, "I'll get even with him!" A phrase, it must be said, which Ellen had never used before in her life.

Ellen made her preparations with a sort of loving care that might well have been lavished on some more worthy object. When the alarm went off she turned in her sleep and smiled before quite waking up, and, once awake and the alarm turned off, she almost laughed out loud. In her slippers and gown, the clock in her hand, she went across her small apartment to the phone; the number was one she was not soon apt to forget. The dial tone sounded amazingly loud, and for a minute she was almost frightened out of her resolution. Then, setting her teeth, she dialed the number, her hand steady. After a second's interminable wait, the ringing began. The phone at the other end rang three times, four times, with what seemed interminable waits between, as though even the mechanical phone system hesitated at this act. Then, at last, there was an irritable crash at the other end of the line, and a voice said, "Wah?"

"Good morning," said Ellen brightly. "I'm so terribly sorry to disturb you at this hour."

"Wah?"

"This is Ellen Webster," said Ellen still brightly. "I called to tell you that my clock has stopped—"

"Wah?" 50

"—and I wonder if you could tell me what time it is?"

There was a short pause at the other end of the line. Then after a minute, his voice came back: "Tenny minna fah."

"I beg your pardon?"

There was another short pause at the other end of the line, as of someone opening his eyes with a shock. "Twenty minutes after four," he said. "*Twenty minutes after four.*"

"The reason I thought of asking you," Ellen said sweetly, "was that you 55 were so *very* obliging before. About the radio, I mean."

"—calling a person at—"

"Thanks so much," said Ellen. "Good-by."

She felt fairly certain that he would not call her back, but she sat on her bed and giggled a little before she went back to sleep.

Walter's response to this was miserably weak: he contacted a neighboring delicatessen a day or so later, and had an assortment of evil-smelling cheese left in Ellen's apartment while she was out. This, which required persuading the superintendent to open Ellen's apartment so that the package might be left inside, was a poor revenge but a monstrous exercise of imagination upon Walter's part, so that, in one sense, Ellen was already bringing out in him qualities he never knew he had. The cheese, it turned out, more than evened the score: the apartment was small, the day was warm, and Ellen did not get home until late, and long after most of the other tenants on the floor had gone to the superintendent with their complaints about something dead in the woodwork.

Since breaking and entering had thus become one of the rules of their game, 60

Ellen felt privileged to retaliate in kind upon Walter. It was with great joy, some evenings later, that Ellen, sitting in her odorous apartment, heard Walter's scream of pure terror when he put his feet into his slippers and found a raw egg in each.

Walter had another weapon, however, which he had been so far reluctant to use; it was a howitzer of such proportions that Walter felt its use would end warfare utterly. After the raw eggs he felt no compunction whatever in bringing out his heavy artillery.

It seemed to Ellen, at first, as though peace had been declared. For almost a week things went along smoothly; Walter kept his radio turned down almost to inaudibility, so that Ellen got plenty of sleep. She was over her cold, the sun had come out, and on Saturday morning she spent three hours shopping, and found exactly the dress she wanted at less than she expected to pay.

About Saturday noon she stepped out of the elevator, her packages under her arm, and walked briskly down the hall to her apartment, making, as usual, a wide half circle to avoid coming into contact with the area around Walter's door.

Her apartment door, to her surprise, was open, but before she had time to phrase a question in her own mind, she had stepped inside and come face to face with a lady who—not to make any more mysteries—was Walter Nesmith's aunt, and a wicked old lady in her own way, possessing none of Walter's timidity and none of his tact.

"Who?" said Ellen weakly, standing in the doorway.                               65

"Come in and close the door," said the old lady darkly. "I don't think you'll want your neighbors to hear what I have to say. I," she continued as Ellen obeyed mechanically, "am Mrs. Harold Vongarten Nesmith. Walter Nesmith, young woman, is my nephew."

"Then you are in the wrong apartment," said Ellen, quite politely considering the reaction which Walter Nesmith's name was beginning by now to arouse in her. "You want Apartment Three-B, across the hall."

"I do *not*," said the old lady firmly. "I came here to see the designing young woman who has been shamelessly pursuing my nephew, and to warn her"—the old lady shook her gloves menacingly—"to warn her that *not one cent* shall she have from me if she marries Walter Nesmith."

"Marries?" said Ellen, thoughts too great for words in her heart.

"It has long been my opinion that some young woman would be after Walter      70
Nesmith for his money," said Walter's aunt with satisfaction.

"Believe me," said Ellen wholeheartedly, "there is not that much money in the world."

"You deny it?" The old lady leaned back and smiled triumphantly. "I expected something of the sort. Walter," she called suddenly, and then, putting her head back and howling, "Wal-l-l-l-ter."

"Sh-h-h," said Ellen fearfully. "They'll hear you all over."

"I expect them to," said the old lady. "Wal-l-l-l-l—Oh, there you are."

Ellen turned, and saw Walter Nesmith, with triumph in his eyes, peering        75
around the edge of the door. "Did it work?" he asked.

"She denies everything," said his aunt.

"About the eggs?" Walter said, confused. "You mean, she denies about the eggs and the phone call and—"

"Look," Ellen said to Walter, stamping across the floor to look him straight in the eye, "of all the insufferable, conceited, rude, self-satisfied—"

"What?" said Walter.

"I wouldn't want to marry you," said Ellen, "if—if—" She stopped for a word, helpless.

"If he were the last man on earth," Walter's aunt supplied obligingly. "I think she's really after your *money*, Walter."

Walter stared at his aunt. "I didn't tell you to tell her—" he began. He gasped, and tried again. "I mean," he said, "I never thought—" He appealed to Ellen. "I don't want to marry you, either," he said, and he gasped again, and said, "I mean, I told my aunt to come and tell you—"

"If this is a proposal," Ellen said coldly, "I decline."

"All I wanted her to do was scare you," Walter said finally.

"It's a good way," his aunt said complacently. "Turned out to be the only way with your Uncle Charles and a Hungarian adventuress."

"I mean," Walter said desperately to Ellen, "she owns this building. I mean, I wanted her to tell you that if you didn't stop—I mean, I wanted her to scare you—"

"Apartments are too hard to get these days," his aunt said. "That would have been *too* unkind."

"That's how I got my apartment at all, you see," Walter said to Ellen, still under the impression he was explaining something Ellen wanted to understand.

"Since you have an apartment," Ellen said with restraint, "may I suggest that you take your aunt and the both of you—"

The phone rang.

"Excuse me," said Ellen mechanically, moving to answer it. "Hello?" she said.

"Hello, may I speak to Walter, please?"

Ellen smiled rather in the manner that Lady Macbeth might have smiled if she found a run in her stocking.

"It's for you," she said, holding the phone out to Walter.

"For me?" he said, surprised. "Who is it?"

"I really could not say," said Ellen sweetly. "Since you have so many friends that one phone is not adequate to answer all their calls—"

Since Walter made no move to take the phone, she put it gently back on the hook.

"They'll call again," she assured him, still smiling in that terrible fashion.

"I ought to turn you both out," said Walter's aunt. She turned to Ellen. "Young woman," she said, "do you deny that all this nonsense with eggs and telephone calls is an attempt to entangle my nephew into matrimony?"

"Certainly not," Ellen said. "I mean, I *do* deny it."

"Walter Nesmith," said his aunt, "do you admit that all your finagling with cheeses and radios is an attempt to strike up an acquaintance with this young woman?"

"Certainly," said Walter. "I mean, I do *not* admit it."

"Good," said Walter's aunt. "You are precisely the pair of silly fools I would have picked out for each other." She rose with great dignity, motioned Walter away from her, and started for the door. "Remember," she said, shaking her gloves again at Ellen, "not one cent."

She opened the door and started down the hall, her handkerchief over her eyes, and—a sorry thing in such an old lady—laughing until she had to stop and lean against the wall near the elevator.

"I'm sorry," Walter was saying to Ellen, almost babbling, "I'm *really* sorry this time—please believe me, I had *no* idea—I wouldn't for the world—nothing but the most profound respect—a joke, you know—hope you didn't really think—" 105

"I understand perfectly," Ellen said icily. "It is all perfectly clear. It only goes to show what I have always believed about young men who think that all they have to do is—"

The phone rang.

Ellen waited a minute before she spoke. Then she said, "You might as well answer it."

"I'm *terribly* sorry," Walter said, not moving toward the phone. "I mean, I'm *terribly* sorry." He waved his hands in the air. "About what she said about what she thought about what you wanted me to do—" His voice trailed off miserably.

Suddenly Ellen began to giggle. 110

Anger is certainly a problem that will bear much analysis. It is hardly surprising that one person may be angry at another, particularly if these are two people who are gentle, usually, and rarely angry, whose emotions tend to be mild and who would rather be friends with everyone than be enemies with anyone. Such an anger argues a situation so acute that only the most drastic readjustment can remedy it.


Either Walter Nesmith or Ellen Webster could have moved, of course. But, as Walter's aunt had pointed out, apartments are not that easy to come by, and their motives and their telephone numbers were by now so inextricably mixed that on the whole it seemed more reasonable not to bother.

Moreover, Walter's aunt, who still snickers when her nephew's name is mentioned, did not keep them long in suspense, after all. She was not lavish, certainly, but she wrote them a letter which both of them found completely confusing and which enclosed a check adequate for a down payment on the extremely modest house in the country they decided upon without disagreement. They even compromised and had four children—two boys and two girls.


# QUESTIONS

1. Describe Walter and Ellen as characters. How individually are they presented? Are they round or flat? Are there any stereotypical qualities about them? Does their marriage seem sterotypical?

2. Develop a plan or structure for the story. What relationship do the various farcical incidents have upon Jackson's development of the structure?

3. What is the setting of the story? Can it be easily visualized? What way of life do the two principal characters follow, and how does this way make their eventual union possible? What does the fact that all the action takes place on the third floor of the apartment building contribute to the happy mood of the story?

4.  What is the central conflict of the story? Who and/or what are the protagonists and antagonists? How is the complication developed? Where is the crisis of the story, and how is it resolved?

5.  Mrs. Nesmith has a small but vital role in the story. Is she flat or round? How much do you learn about her?

6.  What is the point of view of the story? To which character does it become limited? How completely does the point of view inform us about this character? At the end, does the point of view continue as being limited, or does it become more properly described as dramatic?

7.  In the light of the fact that during most of the story the principal characters are "feuding," describe the irony of the story's resolution. Discuss Jackson's use of the various farcical incidents as one of the means by which she shapes your responses to the story. In terms of tone, how does she keep the little war from being taken too seriously?

8.  What sinister turns might the story have taken (such as getting lawyers, dragging each other into court, suing for damages, and so on)? How does Jackson avoid making Mrs. Nesmith one of these more sinister forces, and how does she keep the story comic?

## WRITING ABOUT TONE

In preparing to write about tone in a story you will, as always, need to begin with a careful reading. As you study, it is important to note those elements of the story that touch particularly on attitudes or authorial consideration. Thus, for example, as you read Collier's "The Chaser," it would be necessary to consider whether the story asks too much of the reader: Is the prediction of the old man really the horror at the end of the road for all romantic loves? In this respect, the story may cause a certain mental squirming. But is this right? Did Collier want this squirming to occur? Perhaps if the question is phrased another way, the tone might be more adequately understood. If "overly possessive love" is substituted for "romantic love," the story may become more satisfactory, less disturbing. In seeking answers like this one, you will find that the author has been directing you and guiding your responses; that is, that the author's control over tone has been firmly, clearly established.

Similarly, the farcical happenings in "About Two Nice People" might more likely produce anger than love. Does the story ask too much of the reader in the way of belief? Perhaps it does, if we were to accept it as realism, but in the farcical story that it is, the tone might be considered as being right. The story is not real, nor was it intended that way.

The same sorts of questions can apply when you study internal qualities such as style and characterization. Do all the speeches seem right for the speakers and the situations? Are all the descriptions appropriate? Are all the actions believable? In other words, does the author seem to be faithful to the established integrity of the characters? For example, this question might be asked about Mathilde and her husband Loisel in De Maupassant's "The Necklace" (p. 75). Is it plausible that they would not have told Jeanne Forrestier about the loss? In the same way, in Tom Whitecloud's "Blue Winds Dancing" (p. 107), is the young Indian narrator's return home to be accepted as a permanent sacrifice of his educational future, or just a manifestation of homesickness? In studying questions of this sort, you are in fact dealing with issues about the attitudes of the author toward the subject and also toward the audience—the substance of a discussion on tone.

## ORGANIZING YOUR ESSAY

**INTRODUCTION.** The introduction should begin with a brief description of the situation in the story that prompts the discussion about tone. The central idea should be a brief statement about the tone—such as that the story is one leading to cynicism, as in "The Chaser," or one leading to delight, as in "About Two Nice People." If there are any particular obstacles to the proper determination of the tone, either in the work or in your personal attitudes, these should also be mentioned in the introduction.

**BODY.** In the body of your theme you should examine all aspects that in your judgment have a bearing on the tone of the work. Some of the things to cover are these:

1. *The audience, situation*, and *characters*. Is any person or group being directly addressed by the author? What attitude toward the audience seems to be expressed (love, respect, condescension, confidentiality, etc.)? What is the basic situation in the work? Is there any irony in it? If so, what type is it? What does the irony show about the author's attitudes (optimism or pessimism, for example)? How does the author use the situation to shape your responses? That is, can any action, situation, or character be seen as an expression of attitude, or as a means of controlling attitude (see, for example, the old man in "The Chaser")? What is the nature of the author's voice or persona? Does the author seem to manipulate this voice to any degree to convey attitudes? How? Does the author seem to respect, admire, dislike, or evidence other feeling about any characters or situations? Through what techniques are these feelings made clear?

2. *Descriptions, diction*. Analysis of these is stylistic, but your concern here is to relate stylistic technique to attitude. Are there any systematic references, such as to colors, sounds, noises, natural scenes, and so on, that collectively show or seem to reflect an attitude? Does the author manipulate connotation to control your responses? Is any special speech or dialect pattern used to indicate an attitude about speakers or their condition of

life? Do the speech patterns conform to normal or standard usage? What can you make of this? Are there any unusual or noteworthy kinds of expression? What is their effect on the apparent attitude of the author? Does the author use verbal irony? To what effect?

3. *Humor*. Is there humor in the work? What is its intensity? Does the humor develop out of incongruous situations or out of language? Is there an underlying basis of attack in the humor, or are the objects of laughter still respected or even loved despite having humor directed against them?

4. *Ideas*. Ideas may be advocated, defended mildly, or attacked. Which do you seem to have in the work you have been studying? How does the author make his or her attitude clear—directly, by statement, or indirectly, through understatement, overstatement, or the language of a character?

5. *Unique characteristics of the work*. Each work has unique properties that may contribute to the tone. Collier's "The Chaser," for example, is developed almost entirely through the dialogue between the old man and Austen. The tone of the story is therefore to be perceived by an awareness of the attitudes of each of the participants. In other works there might be some recurring word or theme that seems special. Mark Twain in "Luck," for example, develops a passage centering on the word *blunder* and thereby makes his attitude clear about the boob hero, Scoresby. When you study any assigned story, be alert for anything unusual or individual that you may use in your essay about tone.

CONCLUSION.    The conclusion may summarize the main points of the essay and from there go on to any concluding thoughts about the tone of the story. Redefinitions, explanations, or afterthoughts might belong here, together with reinforcing ideas in support of earlier points. If there are any personal thoughts, any changes of mind, any awakening awarenesses, a brief account of these would also be appropriate here, as long as you demonstrate that they rose out of your analysis of the story's tone.

## SAMPLE ESSAY

### The Situational and Verbal Irony of Collier's "The Chaser"*

[1]    John Collier's "The Chaser" is based on the situational irony of the unreal hope of youth as opposed to the extreme disillusion of age and experience. Collier builds the brief story almost entirely in dialogue between a young man, Alan Austen, who is deeply in love and wants to possess his sweetheart entirely, and an unnamed old man who believes in a life free of romantic involvement. The situation reflects disillusionment so completely that the story may in fact

* See p. 263 for this story.

be called cynical.° This attitude is made plain by the situation, the old man, and the use of double meaning.□

[2]
The situation between the two men establishes the story's dominant tone of cynicism. Austen, the young man full of illusions and unreal expectations about love, has come to the old man to buy a love potion so that his sweetheart, Diana, will love him with slavelike adoration. Collier makes it clear that the old man has seen many young men like Austen in the grips of romantic desire before, and he therefore knows that their possessive love will eventually bore and anger them. He knows, because he has already seen these disillusioned customers return to buy the "chaser," which is a deadly, untraceable poison, so that they could kill the women for whom they previously bought the love potion. Thus Collier creates the ironic situation of the story—the beginning of an inevitable process in which Austen, like other young men before him, are made to appear so unrealistic and self-defeating that their enthusiastic passion will someday change into hate and murderousness.

[3]
The sales method used by the old man reveals his cynical understanding of men like Austen. Collier makes clear, right at the start, that the old man knows why Austen has come: Before showing his love potion, the old man describes the untraceable poison, which he calls a "glove-cleaner" or "life-cleaner." His aim is actually to sell the expensive poison by using the love potion as inexpensive bait. Thus we see the old man's art of manipulation, for even though Austen is at the moment horrified by the poison, the seed has been planted in his mind. He will always know, when his love for Diana changes, that he will have the choice of "cleaning" his life. This unscrupulous sales method effectively corrupts Austen in advance. Such a calculation on the old man's part is grimly cynical.

[4]
Supporting the tone of cynicism in the old man's sales technique is his use of double meaning. His concluding words, "Au revoir" (i.e., "until I see you again"), for example, carry an ironic double meaning. On the one hand, the words conventionally mean "good bye." On the other hand, however, they suggest that the old man expects a future meeting when Austen will return to buy the poison to kill Diana. The old man's acknowledgement of Austen's gratitude shows the same ironic double edge. He says,

> I like to oblige. . . . Then customers come back, later in life, when they are better off, and want more expensive things.

Clearly the "expensive" thing is "the chaser," the undetectable poison. Through such ironic speeches, the old man is politely but cynically telling Austen that his love will not last and that it will eventually bore, irritate, and then torment him to the point where he will want to murder Diana rather than to continue living with her potion-induced possessiveness.

Before "The Chaser" is dismissed as being hopelessly cynical, however, we should note that Austen's ideas about love must inevitably produce just

---

° Central idea.
□ Thesis sentence.

such cynicism. The old man's descriptions of the total enslavement that Austen has dreamed about would leave no breathing room for either Austen or Diana. This sort of love excludes everything else in life and becomes suffocating rather than pleasing. It is normal to wish freedom from such psychological imprisonment, even if the prison is of one's own making. Under these conditions, the cynical tone of "The Chaser" suggests that the desire to be totally possessing and possessed—to "want nothing but solitude" and the loved one—can lead only to disaster for both man and woman. The old man's cynicism and the young man's desire suggest the need for an ideal of love that permits interchange, individuality, and understanding. Even though this better ideal is not described anywhere in the story, it is compatible with Collier's situational irony. Thus, cynical as the story unquestionably is, it does not exclude an idealism of tolerant and more human love.

[5]

### Commentary on the Essay

This essay presents a way in which you can write about a story of dominating pessimism and cynicism without giving in to the underlying negative situational irony. Therefore the essay illustrates how a consideration of tone can aid the development of objective literary judgment.

The introductory paragraph indicates that the aspect of tone to be discussed will be an ironic situation—youthful but unrealistic hope in the context of aged cynicism. The thesis sentence indicates that the body of the essay will deal with (1) this situation and how it is related to (2) the sales method of a major character—the old man—and (3) his speeches containing double meaning.

The second paragraph establishes the situational irony by describing the desires of Austen and the cynical attitude of the old man. In the third paragraph the topic is the sinister manipulation of Austen as a result of the old man's skillful and subtle salesmanship. By stressing that the old man plants the seeds of corruption in Austen, this paragraph continues the topic of the tone of cynicism which is the thematic basis of the essay. The subject of the fourth paragraph, the last in the body of the essay, is Collier's use of double meaning in the speeches of the old man to emphasize the idea that Austen will someday want to kill his wife.

The concluding paragraph is a reflective one. In view of the cynical tone of the story, this paragraph suggests that a more realistic and optimistic attitude about love is possible—a view that while not perceivable in the story is also not incompatible with it.

# 9

# Symbolism and Allegory: Keys to Extended Meaning

## SYMBOLISM

*Symbolism* and *allegory* are modes of literary expression that are designed to extend meaning. **Symbolism** is derived from a Greek word meaning "to throw together" (*syn*, together, and *ballein*, to throw). In literature, a symbol pulls or draws together (1) a specific thing with (2) ideas, values, persons, or ways of life, in a direct relationship that otherwise would not be apparent. A symbol might also be regarded as a substitute for the elements being signified, much as the flag stands for the ideals of the nation.

In short stories and other types of literature, a symbol is usually a person, thing, place, action, situation, or even thought. It possesses its own reality and meaning and may function at the normal level of reality within a story. There is often a topical or integral relationship between the symbol and things it stands for, but a symbol may also have no apparent connection and therefore may be considered arbitrary. What is important, however, is that the symbol points beyond itself to greater and more complex meaning. When a symbol is introduced, like a key opening a lock, it signifies a specific combination of attitudes, a sustained constancy of meaning, and the potential for wide-ranging application. A symbol might appear over and over again in the same story, yet it always maintains the same meaning. Thus you might think of a symbol as a constant against a background of variables, like a theme with variations.

To determine whether something in a story is symbolic, we must decide if it consistently refers beyond itself to a significant idea, emotion, or quality. For example, the ancient mythological character Sisyphus may be considered as a symbol because he is consistently linked with specific ideas. According to legend, he is doomed in the underworld to roll a large boulder up a high hill forever. Just as he gets it to the top, it rolls

279

down, and he is fated to roll it up again, and again, and again, because the rock always rolls back as he gets it to the top. His plight may be seen as a symbol of the human condition: A person rarely if ever completes anything. Work must always be done over and over in every generation, and the same problems confront humanity in each age without any final solution. In the light of such infinitely fruitless effort, life seems to have little meaning. Nevertheless there is hope. People who meet frustration like that experienced by Sisyphus are involved and active in their work even if they are never more than temporarily successful, and in this way they may find meaning in their lives. A writer using Sisyphus as a symbol would want us to understand these ideas as a result of the reference. Symbolism, as you can see, can be a conventionalized shorthand form of communication.

There are other symbols like Sisyphus that are generally or universally recognized, and authors referring to them rely on this common understanding. These types of symbols are sometimes called **cultural** or **universal** symbols. They embody ideas or emotions that the writer and the reader share in common as a result of their social and cultural heritage. When using these symbols, a writer does not have to take the time to invest objects or people with symbolic resonance within the story; she or he can simply assume that the reader knows what the symbol represents. Thus, water, which is the substance in the sacrament of baptism, is acknowledged to be a symbol of life. When water spouts up in a fountain, it may symbolize optimism (as upwelling, bubbling life). A stagnant pool may symbolize life being polluted or diminished. In terms of psychology, water is often understood as a reference to sexuality. Thus, lovers may meet by a quiet lake, a cascading waterfall, a murmuring stream, a wide river, or a stormy sea. The condition of the water in each instance may be interpreted as a symbol of the lovers' romantic relationship. Another generally recognized universal symbol is the serpent, which is often used to represent the Devil, or simply evil. (It was in the form of a serpent, you remember from Genesis 3: 1–7, that Satan tempted Eve in the Garden of Eden.) In "Young Goodman Brown," Nathaniel Hawthorne describes a walking stick that "bore the likeness of a great black snake," in this way instantly evoking the idea of Satanic evil. However, because the stick "might almost be seen to twist and wriggle itself like a living serpent," it may also symbolize human tendencies to see evil where it does not exist.

Objects and descriptions that are not universally recognized as symbols can be developed as symbols only within an individual work. These types of symbols may be termed **private, authorial,** or **contextual** symbols. Unlike universal symbols, these are not derived from common historical, cultural, or religious ground but gain their symbolic meaning within the *context* of the specific work of fiction. For example, the jug of beer carried by Jackie's grandmother in O'Connor's "First Confession" (p. 172) is one of the things that symbolize the grandmother's peasantlike and boorish habits. Similarly, the chrysanthemums tended by Elisa in Steinbeck's "The Chrysanthemums" (p. 303) seem at first nothing more than deeply prized flowers. As the story progresses, however, the flowers gain symbolic significance. The traveling tinsmith's apparent interest in them is the wedge he uses to get a small mending job from Elisa. Her description of the care needed in planting and tending the flowers suggests that they signify her qualities of kindness, love, orderliness, femininity, and, ultimately, her maternal instincts. When, at the end of the story, the flowers are seen dumped at the side of the road, we may conclude that her values have also been dumped and that she has been used and deceived. In short, the chrysanthemums are a major symbol in the story. If you were to encounter references to porter or chrysanthemums in a context other than "First Confession" and "The Chrysanthemums," however, they would not necessarily be symbolic.

In determining whether a particular object or person in a story is a symbol, you need to make decisions based on your judgment of its total significance. If it appears to be of major importance, you can claim it has symbolic value as long as you can show its scope and sustained reference beyond itself. Thus, at the end of Welty's "A Worn Path" (p. 106), Phoenix plans to buy a toy windmill for her sick grandson. The windmill is a small thing, and she will spend all her money for it. It will break soon under constant use, like her life and that of her grandson, but buying it is her attempt to give the boy a little pleasure despite her poverty and the hopelessness of her life. For all these reasons it is justifiable to interpret the windmill as a symbol of her strong character, generous nature, and pathetic existence.

## ALLEGORY

**Allegory** is like symbolism in that both use one thing to refer to something else. The term is derived from the Greek word *allégorein*, which means "to speak so as to imply other than what is said." Allegory, however, tends to be more complex and sustained than symbolism. An allegory is to a symbol as a motion picture is to a still picture; allegory puts symbols into consistent and sustained action. In form, an allegory is a complete and self-sufficient narrative, but it also signifies another series or level of events or conditions of life as expressed in a habit of thought, a philosophy, or a religion. While some works are allegories from beginning to end, many works that are not allegories contain sections or episodes that may be considered allegories.

Allegories and the allegorical method do not exist simply to enable authors to engage in mysterious literary exercises. Rather it was understood at some point in the past that people might more willingly listen to stories instead of moral lessons. Thus, the allegorical method evolved to entertain and instruct at the same time. In addition, the threat of reprisal or censorship sometimes caused authors to express their views indirectly in the form of allegory rather than to write directly. The double meaning that you will find in allegory is hence quite real.

As you study a work for allegory, you should try to determine how an entire story, or a self-contained episode, may be construed as having an extended, allegorical meaning that points consistently to a system of ideas or events beyond the actual occurrences in the text. The popularity of the film *Star Wars* and its sequels, for example, is attributable at least partly to the fact that it may be taken as an allegory of the conflict between good and evil. Obi Wan Kenobi (intelligence) enlists the aid of Luke Skywalker (heroism, boldness) and instructs him in "the force" (religious faith). Thus armed and guided, Skywalker opposes the strength of Darth Vader (evil) to rescue the Princess Leia (purity and goodness) with the aid of the latest spaceships and weaponry (technology). The story is accompanied by ingenious special effects and almost tactile sound effects and music, and hence as an adventure film it stands by itself. With the clear allegorical overtones, however, it stands for any person's quest for self-fulfillment.

To see how it applies, let us consider that Vader is so strong that he imprisons Skywalker for a time, and Skywalker must exert all his skill and strength to get free and to overcome the evil Vader. In the allegorical application of the episode to people generally, it would not be improper to take the temporary imprisonment to refer to those moments of doubt, discouragement, and depression that often beset people seeking an education, a work goal, the good life, a satisfactory marriage, or whatever.

In one form or another, this allegory has been told over and over again. At one time the substance was the hero who went to far lands to gain the prize of the golden fleece; at another, the knight who braved dangers to overcome the dragon. The allegory, in short, is as old as the capacity of human beings to tell stories. As long as the parallel interpretation is kept close and consistent, as in the *Star Wars* films, an extended allegorical interpretation will have validity.

### Fable, Parable, and Myth

There are three narrative forms that are special types of allegory: *fable*, *parable*, and *myth*.

**FABLE.** A **fable** is a short story, often featuring animals with human traits, to which writers and editors attach "morals" or explanations. Such stories are often called **beast fables.** Fables are a very old literary form and have found a place in the literature of most societies. Aesop (sixth century B.C.) was supposedly a slave who composed beast fables in ancient Greece. His fable of "The Fox and the Grapes," for example, signifies the tendency to belittle those things we cannot have. Joel Chandler Harris (1848–1908) was a black American writer whose "Uncle Remus" stories are also beast fables. Walt Disney's "Mickey Mouse" and Walt Kelly's "Pogo" are part of the tradition.

PARABLE.   A **parable** is really a short, simple allegory. Parables are often associated with Jesus, who used them in his teaching to embody religious insights and truth. Parables like those of the Good Samaritan and the Prodigal Son are interpreted to show God's active love, concern, understanding, and forgiveness for human beings.

MYTH.   A **myth** is a story, like the myth of Sisyphus, that is associated with the religion, philosophy, and collective psychology of various groups of cultures. Myths sometimes embody scientific truths for prescientific societies; they codify the social and cultural values of the civilization in which they were composed. Sometimes, unfortunately, the term *mythical* is used to suggest that something is untrue. This minimizing of the word reflects a limited appreciation of the psychological and social truths embedded in myths. The truths in mythology are not found literally in the stories themselves, but rather in our symbolic or allegorical interpretation of them.

## ALLUSION IN SYMBOLISM AND ALLEGORY

Universal or cultural symbols and allegories often **allude** to other works from our cultural heritage, such as the Bible, Greco-Roman mythology, or classical literature. Sometimes understanding a story may require knowledge of politics and history. Thus, for example, a major character in Hawthorne's "Young Goodman Brown" is Brown's wife, Faith, who stays at home when he leaves to go on his journey. Later, in the forest, when Brown is seeing his vision of sinful human beings, he exclaims, "My Faith is gone." On the primary level of reading, this statement makes perfect sense, because Brown has concluded that his wife has been lost. However, the symbol of his being married to Faith takes on additional meaning when one notes that it is also an allusion to the Biblical book of Ephesians (2:8) and to the Protestant-Calvinist tradition that the virtue faith is a key to salvation:

> For by grace you have been saved through faith; and this is not your own doing, it is the gift of God—

This Biblical passage might easily take a volume of explanation, but in brief the allusion makes clear that Brown's loss of faith also indicates his perception that he has been abandoned by God. Here is an instance where a symbol gains its resonance and impact through allusion.

This example brings up the issue of how much background you need for detecting allusions in symbolism and allegory. You can often rely on your own knowledge. Sometimes, however, an allusion may escape you if you do not pursue the point in a dictionary or other reference work. The scope of your college dictionary will surprise you. If you cannot find an entry in your dictionary, however, try one of the major encyclopedias, or ask your reference librarian about standard guides like *The Oxford Companion to English Literature*, *The Oxford Companion to Classical Literature*, and William Rose Benet's *The Reader's Encyclopaedia*. A useful aid in finding Biblical references is *Cruden's Complete Concordance*, which in various editions has been used by scholars and readers for more than two centuries (since 1737). This work lists all words used in the King James translation of the Bible, so that you may easily locate the chapter and verse of any Biblical quotation. If you still have trouble after using sources like these, see your instructor for more help.

## READING FOR SYMBOLISM AND ALLEGORY

To the extent that literature is true and probable, much of it may be considered symbolic or allegorical. A story is about *one* or *two* persons and those closely associated with them, but if these persons were unlike everyone else in the world, a reading would not promote any extended understanding. Because of similarity to life, a good story therefore lends itself to the kind of reading you will be doing here. Despite this fact, you may be tempted to find symbolism and allegorical meaning where none might exist. Some minor details may be no more significant than being necessary to carry on the story. There will be other significant details, however, that readily bear consideration as symbolism and allegory. In the Parable of the Prodigal Son, for example, the party given by the father might seem like nothing more than a party unless it is taken in conjunction with verse 32 about the rejoicing for the recovery of the son. With this explanation, it is clear that the party is a symbol for the New Testament assertion that God knows human beings, loves them like a parent, sorrows when they lose faith, and rejoices when their faith is restored.

For an allegorical reading the same reservation and care are needed. Thus the story "The Chrysanthemums" operates with total effectiveness as a narrative about an isolated woman on a farm. Her relationship with her husband is relatively inarticulate, and the episode with the traveling tinsmith is a brief awakening of her self-esteem about her own attractiveness and sexuality. To determine whether an allegorical reading is possible, it would be necessary to establish whether her isolation is common to many other married women, whether Henry's seeing her talent with flowers as potentially commercial rather than esthetic is typical of the way husbands see wives, and whether her disappointment is like that experienced by many women. Without a statistical study of many such relationships, perhaps, it would be difficult to claim that the story is broadly allegorical, but it would indeed be possible to claim without such a study that the story of Elisa has many allegorical overtones.

As you read, then, be alert for the ways in which actions, things, and characters may be considered symbolically or allegorically. If something seems special, if there is an allusion, if the author has pointed up something in an unusual or special way, the chances are good that a case for the presence of symbolism or allegory may be made. There is no need to make extravagant claims; following the more obvious leads of the author is enough.

## AESOP

*The Fox and the Grapes*                              (*ca*. *6th C*. B.C.)

A hungry Fox coming into a vineyard where there hung delicious clusters of ripe Grapes, his mouth watered to be at them; but they were nailed up to a trellis so high, that with all his springing and leaping he could not reach a single bunch. At last, growing tired and disappointed, "Let who will take them!" says he, "they are but green and sour; so I'll e'en let them alone."

## QUESTIONS

1. How much do you learn about the characteristics of the fox? How are these characteristics related to the moral or message of the fable?
2. What is the plot of the fable, the principal conflict? What is the resolution of the conflict?
3. In your own words, explain the meaning of the fable. Is the "sour grape" explanation a satisfactory excuse, or is it a rationalization for failure?
4. From your reading of "The Fox and the Grapes," explain the characteristics of the fable as a type of literature.

## THE GOSPEL OF ST. LUKE 15:11–32

*The Parable of the Prodigal Son*                         (*ca*. *80* A.D.)

11 ¶ And he said, A certain man had two sons:
12 And the younger of them said to *his* father, Father, give me the portion of goods that falleth *to me*. And he divided unto them *his* living.°

divided . . . *his living*: one-third of the father's estate; the son had to renounce all further claim.

13 And not many days after the younger son gathered all together, and took his journey into a far country,° and there wasted his substance with riotous living.

14 And when he had spent all, there arose a mighty famine in that land; and he began to be in want.

15 And he went and joined himself to a citizen of that country; and he sent him into his fields to feed swine.°

16 And he would fain have filled his belly with the husks° that the swine did eat: and no man gave unto him.

17 And when he came to himself, he said, How many hired servants of my father's have bread enough and to spare, and I perish with hunger!

18 I will arise and go to my father, and will say unto him, Father, I have sinned against heaven, and before thee,

19 And am no more worthy to be called thy son: make me as one of thy hired servants.

20 And he arose, and came to his father. But when he was yet a great way off, his father saw him, and had compassion, and ran, and fell on his neck, and kissed him.

21 And the son said unto him, Father, I have sinned against heaven, and in thy sight, and am no more worthy to be called thy son.

22 But the father said to his servants, Bring forth the best robe, and put *it* on him; and put a ring on his hand, and shoes on *his* feet:

23 And bring hither the fatted calf,° and kill *it*; and let us eat, and be merry:

24 For this my son was dead, and is alive again; he was lost, and is found. And they began to be merry.

25 Now his elder son was in the field: and as he came and drew nigh to the house, he heard musick and dancing.

26 And he called one of the servants, and asked what these things meant.

27 And he said unto him, Thy brother is come; and thy father hath killed the fatted calf, because he hath received him safe and sound.

28 And he was angry, and would not go in: therefore came his father out, and intreated him.

29 And he answering said to *his* father, Lo, these many years do I serve thee, neither transgressed I at any time thy commandment: and yet thou never gavest me a kid, that I might make merry with my friends:

30 But as soon as this thy son was come, which hath devoured thy living with harlots, thou hast killed for him the fatted calf.

31 And he said unto him, Son, thou art ever with me, and all that I have is thine.

*far country*: countries of the Jewish dispersal, or *diaspora,* in the areas bordering the Mediterranean Sea.

*feed swine*: In Jewish custom, pigs were unclean.

*husks*: pods of the carob tree, the eating of which was thought to be penitential.

*fatted calf*: grain-fed calf.

32 It was meet° that we should make merry, and be glad: for this thy brother was dead, and is alive again; and was lost, and is found.

## QUESTIONS

1. Describe the character of the Prodigal Son. If one considers the parable a story, is this character flat or round, representative or individual? Why is it necessary that the character be considered representatively, even though he has individual characteristics?

2. What is the plot of the parable? What is the force of the antagonism against which the Prodigal Son must contend? Considering the moral and religious point of the parable, why is it necessary that the brother be resentful of the brother's return?

3. What is the resolution of the parable? Why is there no "they lived happily ever after" ending?

4. Using verse numbers, analyze the structure of the parable. What determines your division of the parts? Do these parts coincide with the development of the plot? On the basis of your answer, describe the relationship of plot to structure in the parable.

5. What is the point of view of the parable? Is it consistently applied? How does the emphasis shift with verse 22?

6. On the basis of the fact that there are many characteristics here of many of the stories you have read, write a description of the parable as a type of literature.

## NATHANIEL HAWTHORNE (1804–1864)

*Young Goodman Brown*                                                  *1835*

Young Goodman Brown came forth at sunset, into the street of Salem village,° but put his head back, after crossing the threshold, to exchange a parting kiss with his young wife. And Faith, as the wife was aptly named, thrust her own pretty head into the street, letting the wind play with the pink ribbons of her cap, while she called to Goodman Brown.

"Dearest heart," whispered she, softly and rather sadly, when her lips were close to his ear, "prithee, put off your journey until sunrise, and sleep in your own bed to-night. A lone woman is troubled with such dreams and such thoughts, that she's afeard of herself, sometimes. Pray, tarry with me this night, dear husband, of all nights in the year!"

"My love and my Faith," replied young Goodman Brown, "of all nights in

*meet*: appropriate.
*Salem village*: in Massachusetts.

the year, this one night must I tarry away from thee. My journey, as thou callest it, forth and back again, must needs be done 'twixt now and sunrise. What, my sweet, pretty wife, dost thou doubt me already, and we but three months married!"

"Then God bless you!" said Faith with the pink ribbons, "and may you find all well, when you come back."

"Amen!" cried Goodman Brown. "Say thy prayers, dear Faith, and go to       5
bed at dusk, and no harm will come to thee."

So they parted; and the young man pursued his way, until, being about to turn the corner by the meeting-house, he looked back and saw the head of Faith still peeping after him, with a melancholy air, in spite of her pink ribbons.

"Poor little Faith!" thought he, for his heart smote him. "What a wretch am I, to leave her on such an errand! She talks of dreams, too. Methought, as she spoke, there was trouble in her face, as if a dream had warned her what work is to be done to-night. But no, no! 't would kill her to think it. Well; she's a blessed angel on earth; and after this one night, I'll cling to her skirts and follow her to Heaven."

With this excellent resolve for the future, Goodman Brown felt himself justi-fied in making more haste on his present evil purpose. He had taken a dreary road, darkened by all the gloomiest trees of the forest, which barely stood aside to let the narrow path creep through, and closed immediately behind. It was all as lonely as could be; and there is this peculiarity in such a solitude, that the traveller knows not who may be concealed by the innumerable trunks and the thick boughs overhead; so that, with lonely footsteps, he may yet be passing through an unseen multitude.

"There may be a devilish Indian behind every tree," said Goodman Brown to himself; and he glanced fearfully behind him, as he added, "What if the devil himself should be at my very elbow!"

His head being turned back, he passed a crook of the road, and looking       10
forward again, beheld the figure of a man, in grave and decent attire, seated at the foot of an old tree. He arose at Goodman Brown's approach, and walked onward, side by side with him.

"You are late, Goodman Brown," said he. "The clock of the Old South° was striking, as I came through Boston; and that is full fifteen minutes agone."

"Faith kept me back awhile," replied the young man, with a tremor in his voice, caused by the sudden appearance of his companion, though not wholly unexpected.

It was now deep dusk in the forest, and deepest in that part of it where these two were journeying. As nearly as could be discerned, the second traveller was about fifty years old, apparently in the same rank of life as Goodman Brown, and bearing a considerable resemblance to him, though perhaps more in expression than features. Still, they might have been taken for father and son. And yet, though the elder person was as simply clad as the younger, and as simple in manner too, he had an indescribable air of one who knew the world, and would not have felt abashed at the governor's dinner-table, or in King William's° court, were it possible that his affairs should call him thither. But the only thing about him that

*Old South*: The Old South Church, in Boston, is still there.
*King William*: William IV, King of England from 1830 to 1837.

could be fixed upon as remarkable, was his staff, which bore the likeness of a great black snake, so curiously wrought, that it might almost be seen to twist and wriggle itself like a living serpent. This, of course, must have been an ocular deception, assisted by the uncertain light.

"Come, Goodman Brown!" cried his fellow-traveller, "this is a dull pace for the beginning of a journey. Take my staff, if you are so soon weary."

"Friend," said the other, exchanging his slow pace for a full stop, "having kept covenant by meeting thee here, it is my purpose now to return whence I came. I have scruples, touching the matter thou wot'st of." 15

"Sayest thou so?" replied he of the serpent, smiling apart. 'Let us walk on, nevertheless, reasoning as we go, and if I convince thee not, thou shalt turn back. We are but a little way in the forest, yet."

"Too far, too far!" exclaimed the goodman, unconsciously resuming his walk. "My father never went into the woods on such an errand, nor his father before him. We have been a race of honest men and good Christians, since the days of the martyrs.° And shall I be the first of the name of Brown that ever took this path and kept—"

"Such company, thou wouldst say," observed the elder person, interrupting his pause. "Well said, Goodman Brown! I have been as well acquainted with your family as with ever a one among the Puritans; and that's no trifle to say. I helped your grandfather, the constable, when he lashed the Quaker woman so smartly through the streets of Salem. And it was I that brought your father a pitch-pine knot, kindled at my own hearth, to set fire to an Indian village, in King Philip's war.° They were my good friends, both; and many a pleasant walk have we had along this path, and returned merrily after midnight. I would fain be friends with you, for their sake."

"If it be as thou sayest," replied Goodman Brown, "I marvel they never spoke of these matters. Or, verily, I marvel not, seeing that the least rumor of the sort would have driven them from New England. We are a people of prayer, and good works to boot, and abide no such wickedness."

"Wickedness or not," said the traveller with twisted staff, "I have a very general acquaintance here in New England. The deacons of many a church have drunk the communion wine with me; the selectmen, of divers towns, make me their chairman; and a majority of the Great and General Court are firm supporters of my interest. The governor and I, too—but these are state secrets." 20

"Can this be so!" cried Goodman Brown, with a stare of amazement at his undisturbed companion. "Howbeit, I have nothing to do with the governor and council; they have their own ways, and are no rule for a simple husbandman like me. But, were I to go on with thee, how should I meet the eye of that good old man, our minister, at Salem village? Oh, his voice would make me tremble, both Sabbath-day and lecture-day!"

---

*days of the martyrs*: The martyrdoms of Protestants in England during the reign of Queen Mary (1553–1558).

*King Philip's War* (1675–1676): It resulted in the suppression of Indian tribal life in New England and prepared the way for unlimited settlement of the area by European immigrants. "Philip" was the English name of Chief Metacomet of the Wampanoag Indian Tribe.

Thus far, the elder traveller had listened with due gravity, but now burst into a fit of irrepressible mirth, shaking himself so violently, that his snakelike staff actually seemed to wriggle in sympathy.

"Ha! ha! ha!" shouted he, again and again; then composing himself, "Well, go on, Goodman Brown, go on; but, prithee, don't kill me with laughing!"

"Well, then, to end the matter at once," said Goodman Brown, considerably nettled, "there is my wife, Faith. It would break her dear little heart; and I'd rather break my own!"

"Nay, if that be the case," answered the other, "e'en go thy ways, Goodman Brown. I would not, for twenty old women like the one hobbling before us, that Faith should come to any harm."   25

As he spoke, he pointed his staff at a female figure on the path, in whom Goodman Brown recognized a very pious and exemplary dame, who had taught him his catechism in youth, and was still his moral and spiritual adviser, jointly with the minister and Deacon Gookin.

"A marvel, truly, that Goody° Cloyse should be so far in the wilderness, at nightfall!" said he. "But, with your leave, friend, I shall take a cut through the woods, until we have left this Christian woman behind. Being a stranger to you, she might ask whom I was consorting with, and whither I was going."

"Be it so," said his fellow-traveller. "Betake you to the woods, and let me keep the path."

Accordingly, the young man turned aside, but took care to watch his companion, who advanced softly along the road, until he had come within a staff's length of the old dame. She, meanwhile, was making the best of her way, with singular speed for so aged a woman, and mumbling some indistinct words, a prayer, doubtless, as she went. The traveller put forth his staff, and touched her withered neck with what seemed the serpent's tail.

"The devil!" screamed the pious old lady.   30

"Then Goody Cloyse knows her old friend?" observed the traveller, confronting her, and leaning on his writhing stick.

"Ah, forsooth, and is it your worship, indeed?" cried the good dame. "Yea, truly is it, and in the very image of my old gossip,° Goodman Brown, the grandfather of the silly fellow that now is. But, would your worship believe it? My broomstick hath strangely disappeared, stolen, as I suspect, by that unhanged witch, Goody Cory,° and that, too, when I was all anointed with the juice of smallage and cinque-foil and wolf's-bane—"

"Mingled with fine wheat and the fat of a new-born babe," said the shape of old Goodman Brown.

"Ah, your worship knows the recipe," cried the old lady, cackling aloud. "So, as I was saying, being all ready for the meeting, and no horse to ride on, I made up my mind to foot it; for they tell me there is a nice young man to be

Goody: a shortened form of "goodwife," a respectful name for a married woman of low rank. A "Goody Cloyse" was one of the women sentenced to execution by Hawthorne's great grandfather, Judge John Hathorne.
*gossip*: from "good sib" or "good relative."
*Goody Cory*: the name of a woman who was also sent to execution by Judge Hathorne.

taken into communion to-night. But now your good worship will lend me your arm, and we shall be there in a twinkling."

"That can hardly be," answered her friend. "I will not spare you my arm, 35 Goody Cloyse, but here is my staff, if you will."

So saying, he threw it down at her feet, where, perhaps, it assumed life, being one of the rods which its owner had formerly lent to the Egyptian Magi.° Of this fact, however, Goodman Brown could not take cognizance. He had cast up his eyes in astonishment, and looking down again, beheld neither Goody Cloyse nor the serpentine staff, but his fellow-traveller alone, who waited for him as calmly as if nothing had happened.

"That old woman taught me my catechism!" said the young man; and there was a world of meaning in this simple comment.

They continued to walk onward, while the elder traveller exhorted his companion to make good speed and persevere in the path, discoursing so aptly, that his arguments seemed rather to spring up in the bosom of his auditor, than to be suggested by himself. As they went he plucked a branch of maple, to serve for a walking-stick, and began to strip it of the twigs and little boughs, which were wet with evening dew. The moment his fingers touched them, they became strangely withered and dried up, as with a week's sunshine. Thus the pair proceeded, at a good free pace, until suddenly, in a gloomy hollow of the road, Goodman Brown sat himself down on the stump of a tree, and refused to go any farther.

"Friend," said he, stubbornly, "my mind is made up. Not another step will I budge on this errand. What if a wretched old woman do choose to go to the devil, when I thought she was going to Heaven! Is that any reason why I should quit my dear Faith, and go after her?"

"You will think better of this by and by," said his acquaintance, composedly. 40 "Sit here and rest yourself a while; and when you feel like moving again, there is my staff to help you along."

Without more words, he threw his companion the maple stick, and was as speedily out of sight as if he had vanished into the deepening gloom. The young man sat a few moments by the roadside, applauding himself greatly, and thinking with how clear a conscience he should meet the minister, in his morning walk, nor shrink from the eye of good old Deacon Gookin. And what calm sleep would be his, that very night, which was to have been spent so wickedly, but purely and sweetly now, in the arms of Faith! Amidst these pleasant and praiseworthy meditations, Goodman Brown heard the tramp of horses along the road, and deemed it advisable to conceal himself within the verge of the forest, conscious of the guilty purpose that had brought him thither, though now so happily turned from it.

On came the hoof-tramps and the voices of the riders, two grave old voices, conversing soberly as they drew near. These mingled sounds appeared to pass along the road, within a few yards of the young man's hiding-place; but owing, doubtless, to the depth of the gloom, at that particular spot, neither the travellers nor their steeds were visible. Though their figures brushed the small boughs by the wayside, it could not be seen that they intercepted, even for a moment, the

*lent to the Egyptian Magi*: See Exodus 7:10–12.

faint gleam from the strip of bright sky, athwart which they must have passed. Goodman Brown alternately crouched and stood on tiptoe, pulling aside the branches, and thrusting forth his head as far as he durst, without discerning so much as a shadow. It vexed him the more, because he could have sworn, were such a thing possible, that he recognized the voices of the minister and Deacon Gookin, jogging° along quietly, as they were wont to do, when bound to some ordination or ecclesiastical council. While yet within hearing, one of the riders stopped to pluck a switch.

"Of the two, reverend Sir," said the voice like the deacon's, "I had rather miss an ordination dinner than to-night's meeting. They tell me that some of our community are to be here from Falmouth and beyond, and others from Connecticut and Rhode Island; besides several of the Indian powwows,° who, after their fashion, know almost as much deviltry as the best of us. Moreover, there is a goodly young woman to be taken into communion."

"Mighty well, Deacon Gookin!" replied the solemn old tones of the minister. "Spur up, or we shall be late. Nothing can be done, you know, until I get on the ground."

The hoofs clattered again, and the voices, talking so strangely in the empty air, passed on through the forest, where no church had ever been gathered, nor solitary Christian prayed. Whither, then, could these holy men be journeying, so deep into the heathen wilderness? Young Goodman Brown caught hold of a tree, for support, being ready to sink down on the ground, faint and over-burthened with the heavy sickness of his heart. He looked up to the sky, doubting whether there really was a Heaven above him. Yet, there was the blue arch, and the stars brightening in it.    45

"With Heaven above, and Faith below, I will yet stand firm against the devil!" cried Goodman Brown.

While he still gazed upward, into the deep arch of the firmament, and had lifted his hands to pray, a cloud, though no wind was stirring, hurried across the zenith, and hid the brightening stars. The blue sky was still visible, except directly overhead, where this black mass of cloud was sweeping swiftly northward. Aloft in the air, as if from the depths of the cloud, came a confused and doubtful sound of voices. Once, the listener fancied that he could distinguish the accents of town's-people of his own, men and women, both pious and ungodly, many of whom he had met at the communion-table, and had seen others rioting at the tavern. The next moment, so indistinct were the sounds, he doubted whether he had heard aught but the murmur of the old forest, whispering without a wind. Then came a stronger swell of those familiar tones, heard daily in the sunshine, at Salem village, but never, until now, from a cloud at night. There was one voice, of a young woman, uttering lamentations, yet with an uncertain sorrow, and entreating for some favor, which, perhaps, it would grieve her to obtain. And all the unseen multitude, both saints and sinners, seemed to encourage her onward.

"Faith!" shouted Goodman Brown, in a voice of agony and desperation;

*jogging*: riding a horse at a slow trot.
*powwow*: a Narragansett Indian word describing a ritual ceremony of dancing, incantation, and magic.

and the echoes of the forest mocked him, crying—"Faith! Faith!" as if bewildered wretches were seeking her, all through the wilderness.

The cry of grief, rage, and terror was yet piercing the night, when the unhappy husband held his breath for a response. There was a scream, drowned immediately in a louder murmur of voices fading into far-off laughter, as the dark cloud swept away, leaving the clear and silent sky above Goodman Brown. But something fluttered lightly down through the air, and caught on the branch of a tree. The young man seized it and beheld a pink ribbon.

"My Faith is gone!" cried he, after one stupefied moment. "There is no 50 good on earth, and sin is but a name. Come, devil! for to thee is this world given."

And maddened with despair, so that he laughed loud and long, did Goodman Brown grasp his staff and set forth again, at such a rate, that he seemed to fly along the forest path, rather than to walk or run. The road grew wilder and drearier, and more faintly traced, and vanished at length, leaving him in the heart of the dark wilderness, still rushing onward, with the instinct that guides mortal man to evil. The whole forest was peopled with frightful sounds; the creaking of the trees, the howling of wild beasts, and the yell of Indians; while, sometimes, the wind tolled like a distant church bell, and sometimes gave a broad roar around the traveller, as if all Nature were laughing him to scorn. But he was himself the chief horror of the scene, and shrank not from its other horrors.

"Ha! ha! ha!" roared Goodman Brown, when the wind laughed at him. "Let us hear which will laugh loudest! Think not to frighten me with your deviltry! Come witch, come wizard, come Indian powwow, come devil himself! and here comes Goodman Brown. You may as well fear him as he fear you!"

In truth, all through the haunted forest, there could be nothing more frightful than the figure of Goodman Brown. On he flew, among the black pines, brandishing his staff with frenzied gestures, now giving vent to an inspiration of horrid blasphemy, and now shouting forth such laughter, as set all the echoes of the forest laughing like demons around him. The fiend in his own shape is less hideous, than when he rages in the breast of man. Thus sped the demoniac on his course, until, quivering among the trees, he saw a red light before him, as when the felled trunks and branches of a clearing have been set on fire, and throw up their lurid blaze against the sky, at the hour of midnight. He paused, in a lull of the tempest that had driven him onward, and heard the swell of what seemed a hymn, rolling solemnly from a distance, with the weight of many voices. He knew the tune. It was a familiar one in the choir of the village meeting-house. The verse died heavily away, and was lengthened by a chorus, not of human voices, but of all the sounds of the benighted wilderness, pealing in awful harmony together. Goodman Brown cried out; and his cry was lost to his own ear, by its unison with the cry of the desert.

In the interval of silence, he stole forward, until the light glared full upon his eyes. At one extremity of an open space, hemmed in by the dark wall of the forest, arose a rock, bearing some rude, natural resemblance either to an altar or a pulpit, and surrounded by four blazing pines, their tops aflame, their stems untouched, like candles at an evening meeting. The mass of foliage, that had overgrown the summit of the rock, was all on fire, blazing high into the night, and fitfully illuminating the whole field. Each pendent twig and leafy festoon was in a blaze.

As the red light arose and fell, a numerous congregation alternately shone forth, then disappeared in shadow, and again grew, as it were, out of the darkness, peopling the heart of the solitary woods at once.

"A grave and dark-clad company!" quoth Goodman Brown.                       55

In truth, they were such. Among them, quivering to-and-fro, between gloom and splendor, appeared faces that would be seen, next day, at the council-board of the province, and others which, Sabbath after Sabbath, looked devoutly heavenward, and benignantly over the crowded pews, from the holiest pulpits in the land. Some affirm that the lady of the governor was there. At least, there were high dames well known to her, and wives of honored husbands, and widows a great multitude, and ancient maidens, all of excellent repute, and fair young girls, who trembled lest their mothers should espy them. Either the sudden gleams of light, flashing over the obscure field, bedazzled Goodman Brown, or he recognized a score of the church members of Salem village, famous for their especial sanctity. Good old Deacon Gookin had arrived, and waited at the skirts of that venerable saint, his reverend pastor. But, irreverently consorting with these grave, reputable, and pious people, these elders of the church, these chaste dames and dewy virgins, there were men of dissolute lives and women of spotted fame, wretches given over to all mean and filthy vice, and suspected even of horrid crimes. It was strange to see, that the good shrank not from the wicked, nor were the sinners abashed by the saints. Scattered, also, among their pale-faced enemies, were the Indian priests, or powwows, who had often scared their native forest with more hideous incantations than any known to English witchcraft.

"But, where is Faith?" thought Goodman Brown; and, as hope came into his heart, he trembled.

Another verse of the hymn arose, a slow and mournful strain, such as the pious love, but joined to words which expressed all that our nature can conceive of sin, and darkly hinted at far more. Unfathomable to mere mortals is the lore of fiends. Verse after verse was sung, and still the chorus of the desert swelled between, like the deepest tone of a mighty organ. And, with the final peal of that dreadful anthem, there came a sound, as if the roaring wind, the rushing streams, the howling beasts, and every other voice of the unconverted wilderness were mingling and according with the voice of guilty man, in homage to the prince of all. The four blazing pines threw up a loftier flame, and obscurely discovered shapes and visages of horror on the smoke-wreaths, above the impious assembly. At the same moment, the fire on the rock shot redly forth, and formed a glowing arch above its base, where now appeared a figure. With reverence be it spoken, the apparition bore no slight similitude, both in garb and manner, to some grave divine of the New England churches.

"Bring forth the converts!" cried a voice, that echoed through the field and rolled into the forest.

At the word, Goodman Brown stepped forth from the shadow of the trees,     60
and approached the congregation, with whom he felt a loathful brotherhood, by the sympathy of all that was wicked in his heart. He could have well-nigh sworn, that the shape of his own dead father beckoned him to advance, looking downward from a smoke-wreath, while a woman, with dim features of despair, threw out her hand to warn him back. Was it his mother? But he had no power to retreat one step, nor to resist, even in thought, when the minister and good old Deacon

Gookin seized his arms, and led him to the blazing rock. Thither came also the slender form of a veiled female, led between Goody Cloyse, that pious teacher of the catechism, and Martha Carrier, who had received the devil's promise to be queen of hell. A rampant hag was she! And there stood the proselytes, beneath the canopy of fire.

"Welcome, my children," said the dark figure, "to the communion of your race! Ye have found, thus young, your nature and your destiny. My children, look behind you!"

They turned; and flashing forth, as it were, in a sheet of flame, the fiend-worshippers were seen; the smile of welcome gleamed darkly on every visage.

"There," resumed the sable form, "are all whom ye have reverenced from youth. Ye deemed them holier than yourselves, and shrank from your own sin, contrasting it with their lives of righteousness and prayerful aspirations heavenward. Yet, here are they all, in my worshipping assembly! This night it shall be granted you to know their secret deeds; how hoary-bearded elders of the church have whispered wanton words to the young maids of their households; how many a woman, eager for widow's weeds, has given her husband a drink at bedtime, and let him sleep his last sleep in her bosom; how beardless youths have made haste to inherit their father's wealth; and how fair damsels—blush not, sweet ones!—have dug little graves in the garden, and bidden me, the sole guest, to an infant's funeral. By the sympathy of your human hearts for sin, ye shall scent out all the places—whether in church, bed-chamber, street, field, or forest—where crime has been committed, and shall exult to behold the whole earth one stain of guilt, one mighty blood-spot. Far more than this! It shall be yours to penetrate, in every bosom, the deep mystery of sin, the fountain of all wicked arts, and which inexhaustibly supplies more evil impulses than human power—than my power, at its utmost!—can make manifest in deeds. And now, my children, look upon each other."

They did so; and, by the blaze of the hell-kindled torches, the wretched man beheld his Faith, and the wife her husband, trembling before that unhallowed altar.

"Lo! there ye stand, my children," said the figure, in a deep and solemn   65
tone, almost sad, with its despairing awfulness, as if his once angelic nature could yet mourn for our miserable race. "Depending upon one another's hearts, ye had still hoped that virtue were not all a dream! Now are ye undeceived!—Evil is the nature of mankind. Evil must be your only happiness. Welcome, again, my children, to the communion of your race!"

"Welcome!" repeated the fiend-worshippers, in one cry of despair and triumph.

And there they stood, the only pair, as it seemed, who were yet hesitating on the verge of wickedness, in this dark world. A basin was hollowed, naturally, in the rock. Did it contain water, reddened by the lurid light? or was it blood? or, perchance, a liquid flame? Herein did the Shape of Evil dip his hand, and prepare to lay the mark of baptism upon their foreheads, that they might be partakers of the mystery of sin, more conscious of the secret guilt of others, both in deed and thought, than they could now be of their own. The husband cast one look at his pale wife, and Faith at him. What polluted wretches would the next glance show them to each other, shuddering alike at what they disclosed and what they saw!

"Faith! Faith! cried the husband. "Look up to Heaven, and resist the Wicked One!"

Whether Faith obeyed, he knew not. Hardly had he spoken, when he found himself amid calm night and solitude, listening to a roar of the wind, which died heavily away through the forest. He staggered against the rock, and felt it chill and damp, while a hanging twig, that had been all on fire, besprinkled his cheek with the coldest dew.

The next morning, young Goodman Brown came slowly into the street of    70
Salem village staring around him like a bewildered man. The good old minister was taking a walk along the grave-yard, to get an appetite for breakfast and meditate his sermon, and bestowed a blessing, as he passed, on Goodman Brown. He shrank from the venerable saint, as if to avoid an anathema. Old Deacon Gookin was at domestic worship, and the holy words of his prayer were heard through the open window. "What God doth the wizard pray to?" quoth Goodman Brown. Goody Cloyse, that excellent old Christian, stood in the early sunshine, at her own lattice, catechising a little girl, who had brought her a pint of morning's milk. Goodman Brown snatched away the child, as from the grasp of the fiend himself. Turning the corner by the meetinghouse, he spied the head of Faith, with the pink ribbons, gazing anxiously forth, and bursting into such joy at sight of him that she skipt along the street, and almost kissed her husband before the whole village. But Goodman Brown looked sternly and sadly into her face, and passed on without a greeting.

Had Goodman Brown fallen asleep in the forest, and only dreamed a wild dream of a witch-meeting?

Be it so, if you will. But, alas! it was a dream of evil omen for young Goodman Brown. A stern, a sad, a darkly meditative, a distrustful, if not a desperate man did he become, from the night of that fearful dream. On the Sabbath day, when the congregation were singing a holy psalm, he could not listen, because an anthem of sin rushed loudly upon his ear, and drowned all the blessed strain. When the minister spoke from the pulpit, with power and fervid eloquence, and with his hand on the open Bible, of the sacred truths of our religion, and of saint-like lives and triumphant deaths, and of future bliss or misery unutterable, then did Goodman Brown turn pale, dreading lest the roof should thunder down upon the gray blasphemer and his hearers. Often, awaking suddenly at midnight, he shrank from the bosom of Faith, and at morning or eventide, when the family knelt down at prayer, he scowled, and muttered to himself, and gazed sternly at his wife, and turned away. And when he had lived long, and was borne to his grave, a hoary corpse, followed by Faith, an aged woman, and children and grandchildren, a goodly procession, besides neighbors not a few, they carved no hopeful verse upon his tombstone; for his dying hour was gloom.

## QUESTIONS

1. Who is the protagonist in the story? Who *seems* to be the antagonist? What, if anything, do you think the antagonist really is?
2. What *seems* to be the central conflict in the story? How is this apparent conflict

resolved? How is Goodman Brown's life changed by this resolution? To what extent does this change in Goodman Brown point to another conflict that remains unresolved?

3. Near the end of the story the narrator intrudes to ask the following: "Had Goodman Brown fallen asleep in the forest, and only dreamed a wild dream of a witch-meeting?" What do you think the answer to this question is? If Goodman Brown's visions come out of his own dreams (mind, subconscious), what do they tell us about him?

4. Is Goodman Brown a round or flat character? Individual or representative? To what extent is he designed to serve as a symbolic "everyman" or representative of humankind?

5. What point of view is employed in the story? What are the advantages of using this point of view in this kind of story?

6. Consider Hawthorne's use of symbolism in the story, such as the symbolism of sunset and night, the walking stick, the witches' sabbath, the marriage to Faith, and the vague shadows amid the darkness, together with other symbols that you may find.

7. What details go into the establishment of the two distinct settings in this story? What characterizes Salem? The woods? Why might we be justified in seeing the forest as a symbolic setting?

8. What sort of sin does Goodman Brown discover in most of his friends and neighbors during the night in the woods? What common thread runs through most of this sin?

9. To what extent are the people, objects, and events in Goodman Brown's adventure invested with enough *consistent* symbolic resonance to justify calling his episode in the woods an allegory? Consider Brown's wife, Faith, as an allegorical figure. What do you make of Brown's statements that "I'll cling to her skirts and follow her to Heaven" (paragraph 7) and "Faith kept me back awhile" (paragraph 12). In this same light, consider the other characters Brown meets in the forest, the sunset, the walk into the forest, and the staff "which bore the likeness of a great black snake."

## MARJORIE PICKTHALL (1883–1922)

### *The Worker in Sandalwood*                                                          *1923*

I like to think of this as a true story, but you who read may please yourselves, siding either with the curé,° who says Hyacinthe dreamed it all, and did the carving himself in his sleep, or with Madame. I am sure that Hyacinthe thinks it true, and so does Madame, but then she has the cabinet, with the little birds and the lilies carved at the corners. Monsieur le curé shrugs his patient shoulders; but then he is tainted with the infidelities of cities, good man, having been three times to Montreal, and once, in an electric car, to Saint Anne. He and Madame still talk it over whenever they meet, though it happened so many years ago, and each leaves the other forever unconvinced. Meanwhile the dust gathers in the infinite

*curé*: a parish priest.

fine lines of the little birds' feathers, and softens the lily stamens where Madame's duster may not go; and the wood, ageing, takes on a golden gleam as of immemorial sunsets: that pale red wood, heavy with the scent of the ancient East; the wood that Hyacinthe loved.

It was the only wood of that kind which had ever been seen in Terminaison.° Pierre L'Oreillard brought it into the workshop one morning; a small heavy bundle wrapped in sacking, and then in burlap, and then in fine soft cloths. He laid it on a pile of shavings, and unwrapped it carefully and a dim sweetness filled the dark shed and hung heavily in the thin winter sunbeams.

Pierre L'Oreillard rubbed the wood respectfully with his knobby fingers. "It is sandalwood," he explained to Hyacinthe, pride of knowledge making him expansive; "a most precious wood° that grows in warm countries, thou great goblin. Smell it, *imbécile*. It is sweeter than cedar. It is to make a cabinet for the old Madame at the big house. Thy great hands shall smooth the wood, *nigaud*,° and I—I, Pierre the cabinet-maker, shall render it beautiful." Then he went out, locking the door behind him.

When he was gone, Hyacinthe laid down his plane, blew on his stiff fingers, and shambled slowly over to the wood. He was a great clumsy boy of fourteen, dark-faced, very slow of speech, dull-eyed and uncared for. He was clumsy because it is impossible to move gracefully when you are growing very big and fast on quite insufficient food. He was dull-eyed because all eyes met his unlovingly; uncared for, because none knew the beauty of his soul. But his heavy young hands could carve simple things, like flowers and birds and beasts, to perfection, as the curé pointed out. Simon has a tobacco-jar, carved with pine-cones and squirrels, and the curé has a pipe whose bowl is the bloom of a moccasin-flower, that I have seen. But it is all very long ago. And facts, in these lonely villages, easily become transfigured, touched upon their gray with a golden gleam.

"Thy hands shall smooth the wood, *nigaud*, and I shall render it beautiful," said Pierre L'Oreillard, and went off to drink brandy at the Cinq Chateaux.    5

Hyacinthe knew that the making of the cabinet would fall to him, as most of the other work did. He also touched the strange sweet wood, and at last laid his cheek against it, while the fragrance caught his breath. "How it is beautiful," said Hyacinthe, and for a moment his eyes glowed and he was happy. Then the light passed, and with bent head he shuffled back to his bench through a foam of white shavings curling almost to his knees.

"Madame perhaps will want the cabinet next week, for that is Christmas," said Hyacinthe, and fell to work harder than ever, though it was so cold in the shed that his breath hung like a little silver cloud and the steel stung his hands. There was a tiny window to his right, through which, when it was clear of frost, one looked on Terminaison, and that was cheerful and made one whistle. But to the left, through the ch:nk of the ill-fitting door, there was nothing but the forest and the road dying away in it, and the trees moving heavily under the snow. Yet, from there came all Hyacinthe's dumb dreams and slow reluctant fancies, which he sometimes found himself able to tell—in wood, not in words.

---

*Terminaison*: French for "ending or termination," a town imagined here as a town in French Canada.

*a most precious wood*: Sandalwood is still rare and precious; it is grown mainly in India and yields to exquisite detail in carving and decoration.

*nigaud*: simpleton.

Brandy was good at the Cinq Chateaux, and Pierre L'Oreillard gave Hyacinthe plenty of directions, but no further help with the cabinet.

"That is to be finished for Madame on the festival, *gros escargot!*"° said he, cuffing Hyacinthe's ears furiously, "finished, and with a prettiness about the corners, hearest thou, *ourson?*° I suffer from a delicacy of the constitution and a little feebleness in the legs on these days, so that I cannot handle the tools. I must leave this work to thee, *gacheur.*° See it is done properly, and stand up and touch a hand to thy cap when I address thee, *orvet,*° great slow-worm."

"Yes, monsieur," said Hyacinthe, wearily.                                               10

It is hard, when you do all the work, to be cuffed into the bargain, and fourteen is not very old. He went to work on the cabinet with slow, exquisite skill, but on the eve of Noel, he was still at work, and the cabinet unfinished. It meant a thrashing from Pierre if the morrow came and found it still unfinished, and Pierre's thrashings were cruel. But it was growing into a thing of perfection under his slow hands, and Hyacinthe would not hurry over it.

"Then work on it all night, and show it to me all completed in the morning, or thy bones shall mourn thy idleness," said Pierre with a flicker of his little eyes. And he shut Hyacinthe into the workshop with a smoky lamp, his tools, and the sandalwood cabinet.

It was nothing unusual. The boy had often been left before to finish a piece of work overnight while Pierre went off to his brandies. But this was Christmas Eve, and he was very tired. The cold crept into the shed until the scent of the sandalwood could not make him dream himself warm, and the roof cracked sullenly in the forest. There came upon Hyacinthe one of those awful, hopeless despairs that children know. It seemed to be a living presence that caught up his soul and crushed it in black hands. "In all the world, nothing!" said he, staring at the dull flame; "no place, no heart, no love! O kind God, is there a place, a love for me in another world?"

I cannot endure to think of Hyacinthe, poor lad, shut up despairing in the workshop with his loneliness, his cold, and his hunger, on the eve of Christmas. He was but an overgrown, unhappy child, and for unhappy children no aid, at this season, seems too divine for faith. So Madame says, and she is very old and very wise. Hyacinthe even looked at the chisel in his hand, and thought that by a touch of that he might lose it all, all, and be at peace, somewhere not far from God; only it was forbidden. Then came the tears, and great sobs that sickened and deafened him, so that he scarcely heard the gentle rattling of the latch.

At least, I suppose it came then, but it may have been later. The story is    15
all so vague here, so confused with fancies that have spoiled the first simplicity. I think that Hyacinthe must have gone to the door, opening it upon the still woods and the frosty stars, and the lad who stood outside must have said: "I see you are working late, comrade. May I come in?" or something like it.

Hyacinthe brushed his ragged sleeve across his eyes, and opened the door wider with a little nod to the other to enter. Those little lonely villages strung

*gros escargot*: big snail.
*ourson*: bear cub.
*gacheur*: bungler, spoiler.
*orvet*: blind worm, slow worm.

along the great river see strange wayfarers adrift inland from the sea. Hyacinthe said to himself that surely here was such a one.

Afterwards he told the curé that for a moment he had been bewildered. Dully blinking into the stranger's eyes, he lost for a flash the first impression of youth and received one of some incredible age or sadness. But this also passed and he knew that the wanderer's eyes were only quiet, very quiet, like the little pools in the wood where the wild does went to drink. As he turned within the door, smiling at Hyacinthe and shaking some snow from his fur cap, he did not seem more than sixteen or so.

"It is very cold outside," he said. "There is a big oak tree on the edge of the fields that has split in the frost and frightened all the little squirrels asleep there. Next year it will make an even better home for them. And see what I found close by!" He opened his fingers, and showed Hyacinthe a little sparrow lying unruffled in his palm.

"*Pauvrette!*"° said the dull Hyacinthe. "*Pauvrette!* Is it then dead?" He touched it with a gentle forefinger.

"No," answered the strange boy, "it is not dead. We'll put it here among the shavings, not far from the lamp, and it will be well by morning."°          20

He smiled at Hyacinthe again, and the shambling lad felt dimly as if the scent of sandalwood had deepened, and the lamp-flame burned clearer. But the stranger's eyes were only quiet, quiet.

"Have you come far?" asked Hyacinthe. "It is a bad season for travelling, and the wolves are out in the woods."

"A long way," said the other; "a long, long way. I heard a child cry. . . ."

"There is no child here," answered Hyacinthe, shaking his head. "Monsieur L'Oreillard is not fond of children, he says they cost too much money. But if you have come far, you must be cold and hungry, and I have no food or fire. At the Cinq Chateaux you will find both!"

The stranger looked at him again with those quiet eyes, and Hyacinthe fancied          25 his face was familiar. "I will stay here," he said, "you are very late at work and you are unhappy."

"Why, as to that," answered Hyacinthe, rubbing again at his cheeks and ashamed of his tears, "most of us are sad at one time or another, the good God knows. Stay here and welcome if it pleases you, and you may take a share of my bed, though it is no more than a pile of balsam boughs and an old blanket, in the loft. But I must work at this cabinet, for the drawer must be finished and the handles put on and these corners carved, all by the holy morning; or my wages will be paid with a stick."

"You have a hard master," put in the other boy, "if he would pay you with blows upon the feast of Noel."

"He is hard enough," said Hyacinthe; "but once he gave me a dinner of sausages and white wine, and once, in the summer, melons. If my eyes will stay open, I will finish this by morning, but indeed I am sleepy. Stay with me an hour or so, comrade, and talk to me of your wanderings, so that the time may pass more quickly."

*Pauvrette*: poor little thing.
See Psalms 84:4.

"I will tell you of the country where I was a child," answered the stranger.

And while Hyacinthe worked, he told—of sunshine and dust; of the shadows    30
of vine-leaves on the flat white walls of a house; of rosy doves on the flat roof;
of the flowers that come in the spring, crimson and blue, and the white cyclamen
in the shadow of the rocks; of the olive, the myrtle and almond; until Hyacinthe's
slow fingers ceased working, and his sleepy eyes blinked wonderingly.

"See what you have done, comrade," he said at last; "you have told of such
pretty things that I have done no work for an hour. And now the cabinet will
never be finished, and I shall be beaten."

"Let me help you," smiled the other; "I also was bred a carpenter."°

At first Hyacinthe would not, fearing to trust the sweet wood out of his
own hands, but at length he allowed the stranger to fit in one of the little drawers,
and so deftly was the work done, that Hyacinthe pounded his fists on the bench
in admiration. "You have a pretty knack," he cried; "it seemed as if you did but
hold the drawer in your hands a moment, and hey! ho! it jumped into its place!"

"Let me fit in the other little drawers, while you go and rest a while," said
the wanderer. So Hyacinthe curled up among the shavings, and the stranger fell
to work upon the little cabinet of sandalwood.

Here begins what the curé will have it is a dream within a dream. Sweetest    35
of dreams was ever dreamed, if that is so. Sometimes I am forced to think with
him, but again I see as clearly as with old Madame's eyes, that have not seen the
earthly light for twenty years, and with her and Hyacinthe, I say "Credo."°

Hyacinthe said that he lay upon the shavings in the sweetness of the sandalwood, and was very tired. He thought of the country where the stranger had been
a boy; of the flowers on the hills; of the laughing leaves of aspen, and poplar; of
the golden flowering anise and the golden sun upon the dusty roads, until he
was warm. All the time through these pictures, as through a painted veil, he was
aware of that other boy with the quiet eyes, at work upon the cabinet, smoothing,
fitting, polishing. "He does better work than I," thought Hyacinthe, but he was
not jealous. And again he thought, "It is growing towards morning. In a little
while I will get up and help him." But he did not, for the dream of warmth and
the smell of the sandalwood held him in a sweet drowse. Also he said that he
thought the stranger was singing as he worked, for there seemed to be a sense
of some music in the shed, though he could not tell whether it came from the
other boy's lips, or from the shabby old tools as he used them, or from the stars.
"The stars are much paler," thought Hyacinthe, "and soon it will be morning,
and the corners are not carved yet. I must get up and help this kind one in a
little moment. Only I am so tired, and the music and the sweetness seem to wrap
me and fold me close, so that I may not move."

He lay without moving, and behind the forest there shone a pale glow of
some indescribable colour that was neither green nor blue, while in Terminaison
the church bells began to ring. "Day will soon be here!" thought Hyacinthe, immovable in that deep dream of his, "and with day will come Monsieur L'Oreillard and
his stick. I must get up and help, for even yet the corners are not carved."

. . . *bred a carpenter*: See Matthew 13:55.

*Credo*: "I believe," the opening words of the *Credo* section of the Catholic Mass ("Credo
in unum Deum . . ." ["I believe in one God . . ."].

But he did not get up. Instead, he saw the stranger look at him again, smiling as if he loved him, and lay his brown finger lightly upon the four empty corners of the cabinet. And Hyacinthe saw the little squares of reddish wood ripple and heave and break, as little clouds when the wind goes through the sky. And out of them thrust forth little birds, and after them the lilies, for a moment living, but even while Hyacinthe looked, growing hard and reddish-brown and settling back into the sweet wood. Then the stranger smiled again, and laid all the tools neatly in order, and, opening the door quietly, went away into the woods.

Hyacinthe lay still among the shavings for a long time, and then he crept slowly to the door. The sun, not yet risen, set its first beams upon the delicate mist of frost afloat beneath the trees, and so all the world was aflame with splendid gold. Far away down the road a dim figure seemed to move amid the glory, but the glow and the splendour were such that Hyacinthe was blinded. His breath came sharply as the glow beat in great waves on the wretched shed; on the foam of shavings; on the cabinet with the little birds and the lilies carved at the corners.

He was too pure of heart° to feel afraid. But, "Blessed be the Lord," whispered    40
Hyacinthe, clasping his slow hands, "for He hath visited and redeemed His people.° But who will believe?"

Then the sun of Christ's day rose gloriously, and the little sparrow came from his nest among the shavings and shook his wings to the light.°

*pure of heart*: See Matthew 5:8.
*. . . His people*: See Luke 1:68.
*. . . wings to the light*: See Malachi 4:2.

## QUESTIONS

1. What point of view is employed in the story? Who or what is the narrator? To what extent does the narrator know a great deal more than we might expect? Why does the narrator repeat several times that the events in the story happened "very long ago"?

2. What sort of person is Hyacinthe? How does he deal with his life? How does he react to Pierre L'Oreillard's treatment? Why does the "strange child" with "quiet eyes" appear to him?

3. What is the narrator's attitude toward Hyacinthe? In what ways does this shape your attitude?

4. How does Pickthall control the tone of the story? Why does the narrator stress the quality of Hyacinthe's work in the first and third paragraphs? Why does the narrator stress the possibility that Hyacinthe dreamed the events of the story? To what extent do these points of emphasis keep the story from becoming too fantastic or sentimentalized?

5. What kind of person is Pierre L'Oreillard? How does he treat Hyacinthe? How much work does he do?

6. Are the characters in this story round or flat? Static or dynamic? Individual

or representative? In what way do these choices contribute to the total effect of the story?

7. To what extent does the setting work symbolically to establish mood and tone? Consider the time of year, the specific night, the description of the shed in which Hyacinthe works, the forest, and the animals noted throughout.

8. Consider the symbolism associated with the "quiet" stranger: his homeland, his training as a carpenter, the sparrow he revives, the heightening of the lamp-flame, and the warming of the workshop. What do these details suggest? How consistent is this symbolism?

9. Would you consider this story an allegory, a myth, a fable, a parable, or simply symbolic? Explain your answer.


# JOHN STEINBECK (1902–1968)

## *The Chrysanthemums*                                                    *1937*

The high grey-flannel fog of winter closed off the Salinas Valley° from the sky and from all the rest of the world. On every side it sat like a lid on the mountains and made of the great valley a closed pot. On the broad, level land floor the gang plows bit deep and left the black earth shining like metal where the shares had cut. On the foothill ranches across the Salinas River, the yellow stubble fields seemed to be bathed in pale cold sunshine, but there was no sunshine in the valley now in December. The thick willow scrub along the river flamed with sharp and positive yellow leaves.

It was a time of quiet and of waiting. The air was cold and tender. A light wind blew up from the southwest so that the farmers were mildly hopeful of a good rain before long; but fog and rain do not go together.

Across the river, on Henry Allen's foothill ranch there was little work to be done, for the hay was cut and stored and the orchards were plowed up to receive the rain deeply when it should come. The cattle on the higher slopes were becoming shaggy and rough-coated.

Elisa Allen, working in her flower garden, looked down across the yard and saw Henry, her husband, talking to two men in business suits. The three of them stood by the tractor shed, each man with one foot on the side of the little Fordson.° They smoked cigarettes and studied the machines as they talked.

Elisa watched them for a moment and then went back to her work. She was thirty-five. Her face was lean and strong and her eyes were as clear as water. Her figure looked blocked and heavy in her gardening costume, a man's black hat pulled low down over her eyes, clodhopper shoes, a figured print dress almost completely covered by a big corduroy apron with four big pockets to hold the snips, the trowel and scratcher, the seeds and the knife she worked with. She wore heavy leather gloves to protect her hands while she worked.

5

*the Salinas Valley*: in Monterey County, California, about 50 miles south of San José. Steinbeck was born in Salinas, and his home there is open to the public.
*Fordson*: a tractor manufactured by the Ford Motor Company, with large rear steel lugged wheels.

She was cutting down the old year's chrysanthemum stalks with a pair of short and powerful scissors. She looked down toward the men by the tractor shed now and then. Her face was eager and mature and handsome; even her work with the scissors was over-eager, over-powerful. The chrysanthemum stems seemed too small and easy for her energy.

She brushed a cloud of hair out of her eyes with the back of her glove, and left a smudge of earth on the cheek in doing it. Behind her stood the neat white farm house with red geraniums close-banked around it as high as the windows. It was a hard-swept looking little house, with hard-polished windows, and a clean mud-mat on the front steps.

Elisa cast another glance toward the tractor shed. The strangers were getting into their Ford coupe. She took off a glove and put her strong fingers down into the forest of new green chrysanthemum sprouts that were growing around the old roots. She spread the leaves and looked down among the close-growing stems. No aphids were there, no sowbugs or snails or cutworms. Her terrier fingers destroyed such pests before they could get started.

Elisa started at the sound of her husband's voice. He had come near quietly, and he leaned over the wire fence that protected her flower garden from cattle and dogs and chickens.

"At it again," he said. "You've got a strong new crop coming."    10

Elisa straightened her back and pulled on the gardening glove again. "Yes. They'll be strong this coming year." In her tone and on her face there was a little smugness.

"You've got a gift with things," Henry observed. "Some of those yellow chrysanthemums you had this year were ten inches across. I wish you'd work out in the orchard and raise some apples that big."

Her eyes sharpened. "Maybe I could do it, too. I've a gift with things, all right. My mother had it. She could stick anything in the ground and make it grow. She said it was having planters' hands that knew how to do it."

"Well, it sure works with flowers," he said.

"Henry, who were those men you were talking to?"    15

"Why, sure, that's what I came to tell you. They were from the Western Meat Company. I sold those thirty head of three-year-old steers. Got nearly my own price, too."

"Good," she said. "Good for you."

"And I thought," he continued, "I thought how it's Saturday afternoon, and we might go to Salinas for dinner at a restaurant, and then to a picture show— to celebrate, you see."

"Good," she repeated. "Oh, yes. That will be good."

Henry put on his joking tone. "There's fights tonight. How'd you like to    20 go to the fights?"

"Oh, no," she said breathlessly. "No, I wouldn't like fights."

"Just fooling, Elisa. We'll go to a movie. Let's see. It's two now. I'm going to take Scotty and bring down those steers from the hill. It'll take us maybe two hours. We'll go in town about five and have dinner at the Cominos Hotel. Like that?"

"Of course I'll like it. It's good to eat away from home."

"All right, then. I'll go get up a couple of horses."

She said, "I'll have plenty of time to transplant some of these sets, I guess."   25

She heard her husband calling Scotty down by the barn. And a little later she saw the two men ride up the pale yellow hillside in search of the steers.

There was a little square sandy bed kept for rooting the chrysanthemums. With her trowel she turned the soil over and over, and smoothed it and patted it firm. Then she dug ten parallel trenches to receive the sets. Back at the chrysanthemum bed she pulled out the little crisp shoots, trimmed off the leaves of each one with her scissors and laid it on a small orderly pile.

A squeak of wheels and plod of hoofs came from the road. Elisa looked up. The country road ran along the dense bank of willows and cottonwoods that bordered the river, and up this road came a curious vehicle, curiously drawn. It was an old spring-wagon, with a round canvas top on it like the cover of a prairie schooner. It was drawn by an old bay horse and a little grey-and-white burro. A big stubble-bearded man sat between the cover flaps and drove the crawling team. Underneath the wagon, between the hind wheels, a lean and rangy mongrel dog walked sedately. Words were painted on the canvas in clumsy, crooked letters. "Pots, pans, knives, sisors, lawn mores. Fixed." Two rows of articles and the triumphantly definitive "Fixed" below. The black paint had run down in little sharp points beneath each letter.

Elisa, squatting on the ground, watched to see the crazy, loose-jointed wagon pass by. But it didn't pass. It turned into the farm road in front of her house, crooked old wheels skirling and squeaking. The rangy dog darted from between the wheels and ran ahead. Instantly the two ranch shepherds flew out at him. Then all three stopped, and with stiff and quivering tails, with taut straight legs, with ambassadorial dignity, they slowly circled, sniffing daintily. The caravan pulled up to Elisa's wire fence and stopped. Now the newcomer dog, feeling outnumbered, lowered his tail and retired under the wagon with raised hackles and bared teeth.

The man on the wagon seat called out. "That's a bad dog in a fight when he gets started."   30

Elisa laughed. "I see he is. How soon does he generally get started?"

The man caught up her laughter and echoed it heartily. "Sometimes not for weeks and weeks," he said. He climbed stiffly down, over the wheel. The horse and the donkey drooped like unwatered flowers.

Elisa saw that he was a very big man. Although his hair and beard were greying, he did not look old. His worn black suit was wrinkled and spotted with grease. The laughter had disappeared from his face and eyes the moment his laughing voice ceased. His eyes were dark and they were full of the brooding that gets in the eyes of teamsters and of sailors. The calloused hands he rested on the wire fence were cracked, and every crack was a black line. He took off his battered hat.

"I'm off my general road, ma'am," he said. "Does this dirt road cut over across the river to the Los Angeles highway?"

Elisa stood up and shoved the thick scissors in her apron pocket. "Well,   35 yes, it does, but it winds around and then fords the river. I don't think your team could pull through the sand."

He replied with some asperity, "It might surprise you what them beasts can pull through."

"When they get started?" she asked.

He smiled for a second. "Yes. When they get started."

"Well," said Elisa, "I think you'll save time if you go back to the Salinas road and pick up the highway there."

He drew a big finger down the chicken wire and made it sing. "I ain't in any hurry, ma'am. I go from Seattle to San Diego and back every year. Takes all my time. About six months each way. I aim to follow nice weather."    40

Elisa took off her gloves and stuffed them in the apron pocket with the scissors. She touched the under edge of her man's hat, searching for fugitive hairs. "That sounds like a nice kind of a way to live," she said.

He leaned confidentially over the fence. "Maybe you noticed the writing on my wagon. I mend pots and sharpen knives and scissors. You got any of them things to do?"

"Oh, no," she said quickly. "Nothing like that." Her eyes hardened with resistance.

"Scissors is the worst thing," he explained. "Most people just ruin scissors trying to sharpen 'em, but I know how. I got a special tool. It's a little bobbit kind of thing, and patented. But it sure does the trick."

"No. My scissors are all sharp."    45

"All right, then. Take a pot," he continued earnestly, "a bent pot, or a pot with a hole. I can make it like new so you don't have to buy no new ones. That's a saving for you."

"No," she said shortly. "I tell you I have nothing like that for you to do."

His face fell to an exaggerated sadness. His voice took on a whining undertone. "I ain't had a thing to do today. Maybe I won't have no supper tonight. You see I'm off my regular road. I know folks on the highway clear from Seattle to San Diego. They save their things for me to sharpen up because they know I do it so good and save them money."

"I'm sorry," Elisa said irritably. "I haven't anything for you to do."

His eyes left her face and fell to searching the ground. They roamed about until they came to the chrysanthemum bed where she had been working. "What's them plants, ma'am?"    50

The irritation and resistance melted from Elisa's face. "Oh, those are chrysanthemums, giant whites and yellows. I raise them every year, bigger than anybody around here."

"Kind of a long-stemmed flower? Looks like a quick puff of colored smoke?" he asked.

"That's it. What a nice way to describe them."

"They smell kind of nasty till you get used to them," he said.

"It's a good bitter smell," she retorted, "not nasty at all."    55

He changed his tone quickly. "I like the smell myself."

"I had ten-inch blooms this year," she said.

The man leaned farther over the fence. "Look. I know a lady down the road a piece, has got the nicest garden you ever seen. Got nearly every kind of flower but no chrysanthemums. Last time I was mending a copper-bottom washtub for her (that's a hard job but I do it good), she said to me, 'If you ever run acrost some nice chrysanthemums I wish you'd try to get me a few seeds.' That's what she told me."

Elisa's eyes grew alert and eager. "She couldn't have known much about chrysanthemums. You can raise them from seed, but it's much easier to root the little sprouts you see there."

"Oh," he said. "I s'pose I can't take none to her, then." 60

"Why yes you can," Elisa cried. "I can put some in damp sand, and you can carry them right along with you. They'll take root in the pot if you keep them damp. And then she can transplant them."

"She'd sure like to have some, ma'am. You say they're nice ones?"

"Beautiful," she said. "Oh, beautiful." Her eyes shone. She tore off the battered hat and shook out her dark pretty hair. "I'll put them in a flower pot, and you can take them right with you. Come into the yard."

While the man came through the picket gate Elisa ran excitedly along the geranium-bordered path to the back of the house. And she returned carrying a big red flower pot. The gloves were forgotten now. She kneeled on the ground by the starting bed and dug up the sandy soil with her fingers and scooped it into the bright new flower pot. Then she picked up the little pile of shoots she had prepared. With her strong fingers she pressed them into the sand and tamped around them with her knuckles. The man stood over her. "I'll tell you what to do," she said. "You remember so you can tell the lady."

"Yes, I'll try to remember." 65

"Well, look. These will take root in about a month. Then she must set them out, about a foot apart in good rich earth like this, see?" She lifted a handful of dark soil for him to look at. "They'll grow fast and tall. Now remember this. In July tell her to cut them down, about eight inches from the ground."

"Before they bloom?" he asked.

"Yes, before they bloom." Her face was tight with eagerness. "They'll grow right up again. About the last of September the buds will start."

She stopped and seemed perplexed. "It's the budding that takes the most care," she said hesitantly. "I don't know how to tell you." She looked deep into his eyes, searchingly. Her mouth opened a little, and she seemed to be listening. "I'll try to tell you," she said. "Did you ever hear of planting hands?"

"Can't say I have, ma'am." 70

"Well, I can only tell you what it feels like. It's when you're picking off the buds you don't want. Everything goes right down into your fingertips. You watch your fingers work. They do it themselves. You can feel how it is. They pick and pick the buds. They never make a mistake. They're with the plant. Do you see? Your fingers and the plant. You can feel that, right up your arm. They know. They never make a mistake. You can feel it. When you're like that you can't do anything wrong. Do you see that? Can you understand that?"

She was kneeling on the ground looking up at him. Her breast swelled passionately.

The man's eyes narrowed. He looked away self-consciously. "Maybe I know," he said. "Sometimes in the night in the wagon there—"

Elisa's voice grew husky. She broke in on him. "I've never lived as you do, but I know what you mean. When the night is dark—why, the stars are sharp-pointed, and there's quiet. Why, you rise up and up! Every pointed star gets driven into your body. It's like that. Hot and sharp and—lovely."

Kneeling there, her hand went out toward his legs in the greasy black trousers.    75
Her hesitant fingers almost touched the cloth. Then her hand dropped to the
ground. She crouched low like a fawning dog.

He said, "It's nice, just like you say. Only when you don't have no dinner,
it ain't."

She stood up then, very straight, and her face was ashamed. She held the
flower pot out to him and placed it gently in his arms. "Here. Put it in your
wagon, on the seat, where you can watch it. Maybe I can find something for you
to do."

At the back of the house she dug in the can pile and found two old and
battered aluminum saucepans. She carried them back and gave them to him. "Here,
maybe you can fix these."

His manner changed. He became professional. "Good as new I can fix them."
At the back of his wagon he set a little anvil, and out of an oily tool box dug a
small machine hammer. Elisa came through the gate to watch him while he pounded
out the dents in the kettles. His mouth grew sure and knowing. At a difficult part
of the work he sucked his under-lip.

"You sleep right in the wagon?" Elisa asked.    80

"Right in the wagon, ma'am. Rain or shine. I'm dry as a cow in there."

"It must be nice," she said. "It must be very nice. I wish women could do
such things."

"It ain't the right kind of a life for a woman."

Her upper lip raised a little, showing her teeth. "How do you know? How
can you tell?" she said.

"I don't know ma'am," he protested. "Of course I don't know. Now here's    85
your kettles, done. You don't have to buy no new ones."

"How much?"

"Oh, fifty cents'll do. I keep my prices down and my work good. That's
why I have all them satisfied customers up and down the highway."

Elisa brought him a fifty-cent piece from the house and dropped it in his
hand. "You might be surprised to have a rival some time. I can sharpen scissors,
too. And I can beat the dents out of little pots. I could show you what a woman
might do."

He put his hammer back in the oily box and shoved the little anvil out of
sight. "It would be a lonely life for a woman, ma'am, and a scarey life, too, with
animals creeping under the wagon all night." He climbed over the single-tree,
steadying himself with a hand on the burro's white rump. He settled himself in
the seat, picked up the lines. "Thank you kindly, ma'am," he said. "I'll do like
you told me; I'll go back and catch the Salinas road."

"Mind," she called, "if you're long in getting there, keep the sand damp."    90

"Sand, ma'am? . . . Sand? Oh, sure. You mean round the chrysanthemums.
Sure I will." He clucked his tongue. The beasts leaned luxuriously into their col-
lars. The mongrel dog took his place between the back wheels. The wagon
turned and crawled out the entrance road and back the way it had come, along
the river.

Elisa stood in front of her wire fence watching the slow progress of the
caravan. Her shoulders were straight, her head thrown back, her eyes half-closed,
so that the scene came vaguely into them. Her lips moved silently, forming the

words "Good-bye—good-bye." Then she whispered, "That's a bright direction. There's a glowing there." The sound of her whisper startled her. She shook herself free and looked about to see whether anyone had been listening. Only the dogs had heard. They lifted their heads toward her from their sleeping in the dust, and then stretched out their chins and settled asleep again. Elisa turned and ran hurriedly into the house.

In the kitchen she reached behind the stove and felt the water tank. It was full of hot water from the noonday cooking. In the bathroom she tore off her soiled clothes and flung them into the corner. And then she scrubbed herself with a little block of pumice, legs and thighs, loins and chest and arms, until her skin was scratched and red. When she had dried herself she stood in front of a mirror in her bedroom and looked at her body. She tightened her stomach and threw out her chest. She turned and looked over her shoulder at her back.

After a while she began to dress, slowly. She put on her newest under-clothing and her nicest stockings and the dress which was the symbol of her prettiness. She worked carefully on her hair, pencilled her eyebrows and rouged her lips.

Before she was finished she heard the little thunder of hoofs and the shouts 95 of Henry and his helper as they drove the red steers into the corral. She heard the gate bang shut and set herself for Henry's arrival.

His step sounded on the porch. He entered the house calling "Elisa, where are you?"

"In my room, dressing. I'm not ready. There's hot water for your bath. Hurry up. It's getting late."

When she heard him splashing in the tub, Elisa laid his dark suit on the bed, and shirt and socks and tie beside it. She stood his polished shoes on the floor beside the bed. Then she went to the porch and sat primly and stiffly down. She looked toward the river road where the willow-line was still yellow with frosted leaves so that under the high grey fog they seemed a thin band of sunshine. This was the only color in the grey afternoon. She sat unmoving for a long time. Her eyes blinked rarely.

Henry came banging out of the door, shoving his tie inside his vest as he came. Elisa stiffened and her face grew tight. Henry stopped short and looked at her. "Why—why, Elisa. You look so nice!"

"Nice? You think I look nice? What do you mean by 'nice'?" 100

Henry blundered on. "I don't know. I mean you look different, strong and happy."

"I am strong? Yes, strong. What do you mean 'strong'?"

He looked bewildered. "You're playing some kind of a game," he said helplessly. "It's a kind of a play. You look strong enough to break a calf over your knee, happy enough to eat it like watermelon."

For a second she lost her rigidity. "Henry! Don't talk like that. You didn't know what you said." She grew complete again. "I'm strong," she boasted. "I never knew before how strong."

Henry looked down toward the tractor shed, and when he brought his eyes 105 back to her, they were his own again. "I'll get out the car. You can put on your coat while I'm starting."

Elisa went into the house. She heard him drive to the gate and idle down his motor, and then she took a long time to put on her hat. She pulled it here and pressed it there. When Henry turned the motor off she slipped into her coat and went out.

The little roadster bounced along on the dirt road by the river, raising the birds and driving the rabbits into the brush. Two cranes flapped heavily over the willow-line and dropped into the river-bed.

Far ahead on the road Elisa saw a dark speck. She knew.

She tried not to look as they passed it, but her eyes would not obey. She whispered to herself sadly. "He might have thrown them off the road. That wouldn't have been much trouble, not very much. But he kept the pot," she explained. "He had to keep the pot. That's why he couldn't get them off the road."

The roadster turned a bend and she saw the caravan ahead. She swung full around toward her husband so she could not see the little covered wagon and the mismatched team as the car passed them.    110

In a moment it was over. The thing was done. She did not look back. She said loudly, to be heard above the motor, "It will be good, tonight, a good dinner."

"Now you're changed again," Henry complained. He took one hand from the wheel and patted her knee. "I ought to take you in to dinner oftener. It would be good for both of us. We get so heavy out on the ranch."

"Henry," she asked, "could we have wine at dinner?"

"Sure we could. Say! That will be fine."

She was silent for a little while; then she said, "Henry, at those prize fights,    115
do the men hurt each other very much?"

"Sometimes a little, not often. Why?"

"Well, I've read how they break noses, and blood runs down their chests. I've read how the fighting gloves get heavy and soggy with blood."

He looked around at her. "What's the matter, Elisa? I didn't know you read things like that." He brought the car to a stop, then turned to the right over the Salinas River bridge.

"Do any women ever go to the fights?" she asked.

"Oh, sure, some. What's the matter, Elisa? Do you want to go? I don't think    120
you'd like it, but I'll take you if you really want to go."

She relaxed limply in the seat. "Oh, no. No. I don't want to go. I'm sure I don't." Her face was turned away from him. "It will be enough if we can have wine. It will be plenty." She turned up her coat collar so he could not see that she was crying weakly—like an old woman.

## QUESTIONS

1.  What point of view is used in the story? What are the advantages of using this point of view? What does Steinbeck force us to do by using this point of view?

2.  Summarize the plot of the story. What are the conflicts? Which is the central conflict? Where is the climax of the story? To what extent does it resolve the central conflict?

3.  How fully is Henry Allen described? Is he a round or flat character? Static or dynamic? How well does he understand his wife?

4.  Consider the symbolism of the setting in this story with respect to the Salinas

Valley, the time of year, and the description of the Allen house. What do these things tell us about Elisa Allen and her world?

5. To what extent is Steinbeck's description of Elisa in paragraphs 5 and 6 also symbolic? What is she wearing? What do her clothes hide or suppress? What does this description tell us about Elisa?

6. What is the central symbol in the story?

7. What do the chrysanthemums symbolize for Elisa? What do they symbolize about Elisa? What role do these flowers play in her life?

8. What is Elisa's first reaction to giving the tinker work? How does he change Elisa's attitude? How does Elisa change as she speaks with him? How would you explain this change?

9. How does Elisa's character or sense of self change during the episode in which she washes and dresses for dinner? To what extent is this washing-dressing episode symbolic? How would you explain the symbolism here?

10. Consider the symbolic impact of Elisa's seeing the chrysanthemum sprouts on the side of the road. How does this vision affect Elisa? What does it tell us about Elisa's life and values?

## WRITING ABOUT SYMBOLISM AND ALLEGORY

In preparing to write about symbolism or allegory, you will need to be alert and to employ all facilities that can aid your understanding. In the light of the introductory discussion in this chapter, test the material to determine parallels that may genuinely establish the presence of symbolism or allegory. It is particularly helpful to make a list showing how qualities of symbols may be lined up with qualities of a character or action. Such a list can help you think more deeply about the effectiveness of symbols. Here is such a list for the symbol of the toy windmill in Welty's "A Worn Path":

| QUALITIES IN THE WINDMILL | COMPARABLE QUALITIES IN PHOENIX AND HER LIFE |
|---|---|
| 1. Cheap | 1. Poor, but she gives all she has for the windmill |
| 2. Breakable | 2. Old, and not far from death |
| 3. A gift | 3. Generous |
| 4. Not practical | 4. Needs some relief from reality and practicality |
| 5. Colorful | 5. Same as 4 |

An aid for figuring out an allegory or allegorical passage can work well with a diagram of parallel lines. You can place corresponding characters, actions, things, or ideas along these lines as follows (using the film *Star Wars* as the specimen work):

| STAR WARS | Luke Skywalker | Obi Wan Kenobi | Darth Vader | Princess Leia | Capture | Escape, and defeat of Vader |
|---|---|---|---|---|---|---|
| *ALLEGORICAL APPLICATION TO MORALITY AND FAITH* | Forces of good | Education and faith | Forces of evil | Object to be saved, ideals to be rescued and restored | Doubt, spiritual negligence | Restoration of faith |
| *ALLEGORICAL APPLICATION TO PERSONAL AND GENERAL CONCERNS* | Individual in pursuit of goals | The means by which goals may be reached | Obstacles to be overcome | Occupation, happiness, goals | Temporary failure, depression, discouragement, disappointment | Success |

Lists and schemes like this may have the drawback of being too limiting or reductive. If you were to limit your responses only to the material on such visual aids, you might miss much of the impact and resonance of the story. Nevertheless, the knowledge and understanding you have to use in developing aids of this kind can be quite helpful to you when you are formulating the ways in which symbolism and allegory work, and therefore they can help you in getting together materials for your essay. As you make progress with such a method, you might wish to revise and focus things by crossing out some elements and adding others. As long as you transfer your materials directly to your own writing, you will stay on the right track and even improve the accuracy and forcefulness of your final essay.

In developing a thesis for your essay, it is important to begin by establishing significant general ideas about the story. "Young Goodman Brown," for example, is a work about the darkening of the soul of the major character, Brown. As he goes into the woods, he resolves to "stand firm against the devil," and he then looks up to "heaven above." As he looks, a "black mass of cloud" suddenly appears to hide the "brightening stars." Clearly this symbol is a direct visual representation of what is happening to Brown's character. Out of this relationship you could build a thesis about the relationship of Hawthorne's symbolism to his character development.

Similarly, "The Worker in Sandalwood" describes a miraculous rescue from misery and depression. The concluding sentence describes how the sparrow "shook her wings to the light." Because this bird comes to the story with Biblical resonance, and arrives the night before the miracle, it is to be taken as one of the story's symbols of regeneration. A central idea to be developed from this relationship might ultimately depend on the latter part of the story, to be contrasted with the less optimistic symbols of the earlier part.

As you develop your central idea and plan what materials to use in the body of the essay, it is important to be able to justify the claims that you make about symbolism or allegory. In the Parable of the Prodigal Son, for example, the aim is to demonstrate the extreme lowness to which the Son sinks. His job feeding swine, and his sharing food with them, symbolize this depth of his degradation, for a reference to Jewish religion and custom will establish that pigs and pork are unclean and therefore that the Son has reached the nadir of life both spiritually and economically. A discussion of the swine as a symbol should include reference to this cultural and religious attitude. In the same way, the allegorical aspects of "Young Goodman Brown" would need to be established in the observation that people in life lose their ideals and forsake their principles not because they are evil but because they misperceive and misunderstand the events and people around them.

### *Organizing Your Essay*

**INTRODUCTION.**    The introduction should establish the grounds for the discussion of symbolism and allegory in the story. There may be a recurring symbol, for example, or a regular pattern of symbolism. Or there may be actions that have clear allegorical applications. The central idea will refer to the nature of the symbols or allegory, like the benighting symbols in "Young Goodman Brown" or the regenerative symbols in "The Worker in Sandalwood." The thesis sentence will determine the topics to be developed in the body. These topics may refer to specific things, like the "walking stick," or to classes, like "regenerative symbols."

**BODY.**    There are a number of ways in which you might approach the topic of symbolism and allegory. You might wish to use one exclusively, or a combination. The choice is yours. If your choice is symbols and symbolism, you might consider the following:

1. *The meaning of a major symbol.* Here you interpret the symbol and try to show what it stands for both inside and outside the work. A few of the questions you might pursue are these: How do you determine that the symbol is really a symbol? How do you derive from the work a reasonable interpretation of the meaning of the symbol? What is the extent of the meaning? Does the symbol undergo any modification if it reappears in the work? By the same token, does the symbol affect your understanding of other parts of the work? How? Does the author create any ironies by using the symbol? Does the symbol give any special strength to the work?

2. *The meaning and relationship of a number of symbols.* What are the symbols? Do they have any specific connection or common bond? Do they suggest a unified reading or a contradictory one? Do the symbols seem to have general significance, or do they operate only in the context of the work? Do the symbols control the form of the work? How? For example, in "The Worker in Sandalwood" the concluding episode begins in doubt during the night of Christmas Eve and ends in success on the morning of Christmas Day. By contrast, the conclusion of Joyce's "Araby" (see p. 324) begins in anticipation during the day and ends in disillusionment at night. May these contrasting times be viewed symbolically in relationship to the development of the two stories? Other questions you may consider are whether the symbols fit naturally into the context of the story, or whether they seem to be drawn in artificially. Still another question is whether the writer's use of symbols makes for any unique qualities or excellences.

If you choose to write about allegory, you might address the following:

1. *The application of the allegory.* Does the allegory (fable, parable, myth) refer to anything or anyone specific? Does it refer to an action or particular period of history? Or does the allegory refer to human tendencies or ideas?

Does it illustrate, point by point, particular philosophies or religions? If so, what are these? If the original meaning of the allegory seems outdated, how much can be salvaged for people living today?

2. *The consistency of the allegory.* Is the allegory maintained consistently throughout the work, or is it intermittently used and dropped? Explain and detail this use. Would it be correct to call your work *allegorical* rather than *an allegory*? Can you determine how elements in the story have been especially introduced because of the requirements of the allegory (such as, perhaps, the complaints of the brother in "The Prodigal Son," which prompt the speech of the joyful father)? Positively, does the element seem natural, or, negatively, does it in any way seem unnatural or arbitrary?

CONCLUSION. In your conclusion you might summarize your main points, describe your general impressions, try to describe the impact of the images or symbolic methods, indicate your personal responses, or show what might further be done along the lines you have been developing in the body. You might also try to assess the quality of the symbolism or allegory and to make a statement about the appropriateness of the specific details to the applied ideas.


## SAMPLE ESSAY


### Allegory and Symbolism in Hawthorne's "Young Goodman Brown"*

[1]   It is hard to read beyond the third paragraph of "Young Goodman Brown" without finding allegory and symbolism. The opening seems realistic—Goodman Brown, a young Puritan, leaves his home in colonial Salem to take an overnight trip—but his wife's name, "Faith," immediately suggests a symbolic reading. Before long, Brown's walk into the forest becomes an allegorical trip into evil. The idea that Hawthorne shows by this trip is that rigid belief destroys the best human qualities, such as understanding and love.° He develops this thought in the allegory and in many symbols, particularly the sunset, the walking-stick, and the path.▫

[2]   The allegory is about how people develop destructive ideas. Most of the story is dreamlike and unreal, and therefore the ideas that Brown gains are unreal. After the weird night he thinks of his wife and neighbors not with love, but with hatred for their sins during the "witch meeting" deep in the

---

\* See p. 287 for this story.
° Central idea.
▫ Thesis sentence.

dream forest. Because of his own dream vision, he condemns everyone around him, and he lives out his life in unforgiving harshness. The story thus allegorizes the pursuit of any ideal or system beyond human love and forgiveness.

[3] The attack on such dehumanizing belief is found not just in the allegory, but also in Hawthorne's many symbols. The seventh word in the story, *sunset*, may be seen as a symbol. Sunset indicates the end of the day. Coming at the beginning of the story, however, it suggests that Goodman Brown is beginning the long night of his hatred, his spiritual death. For him the night will never end because his final days are shrouded in "gloom" (p. 296). The story suggests that Brown, like anyone else who gives up on human beings, is cut off from humanity, and is locked in an inner prison of bitterness.

[4] The next symbol, the walking-stick, suggests the ambiguous and arbitrary standard by which Brown judges his neighbors. The stick is carried by the guide who looks like Brown's father. It "might almost be seen to twist and wriggle itself like a living serpent" (p. 289). The serpent is a clear symbol for Satan, who tempted Adam and Eve (Genesis 3:1–7). The staff is also still a walking-stick, however, and in this respect it is innocent. Given this double vision, it symbolizes human tendencies to see evil where evil does not really exist. This double meaning squares with the statement about "the instinct that guides mortal man to evil" (p. 293). This instinct is not just the temptation to do bad things, but also the invention of wrongs for arbitrary reasons, and, more dangerously, the condemnation of those who have "done" these wrongs even though they have done nothing more than lead their own quiet lives.

[5] In the same vein, the path through the forest is a major symbol of the destructive mental confusion that overcomes Brown. As he walks, the path before him grows "wilder and drearier, and more faintly traced," and "at length" it vanishes (p. 293). This is like the description of the "broad" Biblical way that leads "to Destruction" (Matthew 7:13). As a symbol, the path shows that most human acts are bad, while a small number, like the "narrow" way to life (Matthew 7:14), are good. Goodman Brown's path is at first clear, as though sin is at first unique and unusual. Soon, however, it is so indistinct that he can see only sin wherever he turns. The symbol suggests that, as people follow evil, their moral vision becomes blurred and they cannot choose the right way even if it is in front of them. With such vision, they can hardly be anything other than destructive of their best instincts.

[6] Through Hawthorne's allegory and symbols, then, the story presents the paradoxes of how a seemingly good system can lead to bad results and also of how noble beliefs can backfire destructively. Goodman Brown dies in gloom because he believes strongly that his wrong vision is real. This form of evil is the hardest to stop, no matter what outward set of beliefs it takes, because wrongdoers who are convinced of their own goodness are beyond reach. Such a blend of evil and self-righteousness causes Hawthorne to write that "the fiend in his own shape is less hideous than when he rages in the breast of man" (p. 293). Young Goodman Brown thus becomes the central symbol of the story. He is one of those who walk in darkness and have forever barred themselves from the light.

### Commentary on the Essay

The introduction justifies the treatment of allegory and symbolism because of the way in which Hawthorne early in the story invites a symbolic reading. The central idea relates Hawthorne's method to the idea that rigid belief destroys the best human qualities. The thesis sentence outlines two major areas of discussion: (1) allegory, and (2) symbolism.

Paragraph 2 considers the allegory as a criticism of rigid Puritan morality. Paragraphs 3, 4, and 5 deal with three major symbols: the sunset, the walking-stick, and the path. The aim of this discussion is to show the meaning and application of these symbols for Hawthorne's attack on rigidity of belief. Throughout these three paragraphs the central idea—the relationship of rigidity to destructiveness—is stressed. Hawthorne's allusions to both the Old and New Testaments are pointed out in paragraphs 4 and 5. The concluding paragraph raises questions that lead to the idea that Brown himself is a symbol of Hawthorne's idea that the primary cause of evil is the inability to separate reality from unreality.

# 10

# Idea or Theme: The Meaning and the Message in Fiction

The term **idea** is connected to the actions of seeing and knowing; indeed, the words *view* and *wit* (in the sense of knowledge) are close relatives of *idea*. Originally, the term was applied to mental images that, once seen, could be remembered and therefore known. Because of this mental activity, an idea was considered as a conceptual **form** as opposed to external reality. The word is now commonly understood to refer to a concept, thought, opinion, or belief. Some typical ideas as delimited by philosophers and historians of ideas are these: *infinity, justice, right and good, necessity, the problem of evil, causation*, and, not unsurprisingly, *idea* itself. A full consideration of ideas like these requires a good deal of knowledge, understanding, and thought. In this respect, therefore, ideas involve the interrelation of thinking and knowing.

In stories, ideas are likely to be concerned not so much with abstract and speculative definitions as with the human side of things. The ancient Greek philosopher Plato, in his *Republic*, attempted a lengthy definition of the idea of justice. By contrast, in "Flying Home" the black American writer Ralph Ellison created a *story* about justice by showing how a young black Air Force pilot is subject to injustice. When an idea is developed throughout a story in this way, it is often given the name **theme**. This word refers to something laid down, a postulate, a central or unifying idea. Loosely, the *theme* of a work and its *central idea* may be considered as synonymous.

## IDEAS, TOPICS, ASSERTIONS, AND MEANING

Writers often (but not always) work with ideas or themes as they shape literary works. The general **subject** or **topic** of a story indicates the idea or group of ideas that the writer is concerned about. These may be broad topics or classes, like those just mentioned, that may be given titles of single words, such as *love*, *sacrifice*, *justice*, *persecution*, *power*, *honor*, *growth*, *maturity*, and so on. Just the topic alone is not enough, however, for the specific idea or theme must embody an **assertion** that the story makes about the subject. Thus, we might find stories with assertions that love is necessary but also irrational, hatred is built on misunderstanding, slavery is worse than death, power destroys youthful dreams, or growth is difficult but exciting.

In other words, the central idea or theme in a story embodies the work's **meaning.** In answering the question, "What does this, or that, *mean*, the response will usually be in the form of a principle about human nature, conduct, or motivation—in other words, in the form of an idea. In Eudora Welty's "A Worn Path" we might formulate an idea about the character of Phoenix Jackson as follows: "Phoenix illustrates the idea that human beings who are committed to caring for others may actually suffer for this commitment." Similarly, it might be argued that Mabel Pervin in D. H. Lawrence's "The Horse Dealer's Daughter" embodies the idea that "even if a commitment to the dead is strong, the commitment to life is stronger."

In considering a story for ideas, keep in mind that an idea pervades a work just as a key signature dominates a musical composition and therefore governs the notes as part of a clearly established scale. In a story, most things happen only as they have a bearing on the idea. Thus, actions, characters, statements, symbols, and dialogue may be judged in terms of how closely they relate to the idea or theme. In this sense, a theme runs throughout a story and ties things together much like a continuous thread. As readers, we can attempt to trace such threads, with all the patterns or variations that writers may work upon them. In Ellison's "Flying Home," for example, all the events may be seen in relationship to the idea that it is only with difficulty and against opposition that minority blacks can accomplish their goals in a majority white society.

## FORMULATING THE IDEAS IN FICTION

Although an idea may be expressed in a phrase or single word, gaining a full understanding of ideas in a work will be difficult unless they can be formulated in complete sentences. Thus, "love for human beings" may be an idea, but it is not an assertion about anything, and therefore it is not specific enough significantly to help someone studying a work in which love of any sort is illustrated. In dealing with Lawrence's "The Horse Dealer's Daughter," for example, little is accomplished with the statement that the story is about the love between a man and a woman. This topic does little more than identify the area of concern. The process must go a step further and ask what the story *says* about love, because the formulation of ideas in literature, like the development of a thesis in an essay, must move beyond subject to assertion. Thus, it is much more helpful to see Lawrence's story as expressing the idea that the love of a man and a woman is so positive that it can literally rescue people from death. In this story Mabel, one of the two major characters, tries to drown herself. She is close to death but is rescued by Dr. Fergusson. When she recovers consciousness, she and the doctor both realize that they have fallen suddenly in love. The events, in other words, illustrate the idea that we have just formulated about the story. Similarly, the thought that selfless love may lead to bravery against hopeless odds can be shown to be a major idea in Welty's "A Worn Path."

## DISTINGUISHING IDEAS FROM SUMMARIES

It is vitally important to make a distinction between ideas and short descriptions of events, or story summaries. Unfortunately, it is easy to go astray. After reading Frank O'Connor's "First Confession," for example, a reader might want to express the central idea in the story as follows: " 'First Confession' is a story about a young boy's family troubles before going to his first confession." This sentence accounts for many of the actions in the story quite well, but it does not state an idea. For this reason it is not helpful in study or analysis. In fact, the sentence might even get in the way of understanding, since it would direct further thought only toward what happens in the story. It does not provide any guidance for seeing the characters and events as they relate to an idea. A better way of approaching the theme in this story might be to assert that "O'Connor's 'First Confession' shows the limitation of trying to instill religion through fear and punishment." This sentence focuses attention on the behavior and advice of the sister, father, and Mrs. Ryan, and also on how their making Jackie confused illustrates the weakness of their threats of punishment. The end result of the clearer formulation is that thinking may be directed toward the idea and away from the sequential events of the story.

## IDEAS AND VALUES

The idea or ideas that an author expresses are closely tied to his or her **values,** or "value system." Unless an idea is completely abstract, like the idea of a geometric form, it usually carries with it some value judgment. In "Flying Home," for example, one of Ellison's dominant ideas is the very basic one that all human beings are equal regardless of race. His values are made clearly apparent as he directs disapproval against those who are so locked into their own prejudicial habits that they do not help but actually harass an injured fellow human being. It would be almost impossible to analyze Ellison's ideas in the story without considering his value system at the same time. As a general rule, then, we should assume that the ideas of authors grow out of their values, and that values are embodied in their stories along with the ideas.

## FINDING THE IDEAS IN FICTION

To find ideas in fiction, one must read the work carefully, considering the main characters and actions and evaluating such variables as tone, setting, and symbolism. Often, several readings of the story are helpful. At some point in the process, you should be able to begin formulating the story's meaning or message in terms of an idea. There are, of course, many different ways of stating the same general idea, but the result should always assert a specific point about the story's general subject. In dealing with James Joyce's story "Araby," for example, an initial expression of the story's idea might take any of the following forms: (1) The force of sexual attraction is strong and begins early in life. (2) The attraction can lead some individuals to strong idealization, or "pedestalization" of the loved one. (3) Sexual feelings are private and may therefore be a source of embarrassment and shame. (4) The sense of shame may produce ambiguous feelings even among those who are otherwise loyal to what produces the shame (in this case, the Church). Although any one of these choices could be an idea around which to build a study of "Araby," together with others that might be developed, they all have in common the idealization by the narrator of his friend's sister. If, in studying for ideas, you attempt to follow this sort of process, fully stating the idea of a story and then revising it in the light of further analysis, you should be able to deal skillfully with ideas in stories.

Authors may express ideas in many different ways. Although we cannot explain every possible method, we can introduce you to some of the most common. You should remember, however, that the following classifications are neither exhaustive nor restrictive; rather, they are for convenience and reference. In actual practice, all these methods (and more) may be employed at the same time.

### Direct Statements by the Author's Unnamed Speaker

Often the unnamed speaker, who may or may not represent the author's exact views, states ideas directly, by way of **commentary,** to guide us or deepen understanding. These ideas, while helping our reading, might also disrupt our understanding of the story. In the second paragraph of "The Necklace," for example, De Maupassant's authorial voice states the idea that women without strong family connections must rely on their charm and beauty to get on in the world. This idea might seem sexist or patronizing today, but it is nevertheless an accurate restatement of what De Maupassant's speaker says. In considering it as an idea, just as you might consider other ideas expressed directly by any other author's authorial voice, you might want to adapt it somewhat in line with your own understanding of the story. Thus, an adequate restatement of the De Maupassant idea might be this: " 'The Necklace' shows the idea that women, with no power except their charm and beauty, are helpless against chance or bad luck."

### Direct Statements by the Persona

Often the first-person narrators or speakers state their own ideas. (See also Chapter 5, on Point of View.) It is possible that the narrator's ideas may be identical with ideas held by the author or the authorial speaker, for the author may use the speaker as a direct mouthpiece for ideas. There is a danger in making a direct equation, however, for any ideas expressed by a persona speaking within a story may belong only to himself or herself, and the author may genuinely not be underwriting the ideas, but only examining them. Careful consideration is therefore necessary to determine the extent to which the narrator's ideas correspond with or diverge from the author's ideas. Sometimes the narrators speak views that are directly opposed to what the author might stand for. Usually these instances are clear. Jonathan Swift, for example, makes his speaker, Gulliver of *Gulliver's Travels*, say many things that Swift himself would have rejected. In addition, the author may cause the persona to make statements indicating a limited understanding of the situation he or she is telling about. Thus the adult Jackie, in O'Connor's "First Confession," says things that show some of his ideas to be immature.

### Dramatic Statements Made by Characters

In many works, different characters state ideas that are in conflict. The English story writer and novelist Aldous Huxley, for example, frequently introduced "mouthpiece" characters specifically to state ideas related to the fictional story being developed. Authors may thus present thirteen ways of looking at a blackbird and leave the choice up to you. They may provide you with guides for your interpretations, however. For instance, they may create an admirable character whose ideas may be the ones they admire. The reverse would be true for a bad character.

### Figurative Language

Authors often use figurative language to express or reinforce their ideas. As an example, here is a comparison from Joyce's "Araby," where the narrator describes the effect that his youthful admiration for his friend's sister had upon him: "But my body was like a harp and her words and gestures were like fingers running upon the wires." This comparison is based on the thought that young, first love is a powerful, irresistible force that may possess a person not only deeply but overwhelmingly. Joyce's entire story bears out this idea.

### Characters Who Stand for Ideas

Although characters are busy in the action of their respective works, they may also be employed symbolically to stand for ideas or values. Mathilde Loisel in "The Necklace" may be thought of as an embodiment of the idea that women of the nineteenth-century middle class, without the possibility of a career, are hurt by unrealizable dreams of wealth. With two diverse or opposed characters, the ideas they represent may be compared or contrasted. Mrs. Ryan and the priest in O'Connor's "First Confession," for instance, represent opposing ideas about the way in which religion is to be instilled in the young.

In effect, characters who stand for ideas may be considered as symbols. Thus, in Ellison's "Flying Home," the character Todd is symbolic of the black who is trying to gain success but who, like most average human beings, experiences a reversal—his plane crashes. Todd's wish to move ahead is hard for him to fulfill because he is denied the assistance that others are granted by right. Seen in this way, characters like Todd and actions they go through achieve a symbolic status that can be analyzed in the more abstract, less narrative language of ideas.

### The Work Itself as it Represents Ideas

One of the most important ways in which authors express ideas is to render them as an inseparable part of the total impression of the work. All the events and characters may add up to an idea that is made forceful by the impact of the story itself. Thus, although an idea may not be directly stated in so many words, it will be clear after you have finished reading. For example, in "Flying Home," Ellison makes objective the idea that racial barriers separate human beings and make them cruel when it would be to everyone's interest to unite and to be helpful. Although he never states this concept directly, the idea is clearly embodied in the story. Similarly, Shakespeare's *Hamlet* dramatizes the idea that a person doing evil sets strong forces in motion that cannot be stopped until everything in the person's path is destroyed. Even "escape literature," which is ostensibly designed to help readers forget about problems, will develop plots that stem out of conflicts between forces of good and evil, love and hate, good spies and bad, the earthlings versus the aliens, and so on. Such stories in fact *do* embody ideas and themes, even though they admittedly do not set out to strike readers with the boldness or originality of their ideas.

## JAMES JOYCE (1882–1941)

*Araby*                                                                                    *1914*

North Richmond Street,° being blind,° was a quiet street except at the hour when the Christian Brothers' School set the boys free. An uninhabited house of two storeys stood at the blind end, detached from its neighbours in a square ground. The other houses of the street, conscious of decent lives within them, gazed at one another with brown imperturbable faces.

The former tenant of our house, a priest, had died in the back drawing room. Air, musty from having long been enclosed, hung in all the rooms, and the waste room behind the kitchen was littered with old useless papers. Among these I found a few paper-covered books, the pages of which were curled and damp: *The Abbott*, by Walter Scott, *The Devout Communicant*° and *The Memoirs of Vidocq*.° I liked the last best because its leaves were yellow. The wild garden behind the house contained a central apple-tree and a few straggling bushes under one of which I found the late tenant's rusty bicycle-pump. He had been a very charitable priest; in his will he had left all his money to institutions and the furniture of his house to his sister.

When the short days of winter came dusk fell before we had well eaten our dinners. When we met in the street the houses had grown sombre. The space of sky above us was the colour of ever-changing violet and towards it the lamps of the street lifted their feeble lanterns. The cold air stung us and we played till our bodies glowed. Our shouts echoed in the silent street. The career of our play brought us through the dark muddy lanes behind the houses where we ran the gantlet of the rough tribes from the cottages, to the back doors of the dark dripping gardens where odours arose from the ashpits, to the dark odorous stables where a coachman smoothed and combed the horse or shook music from the buckled harness. When we returned to the street light from the kitchen windows had filled the areas. If my uncle was seen turning the corner we hid in the shadow until we had seen him safely housed. Or if Mangan's sister came out on the doorstep to call her brother in to his tea we watched her from our shadow peer up and down the street. We waited to see whether she would remain or go in and, if she remained, we left our shadow and walked up to Mangan's steps resignedly. She was waiting for us, her figure defined by the light from the half-opened door. Her brother always teased her before he obeyed and I stood by the railings looking at her. Her dress swung as she moved her body and the soft rope of her hair tossed from side to side.

Every morning I lay on the floor in the front parlor watching her door. The blind was pulled down within an inch of the sash so that I could not be seen. When she came out on the doorstep my heart leaped. I ran to the hall, seized my books and followed her. I kept her brown figure always in my eye and,

---

*North Richmond Street*: A real Dublin street. As a boy, Joyce lived in a house on it.
*blind*: a dead-end street.
*The Devout Communicant*: A book of meditations by Pacificus Baker, published 1873.
*The Memoirs of Vidocq*: Published 1829, the story of François Vidocq, a Parisian chief of detectives.

when we came near the point at which our ways diverged, I quickened my pace and passed her. This happened morning after morning. I had never spoken to her, except for a few casual words, and yet her name was like a summons to all my foolish blood.

Her image accompanied me even in places the most hostile to romance. On Saturday evenings when my aunt went marketing I had to go to carry some of the parcels. We walked through the flaring street, jostled by drunken men and bargaining women, amid the curses of labourers, the shrill litanies of shop-boys who stood on guard by the barrels of pigs' cheeks, the nasal chanting of street singers, who sang a *come-all-you* about O'Donovan Rossa,° or a ballad about the troubles in our native land. These noises converged in a single sensation of life for me: I imagined that I bore my chalice safely through the throng of foes. Her name sprang to my lips at moments in strange prayers and praises which I myself did not understand. My eyes were often full of tears (I could not tell why) and at times a flood from my heart seemed to pour itself out into my bosom. I thought little of the future. I did not know whether I would ever speak to her or not or, if I spoke to her, how I could tell her of my confused adoration. But my body was like a harp and her words and gestures were like fingers running upon the wires.

One evening I went into the back drawing-room in which the priest had died. It was a dark rainy evening and there was no sound in the house. Through one of the broken panes I heard the rain impinge upon the earth, the fine incessant needles of water playing in the sodden beds. Some distant lamp or lighted window gleamed below me. I was thankful that I could see so little. All my senses seemed to desire to veil themselves and, feeling that I was about to slip from them, I pressed the palms of my hands together until they trembled, murmuring: *O love! O love!* many times.

At last she spoke to me. When she addressed the first words to me I was so confused that I did not know what to answer. She asked me was I going to *Araby*.° I forget whether I answered yes or no. It would be a splendid bazaar, she said; she would love to go.

—And why can't you? I asked.

While she spoke she turned a silver bracelet round and round her wrist. She could not go, she said, because there would be a retreat° that week in her convent. Her brother and two other boys were fighting for their caps and I was alone at the railings. She held one of the spikes, bowing her head towards me. The light from the lamp opposite our door caught the white curve of her neck, lit up her hair that rested there and, falling, lit up the hand upon the railing. It fell over one side of her dress and caught the white border of a petticoat, just visible as she stood at ease.

—It's well for you, she said.

—If I go, I said, I will bring you something.

What innumerable follies laid waste my waking and sleeping thoughts after

5

10

---

*O'Donovan Rossa*: A popular ballad about Jeremiah O'Donovan (1831–1915), a leader in the movement to free Ireland from English control.

*Araby*: A bazaar advertised as "Araby in Dublin," a "Grand Oriental Fete," was held in Dublin from May 14–19, 1894.

*retreat*: a special time of two or more days set aside for concentrated religious instruction, discussion, and prayer.

that evening! I wished to annihilate the tedious intervening days. I chafed against the work of school. At night in my bedroom and by day in the classroom her image came between me and the page I strove to read. The syllables of the word *Araby* were called to me through the silence in which my soul luxuriated and cast an Eastern enchantment over me. I asked for leave to go to the bazaar on Saturday night. My aunt was surprised and hoped it was not some Freemason° affair. I answered few questions in class. I watched my master's face pass from amiability to sternness; he hoped I was not beginning to idle. I could not call my wandering thoughts together. I had hardly any patience with the serious work of life which, now that it stood between me and my desire, seemed to me child's play, ugly monotonous child's play.

On Saturday morning I reminded my uncle that I wished to go to the bazaar in the evening. He was fussing at the hall-stand, looking for the hatbrush, and answered me curtly:

—Yes, boy, I know.

As he was in the hall I could not go into the front parlour and lie at the window. I left the house in bad humour and walked slowly towards the school. The air was pitilessly raw and already my heart misgave me.     15

When I came home to dinner my uncle had not yet been home. Still it was early. I sat staring at the clock for some time and, when its ticking began to irritate me, I left the room. I mounted the staircase and gained the upper part of the house. The high cold empty gloomy rooms liberated me and I went from room to room singing. From the front window I saw my companions playing below in the street. Their cries reached me weakened and indistinct and, leaning my forehead against the cool glass, I looked over at the dark house where she lived. I may have stood there for an hour, seeing nothing but the brown-clad figure cast by my imagination, touched discreetly by the lamplight at the curved neck, at the hand upon the railing and at the border below the dress.

When I came downstairs again I found Mrs Mercer sitting at the fire. She was an old garrulous woman, a pawnbroker's widow, who collected used stamps for some pious purpose. I had to endure the gossip of the tea-table. The meal was prolonged beyond an hour and still my uncle did not come. Mrs Mercer stood up to go: she was sorry she couldn't wait any longer, but it was after eight o'clock and she did not like to be out late, as the night air was bad for her. When she had gone I began to walk up and down the room, clenching my fists. My aunt said:

—I'm afraid you may put off your bazaar for this night of Our Lord.

At nine o'clock I heard my uncle's latchkey in the halldoor. I heard him talking to himself and heard the hall-stand rocking when it had received the weight of his overcoat. I could interpret these signs. When he was midway through his dinner I asked him to give me the money to go to the bazaar. He had forgotten.

—The people are in bed and after their first sleep now, he said.     20

I did not smile. My aunt said to him energetically:

—Can't you give him the money and let him go? You've kept him late enough as it is.

My uncle said he was very sorry he had forgotten. He said he believed in the old saying: *All work and no play makes Jack a dull boy*. He asked me where I was going and, when I had told him a second time he asked me did I know *The Arab's*

---

*Freemason:* and therefore Protestant.

*Farewell to his Steed*.° When I left the kitchen he was about to recite the opening lines of the piece to my aunt.

I held a florin° tightly in my hand as I strode down Buckingham Street towards the station. The sight of the streets thronged with buyers and glaring with gas recalled to me the purpose of my journey. I took my seat in a third-class carriage of a deserted train. After an intolerable delay the train moved out of the station slowly. It crept onward among ruinous houses and over the twinkling river. At Westland Row Station a crowd of people pressed to the carriage doors; but the porters moved them back, saying that it was a special train for the bazaar. I remained alone in the bare carriage. In a few minutes the train drew up beside an improvised wooden platform. I passed out on to the road and saw by the lighted dial of a clock that it was ten minutes to ten. In front of me was a large building which displayed the magical name.

I could not find any sixpenny entrance and, fearing that the bazaar would      25
be closed, I passed in quickly through a turnstile, handing a shilling to a weary-looking man. I found myself in a big hall girdled at half its height by a gallery. Nearly all the stalls were closed and the greater part of the hall was in darkness. I recognized a silence like that which pervades a church after a service. I walked into the centre of the bazaar timidly. A few people were gathered about the stalls which were still open. Before a curtain, over which the words *Café Chantant* were written in coloured lamps, two men were counting money on a salver. I listened to the fall of the coins.

Remembering with difficulty why I had come I went over to one of the stalls and examined porcelain vases and flowered tea-sets. At the door of the stall a young lady was talking and laughing with two young gentlemen. I remarked their English accents and listened vaguely to their conversation.

—O, I never said such a thing!
—O, but you did!
—O, but I didn't!
—Didn't she say that?      30
—Yes I heard her.
—O, there's a . . . fib!

Observing me the young lady came over and asked me did I wish to buy anything. The tone in her voice was not encouraging; she seemed to have spoken to me out of a sense of duty. I looked humbly at the great jars that stood like eastern guards at either side of the dark entrance to the stall and murmured:

—No, thank you.

The young lady changed the position of one of the vases and went back to      35
the two young men. They began to talk of the same subject. Once or twice the young lady glanced at me over her shoulder.

I lingered before her stall, though I knew my stay was useless, to make my interest in her wares seem the more real. Then I turned away slowly and walked down the middle of the bazaar. I allowed the two pennies to fall against the sixpence in my pocket. I heard a voice call from one end of the gallery that the light was out. The upper part of the hall was now completely dark.

*The Arab's Farewell to his Steed*: A poem by Caroline Norton (1808–1877).
*florin*: a two-shilling coin; in the 1890s (when the story takes place), worth perhaps ten dollars in today's money.

Gazing up into the darkness I saw myself as a creature driven and derided by vanity; and my eyes burned with anguish and anger.

## QUESTIONS

1. What is the point of view in the story? Why is this point of view especially effective, given the story's nature?

2. Who is the narrator? About how old is he at the time of the events related in the story? About how old when he tells the story? What effect is produced by this difference in age between narrator-as-character and narrator-as-story-teller?

3. Three specific places are described in detail: the street, the house, and the market. In addition, the weather is frequently noted. How would you characterize these elements of setting? How effectively do the adjectives help to create an atmosphere? To what extent does the setting work against the protagonist's emotions but with the climax and resolution of the story?

4. How might the bazaar, "Araby," be considered symbolically in the story? What does Araby symbolize for the protagonist before he gets there? What does it come to symbolize at the close of the story? To what extent does this symbol embody the story's central idea?

5. How would you characterize the speaker's boyhood feelings about Mangan's sister? Are these feelings unusual in any way, or are they normal? Does the speaker's disappointment at being unable to buy a gift for the girl seem to be sufficient cause for his concluding shame and self-criticism, or is there some other cause or causes that are described or hinted at earlier in the story?

6. Consider the attitude of the speaker toward his home as indicated in the first paragraph. What does he think of the school, and of the houses as they represent the people living in them? Why do you think the speaker chose the word *blind* to describe the dead-end street? Can you relate the speaker's disappointment and humiliation at the end of the story to his attitude as it emerges in the first paragraph?

7. Describe what you consider to be the story's major idea about youthful admiration and love (if you wish, you might consider the speaker to be describing a childhood "crush"). Should such admiration be respected and cherished as a memory? How does the speaker think of himself because of his admiration?

## D. H. LAWRENCE (1885–1930)

*The Horse Dealer's Daughter*                                    1922

"Well, Mabel, and what are you going to do with yourself?" asked Joe, with foolish flippancy. He felt quite safe himself. Without listening for an answer, he turned aside, worked a grain of tobacco to the tip of his tongue, and spat it out. He did not care about anything, since he felt safe himself.

The three brothers and the sister sat round the desolate breakfast table, attempting some sort of desultory consultation. The morning's post had given the final tap to the family fortunes, and all was over. The dreary dining-room itself, with its heavy mahogany furniture, looked as if it were waiting to be done away with.

But the consultation amounted to nothing. There was a strange air of ineffectuality about the three men, as they sprawled at table, smoking and reflecting vaguely on their own condition. The girl was alone, a rather short, sullen-looking young woman of twenty-seven. She did not share the same life as her brothers. She would have been good-looking, save for the impassive fixity of her face, "bull-dog," as her brothers called it.

There was a confused tramping of horses' feet outside. The three men all sprawled round in their chairs to watch. Beyond the dark holly-bushes that separated the strip of lawn from the high-road, they could see a cavalcade of shire horses swinging out of their own yard, being taken for exercise. This was the last time. These were the last horses that would go through their hands. The young men watched with critical, callous look. They were all frightened at the collapse of their lives, and the sense of disaster in which they were involved left them no inner freedom.

Yet they were three fine, well-set fellows enough. Joe, the eldest, was a man 5 of thirty-three, broad and handsome in a hot, flushed way. His face was red, he twisted his black moustache over a thick finger, his eyes were shallow and restless. He had a sensual way of uncovering his teeth when he laughed, and his bearing was stupid. Now he watched the horses with a glazed look of helplessness in his eyes, a certain stupor of downfall.

The great draught-horses swung past. They were tied head to tail, four of them, and they heaved along to where a lane branched off from the highroad, planting their great hoofs floutingly in the fine black mud, swinging their great rounded haunches sumptuously, and trotting a few sudden steps as they were led into the lane, round the corner. Every movement showed a massive, slumbrous strength, and a stupidity which held them in subjection. The groom at the head looked back, jerking the leading rope. And the cavalcade moved out of sight up the lane, the tail of the last horse, bobbed up tight and stiff, held out taut from the swinging great haunches as they rocked behind the hedges in a motionlike sleep.

Joe watched with glazed hopeless eyes. The horses were almost like his own body to him. He felt he was done for now. Luckily, he was engaged to a woman as old as himself, and therefore her father, who was steward of a neighbouring estate, would provide him with a job. He would marry and go into harness. His life was over, he would be a subject animal now.

He turned uneasily aside, the retreating steps of the horses echoing in his ears. Then, with foolish restlessness, he reached for the scraps of bacon-rind from the plates, and making a faint whistling sound, flung them to the terrier that lay against the fender. He watched the dog swallow them, and waited till the creature looked into his eyes. Then a faint grin came on his face, and in a high, foolish voice he said:

"You won't get much more bacon, shall you, you little b———?"

The dog faintly and dismally wagged its tail, then lowered its haunches, 10 circled round, and lay down again.

There was another helpless silence at the table. Joe sprawled uneasily in his seat, not willing to go till the family conclave was dissolved. Fred Henry, the second brother, was erect, clean-limbed, alert. He had watched the passing of the horses with more *sang-froid*.° If he was an animal, like Joe, he was an animal which controls, not one which is controlled. He was master of any horse, and he carried himself with a well-tempered air of mastery. But he was not master of the situations of life. He pushed his coarse brown moustache upwards, off his lip, and glanced irritably at his sister, who sat impassive and inscrutable.

"You'll go and stop with Lucy for a bit, shan't you?" he asked. The girl did not answer.

"I don't see what else you can do," persisted Fred Henry.

"Go as a skivvy,"° Joe interpolated laconically.

The girl did not move a muscle.

"If I was her, I should go in for training for a nurse," said Malcolm, the youngest of them all. He was the baby of the family, a young man of twenty-two, with a fresh, jaunty *museau*.°

But Mabel did not take any notice of him. They had talked at her and round her for so many years, that she hardly heard them at all.

The marble clock on the mantel-piece softly chimed the half-hour, the dog rose uneasily from the hearthrug and looked at the party at the breakfast table. But still they sat on in ineffectual conclave.

"Oh, all right," said Joe suddenly, *à propos* of nothing. "I'll get a move on."

He pushed back his chair, straddled his knees with a downward jerk, to get them free, in horsey fashion, and went to the fire. Still he did not go out of the room; he was curious to know what the others would do or say. He began to charge his pipe, looking down at the dog and saying, in a high, affected voice:

"Going wi' me? Going wi' me are ter? Tha'rt goin' further than tha counts on just now, dost hear?"

The dog faintly wagged its tail, the man stuck out his jaw and covered his pipe with his hands, and puffed intently, losing himself in the tobacco, looking down all the while at the dog, with an absent brown eye. The dog looked up at him in mournful distrust. Joe stood with his knees stuck out, in real horsey fashion.

"Have you had a letter from Lucy?" Fred Henry asked of his sister.

"Last week," came the neutral reply.

"And what does she say?"

There was no answer.

"Does she *ask* you to go and stop there?" persisted Fred Henry.

"She says I can if I like."

"Well, then, you'd better. Tell her you'll come on Monday."

This was received in silence.

"That's what you'l' do then, is it?" said Fred Henry, in some exasperation.

But she made no answer. There was a silence of futility and irritation in the room. Malcolm grinned fatuously.

"You'll have to make up your mind between now and next Wednesday," said Joe loudly, "or else find yourself lodgings on the kerbstone."

*sang-froid:* cold blood; i.e., unconcern.
*skivvy:* British slang for housemaid.
*museau:* muzzle, or snout (as of an animal), a French word.

The face of the young woman darkened, but she sat on immutable.

"Here's Jack Fergusson!" exclaimed Malcolm, who was looking aimlessly out      35
of the window.

"Where?" exclaimed Joe, loudly.

"Just gone past."

"Coming in?"

Malcolm craned his neck to see the gate.

"Yes," he said.      40

There was a silence. Mabel sat on like one condemned, at the head of the
table. Then a whistle was heard from the kitchen. The dog got up and barked
sharply. Joe opened the door and shouted:

"Come on."

After a moment, a young man entered. He was muffled up in overcoat and
a purple woollen scarf, and his tweed cap, which he did not remove, was pulled
down on his head. He was of medium height, his face was rather long and pale,
his eyes looked tired.

"Hello Jack! Well, Jack!" exclaimed Malcolm and Joe. Fred Henry merely
said "Jack!"

"What's doing?" asked the newcomer, evidently addressing Fred Henry.      45

"Same. We've got to be out by Wednesday.—Got a cold?"

"I have—got it bad, too."

"Why don't you stop in?"

"*Me* stop in? When I can't stand on my legs, perhaps I shall have a chance."
The young man spoke huskily. He had a slight Scotch accent.

"It's a knock-out, isn't it," said Joe boisterously, "if a doctor goes round      50
croaking with a cold. Looks bad for the patients, doesn't it?"

The young doctor looked at him slowly.

"Anything the matter with *you*, then?" he asked, sarcastically.

"Not as I know of. Damn your eyes, I hope not. Why?"

"I thought you were very concerned about the patients, wondered if you
might be one yourself."

"Damn it, no, I've never been patient to no flaming doctor, and hope I      55
never shall be," returned Joe.

At this point Mabel rose from the table, and they all seemed to become
aware of her existence. She began putting the dishes together. The young doctor
looked at her, but did not address her. He had not greeted her. She went out of
the room with the tray, her face impassive and unchanged.

"When are you off then, all of you?" asked the doctor.

"I'm catching the eleven-forty," replied Malcolm. "Are you goin' down wi'
th' trap,° Joe?"

"Yes, I've told you I'm going down wi' th' trap, haven't I?"

"We'd better be getting her in then. —So long, Jack, if I don't see you      60
before I go," said Malcolm, shaking hands.

He went out, followed by Joe, who seemed to have his tail between his legs.

"Well, this is the devil's own," exclaimed the doctor, when he was left alone
with Fred Henry. "Going before Wednesday, are you?"

"That's the orders," replied the other.

*trap:* a small wagon.

"Where, to Northampton?"

"That's it."                                                                                             65

"The devil!" exclaimed Fergusson, with quiet chagrin.

And there was silence between the two.

"All settled up, are you?" asked Fergusson.

"About."

There was another pause.                                                                                 70

"Well, I shall miss yer, Freddy boy," said the young doctor.

"And I shall miss thee, Jack," returned the other.

"Miss you like hell," mused the doctor.

Fred Henry turned aside. There was nothing to say. Mabel came in again, to finish clearing the table.

"What are *you* going to do then, Miss Pervin?" asked Fergusson. "Going   75
to your sister's, are you?"

Mabel looked at him with her steady, dangerous eyes, that always made him uncomfortable, unsettling his superficial ease.

"No," she said.

"Well, what in the name of fortune *are* you going to do? Say what you *mean* to do," cried Fred Henry, with futile intensity.

But she only averted her head, and continued her work. She folded the white table-cloth, and put on the chenille cloth.

"The sulkiest bitch that ever trod!" muttered her brother.                                               80

But she finished her task with perfectly impassive face, the young doctor watching her interestedly all the while. Then she went out.

Fred Henry stared after her, clenching his lips, his blue eyes fixing in sharp antagonism, as he made a grimace of sour exasperation.

"You could bray her into bits, and that's all you'd get out of her," he said, in a small, narrowed tone.

The doctor smiled faintly.

"What's she *going* to do then?" he asked.                                                               85

"Strike me if *I* know!" returned the other.

There was a pause. Then the doctor stirred.

"I'll be seeing you to-night, shall I?" he said to his friend.

"Ay—where's it to be? Are we going over to Jessdale?"

"I don't know. I've got such a cold on me. I'll come round to the Moon   90
and Stars, anyway."

"Let Lizzie and May miss their night for once, eh?"

"That's it—if I feel as I do now."

"All's one—"

The two young men went through the passage and down to the back door together. The house was large, but it was servantless now, and desolate. At the back was a small bricked house-yard, and beyond that a big square, gravelled fine and red, and having stables on two sides. Sloping, dank, winter-dark fields stretched away on the open sides.

But the stables were empty. Joseph Pervin, the father of the family, had   95
been a man of no education, who had become a fairly large horse dealer. The stables had been full of horses, there was a great turmoil and come-and-go of horses and of dealers and grooms. Then the kitchen was full of servants. But of

late things had declined. The old man had married a second time, to retrieve his fortunes. Now he was dead and everything was gone to the dogs, there was nothing but debt and threatening.

For months, Mabel had been servantless in the big house, keeping the home together in penury for her ineffectual brothers. She had kept house for ten years. But previously, it was with unstinted means. Then, however brutal and coarse everything was, the sense of money had kept her proud, confident. The men might be foul-mouthed, the women in the kitchen might have bad reputations, her brothers might have illegitimate children. But so long as there was money, the girl felt herself established, and brutally proud, reserved.

No company came to the house, save dealers and coarse men. Mabel had no associates of her own sex, after her sister went away. But she did not mind. She went regularly to church, she attended to her father. And she lived in the memory of her mother, who had died when she was fourteen, and whom she had loved. She had loved her father, too, in a different way, depending upon him, and feeling secure in him, until at the age of fifty-four he married again. And then she had set hard against him. Now he had died and left them all hopelessly in debt.

She had suffered badly during the period of poverty. Nothing, however, could shake the curious sullen, animal pride that dominated each member of the family. Now, for Mabel, the end had come. Still she would not cast about her. She would follow her own way just the same. She would always hold the keys of her own situation. Mindless and persistent, she endured from day to day. Why should she think? Why should she answer anybody? It was enough that this was the end, and there was no way out. She need not pass any more darkly along the main street of the small town, avoiding every eye. She need not demean herself any more, going into the shops and buying the cheapest food. This was at an end. She thought of nobody, not even of herself. Mindless and persistent, she seemed in a sort of ecstasy to be coming nearer to her fulfilment, her own glorification, approaching her dead mother, who was glorified.°

In the afternoon she took a little bag, with shears and sponge and a small scrubbing brush, and went out. It was a grey, wintry day, with saddened, dark-green fields and an atmosphere blackened by the smoke of foundries not far off. She went quickly, darkly along the causeway, heeding nobody, through the town to the churchyard.

There she always felt secure, as if no one could see her, although as a matter of fact she was exposed to the stare of everyone who passed along under the churchyard wall. Nevertheless, once under the shadow of the great looming church, among the graves, she felt immune from the world, reserved within the thick church-yard wall as in another country.    100

Carefully she clipped the grass from the grave, and arranged the pinky-white, small chrysanthemums in the tin cross. When this was done, she took an empty jar from a neighbouring grave, brought water, and carefully, most scrupulously sponged the marble headstone and the coping-stone.

It gave her sincere satisfaction to do this. She felt in immediate contact with the world of her mother. She took minute pains, went through the park in a state bordering on pure happiness, as if in performing this task she came into a subtle,

*who was glorified:* see Romans 8:17,30.

intimate connection with her mother. For the life she followed here in the world was far less real than the world of death she inherited from her mother.

The doctor's house was just by the church. Fergusson, being a mere hired assistant, was slave to the countryside. As he hurried now to attend to the outpatients in the surgery, glancing across the graveyard with his quick eye, he saw the girl at her task at the grave. She seemed so intent and remote, it was like looking into another world. Some mystical element was touched in him. He slowed down as he walked, watching her as if spell-bound.

She lifted her eyes, feeling him looking. Their eyes met. And each looked again at once, each feeling, in some way, found out by the other. He lifted his cap and passed on down the road. There remained distinct in his consciousness, like a vision, the memory of her face, lifted from the tombstone in the churchyard, and looking at him with slow, large, portentous eyes. It *was* portentous, her face. It seemed to mesmerise him. There was a heavy power in her eyes which laid hold of his whole being, as if he had drunk some powerful drug. He had been feeling weak and done before. Now the life came back into him, he felt delivered from his own fretted, daily self.

He finished his duties at the surgery as quickly as might be, hastily filling    105
up the bottles of the waiting people with cheap drugs. Then, in perpetual haste, he set off again to visit several cases in another part of his round, before teatime. At all times he preferred to walk, if he could, but particularly when he was not well. He fancied the motion restored him.

The afternoon was falling. It was grey, deadened, and wintry, with a slow, moist, heavy coldness sinking in and deadening all the faculties. But why should he think or notice? He hastily climbed the hill and turned across the dark-green fields, following the black cinder-track. In the distance, across a shallow dip in the country, the small town was clustered like smouldering ash, a tower, a spire, a heap of low, raw, extinct houses. And on the nearest fringe of the town, sloping into the dip, was Oldmeadow, the Pervins' house. He could see the stables and the outbuildings distinctly, as they lay towards him on the slope. Well, he would not go there many more times! Another resource would be lost to him, another place gone: the only company he cared for in the alien, ugly little town he was losing. Nothing but work, drudgery, constant hastening from dwelling to dwelling among the colliers and the iron-workers. It wore him out, but at the same time he had a craving for it. It was a stimulant to him to be in the homes of the working people, moving as it were through the innermost body of their life. His nerves were excited and gratified. He could come so near, into the very lives of the rough, inarticulate, powerfully emotional men and women. He grumbled, he said he hated the hellish hole. But as a matter of fact it excited him, the contact with the rough, strongly-feeling people was a stimulant applied direct to his nerves.

Below Oldmeadow, in the green, shallow, soddened hollow of fields, lay a square, deep pond. Roving across the landscape, the doctor's quick eye detected a figure in black passing through the gate of the field, down towards the pond. He looked again. It would be Mabel Pervin. His mind suddenly became alive and attentive.

Why was she going down there? He pulled up on the path on the slope above, and stood staring. He could just make sure of the small black figure moving in the hollow of the failing day. He seemed to see her in the midst of such obscurity, that he was like a clairvoyant, seeing rather with the mind's eye than with ordinary sight. Yet he could see her positively enough, whilst he kept his eye attentive. He felt, if he looked away from her, in the thick, ugly falling dusk, he would lose her altogether.

He followed her minutely as she moved, direct and intent, like something transmitted rather than stirring in voluntary activity, straight down the field towards the pond. There she stood on the bank for a moment. She never raised her head. Then she waded slowly into the water.

He stood motionless as the small black figure walked slowly and deliberately    110
towards the centre of the pond, very slowly, gradually moving deeper into the motionless water, and still moving forward as the water got up to her breast. Then he could see her no more in the dusk of the dead afternoon.

"There!" he exclaimed. "Would you believe it?"

And he hastened straight down, running over the wet, soddened fields, pushing through the hedges, down into the depression of callous wintry obscurity. It took him several minutes to come to the pond. He stood on the bank, breathing heavily. He could see nothing. His eyes seemed to penetrate the dead water. Yes, perhaps that was the dark shadow of her black clothing beneath the surface of the water.

He slowly ventured into the pond. The bottom was deep, soft clay, he sank in, and the water clasped dead cold round his legs. As he stirred he could smell the cold, rotten clay that fouled up into the water. It was objectionable in his lungs. Still, repelled and yet not heeding, he moved deeper into the pond. The cold water rose over his thighs, over his loins, upon his abdomen. The lower part of his body was all sunk in the hideous cold element. And the bottom was so deeply soft and uncertain, he was afraid of pitching with his mouth underneath. He could not swim, and was afraid.

He crouched a little, spreading his hands under the water and moving them round, trying to feel for her. The dead cold pond swayed upon his chest. He moved again, a little deeper, and again, with his hands underneath, he felt all around under the water. And he touched her clothing. But it evaded his fingers. He made a desperate effort to grasp it.

And so doing he lost his balance and went under, horribly, suffocating in    115
the foul earthy water, struggling madly for a few moments. At last, after what seemed an eternity, he got his footing, rose again into the air and looked around. He gasped, and knew he was in the world. Then he looked at the water. She had risen near him. He grasped her clothing, and drawing her nearer, turned to take his way to land again.

He went very slowly, carefully, absorbed in the slow progress. He rose higher, climbing out of the pond. The water was now only about his legs; he was thankful, full of relief to be out of the clutches of the pond. He lifted her and staggered on to the bank, out of the horror of wet, grey clay.

He laid her down on the bank. She was quite unconscious and running with water. He made the water come from her mouth, he worked to restore her. He did not have to work very long before he could feel the breathing begin again in her; she was breathing naturally. He worked a little longer. He could feel her live beneath his hands; she was coming back. He wiped her face, wrapped her in his overcoat, looked round into the dim, dark-grey world, then lifted her and staggered down the bank and across the fields.

It seemed an unthinkably long way, and his burden so heavy he felt he would never get to the house. But at last he was in the stable-yard, and then in the house-yard. He opened the door and went into the house. In the kitchen he laid her down on the hearthrug, and called. The house was empty. But the fire was burning in the grate.

Then again he kneeled to attend to her. She was breathing regularly, her eyes were wide open and as if conscious, but there seemed something missing in her look. She was conscious in herself, but unconscious of her surroundings.

He ran upstairs, took blankets from a bed, and put them before the fire to   120
warm. Then he removed her saturated, earthy-smelling clothing, rubbed her dry with a towel, and wrapped her naked in the blankets. Then he went into the dining-room, to look for spirits. There was a little whiskey. He drank a gulp himself, and put some into her mouth.

The effect was instantaneous. She looked full into his face, as if she had been seeing him for some time, and yet had only just become conscious of him.

"Dr. Fergusson?" she said.

"What?" he answered.

He was divesting himself of his coat, intending to find some dry clothing upstairs. He could not bear the smell of the dead, clayey water, and he was mortally afraid for his own health.

"What did I do?" she asked.   125

"Walked into the pond," he replied. He had begun to shudder like one sick, and could hardly attend to her. Her eyes remained full on him, he seemed to be going dark in his mind, looking back at her helplessly. The shuddering became quieter in him, his life came back in him, dark and unknowing, but strong again.

"Was I out of my mind?" she asked, while her eyes were fixed on him all the time.

"Maybe, for the moment," he replied. He felt quiet, because his strength had come back. The strange fretful strain had left him.

"Am I out of my mind now?" she asked.

"Are you?" he reflected a moment. "No," he answered truthfully, "I don't   130
see that you are." He turned his face aside. He was afraid, now, because he felt dazed, and felt dimly that her power was stronger than his, in this issue. And she continued to look at him fixedly all the time. "Can you tell me where I shall find some dry things to put on?" he asked.

"Did you dive into the pond for me?" she asked.

"No," he answered. "I walked in. But I went in overhead as well."

There was silence for a moment. He hesitated. He very much wanted to go upstairs to get into dry clothing. But there was another desire in him. And she seemed to hold him. His will seemed to have gone to sleep, and left him, standing there slack before her. But he felt warm inside himself. He did not shudder at all, though his clothes were sodden on him.

"Why did you?" she asked.

"Because I didn't want you to do such a foolish thing," he said.                    135

"It wasn't foolish," she said, still gazing at him as she lay on the floor, with a sofa cushion under her head. "It was the right thing to do. *I* knew best, then."

"I'll go and shift these wet things," he said. But still he had not the power to move out of her presence, until she sent him. It was as if she had the life of his body in her hands, and he could not extricate himself. Or perhaps he did not want to.

Suddenly she sat up. Then she became aware of her own immediate condition. She felt the blankets about her, she knew her own limbs. For a moment it seemed as if her reason were going. She looked round, with wild eye, as if seeking something. He stood still with fear. She saw her clothing lying scattered.

"Who undressed me?" she asked, her eyes resting full and inevitable on his face.

"I did," he replied, "to bring you round."                    140

For some moments she sat and gazed at him awfully, her lips parted.

"Do you love me then?" she asked.

He only stood and stared at her, fascinated. His soul seemed to melt.

She shuffled forward on her knees, and put her arms round him, round his legs, as he stood there, pressing her breasts against his knees and thighs, clutching him with strange, convulsive certainty, pressing his thighs against her, drawing him to her face, her throat, as she looked up at him with flaring, humble eyes of transfiguration, triumphant in first possession.

"You love me," she murmured, in strange transport, yearning and triumphant    145
and confident. "You love me. I know you love me, I know."

And she was passionately kissing his knees, through the wet clothing, passionately and indiscriminately kissing his knees, his legs, as if unaware of everything.

He looked down at the tangled wet hair, the wild, bare, animal shoulders. He was amazed, bewildered, and afraid. He had never thought of loving her. He had never wanted to love her. When he rescued her and restored her, he was a doctor, and she was a patient. He had had no single personal thought of her. Nay, this introduction of the personal element was very distasteful to him, a violation of his professional honour. It was horrible to have her there embracing his knees. It was horrible. He revolted from it, violently. And yet—and yet—he had not the power to break away.

She looked at him again, with the same supplication of powerful love, and that same transcendent, frightening light of triumph. In view of the delicate flame which seemed to come from her face like a light, he was powerless. And yet he had never intended to love her. He had never intended. And something stubborn in him could not give way.

"You love me," she repeated, in a murmur of deep, rhapsodic assurance. "You love me."

Her hands were drawing him, drawing him down to her. He was afraid,    150
even a little horrified. For he had, really, no intention of loving her. Yet her hands were drawing him towards her. He put out his hand quickly to steady himself, and grasped her bare shoulder. A flame seemed to burn the hand that grasped her soft shoulder. He had no intention of loving her: his whole will was against his yielding. It was horrible— And yet wonderful was the touch of her shoulder,

beautiful the shining of her face. Was she perhaps mad? He had a horror of yielding to her. Yet something in him ached also.

He had been staring away at the door, away from her. But his hand remained on her shoulder. She had gone suddenly very still. He looked down at her. Her eyes were now wide with fear, with doubt, the light was dying from her face, a shadow of terrible greyness was returning. He could not bear the touch of her eyes' question upon him, and the look of death behind the question.

With an inward groan he gave way, and let his heart yield towards her. A sudden gentle smile came on his face. And her eyes, which never left his face, slowly, slowly filled with tears. He watched the strange water rise in her eyes, like some slow fountain coming up. And his heart seemed to burn and melt away in his breast.

He could not bear to look at her any more. He dropped on his knees and caught her head with his arms and pressed her face against his throat. She was very still. His heart, which seemed to have broken, was burning with a kind of agony in his breast. And he felt her slow, hot tears wetting his throat. But he could not move.

He felt the hot tears wet his neck and the hollows of his neck, and he remained motionless, suspended through one of man's eternities. Only now it had become indispensable to him to have her face pressed close to him; he could never let her go again. He could never let her head go away from the close clutch of his arm. He wanted to remain like that for ever, with his heart hurting him in a pain that was also life to him. Without knowing, he was looking down on her damp, soft brown hair.

Then, as it were suddenly, he smelt the horrid stagnant smell of that water. 155 And at the same moment she drew away from him and looked at him. Her eyes were wistful and unfathomable. He was afraid of them, and he fell to kissing her, not knowing what he was doing. He wanted her eyes not to have that terrible, wistful, unfathomable look.

When she turned her face to him again, a faint delicate flush was glowing, and there was again dawning that terrible shining of joy in her eyes, which really terrified him, and yet which he now wanted to see, because he feared the look of doubt still more.

"You love me?" she said, rather faltering.

"Yes." The word cost him a painful effort. Not because it wasn't true. But because it was too newly true, the *saying* seemed to tear open again his newly-torn heart. And he hardly wanted it to be true, even now.

She lifted her face to him, and he bent forward and kissed her on the mouth gently, with the one kiss that is an eternal pledge. And as he kissed her his heart strained again in his breast. He never intended to love her. But now it was over. He had crossed over the gulf to her, and all that he had left behind had shrivelled and become void.

After the kiss, her eyes again slowly filled with tears. She sat still, away from 160 him, with her face drooped aside, and her hands folded in her lap. The tears fell very slowly. There was complete silence. He too sat there motionless and silent on the hearthrug. The strange pain of his heart that was broken seemed to consume him. That he should love her? That this was love! That he should be ripped open in this way!—Him, a doctor!—How they would all jeer if they knew!—It was agony to him to think they might know.

In the curious naked pain of the thought he looked again to her. She was sitting there drooped into a muse. He saw a tear fall, and his heart flared hot. He saw for the first time that one of her shoulders was quite uncovered, one arm bare, he could see one of her small breasts; dimly, because it had become almost dark in the room.

"Why are you crying?" he asked, in an altered voice.

She looked up at him, and behind her tears the consciousness of her situation for the first time brought a dark look of shame to her eyes.

"I'm not crying, really," she said, watching him half frightened.

He reached his hand, and softly closed it on her bare arm.                      165

"I love you! I love you!" he said in a soft, low vibrating voice, unlike himself.

She shrank, and dropped her head. The soft, penetrating grip of his hand on her arm distressed her. She looked up at him.

"I want to go," she said. "I want to go and get you some dry things."

"Why?" he said. "I'm all right."

"But I want to go," she said. "And I want you to change your things."        170

He released her arm, and she wrapped herself in the blanket, looking at him rather frightened. And still she did not rise.

"Kiss me," she said wistfully.

He kissed her, but briefly, half in anger.

Then, after a second, she rose nervously, all mixed up in the blanket. He watched her in her confusion, as she tried to extricate herself and wrap herself up so that she could walk. He watched her relentlessly, as she knew.

And as she went, the blanket trailing, and as he saw a glimpse of her feet   175
and her white leg, he tried to remember her as she was when he had wrapped her in the blanket. But then he didn't want to remember, because she had been nothing to him then, and his nature revolted from remembering her as she was when she was nothing to him.

A tumbling muffled noise from within the dark house startled him. Then he heard her voice:—"There are clothes." He rose and went to the foot of the stairs, and gathered up the garments she had thrown down. Then he came back to the fire, to rub himself down and dress. He grinned at his own appearance, when he had finished.

The fire was sinking, so he put on coal. The house was now quite dark, save for the light of a street-lamp that shone in faintly from beyond the holly trees. He lit the gas with matches he found on the mantel-piece. Then he emptied the pockets of his own clothes, and threw all his wet things in a heap into the scullery. After which he gathered up her sodden clothes, gently, and put them in a separate heap on the copper-top in the scullery.

It was six o'clock on the clock. His own watch had stopped. He ought to be back to the surgery. He waited, and still she did not come down. So he went to the foot of the stairs and called:

"I shall have to go."

Almost immediately he heard her coming down. She had on her best dress   180
of black voile, and her hair was tidy, but still damp. She looked at him—and in spite of herself, smiled.

"I don't like you in those clothes," she said.

"Do I look a sight?" he answered.

They were shy of one another.

"I'll make you some tea," she said.

"No, I must go."                                                                                            185

"Must you?" And she looked at him again with the wide, strained, doubtful eyes. And again, from the pain of his breast, he knew how he loved her. He went and bent to kiss her, gently, passionately, with his heart's painful kiss.

"And my hair smells so horrible," she murmured in distraction. "And I'm so awful, I'm so awful! Oh, no, I'm too awful." And she broke into bitter, heartbroken sobbing. "You can't want to love me, I'm horrible."

"Don't be silly, don't be silly," he said, trying to comfort her, kissing her, holding her in his arms. "I want you, I want to marry you, we're going to be married, quickly, quickly—to-morrow if I can."

But she only sobbed terribly, and cried.

"I feel awful. I feel awful. I feel I'm horrible to you."                                                   190

"No, I want you, I want you," was all he answered, blindly, with that terrible intonation which frightened her almost more than her horror lest he should *not* want her.

## QUESTIONS

1.  What has happened to the Pervin family as the story begins? How does the initial description of the setting (especially the adjectives) reinforce the mood associated with these events?

2.  How is Joe Pervin described? In what ways is he like the horses that he is watching? What is Fred Henry Pervin like? To what extent is he also compared to horses?

3.  What kind of person is Mabel Pervin? How old is she? How do her brothers treat her? What is her attitude toward her brothers? What dilemma does she face as the story begins?

4.  To what extent does Mabel seem committed to the past rather than the present and to death rather than life?

5.  What is Dr. Fergusson like? What does his initial attitude toward Mabel seem to be like?

6.  Fergusson watches Mabel in the churchyard and at the pond. How does she affect him in both instances? What does this effect suggest about Fergusson?

7.  What does Mabel try to do at the pond? What does Fergusson do? How does the setting here reinforce both the actions and the mood at this point in the story?

8.  What do Mabel and Fergusson realize about themselves and each other in the Pervin home as he tries to warm her? What is Mabel's attitude toward this realization? Fergusson's attitude?

9.  Why does the narrator keep telling us at the end of the story that Fergusson "had no intention of loving" Mabel? What idea about love does this repeated assertion convey?

10. Often in stories, when authors describe how people fall in love, there is

little further detail beyond the declarations and a concluding "they lived happily ever after." In "The Horse Dealer's Daughter," however, there is a relatively extensive portrayal of the ambiguous feelings of both Dr. Fergusson and Mabel Pervin. Explain what you think are the reasons for which Lawrence explores these feelings so extensively.

11. Consider the narrator's comparison of Joe Pervin and the draft horses. In light of the fact that the horses have great strength but no individuality, being guided and controlled by those with the reins, can this comparison be extended to other characters in the story? To what degree is the love that emerges between Mabel and Dr. Fergusson within their control? Do you think Lawrence believes that love is generally within the control of people falling in love?

## RALPH ELLISON (b. 1914)

*Flying Home*°                                                            *1944*

When Todd came to,° he saw two faces suspended above him in a sun so hot and blinding that he could not tell if they were black or white. He stirred, feeling a pain that burned as though his whole body had been laid open to the sun which glared into his eyes. For a moment an old fear of being touched by white hands seized him. Then the very sharpness of the pain began slowly to clear his head. Sounds came to him dimly. He done come to. Who are they? he thought. Naw he ain't, I coulda sworn he was white. Then he heard clearly:

"You hurt bad?"

Something within him uncoiled. It was a Negro sound.

"He's still out," he heard.

"Give 'im time. . . . Say, son, you hurt bad?"                               5

Was he? There was that awful pain. He lay rigid, hearing their breathing and trying to weave a meaning between them and his being stretched painfully upon the ground. He watched them warily, his mind traveling back over a painful distance. Jagged scenes, swiftly unfolding as in a movie trailer, reeled through his mind, and he saw himself piloting a tailspinning plane and landing and falling from the cockpit and trying to stand. Then, as in a great silence, he remembered the sound of crunching bone, and now, looking up into the anxious faces of an old Negro man and a boy from where he lay in the same field, the memory sickened him and he wanted to remember no more.

"How you feel, son?"

Todd hesitated, as though to answer would be to admit an inacceptable weakness. Then, "It's my ankle," he said.

"Which one?"

"Flying Home" is the title of a song made popular by Glenn Miller in the early 1940s.

*When Todd came to*: Todd is a military pilot in training during World War II (1941–1945). He is black and has just crashed in the south in a field owned by a white man.

"The left."                                                                    10

With a sense of remoteness he watched the old man bend and remove his boot, feeling the pressure ease.

"That any better?"

"A lot. Thank you."

He had the sensation of discussing someone else, that his concern was with some far more important thing, which for some reason escaped him.

"You done broke it bad," the old man said. "We have to get you to a doctor."      15

He felt that he had been thrown into a tailspin. He looked at his watch; how long had he been here? He knew there was but one important thing in the world, to get the plane back to the field before his officers were displeased.

"Help me up," he said. "Into the ship."

"But it's broke too bad. . . ."

"Give me your arm!"

"But, son . . ."                                                               20

Clutching the old man's arm he pulled himself up, keeping his left leg clear, thinking, "I'd never make him understand," as the leather-smooth face came parallel with his own.

"Now, let's see."

He pushed the old man back, hearing a bird's insistent shrill. He swayed giddily. Blackness washed over him, like infinity.

"You best sit down."

"No, I'm OK."                                                                  25

"But, son. You jus' gonna make it worse. . . ."

It was a fact that everything in him cried out to deny, even against the flaming pain in his ankle. He would have to try again.

"You mess with that ankle they have to cut your foot off," he heard.

Holding his breath, he started up again. It pained so badly that he had to bite his lips to keep from crying out and he allowed them to help him down with a pang of despair.

"It's best you take it easy. We gon' git you a doctor."                        30

Of all the luck, he thought. Of all the rotten luck, now I have done it. The fumes of high-octane gasoline clung in the heat, taunting him.

"We kin ride him into town on old Ned." the boy said.

Ned? He turned, seeing the boy point toward an ox team browsing where the buried blade of a plow marked the end of a furrow. Thoughts of himself riding an ox through the town, past streets full of white faces, down the concrete runways of the airfield made swift images of humiliation in his mind. With a pang he remembered his girl's last letter. "Todd," she had written, "I don't need the papers to tell me you had the intelligence to fly. And I have always known you to be as brave as anyone else. The papers annoy me. Don't you be contented to prove over and over again that you're brave or skillful just because you're black, Todd. I think they keep beating that dead horse because they don't want to say why you boys are not yet fighting. I'm really disappointed, Todd. Anyone with brains can learn to fly, but then what? What about using it, and who will you use it for? I wish, dear, you'd write about this. I sometimes think they're playing a trick on us. It's very humiliating. . . ." He wiped cold sweat from his face, thinking, What does she know of humiliation? She's never been down South. Now the humiliation

would come. When you must have them judge you, knowing that they never accept
your mistakes as your own, but hold it against your whole race—that was humiliation.
Yes, and humiliation was when you could never be simply yourself, when you
were always a part of this old black ignorant man. Sure, he's all right. Nice and
kind and helpful. But he's not you. Well, there's one humiliation I can spare myself.

"No," he said, "I have orders not to leave the ship. . . ."

"Aw," the old man said. Then turning to the boy, "Teddy, then you better      35
hustle down to Mister Graves and get him to come. . . ."

"No, wait!" he protested before he was fully aware. Graves might be white.
"Just have him get word to the field, please. They'll take care of the rest."

He saw the boy leave, running.

"How far does he have to go?"

"Might' nigh a mile."

He rested back, looking at the dusty face of his watch. But now they know      40
something has happened, he thought. In the ship there was a perfectly good radio,
but it was useless. The old fellow would never operate it. That buzzard knocked
me back a hundred years, he thought. Irony danced with him like the gnats circling
the old man's head. With all I've learned I'm dependent upon this "peasant's"
sense of time and space. His leg throbbed. In the plane, instead of time being
measured by the rhythms of pain and a kid's legs, the instruments would have
told him at a glance. Twisting upon his elbows he saw where dust had powdered
the plane's fuselage, feeling the lump form in his throat that was always there
when he thought of flight. It's crouched there, he thought, like the abandoned
shell of a locust. I'm naked without it. Not a machine, a suit of clothes you wear.
And with a sudden embarrassment and wonder he whispered, "It's the only dignity
I have. . . ."

He saw the old man watching, his torn overalls clinging limply to him in
the heat. He felt a sharp need to tell the old man what he felt. But that would
be meaningless. If I tried to explain why I need to fly back, he'd think I was
simply afraid of white officers. But it's more than fear . . . a sense of anguish
clung to him like the veil of sweat that hugged his face. He watched the old man,
hearing him humming snatches of a tune as he admired the plane. He felt a furtive
sense of resentment. Such old men often came to the field to watch the pilots
with childish eyes. At first it had made him proud; they had been a meaningful
part of a new experience. But soon he realized they did not understand his accom-
plishments and they came to shame and embarrass him, like the distasteful praise
of an idiot. A part of the meaning of flying had gone then, and he had not been
able to regain it. If I were a prizefighter I would be more human, he thought.
Not a monkey doing tricks, but a man. They were pleased simply that he was a
Negro who could fly, and that was not enough. He felt cut off from them by age,
by understanding, by sensibility, by technology and by his need to measure himself
against the mirror of other men's appreciation. Somehow he felt betrayed, as he
had when as a child he grew to discover that his father was dead. Now for him
any real appreciation lay with his white officers; and with them he could never
be sure. Between ignorant black men and condescending whites, his course of
flight seemed mapped by the nature of things away from all needed and natural
landmarks. Under some sealed orders, couched in ever more technical and mysterious terms, his path curved swiftly away from both the shame the old man symbolized

and the cloudy terrain of white men's regard. Flying blind, he knew but one point of landing and there he would receive his wings. After that the enemy would appreciate his skill and he would assume his deepest meaning, he thought sadly, neither from those who condescended nor from those who praised without understanding, but from the enemy who would recognize his manhood and skill in terms of hate. . . .

He sighed, seeing the oxen making queer, prehistoric shadows against the dry brown earth.

"You just take it easy, son," the old man soothed. "That boy won't take long. Crazy as he is about airplanes."

"I can wait," he said.

"What kinda airplane you call this here'n?"                                          45

"An Advanced Trainer," he said, seeing the old man smile. His fingers were like gnarled dark wood against the metal as he touched the low-slung wing.

"'Bout how fast can she fly?"

"Over two hundred an hour."

"Lawd! That's so fast I bet it don't seem like you moving!"

Holding himself rigid, Todd opened his flying suit. The shade had gone          50
and he lay in a ball of fire.

"You mind if I take a look inside? I was always curious to see. . . ."

"Help yourself. Just don't touch anything."

He heard him climb upon the metal wing, grunting. Now the questions would start. Well, so you don't have to think to answer. . . .

He saw the old man looking over into the cockpit, his eyes bright as a child's.

"You must have to know a lot to work all these here things."                       55

He was silent, seeing him step down and kneel beside him.

"Son, how come you want to fly way up there in the air?"

Because it's the most meaningful act in the world . . . because it makes me less like you, he thought.

But he said: "Because I like it, I guess. It's as good a way to fight and die as I know."

"Yeah? I guess you right," the old man said. "But how long you think before    60
they gonna let you all fight?"

He tensed. This was the question all Negroes asked, put with the same timid hopefulness and longing that always opened a greater void within him than that he had felt beneath the plane the first time he had flown. He felt light-headed. It came to him suddenly that there was something sinister about the conversation, that he was flying unwillingly into unsafe and uncharted regions. If he could only be insulting and tell this old man who was trying to help him to shut up!

"I bet you one thing. . . ."

"Yes?"

"That you was plenty scared coming down."

He did not answer. Like a dog on a trail the old man seemed to smell out          65
his fears, and he felt anger bubble within him.

"You sho' scared me. When I seen you coming down in that thing with it a-rolling' and a-jumpin' like a pitchin' hoss, I thought sho' you was a goner. I almost had me a stroke!"

He saw the old man grinning. "Ever'thin's been happening round here this morning, come to think of it."

"Like what?" he asked.

"Well, first thing I know, here come two white fellers looking for Mister Rudolph, that's Mister Graves's cousin. That got me worked up right away. . . ."

"Why?"

"Why? 'Cause he done broke outta the crazy house, that's why. He liable to kill somebody," he said. "They oughta have him by now though. Then here you come. First I think it's one of them white boys. Then doggone if you don't fall outta there. Lawd, I'd done heard about you boys but I haven't never seen one o' you-all. Cain't tell you how it felt to see somebody what look like me in a airplane!"

The old man talked on, the sound streaming around Todd's thoughts like air flowing over the fuselage of a flying plane. You were a fool, he thought, remembering how before the spin the sun had blazed bright against the billboard signs beyond the town, and how a boy's blue kite had bloomed beneath him, tugging gently in the wind like a strange, odd-shaped flower. He had once flown such kites himself and tried to find the boy at the end of the invisible cord. But he had been flying too high and too fast. He had climbed steeply away in exultation. Too steeply, he thought. And one of the first rules you learn is that if the angle of thrust is too steep the plane goes into a spin. And then, instead of pulling out of it and going into a dive you let a buzzard panic you. A lousy buzzard!

"Son, what made all that blood on the glass?"

"A buzzard," he said, remembering how the blood and feathers had sprayed back against the hatch. It had been as though he had flown into a storm of blood and blackness.

"Well, I declare! They's lots of 'em around here. They after dead things. Don't eat nothing what's alive."

"A little bit more and he would have made a meal out of me," Todd said grimly.

"They bad luck all right. Teddy's got a name for 'em, calls 'em jimcrows,"° the old man laughed.

"It's a damned good name."

"They the damnedest birds. Once I seen a hoss all stretched out like he was sick, you know. So I hollers, 'Gid up from there, suh!' Just to make sho! An' doggone, son, if I don't see two ole jimcrows come flying right up outa that hoss's insides! yessuh! The sun was shinin' on 'em and they couldn't a been no greasier if they'd been eating barbecue."

Todd thought he would vomit, his stomach quivered.

"You made that up," he said.

"Nawsuh! Saw him just like I see you."

"Well, I'm glad it was you."

"You see lots a funny things down here, son."

"No, I'll let you see them," he said.

"By the way, the white folks round here don't like to see you boys up there in the sky. They ever bother you?"

"No."

"Well, they'd like to."

---

*jimcrows:* an insulting slang term for blacks and for the customs and laws segregating blacks.

"Someone always wants to bother someone else," Todd said. "How do you know?"

"I just know."                                                               90

"Well," he said defensively, "no one has bothered us."

Blood pounded in his ears as he looked away into space. He tensed, seeing a black spot in the sky, and strained to confirm what he could not clearly see.

"What does that look like to you?" he asked excitedly.

"Just another bad luck, son."

Then he saw the movement of wings with disappointment. It was gliding       95
smoothly down, wings outspread, tail feathers gripping the air, down swiftly—gone behind the green screen of trees. It was like a bird he had imagined there, only the sloping branches of the pines remained, sharp against the pale stretch of sky. He lay barely breathing and stared at the point where it had disappeared, caught in a spell of loathing and admiration. Why did they make them so disgusting and yet teach them to fly so well? It's like when I was up in heaven, he heard, starting.

The old man was chuckling, rubbing his stubbled chin.

"What did you say?"

"Sho', I died and went to heaven . . . maybe by time I tell you about it they be done come after you."

"I hope so," he said wearily.

"You boys ever sit around and swap lies?"                                   100

"Not often. Is this going to be one?"

"Well, I ain't so sho', on account of it took place when I was dead."

The old man paused, "That wasn't no lie 'bout the buzzards, though."

"All right," he said.

"Sho' you want to hear 'bout heaven?"                                       105

"Please," he answered, resting his head upon his arm.

"Well, I went to heaven and right away started to sproutin' me some wings. Six good ones, they was. Just like them the white angels had. I couldn't hardly believe it. I was so glad that I went off on some clouds by myself and tried 'em out. You know, 'cause I didn't want to make a fool outta myself the first thing. . . ."

It's an old tale, Todd thought. Told me years ago. Had forgotten. But at least it will keep him from talking about buzzards.

He closed his eyes, listening.

". . . First thing I done was to git up on a low cloud and jump off. And    110
doggone, boy, if them wings didn't work! First I tried the right; then I tried the left; then I tried 'em both together. Then Lawd, I started to move on out among the folks. I let 'em see me. . . ."

He saw the old man gesturing flight with his arms, his face full of mock pride as he indicated an imaginary crowd, thinking, It'll be in the newspapers, as he heard, ". . . so I went and found me some colored angels—somehow I didn't believe I was an angel till I seen a real black one, ha, yes! Then I was sho'—but they tole me I better come down 'cause us colored folks had to wear a special kin' a harness when we flew. That was how come they wasn't flyin'. Oh yes, an' you had to be extra strong for a black man even, to fly with one of them harnesses. . . ."

This is a new turn, Todd thought, what's he driving at?

"So I said to myself, I ain't gonna be bothered with no harness! Oh naw! 'Cause if God let you sprout wings you oughta have sense enough not to let nobody make you wear something what gits in the way of flyin'. So I starts to flyin'. Heck, son," he chuckled, his eyes twinkling, "you know I had to let eve'ybody know that old Jefferson could fly good as anybody else. And I could too, fly smooth as a bird! I could even loop-the-loop—only I had to make sho' to keep my long white robe down roun' my ankles. . . ."

Todd felt uneasy. He wanted to laugh at the joke, but his body refused, as of an independent will. He felt as he had as a child when after he had chewed a sugar-coated pill which his mother had given him, she had laughed at his efforts to remove the terrible taste.

". . . Well," he heard, "I was doing all right 'til I got to speeding. Found    115
out I could fan up a right strong breeze, I could fly so fast. I could do all kin'sa stunts too. I started flying up to the stars and divin' down and zooming roun' the moon. Man, I like to scare the devil outa some ole white angels. I was raisin' hell. Not that I meant any harm, son. But I was just feeling good. It was so good to know I was free at last. I accidentally knocked the tips offa some stars and they tell me I caused a storm and a coupla lynchings down here in Macon County— though I swear I believe them boys what said that was making up lies on me. . . ."

He's mocking me, Todd thought angrily. He thinks it's a joke. Grinning down at me. . . . His throat was dry. He looked at his watch; why the hell didn't they come? Since they had to, why? One day I was flying down one of them heavenly streets. You got yourself into it, Todd thought. Like Jonah in the whale.

"Justa throwin' feathers in everybody's face. An' ole Saint Peter called me in. Said, 'Jefferson, tell me two things, what you doin' flyin' without a harness; an' how come you flyin' so fast?' So I tole him I was flyin' without a harness 'cause it got in my way, but I couldn'ta been flyin' so fast, 'cause I wasn't usin' but one wing. Saint Peter said, 'You wasn't flyin' with but one wing?' 'Yessuh,' I says, scared-like. So he says, 'Well, since you got sucha extra fine pair of wings you can leave off yo' harness awhile. But from now on none of that there one-wing flyin', 'cause you gittin' up too damn much speed!"

And with one mouth full of bad teeth you're making too damned much talk, thought Todd. Why don't I send him after the boy? His body ached from the hard ground and seeking to shift his position he twisted his ankle and hated himself for crying out.

"It gittin' worse?"

"I. . . . I twisted it," he groaned.    120

"Try not to think about it, son. That's what I do."

He bit his lip, fighting pain with counter-pain as the voice resumed its rhythmical droning. Jefferson seemed caught in his own creation.

". . . After all that trouble I just floated roun' heaven in slow motion. But I forgot, like colored folks will do, and got to flyin' with one wing again. This time I was restin' my old broken arm and got to flyin' fast enough to shame the devil. I was comin' so fast, Lawd, I got myself called befo' ole Saint Peter again. He said, 'Jeff, didn't I warn you 'bout that speedin'?' 'Yessuh,' I says, 'but it was an accident.' He looked at me sadlike and shook his head and I knowed I was gone. He said, 'Jeff, you and that speedin' is a danger to the heavenly community. If I was to let you keep on flyin', heaven wouldn't be nothin' but uproar. Jeff, you got to go!' Son, I argued and pleaded with that old white man, but it didn't do a bit of good. They rushed me straight to them pearly gates and gimme a parachute and a map of the state of Alabama. . . ."

Todd heard him laughing so that he could hardly speak, making a screen between them upon which his humiliation glowed like fire.

"Maybe you'd better stop awhile," he said, his voice unreal.    125

"Ain't much more," Jefferson laughed. "When they gimme the parachute ole Saint Peter ask me if I wanted to say a few words before I went. I felt so bad I couldn't hardly look at him, specially with all them white angels standin' around. Then somebody laughed and made me mad. So I tole him, 'Well, you done took my wings. And you puttin' me out. You got charge of things so's I can't do nothin' about it. But you got to admit just this: While I was up here I was the flyinest sonofabitch what ever hit heaven!' "

At the burst of laughter Todd felt such an intense humiliation that only great violence would wash it away. The laughter which shook the old man like a boiling purge set up vibrations of guilt within him which not even the intricate machinery of the plane would have been adequate to transform and he heard himself screaming, "Why do you laugh at me this way?"

He hated himself at that moment, but he had lost control. He saw Jefferson's mouth fall open, "What—?"

"Answer me!"

His blood pounded as though it would surely burst his temples and he tried    130
to reach the old man and fell, screaming, "Can I help it because they won't let us actually fly? Maybe we are a bunch of buzzards feeding on a dead horse, but we can hope to be eagles, can't we? Can't we?"

He fell back, exhausted, his ankle pounding. The saliva was like straw in his mouth. If he had the strength he would strangle this old man. This grinning, gray-headed clown who made him feel as he felt when watched by the white officers at the field. And yet this old man had neither power, prestige, rank nor technique. Nothing that could rid him of this terrible feeling. He watched him, seeing his face struggle to express a turmoil of feeling.

"What you mean, son? What you talking 'bout . . . ?"

"Go away. Go tell your tales to the white folks."

"But I didn't mean nothing like that . . . I . . . I wasn't tryin' to hurt your feelings. . . ."

"Please. Get the hell away from me!"

"But I didn't, son. I didn't mean all them things a-tall."    135

Todd shook as with a chill, searching Jefferson's face for a trace of the mockery he had seen there. But now the face was somber and tired and old. He was confused. He could not be sure that there had ever been laughter there, that Jefferson had ever really laughed in his whole life. He saw Jefferson reach out to touch him and shrank away, wondering if anything except the pain, now causing his vision to waver, was real. Perhaps he had imagined it all.

"Don't let it get you down, son," the voice said pensively.

He heard Jefferson sigh wearily, as though he felt more than he could say. His anger ebbed, leaving only the pain.

"I'm sorry," he mumbled.    140

"You just wore out with pain, was all. . . ."

He saw him through a blur, smiling. And for a second he felt the embarrassed silence of understanding flutter between them.

"What you was doin' flyin' over this section, son? Wasn't you scared they might shoot you for a cow?"

Todd tensed. Was he being laughed at again? But before he could decide, the pain shook him and a part of him was lying calmly behind the screen of pain that had fallen between them, recalling the first time he had ever seen a plane. It was as though an endless series of hangars had been shaken ajar in the air base of his memory and from each, like a young wasp emerging from its cell, arose the memory of a plane.

The first time I ever saw a plane I was very small and planes were new in    145
the world. I was four-and-a-half and the only plane that I had ever seen was a model suspended from the ceiling of the automobile exhibit at the State Fair. But I did not know that it was only a model. I did not know how large a real plane was, nor how expensive. To me it was a fascinating toy, complete in itself, which my mother said could only be owned by rich little white boys. I stood rigid with admiration, my head straining backwards as I watched the gray little plane describing arcs above the gleaming tops of the automobiles. And I vowed that, rich or poor, someday I would own such a toy. My mother had to drag me out of the exhibit and not even the merry-go-round, the Ferris wheel, or the racing horse could hold my attention for the rest of the Fair. I was too busy imitating the tiny drone of the plane with my lips, and imitating with my hands the motion, swift and circling, that it made in flight.

After that I no longer used the pieces of lumber that lay about our back yard to construct wagons and autos . . . now it was used for airplanes. I built biplanes, using pieces of board for wings, a small box for the fuselage, another piece of wood for the rudder. The trip to the Fair had brought something new into my small world. I asked my mother repeatedly when the Fair would come back again. I'd lie in the grass and watch the sky, and each fighting bird became a soaring plane. I would have been good a year just to have seen a plane again. I became a nuisance to everyone with my questions about airplanes. But planes were new to the old folks, too, and there was little that they could tell me. Only my uncle knew some of the answers. And better still, he could carve propellers from pieces of wood that would whirl rapidly in the wind, wobbling noisily upon oiled nails.

I wanted a plane more than I'd wanted anything; more than I wanted the red wagon with rubber tires, more than the train that ran on a track with its train of cars. I asked my mother over and over again:

"Mamma?"

"What do you want, boy?" she'd say.

"Mamma, will you get mad if I ask you?" I'd say.    150

"What do you want now? I ain't got time to be answering a lot of fool questions. What you want?"

"Mamma, when you gonna get me one . . ?" I'd ask.

"Get you one what?" she'd say.

"You know, Mamma; what I been asking you. . . ."

"Boy," she'd say, "if you don't want a spanking you better come on an'    155
tell me what you talking about so I can get on with my work."

"Aw, Mamma, you know. . . ."

"What I just tell you?" she'd say.

"I mean when you gonna buy me a airplane."

"AIRPLANE! Boy, is you crazy? How many times I have to tell you to stop that foolishness. I done told you them things cost too much. I bet I'm gon' wham the living daylight out of you if you don't quit worrying me 'bout them things!"

But this did not stop me, and a few days later I'd try all over again.          160

Then one day a strange thing happened. It was spring and for some reason I had been hot and irritable all morning. It was a beautiful spring. I could feel it as I played barefoot in the backyard. Blossoms hung from the thorny black locust trees like clusters of fragrant white grapes. Butterflies flickered in the sunlight above the short new dew-wet grass. I had gone in the house for bread and butter and coming out I heard a steady unfamiliar drone. It was unlike anything I had ever heard before. I tried to place the sound. It was no use. It was a sensation like that I had when searching for my father's watch, heard ticking unseen in a room. It made me feel as though I had forgotten to perform some task that my mother had ordered. . . . then I located it, overhead. In the sky, flying quite low and about a hundred yards off was a plane! It came so slowly that it seemed barely to move. My mouth hung wide; my bread and butter fell into the dirt. I wanted to jump up and down and cheer. And when the idea struck I trembled with excitement: "Some little white boy's plane's done flew away and all I got to do is stretch out my hands and it'll be mine!" It was a little plane like that at the Fair, flying no higher than the eaves of our roof. Seeing it come steadily forward I felt the world grow warm with promise. I opened the screen and climbed over it and clung there, waiting. I would catch the plane as it came over and swing down fast and run into the house before anyone could see me. Then no one could come to claim the plane. It droned nearer. Then when it hung like a silver cross in the blue directly above me I stretched out my hand and grabbed. It was like sticking my finger through a soap bubble. The plane flew on, as though I had simply blown my breath after it. I grabbed again, frantically, trying to catch the tail. My fingers clutched the air and disappointment surged tight and hard in my throat. Giving one last desperate grasp, I strained forward. My fingers ripped from the screen. I was falling. The ground burst hard against me. I drummed the earth with my heels and when my breath returned, I lay there bawling.

My mother rushed through the door.

"What's the matter, chile! What on earth is wrong with you?"

"It's gone! It's gone!"

"What gone?"          165

"The airplane. . . ."

"Airplane?"

"Yessum, jus' like the one at the Fair. . . . I . . . I tried to stop it an' it kep' right on going. . . ."

"When, boy?"

"Just now," I cried, through my tears.          170

"Where it go, boy, what way?"

"Yonder, there . . ."

She scanned the sky, her arms akimbo and her checkered apron flapping in the wind as I pointed to the fading plane. Finally she looked down at me, slowly shaking her head.

"It's gone! It's gone!" I cried.

"Boy, is you a fool?" she said. "Don't you see that there's a real airplane   175
'stead of one of them toy ones?"

"Real. . . ?" I forgot to cry. "Real?"

"Yass, real. Don't you know that thing you reaching for is bigger'n a auto?
You here trying to reach for it and I bet it's flying 'bout two hundred miles higher'n
this roof." She was disgusted with me. "You come on in this house before somebody
else sees what a fool you done turned out to be. You must think these here lil
ole arms of you'n is mighty long. . . ."

I was carried into the house and undressed for bed and the doctor was called.
I cried bitterly, as much from the disappointment of finding the plane so far beyond
my reach as from the pain.

When the doctor came I heard my mother telling him about the plane and
asking if anything was wrong with my mind. He explained that I had had a fever
for several hours. But I was kept in bed for a week and I constantly saw the plane
in my sleep, flying just beyond my fingertips, sailing so slowly that it seemed barely
to move. And each time I'd reach out to grab it I'd miss and through each dream
I'd hear my grandma warning:

> Young man, young man,
> Yo' arms too short
> To box with God. . . .

"Hey, son!"   180

At first he did not know where he was and looked at the old man pointing,
with blurred eyes.

"Ain't that one of you-all's airplanes coming after you?"

As his vision cleared he saw a small black shape above a distant field, soaring
through waves of heat. But he could not be sure and with the pain he feared
that somehow a horrible recurring fantasy of being split in twain by the whirling
blades of a propeller had come true.

"You think he sees us?" he heard.

"See? I hope so."   185

"He's coming like a bat outa hell!"

Straining, he heard the faint sound of a motor and hoped it would soon be
over.

"How you feeling?"

"Like a nightmare," he said.

"Hey, he's done curved back the other way!"   190

"Maybe he saw us," he said. "Maybe he's gone to send out the ambulance
and ground crew." And, he thought with despair, maybe he didn't even see us.

"Where did you send the boy?"

"Down to Mister Graves," Jefferson said. "Man what owns this land."

"Do you think he phoned?"

Jefferson looked at him quickly.   195

"Aw sho'. Dabney Graves is got a bad name on accounta them killings but
he'll call though. . . ."

"What killings?"

"Them five fellers . . . ain't you heard?" he asked with surprise.

"No."

"Everybody knows 'bout Dabney Graves, especially the colored. He done     200
killed enough of us."

Todd had the sensation of being caught in a white neighborhood after dark.

"What did they do?" he asked.

"Thought they was men," Jefferson said, "An' some he owed money, like
he do me. . . ."

"But why do you stay here?"

"You black, son."                                                          205

"I know, but . . ."

"You have to come by the white folks, too."

He turned away from Jefferson's eyes, at once consoled and accused. And
I'll have to come by them soon, he thought with despair. Closing his eyes, he
heard Jefferson's voice as the sun burned blood-red upon his lips.

"I got nowhere to go," Jefferson said, "an' they'd come after me if I did.
But Dabney Graves is a funny fellow. He's all the time making jokes. He can be
mean as hell, then he's liable to turn right around and back the colored against
the white folks. I seen him do it. But me, I hates him for that more'n anything
else. 'Cause just as soon as he gits tired helping a man he don't care what happens
to him. He just leaves him stone cold. And then the other white folks is double
hard on anybody he done helped. For him it's just a joke. He don't give a hilla
beans for nobody—but hisself. . . ."

Todd listened to the thread of detachment in the old man's voice. It was     210
as though he held his words arm's length before him to avoid their destructive
meaning.

"He'd just as soon do you a favor and then turn right around and have     10
you strung up. Me, I stays outa his way 'cause down here that's what you
gotta do."

If my ankle would only ease for a while, he thought. The closer I spin toward
the earth the blacker I become, flashed through his mind. Sweat ran into his eyes
and he was sure that he would never see the plane if his head continued whirling.
He tried to see Jefferson, what it was that Jefferson held in his hand. It was a
little black man, another Jefferson! A little black Jefferson that shook with fits of
belly-laughter while the other Jefferson looked on with detachment. Then Jefferson
looked up from the thing in his hand and turned to speak, but Todd was far
away, searching the sky for a plane in a hot dry land on a day and age he had
long forgotten. He was going mysteriously with his mother through empty streets
where black faces peered from behind drawn shades and someone was rapping
at a window and he was looking back to see a hand and a frightened face frantically
beckoning from a cracked door and his mother was looking down the empty perspective of the street and shaking her head and hurrying him along and at first it was
only a flash he saw and a motor was droning as through the sun-glare he saw it
gleaming silver as it circled and he was seeing a burst like a puff of white smoke
and hearing his mother yell, Come along, boy, I got no time for them fool airplanes,
I got no time, and he saw it a second time, the plane flying high, and the burst
appeared suddenly and fell slowly, billowing out and sparkling like fireworks and
he was watching and being hurried along as the air filled with a flurry of white
pinwheeling cards that caught in the wind and scattered over the rooftops and
into the gutters and a woman was running and snatching a card and reading it
and screaming and he darted into the shower, grabbing as in winter he grabbed

for snowflakes and bounding away at his mother's, Come on here, boy! Come on, I say! and he was watching as she took the card away, seeing her face grow puzzled and turning taut as her voice quavered, "Niggers Stay From the Polls," and died to a moan of terror as he saw the eyeless sockets of a white hood staring at him from the card and above he saw the plane spiraling gracefully, agleam in the sun like a fiery sword. And seeing it soar he was caught, transfixed between a terrible horror and a horrible fascination.

The sun was not so high now, and Jefferson was calling and gradually he saw three figures moving across the curving roll of the field.

"Look like some doctors, all dressed in white," said Jefferson.

They're coming at last, Todd thought. And he felt such a release of tension      215
within him that he thought he would faint. But no sooner did he close his eyes than he was seized and he was struggling with three white men who were forcing his arms into some kind of coat. It was too much for him, his arms were pinned to his sides and as the pain blazed in his eyes, he realized that it was a straitjacket. What filthy joke was this?

"That oughta hold him, Mister Graves," he heard.

His total energies seemed focused in his eyes as he searched their faces. That was Graves: the other two wore hospital uniforms. He was poised between two poles of fear and hate as he heard the one called Graves saying, "He looks kinda purty in that there suit, boys. I'm glad you dropped by."

"This boy ain't crazy, Mister Graves," one of the others said. "He needs a doctor, not us. Don't see how you led us way out here anyway. It might be a joke to you, but your cousin Rudolph liable to kill somebody. White folks or niggers, don't make no difference. . . ."

Todd saw the man turn red with anger. Graves looked down upon him, chuckling.

"This nigguh belongs in a straitjacket, too, boys. I knowed that the minit      220
Jeff's kid said something 'bout a nigguh flyer. You all know you cain't let the nigguh git up that high without his going crazy. The nigguh brain ain't built right for high altitudes. . . ."

Todd watched the drawling red face, feeling that all the unnamed horror and obscenities that he had ever imagined stood materialized before him.

"Let's git outta here," one of the attendants said.

Todd saw the other reach toward him, realizing for the first time that he lay upon a stretcher as he yelled.

"Don't put your hands on me!"

They drew back, surprised.      225

"What's that you say, nigguh?" asked Graves.

He did not answer and thought that Graves's foot was aimed at his head. It landed on his chest and he could hardly breathe. He coughed helplessly, seeing Graves's lips stretch taut over his yellow teeth, and tried to shift his head. It was as though a half-dead fly was dragging slowly across his face and a bomb seemed to burst within him. Blasts of hot, hysterical laughter tore from his chest, causing his eyes to pop and he felt that the veins in his neck would surely burst. And then a part of him stood behind it all, watching the surprise in Graves's red face and his own hysteria. He thought he would never stop, he would laugh himself to death. It rang in his ears like Jefferson's laughter and he looked for him, centering his eyes desperately upon his face, as though somehow he had become his sole salvation in an insane world of outrage and humiliation. It brought a certain relief. He was suddenly aware that although his body was still contorted it was an echo that no longer rang in his ears. He heard Jefferson's voice with gratitude.

"Mister Graves, the Army done tole him not to leave his airplane."

"Nigguh, Army or no, you gittin' off my land! That airplane can stay 'cause it was paid for by taxpayers' money. But you gittin' off. An' dead or alive, it don't make no difference to me."

Todd was beyond it now, lost in a world of anguish.                                               230

"Jeff," Graves said, "you and Teddy come and grab holt. I want you to take this here black eagle over to that nigguh airfield and leave him."

Jefferson and the boy approached him silently. He looked away, realizing and doubting at once that only they could release him from his overpowering sense of isolation.

They bent for the stretcher. One of the attendants moved toward Teddy.

"Think you can manage it, boy?"

"I think I can, suh," Teddy said.                                                                 235

"Well, you better go behind then, and let yo' pa go ahead so's to keep that leg elevated."

He saw the white men walking ahead as Jefferson and the boy carried him along in silence. Then they were pausing and he felt a hand wiping his face; then he was moving again. And it was as though he had been lifted out of his isolation, back into the world of men. A new current of communication flowed between the man and boy and himself. They moved him gently. Far away he heard a mocking-bird liquidly calling. He raised his eyes, seeing a buzzard poised unmoving in space. For a moment the whole afternoon seemed suspended and he waited for the horror to seize him again. Then like a song within his head he heard the boy's soft humming and saw the dark bird glide into the sun and glow like a bird of flaming gold.

## QUESTIONS

1. What is the point of view in "Flying Home"? What advantages does this point of view give the author? Whose thoughts are accessible to us?

2. Who is the protagonist in the story? Who or what is the antagonist? What is the central conflict?

3. What is the climax of the story? To what extent is the central conflict resolved? Do you think the protagonist is completely victorious, completely defeated, or something in between? What sorts of ideas does the climax suggest?

4. What do flying and airplanes symbolize for Todd? How is this symbolism developed in the long digression in which Todd remembers his childhood feelings about airplanes (paragraphs 146 through 179)? What ideas do these symbols embody?

5. To what extent are animals and setting used symbolically to express ideas? Consider especially the dust, the sun, mule, oxen, and the buzzard. Why does Ellison (through Jefferson) carefully point out that buzzards are called "jimcrows"?

6. How would you describe Jefferson and the black boy? Are they round or flat characters? Static or dynamic? Individual or representative? How do they help establish the ideas of the story?

7. To what extent can Jefferson's story about his experiences in heaven be considered an allegory of the plight of blacks in twentieth-century America? What ideas about life can be derived from this episode?

8. The story contains two long digressions—Jefferson's story about heaven and Todd's childhood memories. How effectively are these worked into the story? How do they advance the story's message or meaning?

9. What is Todd's attitude toward white officers? What is Jefferson's attitude toward white landowners? How are these attitudes similar? How might you account for these attitudes?

10. How is the symbolism of flying associated with Todd modified and even undercut by the crash, the image of the soaring buzzard, and Jefferson's story about heaven? What ideas emerge from the interaction of all these symbols and episodes?

11. What do we learn about Dabney Graves? What type of character is he (round or flat, static or dynamic, individual or representative)? How do his presence and behavior clarify the story's message?

12. To what extent is the straitjacket put on Todd at the end of the story symbolic? What ideas are expressed with this object?

## WRITING ABOUT MEANING IN FICTION

When you prepare to write an essay about ideas in fiction, you should explore all the methods of expressing ideas described earlier and use as many as you think will best provide you with useful information. You may rely most heavily on the direct statements of the authorial voice or on a combination of these and your interpretation of characters and actions. Or you might focus exclusively on a persona or speaker and use his or her ideas as a means of determining those of the author, as nearly as they can be determined.

In your prewriting and early drafts, as in your final essay, make a point of stating the sources of facts. Thus, your sentences might be like these:

> In "The Horse Dealer's Daughter," Lawrence's anonymous narrator describes the reservations that Mabel and Dr. Fergusson have about their new-found love. This description illustrates his idea that love not only creates the excitement of anticipated joy, but also brings out resistance to the possibility of being as controlled as a draught animal in harness. [Here the first sentence refers to a statement by the author's unnamed persona. The second sentence interprets this statement.]

> In one of the last speeches in "The Chaser," the old man implies that his clients will someday return for his expensive poison so that they may eliminate

the wives for whom they had felt such youthful infatuation. It is clear that Collier introduces this speech to demonstrate the idea that life sometimes leads to unconquerable cynicism and evil. [Here the source of the detail in the first sentence is a dramatic statement by a character in the story. The second sentence is interpretive.]

The speaker in "Araby" states that the boys from the Christian Brothers School are like inmates just released from prison when school lets out for the day. This comparison, coming as it does right at the beginning, establishes a slightly comic tone that emphasizes the childish, rather embarrassed confession that the speaker goes on to make in the story. [Here the first sentence locates the source as the first-person narrator, while the second is interpretive.]

In "First Confession," the priest's thoughtful, good-humored treatment of Jackie, as contrasted with the harsh, punishing treatment by the others, shows the idea that religious incentive is best implanted by kindness and understanding, not by fear. [Here the idea, expressed as a single sentence, is derived from a consideration of the work as a whole].

Recognizing sources in this way keeps the lines of your conclusions clear. Thereby you will help your reader in verifying and following your arguments.

In developing and writing your essay, you can help yourself by answering questions like these: What is the best wording of the idea that you can make? What has the author done with the idea? How can the actions be related to the idea as you have stated it? Might any characters be measured according to whether they do or do not live up to the idea? What values does the idea seem to suggest? Does the author seem to be proposing a particular cause? Is this cause personal, social, economic, political, scientific, ethical, esthetic, or religious? Can the idea be shown to affect the organization of the work? How? Does imagery or symbolism develop or illustrate the idea?

### Organizing Your Essay

**INTRODUCTION.**   In your introduction you might state any special circumstances in the work that affect ideas generally or your idea specifically. Your statement of the idea will serve as the central idea for your essay. Your thesis sentence should indicate the particular parts or aspects of the story that you will examine.

**BODY.**   The exact form of your essay will be controlled by your goals, which are (1) to define the idea, and (2) to show its importance in the work. Each story will invite its own approach, but here are a number of areas and strategies that might be helpful in the development of the body of your essay:

1.  *The form of the work as a plan, scheme, or logical format.* Example: "The idea makes for a two-part work, the first showing religion as punishment and the second showing religion as kindness and reward."

2.  *A speech or speeches.* Example: "The priest's conversation and responses to Jackie show in operation the idea that kindness and understanding are the best means to encourage religious commitment."

3.  *A character or characters.* Example: "Todd is an embodiment of the idea that black Americans can achieve success and recognition only through their own efforts, and then only against many obstacles."

4.  *An action or actions.* Example: "Dr. Ferguson's saving Mabel from drowning indicates the story's idea that love is an outgoing, physical force that almost literally rescues human lives."

5.  *Shades or variations of the idea.* Example: "The idea of punishment as a corrective is brought out through the simplicity of the father's 'flaking' of Jackie, the spitefulness of Nora, and the sadistic threats of pain and cosmic intimidation by Mrs. Ryan."

6.  *A combination of these together with any other aspect relevant to the work.* Example: "The idea in 'Araby' that devotion is complex and contradictory is shown in the narrator's romantic mission as a carrier of parcels, his outcries to love in the backroom of his house, and his self-reproach and shame at the story's end. [Here the idea is to be traced as action, speech, and character in the story would reflect upon it.]

CONCLUSION.    You might wish to begin your conclusion with a summary of ideas as appropriate to what you have written in the body of the essay. You might also add your own thoughts, such as your evaluation of the validity or force of the idea. If you are convinced, you might wish to say that the author has expressed the idea forcefully and convincingly, or else to show possible application of the idea to current conditions. If you are not convinced, it is never enough just to say that you disagree; you should try to show the reasons for your disagreement, or to demonstrate the shortcomings or limitations of the idea. If you wish to mention an idea related to the one you have discussed, you might introduce that here, being sure to stress the connections.

## SAMPLE ESSAY

### The Idea in D. H. Lawrence's "The Horse Dealer's Daughter"* That Human Destiny Is to Love

There are many ideas in "The Horse Dealer's Daughter" about the love between men and women. The story suggests that love is a part of the uncontrollable and emotional side of human life, and that love cannot exist without a

* See p. 328 for this story.

[1] physical basis. It also suggests that love transforms life into something new, that love gives security, that only love gives meaning to life, and that love is not only something to live for but something to be feared. The one idea that takes in all these is that loving is an essential part of human nature and that it is human destiny to love.° This idea controls the form of Lawrence's story, and the characters are judged on the standard of how they live up to it. The idea is embodied negatively in characters who are without love, and positively in characters who find love.□

[2] In the first part of the story, loveless characters are negative and incomplete. Their lack of love causes them to be frustrated, sullen, argumentative, and even cruel. Their lives are similar to those of the draught horses on the Pervin farm, who move with "a massive, slumbrous strength, and a stupidity which [holds] . . . them in subjection" (p. 329). The idea is brought across with great force, for the story implies that time is running out on people in this condition, and unless they find love they are doomed to misery. And the love they find must be real, for the underlying theme is that anything short of that is an evasion and will hasten their doom. Joe, the eldest of the Pervin brothers, is the major example of what can happen without love, for even though he is planning to marry, he is doing so without love. His motives are destroying him; as the narrator says, Joe's "life was over, he would be a subject animal" like the horses (p. 329).

[3] The thought that life is impossible without love is exemplified most fully in Mabel Pervin. She is alone among the males in the Pervin family and the character for whom the story is named. Just as the death of the father is breaking up the family, so is it forcing her to drastic action. She clearly assumes that the loss of first her mother and now her father has deprived her of all love. Therefore, her attempted suicide symbolically demonstrates the futility of the loveless, purposeless life.

[4] Rather than ending Mabel's life, however, the pond really begins it, for it is the occasion of her finding love. Dr. Fergusson, who rescues her, is in fact her destiny. He has been introduced previously as a person leading a life of quiet desperation. His common cold, which is pointedly mentioned when he first appears in the Pervin home, may be seen as an indication of the sickness of the soul without love. When he leaves the house his route is aimless and without any eagerly sought goal, and his seeing Mabel go into the water is clearly not deliberate but accidental. When he acts heroically, therefore, he saves not only Mabel, but himself too. The rescue thus suggests the idea that once love is attained, it restores life.

[5] But love is also complex, and it creates new problems once it has been found. It brings out new and strange emotions, and it upsets the habits and attitudes of a lifetime. Indeed, there is a strong element of fear in love; it changes life so completely that no one can ever be the same after experiencing it. We see this kind of fearful change in Doctor Fergusson. The narrator tells us that the doctor "had no intention of loving" Mabel, but that destiny drives him into this state. The final paragraph of the story indicates the mixture of desire and terror that love and change can produce:

° Central idea.
□ Thesis sentence.

"No, I want you, I want you," was all he answered, blindly, with that terrible intonation which frightened her almost more than the horror lest he should *not* want her (p. 340).

Thus, the story suggests that the human destiny that drives people toward love is both joyful and fearful at the same time.

[6] <u>This realistic presentation of human emotions raises Lawrence's treatment of his idea above the level of the popular or romantic conception of love.</u> Love itself creates problems as great as those it solves, but it also builds a platform of emotional strength from which these new problems can be attacked. This strength can be achieved only when men and women know love, because only then are they living life as it was designed. The problems facing them then are the real ones that men and women should face, since such problems are a natural result of destiny. By contrast, men and women without love, like those at the beginning of the story, have never reached fulfillment. Consequently, they face problems that, though certainly severe and immediate, are really irrelevant to life as it should be lived. The entire story of Mabel and Jack is an illustration of the idea that it is the destiny of men and women to love.

### Commentary on the Essay

The introductory paragraph first illustrates the many formulations of the ideas about love that the story suggests and then produces a comprehensive statement of the theme which is made the central idea of the essay. This assertion is developed as it applies (1) to characters without love and (2) to those who find it. In the body of the essay, paragraphs 2 and 3 emphasize the emptiness of the lives of characters without love. The relationship of these two paragraphs to the main idea is that if the characters are not living in accord with human destiny, they are cut off from life. Thus Joe is dismissed in the story as a "subject animal," and Mabel, his sister, attempts suicide. These details are brought out in support of the essay's central idea. Paragraphs 4 and 5 treat the positive aspects of the main idea, focusing on the renewing effect of love on both Mabel and Dr. Fergusson, but also on the complexity of their emotional response to their new love. The last paragraph evaluates the idea or theme of the story and concludes that it is realistic and well balanced.

# Additional Stories

**JOHN CHEEVER (1912–1982)**

*The Season of Divorce* 1973

My wife has brown hair, dark eyes, and a gentle disposition. Because of her gentle disposition, I sometimes think that she spoils the children. She can't refuse them anything. They always get around her. Ethel and I have been married for ten years. We both come from Morristown, New Jersey, and I can't even remember when I first met her. Our marriage has always seemed happy and resourceful to me. We live in a walk-up in the East Fifties. Our son, Carl, who is six, goes to a good private school, and our daughter, who is four, won't go to school until next year. We often find fault with the way we were educated, but we seem to be struggling to raise our children along the same lines, and when the time comes, I suppose they'll go to the same school and colleges that we went to.

Ethel graduated from a women's college in the East, and then went for a year to the University of Grenoble. She worked for a year in New York after returning from France, and then we were married. She once hung her diploma above the kitchen sink, but it was a short-lived joke and I don't know where the diploma is now. Ethel is cheerful and adaptable, as well as gentle, and we both come from that enormous stratum of the middle class that is distinguished by its ability to recall better times. Lost money is so much a part of our lives that I am sometimes reminded of expatriates, of a group who have adapted themselves energetically to some alien soil but who are reminded, now and then, of the escarpments of their native coast. Because our lives are confined by my modest salary, the surface of Ethel's life is easy to describe.

She gets up at seven and turns the radio on. After she is dressed, she rouses the children and cooks the breakfast. Our son has to be walked to the school bus at eight o'clock. When Ethel returns from this trip, Carol's hair has to be braided. I leave the house at eight-thirty, but I know that every move that Ethel makes for the rest of the day will be determined by the housework, the cooking, the shopping, and the demands of the children. I know that on Tuesdays and Thursdays she will be at the the A & P between eleven and noon, that on every clear afternoon she will be on a certain bench in a playground from three until five, that she cleans the house on Mondays, Wednesdays, and Fridays, and polishes the silver when it rains. When I return at six, she is usually cleaning the vegetables or making some other preparation for dinner. Then when the children have been fed and bathed, when the dinner is ready, when the table in the living room is set with food and china, she stands in the middle of the room as if she has lost or forgotten something, and this moment of reflection is so deep that she will not hear me if I speak to her, or the children if they call. Then it is over. She lights the four white candles in their silver sticks, and we sit down to a supper of corned-beef hash or some other modest fare.

We go out once or twice a week and entertain about once a month. Because of practical considerations, most of the people we see live in our neighborhood. We often go around the corner to the parties given by a generous couple named Newsome. The Newsomes' parties are large and confusing, and the arbitrary impulses of friendship are given a free play.

We became attached at the Newsomes' one evening, for reasons that I've never understood, to a couple named Dr. and Mrs. Trencher. I think that Mrs. Trencher was the aggressor in this friendship, and after our first meeting she telephoned Ethel three or four times. We went to their house for dinner, and they came to our house, and sometimes in the evening when Dr. Trencher was walking their old dachshund, he would come up for a short visit. He seemed like a pleasant man to have around. I've heard other doctors say that he's a good physician. The Trenchers are about thirty; at least he is. She is older.  5

I'd say that Mrs. Trencher is a plain woman, but her plainness is difficult to specify. She is small, she has a good figure and regular features, and I suppose that the impression of plainness arises from some inner modesty, some needlessly narrow view of her chances. Dr. Trencher doesn't smoke or drink, and I don't know whether there's any connection or not, but the coloring in his slender face is fresh—his cheeks are pink, and his blue eyes are clear and strong. He has the singular optimism of a well-adjusted physician—the feeling that death is a chance misfortune and that the physical world is merely a field for conquest. In the same way that his wife seems plain, he seems young.

The Trenchers live in a comfortable and unpretentious private house in our neighborhood. The house is old-fashioned; its living rooms are large, its halls are gloomy, and the Trenchers don't seem to generate enough human warmth to animate the place, so that you sometimes take away from them, at the end of an evening, an impression of many empty rooms. Mrs. Trencher is noticeably attached to her possessions—her clothes, her jewels, and the ornaments she's bought for the house—and to Fräulein, the old dachshund. She feeds Fräulein scraps from the table, furtively, as if she has been forbidden to do this, and after dinner Fräulein lies beside her on the sofa. With the play of green light from a television set on her drawn features and her thin hands stroking Fräulein, Mrs. Trencher looked to me one evening like a good-hearted and miserable soul.

Mrs. Trencher began to call Ethel in the mornings for a talk or to ask her for lunch or a matinee. Ethel can't go out in the day and she claims to dislike long telephone conversations. She complained that Mrs. Trencher was a tireless and aggressive gossip. Then late one afternoon Dr. Trencher appeared at the playground where Ethel takes our two children. He was walking by, and he saw her and sat with her until it was time to take the children home. He came again a few days later, and then his visits with Ethel in the playground, she told me, became a regular thing. Ethel thought that perhaps he didn't have many patients and that with nothing to do he was happy to talk with anyone. Then, when we were washing dishes one night, Ethel said thoughtfully that Trencher's attitude toward her seemed strange. "He stares at me," she said. "He sighs and stares at me." I know what my wife looks like in the playground. She wears an old tweed coat, overshoes, and Army gloves, and a scarf is tied under her chin. The playground is a fenced and paved lot between a slum and the river. The picture of the well-dressed, pink-cheeked doctor losing his heart to Ethel in this environment was hard to take seriously. She didn't mention him then for several days, and I guessed that he had stopped his visits. Ethel's birthday came at the end of the month, and I forgot about it, but when I came home that evening, there were a lot of roses in the living room. They were a birthday present from Trencher, she told me. I was cross at myself for having forgotten her birthday, and Trencher's roses made me angry. I asked her if she'd seen him recently.

"Oh, yes," she said, "he still comes to the playground nearly every afternoon. I haven't told you, have I? He's made his declaration. He loves me. He can't live without me. He'd walk through fire to hear the notes of my voice." She laughed. "That's what he said."

"When did he say this?"                                                        10

"At the playground. And walking home. Yesterday."

"How long has he known?"

"That's the funny part about it," she said. "He knew before he met me at the Newsomes' that night. He saw me waiting for a crosstown bus about three weeks before that. He just saw me and he said that he knew then, the minute he saw me. Of course, he's crazy."

I was tired that night and worried about taxes and bills, and I could think of Trencher's declaration only as a comical mistake. I felt that he was a captive of financial and sentimental commitments, like every other man I know, and that he was no more free to fall in love with a strange woman he saw on a street corner than he was to take a walking trip through French Guiana or to recommence his life in Chicago under an assumed name. His declaration, the scene in the playground, seemed to me to be like those chance meetings that are a part of the life of any large city. A blind man asks you to help him across the street, and as you are about to leave him, he seizes your arm and regales you with a passionate account of his cruel and ungrateful children; or the elevator man who is taking you up to a party turns to you suddenly and says that his grandson has infantile paralysis. The city is full of accidental revelation, half-heard cries for help, and strangers who will tell you everything at the first suspicion of sympathy, and Trencher seemed to me like the blind man or the elevator operator. His declaration had no more bearing on the business of our lives than these interruptions.

Mrs. Trencher's telephone conversations had stopped, and we had stopped        15 visiting the Trenchers, but sometimes I would see him in the morning on the crosstown bus when I was late going to work. He seemed understandably embarrassed whenever he saw me, but the bus was always crowded at that time of day, and it was no effort to avoid one another. Also, at about that time I made a mistake in business and lost several thousand dollars for the firm I work for. There was not much chance of my losing my job, but the possibility was always at the back of my mind, and under this and under the continuous urgency of making more money the memory of the eccentric doctor was buried. Three weeks passed without Ethel's mentioning him, and then one evening, when I was reading, I noticed Ethel standing at the window looking down into the street.

"He's really there," she said.

"Who?"

"Trencher. Come here and see."

I went to the window. There were only three people on the sidewalk across the street. It was dark and it would have been difficult to recognize anyone, but because one of them, walking toward the corner, had a dachshund on a leash, it could have been Trencher.

"Well, what about it?" I said. "He's just walking the dog." 20

"But he wasn't walking the dog when I first looked out of the window. He was just standing there, staring up at this building. That's what he says he does. He says that he comes over here and stares up at our lighted windows."

"When did he say this?"

"At the playground."

"I thought you went to another playground."

"Oh, I do, I do, but he followed me. He's crazy, darling. I know he's crazy, 25 but I feel so sorry for him. He says that he spends night after night looking up at our windows. He says that he sees me everywhere—the back of my head, my eyebrows—that he hears my voice. He says that he's never compromised in his life and that he isn't going to compromise about this. I feel so sorry for him, darling. I can't help but feel sorry for him."

For the first time then, the situation seemed serious to me, for in his helplessness I knew that he might have touched an inestimable and wayward passion that Ethel shares with some other women—an inability to refuse any cry for help, to refuse any voice that sounds pitiable. It is not a reasonable passion, and I would almost rather have had her desire him than pity him. When we were getting ready for bed that night, the telephone rang, and when I picked it up and said hello, no one answered. Fifteen minutes later, the telephone rang again, and when there was no answer this time, I began to shout and swear at Trencher, but he didn't reply—there wasn't even the click of a closed circuit—and I felt like a fool. Because I felt like a fool, I accused Ethel of having led him on, of having encouraged him, but these accusations didn't affect her, and when I finished them, I felt worse, because I knew that she was innocent, and that she had to go out on the street to buy groceries and air the children, and that there was no force of law that could keep Trencher from waiting for her there, or from staring up at our lights.

We went to the Newsomes' one night the next week, and while we were taking off our coats, I heard Trencher's voice. He left a few minutes after we arrived, but his manner—the sad glance he gave Ethel, the way he sidestepped me, the sorrowful way that he refused the Newsomes when they asked him to stay longer, and the gallant attentions he showed his miserable wife—made me angry. Then I happened to notice Ethel and saw that her color was high, that her eyes were bright, and that while she was praising Mrs. Newsome's new shoes, her mind was not on what she was saying. When we came home that night, the baby-sitter told us crossly that neither of the children had slept. Ethel took their temperatures. Carol was all right, but the boy had a fever of a hundred and four. Neither of us got much sleep that night, and in the morning Ethel called me at the office to say that Carl had bronchitis. Three days later, his sister came down with it.

For the next two weeks, the sick children took up most of our time. They had to be given medicine at eleven in the evening and again at three in the morning, and we lost a lot of sleep. It was impossible to ventilate or clean the house, and when I came in, after walking through the cold from the bus stop, it stank of cough syrups and tobacco, fruit cores and sickbeds. There were blankets and pillows, ashtrays, and medicine glasses everywhere. We divided the work of sickness reasonably and took turns at getting up in the night, but I often fell asleep at my desk during the day, and after dinner Ethel would fall asleep in a chair in the living room. Fatigue seems to differ for adults and children only in that adults recognize it and so are not overwhelmed by something they can't name; but even with a name for it they are overwhelmed, and when we were tired, we were unreasonable, cross, and the victims of transcendent depressions. One evening after the worst of the sickness was over, I came home and found some roses in the living room. Ethel said that Trencher had brought them. She hadn't let him in. She had closed the door in his face. I took the roses and threw them out. We didn't quarrel. The children went to sleep at nine, and a few minutes after nine I went to bed. Sometime later, something woke me.

A light was burning in the hall. I got up. The children's room and the living room were dark. I found Ethel in the kitchen sitting at the table, drinking coffee.

"I've made some fresh coffee," she said. "Carol felt croupy again, so I steamed    30
her. They're both asleep now."

"How long have you been up?"

"Since half past twelve," she said. "What time is it?"

"Two."

I poured myself a cup of coffee and sat down. She got up from the table and rinsed her cup and looked at herself in a mirror that hangs over the sink. It was a windy night. A dog was wailing somewhere in an apartment below ours, and a loose radio antenna was brushing against the kitchen window.

"It sounds like a branch," she said.    35

In the bare kitchen light, meant for peeling potatoes and washing dishes, she looked very tired.

"Will the children be able to go out tomorrow?"

"Oh, I hope so," she said. "Do you realize that I haven't been out of this apartment in over two weeks?" She spoke bitterly and this startled me.

"It hasn't been quite two weeks."

"It's been over two weeks," she said.    40

"Well, let's figure it out," I said. "The children were taken sick on a Saturday night. That was the fourth. Today is the—"

"Stop it, stop it," she said. "I know how long it's been. I haven't had my shoes on in two weeks."

"You make it sound pretty bad."

"It is. I haven't had on a decent dress or fixed my hair."

"It could be worse."    45

"My mother's cooks had a better life."

"I doubt that."

"My mother's cooks had a better life," she said loudly.

"You'll wake the children."

"My mother's cooks had a better life. They had pleasant rooms. No one    50
could come into the kitchen without their permission." She knocked the coffee
grounds into the garbage and began to wash the pot.

"How long was Trencher here this afternoon?"

"A minute. I've told you."

"I don't believe it. He was in here."

"He was not. I didn't let him in. I didn't let him in because I looked so
badly. I didn't want to discourage him."

"Why not?"    55

"I don't know. He may be a fool. He may be insane but the things he's
told me have made me feel marvelously, he's made me feel marvelously."

"Do you want to go?"

"Go? Where would I go?" She reached for the purse that is kept in the
kitchen to pay for groceries and counted out of it two dollars and thirty-five cents.
"Ossining? Montclair?"

"I mean with Trencher."

"I don't know, I don't know," she said, "but who can say that I shouldn't?    60
What harm would it do? What good would it do? Who knows. I love the children
but that isn't enough, that isn't nearly enough. I wouldn't hurt them, but would
I hurt them so much if I left you? Is divorce so dreadful and of all the things
that hold a marriage together how many of them are good?" She sat down at
the table.

"In Grenoble," she said, "I wrote a long paper on Charles Stuart in French.
A professor at the University of Chicago wrote me a letter. I couldn't read a French
newspaper without a dictionary today, I don't have the time to follow any newspaper,
and I am ashamed of my incompetence, ashamed of the way I look. Oh, I guess
I love you, I do love the children, but I love myself, I love my life, it has some
value and some promise for me and Trencher's roses make me feel that I'm losing
this, that I'm losing my self-respect. Do you know what I mean, do you understand
what I mean?"

"He's crazy," I said.

"Do you know what I mean? Do you understand what I mean?"

"No," I said. "No."

Carl woke up then and called for his mother. I told Ethel to go to bed. I    65
turned out the kitchen light and went into the children's room.

The children felt better the next day, and since it was Sunday, I took them
for a walk. The afternoon sun was clement and pure, and only the colored shadows
made me remember that it was midwinter, that the cruise ships were returning,
and that in another week jonquils would be twenty-five cents a bunch. Walking
down Lexington Avenue, we heard the drone bass of a church organ sound from
the sky, and we and the others on the sidewalk looked up in piety and bewilderment,
like a devout and stupid congregation, and saw a formation of heavy bombers
heading for the sea. As it got late, it got cold and clear and still, and on the
stillness the waste from the smokestacks along the East River seemed to articulate,

as legibly as the Pepsi-Cola plane, whole words and sentences. Halcyon. Disaster. They were hard to make out. It seemed the ebb of the year—an evil day for gastritis, sinus, and respiratory disease—and remembering other winters, the markings of the light convinced me that it was the season of divorce. It was a long afternoon, and I brought the children in before dark.

I think that the seriousness of the day affected the children, and when they returned to the house, they were quiet. The seriousness of it kept coming to me with the feeling that this change, like a phenomenon of speed, was affecting our watches as well as our hearts. I tried to remember the willingness with which Ethel had followed my regiment during the war, from West Virginia to the Carolinas and Oklahoma, and the day coaches and rooms she had lived in, and the street in San Francisco where I said goodbye to her before I left the country, but I could not put any of this into words, and neither of us found anything to say. Sometime after dark, the children were bathed and put to bed, and we sat down to our supper. At about nine o'clock, the doorbell rang, and when I answered it and recognized Trencher's voice on the speaking tube, I asked him to come up.

He seemed distraught and exhilarated when he appeared. He stumbled on the edge of the carpet. "I know that I'm not welcome here," he said in a hard voice, as if I were deaf. "I know that you don't like me here. I respect your feelings. This is your home. I respect a man's feelings about his home. I don't usually go to a man's home unless he asks me. I respect your home. I respect your marriage. I respect your children. I think everything ought to be aboveboard. I've come here to tell you that I love your wife."

"Get out," I said.

"You've got to listen to me," he said. "I love your wife. I can't live without her. I've tried and I can't. I've even thought of going away—of moving to the West Coast—but I know that it wouldn't make any difference. I want to marry her. I'm not romantic. I'm matter-of-fact. I'm very matter-of-fact. I know that you have two children and that you don't have much money. I know that there are problems of custody and property and things like that to be settled. I'm not romantic. I'm hardheaded. I've talked this all over with Mrs. Trencher, and she's agreed to give me a divorce. I'm not underhanded. Your wife can tell you that. I realize all the practical aspects that have to be considered—custody, property, and so forth. I have plenty of money. I can give Ethel everything she needs, but there are the children. You'll have to decide about them between yourselves. I have a check here. It's made out to Ethel. I want her to take it and go to Nevada. I'm a practical man and I realize that nothing can be decided until she gets her divorce."

"Get out of here!" I said. "Get the hell out of here!"

He started for the door. There was a potted geranium on the mantelpiece, and I threw this across the room at him. It got him in the small of the back and nearly knocked him down. The pot broke on the floor. Ethel screamed. Trencher was still on his way out. Following him, I picked up a candlestick and aimed it at his head, but it missed and bounced off the wall. "Get the hell out of here!" I yelled, and he slammed the door. I went back into the living room. Ethel was pale but she wasn't crying. There was a loud rapping on the radiator, a signal from the people upstairs for decorum and silence—urgent and expressive, like the communications that prisoners send to one another through the plumbing in a penitentiary. Then everything was still.

70

We went to bed, and I woke sometime during the night. I couldn't see the clock on the dresser, so I don't know what time it was. There was no sound from the children's room. The neighborhood was perfectly still. There were no lighted windows anywhere. Then I knew that Ethel had wakened me. She was lying on her side of the bed. She was crying.

"Why are you crying?" I asked.

"Why am I crying?" she said. "Why am I crying?" And to hear my voice    75 and to speak set her off again, and she began to sob cruelly. She sat up and slipped her arms into the sleeves of a wrapper and felt along the table for a package of cigarettes. I saw her wet face when she lighted a cigarette. I heard her moving around in the dark.

"Why do you cry?"

"Why do I cry? Why do I cry?" she asked impatiently. "I cry because I saw an old woman cuffing a little boy on Third Avenue. She was drunk. I can't get it out of my mind." She pulled the quilt off the foot of our bed and wandered with it toward the door. "I cry because my father died when I was twelve and because my mother married a man I detested or thought that I detested. I cry because I had to wear an ugly dress—a hand-me-down dress—to a party twenty years ago, and I didn't have a good time. I cry because of some unkindness that I can't remember. I cry because I'm tired—because I'm tired and I can't sleep." I heard her arrange herself on the sofa and then everything was quiet.

I like to think that the Trenchers have gone away, but I still see Trencher now and then on a crosstown bus when I'm late going to work. I've also seen his wife, going into the neighborhood lending library with Fräulein. She looks old. I'm not good at judging ages, but I wouldn't be surprised to find that Mrs. Trencher is fifteen years older than her husband. Now when I come home in the evenings, Ethel is still sitting on the stool by the sink cleaning vegetables. I go with her into the children's room. The light there is bright. The children have built something out of an orange crate, something preposterous and ascendant, and their sweetness, their compulsion to build, the brightness of the light are reflected perfectly and increased in Ethel's face. Then she feeds them, bathes them, and sets the table, and stands for a moment in the middle of the room, trying to make some connection between the evening and the day. Then it is over. She lights the four candles, and we sit down to our supper.

## ANTON CHEKHOV (1860–1904 )

*Lady with Lapdog*                                                    *1899*

Translated by David Magarshack.

### I

The appearance on the front of a new arrival—a lady with a lapdog—became the topic of general conversation. Dmitry Dmitrich Gurov, who had been a fortnight in Yalta and got used to its ways, was also interested in new arrivals. One day, sitting on the terrace of Vernet's restaurant, he saw a young woman walking along the promenade; she was fair, not very tall, and wore a toque; behind her trotted a white pomeranian.

Later he came across her in the park and in the square several times a day. She was always alone, always wearing the same toque, followed by the white pomeranian. No one knew who she was, and she became known simply as the lady with the lapdog.

"If she's here without her husband and without any friends," thought Gurov, "it wouldn't be a bad idea to strike up an acquaintance with her."

He was not yet forty, but he had a twelve-year-old daughter and two schoolboy sons. He had been married off when he was still in his second year at the university, and his wife seemed to him now to be almost twice his age. She was a tall, black-browed woman, erect, dignified, austere, and, as she liked to describe herself, a "thinking person." She was a great reader, preferred the new "advanced" spelling, called her husband by the more formal "Dimitry" and not the familiar "Dmitry"; and though he secretly considered her not particularly intelligent, narrow-minded, and inelegant, he was afraid of her and disliked being at home. He had been unfaithful to her for a long time, he was often unfaithful to her, and that was why, perhaps, he almost always spoke ill of women, and when men discussed women in his presence, he described them as *the lower breed*.

He could not help feeling that he had had enough bitter experience to have the right to call them as he pleased, but all the same without *the lower breed* he could not have existed a couple of days. He was bored and ill at ease among men, with whom he was reticent and cold, but when he was among women he felt at ease, he knew what to talk about with them and how to behave, even when he was silent in their company he experienced no feeling of constraint. There was something attractive, something elusive in his appearance, in his character and his whole person that women found interesting and irresistible; he was aware of it, and was himself drawn to them by some irresistible force. 5

Long and indeed bitter experience had taught him that every new affair, which at first relieved the monotony of life so pleasantly and appeared to be such a charming and light adventure, among decent people and especially among Muscovites, who are so irresolute and so hard to rouse, inevitably developed into an extremely complicated problem and finally the whole situation became rather cumbersome. But at every new meeting with an attractive woman he forgot all about this experience, he wanted to enjoy life so badly and it all seemed so simple and amusing.

And so one afternoon, while he was having dinner at a restaurant in the park, the woman in the toque walked in unhurriedly and took a seat at the table next to him. The way she looked, walked and dressed, wore her hair, told him that she was of good social standing, that she was married, that she was in Yalta for the first time, that she was alone and bored. . . . There was a great deal of exaggeration in the stories about the laxity of morals among the Yalta visitors, and he dismissed them with contempt, for he knew that such stories were mostly made up by people who would gladly have sinned themselves if they had had any idea how to go about it; but when the woman sat down at the table three yards away from him he remembered these stories of easy conquests and excursions to the mountains and the tempting thought of a quiet and fleeting affair, an affair with a strange woman whose very name he did not know, suddenly took possession of him.

He tried to attract the attention of the dog by calling softly to it, and when the pomeranian came up to him he shook a finger at it. The pomeranian growled. Gurov again shook a finger at it.

The woman looked up at him and immediately lowered her eyes.

"He doesn't bite," she said and blushed.

"May I give him a bone?" he asked, and when she nodded, he said amiably: "Have you been long in Yalta?"

"About five days."

"And I am just finishing my second week here."

They said nothing for the next few minutes.

"Time flies," she said without looking at him, "and yet it's so boring here."

"That's what one usually hears people saying here. A man may be living in Belev and Zhizdra or some other God-forsaken hole and he isn't bored, but the moment he comes here all you hear from him is "Oh, it's so boring! Oh, the dust!" You'd think he'd come from Granada!"

She laughed. Then both went on eating in silence, like complete strangers; but after dinner they strolled off together, and they embarked on the light playful conversation of free and contented people who do not care where they go or what they talk about. They walked, and talked about the strange light that fell on the sea; the water was of such a soft and warm lilac, and the moon threw a shaft of gold across it. They talked about how close it was after a hot day. Gurov told her that he lived in Moscow, that he was a graduate in philology but worked in a bank, that he had at one time thought of singing in a private opera company but had given up the idea, that he owned two houses in Moscow. . . . From her he learnt that she had grown up in Petersburg, but had got married in the town of S——, where she had been living for the past two years, that she would stay another month in Yalta, and that her husband, who also needed a rest, might join her. She was quite unable to tell him what her husband's job was, whether he served in the offices of the provincial governor or the rural council, and she found this rather amusing herself. Gurov also found out that her name and patronymic were Anna Sergeyevna.

Later, in his hotel room, he thought about her and felt sure that he would meet her again the next day. It had to be. As he went to bed he remembered that she had only recently left her boarding school, that she had been a schoolgirl like his own daughter; he recalled how much diffidence and angularity there was in her laughter and her conversation with a stranger—it was probably the first time in her life she had found herself alone, in a situation when men followed her, looked at her, and spoke to her with only one secret intention, an intention she could hardly fail to guess. He remembered her slender, weak neck, her beautiful grey eyes.

"There's something pathetic about her, all the same," he thought as he fell asleep.

## II

A week had passed since their first meeting. It was a holiday. It was close indoors, while in the streets a strong wind raised clouds of dust and tore off people's hats. All day long one felt thirsty, and Gurov kept going to the terrace of the restaurant, offering Anna Sergeyevna fruit drinks and ices. There was nowhere to go.

In the evening, when the wind had dropped a little, they went to the pier to watch the arrival of the steamer. There were a great many people taking a walk on the landing pier; some were meeting friends, they had bunches of flowers in their hands. It was there that two peculiarities of the Yalta smart set at once arrested attention: the middle-aged women dressed as if they were still young girls and there was a great number of generals.

Because of the rough sea the steamer arrived late, after the sun had set, and she had to swing backwards and forwards several times before getting alongside the pier. Anna Sergeyevna looked at the steamer and the passengers through her lorgnette, as though trying to make out some friends, and when she turned to Gurov her eyes were sparkling. She talked a lot, asked many abrupt questions, and immediately forgot what it was she had wanted to know; then she lost her lorgnette in the crowd of people.

The smartly dressed crowd dispersed; soon they were all gone, the wind had dropped completely, but Gurov and Anna were still standing there as though waiting to see if someone else would come off the boat. Anna Sergeyevna was no longer talking. She was smelling her flowers without looking at Gurov.

"It's a nice evening," he said. "Where shall we go now? Shall we go for a drive?"

She made no answer.                                                          25

Then he looked keenly at her and suddenly put his arms round her and kissed her on the mouth. He felt the fragrance and dampness of the flowers and immediately looked round him fearfully: had anyone seen them?

"Let's go to your room," he said softly.

And both walked off quickly.

It was very close in her hotel room, which was full of the smell of the scents she had bought in a Japanese shop. Looking at her now, Gurov thought: "Life is full of strange encounters!" From his past he preserved the memory of carefree, good-natured women, whom love had made gay and who were grateful to him for the happiness he gave them, however short-lived; and of women like his wife, who made love without sincerity, with unnecessary talk, affectedly, hysterically, with such an expression, as though it were not love or passion, but something much more significant; and of two or three very beautiful, frigid women, whose faces suddenly lit up with a predatory expression, an obstinate desire to take, to snatch from life more than it could give; these were women no longer in their first youth, capricious, unreasoning, despotic, unintelligent women, and when Gurov lost interest in them, their beauty merely aroused hatred in him and the lace trimmings on their négligés looked to him then like the scales of a snake.

But here there was still the same diffidence and angularity of inexperienced   30
youth—an awkward feeling; and there was also the impression of embarrassment, as if someone had just knocked at the door. Anna Sergeyevna, this lady with the lapdog, apparently regarded what had happened in a peculiar sort of way, very seriously, as though she had become a fallen woman—so it seemed to him, and he found it odd and disconcerting. Her features lengthened and drooped, and her long hair hung mournfully on either side of her face; she sank into thought in a despondent pose, like a woman taken in adultery in an old painting.

"It's wrong," she said. "You'll be the first not to respect me now."

There was a water-melon on the table. Gurov cut himself a slice and began to eat it slowly. At least half an hour passed in silence.

Anna Sergeyevna was very touching; there was an air of a pure, decent, naïve woman about her, a woman who had very little experience of life; the solitary candle burning on the table scarcely lighted up her face, but it was obvious that she was unhappy.

"But, darling, why should I stop respecting you?" Gurov asked. 'You don't know yourself what you're saying."

"May God forgive me," she said, and her eyes filled with tears. "It's terrible."      35

"You seem to wish to justify yourself."

"How can I justify myself? I am a bad, despicable creature. I despise myself and have no thought of justifying myself. I haven't deceived my husband, I've deceived myself. And not only now. I've been deceiving myself for a long time. My husband is, I'm sure, a good and honest man, but, you see, he is a flunkey. I don't know what he does at his office, all I know is that he is a flunkey. I was only twenty when I married him, I was eaten up by curiosity, I wanted something better. There surely must be a different kind of life, I said to myself. I wanted to live. To live, to live! I was burning with curiosity. I don't think you know what I am talking about, but I swear I could no longer control myself, something was happening to me, I could not be held back, I told my husband I was ill, and I came here. . . . Here too I was going about as though in a daze, as though I was mad, and now I've become a vulgar worthless woman whom everyone has a right to despise."

Gurov could not help feeling bored as he listened to her; he was irritated by her naïve tone of voice and her repentance, which was so unexpected and so out of place; but for the tears in her eyes, he might have thought that she was joking or play-acting.

"I don't understand," he said gently, "what it is you want."

She buried her face on his chest and clung close to him.      40

"Please, please believe me," she said. "I love a pure, honest life. I hate immorality. I don't know myself what I am doing. The common people say "the devil led her astray," I too can now say about myself that the devil has led me astray."

"There, there . . ." he murmured.

He gazed into her staring, frightened eyes, kissed her, spoke gently and affectionately to her, and gradually she calmed down and her cheerfulness returned; both of them were soon laughing.

Later, when they went out, there was not a soul on the promenade, the town with its cypresses looked quite dead, but the sea was still roaring and dashing itself against the shore; a single launch tossed on the waves, its lamp flickering sleepily.

They hailed a cab and drove to Oreanda.      45

"I've just found out your surname, downstairs in the lobby," said Gurov. "Von Diederitz. Is your husband a German?"

"No. I believe his grandfather was German. He is of the Orthodox faith himself."

In Oreanda they sat on a bench not far from the church, looked down on the sea, and were silent. Yalta could scarcely be seen through the morning mist. White clouds lay motionless on the mountain tops. Not a leaf stirred on the trees, the cicadas chirped, and the monotonous, hollow roar of the sea, coming up from below, spoke of rest, of eternal sleep awaiting us all. The sea had roared like that down below when there was no Yalta or Oreanda, it was roaring now, and it would go on roaring as indifferently and hollowly when we were here no more. And in this constancy, in this complete indifference to the life and death of each one of us, there is perhaps hidden the guarantee of our eternal salvation, the never-ceasing movement of life on earth, the never-ceasing movement towards perfection. Sitting beside a young woman who looked so beautiful at the break of day, soothed and enchanted by the sight of all that fairy-land scenery—the sea, the mountains, the clouds, the wide sky—Gurov reflected that, when you came to think of it, everything in the world was really beautiful, everything but our own thoughts and actions when we lose sight of the higher aims of existence and our dignity as human beings.

Someone walked up to them, a watchman probably, looked at them, and went away. And there seemed to be something mysterious and also beautiful in this fact, too. They could see the Theodosia boat coming towards the pier, lit up by the sunrise, and with no lights.

"There's dew on the grass," said Anna Sergeyevna, breaking the silence.  50

"Yes. Time to go home."

They went back to the town.

After that they met on the front every day at twelve o'clock, had lunch and dinner together, went for walks, admired the sea. She complained of sleeping badly and of her heart beating uneasily, asked the same questions, alternately worried by feelings of jealousy and by fear that he did not respect her sufficiently. And again and again in the park or in the square, when there was no one in sight, he would draw her to him and kiss her passionately. The complete idleness, these kisses in broad daylight, always having to look round for fear of someone watching them, the heat, the smell of the sea, and the constant looming into sight of idle, well-dressed, and well-fed people seemed to have made a new man of him; he told Anna Sergeyevna that she was beautiful, that she was desirable, made passionate love to her, never left her side, while she was often lost in thought and kept asking him to admit that he did not really respect her, that he was not in the least in love with her and only saw in her a vulgar woman. Almost every night they drove out of town, to Oreanda or to the waterfall; the excursion was always a success, and every time their impressions were invariably grand and beautiful.

They kept expecting her husband to arrive. But a letter came from him in which he wrote that he was having trouble with his eyes and implored his wife to return home as soon as possible. Anna Sergeyevna lost no time in getting ready for her journey home.

"It's a good thing I'm going," she said to Gurov. "It's fate."  55

She took a carriage to the railway station, and he saw her off. The drive took a whole day. When she got into the express train, after the second bell, she said:

"Let me have another look at you. . . . One last look. So."

She did not cry, but looked sad, just as if she were ill, and her face quivered.

"I'll be thinking of you, remembering you," she said. "Good-bye. You're staying, aren't you? Don't think badly of me. We are parting for ever. Yes, it must be so, for we should never have met. Well, good-bye. . . ."

The train moved rapidly out of the station; its lights soon disappeared, and  60 a minute later it could not even be heard, just as though everything had conspired to put a quick end to this sweet trance, this madness. And standing alone on the platform gazing into the dark distance, Gurov listened to the churring of the grasshoppers and the humming of the telegraph wires with a feeling as though he had just woken up. He told himself that this had been just one more affair in his life, just one more adventure, and that it too was over, leaving nothing but a memory. He was moved and sad, and felt a little penitent that the young woman, whom he would never see again, had not been happy with him; he had been amiable and affectionate with her, but all the same in his behaviour to her, in the tone of his voice and in his caresses, there was a suspicion of light irony, the somewhat coarse arrogance of the successful male, who was, moreover, almost twice her age. All the time she called him good, wonderful, high-minded; evidently she must have taken him to be quite different from what he really was, which meant that he had involuntarily deceived her.

At the railway station there was already a whiff of autumn in the air; the evening was chilly.

"Time I went north, too," thought Gurov, as he walked off the platform. "High time!"

III

At home in Moscow everything was already like winter: the stoves were heated, and it was still dark in the morning when the children were getting ready to go to school and having breakfast, so that the nurse had to light the lamp for a short time. The frosts had set in. When the first snow falls and the first day one goes out for a ride in a sleigh, one is glad to see the white ground, the white roofs, the air is so soft and wonderful to breathe, and one remembers the days of one's youth. The old lime trees and birches, white with rime, have such a benignant look, they are nearer to one's heart than cypresses and palms, and beside them one no longer wants to think of mountains and the sea.

Gurov had been born and bred in Moscow, and he returned to Moscow on a fine frosty day; and when he put on his fur coat and warm gloves and took a walk down Petrovka Street, and when on Saturday evening he heard the church bells ringing, his recent holiday trip and the places he had visited lost their charm for him. Gradually he became immersed in Moscow life, eagerly reading three newspapers a day and declaring that he never read Moscow papers on principle. Once more, he could not resist the attraction of restaurants, clubs, banquets, and anniversary celebrations, and once more he felt flattered that well-known lawyers and actors came to see him and that in the Medical Club he played cards with a professor as his partner. Once again he was capable of eating a whole portion of the Moscow speciality of sour cabbage and meat served in a frying-pan. . . .

Another month and, he thought, nothing but a memory would remain of Anna Sergeyevna; he would remember her as through a haze and only occasionally dream of her with a wistful smile, as he did of the others before her. But over a month passed, winter was at its height, and he remembered her as clearly as though he had only parted from her the day before. His memories haunted him more and more persistently. Every time the voices of his children doing their homework

65

reached him in his study in the stillness of the evening, every time he heard a popular song or some music in a restaurant, every time the wind howled in the chimney—it all came back to him: their walks on the pier, early morning with the mist on the mountains, the Theodosia boat, and the kisses. He kept pacing the room for hours remembering it all and smiling, and then his memories turned into daydreams and the past mingled in his imagination with what was going to happen. He did not dream of Anna Sergeyevna, she accompanied him everywhere like his shadow and followed him wherever he went. Closing his eyes, he saw her as clearly as if she were before him, and she seemed to him lovelier, younger, and tenderer than she had been; and he thought that he too was much better than he had been in Yalta. In the evenings she gazed at him from the bookcase, from the fireplace, from the corner—he heard her breathing, the sweet rustle of her dress. In the street he followed women with his eyes, looking for anyone who resembled her. . . .

He was beginning to be overcome by an overwhelming desire to share his memories with someone. But at home it was impossible to talk of his love, and outside his home there was no one he could talk to. Not the tenants who lived in his house, and certainly not his colleagues in the bank. And what was he to tell them? Had he been in love then? Had there been anything beautiful, poetic, edifying, or even anything interesting about his relations with Anna Sergeyevna? So he had to talk in general terms about love and women, and no one guessed what he was driving at, and his wife merely raised her black eyebrows and said:

"Really, Dimitry, the role of a coxcomb doesn't suit you at all!"

One evening, as he left the Medical Club with his partner, a civil servant, he could not restrain himself, and said:

"If you knew what a fascinating woman I met in Yalta!"

The civil servant got into his sleigh and was about to be driven off, but suddenly he turned round and called out: 70

"I say!"

"Yes?"

"You were quite right: the sturgeon *was* a bit off."

These words, so ordinary in themselves, for some reason hurt Gurov's feelings: they seemed to him humiliating and indecent. What savage manners! What faces! What stupid nights! What uninteresting, wasted days! Crazy gambling at cards, gluttony, drunkenness, endless talk about one and the same thing. Business that was of no use to anyone and talk about one and the same thing absorbed the greater part of one's time and energy, and what was left in the end was a sort of dock-tailed, barren life, a sort of nonsensical existence, and it was impossible to escape from it, just as though you were in a lunatic asylum or a convict chain-gang!

Gurov lay awake all night, fretting and fuming, and had a splitting headache 75 the whole of the next day. The following nights too he slept badly, sitting up in bed thinking, or walking up and down his room. He was tired of his children, tired of the bank, he did not feel like going out anywhere or talking about anything.

In December, during the Christmas holidays, he packed his things, told his wife that he was going to Petersburg to get a job for a young man he knew, and set off for the town of S——. Why? He had no very clear idea himself. He wanted to see Anna Sergeyevna, to talk to her, to arrange a meeting, if possible.

He arrived in S—— in the morning and took the best room in a hotel, with a fitted carpet of military grey cloth and an inkstand grey with dust on the table, surmounted by a horseman with raised hand and no head. The hall porter supplied him with all the necessary information: Von Diederitz lived in a house of his own in Old Potter's Street, not far from the hotel. He lived well, was rich, kept his own carriage horses, the whole town knew him. The hall-porter pronounced the name: Dridiritz.

Gurov took a leisurely walk down Old Potter's Street and found the house. In front of it was a long grey fence studded with upturned nails.

"A fence like that would make anyone wish to run away," thought Gurov, scanning the windows and the fence.

As it was a holiday, he thought, her husband was probably at home. It did not matter either way, though, for he could not very well embarrass her by calling at the house. If he were to send in a note it might fall into the hands of the husband and ruin everything. The best thing was to rely on chance. And he kept walking up and down the street and along the fence, waiting for his chance. He watched a beggar enter the gate and the dogs attack him; then, an hour later, he heard the faint indistinct sounds of a piano. That must have been Anna Sergeyevna playing. Suddenly the front door opened and an old woman came out, followed by the familiar white pomeranian. Gurov was about to call to the dog, but his heart began to beat violently and in his excitement he could not remember its name.

He went on walking up and down the street, hating the grey fence more and more, and he was already saying to himself that Anna Sergeyevna had forgotten him and had perhaps been having a good time with someone else, which was indeed quite natural for a young woman who had to look at that damned fence from morning till night. He went back to his hotel room and sat on the sofa for a long time, not knowing what to do, then he had dinner and after dinner a long sleep.

"How stupid and disturbing it all is," he thought, waking up and staring at the dark windows: it was already evening. "Well, I've had a good sleep, so what now? What am I going to do tonight?"

He sat on a bed covered by a cheap grey blanket looking exactly like a hospital blanket, and taunted himself in vexation:

"A *lady* with a lapdog! Some adventure, I must say! Serves you right!"

At the railway station that morning he had noticed a poster announcing in huge letters the first performance of *The Geisha Girl* at the local theatre. He recalled it now, and decided to go to the theatre.

"Quite possibly she goes to first nights," he thought.

The theatre was full. As in all provincial theatres, there was a mist over the chandeliers and the people in the gallery kept up a noisy and excited conversation; in the first row of the stalls stood the local dandies with their hands crossed behind their backs; here, too, in the front seat of the Governor's box, sat the Governor's daughter, wearing a feather boa, while the Governor himself hid modestly behind the portière so that only his hands were visible; the curtain stirred, the orchestra took a long time tuning up. Gurov scanned the audience eagerly as they filed in and occupied their seats.

Anna Sergeyevna came in too. She took her seat in the third row, and when

Gurov glanced at her his heart missed a beat and he realized clearly that there was no one in the world nearer and dearer or more important to him than that little woman with the stupid lorgnette in her hand, who was in no way remarkable. That woman lost in a provincial crowd now filled his whole life, was his misfortune, his joy, and the only happiness that he wished for himself. Listening to the bad orchestra and the wretched violins played by second-rate musicians, he thought how beautiful she was. He thought and dreamed.

A very tall, round-shouldered young man with small whiskers had come in with Anna Sergeyevna and sat down beside her; he nodded at every step he took and seemed to be continually bowing to someone. This was probably her husband, whom in a fit of bitterness at Yalta she had called a flunkey. And indeed there was something of a lackey's obsequiousness in his lank figure, his whiskers, and the little bald spot on the top of his head. He smiled sweetly, and the gleaming insignia of some scientific society which he wore in his buttonhole looked like the number on a waiter's coat.

In the first interval the husband went out to smoke and she was left in her seat. Gurov, who also had a seat in the stalls, went up to her and said in a trembling voice and with a forced smile:      90

"Good evening!"

She looked up at him and turned pale, then looked at him again in panic, unable to believe her eyes, clenching her fan and lorgnette in her hand and apparently trying hard not to fall into a dead faint. Both were silent. She sat and he stood, frightened by her embarrassment and not daring to sit down beside her. The violinists and the flautist began tuning their instruments, and they suddenly felt terrified, as though they were being watched from all the boxes. But a moment later she got up and walked rapidly towards one of the exits; he followed her, and both of them walked aimlessly along corridors and up and down stairs. Figures in all sorts of uniforms—lawyers, teachers, civil servants, all wearing badges—flashed by them; ladies, fur coats hanging on pegs, the cold draught bringing with it the odour of cigarette-ends. Gurov, whose heart was beating violently, thought:

"Oh, Lord, what are all these people, that orchestra, doing here?"

At that moment, he suddenly remembered how after seeing Anna Sergeyevna off he had told himself that evening at the station that all was over and that they would never meet again. But how far they still were from the end!

She stopped on a dark, narrow staircase with a notice over it: "To the Upper      95
Circle."

"How you frightened me!" she said, breathing heavily, still looking pale and stunned. "Oh, dear, how you frightened me! I'm scarcely alive. Why did you come? Why?"

"But, please, try to understand, Anna," he murmured hurriedly. "I beg you, please, try to understand. . . ."

She looked at him with fear, entreaty, love, looked at him intently, so as to fix his features firmly in her mind.

"I've suffered so much," she went on, without listening to him. "I've been thinking of you all the time. The thought of you kept me alive. And yet I tried so hard to forget you—why, oh, why did you come?"

On the landing above two schoolboys were smoking and looking down, but      100

Gurov did not care. He drew Anna Sergeyevna towards him and began kissing her face, her lips, her hands.

"What are you doing? What are you doing?" she said in horror, pushing him away. "We've both gone mad. You must go back tonight, this minute. I implore you, by all that's sacred . . . Somebody's coming!"

Somebody was coming up the stairs.

"You must go back," continued Anna Sergeyevna in a whisper. "Do you hear? I'll come to you in Moscow. I've never been happy, I'm unhappy now, and I shall never be happy, never! So please don't make me suffer still more. I swear I'll come to you in Moscow. But now we must part. Oh, my sweet, my darling, we must part!"

She pressed his hand and went quickly down the stairs, looking back at him all the time, and he could see from the expression in her eyes that she really was unhappy. Gurov stood listening for a short time, and when all was quiet he went to look for his coat and left the theatre.

## IV

Anna Sergeyevna began going to Moscow to see him. Every two or three months she left the town of S——, telling her husband that she was going to consult a Moscow gynaecologist, and her husband believed and did not believe her. In Moscow she stayed at the Slav Bazaar and immediately sent a porter in a red cap to inform Gurov of her arrival. Gurov went to her hotel, and no one in Moscow knew about it.

One winter morning he went to her hotel as usual (the porter had called with his message at his house the evening before, but he had not been in). He had his daughter with him, and he was glad of the opportunity of taking her to school, which was on the way to the hotel. Snow was falling in thick wet flakes.

"It's three degrees above zero," Gurov was saying to his daughter, "and yet it's snowing. But then, you see, it's only warm on the earth's surface, in the upper layers of the atmosphere the temperature's quite different."

"Why isn't there any thunder in winter, Daddy?"

He explained that, too. As he was speaking, he kept thinking that he was going to meet his mistress and not a living soul knew about it. He led a double life: one for all who were interested to see, full of conventional truth and conventional deception, exactly like the lives of his friends and acquaintances; and another which went on in secret. And by a kind of strange concatenation of circumstances, possibly quite by accident, everything that was important, interesting, essential, everything about which he was sincere and did not deceive himself, everything that made up the quintessence of his life, went on in secret, while everything that was a lie, everything that was merely the husk in which he hid himself to conceal the truth, like his work at the bank, for instance, his discussions at the club, his ideas of the lower breed, his going to anniversary functions with his wife—all that happened in the sight of all. He judged others by himself, did not believe what he saw, and was always of the opinion that every man's real and most interesting life went on in secret, under cover of night. The personal, private life of an individual was kept a secret, and perhaps that was partly the reason

105

why civilized man was so anxious that his personal secrets should be respected.

Having seen his daughter off to her school, Gurov went to the Slav Bazaar.    110
He took off his fur coat in the cloakroom, went upstairs, and knocked softly on
the door. Anna Sergeyevna, wearing the grey dress he liked most, tired out by
her journey and by the suspense of waiting for him, had been expecting him since
the evening before; she was pale, looked at him without smiling, but was in his
arms the moment he went into the room. Their kiss was long and lingering, as if
they had not seen each other for two years.

"Well," he asked, "how are you getting on there? Anything new?"

"Wait, I'll tell you in a moment. . . . I can't . . ."

She could not speak because she was crying. She turned away from him
and pressed her handkerchief to her eyes.

"Well, let her have her cry," he thought, sitting down in an armchair. "I'll
wait."

Then he rang the bell and ordered tea; while he was having his tea, she    115
was still standing there with her face to the window. She wept because she could
not control her emotions, because she was bitterly conscious of the fact that their
life was so sad: they could only meet in secret, they had to hide from people,
like thieves! Was not their life ruined?

"Please stop crying!" he said.

It was quite clear to him that their love would not come to an end for a
long time, if ever. Anna Sergeyevna was getting attached to him more and more
strongly, she worshipped him, and it would have been absurd to tell her that all
this would have to come to an end one day. She would not have believed it, anyway.

He went up to her and took her by the shoulders, wishing to be nice to
her, to make her smile; and at that moment he caught sight of himself in the
looking glass.

His hair was already beginning to turn grey. It struck him as strange that
he should have aged so much, that he should have lost his good looks in the last
few years. The shoulders on which his hands lay were warm and quivering. He
felt so sorry for this life, still so warm and beautiful, but probably soon to fade
and wilt like his own. Why did she love him so? To women he always seemed
different from what he was, and they loved in him not himself, but the man their
imagination conjured up and whom they had eagerly been looking for all their
lives; and when they discovered their mistake they still loved him. And not one
of them had ever been happy with him. Time had passed, he had met women,
made love to them, parted from them, but not once had he been in love; there
had been everything between them, but no love.

It was only now, when his hair was beginning to turn grey, that he had    120
fallen in love properly, in good earnest—for the first time in his life.

He and Anna Sergeyevna loved each other as people do who are very dear
and near, as man and wife or close friends love each other; they could not help
feeling that fate itself had intended them for one another, and they were unable
to understand why he should have a wife and she a husband; they were like two
migrating birds, male and female, who had been caught and forced to live in separate
cages. They had forgiven each other what they had been ashamed of in the past,
and forgave each other everything in their present, and felt that this love of theirs
had changed them both.

Before, when he felt depressed, he had comforted himself by all sorts of arguments that happened to occur to him on the spur of the moment, but now he had more serious things to think of, he felt profound compassion, he longed to be sincere, tender. . . .

"Don't cry, my sweet," he said. "That'll do, you've had your cry. . . . Let's talk now, let's think of something."

Then they had a long talk. They tried to think how they could get rid of the necessity of hiding, telling lies, living in different towns, not seeing one another for so long. How were they to free themselves from their intolerable chains?

"How? How?" he asked himself, clutching at his head. "How?"     125

And it seemed to them that in only a few more minutes a solution would be found and a new, beautiful life would begin; but both of them knew very well that the end was still a long, long way away and that the most complicated and difficult part was only just beginning.

## JOSEPH CONRAD (1857–1924)

*Youth*                                                                1902

This could have occurred nowhere but in England, where men and sea interpenetrate, so to speak—the sea entering into the life of most men, and the men knowing something or everything about the sea, in the way of amusement, of travel, or of breadwinning.

We were sitting round a mahogany table that reflected the bottle, the claret glasses, and our faces as we leaned on our elbows. There was a director of companies, an accountant, a lawyer, Marlow, and myself. The director had been a *Conway*° boy, the accountant had served four years at sea, the lawyer—a fine crusted Tory, High Churchman, the best of old fellows, the soul of honor—had been chief officer in the P. & O.° service in the good old days when mailboats were square-rigged at least on two masts, and used to come down the China Sea before a fair monsoon with stun'sails set alow and aloft. We all began life in the merchant service. Between the five of us there was the strong bond of the sea, and also the fellowship of the craft, which no amount of enthusiasm for yachting, cruising, and so on can give, since one is only the amusement of life and the other is life itself.

Marlow (at least I think that is how he spelt his name) told the story, or rather the chronicle, of a voyage:

"Yes, I have seen a little of the Eastern seas; but what I remember best is my first voyage there. You fellows know there are those voyages that seem ordered for the illustration of life, that might stand for a symbol of existence. You fight, work, sweat, nearly kill yourself, sometimes do kill yourself, trying to accomplish something—and you can't. Not from any fault of yours. You simply can do nothing, neither great nor little—not a thing in the world—not even marry an old maid, or get a wretched 600-ton cargo of coal to its port of destination.

"It was altogether a memorable affair. It was my first voyage to the East,     5 and my first voyage as second mate; it was also my skipper's first command. You'll

*Conway*: The Merchant Navy Cadet School in Angelsey, a training academy for naval officers.

*P & O*: The Pacific and Orient Line, still in existence.

admit it was time. He was sixty if a day; a little man, with a broad, not very straight back, with bowed shoulders and one leg more bandy than the other, he had that queer twisted-about appearance you see so often in men who work in the fields. He had a nutcracker face—chin and nose trying to come together over a sunken mouth—and it was framed in iron-gray fluffy hair, that looked like a chinstrap of cotton-wool sprinkled with coaldust. And he had blue eyes in that old face of his, which were amazingly like a boy's, with that candid expression some quite common men preserve to the end of their days by a rare internal gift of simplicity of heart and rectitude of soul. What induced him to accept me was a wonder. I had come out of a crack Australian clipper, where I had been third officer, and he seemed to have a prejudice against crack clippers as aristocratic and high-toned. He said to me, 'You know, in this ship you will have to work.' I said I had to work in every ship I had ever been in. 'Ah, but this is different, and you gentlemen out of them big ships; . . . but there! I dare say you will do. Join tomorrow.'

"I joined tomorrow. It was twenty-two years ago; and I was just twenty. How time passes! It was one of the happiest days of my life. Fancy! Second mate for the first time—a really responsible officer! I wouldn't have thrown up my new billet for a fortune. The mate looked me over carefully. He was also an old chap, but of another stamp. He had a Roman nose, a snow-white, long beard, and his name was Mahon, but he insisted that it should be pronounced Mann. He was well connected; yet there was something wrong with his luck, and he had never got on.

"As to the captain, he had been for years in coasters, then in the Mediterranean, and last in the West Indian trade. He had never been round the Capes. He could just write a kind of sketchy hand, and didn't care for writing at all. Both were thorough good seamen of course, and between those two old chaps I felt like a small boy between two grandfathers.

"The ship also was old. Her name was the *Judea*. Queer name, isn't it? She belonged to a man Wilmer, Wilcox—some name like that; but he has been bankrupt and dead these twenty years or more, and his name don't matter. She had been laid up in Shadwell basin for ever so long. You may imagine her state. She was all rust, dust, grime—soot aloft, dirt on deck. To me it was like coming out of a palace into a ruined cottage. She was about 400 tons, had a primitive windlass, wooden latches to the doors, not a bit of brass about her, and a big square stern. There was on it, below her name in big letters, a lot of scrollwork, with the gilt off, and some sort of coat of arms, with the motto 'Do or Die' underneath. I remember it took my fancy immensely. There was a touch of romance in it, something that made me love the old thing—something that appealed to my youth!

"We left London in ballast—sand ballast—to load a cargo of coal in a northern port for Bangkok. Bangkok! I thrilled. I had been six years at sea, but had only seen Melbourne and Sydney, very good places, charming places in their way—but Bangkok!

"We worked out of the Thames under canvas,° with a North Sea pilot on board. His name was Jermyn, and he dodged all day long about the galley drying his handkerchief before the stove. Apparently he never slept. He was a dismal man, with a perpetual tear sparkling at the end of his nose, who either had been in trouble, or was in trouble, or expected to be in trouble—couldn't be happy

10

*under canvas*: The *Judea* is powered totally by sail, as contrasted with the *Somerville* (paragraph 69) which is a steamer. The story is presumably taking place at a time of transition from sail to steam.

unless something went wrong. He mistrusted my youth, my common sense, and my seamanship, and made a point of showing it in a hundred little ways. I dare say he was right. It seems to me I knew very little then, and I know not much more now; but I cherish a hate for that Jermyn to this day.

"We were a week working up as far as Yarmouth Roads, and then we got into a gale—the famous October gale of twenty-two years ago. It was wind, lightning, sleet, snow, and a terrific sea. We were flying light, and you may imagine how bad it was when I tell you we had smashed bulwarks and a flooded deck. On the second night she shifted her ballast into the lee bow, and by that time we had been blown off somewhere on the Dogger Bank. There was nothing for it but go below with shovels and try to right her, and there we were in that vast hold, gloomy like a cavern, the tallow dips stuck and flickering on the beams, the gale howling above, the ship tossing about like mad on her side; there we all were, Jermyn, the captain, everyone, hardly able to keep our feet, engaged on that grave-digger's work, and trying to toss shovelfuls of wet sand up to windward. At every tumble of the ship you could see vaguely in the dim light men falling down with a great flourish of shovels. One of the ship's boys (we had two), impressed by the weirdness of the scene, wept as if his heart would break. We could hear him blubbering somewhere in the shadows.

"On the third day the gale died out, and by and by a north-country tug picked us up. We took sixteen days in all to get from London to the Tyne! When we got into dock we had lost our turn for loading, and they hauled us off to a pier where we remained for a month. Mrs. Beard (the captain's name was Beard) came from Colchester to see the old man. She lived on board. The crew of runners had left, and there remained only the officers, one boy and the steward, a mulatto who answered to the name of Abraham. Mrs. Beard was an old woman, with a face all wrinkled and ruddy like a winter apple, and the figure of a young girl. She caught sight of me once, sewing on a button, and insisted on having my shirts to repair. This was something different from the captains' wives I had known on board crack clippers. When I brought her the shirts, she said: 'And the socks? They want mending, I am sure, and John's—Captain Beard's—things are all in order now. I would be glad of something to do.' Bless the old woman. She over-hauled my outfit for me, and meantime I read for the first time *Sartor Resartus* and Burnaby's *Ride to Khiva*. I didn't understand much of the first then; but I remembered I preferred the soldier to the philosopher at the time; a preference which life has only confirmed. One was a man, and the other was either more—or less. However, they are both dead and Mrs. Beard is dead, and youth, strength, genius, thoughts, achievements, simple hearts—all dies. . . . No matter.

"They loaded us at last. We shipped a crew. Eight able seamen and two boys. We hauled off one evening to the buoys at the dock gates, ready to go out, and with a fair prospect of beginning the voyage next day. Mrs. Beard was to start for home by a late train. When the ship was fast we went to tea. We sat rather silent through the meal—Mahon, the old couple, and I. I finished first, and slipped away for a smoke, my cabin being in a deckhouse just against the poop. It was high water, blowing fresh with a drizzle; the double dock gates were opened, and the steam colliers were going in and out in the darkness with their lights burning bright, a great plashing of propellers, rattling of winches, and a lot of hailing on the pierheads. I watched the procession of headlights gliding high and of green lights gliding low in the night, when suddenly a red gleam flashed at me, vanished, came into view again, and remained. The fore end of a steamer loomed up close. I shouted down the cabin, 'Come up, quick!' and then heard a startled voice saying afar in the dark, 'Stop her, sir.' A bell jingled. Another voice cried warningly, 'We are going right into that bark, sir.' The answer to this was a gruff 'All right,' and the next thing was a heavy crash as the steamer struck a glancing blow with the bluff of her bow about our forerigging. There was a moment of confusion, yelling, and running about. Steam roared. Then somebody was heard saying, 'All clear, sir.' . . . . 'Are you all right?' asked the gruff voice. I had jumped forward to see the damage, and hailed back, 'I think so.' 'Easy astern,' said the gruff voice. A bell jingled. 'What steamer is that?' screamed Mahon. By that time she was no more to us than a bulky shadow maneuvering a little way off. They shouted at us some name—a woman's name, Miranda or Melissa—or some such thing. 'This means another month in this beastly hole,' said Mahon to me, as we peered with lamps about the splintered bulwarks and broken braces. 'But where's the captain?'

'We had not heard or seen anything of him all that time. We went aft to look. A doleful voice arose hailing somewhere in the middle of the dock, '*Judea* ahoy!' . . . How the devil did he get there? . . . 'Hallo!' we shouted. 'I am adrift in our boat without oars,' he cried. A belated water-man offered his services, and Mahon struck a bargain with him for a half crown to tow our skipper alongside; but it was Mrs. Beard that came up the ladder first. They had been floating about the dock in that mizzly cold rain for nearly an hour. I was never so surprised in my life.

"It appears that when he heard my shout 'Come up' he understood at once 15 what was the matter, caught up his wife, ran on deck, and across, and down into our boat, which was fast to the ladder. Not bad for a sixty-year-old. Just imagine that old fellow saving heroically in his arms that old woman—the woman of his life. He set her down on a thwart, and was ready to climb back on board when the painter came adrift somehow, and away they went together. Of course in the confusion we did not hear him shouting. He looked abashed. She said cheerfully, 'I suppose it does not matter my losing the train now?' 'No, Jenny—you go below and get warm,' he growled. Then to us: 'A sailor has no business with a wife—I say. There I was, out of the ship. Well, no harm done this time. Let's go and look at what that fool of a steamer smashed.'

"It wasn't much, but it delayed us three weeks. At the end of that time, the captain being engaged with his agents, I carried Mrs. Beard's bag to the railway station and put her all comfy into a third-class carriage. She lowered the window to say, 'You are a good young man. If you see John—Captain Beard—without his muffler at night, just remind him from me to keep his throat well wrapped up.' 'Certainly, Mrs. Beard,' I said. 'You are a good young man; I noticed how attentive you are to John—to Captain——' The train pulled out suddenly; I took my cap off to the old woman: I never saw her again. . . . Pass the bottle.

"We went to sea next day. When we made that start for Bangkok we had been already three months out of London. We had expected to be a fortnight or so—at the outside.

"It was January, and the weather was beautiful—the beautiful sunny winter weather that has more charm than in the summertime, because it is unexpected, and crisp, and you know it won't, it can't, last long. It's like a windfall, like a godsend, like an unexpected piece of luck.

"It lasted all down the North Sea, all down Channel; and it lasted till we were three hundred miles or so to the westward of the Lizards; then the wind went round to the sou'west and began to pipe up. In two days it blew a gale. The *Judea*, hove to, wallowed on the Atlantic like an old candle-box. It blew day after day: it blew with spite, without interval, without mercy, without rest. The world was nothing but an immensity of great foaming waves rushing at us, under a sky low enough to touch with the hand and dirty like a smoked ceiling. In the stormy space surrounding us there was as much flying spray as air. Day after day and night after night there was nothing round the ship but the howl of the wind, the tumult of the sea, the noise of water pouring over her deck. There was no rest for her and no rest for us. She tossed, she pitched, she stood on her head, she sat on her tail, she rolled, she groaned, and we had to hold on while on deck and cling to our bunks when below, in a constant effort of body and worry of mind.

"One night Mahon spoke through the small window of my berth. It opened right into my very bed, and I was lying there sleepless, in my boots, feeling as though I had not slept for years, and could not if I tried. He said excitedly:

" 'You got the sounding rod in here, Marlow? I can't get the pumps to suck. By God! It's no child's play.'

"I gave him the sounding rod and lay down again, trying to think of various things—but I thought only of the pumps. When I came on deck they were still at it, and my watch relieved at the pumps. By the light of the lantern brought on deck to examine the sounding rod I caught a glimpse of their weary, serious faces. We pumped all the four hours. We pumped all night, all day, all the week—watch and watch. She was working herself loose, and leaked badly—not enough to drown us at once, but enough to kill us with the work at the pumps. And while we pumped the ship was going from us piecemeal: the bulwarks went, the stanchions were torn out, the ventilators smashed, the cabin door burst in. There was not a dry spot in the ship. She was being gutted bit by bit. The longboat changed, as if by magic, into matchwood where she stood in her gripes. I had lashed her myself, and was rather proud of my handiwork, which had withstood so long the malice of the sea. And we pumped. And there was no break in the weather. The sea was white like a sheet of foam, like a caldron of boiling milk; there was not a break in the clouds, no—not the size of a man's hand—no, not for so much as ten seconds. There was for us no sky, there were for us no stars, no sun, no universe—nothing but angry clouds and an infuriated sea. We pumped watch and watch, for dear life; and it seemed to last for months, for years, for all eternity, as though we had been dead and gone to a hell for sailors. We forgot the day of the week, the name of the month, what year it was, and whether we had ever been ashore. The sails blew away, she lay broadside on under a weather cloth, the ocean poured over her, and we did not care. We turned those handles, and had the eyes of idiots. As soon as we had crawled on deck I used to take a round turn with a rope about the men, the pumps, and the mainmast, and we turned, we turned incessantly, with the water to our waists, to our necks, over our heads. It was all one. We had forgotten how it felt to be dry.

"And there was somewhere in me the thought: By Jove! This is the deuce of an adventure—something you read about; and it is my first voyage as second mate—and I am only twenty—and here I am lasting it out as well as any of these men, and keeping my chaps up to the mark. I was pleased. I would not have

20

given up the experience for worlds. I had moments of exultation. Whenever the old dismantled craft pitched heavily with her counter high in the air, she seemed to me to throw up, like an appeal, like a defiance, like a cry to the clouds without mercy, the words written on her stern: '*Judea*, London. Do or Die.'

"O youth! The strength of it, the faith of it, the imagination of it! To me she was not an old rattletrap carting about the world a lot of coal for a freight— to me she was the endeavor, the test, the trial of life. I think of her with pleasure, with affection, with regret—as you would think of someone dead you have loved. I shall never forget her. . . . Pass the bottle.

"One night when tied to the mast, as I explained, we were pumping on,   25 deafened with the wind, and without spirit enough in us to wish ourselves dead, a heavy sea crashed aboard and swept clean over us. As soon as I got my breath I shouted, as in duty bound, 'Keep on, boys!' when suddenly I felt something hard floating on deck strike the calf of my leg. I made a grab at it and missed. It was so dark we could not see each other's faces within a foot—you understand.

"After that thump the ship kept quiet for a while, and the thing, whatever it was, struck my leg again. This time I caught it—and it was a saucepan. At first, being stupid with fatigue and thinking of nothing but the pumps, I did not understand what I had in my hand. Suddenly it dawned upon me, and I shouted, 'Boys, the house on deck is gone. Leave this, and let's look for the cook.'

"There was a deckhouse forward, which contained the galley, the cook's berth, and the quarters of the crew. As we had expected for days to see it swept away, the hands had been ordered to sleep in the cabin—the only safe place in the ship. The steward, Abraham, however, persisted in clinging to his berth, stupidly, like a mule—from sheer fright I believe, like an animal that won't leave a stable falling in an earthquake. So we went to look for him. It was chancing death, since once out of our lashings we were as exposed as if on a raft. But we went. The house was shattered as if a shell had exploded inside. Most of it had gone overboard—stove, men's quarters, and their property, all was gone; but two posts, holding a portion of the bulkhead to which Abraham's bunk was attached, remained as if by a miracle. We groped in the ruins and came upon this, and there he was, sitting in his bunk, surrounded by foam and wreckage, jabbering cheerfully to himself. He was out of his mind; completely and forever mad, with this sudden shock coming upon the fag-end of his endurance. We snatched him up, lugged him aft, and pitched him headfirst down the cabin companion. You understand there was no time to carry him down with infinite precautions and wait to see how he got on. Those below would pick him up at the bottom of the stairs all right. We were in a hurry to go back to the pumps. That business could not wait. A bad leak is an inhuman thing.

"One would think that the sole purpose of that fiendish gale had been to make a lunatic of that poor devil of a mulatto. It eased before morning, and next day the sky cleared, and as the sea went down the leak took up. When it came to bending a fresh set of sails the crew demanded to put back—and really there was nothing else to do. Boats gone, decks swept clean, cabin gutted, men without a stitch but what they stood in, stores spoiled, ship strained. We put her head for home, and—would you believe it? The wind came east right in our teeth. It blew fresh, it blew continuously. We had to beat up every inch of the way, but she did not leak so badly, the water keeping comparatively smooth. Two hours' pumping in every four is no joke—but it kept her afloat as far as Falmouth.

"The good people there live on casualties of the sea, and no doubt were glad to see us. A hungry crowd of shipwrights sharpened their chisels at the sight of that carcass of a ship. And, by Jove! they had pretty pickings off us before they were done. I fancy the owner was already in a tight place. There were delays. Then it was decided to take part of the cargo out and calk her topsides. This was done, the repairs finished, cargo reshipped; a new crew came on board, and we went out—for Bangkok. At the end of a week we were back again. The crew said they weren't going to Bangkok—a hundred and fifty days' passage—in a something hooker that wanted pumping eight hours out of the twenty-four; and the nautical papers inserted again the little paragraph: '*Judea*. Bark. Tyne to Bangkok; coals; put back to Falmouth leaky and with crew refusing duty.'

"There were more delays—more tinkering. The owner came down for a day, and said she was as right as a little fiddle. Poor old Captain Beard looked like the ghost of a Geordie skipper—through the worry and humiliation of it. Remember he was sixty, and it was his first command. Mahon said it was a foolish business, and would end badly. I loved the ship more than ever, and wanted awfully to get to Bangkok. To Bangkok! Magic name, blessed name. Mesopotamia wasn't a patch on it. Remember I was twenty, and it was my first second-mate's billet, and the East was waiting for me.

"We went out and anchored in the outer roads with a fresh crew—the third. She leaked worse than ever. It was as if those confounded shipwrights had actually made a hole in her: This time we did not even go outside. The crew simply refused to man the windlass.

"They towed us back to the inner harbor, and we became a fixture, a feature, an institution of the place. People pointed us out to visitors as 'That 'ere bark that's going to Bangkok—has been here six months—put back three times.' On holidays the small boys pulling about in boats would hail, '*Judea*, ahoy!' and if a head showed above the rail shouted, 'Where you bound to?—Bangkok?' and jeered. We were only three on board. The poor old skipper mooned in the cabin. Mahon undertook the cooking, and unexpectedly developed all a Frenchman's genius for preparing nice little messes. I looked languidly after the rigging. We became citizens of Falmouth. Every shopkeeper knew us. At the barber's or tobacconist's they asked familiarly, 'Do you think you will ever get to Bangkok?' Meantime the owner, the underwriters, and the charters squabbled amongst themselves in London, and our pay went on. . .  Pass the bottle.

"It was horrid. Morally it was worse than pumping for life. It seemed as though we had been forgotten by the world, belonged to nobody, would get nowhere, it seemed that, as if bewitched, we would have to live for ever and ever in that inner harbor, a derision and a byword to generations of longshore loafers and dishonest boatmen. I obtained three months' pay and a five days' leave, and made a rush for London. It took me a day to get there and pretty well another to come back—but three months' pay went all the same. I don't know what I did with it. I went to a music hall, I believe, lunched, dined, and supped in a swell place in Regent Street, and was back on time, with nothing but a complete set of Byron's works and a new railway rug to show for three months' work. The boatman who pulled me off to the ship said: 'Hallo! I thought you had left the old thing. *She* will never get to Bangkok.' 'That's all *you* know about it,' I said, scornfully—but I didn't like that prophecy at all.

"Suddenly a man, some kind of agent to somebody, appeared with full powers.

30

He had grog-blossoms all over his face, an indomitable energy, and was a jolly soul. We leaped into life again. A hulk came alongside, took our cargo, and then we went into dry dock to get our copper stripped. No wonder she leaked. The poor thing, strained beyond endurance by the gale, had, as if in disgust, spat out all the oakum of her lower seams. She was recalked, new-coppered, and made as tight as a bottle. We went back to the hulk and reshipped our cargo.

"Then, on a fine moonlight night, all the rats left the ship.                    35

"We had been infested with them. They had destroyed our sails, consumed more stores than the crew, affably shared our beds and our dangers, and now, when the ship was made seaworthy, concluded to clear out. I called Mahon to enjoy the spectacle. Rat after rat appeared on our rail, took a last look over his shoulder, and leaped with a hollow thud into the empty hulk. We tried to count them, but soon lost the tale. Mahon said: 'Well, well! don't talk to me about the intelligence of rats. They ought to have left before, when we had that narrow squeak from foundering. There you have the proof how silly is the superstition about them. They leave a good ship for an old rotten hulk, where there is nothing to eat, too, the fools! . . . I don't believe they know what is safe or what is good for them, any more than you or I.'

"And after some more talk we agreed that the wisdom of rats had been grossly overrated, being in fact no greater than that of men.

The story of the ship was known, by this, all up the Channel from Land's End to the Forelands, and we could get no crew on the south coast. They sent us one all complete from Liverpool, and we left once more—for Bangkok.

"We had fair breezes, smooth water right into the tropics, and the old *Judea* lumbered along in the sunshine. When she went eight knots everything cracked aloft, and we tied our caps to our heads; but mostly she strolled on at the rate of three miles an hour. What could you expect? She was tired—that old ship. Her youth was where mine is—where yours is—you fellows who listen to this yarn; and what friend would throw your years and your weariness in your face? We didn't grumble at her. To us aft, at least, it seemed as though we had been born in her, reared in her, had lived in her for ages, had never known any other ship. I would just as soon have abused the old village church at home for not being a cathedral.

"And for me there was also my youth to make me patient. There was all      40
the East before me, and all life, and the thought that I had been tried in that ship and had come out pretty well. And I thought of men of old who, centuries ago, went that road in ships that sailed no better, to the land of palms, and spices, and yellow sands, and of brown nations ruled by kings more cruel than Nero the Roman, and more splendid than Solomon the Jew. The old bark lumbered on, heavy with her age and the burden of her cargo, while I lived the life of youth in ignorance and hope. She lumbered on through an interminable procession of days; and the fresh gilding flashed back at the setting sun, seemed to cry out over the darkening sea the words painted on her stern, '*Judea*, London, Do or Die.'

"Then we entered the Indian Ocean and steered northerly for Java Head. The winds were light. Weeks slipped by. She crawled on, do or die, and people at home began to think of posting us as overdue.

"One Saturday evening, I being off duty, the men asked me to give them an extra bucket of water or so—for washing clothes. As I did not wish to screw on the fresh-water pump so late, I went forward whistling, and with a key in my hand to unlock the forepeak scuttle, intending to serve the water out of a spare tank we kept there.

"The smell down below was as unexpected as it was frightful. One would have thought hundreds of paraffin lamps had been flaring and smoking in that hole for days. I was glad to get out. The man with me coughed and said, 'Funny smell, sir.' I answered negligently, 'It's good for the health, they say,' and walked aft.

"The first thing I did was to put my head down the square of the midship ventilator. As I lifted the lid a visible breath, something like a thin fog, a puff of faint haze, rose from the opening. The ascending air was hot, and had a heavy, sooty, paraffiny smell. I gave one sniff, and put down the lid gently. It was no use choking myself. The cargo was on fire.

"Next day she began to smoke in earnest. You see it was to be expected, for though the coal was of a safe kind, that cargo had been so handled, so broken up with handling, that it looked more like smithy coal than anything else. Then it had been wetted—more than once. It rained all the time we were taking it back from the hulk, and now with this long passage it got heated, and there was another case of spontaneous combustion.

"The captain called us into the cabin. He had a chart spread on the table, and looked unhappy. He said, "The coast of West Australia is near, but I mean to proceed to our destination. It is the hurricane month, too; but we will just keep her head for Bangkok, and fight the fire. No more putting back anywhere, if we all get roasted. We will try first to stifle this 'ere damned combustion by want of air.'

"We tried. We battened down everything, and still she smoked. The smoke kept coming out through imperceptible crevices; it forced itself through bulkheads and covers; it oozed here and there and everywhere in slender threads, in an invisible film, in an incomprehensible manner. It made its way into the cabin, into the forecastle; it poisoned the sheltered places on the deck; it could be sniffed as high as the mainyard. It was clear that if the smoke came out the air came in. This was disheartening. This combustion refused to be stifled.

"We resolved to try water, and took the hatches off. Enormous volumes of smoke, whitish, yellowish, thick, greasy, misty, choking, ascended as high as the trucks. All hands cleared out aft. Then the poisonous cloud blew away, and we went back to work in a smoke that was no thicker now than that of an ordinary factory chimney.

"We rigged the force pump, got the hose along, and by and by it burst. Well, it was as old as the ship—a prehistoric hose, and past repair. Then we pumped with the feeble head pump, drew water with buckets, and in this way managed in time to pour lots of Indian Ocean into the main hatch. The bright stream flashed in sunshine, fell into a layer of white crawling smoke, and vanished on the black surface of coal. Steam ascended mingling with the smoke. We poured salt water as into a barrel without a bottom. It was our fate to pump in that ship, to pump out of her, to pump into her; and after keeping water out of her to save ourselves from being drowned, we frantically poured water into her to save ourselves from being burnt.

"And she crawled on, do or die, in the serene weather. The sky was a miracle

45

50

of purity, a miracle of azure. The sea was polished, was blue, was pellucid, was sparkling like a precious stone, extending on all sides, all round to the horizon— as if the whole terrestrial globe had been one jewel, one colossal sapphire, a single gem fashioned into a planet. And on the luster of the great calm waters the *Judea* glided imperceptibly, enveloped in languid and unclean vapors, in a lazy cloud that drifted to leeward, light and slow; a pestiferous cloud defiling the splendor of sea and sky.

"All this time of course we saw no fire. The cargo smoldered at the bottom somewhere. Once Mahon, as we were working side by side, said to me with a queer smile: 'Now, if she only would spring a tidy leak—like that time when we first left the Channel—it would put a stopper on this fire. Wouldn't it?' I remarked irrelevantly, 'Do you remember the rats?'

"We fought the fire and sailed the ship too as carefully as though nothing had been the matter. The steward cooked and attended on us. Of the other twelve men, eight worked while four rested. Everyone took his turn, captain included. There was equality, and if not exactly fraternity, then a deal of good feeling. Sometimes a man, as he dashed a bucketful of water down the hatchway, would yell out, 'Hurrah for Bangkok!' and the rest laughed. But generally we were taciturn and serious—and thirsty. Oh! how thirsty! And we had to be careful with the water. Strict allowance. The ship smoked, the sun blazed. . . . Pass the bottle.

"We tried everything. We even made an attempt to dig down to the fire. No good, of course. No man could remain more than a minute below. Mahon, who went first, fainted there, and the man who went to fetch him out did likewise. We lugged them out on deck. Then I leaped down to show how easily it could be done. They had learned wisdom by that time, and contented themselves by fishing for me with a chainhook tied to a broom handle, I believe. I did not offer to go and fetch up my shovel, which was left down below.

"Things began to look bad. We put the longboat into the water. The second boat was ready to swing out. We had also another, a fourteen-foot thing, on davits aft, where it was quite safe.

"Then, behold, the smoke suddenly decreased. We redoubled our efforts to flood the bottom of the ship. In two days there was no smoke at all. Everybody was on the broad grin. This was on a Friday. On Saturday no work, but sailing the ship of course, was done. The men washed their clothes and their faces for the first time in a fortnight, and had a special dinner given them. They spoke of spontaneous combustion with contempt, and implied *they* were the boys to put out combustions. Somehow we all felt as though we each had inherited a large fortune. But a beastly smell of burning hung about the ship. Captain Beard had hollow eyes and sunken cheeks. I had never noticed so much before how twisted and bowed he was. He and Mahon prowled soberly about hatches and ventilators, sniffing. It struck me suddenly poor Mahon was a very, very old chap. As to me, I was pleased and proud as though I had helped to win a great naval battle. O youth!

"The night was fine. In the morning a homewardbound ship passed us hull down—the first we had seen for months; but we were nearing the land at last, Java Head being about 190 miles off, and nearly due north.

"Next day it was my watch on deck from eight to twelve. At breakfast the captain observed, 'It's wonderful how that smell hangs about the cabin.' About

55

ten, the mate being on the poop, I stepped down on the main deck for a moment. The carpenter's bench stood abaft the mainmast: I leaned against it sucking at my pipe, and the carpenter, a young chap, came to talk to me. He remarked, 'I think we have done very well, haven't we?' and then I perceived with annoyance the fool was trying to tilt the bench. I said curtly, 'Don't, Chips,' and immediately became aware of a queer sensation, of an absurb delusion—I seemed somehow to be in the air. I heard all round me like a pent-up breath released—as if a thousand giants simultaneously had said Phoo!—and felt a dull concussion which made my ribs ache suddenly. No doubt about it—I was in the air, and my body was describing a short parabola. But short as it was, I had the time to think several thoughts in, as far as I can remember, the following order: 'This can't be the carpenter—What is it?—Some accident—Submarine volcano?—Coals, gas!—By Jove! We are being blown up—Everybody's dead—I am falling into the afterhatch—I see fire in it.'

"The coaldust suspended in the air of the hold had glowed dull-red at the moment of the explosion. In the twinkling of an eye, in an infinitesimal fraction of a second since the first tilt of the bench, I was sprawling full length on the cargo. I picked myself up and scrambled out. It was quick like a rebound. The deck was a wilderness of smashed timber, lying crosswise like trees in a wood after a hurricane; an immense curtain of solid rags waved gently before me—it was the mainsail blown to strips. I thought: the masts will be toppling over directly; and to get out of the way bolted on all fours towards the poop ladder. The first person I saw was Mahon, with eyes like saucers, his mouth open, and the long white hair standing straight on end round his head like a silver halo. He was just about to go down when the sight of the main deck stirring, heaving up, and changing into splinters before his eyes, petrified him on the top step. I stared at him in unbelief, and he stared at me with a queer kind of shocked curiosity. I did not know that I had no hair, no eyebrows, no eyelashes, that my young mustache was burnt off, that my face was black, one cheek laid open, my nose cut, and my chin bleeding. I had lost my cap, one of my slippers, and my shirt was torn to rags. Of all this I was not aware. I was amazed to see the ship still afloat, the poop deck whole—and, most of all, to see anybody alive. Also the peace of the sky and the serenity of the sea were distinctly surprising. I suppose I expected to see them convulsed with horror. . . . Pass the bottle.

"There was a voice hailing the ship from somewhere—in the air, in the sky— I couldn't tell. Presently, I saw the captain—and he was mad. He asked me eagerly, 'Where's the cabin table?' and to hear such a question was a frightful shock. I had just been blown up, you understand, and vibrated with that experience—I wasn't quite sure whether I was alive. Mahon began to stamp with both feet and yelled at him, 'Good God! don't you see the deck's blown out of her?' I found my voice, and stammered out as if conscious of some gross neglect of duty, 'I don't know where the cabin table is.' It was like an absurd dream.

"Do you know what he wanted next? Well, he wanted to trim the yards. Very placidly, and as if lost in thought, he insisted on having the foreyard squared. 'I don't know if there's anybody alive,' said Mahon, almost tearfully. 'Surely,' he said, gently, 'there will be enough left to square the foreyard.'

"The old chap, it seems, was in his own berth winding up the chronometers when the shock sent him spinning. Immediately it occurred to him—as he said afterwards—that the ship had struck something, and ran out into the cabin. There,

60

he saw, the cabin table had vanished somewhere. The deck being blown up, it had fallen down into the lazarette of course. Where we had our breakfast that morning he saw only a great hole in the floor. This appeared to him so awfully mysterious, and impressed him so immensely, that what he saw and heard after he got on deck were mere trifles in comparison. And, mark, he noticed directly the wheel deserted and his bark off her course—and his only thought was to get that miserable, stripped, undecked, smoldering shell of a ship back again with her head pointing at her port of destination. Bangkok! That's what he was after. I tell you this quiet, bowed, bandy-legged, almost deformed little man was immense in the singleness of his idea and in his placid ignorance of our agitation. He motioned us forward with a commanding gesture, and went to take the wheel himself.

"Yes; that was the first thing we did—trim the yards of that wreck! No one was killed, or even disabled, but everyone was more or less hurt. You should have seen them! Some were in rags, with black faces, like coal heavers, like sweeps, and had bullet heads that seemed closely cropped, but were in fact singed to the skin. Others, of the watch below, awakened by being shot out from their collapsing bunks, shivered incessantly, and kept on groaning even as we went about our work. But they all worked. That crew of Liverpool hard cases had in them the right stuff. It's my experience they always have. It is the sea that gives it—the vastness, the loneliness surrounding their dark stolid souls. Ah! Well! We stumbled, we crept, we fell, we barked our shins on the wreckage, we hauled. The masts stood, but we did not know how much they might be charred down below. It was nearly calm, but a long swell ran from the west and made her roll. They might go at any moment. We looked at them with apprehension. One could not foresee which way they would fall.

"Then we retreated aft and looked about us. The deck was a tangle of planks on edge, of planks on end, of splinters, of ruined woodwork. The masts rose from that chaos like big trees above a matted undergrowth. The interstices of that mass of wreckage were full of something whitish, sluggish, stirring—of something that was like a greasy fog. The smoke of the invisible fire was coming up again, was trailing, like a poisonous thick mist in some valley choked with dead wood. Already lazy wisps were beginning to curl upwards amongst the mass of splinters. Here and there a piece of timber stuck upright, resembled a post. Half of a fife rail had been shot through the foresail, and the sky made a patch of glorious blue in the ignobly soiled canvas. A portion of several boards holding together had fallen across the rail, and one end protruded overboard, like a gangway leading upon nothing, like a gangway leading over the deep sea, leading to death—as if inviting us to walk the plank at once and be done with our ridiculous troubles. And still the air, the sky—a ghost, something invisible was hailing the ship.

"Someone had the sense to look over, and there was the helmsman, who had impulsively jumped overboard, anxious to come back. He yelled and swam lustily like a merman, keeping up with the ship. We threw him a rope, and presently he stood amongst us streaming with water and very crestfallen. The captain had surrendered the wheel, and apart, elbow on rail and chin in hand, gazed at the sea wistfully. We asked ourselves, What next? I thought, Now, this is something like. This is great. I wonder what will happen. O youth!

"Suddenly Mahon sighted a steamer far astern. Captain Beard said, 'We may do something with her yet.' We hoisted two flags, which said in the international     65 language of the sea, 'On fire. Want immediate assistance.' The streamer grew bigger rapidly, and by and by spoke with two flags on her foremast, 'I am coming to your assistance.'

"In half an hour she was abreast, to windward, within hail, and rolling slightly, with her engines stopped. We lost our composure, and yelled all together with excitement, 'We've been blown up.' A man in a white helmet, on the bridge, cried, 'Yes! All right! all right!' and he nodded his head, and smiled, and made soothing motions with his hand as though at a lot of frightened children. One of the boats dropped in the water, and walked towards us upon the sea with her long oars. Four Calashes pulled a swinging stroke. This was my first sight of Malay seamen. I've known them since, but what struck me then was their unconcern: they came alongside, and even the bowman standing up and holding to our main chains with the boathook did not deign to lift his head for a glance. I thought people who had been blown up deserved more attention.

"A little man, dry like a chip and agile like a monkey, clambered up. It was the mate of the steamer. He gave one look, and cried, 'O boys—you had better quit!'

"We were silent. He talked apart with the captain for a time—seemed to argue with him. Then they went away together to the steamer.

"When our skiper came back we learned that the steamer was the *Somerville*, Captain Nash, from West Australia to Singapore via Batavia with mails, and that the agreement was she should tow us to Anjer or Batavia, if possible, where we could extinguish the fire by scuttling, and then proceed on our voyage—to Bangkok! The old man seemed excited. 'We will do it yet,' he said to Mahon, fiercely. He shook his fist at the sky. Nobody else said a word.

"At noon the steamer began to tow. She went ahead slim and high, and   70 what was left of the *Judea* followed at the end of seventy fathom of towrope— followed her swiftly like a cloud of smoke with mastheads protruding above. We went aloft to furl the sails. We coughed on the yards, and were careful about the bunts. Do you see the lot of us there, putting a neat furl on the sails of that ship doomed to arrive nowhere? There was not a man who didn't think that at any moment the masts would topple over. From aloft we could not see the ship for smoke, and they worked carefully, passing the gaskets with even turns. 'Harbor furl—aloft there!' cried Mahon from below.

"You understand this? I don't think one of those chaps expected to get down in the usual way. When we did I heard them saying to each other, 'Well, I thought we would come down overboard, in a lump—sticks and all—blame me if I didn't.' 'That's what I was thinking to myself,' would answer wearily another battered and bandaged scarecrow. And, mind, these were men without the drilled-in habit of obedience. To an onlooker they would be a lot of profane scallywags without a redeeming point. What made them do it—what made them obey me when I, thinking consciously how fine it was, made them drop the bunt of the foresail twice to try and do it better? What? They had no professional reputation— no examples, no praise. It wasn't a sense of duty; they all knew well enough how to shirk, and laze, and dodge—when they had a mind to it—and mostly they had. Was it the two pounds ten a month that sent them there? They didn't think their pay half good enough. No; it was something in them, something inborn and subtle and everlasting. I don't say positively that the crew of a French or German merchantman wouldn't have done it, but I doubt whether it would have been done in the same way. There was a completeness in it, something solid like a principle, and masterful like an instinct—a disclosure of something secret—of that hidden something, that gift of good or evil that makes racial difference, that shapes the fate of nations.

"It was that night at ten that, for the first time since we had been fighting it, we saw the fire. The speed of the towing had fanned the smoldering destruction. A blue gleam appeared forward, shining below the wreck of the deck. It wavered in patches, it seemed to stir and creep like the light of a glowworm. I saw it first, and told Mahon. 'Then the game's up,' he said. 'We had better stop this towing, or she will burst out suddenly fore and aft before we can clear out.' We set up a yell; rang bells to attract their attention; they towed on. At last Mahon and I had to crawl forward and cut the rope with an axe. There was no time to cast off the lashings. Red tongues could be seen licking the wilderness of splinters under our feet as we made our way back to the poop.

"Of course they very soon found out in the steamer that the rope was gone. She gave a loud blast of her whistle, her lights were seen sweeping in a wide circle, she came up ranging close alongside, and stopped. We were all in a tight group on the poop looking at her. Every man had saved a little bundle or a bag. Suddenly a conical flame with a twisted top shot up forward and threw upon the black sea a circle of light, with the two vessels side by side and heaving gently in its center. Captain Beard had been sitting on the gratings still and mute for hours, but now he rose slowly and advanced in front of us, to the mizzen-shrouds. Captain Nash hailed: 'Come along! Look sharp. I have mailbags on board. I will take you and your boats to Singapore.'

" 'Thank you! No! said our skipper. 'We must see the last of the ship.'

" 'I can't stand by any longer,' shouted the other. 'Mails—you know.'    75

" 'Ay! ay! We are all right.'

" 'Very well! I'll report you in Singapore. . . . Good-by!'

"He waved his hand. Our men dropped their bundles quietly. The steamer moved ahead, and passing out of the circle of light, vanished at once from our sight, dazzled by the fire which burned fiercely. And then I knew that I would see the East first as commander of a small boat. I thought it fine; and the fidelity to the old ship was fine. We should see the last of her. Oh, the glamor of youth! Oh, the fire of it, more dazzling than the flames of the burning ship, throwing a magic light on the wide earth, leaping audaciously to the sky, presently to be quenched by time, more cruel, more pitiless, more bitter than the sea—and like the flames of the burning ship surrounded by an impenetrable night.

"The old man warned us in his gentle and inflexible way that it was part of our duty to save for the underwriters as much as we could of the ship's gear. Accordingly we went to work aft, while she blazed forward to give us plenty of light. We lugged out a lot of rubbish. What didn't we save? An old barometer fixed with an absurd quantity of screws nearly cost me my life: a sudden rush of smoke came upon me, and I just got away in time. There were various stores, bolts of canvas, coils of rope; the poop looked like a marine bazaar, and the boats were lumbered to the gunwales. One would have thought the old man wanted to take as much as he could of his first command with him. He was very, very quiet, but off his balance evidently. Would you believe it? He wanted to take a length of old stream-cable and a kedge anchor with him in the longboat. We said, 'Ay, ay, sir,' deferentially, and on the quiet let the things slip overboard. The heavy medicine chest went that way, two bags of green coffee, tins of paint—fancy, paint!—a whole lot of things. Then I was ordered with two hands into the boats to make a stowage and get them ready against the time it would be proper for us to leave the ship.

"We put everything straight, stepped the longboat's mast for our skipper, who was to take charge of her, and I was not sorry to sit down for a moment. My face felt raw, every limb ached as if broken, I was aware of all my ribs, and would have sworn to a twist in the backbone. The boats, fast astern, lay in a deep shadow, and all around I could see the circle of the sea lighted by the fire. A gigantic flame arose forward straight and clear. It flared fierce, with noises like the whirr of wings, with rumbles as of thunder. There were cracks, detonations, and from the cone of flame the sparks flew upwards, as man is born to trouble, to leaky ships, and to ships that burn.

"What bothered me was that the ship, lying broadside to the swell and to such wind as there was—a mere breath—the boats would not keep astern where they were safe, but persisted, in a pigheaded way boats have, in getting under the counter and then swinging alongside. They were knocking about dangerously and coming near the flame, while the ship rolled on them, and, of course, there was always the danger of the masts going over the side at any moment. I and my two boatkeepers kept them off as best we could, with oars and boathooks; but to be constantly at it became exasperating, since there was no reason why we should not leave at once. We could not see those on board, nor could we imagine what caused the delay. The boatkeepers were swearing feebly, and I had not only my share of the work but also had to keep at it two men who showed a constant inclination to lay themselves down and let things slide.

"At last I hailed, 'On deck there,' and somone looked over. 'We're ready here,' I said. The head disappeared, and very soon popped up again. 'The captain says, All right, sir, and to keep the boats well clear of the ship.'

"Half an hour passed. Suddenly there was a frightful racket, rattle, clanking of chain, hiss of water, and millions of sparks flew up into the shivering column of smoke that stood leaning slightly above the ship. The catheads had burned away, and the two red-hot anchors had gone to the bottom, tearing out after them two hundred fathom of red-hot chain. The ship trembled, the mass of flame swayed as if ready to collapse, and the fore-topgallant mast fell. It darted down like an arrow of fire, shot under, and instantly leaping up within an oar's length of the boats, floated quietly, very black on the luminous sea. I hailed the deck again. After some time a man in an unexpectedly cheerful but also muffled tone, as though he had been trying to speak with his mouth shut, informed me, 'Coming directly, sir,' and vanished. For a long time I heard nothing but the whirr and roar of the fire. There were also whistling sounds. The boats jumped, tugged at the painters, ran at each other playfully, knocked their sides together, or, do what we would, swung in a bunch against the ship's side. I couldn't stand it any longer, and swarming up a rope, clambered aboard over the stern.

"It was as bright as day. Coming up like this, the sheet of fire facing me was a terrifying sight, and the heat seemed hardly bearable at first. On a settee cushion dragged out of the cabin Captain Beard, his legs drawn up and one arm under his head, slept with the light playing on him. Do you know what the rest were busy about? They were sitting on deck right aft, round an open case, eating bread and cheese and drinking bottled stout.

"On the background of flames twisting in fierce tongues above their heads     85
they seemed at home like salamanders, and looked like a band of desperate pirates. The fire sparkled in the whites of their eyes, gleamed on patches of white skin seen through the torn shirts. Each had the marks as of a battle about him—bandaged heads, tied-up arms, a strip of dirty rag round a knee—and each man had a bottle between his legs and a chunk of cheese in his hand. Mahon got up. With his handsome and disreputable head, his hooked profile, his long white beard, and with an uncorked bottle in his hand, he resembled one of those reckless sea robbers of old making merry amidst violence and disaster. 'The last meal on board,' he explained solemnly. 'We had nothing to eat all day, and it was no use leaving all this.' He flourished the bottle and indicated the sleeping skipper. 'He said he couldn't swallow anything, so I got him to lie down,' he went on; and as I stared, 'I don't know whether your are aware, young fellow, the man had no sleep to speak of for days—and there will be dam' little sleep in the boats.' 'There will be no boats by and by if you fool about much longer,' I said, indignantly. I walked up to the skipper and shook him by the shoulder. At last he opened his eyes, but did not move. 'Time to leave her, sir,' I said quietly.

'He got up painfully, looked at the flames, at the sea sparkling round the ship, and black, black as ink farther away; he looked at the stars shining dim through a thin veil of smoke in a sky black, black as Erebus.

" 'Youngest first,' he said.

"And the ordinary seaman, wiping his mouth with the back of his hand, got up, clambered over the taffrail, and vanished. Others followed. One, on the point of going over, stopped short to drain his bottle, and with a great swing of his arm flung it at the fire. 'Take this!' he cried.

"The skipper lingered disconsolately, and we left him to commune alone for a while with his first command. Then I went up again and brought him away at last. It was time. The ironwork on the poop was hot to the touch.

"Then the painter of the longboat was cut, and the three boats, tied together,     90
drifted clear of the ship. It was just sixteen hours after the explosion when we abandoned her. Mahon had charge of the second boat, and I had the smallest— the fourteen-foot thing. The longboat would have taken the lot of us; but the skipper said we must save as much property as we could—for the underwriters— and so I got my first command. I had two men with me, a bag of biscuits, a few tins of meat, and a breaker of water. I was ordered to keep close to the longboat, that in case of bad weather we might be taken into her.

"And do you know what I thought? I thought I would part company as soon as I could. I wanted to have my first command all to myself. I wasn't going to sail in a squadron if there were a chance for independent cruising. I would make land by myself. I would beat the other boats. Youth! All youth! The silly, charming, beautiful youth.

"But we did not make a start at once. We must see the last of the ship. And so the boats drifted about that night, heaving and setting on the swell. The men dozed, waked, sighed, groaned. I looked at the burning ship.

"Between the darkness of earth and heaven she was burning fiercely upon a disc of purple sea shot by the blood-red play of gleams; upon a disc of water glittering and sinister. A high, clear flame, an immense and lonely flame, ascended from the ocean, and from its summit the black smoke poured continuously at the sky. She burned furiously; mournful and imposing like a funeral pile kindled in the night, surrounded by the sea, watched over by the stars. A magnificent death had come like a grace, like a gift, like a reward to that old ship at the end of her laborious days. The surrender of her weary ghost to the keeping of stars and sea was stirring like the sight of a glorious triumph. The masts fell just before daybreak, and for a moment there was a burst and turmoil of sparks that seemed to fill with flying fire the night patient and watchful, the vast night lying silent upon the sea. At daylight she was only a charred shell, floating still under a cloud of smoke and bearing a glowing mass of coal within.

"Then the oars were got out, and the boats forming in a line moved round her remains as if in procession—the longboat leading. As we pulled across her stern a slim dart of fire shot out viciously at us, and suddenly she went down, head first, in a great hiss of steam. The unconsumed stern was the last to sink; but the paint had gone, had cracked, had peeled off, and there were no letters, there was no word, no stubborn device that was like her soul, to flash at the rising sun her creed and her name.

"We made our way north. A breeze sprang up, and about noon all the boats came together for the last time. I had no mast or sail in mine, but I made a mast out of a spare oar and hoisted a boat-awning for a sail, with a boathook for a yard. She was certainly over-masted, but I had the satisfaction of knowing that with the wind aft I could beat the other two. I had to wait for them. Then we all had a look at the captain's chart, and, after a sociable meal of hard bread and water, got our last instructions. These were simple: steer north, and keep together as much as possible. 'Be careful with that jury-rig, Marlow,' said the captain: and Mahon, as I sailed proudly past his boat, wrinkled his curved nose and hailed, 'You will sail that ship of yours under water, if you don't look out, young fellow.' He was a malicious old man—and may the deep sea where he sleeps now rock him gently, rock him tenderly to the end of time!

"Before sunset a thick rain-squall passed over the two boats, which were far astern, and that was the last I saw of them for a time. Next day I sat steering my cockleshell—my first command—with nothing but water and sky round me. I did sight in the afternoon the upper sails of a ship far away, but said nothing, and my men did not notice her. You see I was afraid she might be homeward bound, and I had no mind to turn back from the portals of the East. I was steering for Java—another blessed name—like Bangkok, you know. I steered many days.

"I need not tell you what it is to be knocking about in an open boat. I remember nights and days of calm, when we pulled, we pulled, and the boat seemed to stand still, as if bewitched within the circle of the sea horizon. I remember the heat, the deluge of rain-squalls that kept us baling for dear life (but filled our water cask), and I remember sixteen hours on end with a mouth dry as a cinder and a steering oar over the stern to keep my first command head on to a breaking sea. I did not know how good a man I was till then. I remember the drawn faces, the dejected figures of my two men, and I remember my youth and the feeling that will never come back any more—the feeling that I could last forever, outlast the sea, the earth, and all men; the deceitful feeling that lures us on to joys, to

95

perils, to love, to vain effort—to death; the triumphant conviction of strength, the heat of life in the handful of dust, the glow in the heart that with every year grows dim, grows cold, grows small, and expires—and expires, too soon, too soon—before life itself.

"And this is how I see the East. I have seen its secret places and have looked into its very soul; but now I see it always from a small boat, a high outline of mountains, blue and afar in the morning; like faint mist at noon; a jagged wall of purple at sunset. I have the feel of the oar in my hand, the vision of a scorching blue sea in my eyes. And I see a bay, a wide bay, smooth as glass and polished like ice, shimmering in the dark. A red light burns far off upon the gloom of the land, and the night is soft and warm. We drag at the oars with aching arms, and suddenly a puff of wind, a puff faint and tepid and laden with strange odors of blossoms, of aromatic wood, comes out of the still night—the first sigh of the East on my face. That I can never forget. It was impalpable and enslaving, like a charm, like a whispered promise of mysterious delight.

"We had been pulling this finishing spell for eleven hours. Two pulled, and he whose turn it was to rest sat at the tiller. We had made out the red light in that bay and steered for it, guessing it must mark some small coasting port. We passed two vessels, outlandish and high-sterned, sleeping at anchor, and, approaching the light, now very dim, ran the boat's nose against the end of a jutting wharf. We were blind with fatigue. My men dropped the oars and fell off the thwarts as if dead. I made fast to a pile. A current rippled softly. The scented obscurity of the shore was grouped into vast masses, a density of colossal clumps of vegetation, probably—mute and fantastic shapes. And at their foot the semicircle of a beach gleamed faintly, like an illusion. There was not a light, not a stir, not a sound. The mysterious East faced me, perfumed like a flower, silent like death, dark like a grave.

"And I sat weary beyond expression, exulting like a conqueror, sleepless   100 and entranced as if before a profound, a fateful enigma.

"A splashing of oars, a measured dip reverberating on the level of water, intensified by the silence of the shore into loud claps, made me jump up. A boat, a European boat, was coming in. I invoked the name of the dead; I hailed: '*Judea ahoy!*' A thin shout answered.

"It was the captain. I had beaten the flagship by three hours, and I was glad to hear the old man's voice again, tremulous and tired. 'Is it you, Marlow?' 'Mind the end of that jetty, sir,' I cried.

"He approached cautiously, and brought up with the deep-sea lead line which we had saved—for the underwriters. I eased my painter and fell alongside. He sat, a broken figure at the stern, wet with dew, his hands clasped in his lap. His men were asleep already. 'I had a terrible time of it,' he murmured. 'Mahon is behind—not very far.' We conversed in whispers, in low whispers, as if afraid to wake up the land. Guns, thunder, earthquakes would not have awakened the men just then.

"Looking round as we talked, I saw away at sea a bright light traveling in the night. 'There's a steamer passing the bay,' I said. She was not passing, she was entering, and she even came close and anchored. 'I wish,' said the old man, 'you would find out whether she is English. Perhaps they could give us a passage somewhere.' He seemed nervously anxious. So by dint of punching and kicking I started one of my men into a state of somnambulism, and giving him an oar, took another and pulled towards the lights of the steamer.

"There was a murmur of voices in her, metallic hollow clangs of the engine   105
room, footsteps on the deck. Her ports shone, round like dilated eyes. Shapes moved about, and there was a shadowy man high up on the bridge. He heard my oars.

"And then, before I could open my lips, the East spoke to me, but it was in a Western voice. A torrent of words was poured into the enigmatical, the fateful silence; outlandish, angry words, mixed with words and even whole sentences of good English, less strange but even more surprising. The voice swore and cursed violently; it riddled the solemn peace of the bay by a volley of abuse. It began by calling me Pig, and from that went crescendo into unmentionable adjectives—in English. The man up there raged aloud in two languages, and with a sincerity in his fury that almost convinced me I had, in some way, sinned against the harmony of the universe. I could hardly see him, but began to think he would work himself into a fit.

"Suddenly he ceased, and I could hear him snorting and blowing like a porpoise. I said:

" 'What steamer is this, pray?'

" 'Eh? What's this? And who are you?'

" 'Castaway crew of an English bark burnt at sea. We came here tonight. I   110
am the second mate. The captain is in the longboat, and wishes to know if you would give us a passage somewhere.'

" 'Oh, my goodness! I say. . . . This is the *Celestial* from Singapore on her return trip. I'll arrange with your captain in the morning, . . . and, . . . I say, . . . did you hear me just now?'

" 'I should think the whole bay heard you.'

" 'I thought you were a shoreboat. Now, look here—this infernal lazy scoundrel of a caretaker has gone to sleep again—curse him. The light is out, and I nearly ran foul of the end of this damned jetty. This is the third time he plays me this trick. Now, I ask you, can anybody stand this kind of thing? It's enough to drive a man out of his mind. I'll report him. . . . I'll get the Assistant Resident to give him the sack, by—! See—there's no light. It's out, isn't it? I take you to witness the light's out. There should be a light, you know. A red light on the—'

" 'There was a light,' I said, mildly.

" 'But it's out, man! What's the use of talking like this? You can see for   115
yourself it's out—don't you? If you had to take a valuable steamer along this Godforsaken coast you would want a light, too. I'll kick him from end to end of his miserable wharf. You'll see if I don't. I will—'

" 'So I may tell my captain you'll take us?' I broke in.

" 'Yes, I'll take you. Good night,' he said, brusquely.

"I pulled back, made fast again to the jetty, and then went to sleep at last. I had faced the silence of the East. I had heard some of its language. But when I opened my eyes again the silence was as complete as though it had never been broken. I was lying in a flood of light, and the sky had never looked so far, so high, before. I opened my eyes and lay without moving.

"And then I saw the men of the East—they were looking at me. The whole length of the jetty was full of people. I saw brown, bronze, yellow faces, the black eyes, the glitter, the color of an Eastern crowd. And all these beings stared without a murmur, without a sigh, without a movement. They stared down at the boats, at the sleeping men who at night had come to them from the sea. Nothing moved. The fronds of palms stood still against the sky. Not a branch stirred along the shore, and the brown roofs of hidden houses peeped through the green foliage, through the big leaves that hung shining and still like leaves forged of heavy metal. This was the East of the ancient navigators, so old, so mysterious, resplendent and somber, living and unchanged, full of danger and promise. And these were the men. I sat up suddenly. A wave of movement passed through the crowd from end to end, passed along the heads, swayed the bodies, ran along the jetty like a ripple on the water, like a breath of wind on a field—and all was still again. I see it now—the wide sweep of the bay, the glittering sands, the wealth of green infinite and varied, the sea blue like the sea of a dream, the crowd of attentive faces, the blaze of vivid color—the water reflecting it all, the curve of the shore, the jetty, the high-sterned outlandish craft floating still, and the three boats with the tired men from the West sleeping, unconscious of the land and the people and of the violence of sunshine. They slept thrown across the thwarts, curled on bottomboards, in the careless attitudes of death. The head of the old skipper, leaning back in the stern of the longboat, had fallen on his breast, and he looked as though he would never wake. Farther out old Mahon's face was upturned to the sky, with the long white beard spread out on his breast, as though he had been shot where he sat at the tiller; and a man, all in a heap in the bows of the boat, slept with both arms embracing the stemhead and with his cheek laid on the gunwale. The East looked at them without a sound.

"I have known its fascination since; I have seen the mysterious shores, the   120
still water, the lands of brown nations, where a stealthy Nemesis lies in wait, pursues, overtakes so many of the conquering race, who are proud of their wisdom, of their knowledge, of their strength. But for me all the East is contained in that vision of my youth. It is all in that moment when I opened my young eyes on it. I came upon it from a tussle with the sea—and I was young—and I saw it looking at me. And this is all that is left of it! Only a moment; a moment of strength, of romance, of glamor—of youth! . . . A flick of sunshine upon a strange shore, the time to remember, the time for a sigh, and—good-by!—Night—Good-by . . . !"

He drank.

"Ah! The good old time—the good old time. Youth and the sea. Glamor and the sea! The good, strong sea, the salt, bitter sea, that could whisper to you and roar at you and knock your breath out of you."

He drank again.

"By all that's wonderful it is the sea, I believe, the sea itself—or is it youth alone? Who can tell? But you here—you all had something out of life: money, love—whatever one gets on shore—and, tell me, wasn't that the best time, that time when we were young at sea, young and had nothing, on the sea that gives nothing except hard knocks—and sometimes a chance to feel your strength—that only—that you all regret?"

And we all nodded at him: the man of finance, the man of accounts, the   125
man of law, we all nodded at him over the polished table that like a still sheet of brown water reflected our faces, lined, wrinkled; our faces marked by toil, by deceptions, by success, by love; our weary eyes looking still, looking always, looking

anxiously for something out of life, that while it is expected is already gone—has passed unseen, in a sigh, in a flash—together with the youth, with the strength, with the romance of illusions.

## LANGSTON HUGHES (1902–1967)

*Slave on the Block*                                            (*1938*)

They were people who went in for Negroes—Michael and Anne—the Carraways. But not in the social-service, philanthropic sort of way, no. They saw no use in helping a race that was already too charming and naive and lovely for words. Leave them unspoiled and just enjoy them, Michael and Anne felt. So they went in for the Art of Negroes—the dancing that had such jungle life about it, the songs that were so simple and fervent, the poetry that was so direct, so real. They never tried to influence that art, they only bought it and raved over it, and copied it. For they were artists, too.

In their collection they owned some Covarrubias originals. Of course Covarrubias wasn't a Negro, but how he caught the darky spirit! They owned all the Robeson records and all the Bessie Smith. And they had a manuscript of Countee Cullen's. They saw all the plays with or about Negroes, read all the books, and adored the Hall Johnson Singers. They had met Doctor DuBois, and longed to meet Carl Van Vechten. Of course they knew Harlem like their own backyard, that is, all the speakeasies and night clubs and dance halls, from the Cotton Club and the ritzy joints where Negroes couldn't go themselves, down to places like the Hot Dime, where white folks couldn't get in—unless they knew the man. (And tipped heavily.)

They were acquainted with lots of Negroes, too—but somehow the Negroes didn't seem to like them very much. Maybe the Carraways gushed over them too soon. Or maybe they looked a little like poor white folks, although they were really quite well off. Or maybe they tried too hard to make friends, dark friends, and the dark friends suspected something. Or perhaps their house in the Village was too far from Harlem, or too hard to find, being back in one of those queer and expensive little side streets that had once been alleys before the art invasion came. Anyway, occasionally, a furtive Negro might accept their invitation for tea, or cocktails; and sometimes a lesser Harlem celebrity or two would decorate their rather slow parties; but one seldom came back for more. As much as they loved Negroes, Negroes didn't seem to love Michael and Anne.

But they were blessed with a wonderful colored cook and maid—until she took sick and died in her room in their basement. And then the most marvellous ebony boy walked into their life, a boy as black as all the Negroes they'd ever known put together.

"He *is* the jungle," said Anne when she saw him.

"He's 'I Couldn't Hear Nobody Pray,' " said Michael.

For Anne thought in terms of pictures: she was a painter. And Michael thought

5

in terms of music: he was a composer for the piano. And they had a most wonderful idea of painting pictures and composing music that went together, and then having a joint "concert-exhibition" as they would call it. Her pictures and his music. The Carraways, a sonata and a picture, a fugue and a picture. It would be lovely, and such a novelty, people would have to like it. And many of their things would be Negro. Anne had painted their maid six times. And Michael had composed several themes based on the spirituals, and on Louis Armstrong's jazz. Now here was this ebony boy. The essence in the flesh.

They had nearly missed the boy. He had come, when they were out, to gather up the things the cook had left, and take them to her sister in Jersey. It seems that he was the late cook's nephew. The new colored maid had let him in and given him the two suitcases of poor dear Emma's belongings, and he was on his way to the Subway. That is, he was in the hall, going out just as the Carraways, Michael and Anne, stepped in. They could hardly see the boy, it being dark in the hall, and he being dark, too.

"Hello," they said. "Is this Emma's nephew?"

"Yes'm," said the maid. "Yes'm."                                                                  10

"Well, come in," said Anne, "and let us see you. We loved your aunt so much. She was the best cook we ever had."

"You don't know where I could get a job, do you?" said the boy. This took Michael and Anne back a bit, but they rallied at once. So charming and naive to ask right away for what he wanted.

Anne burst out, "You know, I think I'd like to paint you."

Michael said, "Oh, I say now, that would be lovely! He's so utterly Negro."

The boy grinned.                                                                                  15

Anne said, "Could you come back tomorrow?"

And the boy said, "Yes, indeed. I sure could."

The upshot of it was that they hired him. They hired him to look after the garden, which was just about as big as Michael's grand piano—only a little square behind the house. You know those Village gardens. Anne sometimes painted it. And occasionally they set the table there for four on a spring evening. Nothing grew in the garden really, practically nothing. But the boy said he could plant things. And they had to have some excuse to hire him.

The boy's name was Luther. He had come from the South to his relatives in Jersey, and had had only one job since he got there, shining shoes for a Greek in Elizabeth. But the Greek fired him because the boy wouldn't give half his tips over to the proprietor.

"I never heard of a job where I had to pay the boss, instead of the boss        20
paying me," said Luther. "Not till I got here."

"And then what did you do?" said Anne.

"Nothing. Been looking for a job for the last four months."

"Poor boy," said Michael; "poor, dear boy."

"Yes," said Anne. "You must be hungry." And they called the cook to give him something to eat.

Luther dug around in the garden a little bit that first day, went out and        25
bought some seeds, came back and ate some more. They made a place for him to sleep in the basement by the furnace. And the next day Anne started to paint him, after she'd bought the right colors.

"He'll be good company for Mattie," they said. "She claims she's afraid to stay alone at night when we're out, so she leaves." They suspected, though, that Mattie just liked to get up to Harlem. And they thought right. Mattie was not as settled as she looked. Once out, with the Savoy open until three in the morning, why come home? That was the way Mattie felt.

In fact, what happened was that Mattie showed Luther where the best and cheapest hot spots in Harlem were located. Luther hadn't even set foot in Harlem before, living twenty-eight miles away, as he did, in Jersey, and being a kind of quiet boy. But the second night he was there Mattie said, "Come on, let's go. Working for white folks all day, I'm tired. They needn't think I was made to answer telephones all night." So out they went.

Anne noticed that most mornings Luther would doze almost as soon as she sat him down to pose, so she eventually decided to paint Luther asleep. "The Sleeping Negro," she would call it. Dear, natural childlike people, they would sleep anywhere they wanted to. Anyway, asleep, he kept still and held the pose.

And he *was* an adorable Negro. Not tall, but with a splendid body. And a slow and lively smile that lighted up his black, black face, for his teeth were very white, and his eyes, too. Most effective in oil and canvas. Better even than Emma had been. Anne could stare at him at leisure when he was asleep. One day she decided to paint him nude, or at least half nude. A slave picture, that's what she would do. The market at New Orleans for a background. And call it "The Boy on the Block."

So one morning when Luther settled down in his sleeping pose, Anne said, "No," she had finished that picture. She wanted to paint him now representing to the full the soul and sorrow of his people. She wanted to paint him as a slave about to be sold. And since slaves in warm climates had no clothes, would he please take off his shirt.    30

Luther smiled a sort of embarrassed smile and took off his shirt.

"Your undershirt, too," said Anne. But it turned out that he had on a union suit, so he had to go out and change altogether. He came back and mounted the box that Anne said would serve just then for a slave block, and she began to sketch. Before luncheon Michael came in, and went into rhapsodies over Luther on the box without a shirt, about to be sold into slavery. He said he must put him into music right now. And he went to the piano and began to play something that sounded like Deep River in the jaws of a dog, but Michael said it was a modern slave plaint, 1850 in terms of 1933. Vieux Carré° remembered on 135th Street, Slavery in the Cotton Club.

Anne said, "It's too marvellous!" And they painted and played till dark, with rest periods in between for Luther. Then they all knocked off for dinner. Anne and Michael went out later to one of Lew Leslie's new shows. And Luther and Mattie said, "Thank God!" and got dressed up for Harlem.

Funny, they didn't like the Carraways. They treated them nice and paid them well. "But they're too strange," said Mattie, "they makes me nervous."

"They is mighty funny," Luther agreed.    35

They didn't understand the vagaries of white folks, neither Luther nor Mattie, and they didn't want to be bothered trying.

*Vieux Carré*: the old quarter of New Orleans.

"I does my work," said Mattie. "After that I don't want to be painted, or asked to sing songs, nor nothing like that."

The Carraways often asked Luther to sing, and he sang. He knew a lot of southern worksongs and reels, and spirituals and ballads.

*"Dear Ma, I'm in hard luck:*
*Three days since I et,*
*And the stamp on this letter's*
*Gwine to put me in debt."*

The Carraways allowed him to neglect the garden altogether. About all Luther did was pose and sing. And he got tired of that.

Indeed, both Luther and Mattie became a bit difficult to handle as time went on. The Carraways blamed it on Mattie. She had got hold of Luther. She was just simply spoiling a nice simple young boy. She was old enough to know better. Mattie was in love with Luther.

As least, he slept with her. The Carraways discovered this one night about one o'clock when they went to wake Luther up (the first time they'd ever done such a thing) and ask him if he wouldn't sing his own marvellous version of John Henry for a man who had just come from Saint Louis and was sailing for Paris tomorrow. But Luther wasn't in his own bed by the furnace. There was a light in Mattie's room, so Michael knocked softly. Mattie said, "Who's that?" And Michael poked his head in, and here were Luther and Mattie in bed together!

Of course, Anne condoned them. "It's so simple and natural for Negroes to make love." But Mattie, after all, was forty if she was a day. And Luther was only a kid. Besides Anne thought that Luther had been ever so much nicer when he first came than he was now. But from so many nights at the Savoy, he had become a marvellous dancer, and he was teaching Anne the Lindy Hop to Cab Calloway's records. Besides, her picture of "The Boy on the Block" wasn't anywhere near done. And he did take pretty good care of the furnace. So they kept him. At least, Anne kept him, although Michael said he was getting a little bored with the same Negro always in the way.

For Luther had grown a bit familiar lately. He smoked up all their cigarettes, drank their wine, told jokes on them to their friends, and sometimes even came upstairs singing and walking about the house when the Carraways had guests in who didn't share their enthusiasm for Negroes, natural or otherwise.

Luther and Mattie together were a pair. They quite frankly lived with one another now. Well, let that go. Anne and Michael prided themselves on being different; artists, you know, and liberal-minded people—maybe a little scatter-brained, but then (secretly, they felt) that came from genius. They were not ordinary people, bothering about the liberties of others. Certainly, the last thing they would do would be to interfere with the delightful simplicity of Negroes.

But Mattie must be giving Luther money and buying him clothes. He was really dressing awfully well. And on her Thursday afternoons off she would come back loaded down with packages. As far as the Carraways could tell, they were all for Luther.

And sometimes there were quarrels drifting up from the basement. And often, all too often, Mattie had moods. Then Luther would have moods. And it was pretty awful having two dark and glowering people around the house. Anne couldn't paint and Michael couldn't play.

One day, when she hadn't seen Luther for three days, Anne called downstairs and asked him if he wouldn't please come up and take off his shirt and get on the box. The picture was almost done. Luther came dragging his feet upstairs and humming:

> "*Before I'd be a slave*
> *I'd be buried in ma grave*
> *And go home to my Jesus*
> *And be free*."

And that afternoon he let the furnace go almost out.

That was the state of things when Michael's mother (whom Anne had never liked) arrived from Kansas City to pay them a visit. At once neither Mattie nor Luther liked her either. She was a mannish old lady, big and tall, and inclined to be bossy. Mattie, however, did spruce up her service, cooked delicious things, and treated Mrs. Carraway with a great deal more respect than she did Anne.

"I never play with servants," Mrs. Carraway had said to Michael, and Mattie must have heard her.

But Luther, he was worse than ever. Not that he did anything wrong, Anne thought, but the way he did things! For instance, he didn't need to sing now all the time, especially since Mrs. Carraway had said she didn't like singing. And certainly not songs like "You Rascal, You."

But all things end! With the Carraways and Luther it happened like this: One forenoon, quite without a shirt (for he expected to pose) Luther came sauntering through the library to change the flowers in the vase. He carried red roses. Mrs. Carraway was reading her morning scripture from the Health and Life.

"Oh, good morning," said Luther. "How long are you gonna stay in this house?"

"I never liked familiar Negroes," said Mrs. Carraway, over her nose glasses.

"Huh!" said Luther. "That's too bad! I never liked poor white folks."

Mrs. Carraway screamed, a short, loud, dignified scream. Michael came running in bathrobe and pyjamas. Mrs. Carraway grew tall. There was a scene. Luther talked. Michael talked. Anne appeared.

"Never, never, never," said Mrs. Carraway, "have I suffered such impudence from servants—and a nigger servant—in my own son's house."

"Mother, Mother, Mother," said Michael. "Be calm. I'll discharge him." He turned on the nonchalant Luther. "Go!" he said, pointing toward the door. "Go, go!"

"Michael," Anne cried, "I haven't finished 'The Slave on the Block.'" Her husband looked nonplussed. For a moment he breathed deeply.

"Either he goes or I go," said Mrs. Carraway, firm as a rock.

"He goes," said Michael with strength from his mother.

"Oh!" cried Anne. She looked at Luther. His black arms were full of roses he had brought to put in the vases. He had on no shirt. "Oh!" His body was ebony.

"Don't worry 'bout me!" said Luther. "I'll go."

50

55

60

"Yes, we'll go," boomed Mattie from the doorway, who had come up from below, fat and belligerent. "We've stood enough foolery from you white folks! Yes, we'll go. Come on, Luther."

What could she mean, "stood enough"? What had they done to them, Anne and Michael wondered. They had tried to be kind. "Oh!"

"Sneaking around knocking on our door at night," Mattie went on. "Yes,    65
we'll go. Pay us! Pay us! Pay us!" So she remembered the time they had come for Luther at night. That was it.

"I'll pay you," said Michael. He followed Mattie out.

Anne looked at her black boy.

"Good-bye," Luther said. "You fix the vases."

He handed her his armful of roses, glanced impudently at old Mrs. Carraway and grinned—grinned that wide, beautiful, white-toothed grin that made Anne say when she first saw him, "He looks like the jungle." Grinned, and disappeared in the dark hall, with no shirt on his back.

"Oh," Anne moaned distressfully, "my 'Boy on the Block'!"    70

"Huh!" snorted Mrs. Carraway.


## FRANZ KAFKA (1883–1924)

*A Hunger Artist*    (*1924*)

Translated by Willa and Edwin Muir.


During these last decades the interest in professional fasting has markedly diminished. It used to pay very well to stage such great performances under one's own management, but today that is quite impossible. We live in a different world now. At one time the whole town took a lively interest in the hunger artist; from day to day of his fast the excitement mounted; everybody wanted to see him at least once a day; there were people who bought season tickets for the last few days and sat from morning till night in front of his small barred cage; even in the nighttime there were visiting hours, when the whole effect was heightened by torch flares; on fine days the cage was set out in the open air, and then it was the children's special treat to see the hunger artist; for their elders he was often just a joke that happened to be in fashion, but the children stood openmouthed, holding each other's hands for greater security, marveling at him as he sat there pallid in black tights, with his ribs sticking out so prominently, not even on a seat but down among straw on the ground, sometimes giving a courteous nod, answering questions with a constrained smile, or perhaps stretching an arm through the bars so that one might feel how thin it was, and then again withdrawing deep into himself, paying no attention to anyone or anything, not even to the all-important striking of the clock that was the only piece of furniture in his cage, but merely staring into vacancy with half-shut eyes, now and then taking a sip from a tiny glass of water to moisten his lips.

Besides casual onlookers there were also relays of permanent watchers selected by the public, usually butchers, strangely enough, and it was their task to watch the hunger artist day and night, three of them at a time, in case he should have some secret recourse to nourishment. This was nothing but a formality, insti-tuted to reassure the masses, for the initiates knew well enough that during his fast the artist would never in any circumstances, not even under forcible compulsion, swallow the smallest morsel of food; the honor of his profession forbade it. Not every watcher, of course, was capable of understanding this, there were often groups of night watchers who were very lax in carrying out their duties and deliberately huddled together in a retired corner to play cards with great absorption, obviously intending to give the hunger artist the chance of a little refreshment, which they supposed he could draw from some private hoard. Nothing annoyed the artist more than such watchers; they made him miserable; they made his fast seem unen-durable; sometimes he mastered his feebleness sufficiently to sing during their watch for as long as he could keep going, to show them how unjust their suspicions were. But that was of little use; they only wondered at his cleverness in being able to fill his mouth even while singing. Much more to his taste were the watchers who sat close up to the bars, who were not content with the dim night lighting of the hall but focused him in the full glare of the electric pocket torch given them by the impresario. The harsh light did not trouble him at all, in any case he could never sleep properly, and he could always drowse a little, whatever the light, at any hour, even when the hall was thronged with noisy onlookers. He was quite happy at the prospect of spending a sleepless night with such watchers; he was ready to exchange jokes with them, to tell them stories out of his nomadic life, anything at all to keep them awake and demonstrate to them again that he had no eatables in his cage and that he was fasting as not one of them could fast. But his happiest moment was when the morning came and an enormous breakfast was brought them, at his expense, on which they flung themselves with the keen appetite of healthy men after a weary night of wakefulness. Of course there were people who argued that this breakfast was an unfair attempt to bribe the watchers, but that was going rather too far, and when they were invited to take on a night's vigil without a breakfast, merely for the sake of the cause, they made themselves scarce, although they stuck stubbornly to their suspicions.

Such suspicions, anyhow, were a necessary accompaniment to the profession of fasting. No one could possibly watch the hunger artist continuously, day and night, and so no one could produce first-hand evidence that the fast had really been rigorous and continuous; only the artist himself could know that, he was therefore bound to be the sole completely satisfied spectator of his own fast. Yet for other reasons he was never satisfied; it was not perhaps mere fasting that had brought him to such skeleton thinness that many people had regretfully to keep away from his exhibitions, because the sight of him was too much for them, perhaps it was dissatisfaction with himself that had worn him down. For he alone knew, what no other initiate knew, how easy it was to fast. It was the easiest thing in the world. He made no secret of this, yet people did not believe him, at the best they set him down as modest; most of them, however, thought he was out for publicity or else was some kind of cheat who found it easy to fast because he had discovered a way of making it easy, and then had the impudence to admit the fact, more or less. He had to put up with all that, and in the course of time had got used to it, but his inner dissatisfaction always rankled, and never yet, after any term of fasting—this must be granted to his credit—had he left the cage of his own free will. The longest period of fasting was fixed by his impresario at forty days, beyond that term he was not allowed to go, not even in great cities, and there was good reason for it, too. Experience had proved that for about forty days the interest of the public could be stimulated by a steadily increasing pressure of advertisement, but after that the town began to lose interest, sympathetic support began notably to fall off; there were of course local variations as between one town and another or one country and another, but as a general rule forty days marked the limit. So on the fortieth day the flower-bedecked cage was opened, enthusiastic spectators filled the hall, a military band played, two doctors entered the cage to measure the results of the fast, which were announced through a megaphone, and finally two young ladies appeared, blissful at having been selected for the honor, to help the hunger artist down the few steps leading to a small table on which was spread a carefully chosen invalid repast. And at this very moment the artist always turned stubborn. True, he would entrust his bony arms to the outstretched helping hands of the ladies bending over him, but stand up he would not. Why stop fasting at this particular moment, after forty days of it? He had held out for a long time, an illimitably long time; why stop now, when he was in his best fasting form, or rather, not yet quite in his best fasting form? Why should he be cheated of the fame he would get for fasting longer, for being not only the record hunger artist of all time, which presumably he was already, but for beating his own record by a performance beyond human imagination, since he felt that there were no limits to his capacity for fasting? His public pretended to admire him so much, why should it have so little patience with him; if he could endure fasting longer, why shouldn't the public endure it? Besides, he was tired, he was comfortable sitting in the straw, and now he was supposed to lift himself to his full height and go down to a meal the very thought of which gave him a nausea that only the presence of the ladies kept him from betraying, and even that with an effort. And he looked up into the eyes of the ladies who were apparently so friendly and in reality so cruel, and shook his head, which felt too heavy on its strengthless neck. But then there happened yet again what always happened. The impresario came forward, without a word—for the band made speech impossible—lifted his arms in the air above the artist, as if inviting Heaven to look down upon its creature here in the straw, this suffering martyr, which indeed he was, although in quite another sense; grasped him around the emaciated waist, with exaggerated caution, so that the frail condition he was in might be appreciated; and committed him to the care of the blenching ladies, not without secretly giving him a shaking so that his legs and body tottered and swayed. The artist now submitted completely; his head lolled on his breast as if it had landed there by chance; his body was hollowed out; his legs in a spasm of self-preservation clung close to each other at the knees, yet scraped on the ground as if it were not really solid ground, as if they were only trying to find solid ground; and the whole weight of his body, a featherweight after all, relapsed onto one of the ladies, who, looking around for help and panting a little—this post of honor was not at all what she had expected it to be—first stretched her neck as far as she could to keep her face at least free from contact with the artist, then finding this impossible, and her more fortunate companion not coming to her aid but merely holding extended in her own trembling hand the little bunch of knucklebones that was the artist's, to the great delight of the spectators burst into tears and had to be replaced by an attendant who had long been stationed in readiness. Then came the food, a little of which the impresario managed to get between the artist's lips, while he sat in a kind of half-fainting trance, to the accompaniment of cheerful patter designed to distract the public's attention from the artist's condition; after that, a toast was drunk to the public, supposedly prompted by a whisper from the artist in the impresario's ear; the band confirmed it with a mighty flourish, the spectators melted away, and no one had any cause to be dissatisfied with the proceedings, no one except the hunger artist himself, he only, as always.

So he lived for many years, with small regular intervals of recuperation, in visible glory, honored by the world, yet in spite of that troubled in spirit, and all the more troubled because no one would take his trouble seriously. What comfort could he possibly need? What more could he possibly wish for? And if some good-natured person, feeling sorry for him, tried to console him by pointing out that his melancholy was probably caused by fasting, it could happen, especially when he had been fasting for some time, that he reacted with an outburst of fury and to the general alarm began to shake the bars of his cage like a wild animal. Yet the impresario had a way of punishing these outbreaks which he rather enjoyed putting into operation. He would apologize publicly for the artist's behavior, which was only to be excused, he admitted, because of the irritability caused by fasting; a condition hardly to be understood by well-fed people; then by natural transition he went on to mention the artist's equally incomprehensible boast that he could fast for much longer than he was doing; he praised the high ambition, the good will, the great self-denial undoubtedly implicit in such a statement; and then quite simply countered it by bringing out photographs, which were also on sale to the public, showing the artist on the fortieth day of a fast lying in bed almost dead from exhaustion. This perversion of the truth, familiar to the artist though it was, always unnerved him afresh and proved too much for him. What was a consequence of the premature ending of his fast was here presented as the cause of it! To fight against this lack of understanding, against a whole world of nonunderstanding, was impossible. Time and again in good faith he stood by the bars listening to the impresario, but as soon as the photographs appeared he always let go and sank with a groan back onto his straw, and the reassured public could once more come close and gaze at him.

A few years later when the witnesses of such scenes called them to mind, they often failed to understand themselves at all. For meanwhile the aforementioned change in public interest had set in; it seemed to happen almost overnight; there may have been profound causes for it, but who was going to bother about that; at any rate the pampered hunger artist suddenly found himself deserted one fine day by the amusement-seekers, who went streaming past him to other more-favored attractions. For the last time the impresario hurried him over half Europe to discover whether the old interest might still survive here and there; all in vain; everywhere, as if by secret agreement, a positive revulsion from professional fasting was in evidence. Of course it could not really have sprung up so suddenly as all that, and many premonitory symptoms which had not been sufficiently remarked or suppressed during the rush and glitter of success now came retrospectively to mind, but it was now too late to take any countermeasures. Fasting would surely come into fashion again at some future date, yet that was no comfort for those living in the present. What, then, was the hunger artist to do? He had been applauded by thousands in his time and could hardly come down to showing himself

5

in a street booth at village fairs, and as for adopting another profession, he was not only too old for that but too fanatically devoted to fasting. So he took leave of the impresario, his partner in an unparalleled career, and hired himself to a large circus; in order to spare his own feelings he avoided reading the conditions of his contract.

A large circus with its enormous traffic in replacing and recruiting men, animals, and apparatus can always find a use for people at any time, even for a hunger artist, provided of course that he does not ask too much, and in this particular case anyhow it was not only the artist who was taken on but his famous and long-known name as well; indeed considering the peculiar nature of his performance, which was not impaired by advancing age, it could not be objected that here was an artist past his prime, no longer at the height of his professional skill, seeking a refuge in some quiet corner of a circus; on the contrary, the hunger artist averred that he could fast as well as ever, which was entirely credible, he even alleged that if he were allowed to fast as he liked, and this was at once promised him without more ado, he could astound the world by establishing a record never yet achieved, a statement that certainly provoked a smile among the other professionals, since it left out of account the change in public opinion, which the hunger artist in his zeal conveniently forgot.

He had not, however, actually lost his sense of the real situation and took it as a matter of course that he and his cage should be stationed, not in the middle of the ring as a main attraction, but outside, near the animal cages, on a site that was after all easily accessible. Large and gaily painted placards made a frame for the cage and announced what was to be seen inside it. When the public came thronging out in the intervals to see the animals, they could hardly avoid passing the hunger artist's cage and stopping there for a moment, perhaps they might even have stayed longer had not those pressing behind them in the narrow gangway, who did not understand why they should be held up on their way toward the excitements of the menagerie, made it impossible for anyone to stand gazing quietly for any length of time. And that was the reason why the hunger artist, who had of course been looking forward to these visiting hours as the main achievement of his life, began instead to shrink from them. At first he could hardly wait for the intervals; it was exhilarating to watch the crowds come streaming his way, until only too soon—not even the most obstinate self-deception, clung to almost consciously, could hold out against the fact—the conviction was borne in upon him that these people, most of them, to judge from their actions, again and again, without exception, were all on their way to the menagerie. And the first sight of them from the distance remained the best. For when they reached his cage he was at once deafened by the storm of shouting and abuse that arose from the two contending factions, which renewed themselves continuously, of those who wanted to stop and stare at him—he soon began to dislike them more than the others—not out of real interest but only out of obstinate self-assertiveness, and those who wanted to go straight on to the animals. When the first great rush was past, the stragglers came along, and these, whom nothing could have prevented from stopping to look at him as long as they had breath, raced past with long strides, hardly even glancing at him, in their haste to get to the menagerie in time. And all too rarely did it happen that he had a stroke of luck, when some father of a family fetched up before him with his children, pointed a finger at the hunger artist, and explained at length what the phenomenon meant, telling stories of earlier years when he himself had watched similar but much more thrilling performances, and the children, still rather uncomprehending, since neither inside nor outside school had they been sufficiently prepared for this lesson—what did they care about fasting?—yet showed by the brightness of their intent eyes that new and better times might be coming. Perhaps, said the hunger artist to himself many a time, things would be a little better if his cage were set not quite so near the menagerie. That made it too easy for people to make their choice, to say nothing of what he suffered from the stench of the menagerie, the animals' restlessness by night, the carrying past of raw lumps of flesh for the beasts of prey, the roaring at feeding times, which depressed him continually. But he did not dare to lodge a complaint with the management; after all, he had the animals to thank for the troops of people who passed his cage, among whom there might always be one here and there to take an interest in him, and who could tell where they might seclude him if he called attention to his existence and thereby to the fact that, strictly speaking, he was only an impediment on the way to the menagerie.

A small impediment, to be sure, one that grew steadily less. People grew familiar with the strange idea that they could be expected, in times like these, to take an interest in a hunger artist, and with this familiarity the verdict went out against him. He might fast as much as he could, and he did so; but nothing could save him now, people passed him by. Just try to explain to anyone the art of fasting! Anyone who has no feeling for it cannot be made to understand it. The fine placards grew dirty and illegible, they were torn down; the little notice board telling the number of fast days achieved, which at first was changed carefully every day, had long stayed at the same figure, for after the first few weeks even this small task seemed pointless to the staff; and so the artist simply fasted on and on, as he had once dreamed of doing, and it was no trouble to him, just as he had always foretold, but no one counted the days, no one, not even the artist himself, knew what records he was already breaking, and his heart grew heavy. And when once in a while some leisurely passer-by stopped, made merry over the old figure on the board, and spoke of swindling, that was in its way the stupidest lie ever invented by indifference and inborn malice, since it was not the hunger artist who was cheating, he was working honestly, but the world was cheating him of his reward.

Many more days went by, however, and that too came to an end. An overseer's eye fell on the cage one day and he asked the attendants why this perfectly good cage should be left standing there unused with dirty straw inside it; nobody knew, until one man, helped out by the notice board, remembered about the hunger artist. They poked into the straw with sticks and found him in it. "Are you still fasting?" asked the overseer, "when on earth do you mean to stop?" "Forgive me, everybody," whispered the hunger artist; only the overseer, who had his ear to the bars, understood him. "Of course," said the overseer, and tapped his forehead with a finger to let the attendants know what state the man was in, "we forgive you." "I always wanted you to admire my fasting," said the hunger artist. "We do admire it," said the overseer, affably. "But you shouldn't admire it," said the hunger artist. "Well then we don't admire it," said the overseer, "but why shouldn't we admire it?" "Because I have to fast, I can't help it," said the hunger artist. "What a fellow you are," said the overseer, "and why can't you help it?" "Because," said the hunger artist, lifting his head a little and speaking, with his lips pursed, as if for a kiss, right into the overseer's ear, so that no syllable might be lost, "because I couldn't find the food I liked. If I had found it, believe me, I should have made no fuss and stuffed myself like you or anyone else." These were his last words, but in his dimming eyes remained the firm though no longer proud persuasion that he was still continuing to fast.

"Well, clear this out now!" said the overseer, and they buried the hunger    10
artist, straw and all. Into the cage they put a young panther. Even the most insensitive felt it refreshing to see this wild creature leaping around the cage that had so long been dreary. The panther was all right. The food he liked was brought him without hesitation by the attendants; he seemed not even to miss his freedom; his noble body, furnished almost to the bursting point with all that it needed, seemed to carry freedom around with it too; somewhere in his jaws it seemed to lurk; and the joy of life streamed with such ardent passion from his throat that for the onlookers it was not easy to stand the shock of it. But they braced themselves, crowded around the cage, and did not want ever to move away.


# DORIS LESSING (b. 1919)

*The Old Chief Mshlanga*                                                     1951

They were good, the years of ranging the bush over her father's farm which, like every white farm, was largely unused, broken only occasionally by small patches of cultivation. In between, nothing but trees, the long sparse grass, thorn and cactus and gully, grass and outcrop and thorn. And a jutting piece of rock which had been thrust up from the warm soil of Africa unimaginable eras of time ago, washed into hollows and whorls by sun and wind that had travelled so many thousands of miles of space and bush, would hold the weight of a small girl whose eyes were sightless for anything but a pale willowed river, a pale gleaming castle— a small girl singing: "Out flew the web and floated wide, the mirror cracked from side to side . . ."

Pushing her way through the green aisles of the mealie° stalks, the leaves arching like cathedrals veined with sunlight far overhead, with the packed red earth underfoot, a fine lace of red starred witchweed would summon up a black bent figure croaking premonitions: the Northern witch, bred of cold Northern forests, would stand before her among the mealie fields, and it was the mealie fields that faded and fled, leaving her among the gnarled roots of an oak, snow falling thick and soft and white, the woodcutter's fire glowing red welcome through crowding tree trunks.

A white child, opening its eyes curiously on a sun-suffused landscape, a gaunt and violent landscape, might be supposed to accept it as her own, to take the msasa trees and the thorn trees as familiars, to feel her blood running free and responsive to the swing of the seasons.

This child could not see a msasa tree, or the thorn, for what they were. Her books held tales of alien fairies, her rivers ran slow and peaceful, and she knew the shape of the leaves of an ash or an oak, the names of the little creatures that lived in English streams, when the words "the veld"° meant strangeness, though she could remember nothing else.

*mealie*: Southern African word for corn.
*veld*: Also *veldt*, a vast, open grass-covered area used for grazing.

Because of this, for many years, it was the veld that seemed unreal; the sun was a foreign sun, and the wind spoke a strange language.

The black people on the farm were as remote as the trees and the rocks. They were an amorphous black mass, mingling and thinning and massing like tadpoles, faceless, who existed merely to serve, to say "Yes, Baas,"° take their money and go. They changed season by season, moving from one farm to the next, according to their outlandish needs, which one did not have to understand, coming from perhaps hundreds of miles North or East, passing on after a few months—where? Perhaps even as far away as the fabled gold mines of Johannesburg, where the pay was so much better than the few shillings a month and the double handful of mealie meal twice a day which they earned in that part of Africa.

The child was taught to take them for granted: the servants in the house would come running a hundred yards to pick up a book if she dropped it. She was called "Nkosikaas"—Chieftainess, even by the black children her own age.

Later, when the farm grew too small to hold her curiosity, she carried a gun in the crook of her arm and wandered miles a day, from vlei to vlei,° from *kopje* to *kopje*,° accompanied by two dogs: the dogs and the gun were an armour against fear. Because of them she never felt fear.

If a native came into sight along the kaffir° paths half a mile away, the dogs would flush him up a tree as if he were a bird. If he expostulated (in his uncouth language which was by itself ridiculous) that was cheek. If one was in a good mood, it could be a matter for laughter. Otherwise one passed on, hardly glancing at the angry man in the tree.

On the rare occasions when white children met together they could amuse themselves by hailing a passing native in order to make a buffoon of him; they could set the dogs on him and watch him run; they could tease a small black child as if he were a puppy—save that they would not throw stones and sticks at a dog without a sense of guilt.

Later still, certain questions presented themselves in the child's mind; and because the answers were not easy to accept, they were silenced by an even greater arrogance of manner.

It was even impossible to think of the black people who worked about the house as friends, for if she talked to one of them, her mother would come running anxiously: "Come away; you mustn't talk to natives."

It was this instilled consciousness of danger, of something unpleasant, that made it easy to laugh out loud, crudely, if a servant made a mistake in his English of if he failed to understand an order—there is a certain kind of laughter that is fear, afraid of itself.

One evening, when I was about fourteen, I was walking down the side of a mealie field that had been newly ploughed, so that the great red clods showed fresh and tumbling to the vlie beyond, like a choppy red sea; it was that hushed and listening hour, when the birds send long sad calls from tree to tree, and all the colours of earth and sky and leaf are deep and golden. I had my rifle in the curve of my arm, and the dogs were at my heels.

In front of me, perhaps a couple of hundred yards away, a group of three

*Baas*: I.e., "boss."
*vlei*: A slough or pond (valley).
*kopje*: A small hill covered with vegetation and rocks. Usually pronounced "copy."
*kaffir*: A pejorative word for the various Bantu peoples and their languages.

Africans came into sight around the side of a big antheap. I whistled the dogs close in to my skirts and let the gun swing in my hand, and advanced, waiting for them to move aside, off the path, in respect for my passing. But they came on steadily, and the dogs looked up at me for the command to chase. I was angry. It was "cheek" for a native not to stand off a path, the moment he caught sight of you.

In front walked an old man, stooping his weight on to a stick, his hair grizzled white, a dark red blanket slung over his shoulders like a cloak. Behind him came two young men, carrying bundles of pots, assegais, hatchets.

The group was not a usual one. They were not natives seeking work. These had an air of dignity, of quietly following their own purpose. It was the dignity that checked my tongue. I walked quietly on, talking softly to the growling dogs, till I was ten paces away. Then the old man stopped, drawing his blanket close.

"Morning, Nkosikaas," he said, using the customary greeting for any time of the day.

"Good morning," I said. "Where are you going?" My voice was a little truculent.

The old man spoke in his own language, then one of the young men stepped       20
forward politely and said in careful English: "My Chief travels to see his brothers beyond the river."

A Chief! I thought, understanding the pride that made the old man stand before me like an equal—more than an equal, for he showed courtesy, and I showed none.

The old man spoke again, wearing dignity like an inherited garment, still standing ten paces off, flanked by his entourage, not looking at me (that would have been rude) but directing his eyes somewhere over my head at the trees.

"You are the little Nkosikaas from the farm of Baas Jordan?"

"That's right," I said.

"Perhaps your father does not remember," said the interpreter for the old       25
man, "but there was an affair with some goats. I remember seeing you when you were . . ." The young man held his hand at knee level and smiled.

We all smiled.

"What is your name?" I asked.

"This is Chief Mshlanga," said the young man.

"I will tell my father that I met you," I said.

The old man said: "My greetings to your father, little Nkosikaas."        30

"Good morning," I said politely, finding the politeness difficult, from lack of use.

"Morning, little Nkosikaas," said the old man, and stood aside to let me pass.

I went by, my gun hanging awkwardly, the dogs sniffing and growling, cheated of their favorite game of chasing natives like animals.

Not long afterwards I read in an old explorer's book the phrase: "Chief Mshlanga's country." It went like this: "Our destination was Chief Mshlanga's country, to the north of the river; and it was our desire to ask his permission to prospect for gold in his territory."

The phrase "ask his permission" was so extraordinary to a white child, brought       35
up to consider all natives as things to use, that it revived those questions, which could not be suppressed: they fermented slowly in my mind.

On another occasion one of those old prospectors who still move over Africa looking for neglected reefs, with their hammers and tents, and pans for sifting gold from crushed rock, came to the farm and, in talking of the old days, used that phrase again: "This was the Old Chief's country," he said. "It stretched from those mountains over there way back to the river, hundreds of miles of country." That was his name for our district: "The Old Chief's Country"; he did not use our name for it—a new phrase which held no implication of usurped ownership.

As I read more books about the time when this part of Africa was opened up, not much more than fifty years before, I found Old Chief Mshlanga had been a famous man, known to all the explorers and prospectors. But then he had been young; or maybe it was his father or uncle they spoke of—I never found out.

During that year I met him several times in the part of the farm that was traversed by natives moving over the country. I learned that the path up the side of the big red field where the birds sang was the recognized highway for migrants. Perhaps I even haunted it in the hope of meeting him: being greeted by him, the exchange of courtesies, seemed to answer the questions that troubled me.

Soon I carried a gun in a different spirit; I used it for shooting food and not to give me confidence. And now the dogs learned better manners. When I saw a native approaching, we offered and took greetings; and slowly that other landscape in my mind faded, and my feet struck directly on the African soil, and I saw the shapes of tree and hill clearly, and the black people moved back, as it were, out of my life: it was as if I stood aside to watch a slow intimate dance of landscape and men, a very old dance, whose steps I could not learn.

But I thought: this is my heritage, too; I was bred here; it is my country as    40 well as the black man's country; and there is plenty of room for all of us, without elbowing each other off the pavements and roads.

It seemed it was only necessary to let free that respect I felt when I was talking with old Chief Mshlanga, to let both black and white people meet gently, with tolerance for each other's differences: it seemed quite easy.

Then, one day, something new happened. Working in our house as servants were always three natives: cook, houseboy, garden boy. They used to change as the farm natives changed: staying for a few months, then moving on to a new job, or back home to their kraals.° They were thought of as "good" or "bad" natives; which meant: how did they behave as servants? Were they lazy, efficient, obedient, or disrespectful? If the family felt good-humoured, the phrase was: "What can you expect from raw black savages?" If we were angry, we said: "These damned niggers, we would be much better off without them."

One day, a white policeman was on his rounds of the district, and he said laughingly: "Did you know you have an important man in your kitchen?"

"What!" exclaimed my mother sharply. "What do you mean?"

"A Chief's son." The policeman seemed amused. "He'll boss the tribe when    45 the old man dies."

"He'd better not put on a Chief's son act with me," said my mother.

When the policeman left, we looked with different eyes at our cook: he was a good worker, but he drank too much at week-ends—that was how we knew him.

He was a tall youth, with very black skin, like black polished metal, his tightly-growing black hair parted white man's fashion at one side, with a metal comb

*kraals*: Fenced-in native villages.

from the store stuck into it; very polite, very distant, very quick to obey an order. Now that it had been pointed out, we said: "Of course, you can see. Blood always tells."

My mother became strict with him now she knew about his birth and prospects. Sometimes, when she lost her temper, she would say: "You aren't the Chief yet, you know." And he would answer her very quietly, his eyes on the ground: "Yes, Nkosikaas."

One afternoon he asked for a whole day off, instead of the customary half-day, to go home next Sunday.

"How can you go home in one day?"

"It will take me half an hour on my bicycle," he explained.

I watched the direction he took; and the next day I went off to look for this kraal; I understood he must be Chief Mshlanga's successor: there was no other kraal near enough our farm.

Beyond our boundaries on that side the country was new to me. I followed unfamiliar paths past *kopjes* that till now had been part of the jagged horizon, hazed with distance. This was Government land, which had never been cultivated by white men; at first I could not understand why it was that it appeared, in merely crossing the boundary, I had entered a completely fresh type of landscape. It was a wide green valley, where a small river sparkled, and vivid water-birds darted over the rushes. The grass was thick and soft to my calves, the trees stood tall and shapely.

I was used to our farm, whose hundreds of acres of harsh eroded soil bore trees that had been cut for the mine furnaces and had grown thin and twisted, where the cattle had dragged the grass flat, leaving innumerable criss-crossing trails that deepened each season into gullies, under the force of the rains.

This country had been left untouched, save for prospectors whose picks had struck a few sparks from the surface of the rocks as they wandered by; and for migrant natives whose passing had left, perhaps, a charred patch on the trunk of a tree where their evening fire had nestled.

It was very silent: a hot morning with pigeons cooing throatily, the midday shadows lying dense and thick with clear yellow spaces of sunlight between and in all that wide green park-like valley, not a human soul but myself.

I was listening to the quick regular tapping of a woodpecker when slowly a chill feeling seemed to grow up from the small of my back to my shoulders, in a constricting spasm like a shudder, and at the roots of my hair a tingling sensation began and ran down over the surface of my flesh, leaving me goosefleshed and cold, though I was damp with sweat. Fever? I thought; then uneasily, turned to look over my shoulder; and realized suddenly that this was fear. It was extraordinary, even humiliating. It was a new fear. For all the years I had walked by myself over this country I had never known a moment's uneasiness; in the beginning because I had been supported by a gun and the dogs, then because I had learnt an easy friendliness for the Africans I might encounter.

I had read of this feeling, how the bigness and silence of Africa, under the ancient sun, grows dense and takes shape in the mind, till even the birds seem to call menacingly, and a deadly spirit comes out of the trees and the rocks. You move warily, as if your very passing disturbs something old and evil, something dark and big and angry that might suddenly rear and strike from behind. You look at groves of entwined trees, and picture the animals that might be lurking there; you look at the river running slowly, dropping from level to level through the vlei, spreading into pools where at night the bucks come to drink, and the crocodiles rise and drag them by their soft noses into underwater caves. Fear possessed me. I found I was turning round and round, because of that shapeless menace behind me that might reach out and take me; I kept glancing at the files of *kopjes* which, seen from a different angle, seemed to change with every step so that even known landmarks, like a big mountain that had sentinelled my world since I first became conscious of it, showed an unfamiliar sunlit valley among its foothills. I did not know where I was. I was lost. Panic seized me. I found I was spinning round and round, staring anxiously at this tree and that, peering up at the sun which appeared to have moved into an eastern slant, shedding the sad yellow light of sunset. Hours must have passed! I looked at my watch and found that this state of meaningless terror had lasted perhaps ten minutes.

The point was that it was meaningless. I was not ten miles from home: I had only to take my way back along the valley to find myself at the fence; away among the foothills of the *kopjes* gleamed the roof of a neighbor's house, and a couple of hours' walking would reach it. This was the sort of fear that contracts the flesh of a dog at night and sets him howling at the full moon. It had nothing to do with what I thought or felt; and I was more disturbed by the fact that I could become its victim than of the physical sensation itself: I walked steadily on, quietened, in a divided mind, watching my own pricking nerves and apprehensive glances from side to side with a disgusted amusement. Deliberately I set myself to think of this village I was seeking, and what I should do when I entered it—if I could find it, which was doubtful, since I was walking aimlessly and it might be anywhere in the hundreds of thousands of acres of bush that stretched about me. With my mind on that village, I realized that a new sensation was added to the fear: loneliness. Now such a terror of isolation invaded me that I could hardly walk; and if it were not that I came over the crest of a small rise and saw a village below me, I should have turned and gone home. It was a cluster of thatched huts in a clearing among trees. There were neat patches of mealies and pumpkins and millet, and cattle grazed under some trees at a distance. Fowls scratched among the huts, dogs lay sleeping on the grass, and goats friezed a *kopje* that jutted up beyond a tributary of the river lying like an enclosing arm round the village.

As I came close I saw the huts were lovingly decorated with patterns of yellow and red and ochre mud on the walls; and the thatch was tied in place with plaits of straw.

This was not at all like our farm compound, a dirty and neglected place, a temporary home for migrants who had no roots in it.

And now I did not know what to do next. I called a small black boy, who was sitting on a lot playing a stringed gourd, quite naked except for the strings of blue beads round his neck, and said: "Tell the Chief I am here." The child stuck his thumb in his mouth and stared shyly back at me.

For minutes I shifted my feet on the edge of what seemed a deserted village, till at last the child scuttled off, and then some women came. They were draped in bright cloths, with brass glinting in their ears and on their arms. They also stared, silently; then turned to chatter among themselves.

60

I said again: "Can I see Chief Mshlanga?" I saw they caught the name; they    65
did not understand what I wanted. I did not understand myself.

At last I walked through them and came past the huts and saw a clearing
under a big shady tree, where a dozen old men sat cross-legged on the ground,
talking. Chief Mshlanga was leaning back against the tree, holding a gourd in his
hand, from which he had been drinking. When he saw me, not a muscle of his
face moved, and I could see he was not pleased: perhaps he was afflicted with
my own shyness, due to being unable to find the right forms of courtesy for the
occasion. To meet me, on our own farm, was one thing; but I should not have
come here. What had I expected? I could not join them socially: the thing was
unheard of. Bad enough that I, a white girl, should be walking the veld alone as
a white man might: and in this part of the bush where only Government officials
had the right to move.

Again I stood, smiling foolishly, while behind me stood the groups of brightly
clad, chattering women, their faces alert with curiosity and interest, and in front
of me sat the old men, with old lined faces, their eyes guarded, aloof. It was a
village of ancients and children and women. Even the two young men who kneeled
beside the Chief were not those I had seen with him previously: the young men
were all away working on the white men's farms and mines, and the Chief must
depend on relatives who were temporarily on holiday for his attendants.

"The small white Nkosikaas is far from home," remarked the old man at
last.

"Yes," I agreed, "it is far." I wanted to say: "I have come to pay you a
friendly visit, Chief Mshlanga." I could not say it. I might now be feeling an urgent
helpless desire to get to know these men and women as people, to be accepted
by them as a friend, but the truth was I had set out in a spirit of curiosity: I had
wanted to see the village that one day our cook, the reserved and obedient young
man who got drunk on Sundays, would one day rule over.

"The child of Nkosi Jordan is welcome," said Chief Mshlanga.    70

"Thank you," I said, and could think of nothing more to say. There was a
silence, while the flies rose and began to buzz around my head; and the wind
shook a little in the thick green tree that spread its branches over the old men.

"Good morning," I said at last. "I have to return now to my home."

"Morning, little Nkosikaas," said Chief Mshlanga.

I walked away from the indifferent village, over the rise past the staring
amber-eyed goats, down through the tall stately trees into the great rich green
valley where the river meandered and the pigeons cooed tales of plenty and the
woodpecker tapped softly.

The fear was gone; the loneliness had set into stiff-necked stoicism; there    75
was now a queer hostility in the landscape, a cold, hard, sullen indomitability that
walked with me, as strong as a wall, as intangible as smoke; it seemed to say to
me: you walk here as a destroyer. I went slowly homewards, with an empty heart:
I had learned that if one cannot call a country to heel like a dog, neither can
one dismiss the past with a smile in an easy gush of feeling, saying: I could not
help it, I am also a victim.

I only saw Chief Mshlanga once again.

One night my father's big red land was trampled down by small sharp hooves,
and it was discovered that the culprits were goats from Chief Mshlanga's kraal.
This had happened once before, years ago.

My father confiscated all the goats. Then he sent a message to the old Chief that if he wanted them he would have to pay for the damage.

He arrived at our house at the time of sunset one evening, looking very old and bent now, walking stiffly under his regally draped blanket, leaning on a big stick. My father sat himself down in his big chair below the steps of the house; the old man squatted carefully on the ground before him, flanked by his two young men.

The palaver was long and painful, because of the bad English of the young man who interpreted, and because my father could not speak dialect, but only kitchen kaffir.

From my father's point of view, at least two hundred pounds' worth of damage had been done to the crop. He knew he could not get the money from the old man. He felt he was entitled to keep the goats. As for the old Chief, he kept repeating angrily: "Twenty goats! My people cannot lose twenty goats! We are not rich, like the Nkosi Jordan, to lose twenty goats at once."

My father did not think of himself as rich, but rather as very poor. He spoke quickly and angrily in return, saying that the damage done meant a great deal to him, and that he was entitled to the goats.

At last it grew so heated that the cook, the Chief's son, was called from the kitchen to be interpreter, and now my father spoke fluently in English, and our cook translated rapidly so that the old man could understand how very angry my father was. The young man spoke without emotion, in a mechanical way, his eyes lowered, but showing how he felt his position by a hostile uncomfortable set of the shoulders.

It was now in the late sunset, the sky a welter of colours, the birds singing their last songs, and the cattle, lowing peacefully, moving past us towards their sheds for the night. It was the hour when Africa is most beautiful; and here was this pathetic, ugly scene, doing no one any good.

At last my father stated finally: "I'm not going to argue about it. I am keeping the goats."

The old Chief flashed back in his own language: "That means that my people will go hungry when the dry season comes."

"Go to the police, then," said my father, and looked triumphant.

There was, of course, no more to be said.

The old man sat silent, his head bent, his hands dangling helplessly over his withered knees. Then he rose, the young men helping him, and he stood facing my father. He spoke once again, very stiffly; and turned away and went home to his village.

"What did he say?" asked my father of the young man, who laughed uncomfortably and would not meet his eyes.

"What did he say?" insisted my father.

Our cook stood straight and silent, his brows knotted together. Then he spoke. "My father says: All this land, this land you call yours, is his land, and belongs to our people."

Having made this statement, he walked off into the bush after his father, and we did not see him again.

Our next cook was a migrant from Nyasaland, with no expectations of greatness.

Next time the policeman came on his rounds he was told this story. He remarked: "That kraal has no right to be there; it should have been moved long ago. I don't know why no one has done anything about it. I'll have a chat with the Native Commissioner next week. I'm going over for tennis on Sunday, anyway."

Some time later we heard that Chief Mshlanga and his people had been moved two hundred miles east, to a proper Native Reserve; the Government land was going to be opened up for white settlement soon.

I went to see the village again, about a year afterwards. There was nothing there. Mounds of red mud, where the huts had been, had long swathes of rotting thatch over them, veined with the red galleries of the white ants. The pumpkin vines rioted everywhere, over the bushes, up the lower branches of trees so that the great golden balls rolled underfoot and dangled overhead: it was a festival of pumpkins. The bushes were crowding up, the new grass sprang vivid green.

The settler lucky enough to be allotted the lush warm valley (if he chose to cultivate this particular section) would find, suddenly, in the middle of a mealie field, the plants were growing fifteen feet tall, the weight of the cobs dragging at the stalks, and wonder what unsuspected vein of richness he had struck.

## FLANNERY O'CONNOR (1925–1964)

*A Good Man Is Hard to Find*                                                    *1953*

The grandmother didn't want to go to Florida. She wanted to visit some of her connections in east Tennessee and she was seizing at every chance to change Bailey's mind. Bailey was the son she lived with, her only son. He was sitting on the edge of his chair at the table, bent over the orange sports section of the *Journal*. "Now look here, Bailey," she said, "see here, read this," and she stood with one hand on her thin hip and the other rattling the newspaper at his bald head. "Here this fellow that calls himself The Misfit is aloose from the Federal Pen and headed toward Florida and you read here what it says he did to these people. Just you read it. I wouldn't take my children in any direction with a criminal like that aloose in it. I couldn't answer to my conscience if I did."

Bailey didn't look up from his reading so she wheeled around then and faced the children's mother, a young woman in slacks, whose face was as broad and innocent as a cabbage and was tied round with a green head-kerchief that had two points on the top like rabbit's ears. She was sitting on the sofa, feeding the baby his apricots out of a jar. "The children have been to Florida before," the old lady said. "You all ought to take them somewhere else for a change so they would see different parts of the world and be broad. They never have been to east Tennessee."

The children's mother didn't seem to hear her but the eight-year-old boy, John Wesley, a stocky child with glasses, said, "If you don't want to go to Florida, why dontcha stay at home?" He and the little girl, June Star, were reading the funny papers on the floor.

"She wouldn't stay at home to be queen for a day," June Star said without raising her yellow head.

"Yes and what would you do if this fellow, The Misfit, caught you?" the grandmother asked.                                                                                    5

"I'd smack his face," John Wesley said.

"She wouldn't stay at home for a million bucks," June Star said. "Afraid she'd miss something. She has to go everywhere we go."

"All right, Miss," the grandmother said. "Just remember that the next time you want me to curl your hair."

June Star said her hair was naturally curly.

The next morning the grandmother was the first one in the car, ready to go. She had her big black valise that looked like the head of a hippopotamus in one corner, and underneath it she was hiding a basket with Pitty Sing, the cat, in it. She didn't intend for the cat to be left alone in the house for three days because he would miss her too much and she was afraid he might brush against one of the gas burners and accidentally asphyxiate himself. Her son, Bailey, didn't like to arrive at a motel with a cat.

She sat in the middle of the back seat with John Wesley and June Star on either side of her. Bailey and the children's mother and the baby sat in the front and they left Atlanta at eight forty-five with the mileage on the car at 55890. The grandmother wrote this down because she thought it would be interesting to say how many miles they had been when they got back. It took them twenty minutes to reach the outskirts of the city.

The old lady settled herself comfortably, removing her white cotton gloves and putting them up with her purse on the shelf in front of the back window. The children's mother still had on slacks and still had her head tied up in a green kerchief, but the grandmother had on a navy blue straw sailor hat with a bunch of white violets on the brim and a navy blue dress with a small white dot in the print. Her collar and cuffs were white organdy trimmed with lace and at her neckline she had pinned a purple spray of cloth violets containing a sachet. In case of an accident, anyone seeing her dead on the highway would know at once that she was a lady.

She said she thought it was going to be a good day for driving, neither too hot nor too cold, and she cautioned Bailey that the speed limit was fifty-five miles an hour and that the patrolmen hid themselves behind billboards and small clumps of trees and sped out after you before you had a chance to slow down. She pointed out interesting details of the scenery: Stone Mountain; the blue granite that in some places came up to both sides of the highway; the brilliant red clay banks slightly streaked with purple; and the various crops that made rows of green lace-work on the ground. The trees were full of silver-white sunlight and the meanest of them sparkled. The children were reading comic magazines and their mother had gone back to sleep.

"Let's go through Georgia fast so we won't have to look at it much," John Wesley said.

"If I were a little boy," said the grandmother, "I wouldn't talk about my native state that way. Tennessee has the mountains and Georgia has the hills."

"Tennessee is just a hillbilly dumping ground," John Wesley said, "and Georgia is a lousy state too."

"You said it," June Star said.

"In my time," said the grandmother, folding her thin veined fingers, "children were more respectful of their native states and their parents and everything else. People did right then. Oh look at the cute little pickaninny!" she said and pointed to a Negro child standing in the door of a shack. "Wouldn't that make a picture,

10

15

now?" she asked and they all turned and looked at the little Negro out of the back window. He waved.

"He didn't have any britches on," June said.

"He probably didn't have any," the grandmother explained. "Little niggers 20 in the country don't have things like we do. If I could paint, I'd paint that picture," she said.

The children exchanged comic books.

The grandmother offered to hold the baby and the children's mother passed him over the front seat to her. She set him on her knee and bounced him and told him about the things they were passing. She rolled her eyes and screwed up her mouth and stuck her leathery thin face into his smooth bland one. Occasionally he gave her a faraway smile. They passed a large cotton field with five or six graves fenced in the middle of it, like a small island. "Look at the graveyard!" the grandmother said, pointing it out. "That was the old family burying ground. That belonged to the plantation."

"Where's the plantation?" John Wesley asked.

"Gone With the Wind," said the grandmother. "Ha. Ha."

When the children finished all the comic books they had brought, they opened 25 the lunch and ate it. The grandmother ate a peanut butter sandwich and an olive and would not let the children throw the box and the paper napkins out the window. When there was nothing else to do they played a game by choosing a cloud and making the other two guess what shape it suggested. John Wesley took one the shape of a cow and June Star guessed a cow and John Wesley said, no, an automobile, and June Star said he didn't play fair, and they began to slap each other over the grandmother.

The grandmother said she would tell them a story if they would keep quiet. When she told a story, she rolled her eyes and waved her head and was very dramatic. She said once when she was a maiden lady she had been courted by a Mr. Edgar Atkins Teagarden from Jasper, Georgia. She said he was a very good-looking man and a gentleman and that he brought her a watermelon every Saturday afternoon with his initials cut in it, E. A. T. Well, one Saturday, she said, Mr. Teagarden brought the watermelon and there was nobody at home and he left it on the front porch and returned in his buggy to Jasper, but she never got the watermelon, she said, because a nigger boy ate it when he saw the initials, E. A. T.! This story tickled John Wesley's funny bone and he giggled and giggled but June Star didn't think it was any good. She said she wouldn't marry a man that just brought her a watermelon on Saturday. The grandmother said she would have done well to marry Mr. Teagarden because he was a gentleman and had bought Coca-Cola stock when it first came out and that he had died only a few years ago, a very wealthy man.

They stopped at The Tower for barbecued sandwiches. The Tower was a part stucco and part wood filling station and dance hall set in a clearing outside of Timothy. A fat man named Red Sammy Butts ran it and there were signs stuck here and there on the building and for miles up and down the highway saying, TRY RED SAMMY'S FAMOUS BARBECUE. NONE LIKE FAMOUS RED SAMMY'S! RED SAM! THE FAT BOY WITH THE HAPPY LAUGH. A VETERAN! SAMMY'S YOUR MAN!

Red Sammy was lying on the bare ground outside The Tower with his head under a truck while a gray monkey about a foot high, chained to a small chinaberry tree, chattered nearby. The monkey sprang back into the tree and got on the highest limb as soon as he saw the children jump out of the car and run toward him.

Inside, The Tower was a long dark room with a counter at one end and tables at the other and dancing space in the middle. They all sat down at a broad table next to the nickelodeon and Red Sam's wife, a tall burnt-brown woman with hair and eyes lighter than her skin, came and took their order. The children's mother put a dime in the machine and played "The Tennessee Waltz," and the grandmother said that tune always made her want to dance. She asked Bailey if he would like to dance but he only glared at her. He didn't have a naturally sunny disposition like she did and trips made him nervous. The grandmother's brown eyes were very bright. She swayed her head from side to side and pretended she was dancing in her chair. June Star said play something she could tap to so the children's mother put in another dime and played a fast number and June Star stepped out onto the dance floor and did her tap routine.

"Ain't she cute?" Red Sam's wife said, leaning over the counter. "Would         30
you like to come be my little girl?"

"No I certainly wouldn't," June Star said. "I wouldn't live in a broken-down place like this for a million bucks!" and she ran back to the table.

"Ain't she cute?" the woman repeated, stretching her mouth politely.

"Aren't you ashamed?" hissed the grandmother.

Red Sam came in and told his wife to quit lounging on the counter and hurry with these people's order. His khaki trousers reached just to his hip bones and his stomach hung over them like a sack of meal swaying under his shirt. He came over and sat down at a table nearby and let out a combination sigh and yodel. "You can't win," he said. "You can't win," and he wiped his sweating red face off with a gray handkerchief. "These days you don't know who to trust," he said. "Ain't that the truth?"

"People are certainly not nice like they used to be," said the grandmother.         35

"Two fellers come in here last week," Red Sammy said, "driving a Chrysler. It was a old beat-up car but it was a good one and these boys looked all right to me. Said they worked at the mill and you know I let them fellers charge the gas they bought? Now why did I do that?"

"Because you're a good man!" the grandmother said at once.

"Yes'm, I suppose so," Red Sam said as if he were struck with the answer.

His wife brought the orders, carrying the five plates all at once without a tray, two in each hand and one balanced on her arm. "It isn't a soul in this green world of God's that you can trust," she said. "And I don't count anybody out of that, not nobody," she repeated, looking at Red Sammy.

"Did you read about that criminal, The Misfit, that's escaped?" asked the         40
grandmother.

"I wouldn't be a bit surprised if he didn't attact this place right here," said the woman. "If he hears about it being here, I wouldn't be none surprised to see him. If he hears it's two cent in the cash register, I wouldn't be a tall surprised if he . . ."

"That'll do," Red Sam said. "Go bring these people their Co'Colas," and the woman went off to get the rest of the order.

"A good man is hard to find," Red Sammy said. "Everything is getting terrible. I remember the day you could go off and leave your screen door unlatched. Not no more."

He and the grandmother discussed better times. The old lady said that in her opinion Europe was entirely to blame for the way things were now. She said the way Europe acted you would think we were made of money and Red Sam said it was no use talking about it, she was exactly right. The children ran outside into the white sunlight and looked at the monkey in the lacy chinaberry tree. He was busy catching fleas on himself and biting each one carefully between his teeth as if it were a delicacy.

They drove off again into the hot afternoon. The grandmother took cat naps   45 and woke up every few minutes with her own snoring. Outside of Toombsboro she woke up and recalled an old plantation that she had visited in this neighborhood once when she was a young lady. She said the house had six white columns across the front and that there was an avenue of oaks leading up to it and two little wooden trellis arbors on either side in front where you sat down with your suitor after a stroll in the garden. She recalled exactly which road to turn off to get to it. She knew that Bailey would not be willing to lose any time looking at an old house, but the more she talked about it, the more she wanted to see it once again and find out if the little twin arbors were still standing. "There was a secret panel in this house," she said craftily, not telling the truth but wishing that she were, "and the story went that all the family silver was hidden in it when Sherman° came through but it was never found . . ."

"Hey!" John Wesley said, "Let's go see it! We'll find it! We'll poke all the woodwork and find it! Who lives there? Where do you turn off at? Hey Pop, can't we turn off there?"

"We never have seen a house with a secret panel!" June Star shrieked. "Let's go to the house with the secret panel! Hey, Pop, can't we go see the house with the secret panel!"

"It's not far from here, I know," the grandmother said. "It wouldn't take over twenty minutes."

Bailey was looking straight ahead. His jaw was as rigid as a horseshoe. "No," he said.

The children began to yell and scream that they wanted to see the house   50 with the secret panel. John Wesley kicked the back of the front seat and June Star hung over her mother's shoulder and whined desperately into her ear that they never had any fun even on their vacation, and that they could never do what THEY wanted to do. The baby began to scream and John Wesley kicked the back of the seat so hard that his father could feel the blows in his kidney.

"All right!" he shouted, and drew the car to a stop at the side of the road. "Will you all shut up? Will you all just shut up for one second? If you don't shut up, we won't go anywhere."

"It would be very educational for them," the grandmother murmured.

"All right," Bailey said, "but get this: this is the only time we're going to stop for anything like this. This is the one and only time."

"The dirt road that you have to turn down is about a mile back," the grandmother directed. "I marked it when we passed."

"A dirt road," Bailey groaned.   55

___

*Sherman:* William Tecumseh Sherman (1820–1891), Union general during the Civil War.

After they had turned around and were headed toward the dirt road, the grandmother recalled other points about the house, the beautiful glass over the front doorway and the candle-lamp in the hall. John Wesley said that the secret panel was probably in the fireplace.

"You can't go inside this house," Bailey said. "You don't know who lives there."

"While you all talk to the people in front, I'll run around behind and get in a window," John Wesley suggested.

"We'll all stay in the car," his mother said.

They turned onto the dirt road and the car raced roughly along in a swirl of pink dust. The grandmother recalled the times when there were no paved roads and thirty miles was a day's journey. The dirt road was hilly and there were sudden washes in it and sharp curves on dangerous embankments. All at once they would be on a hill, looking down over the blue tops of trees for miles around, then the next minute, they would be in a red depression with the dust-coated trees looking down on them.

"This place had better turn up in a minute," Bailey said, "or I'm going to turn around."

The road looked as if no one had traveled on it in months.

"It's not much farther," the grandmother said and just as she said it, a horrible thought came to her. The thought was so embarrassing that she turned red in the face and her eyes dilated and her feet jumped up, upsetting her valise in the corner. The instant the valise moved, the newspaper top she had over the basket under it rose with a snarl and Pitty Sing, the cat, sprang onto Bailey's shoulder.

The children were thrown to the floor and their mother, clutching the baby, was thrown out the door onto the ground, the old lady was thrown into the front seat. The car turned over once and landed right-side-up in a gulch on the side of the road. Bailey remained in the driver's seat with the cat—gray-striped with a broad white face and an orange nose—clinging to his neck like a caterpillar.

As soon as the children saw they could move their arms and legs, they scrambled out of the car, shouting, "We've had an ACCIDENT!" The grandmother was curled up under the dashboard, hoping she was injured so that Bailey's wrath would not come down on her all at once. The horrible thought she had had before the accident was that the house she had remembered so vividly was not in Georgia but in Tennessee.

Bailey removed the cat from his neck with both hands and flung it out the window against the side of a pine tree. Then he got out of the car and started looking for the children's mother. She was sitting against the side of the red gutted ditch, holding the screaming baby, but she only had a cut down her face and a broken shoulder. "We've had an ACCIDENT!" the children screamed in a frenzy of delight.

"But nobody's killed," June Star said with disappointment as the grandmother limped out of the car, her hat still pinned to her head but the broken front brim standing up at a jaunty angle and the violet spray hanging off the side. They all sat down in the ditch, except the children, to recover from the shock. They were all shaking.

"Maybe a car will come along," said the children's mother hoarsely.

"I believe I have injured an organ," said the grandmother, pressing her side, but no one answered her. Bailey's teeth were clattering. He had on a yellow

60

65

sport shirt with bright blue parrots designed in it and his face was as yellow as the shirt. The grandmother decided that she would not mention that the house was in Tennessee.

The road was about ten feet above and they could see only the tops of the trees on the other side of it. Behind the ditch they were sitting in there were more woods, tall and dark and deep. In a few minutes they saw a car some distance away on top of a hill, coming slowly as if the occupants were watching them. The grandmother stood up and waved both arms dramatically to attract their attention. The car continued to come on slowly, disappeared around a bend and appeared again, moving even slower, on top of the hill they had gone over. It was a big black battered hearse-like automobile. There were three men in it.

It came to a stop just over them and for some minutes, the driver looked down with a steady expressionless gaze to where they were sitting, and didn't speak. Then he turned his head and muttered something to the other two and they got out. One was a fat boy in black trousers and a red sweat shirt with a silver stallion embossed on the front of it. He moved around on the right side of them and stood staring, his mouth partly open in a kind of loose grin. The other had on khaki pants and a blue striped coat and a gray hat pulled down very low, hiding most of his face. He came around slowly on the left side. Neither spoke.

The driver got out of the car and stood by the side of it, looking down at them. He was an older man than the other two. His hair was just beginning to gray and he wore silver-rimmed spectacles that gave him a scholarly look. He had a long creased face and didn't have on any shirt or undershirt. He had on blue jeans that were too tight for him and was holding a black hat and a gun. The two boys also had guns.

"We've had an ACCIDENT!" the children screamed.

The grandmother had the peculiar feeling that the bespectacled man was someone she knew. His face was as familiar to her as if she had known him all her life but she could not recall who he was. He moved away from the car and began to come down the embankment, placing his feet carefully so that he wouldn't slip. He had on tan and white shoes and no socks, and his ankles were red and thin. "Good afternoon," he said. "I see you all had a little spill."

"We turned over twice!" said the grandmother.

"Oncet," he corrected. "We seen it happen. Try their car and see will it run, Hiram," he said quietly to the boy with the gray hat.

"What you got that gun for?" John Wesley asked, "Whatcha gonna do with that gun?"

"Lady," the man said to the children's mother, "would you mind calling them children to sit down by you? Children make me nervous. I want all you all to sit down right together there where you're at."

"What are you telling us what to do for?" June Star asked.

Behind them the line of woods gaped like a dark open mouth. "Come here," said their mother.

"Look here now," Bailey began suddenly, "we're in a predicament! We're in . . ."

The grandmother shrieked. She scrambled to her feet and stood staring. "You're The Misfit!" she said. "I recognized you at once."

"Yes'm," the man said, smiling slightly as if he were pleased in spite of himself to be known, "but it would have been better for all of you, lady, if you hadn't of reckernized me."

Bailey turned his head sharply and said something to his mother that shocked even the children. The old lady began to cry and The Misfit reddened.

"Lady," he said, "don't you get upset: Sometimes a man says things he don't mean. I don't reckon he meant to talk to you thataway."

"You wouldn't shoot a lady, would you?" the grandmother said and removed a clean handkerchief from her cuff and began to slap at her eyes with it.

The Misfit pointed the toe of his shoe into the ground and made a little hole and then covered it up again. "I would hate to have to," he said.

"Listen," the grandmother almost screamed, "I know you're a good man. You don't look a bit like you have common blood. I know you must come from nice people!"

"Yes mam," he said, "finest people in the world." When he smiled he showed a row of strong white teeth. "God never made a finer woman than my mother and my daddy's heart was pure gold," he said. The boy with the red sweat shirt had come around behind them and was standing with his gun at his hip. The Misfit squatted down on the ground. "Watch them children, Bobby Lee," he said. "You know they make me nervous." He looked at the six of them huddled together in front of him and he seemed to be embarrassed as if he couldn't think of anything to say. "Ain't a cloud in the sky," he remarked, looking up at it. "Don't see no sun but don't see no cloud neither."

"Yes, it's a beautiful day," said the grandmother. "Listen," she said, "you shouldn't call yourself The Misfit because I know you're a good man at heart. I can just look at you and tell."

"Hush!" Bailey yelled. "Hush! Everybody shut up and let me handle this!" He was squatting in the position of a runner about to sprint forward but he didn't move.

"I pre-chate that, lady," The Misfit said and drew a little circle in the ground with the butt of his gun.

"It'll take a half a hour to fix this here car," Hiram called, looking over the raised hood of it.

"Well, first you and Bobby Lee get him and that little boy to step over yonder with you," The Misfit said, pointing to Bailey and John Wesley. "The boys want to ask you something," he said to Bailey. "Would you mind stepping back in them woods there with them?"

"Listen," Bailey began, "we're in a terrible predicament. Nobody realizes what this is," and his voice cracked. His eyes were as blue and intense as the parrots in his shirt and he remained perfectly still.

The grandmother reached up to adjust her hat brim as if she were going to the woods with him but it came off in her hand. She stood staring at it and after a second she let it fall on the ground. Hiram pulled Bailey up by the arm as if he were assisting an old man. John Wesley caught hold of his father's hand and Bobby Lee followed. They went off toward the woods and just as they reached the dark edge, Bailey turned and supporting himself against a gray naked pine trunk, he shouted, "I'll be back in a minute, Mamma, wait on me!"

85

90

95

"Come back this instant!" his mother shrilled but they all disappeared into the woods.

"Bailey Boy!" the grandmother called in a tragic voice but she found she was looking at The Misfit squatting on the ground in front of her. "I just know you're a good man," she said desperately. "You're not a bit common!"

"Nome, I ain't a good man," The Misfit said after a second as if he had considered her statement carefully, "but I ain't the worst in the world neither. My daddy said I was different breed of dog from my brothers and sisters. 'You know,' Daddy said, 'it's some that can live their whole life out without asking about it and it's others has to know why it is, and this boy is one of the latters. He's going to be into everything!' " He put on his black hat and looked up suddenly and then away deep into the woods as if he were embarrassed again. "I'm sorry I don't have on a shirt before you ladies," he said, hunching his shoulders slightly. "We buried our clothes that we had on when we escaped and we're just making do until we can get better. We borrowed these from some folks we met," he explained.

"That's perfectly all right," the grandmother said. "Maybe Bailey has an extra shirt in his suitcase."                                    100

"I'll look and see terrectly," the Misfit said.

"Where are they taking him?" the children's mother screamed.

"Daddy was a card himself," the Misfit said. "You couldn't put anything over on him. He never got in trouble with the Authorities though. Just had the knack of handling them."

"You could be honest too if you'd only try," said the grandmother. "Think how wonderful it would be to settle down and live a comfortable life and not have to think about somebody chasing you all the time."

The Misfit kept scratching in the ground with the butt of his gun as if he     105
were thinking about it. "Yes'm, somebody is always after you," he murmured.

The grandmother noticed how thin his shoulder blades were just behind his hat because she was standing up looking down on him. "Do you ever pray?" she asked.

He shook his head. All she saw was the black hat wiggle between his shoulder blades. "Nome," he said.

There was a pistol shot from the woods, followed closely by another. Then silence. The old lady's head jerked around. She could hear the wind move through the tree tops like a long satisfied insuck of breath. "Bailey Boy!" she called.

"I was a gospel singer for a while," The Misfit said. "I been most everything. Been in the arm service, both land and sea, at home and abroad, been twict married, been an undertaker, been with the railroads, plowed Mother Earth, been in a tornado, seen a man burnt alive oncet," and he looked up at the children's mother and the little girl who were sitting close together, their faces white and their eyes glassy; "I even seen a woman flogged," he said.

"Pray, pray," the grandmother began, "pray, pray . . . ."                       110

"I never was a bad boy that I remember of," The Misfit said in an almost dreamy voice, "but somewheres along the line I done something wrong and got sent to the penitentiary. I was buried alive," and he looked up and held her attention to him by a steady stare.

"That's when you should have started to pray," she said. "What did you do to get sent to the penitentiary that first time?"

"Turn to the right, it was a wall," The Misfit said, looking up again at the cloudless sky. "Turn to the left, it was a wall. Look up it was a ceiling, look down it was a floor. I forgot what I done, lady. I set there and set there, trying to remember what it was I done and I ain't recalled it to this day. Oncet in a while, I would think it was coming to me, but it never come."

"Maybe they put you in by mistake," the old lady said vaguely.

"Nome," he said. "It wasn't no mistake. They had the papers on me."    115

"You must have stolen something," she said.

The Misfit sneered slightly. "Nobody had nothing I wanted," he said. "It was a head-doctor at the penitentiary said what I had done was kill my daddy but I know that for a lie. My daddy died in nineteen ought nineteen of the epidemic flu and I never had a thing to do with it. He was buried in the Mount Hopewell Baptist churchyard and you can go there and see for yourself."

"If you would pray," the old lady said, "Jesus would help you."

"That's right," The Misfit said.

"Well then, why don't you pray?" she asked trembling with delight suddenly.    120

"I don't want no hep," he said. "I'm doing all right by myself."

Bobby Lee and Hiram came ambling back from the woods. Bobby Lee was dragging a yellow shirt with bright blue parrots in it.

"Throw me that shirt, Bobby Lee," The Misfit said. The shirt came flying at him and landed on his shoulder and he put it on. The grandmother couldn't name what the shirt reminded her of. "No, lady," The Misfit said while he was buttoning it up. "I found out the crime don't matter. You can do one thing or you can do another, kill a man or take a tire off his car, because sooner or later you're going to forget what it was you done and just be punished for it."

The children's mother had begun to make heaving noises as if she couldn't get her breath. "Lady," he asked, "would you and that little girl like to step off yonder with Bobby Lee and Hiram and join your husband?"

"Yes, thank you," the mother said faintly. Her left arm dangled helplessly    125 and she was holding the baby, who had gone to sleep, in the other. "Hep that lady up, Hiram," The Misfit said as she struggled to climb out of the ditch, "and Bobby Lee, you hold onto that little girl's hand."

"I don't want to hold hands with him," June Star said. "He reminds me of a pig."

The fat boy blushed and laughed and caught her by the arm and pulled her off into the woods after Hiram and her mother.

Alone with The Misfit, the grandmother found that she had lost her voice. There was not a cloud in the sky nor any sun. There was nothing around her but woods. She wanted to tell him that he must pray. She opened and closed her mouth several times before anything came out. Finally she found herself saying, "Jesus, Jesus," meaning Jesus will help you, but the way she was saying it, it sounded as if she might be cursing.

"Yes'm," The Misfit said as if he agreed. "Jesus thown everything off balance. It was the same case with Him as with me except He hadn't committed any crime and they could prove I had committed one because they had the papers on me.

Of course," he said, "they never shown me any papers. That's why I sign myself now. I said long ago, you get you a signature and sign everything you do and keep a copy of it. Then you'll know what you done and you can hold up the crime to the punishment and see do they match and in the end you'll have something to prove you ain't been treated right. I call myself The Misfit," he said, "because I can't make what all I done wrong fit what all I gone through in punishment."

There was a piercing scream from the woods, followed closely by a pistol report. "Does it seem right to you, lady, that one is punished a heap and another ain't punished at all?" 130

"Jesus!" the old lady cried. "You've got good blood! I know you wouldn't shoot a lady! I know you come from nice people! Pray! Jesus, you ought not to shoot a lady: I'll give you all the money I've got!"

"Lady," The Misfit said, looking beyond her far into the woods, "there never was a body that give the undertaker a tip."

There were two more pistol reports and the grandmother raised her head like a parched old turkey hen crying for water and called, "Bailey Boy, Bailey Boy!" as if her heart would break.

"Jesus was the only One that ever raised the dead," The Misfit continued, "and He shouldn't have done it. He thrown everything off balance. If He did what He said, then it's nothing for you to do but thow away everything and follow Him, and if He didn't, then it's nothing for you to do but enjoy the few minutes you got left the best way you can—by killing somebody or burning down his house or doing some other meanness to him. No pleasure but meanness," he said and his voice had become almost a snarl.

"Maybe He didn't raise the dead," the old lady mumbled, not knowing what she was saying and feeling so dizzy that she sank down in the ditch with her legs twisted under her. 135

"I wasn't there so I can't say He didn't," The Misfit said, "I wisht I had of been there," he said, hitting the ground with his fist. "It ain't right I wasn't there because if I had of been there I would of known. Listen lady," he said in a high voice, "if I had of been there I would of known and I wouldn't be like I am now." His voice seemed about to crack and the grandmother's head cleared for an instant. She saw the man's face twisted close to her own as if he were going to cry and she murmured, "Why you're one of my babies. You're one of my own children!" She reached out and touched him on the shoulder. The Misfit sprang back as if a snake had bitten him and shot her three times through the chest. Then he put his gun down on the ground and took off his glasses and began to clean them.

Hiram and Bobby Lee returned from the woods and stood over the ditch, looking down at the grandmother who half-sat and half lay in a puddle of blood with her legs crossed under her like a child's and her face smiling up at the cloudless sky.

Without his glasses, The Misfit's eyes were red-rimmed and pale and defenseless-looking. "Take her off and thow her where you thown the others," he said, picking up the cat that was rubbing itself against his leg.

"She was a talker, wasn't she?" Bobby Lee said, sliding down the ditch with a yodel.

"She would of been a good woman," The Misfit said, "if it had been somebody     140
there to shoot her every minute of her life."

"Some fun!" Bobby Lee said.

"Shut up, Bobby Lee," The Misfit said. "It's no real pleasure in life."

# TILLIE OLSEN (b. 1913)

## I Stand Here Ironing                                    *1953–1954*

I stand here ironing, and what you asked me moves tormented back and forth
with the iron.

"I wish you would manage the time to come in and talk with me about
your daughter. I'm sure you can help me understand her. She's a youngster who
needs help and whom I'm deeply interested in helping."

"Who needs help.". . . Even if I came, what good would it do? You think
because I am her mother I have a key, or that in some way you could use me as
a key? She has lived for nineteen years. There is all that life that has happened
outside of me, beyond me.

And when is there time to remember, to sift, to weigh, to estimate, to total?
I will start and there will be an interruption and I will have to gather it all together
again. Or I will become engulfed with all I did or did not do, with what should
have been and what cannot be helped.

She was a beautiful baby. The first and only one of our five that was beautiful     5
at birth. You do not guess how new and uneasy her tenancy in her now-loveliness.
You did not know her all those years she was thought homely, or see her poring
over her baby pictures, making me tell her over and over how beautiful she had
been—and would be, I would tell her—and was now, to the seeing eye. But the
seeing eyes were few or nonexistent. Including mine.

I nursed her. They feel that's important nowadays. I nursed all the children,
but with her, with all the fierce rigidity of first motherhood, I did like the books
then said. Though her cries battered me to trembling and my breasts ached with
swollenness, I waited till the clock decreed.

Why do I put that first? I do not even know if it matters, or if it explains
anything.

She was a beautiful baby. She blew shining bubbles of sound. She loved
motion, loved light, loved color and music and textures. She would lie on the
floor in her blue overalls patting the surface so hard in ecstasy her hands and
feet would blur. She was a miracle to me, but when she was eight months old I
had to leave her daytimes with the woman downstairs to whom she was no miracle
at all, for I worked or looked for work and for Emily's father, who "could no
longer endure" (he wrote in his good-bye note) "sharing want with us."

I was nineteen. It was the pre-relief, pre-WPA world of the depression. I
would start running as soon as I got off the streetcar, running up the stairs, the
place smelling sour, and awake or asleep to startle awake, when she saw me she
would break into a clogged weeping that could not be comforted, a weeping I
can hear yet.

After a while I found a job hashing at night so I could be with her days,     10 and it was better. But it came to where I had to bring her to his family and leave her.

It took a long time to raise the money for her fare back. Then she got chicken pox and I had to wait longer. When she finally came, I hardly knew her, walking quick and nervous like her father, looking like her father, thin, and dressed in a shoddy red that yellowed her skin and glared at the pockmarks. All the baby loveliness gone.

She was two. Old enough for nursery school they said, and I did not know then what I know now—the fatigue of the long day, and the lacerations of group life in the kinds of nurseries that are only parking places for children.

Except that it would have made no difference if I had known. It was the only place there was. It was the only way we could be together, the only way I could hold a job.

And even without knowing, I knew. I knew the teacher that was evil because all these years it has curdled into my memory, the little boy hunched in the corner, her rasp, "why aren't you outside, because Alvin hits you? that's no reason, go out, scaredy." I knew Emily hated it even if she did not clutch and implore "don't go Mommy" like the other children, mornings.

She always had a reason why we should stay home. Momma, you look sick.    15
Momma, I feel sick. Momma, the teachers aren't there today, they're sick. Momma, we can't go, there was a fire there last night. Momma, it's a holiday today, no school, they told me.

But never a direct protest, never rebellion. I think of our others in their three-, four-year-oldness—the explosions, the tempers, the denunciations, the demands—and I feel suddenly ill. I put the iron down. What in me demanded that goodness in her? And what was the cost, the cost to her of such goodness?

The old man living in the back once said in his gentle way: "You should smile at Emily more when you look at her." What *was* in my face when I looked at her? I loved her. There were all the acts of love.

It was only with the others I remembered what he said, and it was the face of joy, and not of care or tightness or worry I turned to them—too late for Emily. She does not smile easily, let alone almost always as her brothers and sisters do. Her face is closed and sombre, but when she wants, how fluid. You must have seen it in her pantomimes, you spoke of her rare gift for comedy on the stage that rouses a laughter out of the audience so dear they applaud and applaud and do not want to let her go.

Where does it come from, that comedy? There was none of it in her when she came back to me that second time, after I had had to send her away again. She had a new daddy now to learn to love, and I think perhaps it was a better time.

Except when we left her alone nights, telling ourselves she was old enough.    20
"Can't you go some other time, Mommy, like tomorrow?" she would ask. "Will it be just a little while you'll be gone? Do you promise?"

The time we came back, the front door open, the clock on the floor in the hall. She rigid awake. "It wasn't just a little while. I didn't cry. Three times I called you, just three times, and then I ran downstairs to open the door so you could come faster. The clock talked loud. I threw it away, it scared me what it talked."

She said the clock talked loud again that night I went to the hospital to have Susan. She was delirious with the fever that comes before red measles, but she was fully conscious all the week I was gone and the week after we were home when she could not come near the new baby or me.

She did not get well. She stayed skeleton thin, not wanting to eat, and night after night she had nightmares. She would call for me, and I would rouse from exhaustion to sleepily call back: "You're all right, darling, go to sleep, it's just a dream," and if she still called, in a sterner voice, "now go to sleep, Emily, there's nothing to hurt you." Twice, only twice, when I had to get up for Susan anyhow, I went in to sit with her.

Now when it is too late (as if she would let me hold and comfort her like I    25
do the others) I get up and go to her at once at her moan or restless stirring. "Are you awake, Emily? Can I get you something?" And the answer is always the same: "No, I'm all right, go back to sleep, Mother."

They persuaded me at the clinic to send her away to a convalescent home in the country where "she can have the kind of food and care you can't manage for her, and you'll be free to concentrate on the new baby." They still send children to that place. I see pictures on the society page of sleek young women planning affairs to raise money for it, or dancing at the affairs, or decorating Easter eggs or filling Christmas stockings for the children.

They never have a picture of the children so I do not know if the girls still wear those gigantic red bows and the ravaged looks on the every other Sunday when parents can come to visit "unless otherwise notified"—as we were notified the first six weeks.

Oh it is a handsome place, green lawns and tall trees and fluted flower beds. High up on the balconies of each cottage the children stand, the girls in their red bows and white dresses, the boys in white suits and giant red ties. The parents stand below shrieking up to be heard and the children shriek down to be heard, and between them the invisible wall "Not To Be Contaminated by Parental Germs or Physical Affection."

There was a tiny girl who always stood hand in hand with Emily. Her parents never came. One visit she was gone. "They moved her to Rose Cottage" Emily shouted in explanation. "They don't like you to love anybody here."

She wrote once a week, the labored writing of a seven-year-old. "I am fine.    30
How is the baby. If I write my leter nicly I will have a star. Love." There never was a star. We wrote every other day, letters she could never hold or keep but only hear read—once. "We simply do not have room for children to keep any personal possessions," they patiently explained when we pieced one Sunday's shrieking together to plead how much it would mean to Emily, who loved so to keep things, to be allowed to keep her letters and cards.

Each visit she looked frailer. "She isn't eating." they told us.

(They had runny eggs for breakfast or mush with lumps, Emily said later, I'd hold it in my mouth and not swallow. Nothing ever tasted good, just when they had chicken.)

It took us eight months to get her released home, and only the fact that she gained back so little of her seven lost pounds convinced the social worker.

I used to try to hold and love her after she came back, but her body would stay stiff, and after a while she'd push away. She ate little. Food sickened her, and I think much of life too. Oh she had physical lightness and brightness, twinkling by on skates, bouncing like a ball up and down up and down over the jump rope, skimming over the hill; but these were momentary.

She fretted about her appearance, thin and dark and foreign-looking at a time when every little girl was supposed to look or thought she should look a chubby blonde replica of Shirley Temple. The doorbell sometimes rang for her, but no one seemed to come and play in the house or be a best friend. Maybe because we moved so much.

There was a boy she loved painfully through two school semesters. Months later she told me how she had taken pennies from my purse to buy him candy. "Licorice was his favorite and I brought him some every day, but he still liked Jennifer better'n me. Why, Mommy?" The kind of question for which there is no answer.

School was a worry to her. She was not glib or quick in a world where glibness and quickness were easily confused with ability to learn. To her overworked and exasperated teachers she was an overconscientious "slow learner" who kept trying to catch up and was absent entirely too often.

I let her be absent, though sometimes the illness was imaginary. How different from my now-strictness about attendance with the others. I wasn't working. We had a new baby, I was home anyhow. Sometimes, after Susan grew old enough, I would keep her home from school, too, to have them all together.

Mostly Emily had asthma, and her breathing, harsh and labored, would fill the house with a curiously tranquil sound. I would bring the two old dresser mirrors and her boxes of collections to her bed. She would select beads and single earrings, bottle tops and shells, dried flowers and pebbles, old postcards and scraps, all sorts of oddments; then she and Susan would play Kingdom, setting up landscapes and furniture, peopling them with action.

Those were the only times of peaceful companionship between her and Susan. I have edged away from it, that poisonous feeling between them, that terrible balancing of hurts and needs I had to do between the two, and did so badly, those earlier years.

Oh there are conflicts between the others too, each one human, needing, demanding, hurting, taking—but only between Emily and Susan, no, Emily toward Susan that corroding resentment. It seems so obvious on the surface, yet it is not obvious. Susan, the second child, Susan, golden- and curly-haired and chubby, quick and articulate and assured, everything in appearance and manner Emily was not; Susan, not able to resist Emily's precious things, losing or sometimes clumsily breaking them; Susan telling jokes and riddles to company for applause while Emily sat silent (to say to me later: that was *my* riddle, Mother, I told it to Susan); Susan, who for all the five years' difference in age was just a year behind Emily in developing physically.

I am glad for that slow physical development that widened the difference between her and her contemporaries, though she suffered over it. She was too vulnerable for that terrible world of youthful competition, of preening and parading, of constant measuring of yourself against every other, of envy, "If I had that copper hair," "If I had that skin. . . ." She tormented herself enough about not looking like the others, there was enough of the unsureness, the having to be conscious of words before you speak, the constant caring—what are they thinking of me? without having it all magnified by the merciless physical drives.

35

40

Ronnie is calling. He is wet and I change him. It is rare there is such a cry now. That time of motherhood is almost behind me when the ear is not one's own but must always be racked and listening for the child cry, the child call. We sit for a while and I hold him, looking out over the city spread in charcoal with its soft aisles of light. "Shoogily," he breathes and curls closer. I carry him back to bed, asleep. *Shoogily*. A funny word, a family word, inherited from Emily, invented by her to say: *comfort*.

In this and other ways she leaves her seal, I say aloud. And startle at my saying it. What do I mean? What did I start to gather together, to try and make coherent? I was at the terrible, growing years. War years. I do not remember them well. I was working, there were four smaller ones now, there was not time for her. She had to help be a mother, and housekeeper, and shopper. She had to set her seal. Mornings of crisis and near hysteria trying to get lunches packed, hair combed, coats and shoes found, everyone to school or Child Care on time, the baby ready for transportation. And always the paper scribbled on by a smaller one, the book looked at by Susan then mislaid, the homework not done. Running out to that huge school where she was one, she was lost, she was a drop; suffering over the unpreparedness, stammering and unsure in her classes.

There was so little time left at night after the kids were bedded down. She would struggle over books, always eating (it was in those years she developed her enormous appetite that is legendary in our family) and I would be ironing, or preparing food for the next day, or writing V-mail to Bill, or tending the baby. Sometimes, to make me laugh, or out of her despair, she would imitate happenings or types at school.                    45

I think I said once: "Why don't you do something like this in the school amateur show?" One morning she phoned me at work, hardly understandable through the weeping: "Mother, I did it. I won, I won; they gave me first prize; they clapped and clapped and wouldn't let me go."

Now suddenly she was Somebody, and as imprisoned in her difference as she had been in anonymity.

She began to be asked to perform at other high schools, even in colleges, then at city and statewide affairs. The first one we went to, I only recognized her that first moment when thin, shy, she almost drowned herself into the curtains. Then: Was this Emily? The control, the command, the convulsing and deadly clowning, the spell, then the roaring, stamping audience, unwilling to let this rare and precious laughter out of their lives.

Afterwards: You ought to do something about her with a gift like that—but without money or knowing how, what does one do? We have left it all to her, and the gift has as often eddied inside, clogged and clotted, as been used and growing.

She is coming. She runs up the stairs two at a time with her light graceful     50
step, and I know she is happy tonight. Whatever it was that occasioned your call did not happen today.

"Aren't you ever going to finish the ironing, Mother? Whistler painted his mother in a rocker. I'd have to paint mine standing over an ironing board." This is one of her communicative nights and she tells me everything and nothing as she fixes herself a plate of food out of the icebox.

She is so lovely. Why did you want me to come in at all? Why were you concerned? She will find her way.

She starts up the stairs to bed. "Don't get me up with the rest in the morning." "But I thought you were having midterms." "Oh, those," she comes back in, kisses me, and says quite lightly, "in a couple of years when we'll all be atom-dead they won't matter a bit."

She has said it before. She *believes* it. But because I have been dredging the past, and all that compounds a human being is so heavy and meaningful in me, I cannot endure it tonight.

I will never total it all. I will never come in to say: She was a child seldom smiled at. Her father left me before she was a year old. I had to work her first six years when there was work, or I sent her home and to his relatives. There were years she had care she hated. She was dark and thin and foreign-looking in a world where the prestige went to blondeness and curly hair and dimples, she was slow where glibness was prized. She was a child of anxious, not proud, love. We were poor and could not afford for her the soil of easy growth. I was a young mother, I was a distracted mother. There were the other children pushing up, demanding. Her younger sister seemed all that she was not. There were years she did not want me to touch her. She kept too much in herself, her life was such she had to keep too much in herself. My wisdom came too late. She has much to her and probably little will come of it. She is a child of her age, of depression, of war, of fear.

Let her be. So all that is in her will not bloom—but in how many does it? There is still enough left to live by. Only help her to know—help make it so there is cause for her to know—that she is more than this dress on the ironing board, helpless before the iron.

## GRACE PALEY (b. 1922)

### Goodbye and Good Luck   (1959)

I was popular in certain circles, says Aunt Rose. I wasn't no thinner then, only more stationary in the flesh. In time to come, Lillie, don't be surprised—change is a fact of God. From this no one is excused. Only a person like your mama stands on one foot, she don't notice how big her behind is getting and sings in the canary's ear for thirty years. Who's listening? Papa's in the shop. You and Seymour, thinking about yourself. So she waits in a spotless kitchen for a kind word and thinks—poor Rosie. . . .

Poor Rosie! If there was more life in my little sister, she would know my heart is a regular college of feelings and there is such information between my corset and me that her whole married life is a kindergarten.

Nowadays you could find me any time in a hotel, uptown or downtown. Who needs an apartment to live like a maid with a dustrag in the hand, sneezing? I'm in very good with the bus boys, it's more interesting than home, all kinds of people, everybody with a reason. . . .

And my reason, Lillie, is a long time ago I said to the forelady, "Missus, if I can't sit by the window, I can't sit." "If you can't sit, girlie," she says politely, "go stand on the street corner." And that's how I got unemployed in novelty wear.

For my next job I answered an ad which said: "Refined young lady, medium

salary, cultural organization." I went by trolley to the address, the Russian Art
Theater of Second Avenue where they played only the best Yiddish plays. They
needed a ticket seller, someone like me, who likes the public but is very sharp
on crooks. The man who interviewed me was the manager, a certain type.

Immediately he said: "Rosie Lieber, you surely got a build on you!"

"It takes all kinds, Mr. Krimberg."

"Don't misunderstand me, little girl," he said. "I appreciate, I appreciate.
A young lady lacking fore and aft, her blood is so busy warming the toes and
the finger tips, it don't have time to circulate where it's most required."

Everybody likes kindness. I said to him: "Only don't be fresh, Mr. Krimberg,
and we'll make a good bargain."

We did: Nine dollars a week, a glass of tea every night, a free ticket once a    10
week for Mama, and I could go watch rehearsals any time I want.

My first nine dollars was in the grocer's hands ready to move on already,
when Krimberg said to me, "Rosie, here's a great gentleman, a member of this
remarkable theater, wants to meet you, impressed no doubt by your big brown
eyes."

And who was it, Lillie? Listen to me, before my very eyes was Volodya Vlashkin, called by the people of those days the Valentino of Second Avenue. I took
one look, and I said to myself: Where did a Jewish boy grow up so big? "Just
outside Kiev," he told me.

How? "My mama nursed me till I was six. I was the only boy in the village
to have such health."

"My goodness, Vlashkin, six years old! She must have had shredded wheat
there, not breasts, poor woman."

"My mother was beautiful," he said. "She had eyes like stars."    15

He had such a way of expressing himself, it brought tears.

To Krimberg, Vlashkin said after this introduction: "Who is responsible for
hiding this wonderful young person in a cage?"

"That is where the ticket seller sells."

"So, David, go in there and sell tickets for a half hour. I have something in
mind in regards to the future of this girl and this company. Go, David, be a good
boy. And you, Miss Lieber, please, I suggest Feinberg's for a glass of tea. The
rehearsals are long. I enjoy a quiet interlude with a friendly person."

So he took me there, Feinberg's, then around the corner, a place so full of    20
Hungarians, it was deafening. In the back room was a table of honor for him.
On the tablecloth embroidered by the lady of the house was "Here Vlashkin Eats."
We finished one glass of tea in quietness, out of thirst, when I finally made up
my mind what to say.

"Mr. Vlashkin, I saw you a couple weeks ago, even before I started working
here, in *The Sea Gull*. Believe me, if I was that girl, I wouldn't look even for a
minute on the young bourgeois fellow. He could fall out of the play altogether.
How Chekhov could put him in the same play as you, I can't understand."

"You liked me?" he asked, taking my hand and kindly patting it. "Well,
well, young people still like me . . . so, and you like the theater too? Good. And
you, Rose, you know you have such a nice hand, so warm to the touch, such a
fine skin, tell me, why do you wear a scarf around your neck? You only hide your
young, young throat. These are not olden times, my child, to live in shame."

"Who's ashamed?" I said, taking off the kerchief, but my hand right away went to the kerchief's place, because the truth is, it really was olden times, and I was still of a nature to melt with shame.

"Have some more tea, my dear."

"No, thank you, I am a samovar already."                                    25

"Dorfmann!" he hollered like a king. "Bring this child a seltzer with fresh ice!"

In weeks to follow I had the privilege to know him better and better as a person—also the opportunity to see him in his profession. The time was autumn; the theater full of coming and going. Rehearsing without end. After *The Sea Gull* flopped *The Salesman from Istanbul* played, a great success.

Here the ladies went crazy. On the opening night, in the middle of the first scene, one missus—a widow or her husband worked too long hours—began to clap and sing out, "Oi, oi, Vlashkin." Soon there was such a tumult, the actors had to stop acting. Vlashkin stepped forward. Only not Vlashkin to the eyes . . . a younger man with pitch-black hair, lively on restless feet, his mouth clever. A half a century later at the end of the play he came out again, a gray philosopher, a student of life from only reading books, his hands as smooth as silk. . . . I cried to think who I was—nothing—and such a man could look at me with interest.

Then I got a small raise, due to he kindly put in a good word for me, and also for fifty cents a night I was given the pleasure together with cousins, in-laws, and plain stage-struck kids to be part of a crowd scene and to see like he saw every single night the hundreds of pale faces waiting for his feelings to make them laugh or bend down their heads in sorrow.

The sad day came, I kissed my mama goodbye. Vlashkin helped me to get        30
a reasonable room near the theater to be more free. Also my outstanding friend would have a place to recline away from the noise of the dressing rooms. She cried and she cried. "This is a different way of living, Mama," I said. "Besides, I am driven by love."

"You! You, a nothing, a rotten hole in a piece of cheese, are you telling me what is life?" she screamed.

Very insulted, I went away from her. But I am good-natured—you know fat people are like that—kind, and I thought to myself, poor Mama . . . it is true she got more of an idea of life than me. She married who she didn't like, a sick man, his spirit already swallowed up by God. He never washed. He had an unhappy smell. His teeth fell out, his hair disappeared, he got smaller, shriveled up little by little, till goodbye and good luck he was gone and only came to Mama's mind when she went to the mailbox under the stairs to get the electric bill. In memory of him and out of respect for mankind, I decided to live for love.

Don't laugh, you ignorant girl.

Do you think it was easy for me? I had to give Mama a little something. Ruthie was saving up together with your papa for linens, a couple knives and forks. In the morning I had to do piecework if I wanted to keep by myself. So I made flowers. Before lunch time every day a whole garden grew on my table.

This was my independence, Lillie dear, blooming, but it didn't have no roots       35
and its face was paper.

Meanwhile Krimberg went after me too. No doubt observing the success of Vlashkin, he thought, "Aha, open sesame . . ." Others in the company similar. After me in those years were the following: Krimberg I mentioned. Carl Zimmer, played innocent young fellows with a wig. Charlie Peel, a Christian who fell in the soup by accident, a creator of beautiful sets. "Color is his middle name," says Vlashkin, always to the point.

I put this in to show you your fat old aunt was not crazy out of loneliness. In those noisy years I had friends among interesting people who admired me for reasons of youth and that I was a first-class listener.

The actresses—Raisele, Marya, Esther Leopold—were only interested in tomorrow. After them was the rich men, producers, the whole garment center; their past is a pincushion, future the eye of a needle.

Finally the day came, I no longer could keep my tact in my mouth. I said: "Vlashkin, I hear by carrier pigeon you have a wife, children, the whole combination."

"True, I don't tell stories. I make no pretense."                                    40

"That isn't the question. What is this lady like? It hurts me to ask, but tell me, Vlashkin . . . a man's life is something I don't clearly see."

"Little girl, I have told you a hundred times, this small room is the convent of my troubled spirit. Here I come to your innocent shelter to refresh myself in the midst of an agonized life."

"Ach, Vlashkin, serious, serious, who is this lady?"

"Rosie, she is a fine woman of the middle classes, a good mother to my children, three in number, girls all, a good cook, in her youth handsome, now no longer young. You see, could I be more frank? I entrust you, dear, with my soul."

It was some few months later at the New Year's ball of the Russian Artists      45
Club, I met Mrs. Vlashkin, a woman with black hair in a low bun, straight and too proud. She sat at a small table speaking in a deep voice to whoever stopped a moment to converse. Her Yiddish was perfect, each word cut like a special jewel. I looked at her. She noticed me like she noticed everybody, cold like Christmas morning. Then she got tired. Vlashkin called a taxi and I never saw her again. Poor woman, she did not know I was on the same stage with her. The poison I was to her role, she did not know.

Later on that night in front of my door I said to Vlashkin, "No more. This isn't for me. I am sick from it all. I am no home breaker."

"Girlie," he said, "don't be foolish."

"No, no, goodbye, good luck," I said. "I am sincere."

So I went and stayed with Mama for a week's vacation and cleaned up all the closets and scrubbed the walls till the paint came off. She was very grateful, all the same her hard life made her say, "Now we see the end. If you live like a bum, you are finally a lunatic."

After this few days I came back to my life. When we met, me and Vlashkin,      50
we said only hello and goodbye, and then for a few sad years, with the head we nodded as if to say, "Yes, yes, I know who you are."

Meanwhile in the field was a whole new strategy. Your mama and your grandmama brought around—boys. Your own father had a brother, you never even seen him. Ruben. A serious fellow, his idealism was his hat and his coat, "Rosie, I offer you a big new free happy unusual life." How? "With me, we will raise up the sands of Palestine to make a nation. That is the land of tomorrow for us Jews." "Ha-ha, Ruben, I'll go tomorrow then." "Rosie!" says Ruben. "We need strong women like you, mothers and farmers." "You don't fool me, Ruben, what you need is dray horses. But for that you need more money." "I don't like your attitude, Rose." "In that case, go and multiply. Goodbye."

Another fellow: Yonkel Gurstein, a regular sport, dressed to kill, with such an excitable nature. In those days—it looks to me like yesterday—the youngest girls wore undergarments like Battle Creek, Michigan. To him it was a matter of seconds. Where did he practice, a Jewish boy? Nowadays I suppose it is easier, Lillie? My goodness, I ain't asking you nothing—touchy, touchy. . . .

Well, by now you must know yourself, honey, whatever you do, life don't stop. It only sits a minute and dreams a dream.

While I was saying to all these silly youngsters "no, no, no," Vlashkin went to Europe and toured a few seasons . . . Moscow, Prague, London, even Berlin—already a pessimistic place. When he came back he wrote a book, you could get from the library even today, *The Jewish Actor Abroad.* If someday you're interested enough in my lonesome years, you could read it. You could absorb a flavor of the man from the book. No, no, I am not mentioned. After all, who am I?

When the book came out I stopped him in the street to say congratulations.     55
But I am not a liar, so I pointed out, too, the egotism of many parts—even the critics said something along such lines.

"Talk is cheap," Vlashkin answered me. "But who are the critics? Tell me, do they create? Not to mention," he continues, "there is a line in Shakespeare in one of the plays from the great history of England. It says, 'Self-loving is not so vile a sin, my liege, as self-neglecting.' This idea also appears in modern times in the moralistic followers of Freud. . . . Rosie, are you listening? You asked a question. By the way, you look very well. How come no wedding ring?"

I walked away from this conversation in tears. But this talking in the street opened the happy road up for more discussions. In regard to many things. . . . For instance, the management—very narrow-minded—wouldn't give him any more certain young men's parts. Fools. What youngest man knew enough about life to be as young as him?

"Rosie, Rosie," he said to me one day, "I see by the clock on your rosy, rosy face you must be thirty."

"The hands are slow, Vlashkin. On a week before Thursday I was thirty-four."

"Is that so? Rosie, I worry about you. It has been on my mind to talk to     60
you. You are losing your time. Do you understand it? A woman should not lose her time."

"Oi, Vlashkin, if you are my friend, what is time?"

For this he had no answer, only looked at me surprised. We went instead, full of interest but not with our former speed, up to my new place on Ninety-fourth Street. The same pictures on the wall, all of Vlashkin, only now everything painted red and black, which was stylish, and new upholstery.

A few years ago there was a book by another member of that fine company, an actress, the one that learned English very good and went uptown—Marya Kavkaz, in which she says certain things regarding Vlashkin. Such as, he was her lover for eleven years, she's not ashamed to write this down. Without respect for him, his wife and children, or even others who also may have feelings in the matter.

Now, Lillie, don't be surprised. This is called a fact of life. An actor's soul must be like a diamond. The more faces it got the more shining is his name. Honey, you will no doubt love and marry one man and have a couple kids and be happy forever till you die tired. More than that, a person like us don't have to know. But a great artist like Volodya Vlashkin . . . in order to make a job on the stage, he's got to practice. I understand it now, to him life is like a rehearsal.

Myself, when I saw him in *The Father-in-law*—an older man in love with a darling young girl, his son's wife, played by Raisele Maisel—I cried. What he said to this girl, how he whispered such sweetness, how all his hot feelings were on his face . . . Lillie, all this experience he had with me. The very words were the same. You can imagine how proud I was.

So the story creeps to an end.

I noticed it first on my mother's face, the rotten handwriting of time, scribbled up and down her cheeks, across her forehead back and forth—a child could read— it said, old, old, old. But it troubled my heart most to see these realities scratched on Vlashkin's wonderful expression.

First the company fell apart. The theater ended. Esther Leopold died from being very aged. Krimberg had a heart attack. Marya went to Broadway. Also Raisele changed her name to Roslyn and was a big comical hit in the movies. Vlashkin himself, no place to go, retired. It said in the paper, "an actor without peer, he will write his memoirs and spend his last years in the bosom of his family among his thriving grandchildren, the apple of his wife's doting eye."

This is journalism.

We made for him a great dinner of honor. At this dinner I said to him, for the last time, I thought, "Goodbye, dear friend, topic of my life, now we part." And to myself I said further: Finished. This is your lonesome bed. A lady what they call fat and fifty. You made it personally. From this lonesome bed you will finally fall to a bed not so lonesome, only crowded with a million bones.

And now comes? Lillie, guess.

Last week, washing my underwear in the basin, I get a buzz on the phone. "Excuse me, is this the Rose Lieber formerly connected with the Russian Art Theater?"

"It is."

"Well, well, how do you do, Rose? This is Vlashkin."

"Vlashkin! Volodya Vlashkin?"

"In fact. How are you, Rose?"

"Living, Vlashkin, thank you."

"You are all right? Really, Rose? Your health is good? You are working?"

"My health, considering the weight it must carry, is first-class. I am back for some years now where I started, in novelty wear."

"Very interesting."

"Listen, Vlashkin, tell me the truth, what's on your mind?"

"My mind? Rosie, I am looking up an old friend, an old warmhearted companion of more joyful days. My circumstances, by the way, are changed. I am retired, as you know. Also I am a free man."

"What? What do you mean?"

"Mrs. Vlashkin is divorcing me."

"What come over her? Did you start drinking or something from melancholy?"

"She is divorcing me for adultery."

"But, Vlashkin, you should excuse me, don't be insulted, but you got maybe seventeen, eighteen years on me, and even me, all this nonsense—this daydreams and nightmares—is mostly for the pleasure of conversation alone."

"I pointed all this out to her. My dear, I said, my time is past, my blood is as dry as my bones. The truth is, Rose, she isn't accustomed to have a man around all day, reading out loud from the papers the interesting events of our time, waiting for breakfast, waiting for lunch. So all day she gets madder and madder. By nighttime a furious old lady gives me my supper. She has information from the last fifty years to pepper my soup. Surely there was a Judas in that theater, saying every day, 'Vlashkin, Vlashkin, Vlashkin . . .' and while my heart was circulating with his smiles he was on the wire passing the dope to my wife."

"Such a foolish end, Volodya, to such a lively story. What is your plans?"

"First, could I ask you for dinner and the theater—uptown, of course? After this . . . we are old friends. I have money to burn. What your heart desires. Others are like grass, the north wind of time has cut out their heart. Of you, Rosie, I recreate only kindness. What a woman should be to a man, you were to me. Do you think, Rosie, a couple of old pals like us could have a few good times among the material things of this world?"                                                                                   90

My answer, Lillie, in a minute was altogether. "Yes, yes, come up," I said. "Ask the room by the switchboard, let us talk."

So he came that night and every night in the week, we talked of his long life. Even at the end of time, a fascinating man. And like men are, too, till time's end, trying to get away in one piece.

"Listen, Rosie," he explains the other day. "I was married to my wife, do you realize, nearly half a century. What good was it? Look at the bitterness. The more I think of it, the more I think we would be fools to marry."

"Volodya Vlashkin," I told him straight, "when I was young I warmed your cold back many a night, no questions asked. You admit it, I didn't make no demands. I was softhearted. I didn't want to be called Rosie Lieber, a breaker up of homes. But now, Vlashkin, you are a free man. How could you ask me to go with you on trains to stay in strange hotels, among Americans, not your wife? Be ashamed."

So now, darling Lillie, tell this story to your mama from your young mouth.          95
She don't listen to a word from me. She only screams, "I'll faint, I'll faint." Tell her after all I'll have a husband, which, as everybody knows, a woman should have at least one before the end of the story.

My goodness, I am already late. Give me a kiss. After all, I watched you grow from a plain seed. So give me a couple wishes on my wedding day. A long and happy life. Many years of love. Hug Mama, tell her from Aunt Rose, goodbye and good luck.

# Appendix A: Evaluating Fiction

*Evaluation* means the act of deciding what is good, bad, or mediocre. It requires a steady pursuit of the best—to be satisfied with less is to deny the best efforts of our greatest writers. Evaluation implies that there are ideal standards of excellence by which decisions about quality can be made, but it must be remembered that these standards are flexible, and may be applicable to works of literature written in all places and ages.

An evaluation is different from an essay on what you might like or dislike in a work (see Chapter 1, pp. 1–57). While your preferences are important in your evaluation, they are not as important as your judgment, and your judgment may lead you into positions that seem contrary to your preferences. In other words, it is possible to grant the excellence of a work or writer that you personally may not like.

This claim is not as contradictory as it may at first seem, for perceptions about literary works constantly change. You may have found that works others judge as good do not seem good to you. If such has been the case, you should try to live with the work for a time. You will learn to understand and like a good work of art when you give it enough time. If, however, you find that despite prolonged exposure to the work, you still do not concur in the general favorable judgment, be as certain as you can that your reaction is based on rational and logically defensible grounds.

## STANDARDS FOR EVALUATION

There is no precise answer to the problem of how to justify an evaluation. Evaluation is the most abstract, philosophical, and difficult writing you will do about literature. Standards of taste, social mores, and even morals differ from society to society and age to age; nonetheless, some works of art have been judged as great by generation after generation in many cultures. There are many standards to help you evaluate a literary work. Some of the major ones are described below, and many have been suggested in earlier chapters.

### Truth

Although *truth* or *truthful* is often used in speaking of literature to mean *realism* or *realistic,* its meaning here is carefully restricted. To speak of the truth is to imply generality and universality. Let us take some concrete illustrations.

Both Aesop's "The Fox and the Grapes" (p. 285) and St. Luke's "The Parable of the Prodigal Son" (p. 285) are among the oldest works of prose fiction included in this anthology. They were generated in social contexts that no longer exist and concern circumstances that are difficult to imagine in the twentieth century. Nevertheless, they remain as true (and relevant) for our time as they were when they were written. This is because both embody situations that human beings have always and will always face; both reflect patterns of human behavior that are as valid today as they were 2,500 years ago in Greece and 1,900 years ago in Palestine.

While most short stories cannot claim to have withstood this sort of extended test of time, those that survive and prosper beyond their initial publication do so because they, too, embody some essential fragment of truth about the human condition. Such stories measure up to one standard we use in deciding whether a work of art is good or bad, great or mediocre.

### Affirmativeness

*Affirmativeness* means here that human beings are worth caring about and writing about, no matter how debased the condition in which they live or how totally they abuse their state. All art should be affirmative. Although many works apparently say "no" to life, most say "yes," and a good argument can be made that the "no" works indirectly present a "yes." Thus, if a character like Dmitry Gurov (in Chekhov's "Lady with Lapdog") undergoes great psychological pain, the author must demonstrate that such suffering has value and meaning. If a character is happy at the end of the work, the author must show that this character's qualities have justified such good fortune. Life is again affirmed. If an unworthy character is fortunate at the end, the author still affirms human worth by suggesting a world in which such worth may become triumphant. In short, authors may portray the use and abuse of life, the love and the hate, the heights and the depths, but their vision is always that life is valuable and worthy of respect and dignity. The best works are those that make this affirmation forcefully, without being platitudinous or didactic.

### "The Joint Force and Full Result of All"

Alexander Pope discusses literary evaluation at length in *The Essay on Criticism*. He insists that a critic should not judge a work simply by its parts but should judge the *whole*—"the joint force and full result of all." You can profit from Pope's wisdom. You should consider the total effect of the work, both as an artistic form and as a cause of impressions and emotions in yourself. Bear in mind that a great work may contain imperfections, but if the sum total of the work is impressive, the flaws assume minor importance.

By the same token, excellent technique in itself does not justify a claim for excellence. An interesting plot, a balanced and carefully handled structure, a touching love story, a valid or important moral—none of these attributes alone can support a total judgment of "good" unless everything in the work is balanced.

Another important phase of the "joint force and full result of all" is the way in which you become involved as you read. Most of what you read, if it has merit, will cause you to become emotionally involved with the characters and actions. You have perhaps observed that characters in some works seem real to you or that incidents are described so vividly that you feel as though you had witnessed them. In these cases you were experiencing the pleasure of involvement. The problem here is whether your pleasure was fleeting and momentary or whether it has assumed more permanence.

### Vitality

A good work of literature has a life of its own and can be compared to a human being. A work can grow in the sense that your repeated experience with it will produce insights that you did not have in your previous readings. Examples of such stories include Poe's "The Masque of the Red Death" and Jackson's "The Lottery." Readers and critics alike constantly find new insights and beauties in these works.

### Beauty

Beauty is closely allied with unity, symmetry, harmony, and proportion. To discover the relationship of parts to whole—their logical and chronological and associational functions within the work—is to perceive beauty in a work. In the eighteenth century people believed that "variety within order" constituted beauty; the extent to which Pope's couplets vary within the pattern of the neoclassic couplet is an illustration of this ideal. The Romantic and post-Romantic periods held that beauty could be found only through greater freedom. This belief in freedom has produced such characteristics of modern literature as originality for its own sake, experimentation in verse and prose forms, freedom of syntax, stream-of-consciousness narration, and personal diction. Despite the apparent change of emphasis, however, the concepts of unity and proportion are still valid and applicable. Studies of style, structure, point of view, and tone are therefore all means to the goal of determining whether stories are beautiful. Any one of these studies is an avenue toward evaluation. Remember, however, that an excellence in any one of them does not make a story excellent.

## WRITING AN EVALUATION ESSAY

### *Organizing Your Essay*

In your essay you will attempt to answer the question of whether the work you have studied is good or not. If so, why? If not, why not? The grounds for your evaluation must be artistic. Although some works may be good pieces of political argument, or successfully controversial, your goal is to judge them as works of art.

**INTRODUCTION.**   In the introduction you can briefly summarize your evaluation, which will be your central idea, and list the points by which you expect to demonstrate the validity of your assessment. To assist your reader's comprehension of your ideas, you should note any unique facts or background about the work you are evaluating.

**BODY.**   In the body, demonstrate the grounds for your judgment; your principal points will be the positive or negative features of the work you are evaluating. Positive features include qualities of style, idea, structure, character, logic, point of view, and so on. Your discussion will analyze the probability, truth, force, or power with which the work embodies these positive aspects.

Avoid analysis for its own sake, and do not merely retell stories. If you are showing the excellence or deficiency of a character portrayal, you can include a description of the character, but remember that your discussion is to be pointed toward *evaluation,* not *description.* Therefore you must select details for discussion that will illustrate whether the work is good or bad. If you remember to keep your thematic purpose foremost, you should have little difficulty in making your discussion relate to your central idea.

CONCLUSION.    The conclusion should be a statement on the total result of the work you are evaluating. Your concern here is with total impressions. This part of evaluation should reemphasize your central idea.


## SAMPLE ESSAY

### An Evaluation of "The Chaser,"* by John Collier

[1]    Collier's "The Chaser" contrasts the dreams of youth with the cynicism of age. Because cynicism is dominant at the end, the story might be considered too negative, too bleak, and it might be criticized for this reason. To dismiss "The Chaser" without further thought, however, would be hasty; a careful reading shows that the story has genuine merit.° While a case may be made that the story is cynical and negative, a better case is that it is satirical and positive, demonstrating a corresponding excellence of technique.▫

[2]    The reason for considering "The Chaser" negatively as only a grim joke is the mistaken judgment that the old man has great wisdom along with his cynicism. It is true that he has seen people such as Alan Austen before. They have come to him wanting to make their sweethearts love them passionately, completely, worshipfully, and dependently. For such young people, the old man keeps a supply of inexpensive but infallible love potion. Beyond this, when they grow older and become tired of their potion-induced love, the old man also keeps an expensive and also infallible supply of untraceable poison— the "glove cleaner" or "life cleaner." The concluding words of the old man, "Au revoir," ("until we meet again"), indicate his knowledge that Austen will return someday for the poison. This cynicism, while justified in the light of Austen's character, seems too jarring a contrast to the enthusiasm of Austen's current passion for his lady, Diana. If the story were to do no more than show that young love ends in boredom and hatred, it would indeed be totally negative, and therefore would deserve to be dismissed.

[3]    While one may grant that the old man's judgment is right, and that Austen will grow discontented with the woman he now most enjoys, it by no means follows that "The Chaser" is bad literature. In fact, the story should be seen positively as a satirical attack on the shortsightedness of Austen and of the view that he represents. The old man tantalizes Austen with the following description of the love he is seeking:

> "For indifference," said the old man, "they [women who are scornful] substitute devotion. For scorn, adoration. Give one tiny measure of this to the young lady—its flavour is imperceptible in orange juice, soup, or cocktails—and however gay and giddy she is, she will change altogether. She will want nothing but solitude and you."

* See p. 263 for this story.
° Central Idea
▫ Thesis Sentence

This description suggests not love but enslavement—a fawning devotion that dehumanizes the woman and also makes a monster of the man who expects or demands such attention for himself. The old man's foreknowledge of Austen's eventual return demonstrates the depravity of this misinterpretation of love as total possessiveness. Rather than being held up as a typical, model young man, in other words, Collier satirically shows Austen as one who is corrupt right from the start.

[4]

The technique of the story is geared toward this satirical revelation of Austen's weakness and shortsightedness. After the first few paragraphs of exposition to make the situation clear, Collier develops the rest of the story using a dramatic point of view. There is no sympathetic voice explaining Austen's emotions. Instead, Austen speaks for himself, revealing his own flawed, shallow character while the old man plays the cynical, grimly insinuating game of salesmanship upon him. Because Collier gives the old man much of the dialogue, with Austen's words being mainly in response, Austen is unable to speak of any warm personal relationships, even if he were able to conceive of them. Instead, the talk is all of control and possession. In this way Collier uses technique to reveal Austen's shortcomings, and therefore to rule him out as a complete human being. The truth that Collier is stressing is symbolized by the old man's "glove cleaner," which represents the demeaning and destructive nature of the master-slave bond that Austen so earnestly seeks.

[5]

On balance, therefore, the story is a good one. As a satire, it is more affirmative than it may at first seem, for the positive basis against which Austen and the old man should be measured is a humanized love relationship entered into freely by equals. The bonding in such a relationship is not one of master-slave, but is instead one of mutual consent. Fidelity is freely given and is not extracted either by force, like that produced by the potion Austen comes to buy, or expectation. Through this means of satirical contrast, Collier's dramatic rendering of character and his attack on possessiveness make "The Chaser" true and affirmative. "The Chaser" is a fine and memorable story.

### Commentary on the Essay

The strategy of this evaluative essay is to use an apparent weakness of Collier's "The Chaser" as the basis of an argument asserting the strength and quality of the story. The logic of the essay is that the value of Collier's work may be found in his use of satire. The essay therefore demonstrates the principle that all aspects of a work should be considered when one is making an evaluation. Although a number of ideas and techniques are considered in the essay, these are not used as ends in themselves, but instead are introduced as evidence in the argument for the merits of the story.

Paragraph 1, the introductory paragraph, brings up the issue that the story might be dismissed after no more than a hasty reading; it also asserts the need for an evaluation based on more thought. The points to be developed in the body are stressed in the thesis sentence.

In the body of the essay, paragraph 2 deals with the uncritical, hasty reading that would make the story seem intolerably negative. The strategy here is one of concession, namely, that if the old man were to be considered authoritative, the story would be generally untrue, and would be weak for that reason. Paragraph 3 deals with the idea that "The Chaser" is in fact a satire and that it therefore should be read as a positive work in which the main characters are not admired but attacked. Paragraph 4 demonstrates how Collier's technique complements this satiric thrust. Collier's handling of the story underscores his satiric revelation. In the light of the argument carried out in the body of the essay, the concluding paragraph emphasizes again the "The Chaser" is a good story. The basis for this conclusion is that the view of love in "The Chaser" (developed in three sentences of this last paragraph) is the opposite of what the characters represent.

# Appendix B: Comparison-Contrast and Extended Comparison-Contrast

The comparison essay may be used to compare and contrast different authors, two or more works by the same author, different drafts of the same work, or characters, incidents, and ideas within the same work or in different works. Not only is comparison-contrast popular in literature courses, but it is one of the commonest approaches you will find in other disciplines.

## CLARIFY YOUR INTENTION

Your first problem in planning a comparison-contrast is to decide on a goal, for you may use the comparison-contrast method in a number of ways. One objective can be the equal and mutual illumination of two (or more) works. Thus, an essay comparing Frank O'Connor's "First Confession" (p. 172) and Nathaniel Hawthorne's "Young Goodman Brown" (p. 287) might be designed (1) to compare ideas, characters, or methods in these stories equally, without stressing or favoring either. But you might also wish (2) to emphasize "Young Goodman Brown," and therefore you would use "First Confession" as material for highlighting Hawthorne's work. You might also use the comparison-contrast method (3) to show your liking of one work (at the expense of another), or (4) to emphasize a method or idea that you think is especially noteworthy or appropriate. Your first task is therefore to decide where to place your emphasis.

## FIND COMMON GROUNDS FOR COMPARISON

The second stage in prewriting is to select the proper material—the grounds of your discussion. It is useless to try to compare dissimilar things. You need to put the works or writers you are comparing onto common ground. Compare like with like: idea with idea, characterization with characterization, symbolism with symbolism. Nothing can be learned from a comparison of "Welty's view of courage and Chekhov's view of love," but a comparison of "The relationship of love to stability and courage in Chekhov and Welty" suggests common ground, with points of both likeness and difference.

In searching for common ground, you may have to use your ingenuity a bit. Guy De Maupassant's "The Necklace" (p. 75) and Anton Chekhov's "Lady with Lapdog" (p. 367) at first may seem to be as different as they can be. Yet common grounds do exist for these works, such as "The Treatment of Self-Deceit," "The Effects of Chance on Human Affairs," or "The View of Women." As you can see, apparently unlike works can be put into a frame of reference that permits analytical comparison and contrast.

## METHODS OF COMPARISON

Let us assume that you have decided on your purpose and on the basis or bases of your comparison: You have done your reading, taken your notes, and formulated your argument. The remaining problem is the treatment of your material. Here are two acceptable ways.

One common method is to make your points first about one work and then for the other. This method can make your paper seem like two big lumps, and it also involves much repetition because you must repeat the same points as you treat your second subject.

A more effective method is to treat your main idea in its major aspects and to make references to the two (or more) works as the reference illustrates and illuminates your main idea. Thus you would be constantly referring to both works, sometimes within the same sentence, and would be reminding the reader of the point of your discussion. There are reasons for the superiority of the second method: (1) you do not repeat your points needlessly, for you document them as you raise them; (2) by constantly referring to the two works in relation to your common ground of comparison, you make your points without requiring a reader with a poor memory to reread previous sections.

### Avoid the "Tennis-Ball" Method

As you make your comparisons, do not confuse an interlocking method with a "tennis-ball" method, in which you bounce your subjects back and forth constantly and repetitively. The tennis-ball method is shown in the following excerpt from an essay on prejudice that compares Irwin Shaw's "Act of Faith" (p. 204) and Ralph Ellison's "Flying Home" (p. 301):

> In Shaw's story about anti-semitism, Jacob fears that he is being attacked by "new rocket bombs . . . for the Jews"(p. 210). Todd, in Ellison's story about racial hatred, fears being touched by the hands of white men (p. 353).

Shaw includes the incident of a Jewish writer severely beaten by hoodlums in Los Angeles on V-E Day (p. 211). Ellison includes the chilling fact that Mister Graves has personally killed five blacks. Shaw notes several times in the story that people believe that "the Jews were getting rich out of this war" (p. 211). Ellison repeatedly has his protagonist observe that black men are not allowed into combat. Shaw highlights the incident of the naval officer who claimed that "the Constitution of the United States says I have to serve in the same navy with Jews, but it doesn't say I have to eat at the same table with them" (p. 214). Ellison focuses on Mister Graves's assertion that "the nigguh brain ain't built right for high altitudes" (p. 353).

Imagine the effect of reading an entire essay presented in this fashion. Aside from its power to bore, the tennis-ball method does not give you the chance to develop your points. You should not feel so cramped that you cannot take several sentences to develop a point about one writer or subject before you bring in comparison with another.

A simple comparison-contrast essay may consider points of similarity or contrast in as few as two short stories. Such an essay might compare (or contrast) the use of the first-person speaker in "Blue Winds Dancing" (p. 107) and "First Confession" (p. 172), the character of the strong female protagonist in "A Worn Path" (p. 101) and in "María Concepción" (p. 125), the treatment of racial prejudice in "Flying Home" (p. 341) and "Slave on the Block" (p. 399), or any other common area of exploration that can be exemplified in two or three short stories.

In such a limited essay, you might consider treating each story in sequence, bringing each discussion back to the point of comparison (or contrast) in the topic sentences. Thus, an essay dealing with prejudice might consider Shaw's "Act of Faith," Ellison's "Flying Home," and Hughes's "Slave on the Block" in a series of discrete paragraphs, each of which takes up a different story and considers specific aspects such as character, setting, and symbol. The risk, with such an organization, is that your essay might break into three separate mini-essays, each of which exists without reference to the other two. One way to avoid this dilemma is to bring each section back to the comparative (or contrasting) topic in both the topic sentence and the body of the paragraph(s). Another way to avoid this sort of breakdown of unity is to organize the essay along different lines, treating each element under consideration in all three stories as a major topic. Thus, the essay might consider character, setting, and then symbol as they relate to or express prejudice in all three stories.

## THE EXTENDED COMPARISON-CONTRAST

For a longer essay, such as a limited research paper or the sort of extended essay required at the end of the semester, the technique of comparison-contrast may be used for many works. For essays of this larger scope, you will still need to develop common grounds for comparison, although with more works to discuss you will need to modify the method.

Let us assume that you have been asked to deal with five or six stories. You need first to find a common ground among them that you can use as your central, unifying idea. When you take your notes, sketch out your ideas, make your early drafts, and rearrange and shape your developing materials, try to bring all the works together on the common ground of this idea. Thus, in the following sample essay, all the works are treated on the common basis that they speak about the role of women in marriage and society.

When you contrast the works, you should try to form groups based on variations or differences. If three or four works treat a topic in one way while one or two do it in another, you can treat the topic itself in a straightforward contrast method and use details from the groups on either side of the issue to support your points. Again, it is desirable to use the analysis of a particular point based on one work so that you can make your essay concrete and vivid. But once you have exemplified your point, there is no need to go into any more detail from the other works than seems necessary to get your point across. In this way, you can keep your essay within limits; if you group your works on points of similarity, you do not need to go into excessive and unproductive detail.

## DOCUMENTATION AND THE EXTENDED COMPARISON-CONTRAST ESSAY

For the longer comparison-contrast essay you may find a problem in documentation. Generally you will not need to locate page numbers for references to major traits, ideas, or actions. But if you are quoting lines or passages, or if you are making any special or unusual reference, you may need to use footnotes or parenthetical references. For page numbers, the sample essay uses the parenthetical abbreviation system described in Appendix C. Be guided by this principle: If you make a specific reference, provide the page number. If you are referring to minor details that might easily be forgotten or not noticed, supply the page number. In dealing with larger events or more general points, you need not supply a specific citation.

## WRITING COMPARISON-CONTRAST ESSAYS

In the prewriting stage, you can begin by looking for groups of stories that share a common *subject*, *technique*, or *element*. Unless the topic of the essay is assigned, you can move in any direction that seems fruitful. You might, for example, find five stories that are written in the first person protagonist point of view. An essay developed out of this grouping might compare and contrast the ways each author uses this point of view to achieve similar (or quite distinct) effects. Or, you might identify four or five stories that make extensive use of symbolism, allegory, or irony. In these cases, you could begin to develop an essay that compares and contrasts the authors' uses of such devices. Sometimes, this process can be as simple as locating four stories with female protagonists and comparing the way each author develops his or her heroine. Another approach to the investigations and organizing of the prewriting process is available through *subject* (as opposed to *theme*). You might be able to identify a group of stories that deal directly or obliquely with such general subjects as love, death, youth, or war. Such groups provide an ideal opportunity for the comparison and contrasting of ideas.

Once you have identified both a general organizing principle (such as a shared type of character, technique, or subject) and a relevant group of stories, you can begin to refine and focus the direction that the essay will take. As you investigate each story, begin to note common or contrasting effects. In this process, you will begin to develop the central idea for the essay. At the same time, you can begin to select the most illustrative stories and separate them into similar and contrasting groups. In the sample essay which follows, for example, the subject of marriage is the common ground. The text provides thirteen stories that deal with marriage to some degree. Thus, each of these stories can be examined during the prewriting phase for comparative or contrasting ideas about marriage. Put as briefly as possible, such an examination might yield the following list of topics:

Petronius, "Widow of Ephesus": Infidelity, Faithfulness, Sexuality

Doyle, "Speckled Band": Liberation, Money

De Maupassant, "Necklace": Money, Class, Dissatisfaction

Crane, "Yellow Sky": New Marriage

Porter, "Concepción": Infidelity, Class, Community, Death

Collier, "Chaser": Servitude, Constriction, Boredom, Death

Jackson, "Nice People": New Marriage, Class, Conventionality

Steinbeck, "Chrysanthemums": Constriction, Defeat, Frustration

Lawrence, "Daughter": Liberation, New Marriage, Death, Money

Cheever, "Divorce": Constriction, Defeat, Class, Infidelity

Chekhov, "Lapdog": Constriction, Infidelity, Age

Olsen, "Ironing": Constriction, Money, Class, Children

Paley, "Good Luck": Infidelity, New Marriage, Conventionality

As such a schematic (and admittedly reductive) list is examined, a number of possible focuses should begin to emerge. You might, for example, deal with infidelity in marriage in connection with stories by Petronius, Porter,

Cheever, and Chekhov. Similarly, you might opt to explore the impact of class and money on marriage in stories by Doyle, De Maupassant, Lawrence, and Olsen. Whatever focus you choose, such an organizational process will bring you to the point where writing can begin.

### Organizing Your Essay

First you must narrow your subject into a topic that you can handle conveniently within the limits of the assignment. If you decide to write about the impact of marriage on female protagonists, for example, it would be foolish to try to deal with all thirteen relevant stories in the text. Rather, isolate a discrete subject and a reasonable number of stories that can illustrate the topic. Your instructor may assign specific authors, stories, or a specific number of stories for coverage. If this is not the case, you would be well advised to deal with no more than four or five different works.

**INTRODUCTION.**    You can begin with a general (but not too general) assertion about the element(s) or ideas that your essay will cover. However you begin, the introduction should state what works, authors, and elements or ideas are under consideration and should explain how you have narrowed the basis of your comparison. Your central idea will be a brief statement of what can be learned from your paper: the general similarities and differences that you have observed from your comparison and/or the superiority of one work or author over another. Your thesis sentence should anticipate the body of your essay.

**BODY.**    The body of your essay depends on the points you have chosen for comparison. You might be comparing a number of stories on the basis of *point of view* or *symbolism*, authors on *ideas*, or characters on *character traits*. In your discussion you would necessarily use the same methods that you would use in writing about a single work, except that here (1) you are exemplifying your points by reference to more subjects than one, and (2) your main purpose is to shed light on the subjects on which your comparison is based. In this sense, the methods you use in talking about point of view or symbolism are not "pure" but are instead subordinate to your aims of comparison-contrast.

**CONCLUSION.**    Here you are comparatively free to reflect on other ideas in the works you have compared, to make observations on comparative qualities, or to summarize briefly the basic grounds of your comparison. The conclusion of an extended comparison-contrast essay should represent a final bringing together of the materials. In the body of the essay you may not have referred to all the works in each paragraph; however, in the conclusion you should try to refer to them all, if possible.

If your writers belonged to any "period" or "school," you also might wish to show in your conclusion how they relate to these larger movements. References of this sort provide a natural common ground for comparison. Alternatively, you might use the conclusion to introduce a new idea or perspective that pulls most of the stories together and reinforces the points made in the essay.

## SAMPLE ESSAY
## (EXTENDED COMPARISON-CONTRAST)

### Marriage as a Force for Liberation or Imprisonment in Five Short Stories*

[1]
The popular image of marriage in America has long been one of perfect and idealized joy. Middle class marriage is presented by the mass media as a placid and pleasant experience punctuated by minor and amusing domestic dilemmas. Fathers happily go off to ill-defined but lucrative jobs; mothers cheerfully stay home and manage the details of domestic bliss. Such is not the case in much prose fiction. Here, we are shown a different and more realistic image of marriage. In some stories, marriage provides women with a means of escape from intolerable conditions, but in many others it is presented as a prisonhouse of lost potential, frustration, and despair.° These contrasting images of marriage can be traced in a comparison of five short stories: Arthur Conan Doyle's "The Adventure of the Speckled Band," D. H. Lawrence's "The Horse Dealer's Daughter," John Steinbeck's "The Chrysanthemums," Tillie Olsen's "I Stand Here Ironing," and John Cheever's "The Season of Divorce." While the marriages (or potential marriages) in these stories are quite different from each other, they all share a pattern that suggests either liberation or imprisonment. This pattern may be seen in an examination of the nature of the protagonists' lives and the symbolic settings in each story.□

[2]
For both Helen Stoner, in Doyle's "The Speckled Band," and Mabel Pervin, in Lawrence's "The Horse Dealer's Daughter," marriage represents escape from life-threatening situations and emotional imprisonment. Helen Stoner exists at the mercy of her vicious stepfather, Dr. Grimesby Roylott. She is virtually imprisoned in the crumbling ancestral mansion, Stoke Moran. Roylott treats Helen with cruel brutality; Sherlock Holmes notices the "five little livid spots, the marks of four fingers and a thumb" on Helen's wrist, and he deduces that she has "been cruelly used" (p. 37). Additionally, Roylott controls Helen financially, and this form of imprisonment will also be ended with marriage: Helen Stoner's mother "had not less than 1000 pounds a year—and this she

---

\* For the texts of these stories, please see the following pages: "The Speckled Band," p. 31; "The Horse Dealer's Daughter," p. 328; "The Chrysanthemums," p. 303; "I Stand Here Ironing," p. 429; "The Season of Divorce," p. 360.

° Central Idea

□ Thesis sentence

bequeathed to Dr. Roylott entirely while we resided with him, with a provision that a certain annual sum should be allowed to each of us in the event of our marriage" (p. 34). This "certain annual sum" turns out to be the motive for Roylott's consummate acts of villainy—the murder of Julia Stoner and the attempted murder of Helen.

[3] Like Helen Stoner, marriage for Mabel Pervin offers an escape from a psychological and economic prison of despair. Throughout most of the story, Helen is trapped in the bleak world of poverty and failure; indeed, Lawrence describes her as being "like one condemned" (p. 331). Her world is bounded by three settings all associated with despair and death: the "brutal and coarse" life in the Pervin household, the churchyard, and the "dead water" of the pond. Fergusson's passionate declaration of love—"I want you, I want to marry you, we're going to be married, quickly, quickly—to-morrow if I can"—redeems Mabel from these three worlds of death (p. 340).

[4] In contrast to these women, the female protagonists in Steinbeck's "The Chrysanthemums," Olsen's "I Stand Here Ironing," and Cheever's "The Season of Divorce" are all suppressed and imprisoned by marriage. Elisa Allen, in "The Chrysanthemums," is literally kept down on the farm; her marriage and her life are made more desperate and repressive by the limitations placed on women by society and by a kind but dull husband who simply does not understand Elisa's needs. Elisa longs for a life of passion, freedom, and creativity; she expresses these desires in her response to the tinker's description of his life on the open road: "It must be very nice. I wish women could do such things" (p. 308). The tinker's reply—"It ain't the right kind of life for a woman"—voices the strictures of marriage and society.

Like Elisa Allen, the protagonist-narrator in "I Stand Here Ironing" has led a life of constrained duty and limitation, a life imposed by marriage, family, and poverty. Marriage has not kept her at home. To the contrary, poverty and an irresponsible husband forced her to go to work (or to look for work) and to leave the rearing of her eldest daughter to others. The despair of marriage for this woman is reflected in the massive guilt she feels about her oldest daughter. The suffering and despair of the mother are summed up in what she will never say to the daughter:

[5]
> I will never total it all. I will never come in and say: She was a child seldom smiled at. Her father left me before she was a year old. I had to work her first six years when there was work, or I sent her home and to his relatives. There were years she had care she hated. . . . We were poor and could not afford for her the soil of easy growth. I was a young mother. (p. 434)

Such a life, and such marriages, have put "wrinkles" of pain and guilt on both mother and daughter, wrinkles that no amount of spiritual "ironing" will ever smooth out.

Ethel, the wife of the narrator in Cheever's "The Season of Divorce," shares with Elisa Allen and with Olsen's narrator a life of lost potential, suppression, and despair. Marriage and children have turned her existence into one of deadly routine and alienation. Like Elisa Allen, Ethel is fully aware of the trap and the lost opportunities that marriage embodies:

[6]    "In Grenoble," she said, "I wrote a long paper on Charles Stuart in French. A professor at the University of Chicago wrote me a letter. I couldn't read a French newspaper without a dictionary today, I don't have the time to follow any newspaper, and I am ashamed of my incompetence, ashamed of the way I look. Oh, I guess I love you, I do love the children, but I love myself, I love my life, it has some value and some promise for me and Trencher's roses make me feel that I'm losing this, that I'm losing my self-respect. Do you know what I mean, do you understand what I mean?" (p. 365)

The passage reflects Ethel's awareness that marriage has eroded her potential and that she has been forced to surrender her own competence and self-respect for her husband and children; it rings with a sense of lost hopes and chances. Ethel's husband, like Henry Allen, has no real sense of his wife's agony or despair; he answers her questions about understanding with a simple "no."

[7]    While marriage may represent liberation for two of these women and imprisonment for the other three, the settings in these short stories consistently suggest and symbolize constraint and enclosure. Thus, in "The Speckled Band" and "The Horse Dealer's Daughter," the settings represent the constriction that the female protagonists will escape through marriage. Conversely, the settings in the other three stories emphasize the prisonhouse that marriage has become for Elisa, Olsen's unnamed narrator, and Ethel.

[8]    The setting for much of "The Speckled Band," the Roylott estate called Stoke Moran, reflects the degree to which Helen Stoner is imprisoned and threatened by her stepfather. The house is described as being made of "gray, lichen-blotched stone"; the windows are "small" and "narrow," and covered with iron shutters (p. 41). The sense of imprisonment conveyed by the forbidding stone house and the narrow windows is augmented by the fact that the bedroom doors are locked every night and that Roylott keeps "a cheetah and a baboon, which wander freely over his grounds" (p. 34). This claustrophobic world serves as the setting in which Roylott threatens Helen Stoner's life; marriage (and the help of Sherlock Holmes) free her from this prison.

[9]    Mabel Pervin's world, though less blatantly prison-like, is no less deadly and constricting. Throughout the story, Mabel is linked with three key settings: the Pervin house, the churchyard, and the pond. All three reflect the morbid and constricted world from which marriage will release Mabel. The house, a world of "brutal and coarse" masculine pursuits, offers little hope for release; the dominant symbol associated with this house is draught horses in harness. The churchyard is the one place where Mabel feels secure: "she felt immune from the world, reserved within the thick churchyard wall as in another country" (p. 333). This setting, however, represents another kind of imprisonment—the constricting power of the past and death. And if the churchyard symbolizes the constrictions of death, the pond literally offers such enclosure. The "square, deep pond" has a bottom of "cold, rotten clay that fouled up into the water" (p. 335). Just as Fergusson's efforts literally save Mabel from the "dead cold pond," so his proposal saves her from the deadly constrictions that all three settings imply.

The settings in the remaining three stories are equally symbolic of imprisonment, despair, and lost potential. In these, however, the settings directly reinforce the numbing limitations imposed by marriage. In "The Chrysanthemums," Steinbeck carefully fashions a setting that symbolizes Elisa's narrow and frustrating world. The land and the sky initially suggest imprisonment: "The high grey-flannel fog of winter closed off the Salinas Valley from the sky and from all the rest of the world. On every side it sat like a lid on the mountains and made of the great valley a closed pot" (p. 303). Moving inward, toward the center of this "closed off" world, we see Elisa fenced in with her chrysanthemums, separated from the masculine world of animals and tractors; she is *inside* "the wire fence that protected her flower garden from cattle" (p. 304). If we extend the sense of setting to include Elisa's clothing, we can see that [10] Steinbeck draws the tightening web of imprisonment and suppression inward to Elisa's body:

> [Elisa's] figure looked blocked and heavy in her gardening costume, a man's black hat pulled low down over her eyes, clodhopper shoes, a figured print dress almost completely covered by a big corduroy apron with four big pockets . . . She wore heavy leather gloves to protect her hands while she worked. (p. 303)

Setting and clothing thus suggest constraint and limitation here; Elisa is revealed inside bulky and asexual clothing within the fenced garden and inside the "closed pot" of the Salinas Valley.

The setting in "I Stand Here Ironing" is more temporal and atmospheric than it is physical, but it is just as constrictive and destructive as Elisa Allen's farm or Ethel's apartment. Olsen's protagonist was, in the past of the story, trapped in a world of overwhelming poverty and responsibility. Marriage gave her an irresponsible husband who abandoned her, a child she could neither support nor nurture, and a need to "work or look for work and for Emily's father who 'could no longer endure' (he wrote in his good-bye note) sharing want with us" (p. 429). The circumstances of her marriage destroyed this woman's hopes of having a close and loving relationship with her daughter, Emily. Thus, the destructive forces of the marriage affected the mother and daughter [11] equally. As a result, the one clearly symbolic setting that reflects imprisonment and dehumanization is linked primarily to Emily; it is the convalescent home in the country where she was sent when she was seven. The narrator describes this place as Emily's prison, but the chains inherent in setting and situation clearly work on both women. Parents are allowed to visit children only once every two weeks, when they "stand below shrieking up to be heard and the children shriek down to be heard and between them the invisible wall 'Not To Be Contaminated by Parental Germs or Physical Affection' " (p. 431). The narrator notes that it took her eight months to get Emily "released" from this place.

Like Elisa Allen and Olsen's narrator, the wife-protagonist in Cheever's "The Season of Divorce" exists in settings that symbolize her imprisonment and eroded potential. The primary setting, a "walk-up in the East Fifties," shares images of constriction with Elisa Allen's world and images of poverty with the setting in "I Stand Here Ironing." We get the clearest sense of marriage here

as a prisonhouse when the husband-narrator describes the apartment during
[12]   the children's sickness: "It was impossible to ventilate or clean the house,
and when I came in, after walking through the cold from the bus stop, it stank
of cough syrup and tobacco, fruit cores and sickbeds. There were blankets
and pillows, ashtrays, and medicine glasses everywhere" (p. 364). The sense
of isolated constriction is brought into focus when Ethel "bitterly" complains
that "I haven't been out of this apartment in over two weeks . . . I know how
long it's been. I haven't had my shoes on in two weeks" (p. 364).

Other settings in "The Season of Divorce" are equally suggestive and
symbolic of the prisonhouse of marriage. New York City comes across as a
dingy and depressing enclosure: "the waste from the smokestacks along the
East River seemed to articulate, as legibly as the Pepsi-Cola plane, whole words
and sentences. Halcyon. Disaster" (pp. 365–366). More significantly, the playground where Ethel takes the children each day seems to be another version
of the prison that the apartment has become:

> I know what my wife looks like in the playground. She wears an old
> tweed coat, overshoes, and Army gloves, and a scarf is tied under her
[13]    chin. The playground is a fenced and paved lot between a slum and
> the river. (p. 362)

Ethel is trapped between the "slum and the river," between responsibility and
frustrated potential. As with Elisa Allen, her clothing is an extension of the
repressive setting, whether it be the presence of Army gloves or the absence
of shoes. The constrictions inherent in Ethel's marriage are defined by her
daily and habitual cycle from the apartment to the grocery store and the playground; her imprisonment is symbolized in the settings and the predictable
habits of marriage and motherhood that bring her to despair.

The five stories examined in this essay show us that marriage can be
liberating or constraining. The five women protagonists share symbolic settings
that suggest imprisonment, subjection, and lost potential. The liberations of
Helen Stoner and Mabel Pervin are balanced against the despairing imprisonment of Elisa Allen, Olsen's narrator, and Ethel. In these last three cases, other
symbols are used to suggest the chains of marriage and lost hopes of fulfillment.
[14]    Elisa's chrysanthemums and the roses that Dr. Trencher gives Ethel both symbolize the loss of hope and ultimate resignation to the bonds of habit and custom
imposed by marriage. Similarly, the narrator's ironing in "I Stand Here Ironing"
symbolizes both the chains of domestic service and the futile attempt to "iron
out" the pain of the past.

### Commentary on the Essay

This essay compares and contrasts five short stories on the common
ground or central idea of the liberating or constricting power of marriage.
Three of the stories, which illustrate that marriage can become a prison
of despair and failure, are compared with each other and contrasted with
the other two. In these others, marriage is seen as a way out of intolerable

circumstances. The essay thus illustrates both comparison and contrast as organizational strategies. In writing such an essay, you always have the option (unless told otherwise by your instructor) of using only comparison to organize the paper.

The introduction begins with a general statement about images of marriage, and moves quickly to fiction and then to the five stories discussed in the essay. The central idea—that marriage can be liberating or imprisoning—is stated in the fifth sentence. Sentence 6 announces the specific works (and authors) that will be discussed in the essay, and sentence 8 lists the topics in the order in which the essay will consider them. This topic sentence tells the reader that the essay will examine the role of marriage in the protagonist's life in each story and then the impact of symbolic setting as it relates to marriage.

The plan articulated in the introduction is carried out in the body of the essay (paragraphs 2–13). All five short stories are discussed in paragraphs 1, 7, and 14. For the most part, however, each paragraph in the body considers only one story. Comparison and contrast thus occur from paragraph to paragraph rather than in a single paragraph. Nevertheless, comparative or contrasting perspectives are consistently introduced in the transitional topic sentences that begin almost every paragraph (see the first sentence in paragraphs 2–7 and 9–12). These transitional sentences supply both continuity and comparison (or contrast) and signal these strategies to the reader through phrases like *for both* and *in contrast to*.

The organization of the body follows the plan announced in the topic sentence of the introduction. Thus paragraphs 2–6 deal in sequence with the life of the female protagonist and the role of marriage in each story. The women whom marriage liberates (in Doyle and Lawrence) are compared with each other. Similarly, the three protagonists imprisoned by marriage (in Steinbeck, Olsen, and Cheever) are compared with each other and contrasted with the first two. Paragraph 7 is transitional; it reintroduces from the introduction the idea that setting can symbolize the constraint that women either escape or gain in marriage. The remaining paragraphs of the body (8–13) consider the setting(s) of each story in the same order in which the stories were discussed in paragraphs 2–6. The danger inherent in this kind of organization is that the essay will break in half at paragraph 7, producing two miniature essays that are unrelated to each other. This essay avoids that problem by stressing the connection between marriage and symbolic setting in paragraphs 1 and 7–13.

The essay sticks to its topics with a good deal of rigor. We are told just enough about the protagonists' lives and about the settings to see the pattern of liberation or imprisonment. The essay avoids providing too much information about any one character or setting. In this way, it also avoids becoming simply a summary of plot or a description of setting. It is this technique of limiting the amount of information that permits the essay to deal with three separate settings in "The Horse Dealer's Daughter" in a single paragraph.

The conclusion (paragraph 14) summarizes the points made in the body of the essay and draws all five stories together again in its first three sentences. The remainder of the conclusion briefly introduces a new area of investigation (symbolism) that reinforces the observations already made in the essay. In this way, the conclusion suggests that elements of the short stories other than setting might have been examined to support the essay's central idea.

# Appendix C: Writing and Documenting the Research Essay

Research, as distinguished from pure criticism, refers to using primary and secondary sources for assistance in solving a literary problem. That is, in criticizing a work, pure and simple, you consult only the work in front of you (the primary source), whereas in doing research on the work, you consult not only the work but many other works that were written about it or that may shed light on it (secondary sources). Typical research tasks are to find out more about the historical period in which a story was written or about prevailing opinions of the times or about what modern (or earlier) critics have said about the work. It is obvious that a certain amount of research is always necessary in any critical job, or in any essay about a story. Looking up words in a dictionary, for example, is only minimal research; more vigorous research, and the type we are considering here, involves the use of introductions, critical articles, encyclopedias, biographies, critical studies, histories, and the like.

It is necessary that you put research in perspective. In general, students and scholars do research in order to uncover some of the accumulated "lore" of our civilization. This lore—the knowledge that presently exists—may be compared to a large cone that is constantly being filled. At the beginnings of human existence there was little knowledge of anything, and the cone was at its narrowest point. As civilization progressed, more and more knowledge appeared, and the cone thus began to fill. Each time a new piece of information or a new conclusion was recorded, a little more knowledge or lore was in effect poured into the cone, which accordingly became slightly fuller and wider. Though at present our cone of knowledge is quite full, it appears to be capable of infinite growth. Knowledge keeps piling up and new disciplines keep developing. It becomes more and more difficult for one person to accumulate more than a small portion of the entirety. Indeed, historians generally agree that the last person to know virtually everything about every existing discipline was Aristotle—2400 years ago.

If you grant that you cannot learn everything, you can make a positive start by recognizing that research can provide two things: (1) a systematic understanding of a portion of the knowledge filling the cone, and (2) an understanding of, and ability to handle, the methods by which you might someday be able to make your own contributions to the filling of the cone.

Thus far we have been speaking broadly about the relevance of research to any discipline. Our problem here, however, is literary research, the systematic study of library sources in order to illuminate a topic connected with a work of fiction.

## SELECTING A TOPIC

Frequently your instructor will ask for a research essay on a specific topic. However, if you have only a general research assignment, your first problem is to make your own selection. It may be helpful to have a general notion of the kind of research essay you would find most congenial. Here are some possibilities.

1. *An essay on a particular story.* You might treat character (for example, "The Character of Elisa in 'The Chrysanthemums'" or "The Question of Whether Young Goodman Brown Is a Hero or a Dupe"), or tone, point of view, setting, structure, and the like. A research paper on a single story is similar to an essay on the same story, except that the research paper takes into account more views and facts than those you are likely to have without the research. Please see the sample research essay, on Katherine Mansfield's "Miss Brill," to see how materials may be handled for such an assignment.

2. *An essay on a particular author.* The paper could be about an idea or some facet of style, imagery, setting, or tone of the author, tracing the origins and development of the topic through a number of different stories. An example might be "The Idea of the Individual as Developed by Hemingway in His Early Writing Career." This type of paper is particularly suitable for a number of shorter stories, though a topic like "Conrad's Idea of the Relationship Between Self-Esteem and Work" would be desirable as a topic for a longer story.

3. *An essay based on comparison and contrast.* There are two types:
    a. *A theme or artistic quality common to two or more authors.* Your intention might be to show points of similarity or contrast to show that one author's work may be read as a criticism of another's. A possible subject of one such paper might be "The Use of the First-Person Point of View by Joyce and Conrad," or "The Theme of Love and Sexuality in Jackson, Chekhov, and Lawrence."
    b. *Contrasting or opposing critical views of a particular work or body of works.* Sometimes much is to be gained from an examination of differing critical opinions on topics like "The Meaning of Shirley Jackson's 'The Lottery,'" "The Interpretations of Hawthorne's 'Young Goodman Brown,'" or "The Question of Steinbeck's Attitude Toward Women as Seen in 'The Chrysanthemums.'" Such a study would attempt to

determine the critical opinion and taste to which a story does or does not appeal, and it might also aim at conclusions about whether the work was/is in the advance or rear guard of its time.

4. *An essay showing the influence of an idea, an author, a philosophy, a political situation, or an artistic movement on specific works of an author or authors.* A paper on influences can be fairly direct, as in "Details of Early Twentieth-Century Mexican-American Culture as Reflected in Parédes's 'The Hammon and the Beans,' " or else it can be more abstract and critical, as in "The Influence of Early Twentieth-Century Oppression of Mexican Americans on the Narrator of 'The Hammon and the Beans.' "

5. *An essay on the origins of a particular work or type of work.* One avenue of research for such a paper might be to examine an author's biography to discover the germination and development of a work—for example, " 'The Old Chief Mshlanga' as an Outgrowth of Lessing's Life in Rhodesia-Zimbabwe." Another way of discovering origins might be to relate a work to a particular type or tradition: " 'Goodbye and Good Luck' and the Yiddish Tradition in Literature," or " 'Youth' and Its Relationship to Classical Stories about the Underworld."

If you consider these types, an idea of what to write may come to you. Perhaps you have particularly liked one author, or several authors. If so, you might start to think along the lines of types 1, 2, and 3. If you are interested in influences or in origins, then types 4 or 5 may suit you better.

If you still have not decided on a topic after rereading the works you have liked, then you should carry your search for a topic into your school library. Look up your author or authors in the card or computer catalogue. Usually the works written by the authors are included first, followed by works written about the authors. Your first goal should be to find a relatively recent book-length critical study published by a university press. Use your judgment here: Look for a title indicating that the book is a general one dealing with the author's major works rather than just one work. Study those chapters relevant to your primary story. Most writers of critical studies describe their purpose and plan in their introductions or first chapters, so begin with the first part of the book. If there is no separate chapter on the primary text, use the index and go to the relevant pages. Reading in this way should soon supply you with sufficient knowledge about the issues and ideas raised about the work to enable you to select a topic you will wish to study further. Once you have made your decision, you are ready to go ahead and develop a working bibliography.

## SETTING UP A BIBLIOGRAPHY

The best way to develop a working bibliography of books and articles is to begin with major critical studies of the writer or writers. Again, go to the catalogue and pick out books that have been published by university presses. These books will usually contain selective bibliographies. Be particularly careful to read the chapters on your primary story or stories and to look for the footnotes or endnotes. Quite often you can save time if you record the names of books and articles listed in these notes. Then refer to the bibliographies included at the ends of the books, and select any likely looking titles. Now, look at the dates of publication of the critical books you have been using. Let us suppose that you have been looking at three, published in 1951, 1963, and 1982. The chances are that the bibliography in a book published in 1982 will be fairly complete up through about 1979 or 1980, for the writer will usually have completed the manuscript two or three years before the book actually was published. What you should do then is to gather a bibliography of works published since 1979; you may assume that writers of critical works will have done the selecting for you of the most relevant works published before that time.

### Bibliographical Guides

Fortunately for students doing literary research, the Modern Language Association (MLA) of America has been providing a virtually complete bibliography of literary studies for years, not just in English and American literatures, but in the literatures of most modern foreign languages. The MLA started achieving completeness in the late 1950's, and by 1969 had reached such an advanced state that it divided the bibliography into four parts. All four parts are bound together in library editions. Most university and college libraries have a set of these bibliographies readily available on open shelves or tables. There are, of course, many other bibliographies useful for students doing literary research, such as the *Essay and General Literature Index*, the *International Index*, and various specific indexes. There are many more than can be mentioned here meaningfully. For most purposes, however, the *MLA International Bibliography* is more than adequate. Remember that as you progress in your reading, the notes and bibliographies in the works you consult also will constitute an unfolding bibliography. For the sample research essay in this Appendix, for example, a number of entries were discovered not on the first study of bibliographies, but from a study of the reference lists provided by writers of critical works.

The *MLA International Bibliography* is conveniently organized by period and author. If your author is Katherine Mansfield, for example, look her up under "English Literature X. Twentieth Century," the relevant listing for all twentieth-century English writers. If your author is Hawthorne, refer to "American Literature III. Nineteenth Century, 1800–1870." You will find most of your needed list of books and articles under the author's last name. For special help for students and researchers, the MLA has recently developed an exhaustive topics list that is keyed to the bibliographical entries. Using these topics you may locate important and relevant works that you might not have found with only the authors list. In the MLA bibliographies, journal references are abbreviated, but a lengthy list explaining abbreviations appears at the beginning of the volume. Using the MLA bibliographies, you should begin with the most recent one and then go backward to your stopping point. Be sure to get the complete information, especially volume numbers and years of publication, for each article and book you wish to consult. You are now ready to find your sources and to take notes.

## TAKING NOTES AND PARAPHRASING MATERIAL

There are many ways of taking notes, but the consensus is that the best method is to use note cards. If you have never used cards before, you might profit from consulting any one of a number of handbooks and special workbooks on research. A lucid and methodical explanation of taking notes on cards can be found in Glenn Leggett, et al. *Prentice-Hall Handbook for Writers*, 9th ed., pp. 440–46. (Englewood Cliffs: Prentice-Hall, 1985). The principal virtue of cards, aside from the fact that they stack neatly and do not tear easily, is that they may be classified, numbered, renumbered, shuffled, tried out in one place, rejected, and then used in another place (or thrown away), and arranged in order when you start to write.

### Taking Notes

**WRITE THE SOURCE ON EACH CARD.**   As you take notes, write down the source of your information on each card. This may sound like a lot of bother, but it is easier than finding out when you finally begin writing your research essay that you will need to go back to the library to get the correct source. You can save time if you take the complete data on one card—a "master card" for that source—and then make up an abbreviation to be used in your notes. Here is an example. Observe that the author's last name appears first:

---

Donovan, Josephine, ed. Feminist Literary Criticism: Explorations in Theory. Lexington: The University Press of Kentucky, 1975.

DONOVAN

---

If you plan to write many notes from this book, then the name "Donovan" will serve as a shorthand identification on each card. Be sure not to lose your complete master card, because you will need it in preparing your list of works cited.

**RECORD THE PAGE NUMBER FOR EACH NOTE.**   It would be hard to guess how much exasperation has been caused by the failure to record page numbers of notes. Be sure to get the page number down first, *before* you begin to take your note. If the detail you are noting goes from one page to the next in your source, record the exact spot where the page changes, as in this example:

---

Heilbrun and Stimson, in DONOVAN, pp. 63–64

63 After the raising of the feminist consciousness it is necessary to develop/ 64 "the growth of moral perception" through anger and the correction of social inequity.

---

The reason for being so careful is that you may wish to use only a part of a note you have taken, and when there are two pages you will need to be accurate in your location of what goes where.

**RECORD ONLY ONE FACT OR OPINION PER CARD.**   Record only one thing on each card—one quotation, one paraphrase, one observation—never two or more. You might be tempted to fill up the entire card, but such a try at economy often causes trouble because you might want to use different details recorded on the same card in different places as you write your research paper.

**USE QUOTATION MARKS FOR ALL QUOTED MATERIAL.**   A major problem in taking notes is to distinguish copied material from your own words. Here you must be extremely cautious. Always put quotation marks around *every direct quotation you copy verbatim from a source*. Make the quotation marks immediately, before you forget, so that you will always know that the words of your notes within quotation marks are the words of another writer.

Often, as you take a note, you may use some of your own words and some of the words from your source. In cases like this it is even more important to be cautious. Put quotation marks around *every word* that you take directly from the source, even if you find yourself literally with a note that resembles a picket fence. Later, when you begin writing your paper, your memory of what is yours and not yours will become dim, and if you use another's words in your own paper but do not grant recognition, you lay yourself open to the charge of plagiarism. Statistics are not available, but it seems clear that a great deal of outright plagiarism has been caused not by deliberate deception but rather by sloppy note-taking habits.

### Paraphrasing

When you take notes, it is best to paraphrase the sources. A paraphrase is a restatement in your own words, and because of this it is actually a first step in the writing of the essay. Chapter 2 in this book has a full treatment on making a précis or abstract (pp. 82–86). If you work on this technique, you will be well prepared to paraphrase for your research essay.

A big problem in paraphrasing is to capture the idea in the source without duplicating the words. The best way to do this is to read and reread the passage you are noting. Turn over the book or journal and write out the idea *in your own words* as accurately as you can. Once you have this note, compare it with the original and make corrections to improve your thought and emphasis. Add a short quotation if you believe it is needed, but be sure to use quotation marks. If your paraphrase is too close to the original, throw out the note and try again in your own words. It is worth making this effort, because often you can transform much of your note directly to the appropriate place in your research paper.

To see the problems of paraphrase, let us look at a paragraph of criticism and then see how a student doing research might take notes on it. The paragraph is by Richard F. Peterson, from an essay entitled "The Circle of Truth: The Stories of Katherine Mansfield and Mary Lavin," which was published in *Modern Fiction Studies*, 24 (1978): 383–394. In the passage to be quoted, Peterson is considering the structures of two Mansfield stories, "Bliss" and "Miss Brill":

Peterson 385

"Bliss" and "Miss Brill" are flawed stories, but not because the truth they reveal about their protagonists is too brutal or painful for the tastes of the common reader. In each story, the climax of the narrative suggests an arranged reality that leaves a lasting impression, not of life, but of the author's cleverness. This strategy of arrangement for dramatic effect or revelation, unfortunately, is common in Katherine Mansfield's fiction. Too often in her stories a dropped remark at the right or wrong moment, a chance meeting or discovery, an intrusive figure in the shape of a fat man at a ball or in the Café de Madrid, a convenient death of a hired man or a stranger dying aboard a ship, or a *deus ex machina* in the form of two doves, a dill pickle, or a fly plays too much of a role in / 386 creating a character's dilemma or deciding the outcome of the narrative. 385–386

Because the task of taking notes necessarily forces a shortening of this or any criticism, it also requires you to select and interpret. Taking notes therefore requires discrimination and judgment; good note taking is no easy task. There are some things that can guide you, however, when you go about the business of assimilating the large amount of inspecting and studying that you need to do when using your sources.

**THINK OF THE PURPOSE OF YOUR RESEARCH PAPER.**   You may not know exactly what you are "fishing for" when you start to take notes, for you cannot prejudge what your essay will contain. Research is a form of discovery. But soon you will notice patterns or large topics that your sources constantly explore. If you can accept one of these as your major topic, or focus of interest, you should use that as your guide in all your note taking.

For example, suppose you have started to take notes on criticism about Katherine Mansfield's "Miss Brill," and after a certain amount of reading you have decided to focus on the topic of structure in the story. This decision would prompt you to take a note about Peterson's disapproval of Mansfield's technique of arranging climaxes in her stories. In this instance, the following note would be adequate as a brief reminder of the content in the passage:

---

Peterson 385                                                            structure: negative

    Peterson claims that Mansfield creates climaxes that are too artificial, too unlifelike, giving the impression not of reality but of Mansfield's own "cleverness." 385

---

Let us now suppose that you wanted a fuller note in the expectation that you would need not just Peterson's general idea but also some of his supporting detail. Such a note might look like this:

---

Peterson 385                                                   structure: negative

    Peterson thinks that "Bliss" and "Miss Brill" are "flawed" because they have contrived endings that give the impression "not of life but of" Mansfield's "cleverness." She arranges things artificially, according to Peterson, to cause the endings in many other stories. Some of these things are chance remarks, discoveries, or meetings, together with other unexpected or chance incidents and objects. These contrivances make their stories imperfect. 385

---

When the actual essay is being written, any part of this note would be useful. The words are almost all the note taker's own, and the few quotations are within quotation marks. Note that Peterson, the critic, is properly recognized as the source of the criticism, so that the note could be adapted readily to a research paper. The key here is that your taking of notes should be guided by your developing plan for your essay.

**TITLE YOUR NOTES.** To help plan and develop the various parts of your essay, write a title for each of your notes as in the examples in this chapter. This practice is a form of outlining. Let us continue discussing the structure of Mansfield's "Miss Brill," the actual subject of the sample research essay (pp. 481–489). As you do your research, you discover that there is a divergence of judgment about how the ending of the story should be understood. Here is a note about one of the diverging interpretations:

Daly 90                                                  last sentence

    Miss Brill's "complete" "identification" with the shabby fur piece at the very end may cause readers to conclude that she is the one in tears but bravely does not recognize this fact, and also to conclude that she may never use the fur in public again because of her complete defeat. Everything may be for "perhaps the very last time." 90

Notice that the title classifies the topic of the note. If you use such classifications while taking notes, a number of like-titled cards could form the substance of a section in your essay about the way to understand the concluding sentence of "Miss Brill." In addition, once you decide that "last sentence" is one of the topics you plan to explore, the topic itself will guide you in further study and additional note taking. Please see the sample research essay, in which paragraphs 19–24 are devoted to this subject.

    **Write down your own thoughts as they occur to you.**  As you take your notes, you will develop many thoughts of your own. Do not let these go, to be remembered later (maybe), but write them down immediately. Often you may notice a detail that your source does not mention, or you may get a hint for an idea that the critic does not develop. Often, too, you may get thoughts which can serve as "bridges" between details in your notes or as introductions or concluding observations. Be sure to title your comment and also to mark it as your own thought. Here is such a note, which is concerned with the relative lack of action in "Miss Brill" as opposed to the emphasis in the story on the psychological state of the heroine:

My Own                                                   Last Sentence

Mansfield's letter of Jan. 17, 1921, indicates that action as such was less significant in her scheme for the story than the sympathetic evocation of Miss Brill's observations, impressions, and moods. She wanted to reveal character.

Please observe that in paragraph 5 of the sample research essay, the substance of this note, and a good deal of the language, is used to introduce new material once the passage from the Mansfield letter has been quoted (p. 483).

**Sort your cards into groups.**    If you have taken your notes well, your essay will have been taking shape in your mind already. The titles of your cards will suggest areas to be developed as you do your planning and prewriting. Once you have assembled a stack of note cards derived from a reasonable number of sources (your instructor may have assigned the minimum number), you can sort them into groups according to the topics and titles. For the sample essay, after some shuffling and retitling, the following groups of cards were distributed:

1.   Writing and publication
2.   The title: amusement and seriousness
3.   General structure
4.   Specific structures: season, time of day, levels of cruelty, Miss Brill's own "hierarchies" of unreality
5.   The concluding paragraphs, especially the last sentence
6.   Concluding remarks

If you look at the major sections of the sample essay, you will see that the topics are adapted with only slight changes from these groups of cards.

In other words, the arrangement of the cards is an effective means of outlining and organizing a research essay.

**ARRANGE THE CARDS IN EACH GROUP.**  There is still much to be done with these individual groups. You cannot use the details as they happen to fall randomly in your "deal." You need to decide which notes are relevant. You might also need to retitle some cards and use them elsewhere. Of those that remain in the group, you will need to lay them out in a logical progression in which they may be used in the essay.

Once you have your cards in order, you can write whatever comments or transitions are needed to move from detail to detail. Write this material directly on the cards, and be sure to use a different color ink so that you will be able to know what was on the original card and what you added at this stage of your composing process. Here is an example of such a "developed" note card:

---

Magalaner 39                                              Structure, general

Speaking of Mansfield's sense of form, and referring to "Miss Brill" as an example, Magalaner states that Mansfield has power to put together stories from "a myriad of threads into a rigidly patterned whole."

*Some of these "threads" are the fall season, the time of day, examples of unkindness, the park bench sitters from the cupboards, and Miss Brill's stages of unreality (see Thorpe 661). Each of these is separate, but all work together to unify the story.*

---

By adding such commentary to your note cards, you will facilitate the actual writing of the first draft. In many instances, the note and the comment may be moved directly into the paper with minor adjustments (some of the content of this note appears in paragraph 6 of the sample essay, and almost all the topics introduced here are developed in paragraphs 9–14).

**BE CREATIVE AND ORIGINAL IN RESEARCH PAPERS.**  This is not to say you can always settle for the direct movement of the cards into your essay. The major trap to avoid in a research paper is that your use of sources can become an end in itself and therefore a shortcut for your own thinking and writing. Quite often students introduce details in a research paper the way a master of ceremonies introduces performers in a variety show. This is unfortunate because it is the student whose essay will be judged, even though the sources, like the performers, do all the work. Thus, it is important to be creative and original in a research essay, and do your own thinking and writing, even though you are relying heavily on sources. Here are four ways in which research essays may offer chances for originality:

1.  *Selection*. In each major section of your essay you will include a number of details from your sources. To be creative you should select different but related details and avoid overlapping or repetition. The essay will be judged on the basis of the thoroughness with which you make your point with different details (which in turn will represent the completeness of your research). Even though you are relying on published materials and cannot be original on that score, your selection is original because you are bringing the materials together for the first time.

2.  *Development*. A closely related way of being original is the development of various points. Your arrangement is an obvious area of originality: one detail seems naturally to follow another, and certain conclusions stem out of certain details. As you present the details, conclusions, and arguments from your sources, you may also add your own original stamp by using supporting details that are different from those in your sources. You may also wish to add your own emphasis to particular points—an emphasis that you do not find in your sources.

    Naturally, the words that you use will be original with you. Your topic sentences, for example, all will be your own. As you introduce details and conclusions, you will need to write "bridges" to get yourself from point to point. These may be introductory remarks or transitions. In other words, as you write, you are not just stringing things out but are actively tying thoughts together in a variety of creative ways. Your success in these efforts will constitute the area of your greatest originality.

3.  *Explanation of controversial views*. Also closely related to selection is the fact that in your research you may have found conflicting or differing views on a topic. It is original for you, as you describe and distinguish these views, to explain the reasons for the differences. In other words, as you explain a conflict or difference, you are writing an original analysis. To see how differing views may be handled, see paragraphs 19–21 of the sample essay.

4.  *Creation of your own insights and positions*. There are three possibilities here, all related to how well you have learned the primary texts on which your research in secondary sources is based.
    a.  *Your own interpretations and ideas*. Remember that an important part of taking notes is to make your own points precisely when they occur to you. Often you can expand these as truly original parts of your essay. Your originality does not need to be extensive; it may consist of no

more than a single insight. Here is such a card, which was written during the research on the structure of "Miss Brill":

---

My Own                                            Miss Brill's unreality

It is ironic that the boy and girl sit down on the bench next to Miss Brill just when she is at the height of her fancies. By allowing her to overhear their insults, they introduce objective reality to her. The result is that she is plunged instantly from the height of rapture to the depth of pain.

---

The originality here is built around the contrast between Miss Brill's exhilaration and her rapid and cruel deflation. The observation is not particularly unusual or startling, but it nevertheless represents an attempt at original thought about the subject. When modified and adapted, the material of the note supplies much of paragraph 18 of the sample essay. You can see that here the development of a "my own" note card is an important part of the prewriting stage for a research essay.

b. *Gaps in the sources*. As you read your secondary sources it may dawn on you that a certain, obvious conclusion is not being made, or that a certain detail is not being stressed. Here is an area which you can develop on your own. Your conclusions may involve a particular interpretation or major point of comparison, or they may rest on a particularly important but understressed word or fact. For example, paragraphs 21–24 form an argument based on observations that critics have overlooked, or neglected to mention, about the conclusion of the story. In your research, whenever you find such a critical "vacuum" (assuming that you cannot read all the articles about some of your topics, where your discovery may already have been made a number of times), it is right to move in with whatever is necessary to fill it. A great deal of scholarship is created in this way.

c. *Disputes with the sources*. You may also find that your sources present certain arguments that you wish to dispute. As you develop your disagreement, you will be arguing originally, for you will be using details in a different way from that of the critic or critics whom you are disputing, and your conclusions will be your own. This area of originality is similar to the laying out of controversial critical views, except that you furnish one of the opposing views yourself. The approach is limited, because it is difficult to find many substantive points of interpretation on which there are not already clearly delineated opposing views. Paragraph 13 of the sample research essay (about the woman with the ermine toque) shows how a disagreement can lead to a different, if not original, interpretation.

## DOCUMENTATION: NOTES AND PARENTHETICAL REFERENCES

It is essential to acknowledge—to document—all sources from which you have quoted *or* paraphrased factual and interpretive information. If you do not grant recognition, you run the risk of being challenged for representing as your own the results of others' work; this is plagiarism. As the means of documentation, there are many reference systems, some using parenthetical references, and others using footnotes or endnotes. Whatever the system, they have in common a carefully prepared bibliography or list of works cited. We shall first discuss the list of works cited, and then the two major systems for referring to this list within a research paper. The first system, which uses parenthetical references, is described in detail in the *MLA Handbook for Writers of Research Papers*, 2nd ed., 1984, which we recommend to you. The second system, which features footnotes or endnotes, is still widely used. Because this system was *the* MLA system until 1984, we will review it here also.

Before discussing the two major systems, we should mention that because of the nature of this book and the types of sample essays we have presented, we have not used a formal list of works cited. We have simply indicated in a note at the beginning of each essay the location within this book of the story being discussed. Parenthetical page numbers within a given essay refer to this book, and paragraph numbers, when pertinent, refer to our own apparatus.

## LIST OF WORKS CITED

The key to any reference system is a carefully prepared list of works cited that is included at the end of the essay. If footnotes or endnotes are used to cite sources, however, a list of works cited may not be required. Check your instructor's preference. It is important to include all the following information in each entry:

### For a Book

1. The author's name, last name first, period.
2. Title, underlined, period.
3. City of publication (not state), colon; publisher (easily recognized abbreviations may be used, comma; date, period.

### For an Article

1. The author's name, last name first, period.
2. Title of article in quotation marks, period.
3. Name of journal or periodical, underlined, followed by volume number in Arabic (not Roman) numbers with no punctuation, followed by the year of publication within parentheses (including month and day of weekly or daily issues), colon. Inclusive page numbers, period (without any preceding "pp.").

The list of works consulted should be arranged alphabetically by author, with unsigned articles being listed by title. Bibliographical lists are begun at the left margin, with subsequent lines being indented, so that the key to locating a particular work—usually the author's last name—may be easily seen. The many complex combinations possible in the compilation of a bibliographical list, including ways to describe works of art, musical or other performances, and films, are detailed extensively in the *MLA Handbook* (75–135). Here are two model entries:

> BOOK:   Alpers, Antony. *Katherine Mansfield, A Biography.* New York: Knopf, 1953.
> ARTICLE:   Hankin, Cherry. "Fantasy and the Sense of an Ending in the Work of Katherine Mansfield." *Modern Fiction Studies* 24 (1978): 465–474.

### Parenthetical References to the List of Works Cited

Within the text of the essay, you may refer parenthetically to the list of works cited. The parenthetical reference system recommended in the *MLA Handbook* (137–158) involves the insertion of the author's last name and the relevant page number or numbers into the body of the essay. If the author's name is mentioned in the discussion, only the page number or numbers are given in parentheses. Here are two examples:

> Mansfield shaped the story "Miss Brill" as a development from pleasant daydreams to wakefulness, accompanied by the downfall of hope and imagination (Hankin 472).

> Cherry Hankin points out that Mansfield shaped the story "Miss Brill" as a development from daydreams to wakefulness, accompanied by the downfall of hope and imagination (472).

For a full discussion of the types of in-text references and the format to be used, see the *MLA Handbook*.

### Footnotes and Endnotes

The most formal system of documentation still most widely used is that of footnotes (references at the bottom of each page) or endnotes (references listed numerically at the end of the essay). If your instructor wants you to use one of these formats, do the following: The first time you quote or refer to the source, make a note with the details in this order:

### For a Book

1. The author's name, first name or initials first, comma.
2. The title: underlined for a book, no punctuation. If you are referring to a story found in a collection, use quotation marks for that, but underline the title of the book. (Use a comma after the title if an editor, translator, or edition follows.)
3. The name of the editor or translator, if relevant. Abbreviate "editor" or "edited by" as *ed*.; "editors" as *eds*. Use *trans*. for "translator" or "translated by."
4. The edition (if indicated), abbreviated thus: *2nd ed*., *3rd ed*., and so on.
5. The publication facts should be given in parentheses, without any preceding or following punctuation, in the following order:
   a. City (but *not* the state) of publication, colon.
   b. Publisher (clear abbreviations are acceptable), comma.
   c. Year of publication.
6. The page number(s), for example, 65, 65f., 6–10. If you are referring to longer works, such as novels or longer stories that may have division or chapter numbers, include these numbers for readers who may be using an edition different from yours.

### For an Article

1. The author, first name or initials first, comma.
2. The title of the article, in quotation marks, comma.
3. The name of the journal, underlined, no punctuation.
4. The volume number, in Arabic numbers, no punctuation.
5. The year of publication in parentheses, colon.
6. The page number(s); for example, 65, 65 f., 6–10.

For later notes to the same work, use the last name of the author as the reference unless you are referring to two or more works by the same author. Thus, if you refer to only one work by, say, Joseph Conrad, the name

"Conrad" will be enough for all later references. Should you be referring to other works by Conrad, however, you will also need to make a short reference to the specific works to distinguish them, such as "Conrad, 'Youth,' " and "Conrad, 'The Secret Sharer.' "

*Footnotes* are placed at the bottom of each page, separated from your essay by a line; *endnotes* are included at the end of the essay in a list keyed to the endnote numbers in the essay. Ask your instructor about the practice you should adopt.

The first lines of both footnotes and endnotes should be paragraph indented, and continuing lines should be flush with the left margin. Footnote numbers are positioned slightly above the line (as superior numbers), like this [5] ). Generally, you may single-space such notes, but be sure to ask your instructor about which method to follow.

**SAMPLE FOOTNOTES.**    In the examples below, book titles and periodicals, which are usually italicized in print, are shown underlined, as they would be in your typewritten or carefully handwritten essay.

[1]Andre Maurois, Points of View from Kipling to Graham Greene (New York: Ungar, 1968) 342.

[2]Susan Gubar, "The Birth of the Artist as Heroine: (Re)production, the Künstlerroman Tradition, and the Fiction of Katherine Mansfield," in The Representation of Women in Fiction, eds. Carolyn G. Heilbrun and Margaret R. Higonnet. Selected Papers from the English Institute, 1981 (Baltimore: Johns Hopkins U.P., 1983) 25.

[3]Ann L. McLaughlin, "The Same Job: The Shared Writing Aims of Katherine Mansfield and Virginia Woolf," Modern Fiction Studies 24 (1978): 375.

[4]Gubar 55.

[5]Maurois 344.

[6]McLaughlin 381.

As a general principle, you do not need to repeat in a note any material that you have already included in your essay. For example, if you mention the author and title of your source in the essay, then the note should merely give the data about publication. Here is an example:

> In *The Fiction of Katherine Mansfield*, Marvin Magalaner points out that Mansfield was as skillful in the development of epiphanies (that is, the use of highly significant though perhaps unobstrusive actions or statements to reveal the depths of a particular character) as Joyce himself, the "inventor" of the technique.[16]

[16](Carbondale: Southern Illinois U.P., 1971) 130.

## FINAL WORDS

As long as all that you want from a reference is the page number of a quotation or of a paraphrase, the parenthetical system is suitable and easy. It saves your reader the trouble of searching the bottom of the page or of thumbing through pages to find a reference in a long list of notes. However, you may wish to use footnotes or endnotes if you need to add more details or refer your readers to other materials that you are not using in your essay.

Whatever method you use, there is an unchanging need to grant recognition to sources. Remember that whenever you begin to write and to make references, you might forget a number of specific details about documentation, and you will certainly discover that you have many questions. Be sure then to ask your instructor, who is your final authority.

## ORGANIZING YOUR ESSAY

### Introduction

In planning, keep in mind that for a research essay, the introduction may be expanded beyond the length of an ordinary essay because of the need to relate the research to your topic. You may wish to bring in relevant historical or biographical information (see, for example, the introduction of the sample essay). You might also wish to summarize critical opinion or to describe any particular critical problems as they pertain to your subject. The idea is to introduce interesting and significant materials that you have found during your research. Obviously, you should plan to include your usual guides—your central idea and your thesis sentence.

Because of the greater length of most research essays, some instructors require a topic outline, which is in effect a brief table of contents. This pattern is observed in the sample essay. Inasmuch as the inclusion of any outline is a matter of choice with various instructors, be sure that you understand whether your instructor requires it.

### Body, Conclusion

Your development both for the body and the conclusion will be governed by your choice of subject. Please consult the relevant chapters in this book about what to include for whatever approach or approaches you select (setting, point of view, character, tone, or any other).

In length, the research essay may be anywhere from five to fifteen or more pages. It seems reasonable to assume that an essay based on only one work may be shorter than one based on two or more. If you narrow the scope of your topic, as suggested in the approaches described above, you can readily keep your essay within the assigned length. The sample research essay, for example, illustrates the first approach by being limited to the structural aspects of one story. Were you to write on characteristic structures in a number of other stories by Mansfield or any other writer (the second approach), you could limit your total number of pages by stressing comparative treatments and by avoiding excessive detail about problems pertaining to each and every story. In short, you will decide to include or exclude materials by compromising between the importance of the materials and the limits of your assignment.

Although you limit your topic yourself in consultation with your instructor, you may encounter problems because you will be dealing not with one text alone but with many. Naturally the sources will provide you with details and also with many of your ideas. The problem is to handle the many strands without piling on too many details, and also without being led into digressions. It is important therefore to keep your central idea foremost, for the constant stressing of your central idea will help you both in selecting relevant materials and rejecting irrelevant ones.

Because of the sources, there is a problem about authority, and that problem is to quote, paraphrase, and otherwise adapt the materials of others without plagiarism. Your reader will automatically assume that everything you write is your own unless you indicate otherwise. You leave yourself open to a charge of plagiarism, however, if you give no recognition to details, interpretations, or specific language that you clearly derive from a source. To handle this problem, you must be especially careful in the use of quotation marks and in the granting of recognition. Most commonly, if you are simply presenting details and facts, you can write straightforwardly and let parenthetical references suffice as your authority, as the following sentence from the sample essay will show:

> Because Katherine Mansfield's "Miss Brill"—one of the eighty-eight short stories and fragments she wrote in her brief life (Magalaner 5)—succeeds so well as a protrait of the protagonist's inner life, it has become well known and frequently anthologized (Gargano).

Here the parenthetical references to secondary texts adequately recognize the authority beyond your own (the Gargano reference, incidentally, contains no page number because it is an unpaginated one-page article).

If you are using an interpretation that is unique to a particular writer or writers, however, or if you are relying on a significant quotation from your source, you should grant recognition and use quotation marks as an essential part of your discussion, as in this sentence:

> While Cherry Hankin suggests that the structuring is perhaps more "instinctive" than deliberate (474), Marvin Magalaner, using "Miss Brill" as an exam-

ple, speaks of Mansfield's power to weave "a myriad of threads into a rigidly patterned whole" (39).

Here there can be no question about plagiarism, for the names of the authorities are acknowledged in full, the page numbers are specific, and the quotation marks clearly show the important word and phrase that are introduced from the sources. If you grant recognition as recommended here, no confusion can possibly result about the authority underlying your essay.

## SAMPLE RESEARCH ESSAY

### The Structure of Mansfield's "Miss Brill"

### I.  Introduction

#### A.  The Writing of "Miss Brill"

Because Katherine Mansfield's "Miss Brill"—one of the eighty-eight short stories and fragments she wrote in her brief life (Magalaner 5)—succeeds so well as a portrait of the protagonist's inner life, it has become well known and frequently anthologized (Gargano). She apparently wrote it on the evening of November 11, 1920, when she was staying at Isola Bella, an island retreat in north Italy where she had gone in her desperate search to overcome tuberculosis. In her own words, she describes the night of composition:

[1]
> Last night I walked about and saw the new moon with the old moon in her arms and the lights in the water and the hollow pools filled with stars—and lamented there was no God. But I came in and wrote Miss Brill instead; which is my insect Magnificat now and always (Letters 594).

Her husband, J. Middleton Murry, who had remained in London, published the story in the November 26, 1920 issue of the journal Athenaeum, which he was then editing. In 1922, Mansfield included "Miss Brill" in her collection entitled The Garden Party and Other Stories (Daly 134).

[2] She was particularly productive at the time of "Miss Brill" despite her illness, for she wrote a number of superb stories then. The others, as reported by her biographer Antony Alpers, were "The Lady's Maid," "The Young Girl," "The Daughters of the Late Colonel," and "The Life of Ma Parker" (304–305). All these stories share the common bond of "love and pity" rather than the "harshness or satire" that typifies many of her earlier stories (Alpers 305).

## B. The Choice of the Name "Brill"

[3] "Miss Brill," however, does contain at least a minor element of humor. James W. Gargano notes that the title character, Miss Brill, is named after a lowly flatfish, the brill. This fish, with notoriously poor vision, is related to the turbot and the whiting (it is the whiting that the rude girl compares to Miss Brill's fur piece). The Oxford English Dictionary records that the brill is "inferior in flavour" (sic) to the turbot. One may conclude that Mansfield, in choosing the name, wanted to minimize her heroine.

[4] While Mansfield's use of the name suggests a small trick on poor Miss Brill, the story is anything but amusing. Miss Brill is not mocked as an "alien-ated city character" symbolizing contemporary decay, but rather is a model of a genuine human being, a person to pity and with whom to identify (Kaplan 165). She is a part of the "feminine world" (Maurois 337), and for this reason is one of those who have been excluded from "public history" (Gubar 31). Her main concerns are not power and greatness but the privacy of personal moments (Gubar 38) which may be upset by no more than a contemptuous giggle. The poignancy of the story stems from everyday callousness and "inhu-manity," to quote Sydney Kaplan in specific reference to "Miss Brill," and also from the close identification, in the presentation, of the speaker and the main character (165). The story's power may be explained as a result of the feeling with which Mansfield renders the "inarticulate longings and the tumultu-ous feelings that lie beneath the surface of daily life" (McLaughlin 381). A mark of skill here is the way in which Mansfield has entered the soul of her heroine and turned it "outward, for her reader to see and understand" (Magill 710). Her friend (but not firm supporter) Virginia Woolf noticed a want of "rich-ness and depth" (75) in Mansfield's work. But Mansfield's own description of her method in composing and revising "Miss Brill" contradicts Woolf, for it demonstrates, in this story at least, how deeply she considered the inner life of her major character:

> In Miss Brill I choose not only the length of every sentence, but even the sound of every sentence. I choose the rise and fall of every paragraph to fit her, and to fit her on that day at that very moment. After I'd written it I read it aloud—numbers of times—just as one would play over a musical composition—trying to get it nearer to the expression of Miss Brill—until it fitted her. (Letter to Richard Murry of January 17, 1921, qtd. in Sewell, 5–6).

## C. The Nature of the Story's Structure

[5] Mansfield's description strongly indicates that action in the story was less significant in her scheme than the sympathetic evocation of Miss Brill's moods and impressions—in other words, the depths of her character. Such a design might lead readers to conclude that the story is not so much formed as forming, a free rather than planned development. In reference to Mansfield's talent generally, Edward Wagenknecht reflects that the stories, including "Miss Brill," are "hardly even episodes or anecdotes. They offer reflections [instead] of some aspect of experience or express a mood" (163). In many ways, Wagenknecht's observation is true of "Miss Brill." The story seems to be built up from within the character, and it leaves the impression of an individual who experiences a "crisis in miniature," a "deep cut into time" in which life changes and all hopes and expectations are reversed (Hankin 465).

[6] It is therefore clear that Mansfield's achievement in "Miss Brill" is to fashion a credible character in a pathetic and quite shattering moment of life, but the story embodies an intricate set of structures which simultaneously complement the movement downward. Mansfield's control over form is strong. While Cherry Hankin suggests that the structuring is perhaps more "instinctive" than deliberate (474), Marvin Magalaner, using "Miss Brill" as an example, speaks of Mansfield's power to weave "a myriad of threads into a rigidly patterned whole" (39). These complementary threads, stages, or "levels" of "unequal length" (Harmat uses the terms "niveaux" and "longueur inégale," 49, 51) are the fall season, the time of day, insensitive or cruel actions, Miss Brill's own unreal perceptions, and the final section or denouement.

## II. The Seasonal Setting as Structure

[7] The first aspect of structure, on the level of setting, is the autumnal, seasonal backdrop, which is integral to the deteriorating circumstances of Miss Brill. In the very first paragraph we learn that there is a "faint chill" in the air (is the word "chill" chosen to rhyme with "Brill"?), and this phrase is repeated in paragraph 10. Thus the author establishes autumn and the approaching end of the year as the beginning of the movement toward dashed hopes. This seasonal reference is also carried out when we read that "yellow leaves" are "down drooping" in the park, or Jardins Publiques (paragraph 6), and that leaves are drifting "now and again" from almost "nowhere, from the sky" (paragraph 1). It is of course the autumn cold that has caused Miss Brill to take out her bedraggled fur piece at which the young girl later is so amused. Thus the chill, together with the fur, forms a structural setting integrated both with the action and mood of the story. In a real way, the story begins and ends with the fur (Sewell 25), which is almost literally the direct cause of Miss Brill's deep hurt at the end.

### III.   The Time of Day as Structure

[8]
Like this seasonal structuring, the times of day parallel the darkening existence of Miss Brill. At the beginning, the day is "brilliantly fine—the blue sky powdered with gold" (did Mansfield choose "brilliantly" because it contains the name of her heroine?), and the light is "like white wine." This metaphorical language (also containing assonance) suggests the brightness and crispness of full sunlight. In paragraph 6, where we also learn of the yellow leaves, "the blue sky with gold-veined clouds" indicates that time has been passing as clouds drift in during late afternoon. By the end of the story, Miss Brill has returned to her "little dark room" (paragraph 18). In other words, the time moves from day to evening, from light to darkness, as an accompaniment to the psychological pain of Miss Brill.

### IV.   Insensitive or Cruel Actions as Structure

[9]
What seems to be Mansfield's most significant structural device, which is nevertheless not emphasized by critics, is the introduction of insensitive or cruel actions. It is as though the hurt experienced by Miss Brill on the bright Sunday afternoon in the Public Gardens is also being experienced by many others. Because she is the spectator who is closely related to Mansfield's narrative voice, Miss Brill is the filter through whom these negative examples reach the reader. Considering the patterns that emerge, one may conclude that Mansfield intends the beauty of the day and the joyousness of the band as an ironic contrast to the pettiness and insensitivity of people in the park.

[10]
The first characters are the silent couple on Miss Brill's bench (paragraph 3), and the incompatible couple of the week before (paragraph 4). Because these seem no more than ordinary, they are not at first perceived as a part of the story's pattern of cruelty and rejection. But the incompatibility suggested by their silence and one-way complaining establishes a structural parallel with the young and insensitive couple who insult Miss Brill. Thus the first two couples prepare the way for the third, and all exhibit behavior of increasing insensitivity.

[11]
Almost unnoticed as a second level of negative life is the vast group of "odd, silent, nearly all old" people filling "the benches and green chairs" (paragraph 5). These people are nevertheless significant structurally because the "dark little rooms—or even cupboards" that Miss Brill associates with them describe her circumstances at the story's end (paragraph 18). The reader may conclude from Miss Brill's silent, eavesdropping behavior that she herself is one of these nameless and faceless ones.

[12]
Once Mansfield has set these levels for her heroine, she introduces examples of more active rejection and cruelty. The beautiful woman of paragraph 8, who throws down the bunch of violets, is the first of these. The causes of her scorn are not made clear, and Miss Brill does not know what to make of the incident, but the woman's actions indicate that she has been involved in a relationship that has ended bitterly.

Perhaps the major figure involved in rejection, who is so important that

[13] she may be considered a structural double of Miss Brill, is the woman wearing the ermine toque (paragraph 8). She does her best to please the "gentleman in grey," but this man insults her by blowing smoke in her face as he leaves. It could be, as Peter Thorpe observes, that the woman is "obviously a prostitute" (661). More likely, however, from the content of their conversation overheard by Miss Brill, is that the toque-wearing woman has had a broken relationship with the gentleman. Being familiar with his Sunday habits, she deliberately comes to the park to meet him, as though by accident, in order to attempt a reconciliation. After her rejection, her hurrying off to meet someone "much nicer" (there is no such person, for Mansfield uses the phrase "as though" to introduce the ermine toque's departure) is her way of masking her hurt. Regardless of the precise situation, however, Mansfield makes plain that the encounter is characterized by vulnerability, unkindness, and pathos.

[14] Once Mansfield has established this major incident, she introduces two additional examples of insensitivity. At the end of paragraph 8, the hobbling old man "with long whiskers" is nearly knocked over by the troupe of four girls—arrogance if not contempt. The final examples involve Miss Brill herself. These are the apparent indifference of her students, together with the old invalid gentleman "who habitually sleeps" when Miss Brill reads to him.

[15] Although "Miss Brill" is a brief story, Mansfield creates a surprisingly large number of structural parallels to the sudden climax brought about by the insulting young couple. The boy and girl do not appear until the very end, in other words (paragraphs 11–14), but actions like theirs have been anticipated structurally throughout the entire narrative. The story does not take us to the homes of the other victims as we follow Miss Brill, but readers may conclude that the silent couple, the complaining wife and long-suffering husband, the unseen man rejected by the beautiful young woman, the ermine toque, and the funny gentleman, not to mention the many silent and withdrawn people sitting in the park, all return to somewhat similar loneliness and various degrees of personal pain.

## V. Miss Brill's "Hierarchy of Unrealities" as Structure

[16] The intricacy of the structure of "Miss Brill" does not end here. Of great importance is the structural development of the heroine herself. Peter Thorpe notes a "hierarchy of unrealities" which governs the reader's increasing awareness of her plight (661). By this measure, the story's actions progressively bring out Miss Brill's failures of perception and understanding—failures which in this respect make her like her namesake fish, the brill (Gargano).

[17] These unrealities begin with Miss Brill's fanciful but harmless imaginings about her shabby fur piece. This beginning sets up the pattern of her pathetic inner life. When she imagines that the park band is a "single, responsive, and very sensitive creature" (Thorpe 661), we are to realize that she is simply making a great deal out of nothing more than an ordinary band. Though she cannot interpret the actions of the beautiful young woman with the violets, she does see the encounter between the ermine toque and the gentleman in grey as an instance of rejection. Her response is certainly correct, but then her belief that the band's drumbeats are sounding out "The Brute! The Brute!"

indicates her vivid overdramatization of the incident. The "top of the hierarchy of unrealities" (Thorpe 661) is her fancy that she is an actor with a vital part in a gigantic drama played by all the people in the park. The most poignant aspect of this daydream is her imagining that someone would miss her if she were absent, for this fancy shows how far she is from reality.

With regard to this structure or hierarchy of unrealities, it is ironic that the boy and girl sit down next to her just when she is at the height of her fancy about her own importance in life. By allowing her to overhear their insults, [18]    the couple introduces objective reality to her with a vengeance, and she is plunged from rapture to pain. The following, and final, two paragraphs hence form a rapid denouement which reflects her loneliness and despair.

## VI.  The Story's Conclusion

Of unique importance in the structure of the story are the final two paragraphs—the conclusion or denouement—in which Miss Brill returns to her miserable little dark room. This conclusion may easily be understood as a total, final defeat. For example, Saralyn Daly, referring to Miss Brill as one of Mansfield's "isolatoes"—that is, solitary persons cut off from normal human contacts (88)—fears that the couple's callous insults have caused Miss Brill to face the outside world with her fur piece "perhaps for the very last time" (90). [19]    Eudora Welty points out that Miss Brill is "defenseless and on the losing side" and that her defeat may be for "always" (87). Miss Brill has experienced a pattern described by Zinman as common in Mansfield's stories, in which the old are destroyed "by loneliness and sickness, by fear of death, by the thoughtless energy of the younger world around them" (457). With this disaster for the major character, the story may be fitted to the structuring of Mansfield stories observed by André Maurois: "moments of beauty suddenly broken by contact with ugliness, cruelty, or death" (342–343).

Because some critics have stated that Miss Brill's downfall is illogically sudden, they have criticized the conclusion. Peterson, for example, complains that the ending is artificial and contrived because of the improbability that the [20]    young couple would appear at just that moment to make their insults (385). On much the same ground, Berkman declares that the ending is excessive, mechanical, and obvious (162, 175).

Cherry Hankin, however, suggests another way in which the conclusion may be taken, a way which makes the story seem both ironic and grimly humorous. In describing patterns to be found in Mansfield's stories, Hankin notes the following situation that may account for the ending of "Miss Brill":

[21]        . . . an impending disillusionment or change in expectations may be deflected by the central character's transmutation of the experience into something positive (466).

There is no question of course that Mansfield's ending indicates that Miss Brill has been totally shattered. Her long, silent, dejected sitting on the bed testifies to the extent of her deflation.

Mansfield's last sentence, however, may be interpreted as a way of indicating that Miss Brill is going back to her earlier habit of making reality over to fit her own needs:

> But when she put the lid on she thought she heard something crying (paragraph 18).

[22] It is hard to read this last sentence without finding irony and pathos. By hearing "something crying," Miss Brill may likely be imagining that the fur piece, and not she, has been hurt. One might remember that the thoughtless young girl has laughed at the fur because it resembles a "fried whiting" (paragraph 14). The irony here is that Miss Brill, like the Boss in another Mansfield story, "The Fly," is forgetting about the pain of remembrance and slipping back into customary defensive behavior.

This pattern of evasion is totally in keeping with Miss Brill's character. Despite her poverty and loneliness, she has been holding a job (as a teacher of English, presumably to French pupils), and has also been regularly performing her voluntary task of reading to the infirm old man. She has clearly not had a life filled with pleasure, but her Sunday afternoons of eavesdropping have enabled her to share in the lives of many other people. This vicarious sociability

[23] is established by Mansfield as Miss Brill's major way of coming to grips with life. Her method may make her seem strange as well as pathetic, but nevertheless Miss Brill has been getting along; she is presented as a person who is able to function. Within such a framework, the deflating insults of paragraphs 13 and 14, hurtful as they are, may be seen as another incentive for her to adjust by strengthening her flights of fancy, not abandoning them.

This is not to interpret the story's conclusion as an indication that Miss Brill has shaken off the effects of the couple's insults. She is first and foremost a "victim" (Zinman 457), if not of others, then of her own reality-modifying imagination. But she is presented as a character who has positive qualities. Indeed, Mansfield herself expressed her own personal liking of Miss Brill (despite her use of the name "brill"). Her husband, J. Middleton Murry, shortly after receiving the story from her for publication, sent her a letter in which he expressed his fondness for the heroine. In a letter to him of November 21, 1920, Mansfield wrote that she shared this fondness. She went on in the same letter to say:

[24]

> One writes (one reason why is) because one does care so passionately that one must show it—one must declare one's love (qtd. in Magalaner 17).

Surely the author could love her creation out of pity alone, but if she had added an element of strength, such as the brave even if sad ability to cope and adjust to "impossible and intolerable conditions" in life (Zinman 457), then her love would have an additional cause. Therefore it seems plausible to understand the last sentence of "Miss Brill" as the resumption of the heroine's ways of surviving despite her obvious pain.

## VII.  Conclusion

[25]
"Miss Brill" is a compact story intricately built up from a number of coexisting structures. It is alive, so much so that it justifies the tribute of Antony Alpers that it is a "minor masterpiece" (305). The structural contrast between the heroine and the world around her is derived from a deeply felt dichotomy about life attributed to Mansfield herself, a sense that the human soul is beautiful, on the one hand, but that people are often vile, on the other (Moore 245). It is the vileness from which Miss Brill seems to be escaping at the end.

[26]
The greater structure of "Miss Brill" is therefore a hard, disillusioned view of life itself, in which the lonely, closed out, and hurt are wounded even more. This pattern of exclusion affects not only the restricted lives of the lonely, but it also reaches directly into their minds and souls. Miss Brill's response is to retreat further and further into an inner world of unreality, but also to continue life, even at an almost totally subdued level, within these confines. It is Mansfield's "almost uncanny psychological insight" (Hankin 467) into the operation of this characteristic response that gives "Miss Brill" its structure and also accounts for its excellence as a story.

## A List of References Consulted

Alpers, Antony. Katherine Mansfield, A Biography. New York: Knopf, 1953.

Berkman, Sylvia. Katherine Mansfield, A Critical Study. New Haven: Yale U. P. (for Wellesley College), 1951.

Daly, Saralyn R. Katherine Mansfield. New York: Twayne, 1965.

Gargano, James W. "Mansfield's MISS BRILL." Explicator 19, No. 2 (Nov., 1960): item 10 (one page, unpaginated).

Gubar, Susan. "The Birth of the Artist as Heroine: (Re)production, the Kunstlerroman Tradition, and the Fiction of Katherine Mansfield." The Representation of Women in Fiction. Eds. Carolyn Heilbrun and Margaret R. Higonnet. Selected Papers from the English Institute, 1981. Baltimore: Johns Hopkins U.P., 1983. 19–59.

Hankin, Cherry. "Fantasy and the Sense of an Ending in the Work of Katherine Mansfield." Modern Fiction Studies 24 (1978): 465–474.

Harmat, Andrée-Marie. "Essai D'Analyse Structurale D'Une Nouvelle Lyrique Anglaise: 'Miss Brill' de Katherine Mansfield." Les Cahiers de la Nouvelle 1 (1983): 49–74.

Heiney, Donald W. Essentials of Contemporary Literature. Great Neck: Barron's, 1954.

Kaplan, Sydney Janet. " 'A Gigantic Mother': Katherine Mansfield's London." Women Writers and the City: Essays in Feminist Literary Criticism. Knoxville: U. of Tennessee P., 1984. 161–175.

Magalaner, Marvin. The Fiction of Katherine Mansfield. Carbondale: Southern Illinois U. P., 1971.

Magill, Frank N., Ed. English Literature: Romanticism to 1945. Pasadena: Salem Softbacks, 1981.

Mansfield, Katherine. Katherine Mansfield's Letters to John Middleton Murry, 1913–1922. Ed. John Middleton Murry. New York: Knopf, 1951. Cited as "Letters."

———. The Short Stories of Katherine Mansfield. New York: Knopf, 1967.

Maurois, André. Points of View from Kipling to Graham Greene. New York: Ungar, 1935, rpt. 1968.

McLaughlin, Ann L. "The Same Job: The Shared Writing Aims of Katherine Mansfield and Virginia Woolf." Modern Fiction Studies 24 (1978): 369–382.

Moore, Virginia. Distinguished Women Writers. Port Washington: Kennikat, 1934, rpt. 1962.

Peterson, Richard F. "The Circle of Truth: The Stories of Katherine Mansfield and Mary Lavin." Modern Fiction Studies 24 (1978): 383–394.

Sewell, Arthur. Katherine Mansfield: A Critical Essay. Auckland: Unicorn, 1936.

Thorpe, Peter. "Teaching 'Miss Brill'." College English 23 (1962): 661–663.

Wagenknecht, Edward. A Preface to Literature. New York: Holt, 1954.

Welty, Eudora. The Eye of the Story: Selected Essays and Reviews. New York: Random House, 1977. 85–106.

Woolf, Virginia. "A Terribly Sensitive Mind." Granite and Rainbow. New York: Harcourt Brace, 1958. 73–75.

Zinman, Toby Silverman. "The Snail under the Leaf: Katherine Mansfield's Imagery." Modern Fiction Studies 24 (1978): 457–464.

## Commentary on the Essay

This essay fulfills an assignment of 2500–3000 words, with 15–25 sources. The bibliography was developed from a college library card catalogue, together with lists of references in some of the critical books (Magalaner, Daly, Berkman), the *MLA International Bibliography*, and the *Essay and General Literature Index*. The sources were contained in a college library with selective, not exhaustive, holdings, supplemented by the use of a local public library. There is only one rare source, an article (Harmat) which was obtained on Xerox through Interlibrary Loan from one of only two United States libraries holding the journal in which it appears. For most quarterly or semester-long classes, you will likely not have the time to extend your sources by this method, but the article in question refers specifically to "Miss Brill," and it was therefore desirable to examine it.

The sources for the sample essay consist of a mixture of books, articles, and chapters or portions of books. Although a reference is made to an entry in the *Oxford English Dictionary*, it is not necessary to list this work in the sources. One article (Sewell) is published as a separate short monograph. Also a part of the sources is the story "Miss Brill" itself, from this anthology (with locations made by paragraph number), together with editions of Mansfield's letters and stories. The sources are used in the essay for facts, interpretations, reinforcement of conclusions, and general guidance and authority. The essay also contains passages taking issue with some specific matters in certain of the sources. All necessary thematic devices, including overall organization and transitions, are unique to the sample essay. Additional particulars about the handling of sources and developing a research essay are included in the discussion of note taking and related matters in the previous part of this appendix.

The introduction to the sample essay contains essential details about the writing of the story and the title, and it also contains a pointed summary of critical appraisals of the story itself. The idea explored here is that the story dramatizes the heroine's emotional responses first to exhilarating and then to deflating experiences. The central idea (paragraph 6) is built out of this idea, explaining that the movement of emotions is accompanied by an intricate and complementary set of structures. The thesis sentence, at the end of paragraph 6, presents the topics to be developed in the body.

Sections II–VI examine various elements of the story for their structural relationship to Miss Brill's emotions. Sections II and III detail the structural uses of the settings of autumn and daylight-darkness, pointing out how they parallel the experiences of Miss Brill. The longest section in the body is part IV (paragraphs 9–18), which is based on an idea not found in the sources. The aspect of the central idea stressed here is that the story is filled with persons going through disappointments that are more or less similar to those of Miss Brill. Paragraph 10 cites the three couples of the story; paragraph 11, the silent old people; and paragraph 12 the woman with violets. The major figure parallel to Miss Brill, the woman wearing the ermine toque, is discussed in paragraph 13. A part of the analysis of the "ermine toque" exemplifies how an original point may be made through the presentation of a view differing from that in a source. Paragraph 14 contains brief descriptions of additional examples of insensitivity, two of them involving Miss Brill herself. Paragraph 15 both concludes and summarizes the instances of insensitivity and cruelty, emphasizing again the "structural parallels" to the situation of the heroine.

Section V (paragraphs 16–18) is based on ideas of the story's structure found in one of the sources (Thorpe). It hence is more derivative than the previous section. Section VI (paragraphs 19–24) is devoted to the denouement of the story. Paragraphs 19 and 20 consider critical disparagements and interpretations of the ending. In paragraph 21, however, a hint found in a source (Hankin) is used to interpret the story's final sentence. An argument in support of this reading is developed in paragraphs 22–

24, concluding with a reference to Manfield's personal approval of the main character.

Section VII, the conclusion of the sample essay (paragraphs 25, 26), relates the central idea to further biographical information and also to Mansfield's achievement in the story. Of the three sources used here, two are used earlier in the essay, and one (Moore) is new.

The list of works cited is the basis of all references in the text of the essay, in accord with the *MLA Handbook for Writers of Research Papers*, 2nd ed. By locating the parenthetical references, a reader might readily examine, verify, and further study any of the ideas and details drawn from the sources and developed in the essay.

# Appendix D:
# Taking Examinations
# on Prose Fiction

Taking an examination on prose fiction is not difficult if you prepare in the right way. Preparing means (1) studying the material assigned, the comments made in class by your instructor and by fellow students, and your own thoughts; (2) anticipating your instructor's questions by writing some of your own questions on the material to be tested and by writing practice answers to these questions; and (3) understanding the precise function of the test in your education.

Tests are not designed to plague you or to hold down your grade. The grade you receive is in fact a reflection of your achievement at a given point in the course. If your grades are low, you can certainly improve them by studying in a coherent and systematic way. Those students who can easily do satisfactory work might do superior work if they improve their method of preparation. From whatever level you begin, you can increase your achievement by improving your method of study.

Your instructor has three major concerns in evaluating your tests (assuming good English): (1) to see the extent of your command over the subject material of the course, (2) to see how well you are able to think about the material, and (3) to see how well you can actually respond to a question or address yourself to an issue.

There are many elements that go into writing good answers on tests, but this last point, about responsiveness, is perhaps the most important. A major cause of low exam grades is that students really do not *answer* the questions asked. The problem is that some students do no more than retell the story, never confronting the issues in the question. Therefore, if you are asked, "Why does . . . ," be sure to emphasize the *why*, and use the *does* only to exemplify the *why*. If the question is about organization, focus on that. If a technical issue is raised, deal with it. In short, always *respond* directly to the question or instruction. Let us compare two answers to the same question:

Question: How important is the setting of Poe's "The Masque of the Red Death" to the plan and action of the story?

1

2

The setting of Poe's "The Masque of the Red Death" is a major element in all aspects of the story. The Prince Prospero invites a thousand of his subjects into his vast "castellated abbey" to be entertained while being shielded from the plague of the red death killing the people in the country. The abbey is surrounded by a high and strong wall, and the gates are all welded shut to prevent all contamination from the plague. The prince lays in much food and wine, and also has musicians, dancers, and other entertainers present and performing constantly so that time can pass well. After a short period he gives a gala, lavish masquerade ball in seven huge rooms of his abbey. Each room has a uniform color scheme—one blue, one purple, one green, one orange, one white, one violet, and one black (with red)—almost all the colors of the rainbow. Over all this a black clock in the black room hourly chimes a frightening, dismal sound that makes the merriment halt momentarily, as though it were a reminder of the brevity of life. At midnight—the ghostliest hour—Death himself appears, costumed as one of those who have died of the red death, to the horror of the guests. The prince runs after Death, into the black room, in reproach and assault. But then Prospero abruptly dies, and so do all the other guests. Everything happens within the abbey. And so the setting is all pervasive in Poe's development of the story.

The setting of Poe's "The Masque of the Red Death" is a major element in all aspects of the story. As a location, Prospero's "castellated abbey" is a focus of human defiance against death. As a cause of action, the walling in of his thousand courtiers is, ironically, the same as insuring that they will all die when Death finally arrives. As a means of achieving probability, the laying in of provisions and entertainment makes the plans of the prince and his "lighthearted friends" seem possible and realistic. As atmosphere, the eerie black clock and the even eerier coloring and lighting of the ballrooms are a commentary on the prince's bizarre and vain attempt to avoid fate. Finally, the setting of the ballrooms, expressively described by the narrator, is the place of the final assault that Prospero makes against the ghoulish, spectral figure of the Red Death, and where he and his followers all die. The setting is therefore all pervasive in Poe's development of the story.

While paragraph 1 relates the action to the various scenes of the story, it does not focus on the relationship. It is also cluttered by details that have no bearing on the question. Paragraph 2, on the other hand, focuses directly on the connection. Because of this emphasis, 2 is shorter than 1. That is, with the focus directly on the issue, there is no need for irrelevant narrative details. Thus, 1 is unresponsive and unnecessarily long, while 2 is responsive and includes only enough detail to exemplify the major points.

## PREPARATION

Your problem is how best to prepare yourself to be knowledgeable and ready for an examination. If you simply cram facts into your head in hopes that you will be able to adjust to whatever questions are asked, you will likely flounder.

### Read and Reread

Above all, keep in mind that your preparation should begin not on the night before the exam but as soon as the course begins. When each assignment is given, you should complete it by the date due, for you will understand your instructor's lecture and the classroom discussion only if you know the material being discussed. Then, about a week before the exam, you should review each assignment, preferably rereading everything completely. With this preparation, your study on the night before the exam will be fruitful, for it might be viewed as a climax of preparation, not the entire preparation itself.

### Make Your Own Questions: Go on the Attack

Rereading is effective but passive preparation. You should instead go on the attack by trying to anticipate the specific conditions of the test. The best way to do this is to compose and answer your own practice questions. Do not waste your time trying to guess the questions you think your instructor might ask. What is of greatest importance is to arrange the subject matter by asking yourself questions that help you get things straight.

How can you make your own questions? It is not as hard as you might think. Your instructor may have announced certain topics or ideas to be tested on the exam. You might develop questions from these. Or you might apply general questions to the specifics of your assignments, as in the following examples:

1.  About a character: What sort of character is *A*? How does *A* grow, or change in the work? What does *A* learn, or not learn, that brings about the conclusion? To what degree is *A* the representative of any particular type?

2.  About the interactions of characters: How does *B* influence *A*? Does a change in *C* bring about any corresponding change in *A*?

3. About events or situations: What relationship does episode *A* have to situation *B*? Does *C*'s thinking about situation *D* have any influence on the outcome of event *E*?

4. About a theme: What ideas does the work explore? How are these established? Which were emphasized in class?

### Adapt Your Notes to Make Questions

Perhaps the best way to construct questions is to use your classroom notes, for notes are the fullest record you have about the way the class approached the material. As you work with your notes, you should reread passages from the texts that were studied by the class or mentioned by your instructor. Remember that it is helpful to work not only with main ideas from your notes, but also with matters such as style, imagery, and organization.

Obviously you cannot make questions from all your notes, and you will therefore need to select from those that seem most important. As an example, here is a short but significant note from a classroom discussion about Walter Van Tilburg Clark's story "The Portable Phonograph" (p. 199): "A particularly timely and modern story. The context is the global, less localized nature of warfare, and the massive destructiveness made possible by modern weapons technology." It is not difficult to adapt this note to make two practice questions:

1. What effects of modern weapons technology make the post-war wasteland setting of "The Portable Phonograph" seem realistic?

2. Why may "The Portable Phonograph" be considered as a particularly timely and modern story?

The first question applies the word *what* to the second part of the note, with the specific focus on the setting of the story. The second applies the word *why* to the phrasing of the first part of the note. Either question would guide you to focused study. The first would require an explanation of the setting of Clark's story realistically mirroring the complete destructiveness made possible by large-scale weapons. The second would emphasize the conditions of modern warfare and their possible effects, with attempts to show how the story reflects these modern conditions. If you were to spend fifteen or twenty minutes writing practice answers to these questions, you could be confident in taking an examination on the material.

### Use Questions Even When Time is Short

Whatever your subject, it is important that you spend as much study time as possible making and answering your own questions. Of course, you will have limited time and will not be able to write extensive answers indefinitely. Even so, do not give up on the question method. If time is too short for full answers, write out the main heads, or topics, of an answer. When time no longer permits you to make even such a brief outline answer, keep thinking of questions, and think about the answers on the way to the exam. Try never to read passively or unresponsively, but always with a creative, question-and-answer goal. Think of studying as a potential writing experience.

### Study with a Fellow Student

Often the thoughts of another person can help you understand the material to be tested. Try to find a fellow student with whom you can work. In view of the need for steady preparation throughout a course, keep in mind that regular conversations are a good idea. Also, you might wish to make your joint study genuinely systematic and thus might set aside a specific evening or afternoon for detailed work sessions.

## TWO BASIC TYPES OF QUESTIONS ABOUT LITERATURE

There are two types of questions that you will find on any examination about prose fiction, and literature generally. Keep them in mind as you prepare. The first type is *factual*, or *mainly objective*, and the second is *general*, *comprehensive*, *broad*, or *mainly subjective*. In a literature course very few questions are purely objective, except multiple-choice questions.

### Factual Questions

**MULTIPLE-CHOICE QUESTIONS.** These are the most purely factual questions. In an introduction to literature course your instructor will most likely reserve them for short quizzes, usually on days when an assignment is due, to make sure that you are keeping up with the reading. Multiple choice can test your knowledge of facts, and it also can test your ingenuity in perceiving subtleties of phrasing in certain choices, but on a literature exam this type of question is rare.

**IDENTIFICATION QUESTION.** These questions test not only your factual knowledge but also your ability to relate this knowledge to your understanding of the work assigned. Typical examples of what you might be asked to identify are:

1. *A character*, for example, Nora in O'Connor's "First Confession." It is necessary to describe briefly the character's position and main activity (that is,

she is Jackie's older sister who gets him in trouble at home and who takes him to his confession). You should then go on to emphasize the character's importance (that is, her values keep Jackie confused throughout most of the story, but by the end it is clear that O'Connor shows that it is really her values that are confused).

2. *Incidents or situations*, which may be illustrated as follows: "A woman tries to drown herself." After giving the location of the situation or incident (Mabel in Lawrence's "The Horse Dealer's Daughter"), try to demonstrate its significance in the work. (That is, Mabel's suicide attempt suggests a belief that the most positive thing she can do, with all her loved ones dead and with her alienation from her brothers, is to join her mother in death. That Dr. Jack Fergusson sees her and rescues her prompts the two to declare a powerful love for each other. The incident therefore illustrates the overwhelming power of love, a major idea in Lawrence's story.)

3. *Things, places, and dates.* Your instructor may ask you to identify a bottle of poison (Collier's "The Chaser"), a royal palace (Poe's "The Masque of the Red Death"), or the dates of Hemingway's "A Clean, Well-Lighted Place" (1933) or Clark's "The Portable Phonograph" (1942). For dates, you might often be given a leeway of five or ten years if you must guess. What is important about dates is not so much exact precision as historical and intellectual perspective. For example, "The Portable Phonograph" was published during the darkest days of the Second World War, and it consequently reflects foreboding about the destructiveness of total, strategic warfare.

4. *Quotations.* Theoretically, you should remember enough of the text to identify a passage taken from it, or at least to make an informed guess. Generally, you should try to locate the quotation, if you remember it, or else to describe the probable location, and to show the ways in which the quotation is typical of the story you have read, with regard to both content and style. You can often salvage much from a momentary lapse of memory by writing a reasoned and careful explanation of your guess, even if the guess is incorrect.

**TECHNICAL AND ANALYTICAL QUESTIONS AND PROBLEMS.** In a scale of ascending importance, the third and most difficult type of factual question involves technique, analysis, and problems. You might be asked to discuss the *setting*, *images*, *point of view*, or *idea or theme* of a work; you might be asked about the use of a *symbol*; you might be asked to analyze an important paragraph that may or may not be duplicated for your benefit.

The use of technical questions will obviously depend on what you have been studying during the period for which you are being tested. If your instructor has been stressing topics like character, setting, point of view, and metaphors and similes, you should prepare to answer questions involving these techniques. If classroom discussion has been confined to theme and idea, however, your preparation may be focused on these. Most instructors announce their intentions well in advance of the exam; if you have any uncertainties about how to prepare, be sure to ask your instructor.

Technical questions may be fairly long, with from fifteen to twenty-five minutes allowed for each. If you have two or more of these questions, try to space your time sensibly; do not devote 80 percent of your time to one question and leave only 20 percent for the rest.

### Basis of Judging Factual Questions

IDENTIFICATION QUESTIONS.    In all identification questions, your instructor is testing (1) your command of facts and (2) your understanding of the relationships of parts to wholes. Thus, let us suppose that you are asked to identify the incident "A woman stabs another woman." It is correct to begin by saying that Katherine Anne Porter's "María Concepción" is the story, that María Concepción does the stabbing, and that María Rosa is killed. Knowledge of these details clearly establishes your command of the facts. But a strong answer must go further. Even in the brief time available for short answers, a good response should also aim at relating the thing being identified to (1) major causation in the story, (2) major ideas, (3) the organization or structure of the story, and (4) for a quotation, the style. Time is short, and you must be selective, but if you can establish a pattern that moves from the factual to the significant, you will be writing superior answers. Along these lines, let us look at an answer identifying the incident from "María Concepción":

> This incident is from Porter's "María Concepción." María Rosa is the victim, and María Concepción stabs her as an apparent act of revenge for her having run away with Juan Villegas, María Concepción's husband, and having borne his child. The incident is central to the story because it shows the depth of María Concepción's accumulating rage at having been so wronged. Because it also creates a crisis, it produces resolutions. Juan returns immediately to María Concepción and plans to stick by her and defend her. Also, the villagers rally around her during the investigation, and in addition, once she is relieved of suspicion she is able to claim María Rosa's baby to replace her own baby that had died. By the story's end María Concepción is totally safe and has secured her place in the community. The incident is therefore a major element in the characterization, causation, and structure of the story.

Any of the points made in this answer could be more fully developed, but the answer is successful because it both places the incident in perspective and deals with its significance. One thing is clear from this example: *A really superior answer cannot be written if your thinking originates entirely at the time you first see the question.* The more thinking and practicing you do before the exam, the better your answers will be.

LONGER FACTUAL QUESTIONS.    The more extended factual questions also require more thoroughly developed organization. Remember that here your knowledge of essay writing is important, for your writing skills will determine a major share of your instructor's evaluation of your answers. It is therefore best to take several minutes to gather your thoughts together before you begin to write. When the questions are before you, use a sheet of scratch paper to jot down the facts you remember and your ideas about them in relation to the question. Then put them together, phrase a thesis sentence, and use your facts to illustrate or prove your thesis.

Begin your answer pointedly; use key words or phrases from the question or direction if possible, so that your answer will have thematic focus. To be most responsive during the short time available for writing an exam, use the question as your guide for your answer. Let us suppose that you have the following question on your test: "How does Steinbeck use details in 'The Chrysanthemums' to reveal the character of Eliza?" The most common way to go astray on such a question, and the easiest thing to do, is to concentrate on Eliza's character rather than on *how* Steinbeck *uses* detail to bring out her character. The word *how* makes a vast difference, and hence the best thing to do on an exam is to copy key phrases from the question to ensure that the answer will be launched in the right direction. Here is an opening sentence that uses the key words and phrases from the question to provide focus.

> Steinbeck uses details about gardening, farm life, and personal care as symbols to reveal the character of Eliza as a motherly and sexual but repressed and unhappy person.

This sentence sets aims and limits so that the subsequent material will be clearly focused and responsive to the question as it has been asked.

### General or Comprehensive Questions

General or comprehensive questions are particularly important on final examinations, when your instructor is interested in testing your total comprehension of the course material. Considerable time is usually allowed for answering this type of question. They may be phrased in a number of ways:

1. A direct question asking about philosophy, underlying attitudes, main ideas, characteristics of style, backgrounds, and so on. Here are some possible questions in this category: "What use do _____, _____, and _____ make of the topic of _____?" "Define and characterize the short story as a genre of literature." "Explain the use of dialogue by Jackson, Collier, and Hemingway." "Contrast the technique of point of view as used by _____, _____, and _____."

2. A "comment" question, often based on an extensive quotation, borrowed from a critic or written by your instructor for the occasion, about a broad class of writers, or about a literary movement, or the like. Your instructor

may ask you to treat this question broadly (taking in many writers) or else to apply the quotation to a specific writer.

3. A "suppose" question, such as "What might Poe have said about the use of the short story form to bring out political and racial ideas, such as Lessing's 'The Old Chief Mshlanga' and Ellison's 'Flying Home' "? Though "suppose" questions might seem whimsical at first sight, they definitely have a serious and thoughtful design. For example, let us put this question: "Suppose that Abner Snopes of Faulkner's 'Barn Burning' were in the place of Erwin Martin of Thurber's 'The Catbird Seat.' Would he be content to develop a plan of revenge like that of Martin?" Obviously, were these two characters reversed we would have neither story. As a serious proposition, however, the question gets directly at the characters of both Martin and Snopes, and, further, requires conclusions about the degrees to which character and action are interlocked in both stories and in fiction generally.

### Basis of Judging General Questions

When answering broad, general questions you are in fact dealing with an unstructured situation, and you must not only supply an *answer* but—equally as important—you must also create a *structure* within which your answer can have meaning. You might almost say that you make up your own specific question out of the original general question. If you were asked to "Consider the role of women as expressed by Porter, Mansfield, and Paley," for example, you would do well to structure the question by narrowing its limits. A possible way to focus such a question might be this:

> Porter, Mansfield, and Paley present a view of women's individuality and difficult circumstances by dramatizing their resolution, their power of adaptation, and their tenacity.

With this sort of focus you would be able to proceed point by point, introducing supporting data as you form your answer.

As a general rule, the best method for answering a comprehensive question is comparison-contrast. The reason is that in dealing with, say, a general question on Crane, Joyce, Lawrence, and Collier, it is too easy to write *four* separate essays rather than *one*. Thus, you should force yourself to consider a topic like "The treatment of love or infatuation" or "The relationship of men and women," and then to develop your answer point by point rather than writer by writer. By creating your answer in this way, you can bring in references to each or all of the writers as they become relevant to your main idea. But if you were to treat each writer separately, your comprehensive answer would lose focus and effectiveness, and it would be needlessly repetitive.

# Glossary

**Abstract diction**   Language that is far removed from the concrete, and therefore applicable to many rather than few objects, persons, actions, and situations. *223–24*

**Actions, or incidents**   The events or occurrences in a work of literature. *64, 87*

**Accumulation**   See *Cumulatio*.

**Allegory**   A story that may be applied to another, parallel, set of situations while maintaining its own narrative integrity. *69–70, 281–82*

**Allusion**   References (usually unacknowledged) to literary works, persons, sayings, and other elements of our cultural heritage. *283–84*

**Analysis**   See *Commentary*.

**Antagonist**   The character or characters opposing the protagonist. A conflict between a protagonist and an antagonist or non-human force is *antagonism*. *64, 121*

**Antimetabole**   See *Chiasmus*.

**Assertion**   A positive or negative statement about an idea, such as that love [the idea in the subject of the sentence] is necessary but also irrational [the predicate contains the assertion about the idea]. *319*

**Atmosphere**   See *Mood*.

**Authorial symbols**   See *Private symbols*.

**Authorial voice**   The name given to the speaker of a story when this speaker is not identified; used to distinguish between author and speaker. *163*

**Beast fable**   See *Fable*.

**Cause and effect**   The interaction of events and the pattern of causation that produces the tension and therefore the interest of fiction. *64*

**Central idea**   (1) The thesis of an essay; (2) the theme of a literary work. See also *Theme*. *6, 65*

**Character**   An extended verbal representation of a human being, the inner self that determines thought, speech, and behavior—a reasonable facsimile of a human being. *63–64, 119–61*

**Chiasmus**   A rhetorical sentence pattern (or even a larger pattern) repeating in the sequence A-B-B-A, such as:

    *A*       *B*                *B*                     *A*
    "I know she loves me, but she loves to keep me from knowing it." *229*

**Chronology**   The sequence of events in a work, with emphasis upon the logic of cause and effect. *64*

**Climax**   The high point in an action, the third stage of dramatic plot structure, in which the conflict and the consequent tension are brought out to the fullest extent; hence the turning point of a work at which the outcome is determined. *90*

**Commentary**   The use of passages of reflection as a means of explaining the meaning of an action or dialogue. *68, 321–22*

**Complex sentence**   A main clause together with a subordinate or dependent clause. *226*

**Complication**   The onset of the major conflicts in a work. *90*

**Compound-complex sentence**   Two or more independent clauses with which one or more dependent clauses are integrated. *227*

**Compound sentence**   Two simple sentences joined by a conjunction. *226*

**Concrete diction**   Words that describe qualities or conditions, such as an ice cream sundae being "cold," "sweet," and "creamy." Distinguished from *abstract diction*. *223–24*

**Conflict**   The opposition between two characters, between large groups of people, or between individuals and larger forces such as natural objects, ideas, modes of behavior, public opinion, and the like. Conflict may also be internal, involving choices facing a character. It is the essence of *plot*. *64, 87–89*

**Connotation**   The emotional, psychological, or social overtones or implications that words carry in addition to their standard dictionary meaning. *224–25*

**Contextual symbols**   See *Private symbols*.

**Cosmic irony or irony of fate**   Situational irony that is connected to a pessimistic or fatalistic view of life. *256–57*

**Crisis**   The turning point, the separation between what has gone before and what will come after, usually a decision or action undertaken in an effort to resolve the conflict of the work; see also *Climax*. *90*

**Cultural or universal symbols**   Generally or universally recognized symbols embodying ideas or emotions that the writer and the reader share in common as a result of their social and cultural heritage. *280*

**Cumulatio**   The parallel building up of much detail; a short way of introducing a considerable amount of material. Also called *accumulation*. *229*

**Decorum**   A quality of language and behavior that is thought to be appropriate, suitable, or fitting both to the literary medium (such as epic poetry) and also to subject and character. *139–40*

**Denotation**   The standard dictionary meaning of a word. *224–25*

**Dénouement**   See *Resolution*.

**Description**   The exposition of scenes, actions, attitudes, and feelings. *67*

**Dialogue**   A conversation between two or more characters in a story. *67–68*

**Diction**   Word choice, types of words, and the level of language. *221–25*

**Diction, formal**   Proper, elevated, and elaborate language characterized by complex words and a lofty tone. *222*

**Diction, informal or low**   Relaxed, conversational, and colloquial language. *223*

**Diction, middle or neutral**   Correct language and word order without elaborate words or a lofty tone. *222–23*

**Dilemma**   Two choices facing a protagonist, with either one being unacceptable or damaging. *88*

*Donnée*   The given situation or set of assumptions on which a work of literature is based. *62*

**Double-entendre**   Deliberate ambiguity, often sexual. *256*

**Dramatic irony**   A special kind of situational irony in which a character perceives his or her plight in one way while the reader and one or more of the other characters understand it in greater perspective. *69, 257*

**Dramatic point of view**   A third person narration reporting speech and action but rigorously excluding commentary on the action and thoughts of any of the characters. *66, 168*

**Dynamic character**   A character with the capacity to adapt, change, and grow (opposed to *static character*). *121*

**Enclosing method**   See *Framing mode*.

**Epic**   Usually a long narrative poem that features heroic characters, momentous events, and highly elevated diction. *58–59*

**Essay**   A fully developed set of interconnected paragraphs that grow systematically out of a central idea. *6*

**Exposition**   The laying out or putting forth of the materials necessary for an understanding of a work. *89–90*

**Fable**   A short, pointed story illustrating a moral truth, most often associated with the ancient Greek writer Aesop. *59, 282–83*

**Falling action**   The action in a story after the climax—the catastrophe and resolution. *90–91*

**Fantasy**   The creation of events that are dreamlike or fantastic, departing from ordinary understanding of reality because of apparently illogical causation and chronology. *61*

**Fiction**   A prose story based in the imagination of the author, not in literal facts. *58–82*

**First-person point of view**   The "I" narrator who acquires authority because of close involvement in the action or because of being an observer. *66, 164–65, 168*

**Flashback**   A narrative or dramatic episode that presents past action (often through memory) in the present. *91–92*

**Flat character**   A character, usually minor, who is not individual, but rather useful and structural, static and unchanging; compare *round character*. *121–22*

**Form** In the consideration of ideas, a form may be conceptual as opposed to real. Thus the activity of thought, to the degree that it can be remembered or imagined, is a mental *form*. *318*

**Formal diction** See *Diction, formal*.

**Framing mode** The use of a setting at both the beginning and ending of a story so that the story itself is "framed." *193*

**General language** Words referring to broad classes of persons or things. Distinguished from *specific* language. *223–24*

**General symbols** See *Cultural symbols*.

**Hero, heroine** The major character in a work, the protagonist, the human center of interest. Though the term implies that a character be particularly valiant, the fact that a character has a major role is sufficient cause to label him or her *hero* or *heroine*. *121*

**Hyperbole** See *Overstatement*.

**Idea** A broad word referring to a concept, thought, opinion, or belief. Some types of ideas are those of justice, right and good, necessity, and causation. An idea developed throughout a work of literature is called a *theme*. *318–59*

**Idiom** A phrase or style of speaking characteristic of a particular group, class, region, or nation, whose meaning cannot be derived from an analysis of constituent parts.

**Imitation** The idea that literature is derived from life and is an imaginative duplication of life experiences; closely connected to *realism* and *verisimilitude*. *61*

**Incidents, or Actions** The events or occurrences in a work of literature. *64*

**Informal or Low Diction** See *Diction, informal*.

**Interpretation** See *Commentary*.

**Invention** The process of making up situations and stories out of the imagination, derived by the writer from life experiences and thought. *7, 61*

**Irony** The use of language and situations that are widely inappropriate or opposite from what might be ordinarily expected. *69, 255–57*

**Irony of fate** See *Cosmic irony*.

**Limited omniscient point of view** A third-person narration with the focus made on one particular character's activities and thoughts. *66, 166–68*

**Listener** A character or characters imagined as the audience to whom a story is spoken, and as a result one of the influences on the content of the work. *162, 165–66*

**Loose sentence** A straightforward sentence with no climax and no surprises. *227*

**Meaning** The combination of a story's theme, its emotional impact, and the experience it creates for the reader. *319*

**Metaphor** Figurative language in which one thing is directly equated with another, as in "the arts are sisters." *67*

**Mood** The emotional aura evoked by a work, usually as a result of the quality of the descriptions. *67, 193*

**Myth** A story that explains a specific aspect of life or a natural phenomenon, based on the religion, philosophy, and collective psychology of various groups or cultures. *283*

**Narration**   The relating or recounting, usually fictional, of a sequence of events or actions. *58–65*

**Narrative fiction**   See *Prose fiction*.

**Narrator**   See *Speaker*.

**Neutral, or Middle Diction**   See *Diction, middle*.

**Novel**   A long work of prose fiction. *60*

**Objective point of view**   See *Dramatic point of view*.

**Omniscient point of view**   A third person narrative in which the speaker shows knowledge not only of the actions and speeches of all the characters, but also of their thoughts. *66, 166, 168*

**Organic unity**   The interdependence of all elements of a work, including character, actions, speeches, thoughts, and observations. *64*

**Overreacher**   See *Overstatement*.

**Overstatement**   A rhetorical figure in which emphasis is achieved through exaggeration. *256*

**Parable**   Short stories designed to illustrate a religious truth, most often associated with Jesus. *59, 283*

**Parallelism**   A rhetorical figure in which the same grammatical forms are repeated in two or more phrases, lines of verse, or sentences. *227–29*

**Paraphrase**   The brief rewriting of a work in words other than those of the original. *82–86, 467–68*

**Periodic Sentence**   A sentence arranged in an order of climax, sometimes building to a surprising idea. *227*

**Persona**   The narrator or speaker of a story. *66, 162–64*

**Plausibility**   See Probability.

**Plot**   The plan or groundwork for a story, based in conflicting human motivations, with the actions resulting from believable and realistic human responses. It is response, interaction, opposition, and causation that make a plot out of a simple series of actions. *64, 87–118*

**Point of view**   The voice of a story, the speaker who is doing the narration; the means by which the reality and truthfulness of a story are made to seem authentic; the focus or angle of vision from which things are not only seen and reported but also judged. *66–67, 162–89*

**Postulate**   The assumption on which a work of literature is based, such as a level of absolute, literal reality, or as a dreamlike, fanciful set of events; see also *Donné*. *62*

**Précis**   A shortening, or cutting down, of a narrative into its essential parts, a synopsis, abridgement, paraphrase, condensation, or epitome. *82–86*

**Premise**   See *Postulate*.

**Private symbols**   Symbols derived not from common historical, cultural, or religious ground, but from the context of the work in which they are included. Also called *authorial* or *contextual symbols*. *280–81*

**Probability**   The standard of judgment requiring that literature be about what would normally, usually, and probably occur, not by what could possibly occur. Also called *verisimilitude* or *plausibility*. *124–25*

**Prose fiction**   Novels, short stories, and shorter prose works that generally focus on one or a few characters who undergo some sort of change as they encounter other characters or deal with some problem. *3*

**Protagonist**   The principal character in a work, the human center of interest, who is involved in some sort of conflict; see also *antagonist*. *64, 121*

**Realism**   The use of true, lifelike, or probable situations and concerns. Also, the concept underlying the use of reality in literature. *61, 124*

**Realistic character**   The accurate imitation of individualized men and women. *121*

**Representative characters**   Flat characters who are undistinguishable from the groups or classes to which they belong. *121*

**Resolution**   The fifth stage of plot development in which conflicts are resolved, problems are solved, and loose ends are tied up. Also called *dénouement*. *90*

**Rhetoric**   Broadly, the art of persuasive writing and even more broadly, the general art of writing. Short or long sentences, and devices such as parallelism, climax, simile, metaphor, irony, and symbolism are all aspects of rhetoric. *226–29*

**Rising action**   The action in a story before the climax. *89–90*

**Romance**   The name applied to lengthy Spanish and French stories written in the sixteenth and seventeenth centuries. Today, the word is applied to formulaic stories, usually involving the development of a love relationship. *60*

**Round character**   Usually a major figure in a work, with relatively full development and many individual and dynamic traits; compare *flat character*. *120–21*

**Satire**   An attack on human follies or vices, as measured positively against a normative religious, moral, or social standard.

**Second-person point of view**   A narration employing the "you" personal pronoun. *165–66, 168*

**Sequence**   The events in a work as they take place in time, from beginning to end. *64*

**Setting**   The natural and artificial environment in which characters in literature live their lives; the sum total of references to physical and temporal objects and artifacts. *190–220*

**Short story**   A short, concentrated narrative, called by Poe a "brief prose tale," designed to create a powerful, single impression. *60*

**Simile**   Figurative language in which words such as *like* or *as* are used to draw similarities between two apparently unlike things, as in "a family is like a sturdy tree." *230*

**Simple sentence**   A complete sentence containing one subject and one verb, together with modifiers and complements. *226*

**Situational irony**   A type of irony emphasizing that human beings are enmeshed in forces beyond their comprehension or control. *69, 256–57*

**Speaker**   A fictitious observer, the point-of-view narrator of a story, often a totally independent character who is completely imagined and consistently maintained by the author. *66*

**Specific language**   References to a real thing or things that may be readily perceived or imagined; distinguished from *general language*. *223–24*

**Static character**   A character, usually a minor one, who remains the same and undergoes no growth or change in the work; compare *dynamic character*. *121–22*

**Stereotype**   A stock character who seems to have been stamped from a mold; highly conventionalized, unchanging characters. See also *Stock character*. *122*

**Stock character**   A character, usually flat and static, who performs in repeating situations. Examples are the foolish boss, the angry police captain, the lovable drunk, the bewildered or stubborn parent, and the prodigal son. *122*

**Structure**   The arrangement and placement of materials in a work, the actual assemblage of an entire work or part of a work. See also *Form*. *64*, *87*, *89–92*, *115–18*, *481–91*

**Style**   The manipulation of language, the way in which writers tell the story; the placement of words in the service of content. *65–66*, *221–50*

**Subject**   The topic that a literary work addresses, such as love, marriage, war, death, and the like. *318–19*

**Symbol, Symbolism**   A specific thing that may stand for ideas, values, persons, or ways of life; a symbol always points beyond its own meaning toward greater and more complex meaning. *67*, *69–70*

**Theme**   The specific and central idea or ideas that a literary work explores or asserts about its subject. *65*, *318–59*

**Third-person point of view**   A method of narration in which all things are described in the third person and in which the narrator is not introduced as an identifiable persona. *66*, *166–68*

**Tone**   The methods used by writers to convey and control attitude about their material and their readers. *69*, *251–78*

**Topic**   See *Subject*.

**Tragedy**   A literary work, beginning in prosperity and ending in adversity, that recounts the fall of an individual.

**Understatement**   The deliberate underplaying or undervaluing of a thing for purposes of emphasis. *256*

**Universal symbols**   See *Cultural symbols*.

**Value**   A standard by which ideas and customs are measured. *320–21*

**Verbal irony**   Language stating the opposite of what is meant. *69*, *256*

**Verisimilitude**   A characteristic of literature, particularly fiction, that emphasizes the probable and lifelike. *61*, *124–25*

# Credits

# Author and Title Index